PENGUIN COMPASS

THE MASKS OF GOD: CREATIVE MYTHOLOGY

Joseph Campbell was interested in mythology since his childhood in New York, when he read books about American Indians, frequently visited the American Museum of Natural History, and was fascinated by the museum's collection of totem poles. He earned his B.A. and M.A. degrees at Columbia in 1925 and 1927 and went on to study medieval French and Sanskrit at the universities of Paris and Munich. After a period in California, where he encountered John Steinbeck and the biologist Ed Ricketts, he taught at the Canterbury School, then, in 1934, joined the literature department at Sarah Lawrence College, a post he retained for many years. During the 1940s and '50s he helped Swami Nikhilananda to translate the Upanishads and *The Gospel of Sri Ramakrishna*. The many books by Professor Campbell include *The Hero with a Thousand Faces*, *Myths to Live By*, *The Flight of the Wild Gander*, and *The Mythic Image*. He edited *The Portable Arabian Nights*, *The Portable Jung*, and other works. He died in 1987.

JOSEPH CAMPBELL

THE
MASKS of GOD:
CREATIVE
MYTHOLOGY

PENGUIN COMPASS

PENGUIN BOOKS

Published by the Penguin Group

Penguin Group (USA) Inc., 375 Hudson Street, New York, New York 10014, U.S.A.

Penguin Group (Canada), 90 Eglinton Avenue East, Suite 700, Toronto, Ontario,
Canada M4P 2Y3 (a division of Pearson Penguin Canada Inc.)

Penguin Books Ltd, 80 Strand, London WC2R 0RL, England

Penguin Ireland, 25 St Stephen's Green, Dublin 2, Ireland (a division of Penguin Books Ltd)

Penguin Group (Australia), 250 Camberwell Road, Camberwell, Victoria 3124,
Australia (a division of Pearson Australia Group Pty Ltd)

Penguin Books India Pvt Ltd, 11 Community Centre, Panchsheel Park, New Delhi – 110 017, India

Penguin Group (NZ), 67 Apollo Drive, Rosedale, North Shore 0745,
Auckland, New Zealand (a division of Pearson New Zealand Ltd)

Penguin Books (South Africa) (Pty) Ltd, 24 Sturdee Avenue, Rosebank,
Johannesburg 2196, South Africa

Penguin Books Ltd, Registered Offices: 80 Strand, London WC2R 0RL, England

First published in the United States of America by Viking Penguin Inc. 1968
First published in Great Britain by Souvenir Press Ltd 1973
Viking Compass Edition published 1970
Reprinted 1971 (twice), 1973, 1974, 1975
Published in Penguin Books 1976
Published in Arkana Books 1991

26 27 28 29 30

Library of Congress catalog card number: 68-14983

ISBN 978-0-14-019440-1

Printed in the United States of America
Set in Times Roman

The author wishes to acknowledge with gratitude
the generous support of his researches by
the Bollingen Foundation.
Where no translator's name is given in the notes,
the translations throughout this work are the author's.
The selections and illustrations from the works listed opposite and others acknowledged in the
author's reference notes are reprinted in this volume by permission of the holders of copyright
and publication rights. The page following constitutes an extension of this copyright page.

CONTENTS

PART FOUR: NEW WINE

Chapter 9. The Death of "God"

Chapter 10. The Earthly Paradise

ILLUSTRATIONS

Figure

Figure

Figure

Sketches for Figures 3, 4, 9, 10, 11, 12, 14, 23, 24, and 36 are
by John L. Mackey.

Sketches for Figures 16, 17, 18, 28, 32, 40, 45, 51, 52, 56, 57,
and 58 are by Al Burkhardt.

THE MASKS OF GOD:
CREATIVE
MYTHOLOGY

The Masks of God

Looking back today over the twelve delightful years that I spent on this richly rewarding enterprise, I find that its main result for me has been its confirmation of a thought I have long and faithfully entertained: of the unity of the race of man, not only in its biology but also in its spiritual history, which has everywhere unfolded in the manner of a single symphony, with its themes announced, developed, amplified and turned about, distorted, reasserted, and, today, in a grand *fortissimo* of all sections sounding together, irresistibly advancing to some kind of mighty climax, out of which the next great movement will emerge. And I can see no reason why anyone should suppose that in the future the same motifs already heard will not be sounding still—in new relationships indeed, but ever the same motifs. They are all given here, in these volumes, with many clues, besides, suggesting ways in which they might be put to use by reasonable men to reasonable ends—or by poets to poetic ends—or by madmen to nonsense and disaster. For, as in the words of James Joyce in *Finnegans Wake:* "utterly impossible as are all these events they are probably as like those which may have taken place as any others which never took person at all are ever likely to be."

THE ANCIENT VINE

✦✦✦

✦✦✦✦✦✦✦✦✦✦✦✦✦✦✦✦✦ *Chapter 1* ✦✦✦✦✦✦✦✦✦✦✦✦✦✦✦✦✦

EXPERIENCE AND AUTHORITY

✦✦

I. Creative Symbolization

In the earlier volumes of this survey of the historical transformations of those imagined forms that I am calling the "masks" of God, through which men everywhere have sought to relate themselves to the wonder of existence, the myths and rites of the Primitive, Oriental, and Early Occidental worlds could be discussed in terms of grandiose unitary stages. For in the history of our still youthful species, a profound respect for inherited forms has generally suppressed innovation. Millenniums have rolled by with only minor variations played on themes derived from God-knows-when. Not so, however, in our recent West, where, since the middle of the twelfth century, an accelerating disintegration has been undoing the formidable orthodox tradition that came to flower in that century, and with its fall, the released creative powers of a great company of towering individuals have broken forth: so that not one, or even two or three, but a galaxy of mythologies—as many, one might say, as the multitude of its geniuses—must be taken into account in any study of the spectacle of our own titanic age. Even in the formerly dominant, but now distinctly subordinate, sphere of theology there has arisen, since the victories of Luther, Melanchthon, and the Augsburg Confession of 1530, a manifold beyond reckoning of variant readings of the Christian revelation; while in the fields of literature, secular philosophy, and the arts, a totally new type of non-theological revelation, of great scope, great depth, and

3

infinite variety, has become the actual spiritual guide and structuring force of the civilization.

In the context of a traditional mythology, the symbols are presented in socially maintained rites, through which the individual is required to experience, or will pretend to have experienced, certain insights, sentiments, and commitments. In what I am calling "creative" mythology, on the other hand, this order is reversed: the individual has had an experience of his own—of order, horror, beauty, or even mere exhilaration—which he seeks to communicate through signs; and if his realization has been of a certain depth and import, his communication will have the value and force of living myth—for those, that is to say, who receive and respond to it of themselves, with recognition, uncoerced.

Mythological symbols touch and exhilarate centers of life beyond the reach of vocabularies of reason and coercion. The light-world modes of experience and thought were late, very late, developments in the biological prehistory of our species. Even in the life-course of the individual, the opening of the eyes to light occurs only after all the main miracles have been accomplished of the building of a living body of already functioning organs, each with its inherent aim, none of these aims either educed from, or as yet even known to, reason; while in the larger course and context of the evolution of life itself from the silence of primordial seas, of which the taste still runs in our blood, the opening of the eyes occurred only after the first principle of all organic being ("Now I'll eat you; now you eat me!") had been operative for so many hundreds of millions of centuries that it could not then, and cannot now, be undone—though our eyes and what they witness may persuade us to regret the monstrous game.

The first function of a mythology is to reconcile waking consciousness to the *mysterium tremendum et fascinans* of this universe *as it is:* the second being to render an interpretive total image of the same, as known to contemporary consciousness. Shakespeare's definition of the function of his art, "to hold, as 'twere, the mirror up to nature," is thus equally a definition of mythology. It is the revelation to waking consciousness of the powers of its own sustaining source.

A third function, however, is the enforcement of a moral order:

the shaping of the individual to the requirements of his geographically and historically conditioned social group, and here an actual break from nature may ensue, as for instance (extremely) in the case of a *castrato*. Circumcisions, subincisions, scarifications, tattoos, and so forth, are socially ordered brands and croppings, to join the merely natural human body in membership to a larger, more enduring, cultural body, of which it is required to become an organ—the mind and feelings being imprinted simultaneously with a correlative mythology. And not nature, but society, is the alpha and omega of this lesson. Moreover, it is in this moral, sociological sphere that authority and coercion come into play, as they did mightily in India in the maintenance of caste and the rites and mythology of suttee. In Christian Europe, already in the twelfth century, beliefs no longer universally held were universally enforced. The result was a dissociation of professed from actual existence and that consequent spiritual disaster which, in the imagery of the Grail legend, is symbolized in the Waste Land theme: a landscape of spiritual death, a world waiting, waiting—"Waiting for Godot!"—for the Desired Knight, who would restore its integrity to life and let stream again from infinite depths the lost, forgotten, living waters of the inexhaustible source.

The rise and fall of civilizations in the long, broad course of history can be seen to have been largely a function of the integrity and cogency of their supporting canons of myth; for not authority but aspiration is the motivater, builder, and transformer of civilization. A mythological canon is an organization of symbols, ineffable in import, by which the energies of aspiration are evoked and gathered toward a focus. The message leaps from heart to heart by way of the brain, and where the brain is unpersuaded the message cannot pass. The life then is untouched. For those in whom a local mythology still works, there is an experience both of accord with the social order, and of harmony with the universe. For those, however, in whom the authorized signs no longer work—or, if working, produce deviant effects—there follows inevitably a sense both of dissociation from the local social nexus and of quest, within and without, for life, which the brain will take to be for "meaning." Coerced to the social pattern, the individual can only harden to some figure of living death; and if any considerable number of

the members of a civilization are in this predicament, a point of
no return will have been passed.

Jean Jacques Rousseau's *Discours sur les arts et sciences,* published 1749, marked an epoch of this kind. Society was the corruption of man; "back to nature" was the call: back to the state of
the "noble savage" as the model of "natural man"—which the savage, with his tribal imprints, was no more, of course, than was Rousseau himself. For as faith in Scripture waned at the climax of the
Middle Ages, so at the climax of the Age of Enlightenment, did
faith in reason: and today, two centuries later, we have T. S.
Eliot's *The Waste Land* (published 1922, with footnotes): [1] *

> Here is no water but only rock
> Rock and no water and the sandy road
> The road winding above among the mountains
> Which are mountains of rock without water
> If there were water we should stop and drink
> Amongst the rock one cannot stop or think
> Sweat is dry and feet are in the sand
> If there were only water amongst the rock
> Dead mountain mouth of carious teeth that cannot spit
> Here one can neither stand nor lie nor sit
> There is not even silence in the mountains
> But dry sterile thunder without rain
> There is not even solitude in the mountains
> But red sullen faces sneer and snarl
> From doors of mudcracked houses

The fourth and most vital, most critical function of a mythology, then, is to foster the centering and unfolding of the individual
in integrity, in accord with *d*) himself (the microcosm), *c*) his culture (the mesocosm), *b*) the universe (the macrocosm), and *a*)
that awesome ultimate mystery which is both beyond and within
himself and all things:

> Wherefrom words turn back,
> Together with the mind, not having attained.[2]

Creative mythology, in Shakespeare's sense, of the mirror "to show
virtue her own feature, scorn her own image, and the very age and
body of the time his form and pressure," [3] springs not, like theol-

---

* Numbered reference notes begin on page 679.

Figure 1. Orpheus the Savior; Domitilla Catacomb,
Rome, 3rd century A.D.

ogy, from the dicta of authority, but from the insights, sentiments,
thought, and vision of an adequate individual, loyal to his own experience of value. Thus it corrects the authority holding to the
shells of forms produced and left behind by lives once lived. Renewing the act of experience itself, it restores to existence the quality of adventure, at once shattering and reintegrating the fixed, already known, in the sacrificial creative fire of the becoming thing
that is no thing at all but life, not as it *will be* or as it *should be,* as

it *was* or as it *never will be,* but as it *is,* in depth, in process, *here and now,* inside and out.

Figure 1 shows an early Christian painting from the ceiling of the Domitilla Catacomb in Rome, third century A.D. In the central panel, where a symbol of Christ might have been expected, the legendary founder of the Orphic mysteries appears, the pagan poet Orpheus, quelling animals of the wilderness with the magic of his lyre and song. In four of the eight surrounding panels, Old and New Testament scenes can be identified: David with his sling (upper left), Daniel in the lion's den (lower right), Moses drawing water from the rock, Jesus resurrecting Lazarus. Alternating with these are four animal scenes, two exhibiting, among trees, the usual pagan sacrificial beast, the bull; two, the Old Testament ram. Toward the corners are eight sacrificed rams' heads (Christ, the sacrificed "Lamb of God"), each giving rise to a vegetal spray (the New Life), while in each of the corners Noah's dove bears the olive branch telling of the reappearance of land after the Flood. The syncretism is deliberate, uniting themes of the two traditions of which Christianity was the product, and thus pointing through and beyond all three traditions to the source, the source-experience of a truth, a mystery, out of which their differing symbologies arose. Isaiah's prophecy of the Messianic age, when "the wolf shall dwell with the lamb, and the leopard lie down with the kid" (Isaiah 11:6), and the Hellenistic mystery theme of the realization of harmony in the individual soul, are recognized as variants of one and the same idea, of which Christ was conceived to be the fulfillment: the underlying theme in all being of the life transcending death.

We may term such an underlying theme the "archetypal, natural, or elementary idea," and its culturally conditioned inflections "social, historical, or ethnic ideas." [4] The focus of creative thought is always on the former, which then is rendered, necessarily, in the language of the time. The priestly, orthodox mind, on the other hand, is always and everywhere focused upon the local, culturally conditioned rendition.

Figure 2, from a set of pavement tiles from the ruins of Chertsey Abbey (Surrey), c. 1270 A.D., shows the youthful Tristan harping for his Uncle Mark. No one regarding this in its time would have failed to associate the scene with the young David harping for

Figure 2. Tristan Harping for King Mark

King Saul. "Saul," we are told, "was afraid of David because the Lord was with him but had departed from Saul" (I Samuel 18:12). By analogy, as Saul's kingdom went to David, so Mark's queen to his nephew. The ruler according to the order merely of the day (the ethnic sphere), out of touch with the enduring principles of his own nature and the world (the elementary), is displaced in his sovereignty (in his kingdom / in his queen) by the revealer of the concealed harmony of all things.

II. Where Words Turn Back

Figures 3 and 4 show the interior and the central figure of an Orphic sacramental bowl of gold, dating approximately from the period of the Domitilla ceiling. It was unearthed in the year 1837,

Figure 3. Orphic Sacramental Bowl; Rumania, 3rd or 4th century A.D.

Figure 4. Central Figure of the Orphic Bowl

near the town of Pietroasa, in the area of Buzau, Rumania, together with twenty-one other precious pieces; and since one of the
large armbands of the hoard was inscribed with runic characters, a
number of the scholars first examining the treasure suggested that
it might have been buried by the Visigothic king Athanaric when,
in the year 381 A.D., he fled for protection from the Huns to Byzantium. During the First World War the whole collection was
taken to Moscow to be kept from the Germans, where it was
melted down by the Russian Communists for its gold; so that nothing can now be done to establish its origin or precise date. However, during the winter of 1867–1868 it had been on loan for six
months in England, where it was photographed and galvano-
plastically reproduced.

The figures are crude, according to classical standards, and may represent the work of a provincial craftsman. Rumania, it may be recalled, was for centuries occupied by the Roman border legions defending the Empire from the Goths and other Germanic tribes, with, however, increasingly numerous German auxiliaries and even officers of rank. Throughout the area and on into Central Europe shrines of the Mithra mysteries have been discovered in abundance; [5] and as this bowl reveals, the Orphic cult also was known. Moreover, since it was from this province that a continuous stream of Hellenistic influences flowed northward, throughout the Roman period, to the Celtic as well as to the German tribes, and from which, furthermore, in the Middle Ages, a powerful heresy of Gnostic-Manichaean cast flooded westward into southern France (precisely in the century of the rise of the love cult of the troubadours and legends of the Grail), the figures on this Orphic bowl bear especial relevance not only to the religious but also to the literary and artistic traditions of the West. Indeed, already at its first station, showing Orpheus as a fisherman, a host of associations springs to mind.

 1. *Orpheus the Fisherman* is here shown with his fishing pole, the line wound around it, a mesh bag in his elevated hand, and a fish lying at his feet. One thinks of Christ's words to his fishermen apostles, Peter, James, and John: "I shall make you fishers of men"; [6] but also of the Fisher King of the legends of the Grail: and with this latter comes the idea that the central figure of the vessel, seated with a chalice in her hands, may be a prototype of the Grail Maiden in the castle to which the questing knight was directed by the Fisher King. A very early model of the mystic fisherman appears on Babylonian seals in a figure known as the "Warden of the Fish" (Figure 5),[7] while the most significant current reference is on the ring worn by the Pope, the "Fisherman's Ring," which is engraved with a representation of the miraculous draft of fishes that afforded the occasion for Christ's words.

 For the fishing image was appropriate in a special way to the early Christian community, where in baptism the neophyte was drawn from the water like a fish. Figure 6 is an early Christian earthenware lamp showing such a neophyte clothed as a fish, to be born, as it were, a second time, in accordance with Christ's teaching that "unless one is born of water and the Spirit, he cannot enter the kingdom of God." [8] The Hindu legend

Figure 5. The Warden of the Fish; Babylonia, 2nd millennium B.C.

of the birth of the great sage Vyāsa from a fish-born virgin nicknamed Fishy Smell (whose proper name, however, was Truth) may recur to mind at this point;[9] and one thinks also of Jonah reborn from the whale—of whom it is said in the Midrash that in the belly of the fish he typifies the soul of man swallowed by Sheol.[10] Christ himself is symbolized by a fish, and on Friday a fish meal is consumed.

Evidently we have here broken into a context of considerable antiquity, referring to a plunge into abyssal waters, to emerge as though reborn; of which spiritual experience perhaps the best-known ancient legend is of the plunge of the Babylonian King Gilgamesh to pluck the plant of immortality from the floor of the cosmic ocean.[11] Figure 7, from an Assyrian cylinder seal of c. 700 B.C. (the period to which the prophet Jonah is commonly assigned), shows a worshiper with outstretched arms arriving at this immortal plant on the floor of the abyss, where it is found guarded by two fish-men.[12] The god Assur of Nineveh (to which city Jonah was traveling when he was swallowed by the whale) floats wonderfully above the scene. But Gilgamesh,

Figure 6. Christian Neophyte in Fish Garb; early Christian lamp

it is recalled, lost the plant after he had come ashore. It was eaten by a serpent; so that, whereas serpents now can shed their skins to be reborn, man is mortal and must die. As in the words of the God of Eden to Adam after the fall, so here: man is dust and unto dust he shall return.[13]

Such, however, was not the idea of the Greeks of the mystery tradition, who told of God (Zeus) creating man, not from lifeless dust, but from the ashes of the Titans who had consumed his son, Dionysus.[14] Man is in part, therefore, of immortal Dionysian substance, though in part, also, of Titanic, mortal; and in the mystery initiations he is made cognizant of the portion

Figure 7. Fish Gods at the Tree of Life; Assyria, c. 700 B.C.

within him of the ever-living god who died to himself to live manifold in us all.

In the sixteen figures of the once golden sacramental bowl of Figure 3, the sequence of initiatory stages of that inward search is represented. Having been drawn to the mystic gate by Orpheus's fishing line, the neophyte seen at Station 3 commences the night-sea journey, sunwise round the bowl. Like the setting sun, he descends in symbolic death into the earth and at Station 14 reappears to a new day, qualified to experience the "meeting of the eyes" of Hyperborean Apollo at Station 16.

2. *A naked figure in attendance at the entrance,* bearing on his head a sacred chest (*cista mystica*), and with an ear of grain in hand,* offers the contents of the chest to:

3. *A kilted male, the neophyte.* He holds a torch in his left hand, symbol of the goddess Persephone of the netherworld, to whose mystery (the truth about death) he is to be introduced.

_____

* In classical reliefs such figures, bearing sacred chests, are frequently smaller than those around them. We are not to interpret this figure as a child.

Yet his eyes still hold to those of his mystagogue, the Fisher. The raven of death perches on his shoulder,* while with his right hand he lifts from the mystic chest an immense pine cone symbolic of the life-renewing principle of the seed, which the death and decay of its carrier, the cone, are to set free. For, as in the words of Paul, so here: "what you sow does not come to life unless it dies. . . . What is sown is perishable, what is raised is imperishable." [15]

4. *A draped female figure, porteress of the sanctuary,* bearing in her left hand a bowl and in her right a pail, conducts the neophyte within. For as the female power resident in the earth releases the seed-life from the cone, so will the mystery of the goddesses release the mind of this neophyte from its commitment to what Paul (using the language of the mysteries) termed "this body of death." [16] On the early Mesopotamian cylinder seals, porters at the entrances to shrines carried pails, like that of this figure, of the mead of immortal life. [17] The fish-men of Figure 7 also carry such pails. The neophyte is being guided to the sanctuary of the two goddesses:

5. *Demeter enthroned,* in her right hand holding the flowering scepter of terrestrial life, and in her left the open shears by which life's thread is cut; and

6. *Her daughter, Persephone,* as mistress of the netherworld, enthroned beyond the reign of Demeter's scepter and shears. The torch, her emblem, symbolic of the light of the netherworld, is a regenerative spiritual flame.

The neophyte now has learned the meaning of the raven that perched on his shoulder when he entered the mystic way and of the torch and cone that were placed in his hands. We see him next, therefore, as:

7. *The initiated mystes,* standing with his left hand reverently to his breast, holding a chaplet in his right.

8. *Tyche, the goddess of Fortune,* touches the initiate with a wand that elevates his spirit above mortality, holding on her left arm a cornucopia, symbolic of the abundance she bestows.

We are now just halfway around, at the point, as it were, of midnight, where:

---

* Compare the symbolism of the initiations of Mithra. *Occidental Mythology,* p. 225, and the Irish goddess of death, pp. 304–305.

9. *Agathodaemon, the god of Good Fortune,* holding in his right hand, turned downward, the poppy stalk of the sleep of death, and in his left, pointing upward, a large ear of the grain of life, is to introduce the initiate to:

10. *The Lord of the Abyss.* With his hammer in his right hand and on his left arm a cornucopia, this dark and terrible god is enthroned upon a scaly sea-beast, a sort of modified crocodile. His hammer is the instrument of Plato's Divine Artificer, by whom the temporal world is fashioned on the model of eternal forms. But the same hammer is symbolic, also, of the lightning bolt of illumination, by which ignorance concerning this same temporal world is destroyed. Compare the symbolism of the god Zervan Akarana in the initiations of Mithraism;[18] also, the Indian divinities who both create and destroy the world illusion.

The old Sumerian serpent-god Ningizzida is the ultimate archetype of this lord of the watery abyss from which mortal life arises and back to which it returns.[19] Among the Celts, the underworld god Sucellos represented this same dark power;[20] in the classical mythologies he was Hades-Pluto-Poseidon; and in Christian mythology he is, exactly, the Devil.

Figure 8 will show, however, that there is an important difference between the Devil's place in the Christian universe and Ningizzida's or Hades-Pluto-Poseidon's in the pagan. The illustration is from an illuminated twelfth-century handbook of everything worth knowing, called *The Little Garden of Delights* (*Hortulus deliciarum*), compiled by the Abbess Herrad von Landsberg (d. 1195) in her convent in Hohenburg, Alsace, to assist her nuns in their teaching tasks.[21] Its figure is based on a metaphor coined by Gregory the Great, as Pope (590–604), to illustrate the doctrine of salvation that was most favored throughout Christendom for the first twelve hundred years. Known as "the ransom theory of salvation," it is based on the words of the Savior himself, as reported in the Mark and Matthew Gospels: "For the Son of Man came not to be served but to serve, and to give his life as a ransom for many."[22] The second-century Greek bishop of Lyons, Irenaeus (130?–202?) and the Alexandrian theologian Origen (185?–254?) seem to have been among the first to read a theological thesis into this metaphor, which then was accepted even by Augustine (354?–430).[23]

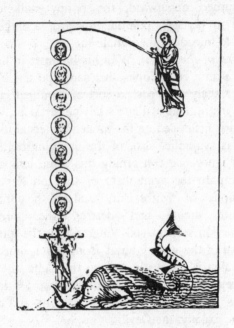

Figure 8. God the Father, Fishing; c. 1180 A.D.

What we see is God the Father in heaven, fishing for the Devil in the form of the monster Leviathan, using for his line the kings of the royal house of David, with the Cross for his hook, and his Son affixed there as bait. For the Devil, through his ruse in the Garden of Eden, had acquired a legal right to man's soul, which God, as a just God, had to honor. However, since the right had been acquired by a ruse, God might justly terminate it by a ruse. He offered as ransom for the soul of man the soul of his own divine Son, knowing, as the Devil did not, that since the Second Person of the Trinity is beyond the touch of corruption, Satan would not be able to lay hold. Christ's humanity was thus the bait at which the Devil snapped like a fish, only to be caught on the hook of the Cross, from which the Son of God, through his resurrection, escaped.

It is little wonder that Saint Anselm (1033–1109) should have thought a new interpretation of the Incarnation desirable.

In his celebrated tract, *Cur deus homo?* ("Why did God become Man?"), which marks an epoch in Christian theology, he proposed that the claimant in the case was not the Devil but the Father, whose command had been disobeyed; and the claim, moreover, was against man. What was required, consequently, was not a ransom rendered to Satan, but atonement rendered to God, in the sense of satisfaction for an injury sustained. The injury, however, had been against the infinite majesty of God, whereas man is finite. Hence, no act or offering by any number of men could ever have cleared the account. And God's whole program for creation was meanwhile being frustrated by this legal impasse. *Cur deus homo?* The answer is suggested in two stages:

1. In Christ, true God and true Man, the species Man had a perfect representative, who at the same time was infinite and consequently adequate to make satisfaction for an infinite offense.

2. Merely living perfectly, as Christ did, however, would not have sufficed to compensate for man's fault, since living perfectly is no more than man's duty and produces no merit to spare. "If man has had a sweet experience in sinning, is it not fitting," Anselm argued "that he should have a hard experience in satisfying? . . . But there is nothing harder or more difficult that a man can suffer *for the honor of God* spontaneously, and not of debt, than death, *and in no way can man give himself more fully to God than when he surrenders himself to death for His honor.*"

Christ's dying was necessary because he willed it; but at the same time was not necessary, because God did not demand it. The Son's death, therefore, was voluntary, and the Father had to recompense him. However, since nothing could be given to the Son, who already had all, Christ passed the benefit earned to mankind; so that God now rejects no one who comes to him in the name of Christ—on condition that he come as Holy Scripture directs.[24]

It is difficult to believe today that anyone could ever have taken seriously either of these attributions of legal mathematics to a God supposed to be transcendent. They are known, respectively, as the "ransom" and the "penal" doctrines of redemption. A third suggestion was offered by Saint Anselm's brilliant contemporary, the lover of Heloise, Abelard (1079–1142), but rejected by the churchmen as unacceptable; namely, that Christ's self-offering was addressed neither to the Devil nor to God, but to man, to prove God's love, to waken love in response, and thus to win man back to God. All that was asked for redemption was a response of love in return, and the power of love then itself would operate to effect the reunion that is mankind's proper end.[25] However, as Professor Etienne Gilson of the Pontifical Institute of Mediaeval Studies, Toronto, points out in his *History of Christian Philosophy in the Middle Ages*,[26] there is throughout Abelard's thinking an indifference to the distinction between natural and supernatural grace, the merely natural virtues of the unbaptized and the priceless gift of God in the sacraments. Abelard was one of those who believed that the unbaptized might be saved; which implied that the sacraments were unnecessary, and natural grace sufficient for salvation. What about the pagan philosophers on whose writings Christian thought itself was grounded? he asked. And what of the prophets and all those who have lived by their words?

"Abélard," writes Professor Gilson, "is here freely indulging in his general tendency to look upon grace as a blossoming of nature, or inversely . . . to conceive Christianity as the total verity which includes all others within it. . . . Christian revelation was never, for him, an impassable barrier dividing the chosen from the condemned and truth from error. . . . One cannot read Abélard without thinking of those educated Christians of the sixteenth century, Erasmus for example, to whom the distance from ancient wisdom to the wisdom of the Gospel will seem so short." [27]

The biblical representation of God as somebody "up there" (rather like the god Assur in Figure 7), not the substance, but the maker of this universe, from which he is distinct, had deprived matter of a divine dimension and reduced it to mere dust. Hence, whatever the pagan world had regarded as evidence of a divine presence in nature, the Church interpreted as of the Devil. Poseidon's trident (which in India is Shiva's) became thus the Devil's popular pitchfork; Poseidon's great bull, sire of the Minotaur (in India, Shiva's bull Nandi) gave the Devil his cloven foot and horns; the very name, Hades, of the god of the underworld became a designation of that inferno which Heinrich Zimmer once described wittily as "Mr. Lucifer's luxury skyscraper apartment-hotel for lifers, plunged top downward in the abyss"; and the creative life-fire of the netherworld, displayed in Persephone's torch, became a reeking furnace of sin.

The simplest way, therefore, to suggest in Christian terms the sense of the Orphic initiation at Station 10 might be to say that here the Devil himself is taken to be the immanent presence of God. However, whereas in the Christian view the Devil, like God, is an independent personage "out there," what the mystes learned at this Orphic station was that the god of the creative sea, the moving *tremendum* of this world, was an aspect of himself, to be experienced within—exactly as in the Indian Tantric tradition, where all the gods and demons, heavens and hells, are discovered and displayed within us—and this ground of being, which is both giver and taker of the forms that appear and disappear in space and time, though dark indeed, cannot be termed evil unless the world itself is to be so termed. The lesson of Hades-Pluto, Poseidon-Neptune-Shiva, is not that our mortal part is ignoble but that within it—or at one with it—is that immortal Person whom the Christians split into God and Devil and think of as "out there."

And so we move to the next station, of:

11. The Mystes, fully initiate. He bears a bowl, as though endowed with a new capacity. His hair is long, and his right hand, on his belly, suggests a woman who has conceived. Yet the chest is clearly male. Thus an androgyne theme is suggested, symbolic of a spiritual experience uniting the opposed ways of knowledge of the male and female; and fused with this idea is that of a new life conceived within. Above the crown of the head, symbolic center of realization, is a pair of spiritual wings. The initiate is now fit to return to the world of normal day. There follow:

12 and 13. Two young men regarding each other. As to the identity of these, there has been considerable academic disagreement. The French archaeologist Charles de Linas believed they represented Castor and Triptolemus.* However, to this the late Professor Hans Leisegang of the University of Jena objected reasonably that in that case Castor would have been separated from his inseparable twin, Pollux.[28] The pair, he suggested, might rather represent two mystes bearing scourges (for in certain mys-

_____
* For Triptolemus, see *Occidental Mythology*, Figure 14.

teries scourging played a part). However, to me this seems unlikely, since if scourging were to have been noticed, we should
have had it earlier in the series, on the way down, not the way
up.

For myself, I cannot see why the two should not be identified as
(12) the immortal twin Pollux and (13) the mortal Castor. For
the mystes, departing from the sanctuary of his experience of an-
drogyny (beyond the opposites not only of femininity and mascu-
linity but also of life and death, time and eternity), must resume
his place in the light world without forfeiting the wisdom gained;
and exactly proper to the sense of such a passage is the dual symbol
of the twins, immortal and mortal, respectively, Pollux and Castor. The legs of the two are straight, the only such in the composition; they touch at the feet, and the two are looking at each
other. Both were horsemen; hence the whips. Furthermore, on
the shoulder of the second the raven again perches that has
not been seen since the passage of the dual-goddess threshold, opposite, where the passage was *into* the realm of knowledge
beyond death, from which we are now emerging. The raven on
the right shoulder and torch in the left hand here correspond
to the raven and torch at Station 3, to which the whip in the right
hand now adds a token of the initiate's acquired knowledge
of his immortal part as a member of the symbolic twin-horsemen
syzygy. And I am encouraged in this interpretation by the view
of Professor Alexander Odobesco of the University of Bucha-
rest, the first scholar to examine this bowl, who identified
these two as the Alci, the German counterparts of Castor and
Pollux; for since both the Greeks and the Romans strove generally to recognize analogies between their own and alien
gods, it is altogether likely that, whether in the hands of
some German chieftain or in those of a Roman officer, the
twin horsemen would have been recognized as readily by their
German as by their Greek or Roman names.

The last three figures of the series return us to the light world:

14. The returning mystes, clothed exactly as at Station 3, now
bears in his left hand a basket of abundance and in his right a sage's
staff. He is conducted by:

15. A draped female figure with pail and bowl, counterpart of the figure at Station 4. Vines and fruit are at her right and left: fulfillment has been attained. She leads the initiate toward the god to whose vision he has at last arrived, on whom his eyes are fixed:

16. *Hyperborean Apollo,* the mythopoetic personification of the *transcendent* aspect of the Being of beings, as the Lord of the Abyss at Station 10 represented the *immanent* aspect of the same. He sits gracefully with lyre in hand and a griffin reposing at his feet: the very god addressed as the Lord of both Day and Night in the Orphic hymns:

> For thou surveyest this boundless ether all,
> And every part of this terrestrial ball
> Abundant, blessed; and thy piercing sight
> Extends beneath the gloomy, silent night;
> The world's wide bounds, all-flourishing, are thine,
> Thyself of all the source and end divine.[29]

Having circled the full round, the mystes now is in possession of the knowledge of that mover beyond the motions of the universe, from whose substance the sun derives its light and the dark its light of another kind. The lyre suggests the Pythagorean "harmony of the spheres," and the griffin at the god's feet, combining the forms of the solar bird and solar beast, eagle and lion, is the counterplayer to the symbolic animal-fish, the crocodile of night. Moreover, the knowledge through these two gods of the mystery beyond duality is the only knowledge adequate to the sense of:

The Great Goddess (Figure 4). By whatever name, she it is within whose universal womb both day and night are enclosed, the worlds both of life, symbolized by Demeter (5), and of death, life's daughter, Persephone (6). The grapevine entwining her throne is matched by that of the outer margin of the bowl; and she holds in both hands a large chalice of the ambrosia of this vine of the universe: the blood of her ever-dying, ever-living slain and resurrected son, Dionysus-Bacchus-Zagreus—or, in the older, Sumero-Babylonian myths, Dumuzi-absu, Tammuz—the "child of the abyss," whose blood, in this chalice to be drunk, is the pagan prototype of the wine of the sacrifice of the Mass, which is transubstantiated by the words of consecration into the blood of the Son of the Virgin.

Figure 9. Orpheos Bakkikos Crucified; c. 300 A.D.

Figure 9 is from a cyclinder seal of 300 A.D.[30] The date is of the general period of both the Domitilla ceiling and the Pietroasa bowl, and as Dr. Eisler, in whose *Orpheus the Fisher* the figure was first published, suggests, it must have belonged to "an Orphic initiate who had turned Christian without giving up completely his old religious beliefs." [31] The inscription is unmistakable: *Orpheos Bakkikos*. The seven stars represent the Pleiades, known to antiquity as the Lyre of Orpheus, and the cross suggests, besides the Christian Cross, the chief stars ⁂ of the constellation Orion, known also as that of Dionysus. The crescent is of the ever-waning and -waxing moon, which is three days dark as Christ was three days in the tomb.

Interpreted in Orphic terms, such a crucified redeemer, in his human character as *Orpheos* (True Man), would have represented precisely that "ultimate surrender of self, in love 'to the uttermost,' " which both the Bishop John A. T. Robinson of Woolwich and the late Dr. Paul Tillich have proposed as the mystic lesson of Christ's crucifixion.[32] But at the same time, in his divine character as *Bakkikos* (True God), the image must have symbolized that coming to us of the personified transcendent "ground of Being," through whose willing self-dismemberment as the substance (not the creator merely) of this world, that which *there* is one becomes these many *here*—"like a felled tree, cut up into logs" (*Rg Veda* I: 32).

It is, however, by way of the Goddess Mother of the universe, whose womb is the apriority of space and time, that the one, there, becomes these many, here. It is she who is symbolized by the Cross; as, for instance, in the astrological-astronomical sign signifying earth ⊕. It is into and through her that the god-substance pours into this field of space and time in a continuous act of world-creative self-giving; and through her, in return—her guidance and her teaching—that these many are led back, beyond her reign, to the light beyond dark from which all come.

Returning, therefore, to Figure 3, we now remark that in the inner circle surrounding her seat there is a reclining human being, apparently a shepherd, by whose legs there lies (or runs) a dog, before whose nose we see a recumbent (or fleeing) donkey colt. The reclining figure, in contrast to those upright in the outer series, suggests sleep, the spiritual state of the uninitiated natural man, who sees without understanding; whereas the knowledge gained by the mystes in the outer circle is of those eternal forms, or Platonic ideas, that are the structuring principles of all things, inherent in all, and to be recognized by the wakened mind.

In this inner circle, at the opposite point to the dreamer, two asses—recumbent and standing—browsing on a plant are themselves about to be consumed by a leopard and a lion. The lesson is the same as that of "The Self-Consuming Power" represented on the old Sumerian seal of c. 3500 B.C. reproduced in a preceding volume of this work, *Oriental Mythology,* Figure 2. The ever-dying, ever-living god, who is the reality of all beings, our eyes see as the consumer and consumed. However, the initiate, who has penetrated the veil of nature, knows that the one life immortal lives in all: namely, the god whose symbol is the vine here growing from the feet of the World Goddess and encircling the composition. Of old he was known as Dionysus-Orpheus-Bacchus; earlier still, Dumuzi-Tammuz; but we hear of him, also, in the words of that one, about to be crucified, who at the banquet of his Last Supper spoke (as quoted in the John Gospel) to his zodiac of apostles: "I am the vine, you are the branches. He who abides in me, and I in him, he it is that bears much fruit, for apart from me you can do nothing." [33]

In a word, then, the same symbols, words, and mysteries were associated with the ancient pagan vine as with the Christian gospel of the new. For the myth of the dead and resurrected god whose being is the life-pulse of the universe had been known to the pagans millenniums before the crucifixion of Christ. In the earliest agricultural communities the image had been rendered in rites of actual human sacrifice, the aim of which had been magical, to make the crops grow. In the later Hellenistic cosmopolitan cities, on the other hand, where a concern for the inner man removed from the stabilizing influences of nature and the soil was more acutely felt than the earlier, for the crops, the ancient myth became interiorized, translated from the syntax of earth-magic to spiritual initiation; from the work of enlivening fields to that of livening the soul.[34] And in this it became joined with Greek philosophy, science, and the arts, to uncover the ways to a knowledge of those intelligible forms that are the "models" (in Platonic terms; or, as Aristotle taught, the "entelechies") of all things: the immanent "thoughts" of that First Mover, called God, who is both separate, "by Himself," and yet identical with the nature of the universe as the order and potential of its parts.[35]

And if we now ask why, in the Domitilla ceiling, it is Orpheus, not Jesus, who holds the central, solar place, the answer, I think, is clear. The Jewish idea of the Messianic age is of a time to come. The earliest Christian notion was that the time had already come. By the end of the second century, however, it was obvious that the end of time had not come. The necessity arose, therefore, to reinterpret the prophecy as referring either to an end postponed to some unspecified future date, or to an end not of the world, as in Hebrew thought, but of delusion, as in Greek. The former was the

orthodox Christian solution, the latter the Orphic-Gnostic, casting
Christ in the role of the mystagogue supreme. And accordingly, as
we have seen, the symbol of Christ as the crucified God-Man had
then to be read not in the way of either Saint Gregory's "ransom"
or Saint Anselm's "penal" doctrine, but of Abelard's, Paul Tillich's, and Bishop Robinson's, of "mutual approach"; namely,
read from there to here, as of the god, the Being of beings, willingly come to the Cross to be dismembered, broken into mortal
fragments, "like a felled tree cut into logs"; and simultaneously
read the other way—here to there—as of the self-noughting
individual abandoning attachment to his mortal portion to rejoin the archetype, thus achieving atonement, not in the
penal sense of a legal "reparation for injury," but in the earlier,
mystical meaning of the term: at-one-ment.

III. The Trackless Way

"What greater misfortune for a state can be conceived than that
honorable men should be sent like criminals into exile, because
they hold diverse opinions which they cannot disguise? What, say
I, can be more hurtful than that men who have committed no
crime or wickedness should, simply because they are enlightened,
be treated as enemies and put to death, and that the scaffold, the
terror of evil-doers, should become the stage where the highest examples of tolerance and virtue are displayed to the people with all
the marks of ignominy that authority can devise?" [36]

These are the words of Benedict Spinoza (1632–1677), a Jew
in refuge from his own synagogue, whom the German romantic
Novalis (1772–1801) was to celebrate as *ein gottbetrunkener
Mensch*, "a God-intoxicated man." In a period of appalling religious massacres, writing, as he declared, "to show that not only is
perfect liberty to philosophize compatible with devout piety and
with the peace of the state, but that to take away such liberty is to
destroy the public peace and even piety itself," Spinoza represents
as courageously and splendidly as anyone in the European record
those principles of enlightenment and integrity that he stood for.
His own writing was denounced in his time as an instrument
"forged in hell by a renegade Jew and the Devil." In a world of
madmen flinging the Bible at one another—French Calvinists,
German Lutherans, Spanish and Portuguese inquisitors, Dutch

rabbis, and miscellaneous others—Spinoza had the spirit to point out (what should have been obvious to all) that the Bible "is in parts imperfect, corrupt, erroneous, and inconsistent with itself," whereas the real "word of God" is not something written in a book but "inscribed on the heart and mind of man."

The world, men had begun to learn, was not a nest of revolving crystalline spheres with the earth at its precious center and man thereon as the chief concern of the moon, the sun, the planets, the fixed stars, and, beyond all these, a King of Kings on a throne of jeweled gold, surrounded by nine rapturous choirs of many-winged luminous seraphim, cherubim, thrones, dominions, virtues, powers, principalities, archangels, and angels. Nor is there anywhere toward the core of this earth a pit of flaming souls, screaming, tortured by devils who are fallen angels all. There never was a Garden of Eden, where the first human pair ate forbidden fruit, seduced by a serpent who could talk, and so brought death into the world; for there had been death here for millenniums before the species Man evolved: the deaths of dinosaurs and of trilobites, of birds, fish, and mammals, and even of creatures that were almost men. Nor could there ever have occurred that universal Flood to float the toy menagerie of Noah's Ark to a summit of the Elburz range, whence the animals, then, would have studiously crawled, hopped, swum, or galloped to their continents: kangaroos and duck-billed platypuses to far-away Australia, llamas to Peru, guinea pigs to Brazil, polar bears to the farthest north, and ostriches to the south. . . . It is hard to believe today that for doubting such extravagances a philosopher was actually burned alive in the Campo dei Fiori in Rome in the Year of Our Lord 1600; or that as late as the year of Darwin's *Origin of Species*, 1859, men of authority still could quote this kind of lore against a work of science.

"The fool says in his heart, 'There is no God' " (Psalms 14:1; 53:1). There is, however, another type of fool, more dangerous and sure of himself, who says in his heart and proclaims to all the world, "There is no God but mine."

Giordano Bruno (1548–1600), the indiscreet philosopher who was burned in the Campo dei Fiori—where his statue by the sculptor Ferrari now stands—was incinerated not because he had said in his heart, "There is no God"; for in fact he had taught and written that there is a God, who is both transcendent and immanent. As transcendent, according to Bruno's understanding, God is outside of and prior to the universe and unknowable by reason; but as immanent, he is the very spirit and nature of the universe, the image in which it is created, and knowable thus by sense, by reason, and by love, in gradual approximation. God is in all and in every part, and in him all opposites, including good and evil, coincide. Bruno was burned alive for teaching the truth that the mathematician Copernicus had demonstrated five years before his birth; namely, that the earth revolves around the sun, not the sun around the earth, which, as all Christian authorities, Catholic and Protestant, as well as Bruno himself, knew, was a doctrine contrary to the Bible. *The actual point in question, throughout the centuries of Christian persecution, has never been faith in God, but faith in the Bible as the word of God, and in the Church* (*this Church or that*) *as the interpreter of that word.* Bruno held that the Old Testament tales teach neither science, history, nor metaphysics, but morality of a kind; and he placed them on a level with Greek mythology, which teaches morality of another kind. He also expressed unorthodox views on the delicate topics of the Virgin Birth of Jesus and the mystery of transubstantiation. The function of a church, he declared, is the same as that of a state; it is social and practical: the security of the community, the prosperity and well-doing of its members. Dissension and strife are dangerous to the state, hence the need of an authoritative doctrine and the enforcement of its acceptance and of outward conformity with it; but the Church has no right to go further, to interfere with the pursuit of knowledge, of truth, which is the object of philosophy or science.[37]

The altogether new thing in the world that was making all the trouble was the scientific method of research, which in that period of Galileo, Kepler, Descartes, Harvey, and Francis Bacon was advancing with enormous strides. All walls, all the limitations, all the certainties of the ages were in dissolution, tottering. There had never been anything like it. In fact this epoch, in which we are participating still, with continually opening vistas, can be compared in magnitude and promise only to that of the eighth to fourth millenniums B.C.: of the birth of civilization in the nuclear Near East, when the inventions of food production, grain agriculture and stockbreeding, released mankind from the primitive condition of foraging and so made possible an establishment of soundly grounded communities: first villages, then towns, then cities, kingdoms, and empires. Leo Frobenius in his *Monumenta Terrarum* [38] wrote of the age that opened at that distant date as the Monumental Age—now closing—and of the age now before us, dawning, as the Global.

"We are concerned no longer with cultural inflections," he declared, "but with a passage from one culture stage to another. In all previous ages, only restricted portions of the surface of the earth were known. Men looked out from the narrowest, upon a somewhat larger neighborhood, and beyond that, a great unknown. They were all, so to say, insular: bound in. Whereas our view is confined no longer to a spot of space on the surface of this earth. It surveys the whole of the planet. And this fact, this lack of horizon, is something new."

Now it has been—as I have already said—chiefly to the scientific method of research that this release of mankind has been due, and along with mankind as a whole, every developed individual has been freed from the once protective but now dissolved horizons of the local land, local moral code, local modes of group thought and sentiment, local heritages of signs. But this scientific method was itself a product of the minds of already self-reliant individuals courageous enough to be free. Moreover, not only in the sciences but in every department of life the will and courage to credit one's own senses and to honor one's own decisions, to name one's own virtues and to claim one's own vision of truth, have been the generative forces of the new age, the enzymes of the fermentation of the wine of this great modern harvest—which is a wine, however, that can be safely drunk only by those with a courage of their own.

For this age is one of unbridled, headlong adventure, not only for those addressed to the outward world, but also for those turned inward, released from the guidance of tradition. Its motto is perhaps most aptly formulated in Albert Einstein's statement of the principle of relativity, set down in the year 1905: "Nature is such that it is impossible to determine absolute motion by any experiment whatsoever." [39] In these fifteen words we find summarized the results of a decade of experiments in various quarters of Europe, to establish some absolute standard of rest, some static envi-

ronment of ether, as a fixed frame of reference against which the
movements of the stars and suns might be measured. None was
found. And this negative result only confirmed what Sir Isaac
Newton (1642–1727) had already suspected when he wrote in his
Principia:

> It is possible that in the remote regions of the fixed stars, or
> perhaps far beyond them, there may be some body absolutely at
> rest, but it is impossible to know from the positions of bodies to
> one another in our regions whether any one of these do not keep
> the same position to that remote body. It follows that absolute
> rest cannot be determined from the position of bodies in our
> region.[40]

It might be said, in fact, that the principle of relativity had been
defined already in mythopoetic, moral, and metaphysical terms in
that sentence from the twelfth-century hermetic *Book of the
Twenty-four Philosophers,* "God is an intelligible sphere, whose
center is everywhere and circumference nowhere," [41] which has
been quoted with relish through the centuries by a significant
number of influential European thinkers; among others, Alan of
Lille (1128–1202), Nicholas Cusanus (1401–1464), Rabelais
(1490?–1553), Giordano Bruno (1548–1600), Pascal (1623–
1662), and Voltaire (1694–1778).

In a sense, then, our recent mathematicians, physicists, and
astronomers have only validated for their own fields a general
principle long recognized in European thought and feeling. Whereas
formerly, in the old Sumerian world view, preserved in the Old
Testament, the notion of a stable cosmological order had prevailed
and was matched by the priestly concept of an established moral
order as well; we now find that, matching our recent cosmological
recognition of the relativity of all measures to the instrument
doing the measuring, there is a growing realization even in the
moral field that all judgments are (to use Nietzsche's words)
"human, all too human."

Oswald Spengler, in *The Decline of the West,* coined the term
"historical pseudomorphosis" to designate, as he explained, "those
cases in which an older alien culture lies so massively over a land
that a young culture, born in this land, cannot get its breath and
fails not only to achieve pure and specific expression forms, but
even to develop fully its own self-consciousness." [42] The figure

was adopted from the terminology of the science of mineralogy, where the word *pseudomorphosis,* "false formation," refers to the deceptive outer shape of a crystal that has solidified within a rock crevice or other mold incongruous to its inner structure. An important part of the Levantine (or, as Spengler termed it, Magian) culture developed in such a way under Greek and Roman pressures; but then suddenly, with Mohammed, it broke free to evolve in its own style the civilization of Islam; [43] and in like manner the North European culture developed throughout its Gothic period under an overlay of both classical Greco-Roman and Levantine biblical forms, in each of which there was the idea of a single law for mankind, from which notion we are only now beginning to break free.

The biblical law was supposed to be of a supernatural order, received by special revelation from a God set apart from nature, who demanded absolute submission of the individual will. But in the classical portion of our dual heritage, too, there is equally the concept of a single normative moral law; a natural law, this time, however, discoverable by reason. Yet if there is any one thing that our modern archives of anthropology, history, physiology, and psychology prove, it is that there is no single human norm.

The British anatomist Sir Arthur Keith testified to the psychosomatic determination of this relativism some thirty-odd years ago. "Within the brain," he wrote in a piece composed for what used to be called the General Reader, "there are some eighteen thousand million of microscopic living units or nerve cells. These units are grouped in myriads of battalions, and the battalions are linked together by a system of communication which in complexity has no parallel in any telephone network devised by man. Of the millions of nerve units in the brain not one is isolated. All are connected and take part in handling the ceaseless streams of messages which flow into the brain from eyes, ears, fingers, feet, limbs, and body." And then he moved to his conclusion:

If nature cannot reproduce the same simple pattern in any two fingers, how much more impossible is it for her to reproduce the same pattern in any two brains, the organization of which is so inconceivably complex! Every child is born with a certain balance of faculties, aptitudes, inclinations, and instinctive leanings. In no two is the balance alike, and each different brain has to deal with a different tide of experience. I marvel, then, not that one man should disagree with another concerning the ultimate realities of life, but that so many, in spite of the diversity of their inborn natures, should reach so large a measure of agreement.[44]

Thus, as in the world without, of Einstein, so in the world within, of Keith, there is no point of absolute rest, no Rock of Ages on which a man of God might stand assured or a Prometheus be impaled. But this too was only something that in the arts and philosophies of post-Gothic Europe had already been recognized; for instance, in metaphysical terms, in the writings of Arthur Schopenhauer (1788–1860). This melancholy genius—touched, like the Buddha, by the spectacle of the world's sorrow—was the first major philosopher of the West to recognize the relevance of Vedantic and Buddhistic thought to his own; yet in his doctrine of the metaphysical ground of the unique character of each and every human individual he stood worlds apart from the indifference of all Indian thought to individuation. The goal in India, whether in Hinduism, Buddhism, or Jainism, is to purge away individuality through insistence first upon the absolute laws of caste (*dharma*), and then upon the long-known, marked-out stages of the way (*mārga*) toward indifference to the winds of time (*nirvāṇa*). The Buddha himself only renewed the timeless teaching of the Buddhas, and all Buddhas, cleansed of individuality, look alike. For Schopenhauer, on the other hand (though indeed in the end he saw the denial of the will-to-life as the highest spiritual goal), not caste or a social order but intelligent, responsible autonomy in the realization of character and in sympathy and well-doing was the criterion of moral worth, having as general guide the formula: "Hurt none; but, as far as possible, benefit all." [45]

For in Schopenhauer's view, the species *Homo sapiens* represents the achievement of a stage in evolution beyond the meaning of the word "species" when applied to animals, since among men each individual is in himself, as it were, a species. "No animals," he states, "exhibit individuality to any such remarkable degree. The higher types, it is true, show traces; yet even there, it is the character of the species that predominates and there is little individuality of physiognomy. Moreover, the farther down we go, the more does every trace of individual character disappear in the

common character of the species, until, at last, only a general physiognomy remains." [46]

In the pictorial arts, Schopenhauer then observes, there is a distinction between the aims of those addressed to the beauty and
grace of a species and those concerned to render the character of
an individual. Animal sculpture and painting are of the former
type; portraiture in sculpture and painting, of the latter. A mid-
ground is to be recognized in the rendition of the nude; for here—
at least in the classical arts—the figure is regarded in terms of the
beauty of its species, not the character of the individual. Where the
individual appears, the figure is naked, not properly a "nude." [47]
However, the nakedness itself may be advanced to the status of
portraiture if the address is to the character of the subject; for, as
Schopenhauer sees, individuality extends to the entire embodiment.[48]

And so we now note that in classical art the culminating
achievement, the apogee, was the beautiful standing nude: a revelation physically of the ideal of the norm of the human species, in
accord with the quest of Greek philosophy for the moral and spiritual norm. Whereas, in contrast, at the apogee of Renaissance and
Baroque achievement the art of portraiture came to flower— in
the canvases, for instance, of Titian, Rembrandt, Dürer, and
Velázquez. Even the nudes in this period are portraits, and in the
large historical canvases, such as Velázquez's "Surrender of Breda"
(in the Prado), portraiture again prevails. The epochs of history
are read not as impersonal, anonymous effects of what are being
called today the "winds of change" (as though history moved of
itself), but as the accomplishments of specific individuals. And in
the little as well as in the great affairs of life the accent remains on
character—as in the paintings of Toulouse-Lautrec from the Mou-
lin Rouge.

The masters of these works, then, are the prophets of the present dawn of the new age of our species, identifying that aspect of
the wonder of the world most appropriate to our contemplation: a
pantheon not of beasts or of superhuman celestials, not even of
ideal human beings transfigured beyond themselves, but of actual
individuals beheld by the eye that penetrates to the presences actually there.

Let me quote again from the philosopher:

As the general human form corresponds to our general human will, so the individual bodily form to the individually inflected will of the personal character; hence, it is in every part characteristic and full of expression.[49]

The ultimate ground of the individual character, Schopenhauer states, in perfect accord with the finding of Sir Arthur Keith, lies beyond research, beyond analysis; it is in the body of the individual as it comes to birth. Hence, the circumstances of the environment in which the individual lives do not *determine* the character. They provide only the furtherances and hindrances of its temporal fulfillment, as do soil and rain the growth and flowering of seed. "The experiences and illuminations of childhood and early youth," he writes in a sentence anticipating much that has been clinically confirmed by others since, "become in later life the types, standards and patterns of all subsequent knowledge and experience, or as it were, the categories according to which all later things are classified—not always consciously, however. And so it is that in our childhood years the foundation is laid of our later view of the world, and therewith as well of its superficiality or depth: it will be in later years unfolded and fulfilled, not essentially changed." [50]

The inborn, or, as Schopenhauer terms it, *intelligible* character is unfolded only gradually and imperfectly through circumstance; and what comes to view in this way he calls the *empirical* (experienced or observed) character. Our neighbors, through observation of this empirical character, often become more aware than ourselves of the intelligible, innate personality that is secretly shaping our life. We have to learn through experience what we are, want, and can do, and "until then," declares Schopenhauer, "we are characterless, ignorant of ourselves, and have often to be thrown back onto our proper way by hard blows from without. When finally we shall have learned, however, we shall have gained what the world calls 'character'—which is to say, *earned* character. And this, in short, is neither more nor less than the fullest possible knowledge of our own individuality." [51]

A great portrait is, then, a revelation, through the "empirical," of the "intelligible" character of a being whose ground is beyond our comprehension. The work is an icon, so to say, of a spirituality true to this earth and to its life, where it is in the creatures of this world that the Delectable Mountains of our Pilgrim's Progress are discovered, and where the radiance of the City of God is recognized as Man. The arts of Shakespeare and Cervantes are revelations, texts and chapters, in this way, of the actual living mythology of our present developing humanity. And since the object of contemplation here is man—not man as species, or as representing some social class, typical situation, passion, or idea (as in Indian literature and art) [52]—but as that specific individual which he is, or was, and no other, it would appear that the pantheon, the gods, of this mythology must be its variously realized individuals, not as they may know or not know themselves, but as the canvas of art reveals them: each in himself (as in Schopenhauer's phrase) "the entire World-as-Will in his own way." The French sculptor Antoine Bourdelle (1861–1929) used to say to the pupils in his studio: *"L'art fait ressortir les grandes lignes de la nature."* James Joyce in *A Portrait of the Artist as a Young Man* writes of "the *whatness* of a thing" as that "supreme quality of beauty" which is recognized when "you see that it is that thing which it is and no other thing." [53] And we have also, again, Shakespeare's figure of "the mirror."

And just as in the past each civilization was the vehicle of its own mythology, developing in character as its myth became progressively interpreted, analyzed, and elucidated by its leading minds, so in this modern world—where the application of science to the fields of practical life has now dissolved all cultural horizons, so that no separate civilization can ever develop again—each individual is the center of a mythology of his own, of which his own intelligible character is the Incarnate God, so to say, whom his empirically questing consciousness is to find. The aphorism of Delphi, "Know thyself," is the motto. And not Rome, not Mecca, not Jerusalem, Sinai, or Benares, but each and every "thou" on earth is the center of this world, in the sense of that formula just quoted from the twelfth-century *Book of the Twenty-four Philosophers,* of God as "an intelligible sphere, whose center is everywhere."

In the marvelous thirteenth-century legend called *La Queste del Saint Graal,* it is told that when the knights of the Round Table set forth, each on his own steed, in quest of the Holy Grail, they departed separately from the castle of King Arthur. "And now each one," we are told, "went the way upon which he had decided, and they set out into the forest at one point and another, there where they saw it to be thickest" (*la ou il la voient plus espesse*); so that each, entering of his own volition, leaving behind the known good company and table of Arthur's towered court, would experience the unknown pathless forest in his own heroic way.[54]

Today the walls and towers of the culture-world that then were in the building are dissolving; and whereas heroes then could set forth of their own will from the known to the unknown, we today, willy-nilly, *must* enter the forest *la ou nos la voions plus espesse:* and, like it or not, the pathless way is the only way now before us.

But of course, on the other hand, for those who can still contrive to live within the fold of a traditional mythology of some kind, protection is still afforded against the dangers of an individual life; and for many the possibility of adhering in this way to established formulas is a birthright they rightly cherish, since it will contribute meaning and nobility to their unadventured lives, from birth to marriage and its duties and, with the gradual failure of powers, a peaceful passage of the last gate. For, as the psalmist sings, "Steadfast love surrounds him who trusts in the Lord" (Psalm 32:10); and to those for whom such protection seems a prospect worthy of all sacrifice, an orthodox mythology will afford both the patterns and the sentiments of a lifetime of good repute.

However, by those to whom such living would be not life, but anticipated death, the circumvallating mountains that to others appear to be of stone are recognized as of the mist of dream, and precisely between their God and Devil, heaven and hell, white and black, the man of heart walks through. Out beyond those walls, in the uncharted forest night, where the terrible wind of God blows directly on the questing undefended soul, tangled ways may lead to madness. They may also lead, however, as one of the greatest poets of the Middle Ages tells, to "all those things that go to make heaven and earth."

IV. Mountain Immortals

"I have undertaken a labor," wrote the poet Gottfried von Strassburg, whose *Tristan,* composed about the year 1210, became the source and model of Wagner's mighty work, "a labor out of love for the world and to comfort noble hearts: those that I hold dear, and the world to which my heart goes out. Not the common world do I mean of those who (as I have heard) cannot bear grief, and desire but to bathe in bliss. (May God then let them dwell in bliss!) Their world and manner of life my tale does not regard: its life and mine lie apart. Another world do I hold in mind, which bears together in one heart its bitter sweet, its dear grief, its heart's delight and its pain of longing, dear life and sorrowful death, its dear death and sorrowful life. In this world let me have my world, to be damned with it, or to be saved." [55]

James Joyce, in *A Portrait of the Artist as a Young Man,* sounded the same bold theme in the words of his twentieth-century Irish Catholic hero, Stephen Dedalus: "I do not fear to be alone. And I am not afraid to make a mistake, even a great mistake, a lifelong mistake, and perhaps as long as eternity too." [56]

It is amazing, really, to think that in our present world with all its sciences and machines, megalopolitan populations, penetrations of space and time, night life and revolutions, so different (it would seem) from the God-filled world of the Middle Ages, young people should still exist among us who are facing in their minds, seriously, the same adventure as thirteenth-century Gottfried: challenging hell. If one could think of the Western World for a moment in terms not of time but of space; not as changing in time, but as remaining in space, with the men of its various eras, each in his own environment, still there as contemporaries discoursing, one could perhaps pass from one to another in a trackless magical forest, or as in a garden of winding ways and little bridges. The utilization by Wagner of both the *Tristan* of Gottfried and the majestic *Parzival* of Gottfried's leading contemporary, Wolfram von Eschenbach, would suggest perhaps a trail; so also the line, very strong indeed, from Gottfried to James Joyce. Then again there is the coincidence (this time in two contemporaries) of James Joyce (1882–1941) and Thomas Mann (1875–1955), proceeding each along his own path, ignoring the other's work, yet marking, in measured pace, the same stages, date by date; as follows:

First, in the *Buddenbrooks* (1902) and "Tonio Kröger" (1903) of Thomas Mann, *Stephen Hero* (1903) and *Portrait of the Artist as a Young Man* (1916) of James Joyce: accounts of the separation of a youth from the social nexus of his birth to strive to realize a personal destiny, the one moving from the Protestant side, the other from the Roman Catholic, yet each resolving his issue through a moment of inspired insight (the inspiring object, in each case, being the figure of a girl), and the definition, then, of an aesthetic theory and decision.

Next, in *Ulysses* (1922) and *The Magic Mountain* (1924), two accounts of quests through all the mixed conditions of a modern civilization for an informing principle substantial to existence, the episodes being rendered in the manner of the naturalistic novel, yet in both works opening backward to reveal mythological analogies: in Joyce's case, largely by way of Homer, Yeats, Blake, Vico, Dante, and the Roman Catholic Mass, with many echoes more; and in Mann's, by way of Goethe's *Faust*, Schopenhauer, Nietzsche, the Venus Mountain of Wagner, and hermetic alchemical lore.

Then, in *Finnegans Wake* (1939) and the tetralogy of *Joseph and His Brothers* (1933–1943), both novelists dropped completely into the well and seas of myth, so that, whereas in the earlier great novels the mythological themes had resounded as memories and echoes, here mythology itself became the text, rendering visions of the mystery of life as different from each other as the brawl at an Irish wake and a conducted visit to a museum, yet, for all that, of essentially the same stuff. And, as in the Domitilla Catacomb the composed syncretic imagery broke the hold upon the mind of the ethnic orders, opening back, beyond, and within, to their source in elementary ideas, so in these really mighty mythic novels (the greatest, without question, yet produced in our twentieth century), the learnedly structured syncrasies conjure, as it were from the infinite resources of the source abyss of all history itself, intimations in unending abundance of the wonder of one's own life as Man.

In the earlier volumes of this survey the mythologies treated are largely of the common world of those who, in the poet Gottfried's words, "can bear no grief and desire but to bathe in bliss": the mythologies, that is to say, of the received religions, great and small. In the present work, on the other hand, I accept the idea proposed by Schopenhauer and confirmed by Sir Arthur Keith, the intention being to regard each of the creative masters of this dawning day and civilization of the individual as absolutely singular, each a species unique in himself. He will have arrived in this world in one place or another, at one time or another, to unfold, in the conditions of his time and place, the autonomy of his nature. And in youth, though early imprinted with one authorized brand or another of the Western religious heritage, in one or another of its known historic states of disintegration, he will have conceived the idea of thinking for himself, peering through his own eyes, heeding the compass of his own heart. Hence the works of the really great of this new age do not and cannot combine in a unified tradition to which followers then can adhere, but are individual and various. They are the works of individuals and, as such, will stand as models for other individuals: not coercive, but evocative. Wagner following Gottfried, Wagner following Wolfram, Wagner following Schopenhauer, follows, finally, no one but himself. Scholars, of course, have nevertheless traced, described, and taught school around traditions; and for scholars as a race such work affords a career. However, it has nothing to do with creative life and less than nothing with what I am here calling creative myth, which springs from the unpredictable, unprecedented experience-in-illumination of an object by a subject, and the labor, then, of achieving communication of the effect. It is in this second, altogether secondary, technical phase of creative art, *communication*, that the general treasury, the dictionary so to say, of the world's infinitely rich heritage of symbols, images, myth motives, and hero deeds, may be called upon—either consciously, as by Joyce and Mann, or unconsciously, as in dream—to render the message. Or on the other hand, local, current, utterly novel themes and images may be used—as again in Joyce and Mann.

But I shall not anticipate here the adventures in these pages beyond pointing out that we shall dwell first upon the mystery of that moment of aesthetic arrest when the possibility of a life in adventure is opened to the mind; review, next, a catalogue of the vehicles of communication available to the Western artist for the celebration of his rapture; and follow, finally, the courses of fulfillment of a certain number of masters, dealing all with that same rich continuum of themes from our deepest, darkest past that has come to boil most recently in the vessel of *Finnegans Wake*. Further, for the giving of heart to those who have entered into other works with hope, only to find in the end dust and ashes, the assurance can also be given that, according to the evidence of these pages, it appears that the soul's release from the matrix of inherited social bondages can actually be attained and, in fact, has already been attained many times: specifically, by those giants of creative thought who, though few in the world on any given day, are in the long course of the centuries of mankind as numerous as mountains on the whole earth, and are, in fact, the great company from whose grace the rest of men derive whatever spiritual strength or virtue we may claim.

Societies throughout history have mistrusted and suppressed these towering spirits. Even the noble city of Athens condemned Socrates to death, and Aristotle, in the end, had to flee its indignation. As Nietzsche could say from experience: "The aim of institutions—whether scientific, artistic, political, or religious—never is to produce and foster exceptional examples; institutions are concerned, rather, for the usual, the normal, the mediocre." And yet, as Nietzsche goes on to affirm, "The goal of mankind is not to be seen in the realization of some terminal state of perfection, but is present in its noblest exemplars."

That the Great Man should be able to appear and dwell among you again, again, and again [he wrote], *that* is the sense of all your efforts here on earth. That there should ever and again be men among you able to elevate you to *your* heights: that is the prize for which you strive. For it is only through the occasional coming to light of such human beings that your own existence can be justified. . . . And if you are not yourself a great exception, well then be a small one at least! and so you will foster on earth that holy fire from which genius may arise.[57]

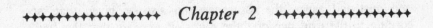

THE WORLD TRANSFORMED

I. The Way of Noble Love

A man a woman, a woman a man,
Tristan Isolt, Isolt Tristan.

"As the glow of love's inward fire increases," the poet Gottfried wrote, "so the frenzy of the lover's suit. But this pain is so full of love, this anguish so enheartening, that no noble heart would dispense with it, once having been so heartened." [1]

Of all the modes of experience by which the individual might be carried away from the safety of well-trodden grounds to the danger of the unknown, the mode of feeling, the erotic, was the first to waken Gothic man from his childhood slumber in authority; and, as Gottfried's language tells, there were those, whom he calls noble, whose lives received from this spiritual fire the same nourishment as the lover of God received from the bread and wine of the sacrament. The poet intentionally echoes, in celebration of his legend, the monkish raptures of Saint Bernard of Clairvaux's famous series of sermons on the Song of Songs:

"I know it," he writes, "as surely as my death, since I have learned from the agony itself: the noble lover loves love stories. Anyone yearning for such a story, then, need fare no farther than here: for I shall story him well of noble lovers who of pure love gave proof enough: he in love, she in love. . . ."

We read their life, we read their death,
And to us it is sweet as bread.
Their life, their death, are our bread.

42

> So lives their life, so lives their death,
> So live they still and yet are dead
> And their death is the bread of the living.[2]

Like the other legends of Arthurian romance, that of Tristan and Isolt had been distilled from a compound of themes derived from pagan Celtic myth, transformed and retold as of Christian knighthood. Hence the force of its allure to the still half-pagan ears that opened to its song in the age of the Crusades, and its appeal to romantic hearts ever since. For, as in all great pagan mythologies, in the Celtic there is throughout an essential reliance on nature; whereas, according to every churchly doctrine, nature had been so corrupted by the Fall of Adam and Eve that there was no virtue in it whatsoever. The Celtic hero, as though moved by an infallible *natural* grace, follows without fear the urges of his heart. And though these may promise only sorrow and pain, danger and disaster—to Christians, even the ultimate disaster of hell for all eternity—when followed for themselves alone, without thought or care for consequence, they can be felt to communicate to a life, if not the radiance of eternal life, at least integrity and truth.

Saint Augustine had established in the early fifth century, against the Irish heretic Pelagius, the doctrine that salvation from the general corruption of the Fall can be attained only through a *super*natural grace that is rendered not by nature but by God, through Jesus crucified, and dispensed only by the clergy of his incorruptible Church, through its seven sacraments. *Extra ecclesiam nulla salus.* And yet within the fold of the Gothic Church of the twelfth and thirteenth centuries the corruption at least of the natural (if not also the supernatural) character of its incorruptible clergy was the outstanding scandal of the age.[3] Arthurian romance suggested to those with ears to hear that there was in corruptible nature a virtue, after all, without which life lacked incorruptible nobility; and it delivered this interesting message, which had been known for eons to the greater part of mankind, simply by clothing Celtic gods and heroes, heroines and goddesses, in the guise of Christian knights and damosels. Hence the challenge in these romances to the Church.

And to make his own recognition of this really serious challenge quite clear, the poet Gottfried described the love grotto in which his lovers took refuge from Isolt's sacramented marriage to King

Mark as a chapel in the heart of nature, with the bed of their consummation of love in the place proper to an altar.

The grotto had been hewn in heathen times into the wild mountain [Gottfried told], when giants ruled, before the coming of Corinaeus.* And there it had been their wont to hide when they wished privacy to make love. Indeed, wherever such a grotto was found, it was closed with a door of bronze and inscribed to Love with this name: *La fossiure a la gent amant,* which is to say, "The Grotto for People in Love."

The name well suited the place. For as its legend lets us know, the grotto was circular, wide, high, and with upright walls, snow-white, smooth and plain. Above, the vault was finely joined, and on the keystone there was a crown, embellished beautifully by the goldsmith's art with an incrustation of gems. The pavement below was of a smooth, shining and rich marble, green as grass. In the center stood a bed, handsomely and cleanly hewn of crystal, high and wide, well raised from the ground, and engraved round about with letters which—according to the legend—proclaimed its dedication to the goddess Love. Aloft, in the ceiling of the grotto, three little windows had been cut, through which light fell here and there. And at the place of entrance and departure was a door of bronze.[4]

Gottfried explains in detail the allegory of these forms.

The circular interior is Simplicity in Love; for Simplicity best beseems Love, which cannot abide any corners: in Love, Malice and Cunning are the corners. The great width is the Power of Love. It is boundless. Height signifies Aspiration, reaching toward the clouds: nothing is too much for it when it strives to rise to where Golden Virtues bind the vault together at the key. . . .

The wall of the grotto is white, smooth, and upright: the character of Integrity. Its luster, uniformly white, must never be colored over; nor should any sort of Suspicion be able to find there bump or dent. The marble floor is Constancy—in its greenness and its hardness, which color and surface are most fitting; for Constancy is ever as freshly green as grass and as level and clear as glass. The bed of crystalline noble Love, at the

* Corinaeus was supposed to have been the eponymous hero of Cornwall. He was so designated in Geoffrey of Monmouth's *History of the Kings of Britain* 1.12, whose source for the name was Virgil's *Aeneid* 9.571 and 12.298.

center, was rightly consecrated to her name, and right well had
the craftsman who carved its crystal recognized her due: for
Love indeed must be crystalline, transparent, and translucent.

Within the cave, across the door of bronze, there ran two
bars; and there was a latch, too, within, let ingeniously through
the wall—exactly where Tristan had found it. A little lever controlled it, which ran in from the outside and moved it this way
and that. Moreover, there was neither lock nor key; and I shall
tell you why.

There was no lock because any device that might be attached
to a door (I mean on the outside) to cause it either to open or
to lock, would signify Treachery. Because, if anyone enters
Love's door when he has not been admitted from within, this
cannot be accounted Love: it is either Deceit or Force. Love's
door is there—Love's door of bronze—to prevent anyone from
entering unless it be by Love: and it is of bronze so that no device, whether of violence or of strength, cunning or mastery,
treachery or lies, should enable one to undo it. Furthermore, the
two bars within, the two seals of Love, are turned toward each
other from each side. One is of cedar, the other ivory. And
now you must learn their meaning:

The cedar bar signifies the Understanding and Reasoning of
Love; the ivory, its Modesty and Purity. And with these two
seals, these two chaste bars, the dwelling of Love is guarded:
Treachery and Violence are locked out.

The little secret lever that was let in to the latch from outside was a rod of tin, and the latch—as it should be—was of
gold. The latch and the lever, this and that: neither could have
been better chosen for qualities. For tin is Gentle Striving in relation to a secret hope, while gold is Success. Thus tin and gold
are appropriate. Everybody can direct his own striving according to his will: narrowly, broadly, briefly or at length, liberally
or strictly, that way or this, this way or that, with little effort—
as with tin; and there is little harm in that. But if he then, with
proper gentleness, can give thought to the nature of Love, his
lever of tin, this humble thing, will carry him forward to golden
success and on to dear adventure.

Now those little windows above, neatly, skillfully, hewn into
the cave right through the rock, admitted the radiance of the
sun. The first is Gentleness, the next Humility, the last Breeding;
and through all three the sweet light smiled of that blessed radi-

ance, Honor, which is of all lights the very best to illuminate our grotto of earthly adventure.

Then finally, it has meaning, as well, that the grotto should lie thus alone in a savage waste. The interpretation must be that Love and her occasions are not to be found abroad in the streets, nor in any open field. She is hidden away in the wild. And the way to her resort is toilsome and austere. Mountains lie all about, with many difficult turns leading here and there. The trails run up and down; we are martyred with obstructing rocks. No matter how well we keep the path, if we miss one single step, we shall never know safe return. But whoever has the good fortune to penetrate that wilderness, for his labors will gain a beatific reward. For he shall find there his heart's delight. The wilderness abounds in whatsoever the ear desires to hear, whatsoever would please the eye; so that no one could possibly wish to be anywhere else.—And this I well know; for I have been there. . . . The little sun-giving windows often have sent their rays into my heart. I have known that grotto since my eleventh year, yet never have I been to Cornwall.[5]

What food sustains the lovers sequestered in that cave? "Obsessed with curiosity and wonder," the poet Gottfried answers, "enough people have puzzled themselves with the question of how that couple, Isolt and Tristan, fed themselves in the Waste Land. I shall now tell and set that curiosity at rest.

"They looked upon each other and nourished themselves with that. The fruit that their eyes bore was the sustenance of both. Nothing but love and their state of mind did they consume. . . . And what better food could they have had, either for spirit or for body? Man was there with Woman, Woman was there with Man. What more could they have wished? They had what they were meant to have and had reached the goal of desire. . . .[6]

"Love's service (*minne*) is without eyes, and love (*liebe*) without fear, when it is sincere."[7]

II. The Devil's Door

"The twelfth and thirteenth centuries, studied in the pure light of political economy, are insane," wrote Henry Adams in his deceptively playful, profoundly serious interpretation of the great high peak of communal creative life in the cathedral-building age, *Mont-Saint-Michel and Chartres:*[8]

"According to statistics, in the single century between 1170 and 1270, the French built eighty cathedrals and nearly five hundred churches of the cathedral class, which would have cost, according to an estimate made in 1840, more than five thousand millions to replace. Five thousand million francs is a thousand million dollars,* and this covered only the great churches of a single century. The same scale of expenditure had been going on since the year 1000, and almost every parish in France had rebuilt its church in stone; to this day France is strewn with the ruins of this architecture, and yet the still preserved churches of the eleventh and twelfth centuries, among the churches that belong to the Romanesque and Transition period, are numbered by hundreds until they reach well into the thousands. The share of this capital which was —if one may use a commerical figure—invested in the Virgin cannot be fixed, any more than the total sum given to religious objects between 1000 and 1300; but in a spiritual and artistic sense, it was almost the whole, and expressed an intensity of conviction never again reached by any passion, whether of religion, of loyalty, of patriotism, or of wealth; perhaps never even paralleled by any single economic effort, except in war." [9]

But we have found—have we not?—that a number of other initial developments in the unfolding of great civilizations also were marked with signs of insanity: the prodigious labors on the pyramids, for instance,[10] and the courtly astronomical mime of the Royal Tombs of Ur.[11] Indeed, as there appeared, and as here we recognize again, civilization, seriously regarded, cannot be described in economic terms. In their peak periods civilizations are mythologically inspired, like youth. Early arts are not, like late, the merely secondary concerns of a people devoted first to economics, politics, comfort, and then, in their leisure time, to aesthetic enjoyment. On the contrary, economics, politics, and even war (crusade) are, in such periods, but functions of a motivating dream of which the arts too are an irrepressible expression. The formative force of a traditional civilization is a kind of compulsion neurosis shared by all members of the implicated domain, and the leading *practical* function of religious (i.e. mythological) education, therefore, is to infect the young with the madness of their eld-

---

* Adams was writing in 1904. Today's equivalent would be something more like ten thousand million dollars.

ers—or, in sociological terms, to communicate to its individuals the "system of sentiments" on which the group depends for survival as a unit. Let me cite to this point, once again, the whole paragraph already quoted in *Primitive Mythology* from the distinguished British anthropologist of Trinity College, Cambridge, the late Professor A. R. Radcliffe-Brown:

> A society depends for its existence on the presence in the minds of its members of a certain system of sentiments by which the conduct of the individual is regulated in conformity with the needs of the society. Every feature of the social system itself and every event or object that in any way affects the well-being or the cohesion of the society becomes an object of this system of sentiments. *In human society the sentiments in question are not innate but are developed in the individual by the action of the society upon him* [italics mine]. The ceremonial customs of a society are a means by which the sentiments in question are given collective expression on appropriate occasions. The ceremonial (i.e. collective) expression of any sentiment serves both to maintain it at the requisite degree of intensity in the mind of the individual and to transmit it from one generation to another. Without such expression the sentiments involved could not exist.[12]

In the great creative period of the cathedrals and crusades the leading muse of the civilization, as Adams correctly saw, was the Virgin Mother Mary, whom Dante, one century later, was to eulogize in the celebrated prayer that marks the culmination of his spiritual adventure through Hell, Purgatory, and the spheres of Paradise, to the beatific vison of the Trinity in the midst of the celestial rose:

> Virgin Mother, daughter of thine own Son, humble and exalted more than any creature, fixed term of the eternal counsel, thou art she who didst so ennoble human nature that its own Maker disdained not to become its creature. Within thy womb was rekindled the Love through whose warmth this flower [the Celestial Rose] has thus blossomed in the eternal peace. Here [in Paradise] thou art to us the noonday torch of charity, and below, among mortals, thou art the living torch of hope. Lady, thou art so great, and so availest, that whoso would have grace, and has not recourse to thee, would have his desire fly without

wings. Thy benignity not only succors him who asks, but often-
times freely foreruns the asking. In thee mercy, in thee pity, in
thee magnificence, in thee whatever goodness there is in any
creature, are united. . . .[13]

As Oswald Spengler has properly noticed, however, the world
of purity, light and utter beauty of soul of the Virgin Mother
Mary—whose coronation in the heavens was one of the earliest
motives of Gothic art, and who is simultaneously both a light-
figure, in white, blue, and gold, surrounded by heavenly hosts, and
an earthly mother bending over her newborn babe, standing at the
foot of his Cross, and holding the corpse of her tortured, murdered
son in resignation on her knees—would have been unimaginable
without the counter-idea, inseparable from it, of Hell, "an idea,"
Spengler writes,

> that constitutes one of the maxima of the Gothic, one of its un-
> fathomable creations—one that the present day forgets and *de-
> liberately* forgets. While she there sits enthroned, smiling in
> her beauty and tenderness, there lies in the background an-
> other world that throughout nature and throughout mankind
> weaves and breeds ill, pierces, destroys, and seduces—the realm,
> namely, of the Devil. . . .
>
> It is not possible to exaggerate either the grandeur of this
> forceful, insistent picture or the depth of sincerity with which it
> was believed in. The Mary-myths and the Devil-myth formed
> themselves side by side, neither possible without the other. Dis-
> belief in either of them was deadly sin. There was a Mary-cult
> of prayer, and a Devil-cult of spells and exorcisms. Man walked
> continuously on the thin crust of a bottomless pit. . . .
>
> For the Devil gained possession of human souls and seduced
> them into heresy, lechery, and black arts. It was war that was
> waged against him on earth, and waged with fire and sword
> upon those who had given themselves up to him. It is easy
> enough for us today to think ourselves out of such notions, but
> if we eliminate this appalling reality from the Gothic, all that re-
> mains is mere romanticism. It was not only the love-glowing
> hymns to Mary, but the cries of countless pyres as well that rose
> up to heaven. Hard by the Cathedral were the gallows and the
> wheel. Every man lived in those days in the consciousness of an
> immense danger, and it was hell, not the hangman, that he
> feared. Unnumbered thousands of witches genuinely imagined

themselves to be so; they denounced themselves, prayed for absolution, and in pure love of truth confessed their night rides and bargains with the Evil One. Inquisitors, in tears and compassion for the fallen wretches, doomed them to the rack in order to save their souls. That is the Gothic myth, out of which came the cathedral, the crusader, the deep and spiritual painting, the mysticism. In its shadow flowered that profound Gothic blissfulness of which today we cannot even form an idea.[14]

Nor did the Devil and his army of night-spirits, werewolves, and witches disappear from the European scene with the waning of the Middle Ages; with the Puritans he was transported to Plymouth Rock and New England and with Cortez went to Mexico to link arms with the powers of the Aztec underworld, Mictlan; for there too the cosmic nightmare was known: there were nine hells and thirteen heavens; however, until the Christian religion arrived, the idea of an *eternal* hell had never been conceived. In the ninth or final Aztec hell, which the voyaging soul would reach after a tortured journey of four years, it either found eternal rest or forever disappeared.

James Joyce, in *A Portrait of the Artist as a Young Man,* has provided an unforgettable reproduction of the standard Jesuit hell sermon, delivered to Catholic schoolboys to this day by retreat masters, to furnish their dreams with nightmare stuff and keep their feet on the straight and narrow path. The scene is the chapel of an Irish Catholic school. The priest is lecturing his young charges quietly and gently, with genuine solicitude:

"Now let us try for a moment to realise, as far as we can, the nature of that abode of the damned which the justice of an offended God has called into existence for the eternal punishment of sinners. Hell is a strait and dark and foulsmelling prison, an abode of demons and lost souls, filled with fire and smoke. The straitness of this prison house is expressly designed by God to punish those who refused to be bound by His laws. In earthly prisons the poor captive has at least some liberty of movement, were it only within the four walls of his cell or in the gloomy yard of his prison. Not so in hell. There, by reason of the great number of the damned, the prisoners are heaped together in their awful prison, the walls of which are said to be four thousand miles thick: and the damned are so utterly bound and helpless that, as a blessed saint, saint Anselm, writes in his

book on similitudes, they are not even able to remove from the
eye a worm that gnaws it.

"They lie in exterior darkness. For, remember, the fire of hell
gives forth no light. As, at the command of God, the fire of the
Babylonian furnace lost its heat but not its light, so, at the command of God, the fire of hell, while retaining the intensity of its
heat, burns eternally in darkness. It is a neverending storm of
darkness, dark flames and dark smoke of burning brimstone,
amid which the bodies are heaped one upon another without
even a glimpse of air. Of all the plagues with which the land of
the Pharaohs was smitten one plague alone, that of darkness,
was called horrible. What name, then, shall we give to the darkness of hell which is to last not for three days alone but for all
eternity?

"The horror of this strait and dark prison is increased by its
awful stench. All the filth of the world, all the offal and scum of
the world, we are told, shall run there as to a vast reeking sewer
when the terrible conflagration of the last day has purged the
world. The brimstone, too, which burns there in such prodigious
quantity fills all hell with its intolerable stench; and the bodies
of the damned themselves exhale such a pestilential odor that,
as saint Bonaventure says, one of them alone would suffice to
infect the whole world. The very air of this world, that pure element, becomes foul and unbearable when it has been long enclosed. Consider then what must be the foulness of the air of
hell. Imagine some foul and putrid corpse that has lain rotting
and decomposing in the grave, a jelly-like mass of liquid corruption. Imagine such a corpse a prey to flames, devoured by
the fire of burning brimstone and giving off dense choking fumes
of nauseous loathsome decomposition. And then imagine this
sickening stench, multiplied a millionfold and a millionfold
again from the millions of fetid carcasses massed together in the
reeking darkness, a huge and rotting human fungus. Imagine all
this, and you will have some idea of the horror of the stench of
hell.

"But this stench is not, horrible though it is, the greatest physical torment to which the damned are subjected. The torment of
fire is the greatest torment to which the tyrant has ever subjected
his fellowcreatures. Place your finger for a moment in the flame
of a candle and you will feel the pain of fire. But our earthly fire
was created by God for the benefit of man, to maintain in him
the spark of life and to help him in the useful arts, whereas the

fire of hell is of another quality and was created by God to torture and punish the unrepentant sinner. Our earthly fire also consumes more or less rapidly according as the object which it attacks is more or less combustible, so that human ingenuity has even succeeded in inventing chemical preparations to check or frustrate its action. But the sulphurous brimstone which burns in hell is a substance which is especially designed to burn for ever and for ever with unspeakable fury. Moreover, our earthly fire destroys at the same time as it burns, so that the more intense it is the shorter is its duration; but the fire of hell has this property, that it preserves that which it burns, and, though it rages with incredible intensity, it rages for ever. . . ." [15]

And so on, for a terrible half-hour.

"Every sense of the flesh is tortured and every faculty of the soul therewith. . . . Consider finally that the torment of this infernal prison is increased by the company of the damned themselves. . . . The damned howl and scream at one another, their torture and rage intensified by the presence of beings tortured and raging like themselves. All sense of humanity is forgotten. . . . Last of all consider the frightful torment to those damned souls, tempters and tempted alike, of the company of the devils. These devils will afflict the damned in two ways, by their presence and by their reproaches. We can have no idea of how horrible these devils are. Saint Catherine of Siena once saw a devil and she has written that, rather than look again for one single instant on such a frightful monster, she would prefer to walk until the end of her life along a track of red coals. . . ."

The young hero of Joyce's novel heard with a knowledge of precocious sins of his own, already committed, and when the priest dismissed the sickened little flock with the wish—"O, my dear little brothers in Christ!"—that they might never hear in God's voice the awful sentence of rejection: *Depart from me, ye cursed, into everlasting fire which was prepared for the devil and his angels!*, the boy rose from his pew and came down the aisle of the chapel, "his legs shaking and the scalp of his head trembling as though it had been touched by ghostly fingers. . . . And at every step he feared that he had already died. . . . He was judged. . . . His brain began to glow." In the classrooom, he leaned back weakly at his desk. "He had not died. God had spared him still.

. . . There was still time. . . . O Mary, refuge of sinners, intercede for him! O Virgin Undefiled, save him from the gulf of death!" [16]

It is against the backdrop of such a nightmare as this, taken infinitely more seriously than the earth itself and the life to be lived on this earth (since the earth and life would pass, but this scene of hell's bedlam, never), that the loves of Isolt and Guinevere, and of the actual women of the age of the great cathedrals, must be understood. Marriage in the Middle Ages was an affair largely of convenience. Moreover, girls betrothed in childhood for social, economic, or political ends, were married very young, and often to much older men, who invariably took their property rights in the women they had married very seriously. They might be away for years on Crusade; the wife was to remain inviolate, and if for any reason the worm Suspicion happened to have entered to gnaw the husband's brain, his blacksmith might be summoned up to fit an iron girdle of chastity to the mortified young wife's pelvic basin. The Church sanctified these sordid property rights, furthermore, with all the weight of Hell, Heaven, eternity, and the coming of Christ in glory on the day of judgment—the day so beautifully pictured in the western rose window of Chartres: that "jeweled sunburst on the Virgin's breast," as Henry Adams called it, "with three large pendants beneath." So that, against all this, the wakening of a woman's heart to love was in the Middle Ages a grave and really terrible disaster, not only for herself, for whom torture and fire were in prospect, but also for her lover; and not only here on earth but also—and more horribly—in the world to come, forever. Hence, in a phrase coined by the early Church Father Tertullian, which long remained a favorite of the pulpits, woman—earthly, actual woman, that is—awakened to her nature, was *janua diaboli,* "the devil's door."

III. Heloise

Abelard was thirty-eight, Heloise eighteen, and the year 1118 A.D. "There was in Paris a young girl named Heloise, the niece of a canon, Fulbert," we read in the rueful autobiographical letter known as Abelard's *Historia calamitatum.*

I had hitherto lived continently, but now was casting my eyes about, and I saw that she possessed every attraction that lovers seek; nor did I regard my success as doubtful, when I considered my fame and my goodly person, and also her love of letters. Inflamed with love, I thought how I could best become intimate with her. It occurred to me to obtain lodgings with her uncle, on the plea that household cares distracted me from study. Friends quickly brought this about, the old man being miserly and yet desirous of instruction for his niece. He eagerly entrusted her to my tutorship, and begged me to give her all the time I could take from my lectures, authorizing me to see her at any hour of the day or night and punish her when necessary. I marveled with what simplicity he confided a tender lamb to a hungry wolf. . . . Well, what need to say more: we were united first by the one roof above us, and then by our hearts.

Now it may or may not be relevant that Abelard, like Tristan of the legend, was born in Celtic Brittany, where, in those years, that oft-told tale of illicit love was in the making which (in Gottfried's phrase) was "bread to all noble hearts." Abelard, like Tristan, was a harpist of renown: his songs composed to Heloise were sung throughout the young Latin Quarter. And, like Tristan, he was given the task of tutoring the young lady, who, like the maid Isolt, was comparable (in the words, again, of Gottfried) "only to the Sirens with their lodestone, who draw to themselves stray ships."

To the agitation of many a heart [wrote Gottfried of the maid Isolt] she sang at once openly and secretly, by the ways of both ear and eye. The melody sung openly, both abroad and with her tutor, was of her own sweet voice and the strings' soft sound that openly and clearly rode through the kingdom of the ears, down deep, into the heart. But the secret song was her marvelous beauty itself, which covertly and silently slipped through the windows of the eyes, and in many noble hearts spread a magic that immediately made thoughts captive and fettered them with yearning and yearning's stress.[17]

Love was in the air in that century of the troubadours, shaping lives no less than tales; but the lives, specifically and only, of those of noble heart, whose courage in their knowledge of love announced the great theme that was in time to become the characteristic signal of our culture: the courage, namely, to affirm against tradition whatever knowledge stands confirmed in one's own controlled experience. For the first of such creative knowledges in the destiny of the West was of the majesty of love, against the super-natural utilitarianism of the sacramental system of the Church. And the second was of reason. So it can be truly said that the first published manifesto of this new age of the world, the age of the self-reliant individual, appeared at the first dawn of the most cre-ative century of the Gothic Middle Ages, in the love and the noble love letters of the lady Heloise to Abelard. For when she dis-covered herself pregnant, her lover, in fear, spirited her off to his sister's place in Brittany; and when she had there given birth to their son—whom they christened Astralabius—Abelard, as the calamitous letter tells, proposed to her that they should marry.

However, as we read, returning to Abelard's words:

She strongly disapproved and urged two reasons against the marriage, to wit, the danger and the disgrace in which it would involve me.

She swore—and so it proved—that no satisfaction would ever appease her uncle. She asked how she was to have any glory through me when she should have made me inglorious, and should have humiliated both herself and me. What penalties would the world exact from her if she deprived it of such a lu-minary; what curses, what damage to the Church, what lamenta-tions of philosophers, would follow on this marriage! How inde-cent, how lamentable would it be for a man whom nature had made for all, to declare that he belonged to one woman, and subject himself to such shame!"

The letter, continuing, next recounts some of the arguments urged by Heloise in dissuasion.

From her soul [wrote Abelard to his reader], she detested this marriage, which would be so utterly ignominious for me, and a burden to me. She expatiated on the disgrace and inconvenience of matrimony for me and quoted the Apostle Paul exhorting men to shun it. If I would not take the apostle's advice or listen to what the saints had said regarding the matrimonial yoke, I should at least pay attention to the philosophers—to Theo-phrastus's words upon the intolerable evils of marriage, and to the refusal of Cicero to take a wife after he had divorced Teren-tia, when he said that he could not devote himself to a wife and philosophy at the same time. "Or," she continued, "laying aside the disaccord between study and a wife, consider what a mar-

ried man's establishment would be to you. What sweet accord
there would be between the schools and domestics, between
copyists and cradles, between books and distaffs, between pen
and spindle! Who, engaged in religious or philosophical meditations, could endure a baby's crying and the nurse's ditties stilling
it, and all the noise of servants? Could you put up with the dirty
ways of children? The rich can, you say, with their palaces and
apartments of all kinds; their wealth does not feel the expense or
the daily care and annoyance. But I say, the state of the rich is
not that of philosophers; nor have men entangled in riches and
affairs any time for the study of Scripture or philosophy. The
renowned philosophers of old, despising the world, fleeing rather
than relinquishing it, forbade themselves all pleasures, and reposed in the embraces of philosophy. . . . If laymen and Gentiles, bound by no profession of religion, lived thus, surely you,
a clerk and canon, should not prefer low pleasures to sacred
duties, nor let yourself be sucked down by this Charybdis and
smothered in filth inextricably. If you do not value the privilege
of a clerk, at least defend the dignity of a philosopher. If reverence for God be despised, still let love of decency temper im-
modesty. . . ."

Finally [Abelard continued to his friend] she said that it
would be dangerous for me to take her back to Paris; it was
more becoming to me, and sweeter to her, to be called my mistress, so that affection alone might keep me hers and not the
binding power of any matrimonial chain; and if we should be
separated for a time, our joys at meeting would be the dearer for
their rarity. When at last with all her persuasions and dissua-
sions she could not turn me from my folly, and could not bear
to offend me, with a burst of tears she ended in these words:
"One thing is left: in the ruin of us both the grief which follows
shall not be less than the love which went before."

"Nor did she here lack the spirit of prophecy," the poor man
added in comment; for the world knows what then occurred. Leaving their son in Brittany in the care of Abelard's sister, the couple
returned to Paris and were married in the presence of the canon
Fulbert, her uncle, who, however, still resenting the seduction, de-
flowering, and marriage of his niece, retaliated like a savage.

"Having bribed my servant," Abelard wrote, "they came upon
me by night, when I was sleeping, and took on me a vengeance as
cruel and irretrievable as it was vile and shameful." The canon

Fulbert and his footpads had turned Abelard into a eunuch—who, however, in the spirit of a true and penitent Christian, finally was able to reflect in his confessional letter, years later: "I thought of my ruined hopes and glory, and then saw that by God's just judgment I was punished where I had most sinned, and that Fulbert had justly avenged treachery with treachery."

That is the first part of this cruel story. The second carries us further; for Abelard, in his shame, entered the monastery of Saint Denis as a monk, and Heloise, in obedience to his wish, the convent of Argenteuil as a nun. Ten years of silence followed, whereafter, from the convent to the monastery came a letter with the following superscription:

> To her master, rather to a father, to her husband, rather to a brother, his maid or rather daughter, his wife or rather sister, to Abelard, Heloise. . . .

And therein the following, among much more of the kind, was to be read:

> Thou knowest, dearest—and who knows not?—how much I lost in thee, and that an infamous act of treachery robbed me of thee and of myself at once. . . . Love turned to madness and cut itself off from hope of that which alone it sought, when I obediently changed my garb and my heart too in order that I might prove thee sole owner of my body as well as of my spirit. God knows, I have ever sought in thee only thyself, desiring simply thee and not what was thine. I asked no matrimonial contract, I looked for no dowry; not my pleasure, not my will, but thine have I striven to fulfill. And if the name of wife seemed holier or more potent, the word mistress [amica] was always sweeter to me, or even—be not angry!—concubine or harlot; for the more I lowered myself before thee, the more I hoped to gain thy favor, and the less I should hurt the glory of thy renown.
>
> I call God to witness that if Augustus, the master of the world, would honor me with marriage and invest me with equal rule, it would still seem to me dearer and more honorable to be called thy strumpet than his empress. He who is rich and powerful is not the better man: that is a matter of fortune, this of merit. And she is venal who marries a rich man sooner than a poor man, and yearns for a husband's riches rather than himself.

Such a woman deserves pay and not affection. She is not seeking
the man but his goods, and would wish, if possible, to prostitute
herself to one still richer.

Thus the female of the species spoke, and one is reminded
strongly of those noble words of an Abyssinian woman that were
quoted in *Primitive Mythology:* "How can a man know what a
woman's life is . . ."; [18] so that once again, as so often in these
pages, the same age-long dialogue of the sexes is heard that was
represented first in the alternating early symbols of the female- and
the male-oriented mythological orders: first the little stone paleolithic Venus figurines of the earliest Aurignacian rock shelters,
which presently had to give way to the magically costumed dancing
males of the painted temple caves; next the numerous ceramic
female figurines that have been found wherever Neolithic man
tilled the soil, and then the sudden appearance of those thunder-
hurling male divinities of the great patriarchal Semitic and Aryan
warrior races. In the old Irish legends of the brazen Queen Meave,
disregarding scornfully the patriarchal claims on her of her kingly
warrior spouse, we have an early Celtic version of the challenge
from the "other side," delivered with a strong barbaric force; [19]
and now, elevated in Heloise to a plane of civilization already centuries in advance of the crudely patriarchal, ecclesiastically sacramentalized moral order of her day, the challenge is again flung
forth, and with equal, though more cautiously and much more gra-
ciously verbalized, scorn. From the opposite side, the nun, now the
abbess of her convent, reviews the young love scenes of the tender
lamb and middle-aged, ravenous wolf: "What queen did not envy
me my joys and couch?" she wrote to her shattered lover of yore.

There were in you two qualities by which you could draw the
soul of any woman, the gift of poetry and the gift of singing,
gifts which other philosophers had lacked. As a distraction from
labor, you composed love-songs both in meter and in rhyme,
which for their sweet sentiment and music have been sung and
resung and have kept your name in every mouth. Your sweet
melodies do not permit even the illiterate to forget you. Because
of these gifts women sighed for your love. And, as these songs
sang of our loves, they quickly spread my name in many lands,
and made me the envy of my sex. What excellence of mind or
body did not adorn your youth?"

That had been the lover then; whereas now, as she reminds him, during the ten years of their separation she has not received from that lover a single written line.

"Tell me," she wrote, "one thing," and here she drove her dart:

Why, after our conversion, commanded by thyself, did I drop into oblivion, to be no more refreshed by speech of thine or letter? Tell me, I say, if you can, or I will say what I feel and what everyone suspects: desire rather than friendship drew you to me, lust rather than love. So when desire ceased, whatever you were manifesting for its sake likewise vanished. This, beloved, is not so much my opinion as the opinion of all. Would it were only mine and that thy love might find defenders to argue away my pain. Would that I could invent some reason to excuse you and also cover my cheapness. Listen, I beg, to what I ask, and it will seem small and very easy to you. Since I am cheated of your presence, at least put vows in words, of which you have a store, and so keep before me the sweetness of thine image. . . . When little more than a girl I took the hard vows of a nun, not from piety but at your command. If I merit nothing from thee, how vain I deem my labor! I can expect no reward from God, as I have done nothing from love of Him. . . . God knows, at your command I would have followed or preceded you to fiery places. For my heart is not with me, but with thee.[20]

As Professor Henry Osborn Taylor, from whose translation I have taken my text, observes: "Remarks upon this letter would seem to profane a shrine. Had the man profaned that shrine?" [21]

Obviously, the man had; and the same man, now a eunuch monk, was about to do so again. For the shrine of the abbess Heloise was to a deity unrecognized by the offices of Abelard's theology: an actual experience, namely, of love, not for an abstraction but for a person; a flame of love in which lust and religion are equally consumed, so that, in fact, Abelard was her god. In her own words—and they may yet be crowned in Heaven as the noblest signature of her century—not the natural, animal urgencies of lust, not the supernatural, angelic desire to glow forever in the beatific vision, but the womanly, purely human experience of love for a specific living being, and the courage to burn for that love were to be the kingdom and the glory of a properly human life. Abelard, however, had never even known of that kingdom. For

all his song-building and philosophy, the urge in his seduction of
the girl had indeed been lust, and the urge behind his command of
her to the nunnery had been fear—both of which emotions she had
transcended through her love; which gives point to the famous line
of the Persian poet of love, Hafiz (1325–1389): "Love's slave
am I, and from both worlds free."

And so what, now, was to be Abelard's reply? A letter addressed as follows: "To Heloise, his beloved sister in Christ, Abelard, her brother in the Same." And, after a number of edifying
paragraphs:

> I have composed this prayer, which I send thee:
> "O God, who formed woman from the side of man and didst
> sanction the sacrament of marriage; who didst bestow upon my
> frailty a cure for its incontinence; do not despise the prayers of
> thy handmaid, and the prayers which I pour out for my sins and
> those of my dear one. Pardon our great crimes, and may the
> enormity of our faults find the greatness of thy ineffable mercy.
> Punish the culprits in the present; spare, in the future. Thou
> hast joined us, Lord, and hast divided us, as it pleased thee.
> Now complete most mercifully what thou hast begun in mercy;
> and those whom thou hast divided in this world, join eternally in
> heaven, thou who art our hope, our portion, our expectation,
> our consolation, Lord blessed forever. Amen."
> Farewell in Christ, spouse of Christ; in Christ farewell and in
> Christ live. Amen.[22]

These two tortured communications, from convent to monastery
and from monastery to convent, reveal the cleavage that in that
period of the apogee of the Gothic separated the truths of human
experience from the articles of enforced faith. The raging heresies
of the time and the fury of their suppression likewise testify to an
incongruity of Credo and Libido. However, these heresies, for the
most part, whether of Manichaean or of Waldensian Christian
type [23]—as well as the coarsely obscene, pathological Black Mass,
which also flourished in these centuries—were as committed as the
Roman Church itself to that dualistic dogma, imported from the
Levant, according to which life in its spontaneity is not innocent
but corrupt. Moreover, even following the inevitable explosion of
the Reformation and the breakaway thereafter of the Lutherans,
Calvinists, Anabaptists, and all, the entire Protestant movement

carried this same dualism onward; so that the rafters of their chapels rang, splintered, cracked, and warped to the fiery preachments of the Fall of Man, atonement, and the reek of Hell.

In contrast, the testament of Heloise was of an actual experience of innocence in love, which erased from her heart the whole appeal of the other myth. One is reminded of the words of the greatest female mystic of Islam, Rabi'a of Basra (d. 801 A.D.), who proclaimed in her poems that her love for God was so great that she was filled with it to the brim, as a cup with wine, so that no place remained in her for either fear of Hell or desire for Paradise, nor for either love or hate of any other being—not the Prophet himself.[24]

Now such a commitment to the beloved as that expressed in the declarations of these two women corresponds perfectly to the ideal of religious fervor that was cultivated in India in those centuries in the popular *bhakti* movement. Religious devotion was there defined as of two orders: 1. liturgical, formal (*vaidhī bhakti*); and 2. impassioned, guided by feeling (*rāgānuga bhakti*). The first, being the usual churchgoing sort of thing, was only by courtesy called devotion; whereas the latter, on the contrary, could not be acquired either by practice or by desire. As though struck by lightning, so is one by love, which is a divine seizure, transmuting the life, erasing every interfering thought. As we read in a Bengali text celebrating this experience: "The self is void, the world is void; heaven, earth, and the space between are void: in this rapture, there is neither virtue nor sin." [25]

The popular Indian Puranic legends of Krishna and the Gopis, and the passionate *Gīta Govinda* of the young love poet Jayadeva (fl. 1170 A.D.) [26] represent the spirit of this tradition of divine rapture. And in the Moslem world as well, the related mystic movement of the Sufis—celebrating *fanā*, the "passing away of the self," and *baqā*, the "unitive life in God"—likewise became the inspiration not only of religiously ecstatic (dervish) orders but also of a mystically toned secular poetry of love,[27] one of the leading centers of which was Moorish Spain.

But here we are on the road back to Abelard and Heloise, Tristan and Isolt; for with the reconquest of Toledo, in the year 1085, by Alfonso the Brave—the Christian King, Alfonso VI of Castile and León—the gates of Oriental poetry and song, mysticism and learning were opened wide to Europe. It is possible that even earlier than this date a flow of ideas may already have been set in motion from Moorish Spain to the north, and in particular by sea to Celtic Ireland, Wales, Cornwall, and Brittany (the lands of the romance of Tristan and Isolt), where a golden age of amalgamated pagan and Christian poetry and learning had glowed with a wild strange light of its own throughout the long grim night of the early Christian Middle Ages.[28] However, the real event was the reconquest of Toledo. And among the first of its great effects were the simultaneous births of the arts of love and love poetry in the lives and works of the troubadours.

The name troubadour itself (Provençal, *trobador*) has been traced with reasonable assurance from the Arabic root TRB (Ta Ra B = "music, song"), plus -*ador,* the usual Spanish agential suffix (as, for instance, in *conquist-ador*); so that *Ta Ra B-ador* would have meant originally simply "song- or music-maker." [29] Professor Philip K. Hitti, who supports this etymology, states in his *History of the Arabs* that "the troubadours resembled Arab singers, not only in sentiment and character, but also in the very forms of their minstrelsy. Certain titles," he avers, "which these Provençal singers gave to their songs are but translations from Arabic titles." [30] And Professor H. A. R. Gibb has likewise remarked the connection of the two traditions, even pointing out that the poems of the first European troubadour, Count William IX of Poitiers, Duke of Aquitaine (1071–1127), were composed in meters sometimes identical with those of his Andalusian Arabic contemporary Ibn Quzman.[31] Moreover, Professor Hitti has further observed that, simultaneously with the rise, at the opening of the twelfth century, of this elite tradition of Arabicized European poetry, the "cult of the dame," likewise "following the Arab precedent," also suddenly appears.[32] Thus we now have evidence of an unbroken, though variously modified, aristocratic tradition of mystically toned erotic lore, extending from India not only eastward (as noted in *Oriental Mythology*) as far as to Lady Murasaki's sentimental Fujiwara court in Kyoto,[33] but also westward into Europe, and even rising to almost simultaneous culmination all the way from Ireland to the Yellow Sea, at exactly the time of the calamitous adventure of Abelard and Heloise; so that the songs that he sang to the world in her name, and which would have drawn, as she declared, the soul of any woman, almost certainly were a northern echo from the gardens of Granada, Tripoli, Baghdad, and Kashmir.

However, whereas in the Orient the ultimate reference of the poetry of love was normally to that unitive rapture epitomized in the cry of the Persian Sufi mystic Bayazid of Bistan (d. 874 A.D.): "I am the Wine-drinker, the Wine, and the Cupbearer!" "Lover, beloved, and love are one!" [34] the European ideal was rather to celebrate specifically the beloved human individual, who, moreover, was normally a woman of high station and developed personality, not, as so often in the Orient, a mere slave girl, professional courtesan, or (in the Indian erotic rituals) a female of inferior caste.[35] In Dante's case, it is true, no personal relationship beyond the meeting of the eyes was ever established here on earth between the poet and his beloved. However, it was Beatrice and she alone—Beatrice Portinari, in her own spiritual character, not as an exemplar merely of the general female power (*śakti*) but as that uniquely beautiful Florentine lady she had been when their eyes met—whose recollection brought home to him, in the decade following her death, the realization of the radiance and beatitude of that "divine Love," as he writes, "which moves the sun and the other stars." [36] Nor was she left behind, dissolved, forgotten, in the rapture of that beatific radiance, but herself was there, at the very feet of God, when the consummation was attained. And the work itself then was composed—the poet tells—in celebration specifically of *her*.

From the Oriental point of view, such a radical shift of accent from the abstract spiritual rapture to its natural earthly term has been generally judged to be a debasement; as it is, for example, in a recent work, *The Sufis,* by the Grand Sheikh Idries Shah, where it is alleged that, on entering the West, "the Sufi stream was partially dammed. . . . Certain elements, necessary to the whole and impossible without a human exemplar of the Sufi Way, remained almost unknown." [37] But, on the other hand, in Europe an Oriental liquidation of oneself in a rapturous realization of the Alone with the Alone has been seldom either desired or intended—or even greatly admired—outside, that is to say, of certain cloisters. For the maintenance even in rapture of a hither-world state of consciousness—and a grateful appreciation thereby of the values of

the personality—has been through most of our centuries the preferred Occidental state of mind. In the words of Nietzsche, "A new
pride, my Ego taught me, and I teach it now to men: no longer to
stick one's head in the sand of celestial things, but to carry it
freely, an earthly head that gives meaning to the earth!" [38]

Something similar may seem to be intended in some of the advanced mystical writings of Japan; the lines, for instance, of the
eighteenth-century Zen master Hakuin (1685–1768):

> Not knowing how near the Truth is,
> People seek it far away: what a pity!

> This very earth is the Lotus Land of Purity,
> And this body is the body of the Buddha.[39]

However, even there, in the youngest, livest nation of the great
East, the ideal—even in the Zen monasteries—is to follow rules of
discipline handed down from the masters of the past for the realization of specified spiritual ends, whereas in the Europe of the
new mythology of self-discovery and -reliance that was coming
into being in the century of Heloise (outside the Church, outside
the monastery), neither rules nor aims were foreknown. The mind
entered the wood, so to say, "where it was thickest," in true adventure, and the unforeseen, unprecedented experience itself then became the opener and dictator of a singular way.

Abelard had been for Heloise such a determinant, and she, in
turn, might have become the like for him, had he possessed the
courage to let her remain unincorporated through marriage in the
context of his already held system of ideas. But instead—alas for
them both!—he clung to his past, his sacraments, Heaven and
Hell, and all was lost. He became what Nietzsche has called "the
pale criminal": "An idea made this man pale. Adequate was he to
his deed when he did it: but the idea of it he could not bear, when
it was done." [40]

And so we may say in summary at this point that the first and
absolutely essential characteristic of the new, secular mythology
that was emerging in the literature of the twelfth and thirteenth
centuries was that its structuring themes were not derived from
dogma, learning, politics, or any current concepts of the general
social good, but were expressions of individual experience: what

I have termed Libido as opposed to Credo. Undoubtedly the myths of all traditions, great and small, must have sprung in the first instance from individual experiences: indeed we possess, in fact, a world of legends telling of the prophets and visionaries through whose personal realizations the cults, sects, and even major religions of mankind were instituted. However, in so far as these then became the authorized and even sanctified vehicles of established cultural heritages, overinterpreted as of divine origin and enforced often on pain of death—representing what the late Professor José Ortega y Gasset well defined as "collective faith" in contrast to "individual faith"—they were no longer determined by, but were rather determinants of, individual experience, feeling, thought, and motivation. In the words of Ortega y Gasset:

> Apart from what individuals as individuals, that is to say, each for himself and on his own account, may believe, there exists always a collective state of belief. This social faith may or may not coincide with that felt by such and such an individual. . . . What constitutes and gives a specific character to collective opinion is the fact that its existence does not depend on its acceptance or rejection by any given individual. From the viewpoint of each individual life, public belief has, as it were, the appearance of a physical object. The tangible reality, so to speak, of collective belief does not consist in its acceptance by you or by me; instead it is *it* which, whether we acquiesce or not, imposes on us its reality and forces us to reckon with it." [41]

Traditional mythologies, that is to say, whether of the primitive or of the higher cultures, antecede and control experience; whereas what I am here calling Creative Mythology is an effect and expression of experience. Its producers do not claim divine authority for their human, all too human, works. They are not saints or priests but men and women of *this* world; and their first requirement is that both their works and their lives should unfold from convictions derived from their own experience.

IV. The Crystalline Bed

Our Tristan poet Gottfried, for instance—who was one of the earliest modern geniuses of first magnitude in the history of Euro-

pean letters—took particular pains to assure his readers that he
knew whereof he spoke when telling of the life-empowering mysteries of love. Indeed, the only statement of this master in which he
lets fall any hint of his personal life follows immediately upon
his description of the love grotto and symbolic wilderness round
about it:

> No one could wish to be anywhere else. And this I well know;
> for I have been there. I, too, have tracked and pursued the wild
> birds and beasts in that wilderness, the deer and other game,
> over many a wooded stream; and yet, having so given my time, I
> never made a real kill. My toils and pains gained no reward.
> I have found the lever and seen the latch of that cave; occa-
> sionally reached even the crystalline bed. In fact, I have danced
> up to it and back frequently and rather well; yet never have
> known rest upon it. The marble floor beside it, hard though it is,
> I have so trodden that were it not continually refreshed by the
> virtue of its greenness—in which its greatest virtue lies and
> through which it is ever renewed—you would see on it Love's
> true tracks. My eyes I have feasted richly on those gleaming
> walls, and with upturned gaze to the medallion, vault, and key-
> stone, full eagerly have I destroyed my sight on the ornaments
> up there, they are so bespangled with Excellence. The little sun-
> giving windows often have sent their rays into my heart.[42]

For the love grotto, like the center of that circle whose circumference is nowhere and center everywhere, can be found as well in
the Rhineland as in the neighborhood of Tintagel; and for those at
rest on its crystalline bed the conditions of time dissolve to eternity. As Gottfried tells of his two lovers there: "They looked upon
each other and nourished themselves with that. . . . Nothing but
their state of mind and love did they consume." * How few, however, have known the purity of that bed!

We may dance toward it and away, achieve glimpses, and even
dwell in its beauty for a time; yet few are those who have been
confirmed in that knowledge of its ubiquity which antiquity called
gnosis and the Orient calls *bodhi:* full awakening to the crystalline
purity of the bed or ground of one's own and the world's true being. Like perfectly transparent crystal, it is there, yet as though not
there; and all things, when seen through it, become luminous in its
light. Moreover, it is hard, endures forever. And the green floor

* Supra, p. 46.

across which one approaches reveals the excellence of time, which is ever-renewing.

In short, the love grotto in its wilderness can be compared to the cave-sanctuary of the classical mysteries of Eleusis, or to the sanctum of the female triad shown at Stations 4–5–6 of the golden mystery-bowl of Figure 3. The female guide to the secret gate (at Station 4) bears in hand a little pail of the ambrosia of eternity, but the raven of death appears first, since all who would know eternity must die to their temporal hopes and fears, and to their name in the world as well. The female guide and guardian marks the way both to the entry into wisdom and to the return with it to the world (Figure 3, Stations 4 and 15). Heloise, it can be truly said, had appeared as such a guide to Abelard.

In the rites of the classical mystery cults the initiatory symbolic shocks were experienced in graduated series by neophytes spiritually ready, who were carried thereby through expanding revelations to whatever sign or event, displayed within the ultimate sanctum, conferred the consummating epiphany. But life too confers initiations, and the most potent of these are of sex and death. Life too communicates revelatory shocks, but they are not pedagogically graded. These initiations are administered both to those prepared and to those who are unprepared, and while the latter either receive from them no instruction or, worse, are left damaged (insane, a bit exploded, defensively hardened, or inert), those ready receive initiations that may not only match but even surpass the revelations of the cults. For since life is itself the background from which the prophets of yore of both the great and the little ceremonial systems derived their initial inspirations, life holds still in store the possibilities of the same enlightenment anew, and of more and greater besides.

v. Aesthetic Arrest

Now, in the language of art such a seizure is termed aesthetic arrest. As characterized by James Joyce in the words of his hero Stephen Dedalus, it is that "enchantment of the heart" by which the mind is arrested and raised above desire and loathing in the luminous stasis of aesthetic pleasure. "This supreme quality is felt by the artist," Stephen declares, "when the esthetic image is first conceived in his imagination." [43] By Dante the moment is described at the opening of his *Vita Nuova,* where Beatrice—then but a child of nine, he also a child of nine—first appeared before his eyes.

At that instant, I say truly, the spirit of life, which dwells in the most secret chamber of the heart, began to tremble with such violence that it appeared fearfully in the least pulses, and, trembling, said these words: *Ecce deus fortior me, qui veniens dominabitur mihi* [Behold a god stronger than I, who coming shall rule over me].

At that instant the spirit of the soul, which dwells in the high chamber to which all the spirits of the senses carry their perceptions, began to marvel greatly, and, speaking especially to the spirit of the sight, said these words: *Apparuit jam beatitudo vestra* [Now has appeared your bliss].

At that instant the natural spirit, which dwells in that part where our nourishment is supplied, began to weep, and, weeping, said these words: *Heu miser! quia frequenter impeditus ero deinceps* [Woe is me, wretched! because often from this time forth shall I be hindered].

I say that from that time forward Love lorded it over my soul, which had been so speedily wedded to him: and he began to exercise over me such control and such lordship, through the power which my imagination gave to him, that it behooved me to do completely all his pleasure.[44]

The whole career of Dante in art unfolded from this instant; for, as he tells at the close of the *Vita Nuova,* having published as a youth the sonnets and canzoni of his emotion, he resolved to speak no more of that blessed one till he could more worthily treat of her. "And to attain to this," he decared, "I study to the utmost of my power, as she truly knows. So that, if it shall please Him through whom all things live, that my life be prolonged for some years, I hope to say of her what was never said of any woman." [45]

James Joyce too writes of such a moment in the youth of his alter-ego, Stephen. He had arrived spiritually in a Waste Land of total disillusionment in the goals and ideals offered him by the society and its church into which he had been born. "Where," asks the author, "was his boyhood now? Where was the soul that had hung back from her destiny, to brood alone upon the shame of her wounds and in her house of squalor and subterfuge . . . ?" Unhappily brooding in this vein, he was strolling barefoot along the

broad beach at Dollymount, north of Dublin, beside a long rivulet
in the strand. "He was alone. He was unheeded, happy and near to
the wild heart of life."

And then, behold!

A girl stood before him in midstream, alone and still, gazing
out to sea. She seemed like one whom magic had changed into
the likeness of a strange and beautiful seabird. Her long slender
bare legs were delicate as a crane's and pure save where an emerald trail of seaweed had fashioned itself as a sign upon the
flesh. Her thighs, fuller and softhued as ivory, were bared almost to her hips, where the white fringes of her drawers were like
feathering of soft white down. Her slateblue skirts were kilted
boldly about her waist and dovetailed behind her. Her bosom
was as a bird's, soft and slight, slight and soft as the breast of
some darkplumaged dove. But her long fair hair was girlish:
and girlish, and touched with the wonder of mortal beauty,
her face.

She was alone and still, gazing out to sea; and when she felt
his presence and the worship of his eyes her eyes turned to him
in quiet sufferance of his gaze, without shame or wantonness.
Long, long she suffered his gaze and then quietly withdrew her
eyes from his and bent them towards the stream, gently stirring
the water with her foot hither and thither. The first faint noise of
gently moving water broke the silence, low and faint and whispering, faint as the bells of sleep; hither and thither, hither and
thither; and a faint flame trembled on her cheek.

—Heavenly God! cried Stephen's soul, in an outburst of profane joy.

He turned away from her suddenly and set off across the
strand. His cheeks were aflame; his body was aglow; his limbs
were trembling. On and on and on and on he strode, far out
over the sands, singing wildly to the sea, crying to greet the
advent of the life that had cried to him.

Her image had passed into his soul for ever and no word had
broken the holy silence of his ecstasy. Her eyes had called him
and his soul had leaped at the call. To live, to err, to fall, to
triumph, to recreate life out of life! A wild angel had appeared
to him, the angel of mortal youth and beauty, an envoy from the
fair courts of life, to throw open before him in an instant of ecstasy the gates of all the ways of error and glory. On and on and
on and on![46]

In the Tristan legend, this moment of the meeting of the eyes and stilling of the world occurred when the couple, sailing from Ireland to Cornwall, drank by accident the magic potion that Isolt's mother had prepared for the maiden's wedding night with King Mark. There has been a difference of opinion among both poets and critics, however, as to whether this draft was merely a catalyst or itself the cause of the passion, and I suppose there must also be lovers who wonder if the wild storm they enjoy would ever have been known to them had they not tarried long—for just one more glass—that night of the moon on Caribbean waters. "The potion," states one authority, "was indeed the true cause of the lovers' passion, and of all that followed from it." [47] "The love-potion," states another, "is a poetic symbol, and Gottfried perhaps kept the love-drink because it made an excellent climax. Love-potion or not—the climax in his Tristan and Isolt was bound to come." [48]

We do not know how the matter stood in the earliest versions of the legend. Many scholars have pointed out, however, that in the earliest extant version—namely that of Thomas of Britain, composed c. 1165–1170—the beautiful maid and heroic youth were already clearly in love before the potion at last unlocked their hearts. [49] In the later version of Eilhart von Oberge (c. 1180–1190) the influence of the magic abates after a period of four years, and in the Norman French version of Béroul (c. 1191–1205), which follows Eilhart's tradition, the period given is three: in both, the drink is declared to be the cause. In Eilhart's words: "For four years, their love was so great they could not be apart for even half a day. Unless they saw each other every day, they fell ill: they were in love because of that drink. And if they had not seen each other for a week, they would have died: the drink was so concocted and of such great strength. Of this you must take full account!" [50] Gottfried (c. 1210), on the other hand, followed Thomas, and Richard Wagner followed Gottfried.

But if the potion is not the cause of love, then what, for these great poets—Thomas, Gottfried, and Wagner—can the meaning of its magic have been?

In Wagner's case we know from his autobiography as well as letters that throughout the years of the composition of his Tristan und Isolde, 1854–1859, he was in rapturous love with the wife,

Mathilde, of his most generous friend and benefactor, Otto Wesendonck; even conceiving of himself as Tristan, Wesendonck as King Mark, and his muse Mathilde as Queen Isolde, in whose arms (according to his own oft repeated words) he desired to die. For, like Gottfried, this incurable lover of other men's wives also had danced rather well and frequently to the crystalline bed and back, yet never had known rest upon it. And in fact, if such poets ever had found that rest, we should never have had their works.

"Because I have never tasted the true bliss of love," Wagner wrote to his friend Franz Liszt in December 1854, "I shall raise a monument to that most beautiful of all dreams, wherein, from beginning to end, this love may for once drink to its full." [51] He had met Mathilde, his Beatrice, two years before. And—what is no less relevant—he had discovered in the language of philosophy, like Dante, the means not only to read in depth the secret of his stricken heart, but also to render the import of its sweetly bitter agony in the timeless metaphors of myth. For, as we learn from his own account in the autobiography, it was in the year of his conception of this monument to a dream that he found the works of Schopenhauer; and, as he declares in so many words: "It was certainly, in part, the serious mood into which Schopenhauer had transposed me and which now was pressing for an ecstatic expression of its structuring ideas, that inspired in me the conception of a *Tristan und Isolde*." [52]

Schopenhauer, it will be recalled, treats of love as the great transforming power that converts the will to live into its opposite and reveals thereby a dimension of truth beyond the world dominion of King Death: beyond the boundaries of space and time and the turbulent ocean, within these bounds, of our life's conflicting centers of self-interest. As he writes in his famous paper on "The Foundation of Morality," crowned in the year 1840 by the Royal Danish Society of Sciences: "If I perform an act wholly and solely in the interest of another, it is then *his* weal and woe that have become my immediate concern—just as in every other act of mine, the interest served is my own. . . .

"But how," he then asks, "can it possibly be that the weal and woe of another should directly move *my* will; that is to say, become *my* motivation, as though the end served were my own: indeed, and even occasionally to such a degree that my own well being and suffering—which are normally my only two springs of conduct—should remain more or less ignored?"

He replies in a fundamental passage that can be read, now, as the grounding theme not only of Wagner's *Tristan* but also of his *Parsifal*—and of the *Ring der Nibelungen* as well:

> Obviously this can occur only because *another* can actually become the final concern of *my* willing—as I am myself its usual concern: that is to say, because I can desire *his* weal and suffer *his* woe as acutely as though they were my own. But this necessarily presupposes that I can actually participate sympathetically in *his* pain, can experience *his* pain as otherwise only my own, and consequently can truly desire *his* good, as otherwise only my own. Which, in turn, demands, however, that I should for a certain time become *identified with him:* demands, that is to say, that the final distinction between me and him, which is the premise of my egoism, should, to some degree at least, be suspended. And since I am not actually *in the skin* of that other, it can be only through my *knowledge* of him, his image *in my head,* that I can become to such a degree identified with him as to act in a way that annuls the difference between us.

Having thus reasoned, Schopenhauer now proceeds to his metaphysical judgment; and in the light of the luminous words that we have just read of Heloise to Abelard, these relatively dispassionate paragraphs of the lucid bachelor philosopher will seem rather to understate than to overstate the message that Wagner echoed and amplified in the mild and gentle swelling strains of Isolde's *"Liebestod."*

> The sort of act that I am here discussing [states Schopenhauer] is not something that I have merely dreamed up or conjured out of thin air, but a reality—in fact, a not unusual reality: it is, namely, the everyday phenomenon of *Mitleid,* compassion, which is to say: immediate participation, released from all other considerations, first, in the pain of another, and then, in the alleviation or termination of that pain . . . : which alone is the true ground of all autonomous righteousness and of all true human love. An act can be said to have genuine moral worth only in so far as it stems from this source; and conversely, an act from any other source has none. The weal and woe of another comes to lie directly on my heart in exactly the same way—though not always to the same degree—as otherwise only my own would

lie, as soon as this sentiment of compassion is aroused, and therewith, the difference between him and me is no longer absolute. And this really is amazing—even mysterious. It is, in fact, the great mystery inherent in all morality, the prime integrant of ethics, and a gate beyond which the only type of speculation that can presume to venture a single step must be metaphysical.[53]

It is fascinating to read in Wagner's account of his studies of these years that, even while engrossed in his volumes of Schopenhauer and settling down to his *Tristan*, he became so deeply interested in Eugène Burnouf's *Introduction à l'histoire du Bouddhisme indien* (1844) that for a time he thought of writing an opera "based on the simple legend," as he tells us, "of the reception of a maiden of an untouchable caste into the exalted mendicant order of Shakyamuni; she having made herself worthy of this, through her most passionately intensified and purified love for the Buddha's chief disciple Ananda." [54] But Schopenhauer had himself already recognized, acknowledged, and even celebrated the relationship of his metaphysics not only to Indian Buddhist and Vedantic thought, but to an ever-present heretical strain in Occidental philosophy as well. As we read, for instance, turning with Wagner once again to the prize essay, "On the Foundation of Morality":

> This doctrine, that plurality is merely illusory, and that in all
> the individuals of this world—no matter how great their number, as they appear beside each other in space and after each other in time—there is made manifest only one, single, truly existent Being, present and ever the same in all, was known to the world, even ages before Kant. In fact, it can be said to have been with us through all time. For, in the first place, it is the chief and fundamental teaching of the oldest books in the world, the sacred Vedas,* the dogmatic portion—or better, esoteric meaning—of which is preserved for us in the Upanishads,†

---

* In Schopenhauer's century, the clay tablets of Sumer had not yet been discovered, nor the Pyramid Texts deciphered; moreover a greatly excessive antiquity was attributed to the Vedas. These texts and their dates are discussed in *Oriental Mythology*.

† "The Upanishads," wrote Schopenhauer in a frequently quoted passage, "afford the most rewarding and exalting reading possible in this world: they are the consolation of my life, as they will be of my death" (*Parerga und Paralipomana* XVI. 187).

throughout which the same great teaching is to be found tire-
lessly restated in endless variation on practically every page, as
well as allegorized in multitudes of similes and figures. That it
was basic, also, to the wisdom of Pythagoras, there can be no
doubt, even in spite of our paucity of information concerning
that philosopher; and practically the entire body of teaching of
the Eleatic school consisted of this doctrine, as everybody
knows. The Neoplatonists were literally soaked in it: "Through
the unity of all," they wrote, "all souls are one" (διὰ τὴν ἑνότητα
ἁπάντων πάσας ψυχὰς μίαν εἶναι: *propter omnium unitatem cunctas
animas unam esse*). Then in Europe, unexpectedly, we see it
emerge in the ninth century in the works of Scotus Erigena,[55]
whom it so excited that he strove to clothe it in the forms and
language of the Christian faith. Among Mohammedans it is
found in the inspired mysticism of the Sufis.[56] And yet in the
more recent Occident, Giordano Bruno had to pay with a
shameful and painful death for his inability to suppress an urge
to proclaim its general truth. The Christian mystics, no matter
when or where they appear, can be seen caught in this realization—even against their will and in spite of every effort. Spinoza's name is identified with it. And in our own day, at last—
now that Kant has blown the old dogmatic theology to bits
and the world stands appalled among the smoking ruins—the
same perception is restated in the eclectic philosophy of Schelling [1775–1854]. Uniting deftly in a single system the doctrines of Plotinus, Spinoza, Kant, and Jacob Boehme, combined
with the findings of modern science, Schelling, to meet the
pressing need of his generation, developed his own variations
on the common themes—so that this knowledge has now gained
general credit among German scholars and is known even
to the educated public. As in the words of Voltaire:

> On peut assez longtemps, chez notre espèce,
> Fermer la porte à la raison.
> Mais, dès qu'elle entre avec adresse,
> Elle reste dans la maison,
> Et bientôt elle en est maîtresse.

The only exceptions today are the university professors, who
face now the difficult assignment of waging war on this so-called
"Pantheism." Placed thereby in a situation of both embarrass-
ment and jeopardy, they are clutching in their heartfelt anxiety
at every sort of pitiful sophism, all kinds of bombastic phraseol-

ogies, from which to piece together an acceptable disguise for their cherished, specially privileged, old cutaway-coat philosophy.

In brief: The Ἐν καὶ πᾶν has been forever the laughingstock of fools and the everlasting meditation of the wise. And yet, no rigorous proof has ever been, or can be, given for it, except by way of the demonstrations of Kant—who, however, did not complete the proof himself, but, like a sharp debater, presented only his premises, leaving to his audience the pleasure of arriving at the necessary conclusion.

For if plurality and distinction belong only to this world of *appearances,* and if one and the same Being is what is beheld in all these living things, well then, the experience that dissolves the distinction between the I and the Not-I cannot be false. On the contrary: its opposite must be false; and indeed, in India we find this opposite denoted by the term *māyā,* meaning "deception, phantasm, illusion," However, as we have just seen, the former experience underlies the mystery of compassion, and stands, in fact, for the reality of which compassion is the prime expression. *That* experience, therefore, must be the metaphysical ground of ethics and consist simply in this: that *one* individual should recognize in *another,* himself in his own true being. . . . Which is the recognition for which the basic formula is the standard Sanskrit expression, "Thou art that," *tat tvam asi.*[57]

VI. The Potion

Wagner's understanding of the love potion of Isolt and Tristan was in large measure inspired by this poetic philosophy of Schopenhauer, and yet, as he one day realized with astonishment and declares in his autobiography, his own creative work had already, of itself, anticipated these metaphysical insights. Schopenhauer, his mystagogue, was to mature his art and lead him on from the love grotto of Tristan to Amfortas's Castle of the Grail, not by any force of indoctrinating authority, but by way of an eagerly desired, freely and gratefully accepted elucidation and validation of his own as yet unconscious motivating idea of love's transfiguration.

As anyone passionately excited by a living experience would have done [he tells us], I pressed on, as fast as I could, to the conclusion of the Schopenhauerian system: but though its aesthetic portion had satisfied me completely, and particularly had astonished me with its notable understanding of music, I was nevertheless shocked—as any in my state of mind would have been—by the moral turn at the end of it all. For there, the extinction of the Will to Life, absolute renunciation, was put forward as our only real and final redemption from the bonds (now for the first time keenly felt) of our individual limitation in understanding and dealing with the world. For such a one as I, who had expected to cull from philosophy a capital justification for political and social agitation in the name of the so-called "free individual," there was here, obviously, nothing to gain: the only offering was a requirement to turn from this road entirely and put down the impulse to a personal career. To me, at first, this had nothing at all to say. Not so readily, I thought, would I allow myself to be moved to renounce the so-called "cheerful" Greek viewpoint, from which I had composed my paper on "The Artwork of the Future" [written 1849, published 1850]. Actually, it was Herwegh,* who, with a weighty thought, first moved me to reconsider my emotion. "All tragedy," he suggested, "is contingent on this insight into the nullity of the sphere of appearance; and every great poet—indeed, every great human being—must inwardly have reconciled himself intuitively to this truth." I looked back to my Nibelungen poem and there, to my amazement, found that what now was giving me such difficulty as a theory had long been familiar to my own poetic imagination. So that I understood now, for the first time, my own "Wotan," and, considerably shaken, returned to Schopenhauer, to commence a more attentive study of his work. I now realized that the most important thing of all was to understand correctly Book I of *The World as Will and Idea,* where he interprets and enlarges upon Kant's doctrine of the mere ideality of this world of space and time, which appears to us so firmly founded; and I believed myself to have taken the first real step along the way to understanding, in as much as I now recognized, at least, how uncommonly difficult this doctrine

* George Herwegh (1817–1875) was a leading revolutionary poet of the "Young German" movement, who, like Wagner, had been implicated in the risings of the year 1848 and was now, like Wagner himself, in political exile for a while in Zurich. Wagner met him there in 1851 in the rooms of another revolutionary littérateur, Adolph Kolatschek, who was editing a German monthly journal dedicated to perpetuating on the mental plane the revolution that had failed on the political (cf. Wagner, *Mein Leben,* (Munich: F. Bruckmann, 1911), pp. 547–48).

actually was. For many years thereafter, the book never left my side, and already by the summer of the following year I had worked through it studiously, four times. The effect that it was gradually taking upon me was extraordinary and, in any case, became decisive for my entire life.[58]

Very, very thinly summarized, in the most elementary terms possible, this "uncommonly difficult" doctrine of the nullity of the apparent world can perhaps be sufficiently suggested for our present reading simply by reminding ourselves of the following obvious fact: namely, that since every sight, sound, smell, taste, and tactile impression necessarily comes to us from some part of space and endures for some period of time, space and time, consequently, are the ineluctable preconditions of all outward experience whatsoever: we have our being in their ambience, as fish in water, and what any state of being independent of time and space might be, we neither know nor can imagine. Nor can we hope to learn from reason; for all thinking is ineluctably conditioned by the laws of grammar and logic. Thus all forms beheld in the outer world and all thoughts entertained about them are removed by the conditions of perception and cogitation from whatever the prime state—or non-state—might be of any Being-in-itself: Kant's *Ding an sich.*

Plato's parable of the Cave,[59] as well as the Indian doctrine of *māyā,*[60] adumbrate the same realization; in Shelley's beautiful lines we recognize it again:

> Life, like a dome of many-colored glass,
> Stains the white radiance of Eternity.[61]

And in Goethe's *Faust,* at the opening of Part II, it is represented where the hero turns, unable to gaze directly into the blinding light of the sun, and sees a waterfall, arched by a rainbow. "So let the sun then remain at my back!" he declares. . . . "We have our life in the colorful reflection." [62]

However—and here is where Schopenhauer steps away from Kant—whereas the eye directed outward to the many-colored manifold beholds apparent phenomenal forms, the gaze turned inward comes to something else. In meditation deepening, going past the dreamlike, remembered forms of outer experience and the abstract concepts derived both from such experience and from the structure of the mind itself, pressing down beyond all this, one comes in touch finally not with forms or thoughts at all, but with what Schopenhauer termed the will (*die Wille*): one's own sheer will to live, which is simply one's own share of the general will to live that is the ground of being of all nature, manifest as well in the physical laws that bring crystals into form and move a magnet, as in the formative energies of the plant world, the animal kingdom, and the bodies, cities, and civilizations of mankind.

"It is what is innermost," states Schopenhauer, "the kernel of each individual thing and equally of the whole. It is manifest in every blindly working force of nature; it is manifest, also, in the considered deeds of men: the great difference between these two being merely a matter of the level of manifestation, not the essence of what is made manifest." [63]

> Up to now [he continues], the concept *will* has been subsumed under the concept *force;* but I am using it just the opposite way, and mean that every force in nature is to be understood as a function of will. And this is no mere squabble over words, or matter of no moment: on the contrary, it is of the greatest significance and importance. For at the back of the concept *force* there is finally our visual knowledge of the objective world, i.e, of some phenomenon, something seen. It is from this that the concept *force* derives. It is an abstraction from the field in which the laws of cause and effect prevail . . . whereas the concept *will*, on the contrary, is the one, among all possible concepts, that does *not* derive from the observation of phenomena, *not* from mere visual knowledge, but comes from inside, emerges from the immediate consciousness of each one of us, in which each is directly aware of his own individuality in terms of his own existence: not as a form, not even in terms of the subject-object relationship, but as that which he himself is; for here the knower and the known are the same. [64]

One recognizes immediately the relationship of this Schopenhauerian concept of the will to the Indian idea of the *brahman*, which is identical with the self (*ātman*) of all beings ("thou art that," *tat tvam asi*). The will, as *brahman*, transcends the object-subject relationship and is therefore non-dual (*nir-dvandva*). Duality (*dvandva*), on the other hand, is an illusion of the sphere of space and time (*māyā*): both our fear of death (*māra*) and our yearning for the pleasures of this world (*kāma*) derive from, and attach us to, this manifold delusion, from which release (*mokṣa*) is achieved only when the fear of death and desire for enjoyment are extinguished in the knowledge (Sanskrit, *bodhi;* Greek, *gnosis*) of non-duality (*nir-dvandva: tat tvam asi*). With that, the veil of delusion dissolves and the realization is immediate that "we are all," as Schopenhauer avers, "one and the same single Being." And the sentiment proper to this selfless realization is compassion (*karuṇā*).

"All individuation is a mere appearance, an effect of space and time, which are themselves nothing more than the forms of my cerebral capacity for knowledge and the conditioning factors, consequently, of all objects of that knowledge. Accordingly, the multitude and variety of individuals, also, is merely an appearance, i.e., a mere effect of my *way of perceiving*. Whereas my true, my inmost being subsists in every living thing as immediately as I can know and experience it only in my own self-conscious self." [65]

And with that we awake to the meaning of the potion in Wagner's Tristan romance. It is neither a cause nor a catalyst of the mighty passion of love; for that love was already present in both hearts before the couple drank, and both, moreover, knew that it was there. The great point of the splendid scene of the drinking of the potion is that the couple believe they are drinking death and have spiritually acquiesced in this act of renunciation; for there is in Wagner's version of the romance a death potion as well as a love potion aboard the bride-ship, which Isolde's mother also has prepared. And Isolde's maid Brangaene (who is in the role here of the porteress at the gate of initiation with the pail of ambrosia, the drink of immortality, in hand) has substituted the love potion for the other in their cup. So that, as they have already renounced psychologically both love as lust and the fear of death, when they drink, and live, and again look upon each other, the veil of *māyā* has fallen.

Isolde throws the cup aside. Both are seized with trembling. They clutch convulsively at their breasts. The music is developing the Love Potion Motive, and, after a stunned, excruciating moment, the two break into wild song:

ISOLDE: Tristan!

TRISTAN: Isolde! . . . What dream was that I had, of Tristan's honor?

ISOLDE: What dream was that I had, of Isolde's shame?

Do we hear an echo of Heloise?

And in Gottfried's poem the marvel wrought by the potion is the
same: for though he had, in his philosophy, no Schopenhauer to
call upon, he had the Greeks and the grace of their Muses—the
same who were to become for the poets and artists of the Renaissance the openers of the senses to the music of the spheres.
When he paused in his work to invoke divine inspiration, it
was not to Jesus, Mary, or any Christian saint that he called, but
to the Muses Nine (the Camenae), and the master of their cosmic
dance, Apollo with his lyre:

> My prayers and entreaties will I now send forth from heart
> and hands aloft to Helicon, to that ninefold throne whence the
> fountains spring from which the gift of words and meaning flow.
> Its host and its nine hostesses are Apollo and the Camenae.
> . . . And could I obtain of it but a single drop, my words
> would be dipped in the glowing crucible of Camenian inspira-
> tion, to be there transmuted into something strangely wonderful,
> made to order, like Arabian gold.[66]

Schopenhauer's theory of art, which so appealed to Wagner that
he took it for his own, elucidates in nineteenth-century terms the
same Hellenistic concept of the Muses here alluded to by Gottfried. It is a concept, moreover, that is in perfect accord with the
representations of both poets of the influence of the potion; for the
waters of the fountains of inspiration dispensed to artists by the
Muses, the liquor in the little pails of the guides and guardians of
the mysteries, the drink of the gods, and the distillate of love are
the same, in various strengths, to wit, ambrosia (Sanskrit, amṛta,
"immortality"), the potion of deathless life experienced here and
now. It is milk, it is wine, it is tea, it is coffee, it is anything you
like, when drunk with a certain insight—life itself, when experienced from a certain depth and height.

For normally, biologically, the animal function of eyes is to be
on the watch for things in the field of space and time that might be
a) desirable or b) dangerous. They are the scouts of an alimentary

canal, inquiring, "Can I eat that, or will that eat me?" And when functioning on this zoological-economic-political level of concern, even the organs of higher knowledge are in the service only of the will to live, "serving," as Schopenhauer states, "merely as means for the preservation of the individual and his species. And having originated so," he continues, "in the service of the Will, for the realization of its aims, knowledge remains practically entirely in that service—at least, in all animals and in nearly all human beings. And yet . . . in some men knowledge can break free of this servitude, release itself from such bondage, and stand free of the Will and its aims, sheerly in and for itself, as a clean clear mirror of the world—which is the order of consciousness of art." [67]

For it is possible, in certain circumstances, to dissociate the act of seeing from the will of the individual to live. It is possible to view an object not in terms of its relationship to the well-being of the viewer, the subject, but in its own being, in and for itself. The object then is seen with the eye not of a temporal individual but of uncommitted consciousness: the world eye, as Schopenhauer calls it—without desire, without fear, absolutely dissociated from the vicissitudes of mortality in space and time and those laws of cause and effect which operate in this field. This is the eye not of man the sleeper at the feet of the central goddess of Figure 3, in the circle of the scared and ravenous beasts, but of Hyperborean Apollo at the summit of Mount Helicon, lyre in hand, beholding those eternal forms which are manifest through all phenomena and which Plato called the universal "ideas."

> This transition from the usual way of perceiving an individual thing to the perception of its informing idea occurs abruptly [states Schopenhauer], when the act of cognition is released from the service of the Will, and the knowing subject consequently ceases to be a mere individual and becomes the willless, pure subject of knowledge: no longer seeking relationships in terms of the laws of cause and effect, but resting and fulfilled in fixed contemplation of the presented object, which is released from its connections with all else.[68]

Or, as James Joyce formulates the same insight in his discussion (in *A Portrait of the Artist as a Young Man*) of the moment of aesthetic arrest in the contemplation of an object: "You see that it is that thing which it is and no other thing. . . . The mind in that mysterious instant Shelley likened to a fading coal." [69]

Science, Schopenhauer declares, is concerned with the laws of cause and effect, which are not the object of art. Mathematics is concerned with the conditions of space and time: these conditions are not the object of art. History is concerned with motivation: motivation is not the object of art. Art is informed by the contemplation of the object in its character as "idea": not as a "concept," abstracted by the intellect, but as a thing regarded in and for itself, dissociated from the temporal flow of causal laws. "And this separate thing," Schopenhauer explains, "which in that general stream has been but the least vanishing particle, becomes, when so regarded, an epiphany of the whole, equivalent to the entire unending manifold of time." [70]

This way of seeing is the way of genius, the way of art, the way of perfect objectivity, the way of the world eye, and is not to be confused either with intellectual abstraction or with allegorical reference. But for those unable to bear its impact, which annihilates momentarily the entire world and world-orientation of the self-protecting, self-advancing biological-political individual, the consequence is madness. Schopenhauer cites from Aristotle a sentence quoted by Seneca: *"Nullum magnum ingenium sine mixtura dementiae fuit."* [71] He cites, too, the lines of Dryden:

> Great wits are sure to madness near allied,
> And thin partitions do their bounds divide.[72]

And he reminds us, finally, of Plato's allegory of the cave,* where the poet-philosopher states that those who have been outside the cave are mocked when they return, since their eyes, disaccustomed to its darkness, no longer rightly see and judge its shadows. The genius, then, may be said to be one who can live simultaneously in two views of the world, that of art and that of the will, without going mad.[73]

According to this philosophy, to which Wagner gave his whole regard, each of the arts is most fittingly applied to one aspect of the cosmic vision. For example, architecture renders the physical strains of the universal harmony: weight, cohesion, rigidity and mass, the play of light and dark, form and symmetry. Landscape-

---

* Plato, *The Republic*, 7; supra, p. 77.

painting and gardening the silent power, in spiritual peace, of the impersonal will in nature; animal sculpture and painting show the character of species. The nude in sculpture and painting renders the grace of the species Man; and portraiture, as said, the intelligible character of the individual as a species in himself. Music, however, has a role apart; for it deals not with forms in space, but with time, sheer time. It is not, like the other arts, a rendition of what Plato calls "ideas," but of the will itself, the world will, of which the "ideas" are but inflections. "One could call the world 'embodied music,' as well as 'embodied Will.' " Schopenhauer wrote, confirming thus the ancient theme of the music of the spheres.

And in the art of Wagner's opera, therefore, the music is meant to render the inward time-sense of the scenes presented on the outward space-field of the stage. It is related to those scenes as the will is to the body, and is equivalent, that is to say, in both sense and effect, to the love potion itself, by which the two wills of Isolt and Tristan were touched, to move as one.

The two believe they are drinking death: their will to live they have canceled. They drink, and hark!—the music of the universe changes:

> ISOLDE: Tristan! From the world released, thou art won to me, Tristan!
> TRISTAN: Isolde! . . . thou art won to me!
> THE TWO TOGETHER: Won to me! Thou, my only thought, love's delight supreme! [74]

Or, as Gottfried, the earlier poet, states:

> Love, the waylayer of all hearts, had stolen in. . . . Those who before had been two and twofold, were now one, single-fold. . . . Each was to the other as translucent as a glass: the two possessed one heart. . . .
>
> When Isolt thought, the only thought she had was neither of this nor of that, but of Love alone and Tristan. . . . For the burgeoning of Love makes lovers ever the more fair. That is the seed of Love, by which it never dies. [75]

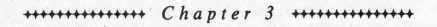

THE WORD BEHIND WORDS

1. Symbolic Speech

The best things cannot be told, the second best are misunderstood. After that comes civilized conversation; after that, mass indoctrination; after that, intercultural exchange. And so, proceeding, we come to the problem of communication: the opening, that is to say, of one's own truth and depth to the depth and truth of another in such a way as to establish an authentic community of existence.

I have already said that the mythology of which we are treating in this volume springs from individual experience, not dogma, learning, political interests, or programs for the renovation of society; and the type of experience of which we have been reading in the words of Heloise and Rabi'a, Gottfried, Dante, Wagner, and Joyce, has been the innocence and majesty of love. I am aware that their experiences differed, and that what Heloise, Gottfried, and Wagner called love, Dante condemned as lust in Canto V of the *Inferno.* However, the innocence and majesty of his own emotion Dante never doubted; and what we are discussing here is not what men have thought of others, but the force of their convictions based on experiences of their own; and this we may well call faith —in Ortega y Gasset's sense of the term, "individual faith," in contrast to "collective": not faith in what one has been told to believe, or in what, for the earning of money, political office, or fame, it may be thought propitious to believe, but faith in one's own experience, whether of feeling, fact, reason, or vision. For, as Ortega remarks, "It is not in man's power to think and believe as he pleases." He continues:

One can want to think otherwise than one really thinks, one can work faithfully to change an opinion and may even be successful. But what we cannot do is to confuse our desire to think in another way with the pretense that we are already thinking as we want to. One of the giants of the Renaissance, the strange Leonardo da Vinci, coined for all time the adage: *"Che non puo quel che vuol, quel che puo voglia"*—he who cannot do what he wants, let him want what he can do.[1]

The socially authorized mythologies and cults of the classical and medieval as well as various primitive and Oriental traditions were intended, and commonly functioned, to inculcate belief; and in salient instances their effectiveness was such that they determined the form and content of the most profound personal experiences. No one has yet reported of a Buddhist arhat surprised by a vision of Christ, or a Christian nun by the Buddha. The image of the vehicle of grace, arriving in vision from untold depths, puts on the guise of the local mythic symbol of the spirit, and as long as such symbols work there can be no quarrel with their retention. They serve no less effectively as guides of the individual than as stays of the social order. However, "collective" mythologies do not always function so. Individuals there have always been in whom the socially enforced forms have produced neither vision nor conviction. Some of these have fallen apart either in solitude or in bedlam; others have been delivered to the stake or firing squad. Today, more fortunately, it is everywhere the collective mythology itself that is going to pieces, leaving even the non-individual (*sauve qui peut!*) to be a light unto himself. It is true that the madhouses are full; psychoanalysts, millionaires. Yet anyone sensible enough to have looked around somewhat outside his fallen church will have seen standing everywhere on the cleared, still clearing, world stage a company of mighty individuals: the great order of those who in the past found, and in the present too are finding, in themselves all the guidance needed. The mythologies of this book are the productions, the revelations—the letters in a bottle, set floating on the sea—of such men and women, who have had the courage to be at one in their wanting and their doing, their knowing and their telling. And we may leave it to God, Dante, and our local priest or newspaper to put them in Heaven or Hell. But better Hell in one's own character than Heaven as someone else; for that would be exactly to make of Hell, Heaven, and of Heaven, Hell.

The profession of views that are not one's own and the living of life according to such views—no matter what the resultant sense of social participation, fulfillment, or even euphoria may be—eventuates inevitably in self-loss and falsification. For in our public roles and conventional beliefs we are—after all!—practically interchangeable. "Out there" we are not ourselves, but at best only what we are expected to be, and at worst what we have got to be. The intent of the old mythologies to integrate the individual in his group, to imprint on his mind the ideals of that group, to fashion him according to one or another of its orthodox stereotypes, and to convert him thus into an absolutely dependable cliché, has become assumed in the modern world by an increasingly officious array of ostensibly permissive, but actually coercive, demythologized secular institutions. A new anxiety in relation to this development is now becoming evident, however; for with the increase, on one hand, of our efficiencies in mass indoctrination and, on the other, of our uniquely modern Occidental interest in the fosterage of authentic individuals, there is dawning upon many a new and painful realization of the depth to which the imprints, stereotypes, and archetypes of the social sphere determine our personal sentiments, deeds, thoughts, and even capacities for experience.

The playwright Ionesco, in his modern "comedy of the absurd" *The Bald Soprano,* brings a properly married British couple into a properly arid British drawing room, where each has the curious presentiment of having met or seen the other somewhere before. They are strangers to each other. And in the same vein T. S. Eliot, in his poem "The Hollow Men" (1925)—as in his earlier piece, *The Waste Land* (1922)—protests that we are all today so emptied of validity that even

> At the hour when we are
> Trembling with tenderness
> Lips that would kiss
> Form prayers to broken stone.[2]

In the expatriate poet's memorable words:

> We are the hollow men
> We are the stuffed men

> Leaning together
> Headpiece filled with straw. Alas!
> Our dried voices, when
> We whisper together
> Are quiet and meaningless
> As wind in dry grass
> Or rats' feet over broken glass
> In our dry cellar
>
> Shape without form, shade without colour,
> Paralyzed force, gesture without motion.[3]

In the primitive and Oriental provinces of collective authority and faith, local customs were always mythologically overinterpreted as of superhuman origin. Among the primitives, generally, the mythological ancestors in the mythological age were believed to have founded, once and for all, the customs by which their descendants would have to abide if they and the world itself were to endure. In the great East, as in ancient Sumer and Akkad, Egypt and Babylon, the orthodox social order was traditionally regarded as of a piece with the order of nature, established—like the movements of the planets—on a context of eternal, impersonal, absolutely implacable cosmic law. And according to our own tradition, the moral orders of both the Old and New Testament issued from the will of a personal Creator God dwelling (as Bishop Robinson has remarked in his bold little volume *Honest to God*) somewhere either out or up "there."

It took the Greeks and Romans and the later Celts and Germans to realize that the laws by which men regulate their lives are of human derivation: conventional, not apodictical, hence alterable by the human will to comport with human aims and means. We count Greek philosophy and Roman law, as well as the modern concept of the secular state, as the great milestones of this release of man from the grip of his own nightmare of a past. And with this demythologization of the regulations of society—their reduction to the status of an expedient, rationally ordered, conventional frame, within the neutral field of which human lives of various kinds should be able to prosper with as little impediment as possible—the modern center of supreme concern has shifted from the social order *as an end* to the individual. A pathological throwback to archaic times and ideals has lately appeared, however, in that vast Eurasian empire of modernized Byzantine despotism (bounded by machine guns turned inward on its own imprisoned population) where the scientific brainwash now has replaced the catechism and confessional, the commissar the bishop, and *Das Kapital* the Bible. The genius Friedrich Nietzsche, as early as 1881, foresaw this possibility and warned of it—even described it—in his chapter on "The New Idol: The State," in his *Thus Spake Zarathustra:*

> The State, that is the coldest of all cold monsters. Coldly, also, it lies; and the lie that creeps from its mouth is this: "I, the State, am the People."
> That is a lie! Those who created peoples were creators, and they hung a faith over them and a love, and so, served life.
> Destroyers are these who lay snares for many and call it the State: they hang a sword over them and a hundred cravings.
> Where people still exist, the State is not understood, but hated as the evil eye and as sin against custom and law.
> I give unto you this sign: every people speaks of good and evil in its own language, which its neighbor does not understand. It has devised its language for itself in customs and in laws.
> But the State lies about good and evil in all tongues; and whatever it says, it lies—and whatever it has, it has stolen.
> Everything in it is false; it bites with stolen teeth—the biter. False even are its bowels. . . .
> But the earth still is free for great souls. Open still are many sites for one alone or for two alone, where the odor floats of quiet seas. . . .
> There where the State leaves off—look but there, my Brother! Do you not see it: the rainbow and the bridge of the Superman? [4]

Two great difficulties, however, confront the questing individual who, alone, would seek beyond the tumult of the state, in the silences of earth and sea and the silence of his heart, the Word beyond words of the mystery of nature and his own potentiality as man—like the knight errant riding forth into the forest "there where he saw it to be thickest." * The first is the difficulty of breaking through and beyond the system of delusion impressed upon and built into his very nerves by the forces—at once moral and

* Supra, p. 37.

linguistic—of his youth. Sigmund Freud has described as a process of introjection the psychological mechanism by which, in infancy, parental commands are imprinted indelibly on the motivating centers of the will; and the comparative linguist Benjamin Lee Whorf has demonstrated through a number of detailed comparisons to what extent the language learned in infancy determines not only the manner in which one's thoughts and feelings have to be expressed, but also the very patterns of those thoughts and feelings themselves.[5] Hence, even in the solitudes of those remotest fastnesses where the state would seem to have left off, the imprintings of our parish are with us, tattooed on the inside of our skins. Therein lies the sense of the enigmatic command of the Japanese Zen master: "Show me the face you had before you were born." In the Chinese Tao Te Ching we read of returning "to the uncarved block." And the Indian Upanishads point in every line to that interior, ineffable source of being, consciousness, and bliss, "wherefrom words turn back, together with the mind, not having attained." [6]

> Self-luminous, fixed, yet known as moving
>   in the secret cavity of the heart,
> That is the great support. Herein abides all
>   that moves and breathes and winks.[7]

And in the West: "O pleasing silence, where all things are still and the voice of the Beloved is heard with the faintest sound!" wrote the interesting Spaniard, Saint Thomas of Villanueva (1488–1555),[8] who as Archbishop of Valencia was a preacher of the mystic way from the pulpit of his see.

But then, when one has actually been vouchsafed an experience of one's own—transcending those categories written by one's people over the face of nature—upon returning, so to say, to the king's court and rejoining there, at the Table Round, those others who likewise in the dark wood were vouchsafed their own experiences, the second difficulty arises, of establishing some kind of life, in terms not of the old "collective faith" but of one's own.

T. S. Eliot, in a footnote to *The Waste Land,* cites a passage from F. H. Bradley's *Appearance and Reality*:

My external sensations [the philosopher had declared] are no less private to myself than are my thoughts or my feelings. In either case my experience falls within my own circle, a circle closed on the outside; and, with all its elements alike, every sphere is opaque to the others which surround it. . . . In brief, regarded as an existence which appears in a soul, the whole world for each is peculiar and private to that soul.[9]

In the light of Freud and Whorf, however, this cannot be altogether true, since the categories according to which our experiences become conscious even to ourselves have been supplied to us by our society and are shared by everybody in it. The really private experiences do not occur until these categories are dissolved; and then the second task emerges of communication: communication that will not immediately drag the whole discourse—and one's life itself—down and back into the now transcended mold.

In the case of the absolute hermit no communication is either attempted or desired; he rests in the state of Nietzsche's "one alone." In the case of a shared seizure of love (Nietzsche's case of "two alone"), as celebrated by Gottfried in his grotto of the crystalline bed, an immediately intelligible secret language of signs and words comes into being, from which the world is automatically excluded. And comparably, in larger context, where a team, a company, a tribe, or a people shares significant common experiences, a language inevitably comes into being that is, in depth, unintelligible to outsiders, even where its rational or pragmatic import may seem to be obvious and translatable.

In *Primitive Mythology* I have employed the term "mythogenetic zone" to designate any geographical area in which such a language of mythic symbols and related rites can be shown to have sprung into being.[10] However, when the forms of the rites and symbols are then diffused to other zones, or passed on to later generations no longer participating in the earlier experience, they lose depth, lose sense, lose heart; so that whereas originally their sense and effect had been spontaneously recognized and rendered—like the sense and effects of bird calls within the range of a species—in later use, having lost force, they are consciously reinterpreted and applied to new and even contrary themes—as occurred in the case, for example, of the serpent symbol in the Near East, when it passed from Sumero-Babylonian mythology to the Bible.[11]

In the modern world of science and the power-driven machine, global commerce, and massive cross-cultural exchanges, the social and physical backgrounds out of which the old symbolic orders arose have disappeared. Moreover, in our present world environment of intermingling religious communities, nationalities and races, social orders and economies, there is no actual community in depth anywhere, even where, for practical ends, agreements may appear to have been achieved. No one who has ever seriously attended an East-West philosophers' congress, an interfaith parley of religions, or a season at the UN will again believe that anything but empty barrels (which, as the proverb tells, make the most noise) can be transferred across a cultural divide. As the old Romans used to say, *"Senatus bestia, senatores boni viri:* The senate is a beast, the senators are good men."* The parliamentary arena has for centuries been understood to be the Devil's own gaming ground of deceit and compromise. And yet—to give the Devil his due—airtight empty barrels are exactly what is required in this new day of new wines. For, as even the most pessimistic eye must recognize, compromise and deceit, *force majeure* and accommodation, are gradually fashioning in this world today (though perhaps—tragically—too slowly) a sort of noncommittal social order, defined in a legal Esperanto, that should serve, in the end, as a demythologized, undecorated, merely practical frame for whatever possibilities of existence one or two alone or companies in consort may yet develop for themselves on this living earth and in the infinite space beyond. There is still the danger, of course, of the new monster idol, the state, with its scientific brainwash and its awesome, gruesome mass product, the non-individual doll of living flesh, moved not from within but by remote control and signal from without, like one of Pavlov's dogs. In the words, again, of T. S. Eliot's "The Hollow Men," *"Mistah Kurtz—he dead."*

> *Here we go round the prickly pear*
> *Prickly pear prickly pear*
> *Here we go round the prickly pear*
> *At five o'clock in the morning.*
>
> Between the idea
> And the reality
> Between the motion
> And the act
> Falls the Shadow
>   *For Thine is the Kingdom*

> Between the conception
> And the creation
> Between the emotion
> And the response
> Falls the Shadow
> > *Life is very long*
>
> Between the desire
> And the spasm
> Between the potency
> And the existence
> Between the essence
> And the descent
> Falls the Shadow
> > *For Thine is the Kingdom*
>
> For Thine is
> Life is
> For Thine is the
>
> *This is the way the world ends*
> *This is the way the world ends*
> *This is the way the world ends*
> *Not with a bang but a whimper.*[12]

And so, proceeding, we come to the question of translating an actual experience of life into the language of these dead—who are, however, not dead, but sleep, and among whom (as even the most pessimistic social critics must know) there move many who are neither dead nor asleep but searching; many others, furthermore, who have already roused within themselves a life more awake, Mr. Critic, than is perhaps dreamt of in your philosophy.

For we move—each—in two worlds: the inward of our own awareness, and an outward of participation in the history of our time and place. The scientist and historian serve the latter: the world, that is to say, of things "out there," where people are interchangeable and language serves to communicate information and commands. Creative artists, on the other hand, are mankind's wakeners to recollection: summoners of our outward mind to conscious contact with ourselves, not as participants in this or that morsel of history, but as spirit, in the consciousness of being. Their task, therefore, is to communicate directly from one

inward world to another, in such a way that an actual shock of experience will have been rendered: not a mere statement for the information or persuasion of a brain, but an effective communication
across the void of space and time from one center of consciousness
to another.

But that, in traditional systems, was the function of myth and
rite. Originating, as I have remarked, in the mythogenetic zone of
some particular place and time, as the depth-language spontaneously shared by all or most of the members of a largely homogeneous community, such a signal code lost force when the conditions
from which it sprang were historically altered and new conditions
arose through which to experience the mystery of existence. All
such codes are today in dissolution; and, given the miscellaneous
composition of our present social bodies and the fact, furthermore,
that in our world there exist no more closed horizons within the
bounds of which an enclave of shared experience might become established, we can no longer look to communities for the
generation of myth.

*The mythogenetic zone today is the individual in contact with his
own interior life, communicating through his art with those "out
there."*

But to this end communicative signs must be employed: words,
images, motions, rhythms, colors, and perfumes, sensations of all
kinds, which, however, come to the creative artist from without
and inevitably bear associations, not only colored by the past but
also relevant to the commerce of the day.

> Between the conception
> And the creation
> Between the creation
> And the response
> Falls the Shadow.

By what means can this intervention be transcended?

Gerhart Hauptmann somewhere has written: *"Dichten heisst,
hinter Worten das Urwort erklingen lassen:* Poetic writing consists
in letting the Word resound behind words."

There are schools of poetic speech that have sought, through
elevated rhetoric untouched by echoes of the marketplace, to bear
the educated mind aloft; others, to renew in us the force of earth

through accents of the soil and woodnotes wild. A few, more recently, have thought to purge away all language, thought, and civilization whatsoever, emitting sounds, syllables, tintinnabulations, pig grunts, eagle screams, baboon howls, and silence, returning thus to the lower Paleolithic for a fresh start. But pig grunts of themselves are no more eloquent of transcendence than are Alexandrian couplets. The art required is to make sounds, words, and forms, whether of base or of noble provenance, open out in back, as it were, to eternity, and this requires of the artist that he should himself, in his individual experience, have touched anew that still point in this turning world of which the immemorial mythic forms are the symbols and guarantee. In fact, if one may judge from the record, the shared secret of all the really great creative artists of the West has been that of letting themselves be wakened by—and then reciprocally reawakening—the inexhaustibly suggestive mythological symbols of our richly compound European heritage of intermixed traditions. Avoiding, on one hand, the popular mistake of reading mythology as a reference to hard historic fact and, on the other hand, the puerility of rejecting the guidance of the centuries and so drowning like a puppy in the shallows of one's own first depth, they have passed, one and all, beyond this general wrecking point of Scylla and Charybdis to that sun door of which the knowers have sung through all ages, each in the language of his own world. Having let their imaginations be roused by the waking power of the symbols, they have followed the echoes of their eloquence within—each opening thus a way of his own to the seat of silence where signals cease. And returning then to the world and its companionship, having learned from their own depths the grammar of symbolic speech, they are competent to touch to new life the museum of the past as well as the myths and dreams of their present—in that way to bring (as in the closing chorus of Wagner's *Parsifal*) "redemption to the Redeemer," causing the petrified, historicized blood of the Savior to flow again as a fountain of spiritual life.

So let us reconsider, now, in brief series, the chief strains of traditional word and symbol that have served our master poets and artists both as guides to the silence of the Word behind words and as the means to communicate its rapture; commencing with the epoch of those bold twelfth- and thirteenth-century poets who were

the first individual authors in a truly modern sense, and coming
down to this present time of our own great masters of the
Word.

II. The Classical Heritage

We have already remarked Gottfried's celebration of Apollo and
the nine Muses on the paradisial summit of Mount Helicon. Dante
also called upon the Muses—at the opening of the *Inferno,* Canto
II—and he was guided both through his Hell and to the paradisial
summit of Mount Purgatory by the pagan Virgil, who throughout
the earlier Middle Ages had already been idealized as *l'altissimo
poeta,* the paramount literary guide. Figure 10 is a quaint conception of Virgil's Dido and Aeneas from a tenth-century manuscript
in the Biblioteca Nazionale, Naples. In form and gesture the figures are not classical but medieval; for as the late Professor
E. R. Curtius states in his formidable study *European Literature
and the Latin Middle Ages,* "The Middle Ages had their own view
of antiquity." No less in philosophy and science than in literature
and art, the authority of the Greco-Roman heritage throughout
even the dark period from the fifth to eleventh centuries was such
that Dr. Curtius could write of a single Classical European tradition extending without break from Homer to Goethe.[13] It was carried by way of two interacting streams. One, above ground, was of
the poets and philosophers, grammarians, scientists, and historians, openly read and taught in the schools. The other, more secret, beneath ground, was of the mystery cults which in the late
Roman centuries had flourished throughout the classical world,
from India and the Upper Nile to the Celtic British Isles.

Figures 11 and 12 show the inside and outside of an alabaster
bowl of about the period of the Pietroasa bowl of Figures 3 and 4.
In the center—where in the other bowl a goddess sits on a throne
entwined by a vine—the forward part of a winged serpent (one
wing lost) coils around a hemispherical mound, from the base of
which radiate spikes of flame. Sixteen figures, nine women, seven
men, all naked, stand in attitudes of worship, with eyes turned toward the serpent, several holding one hand to the chest in the posture of the initiate of Figure 3, Station 7. Five women stand in a
sort of Venus de' Medici pose, suggesting the attitude of the androgyne at Station 11 of the other series; and there—as here—

Figure 10. Dido and Aeneas; 10th century A.D.

sixteen figures are to be seen. The winged serpent, furthermore, combines the wings of the griffin at Station 16 with the reptilian character of the beast at Station 10, which indicates that we are here within such a sanctuary as in the other series must have been entered by the candidate at Station 10: of the mystery beyond the "pairs of opposites," following which, at 11, the initiate stands as an androgyne with the wings above his head of the Holy Spirit.

Now, in the Hellenistic mystery cults initiates entering the holy

Figure 11. The Sanctum of the Winged Serpent;
Orphic bowl, 2nd or 3rd century A.D.

of holies were often required to be naked, and, whereas women
were excluded from Mithraic rites,[14] they were essential to the
Orphic-Dionysian, both as inciters of the mystic rapture and as vehicles of the revelation. Witness their prominence in the Pietroasa
context, both as guides and as divinities. There both they and the
initiates are clothed and everything is in movement: here all is still.
The mound in the center, covered by the winged serpent, is the top
of the Orphic cosmic egg, within which all mortal creatures dwell.

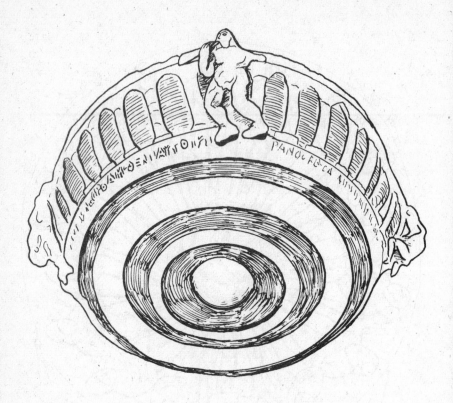

Figure 12. Outside of the Serpent Bowl

This company is *outside* and *above* the egg. They have ascended (spiritually) through the sun door, which opens at the instant of noon at the summit of the sky. The clashing rocks (Symplegades) which separate at that moment have closed again beneath them, and they are now (in knowledge) in eternity, beyond all pairs of opposites: death-birth, male-female, subject-object, good-and-evil, light-and-dark. The normal limitations of human thought and sense, the clothing of the mind, were destroyed in the fiery passage, the purging flames of which are now blazing *at their feet;* and the serpent wrapped around the mound, at which they gaze in silent rapture, combines the forms that would have been seen below as opposites: the serpent crawling on its belly and the bird in winged flight. This figure of transcendent form represents the same world-suffusing power that is symbolized in the other bowl by

the rapture-inspiring potion in the chalice of the Goddess Mother
of all being. Standing in the bowl of the winged serpent, we are
inside that sacramental chalice, drinking with our eyes, so to
say, the intoxicant, there symbolized as wine, of the mystery
of the substance of our being.

Figure 12, the outside of the bowl, is a view of the heavenly
dome from beneath the vault of the ever-turning cosmic shell—the
merely exoteric view made known to us through our eyes and the
instruments of science. Four nude cherubs blowing trumpets and
conchs at the four points of the compass symbolize the four winds
of the round of space and the seasons of the round of time; twenty-
four columns support this space-time structure, as hours support
the day; while beneath, on the floor of heaven, the ceiling of our
world, are the circles of the orbits of the spheres. Moreover, an inscription around the base in slightly incorrect Greek was recognized by the first interpreter of this bowl, Professor Hans Leisegang, as composed of partial quotations from four separate Orphic hymns:

> Hear, Thou who turnest forever the
>   radiant sphere of distant motion. . . .
>
> Originally Heaven and Earth were a single
>   form—the Cosmic Egg. . . .
>
> First, light—Phanes—appeared: named
>   also Dionysus, because it moves in a
>   circle round the infinitely lofty
>   Mount Olympus. . . .
>
> He is glittering Zeus, Father of All the World.[15]

So let us now turn to Figure 13, "The Music of the Spheres,"
from a fifteenth-century Neoplatonic work, Gafurius's *Practica
musice,* published in 1496 in Milan. The figure of the descending
serpent is dramatic. Where it breaks below into the spheres of the
four elements it divides into a triad of animal heads: a lion at the
center, wolf to our left, dog to our right. Gafurius identified this
beast with the guardian dog Cerberus of Hades,[16] which in the
Hellenistic period had been pictured as triple-headed with a serpent tail. In the temple in Alexandria of the Greco-Egyptian syncretic god Serapis (who was identified syncretically with Zeus, Di-

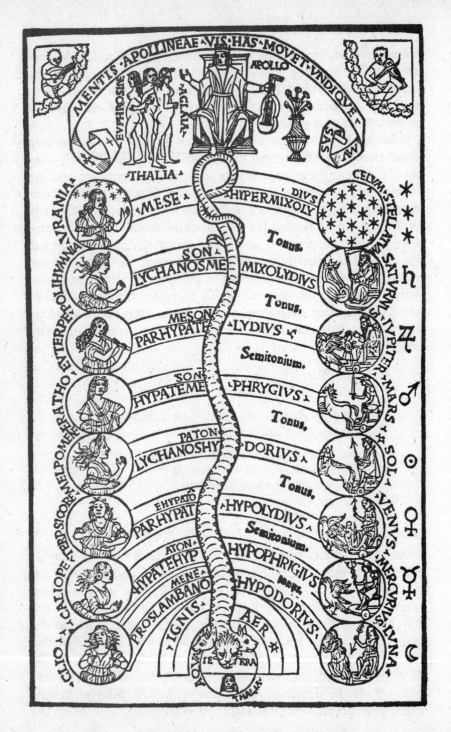

Figure 13. The Music of the Spheres; Italy, 1496

onysus, Phanes, Apollo, Osiris and the Apis bull) the diety sat on
a lofty throne with Cerberus at his feet, as here.[17] The beast's
heads symbolize Devouring Time in its three aspects—Present,
Past, and Future—through which the unchanging presence of the
god is experienced, ever passing, here on earth. As we read in
Macrobius's *Saturnalia* (fifth century A.D.): "The lion, violent and
sudden, expresses the present; the wolf, which drags away its victims, is the image of the past, robbing us of memories; the dog,
fawning on its master, suggests to us the future, which ceaselessly
beguiles us with hope." [18]

At the bottom of Gafurius's plan, breathed upon by the lion's
head, is a female form labeled Thalia, "Abundance," the first of
the nine Muses. The other eight in ascending series appear along
the left, and at the top is again the name of Thalia, here designa-
ting, however, the central member of the triad of Graces, dancing
unclothed on paradisial Mount Helicon before Apollo's throne.

Thalia, in her character as Muse, at the bottom, is the inspiration of Bucolic Poetry and Comedy, and as here represented, *below* the surface of the earth, unseen, she is "Silent Thalia," *surda
Thalia,* the Muse unheard. For men confronted by the frightening
features of time, which they do not penetrate with understanding,
are made blind and deaf to the inspiration of the Muse of the Poetry of Nature, and it is only when one's spirit has been transported
to the summit of wisdom that her glory is disclosed.

Read in terms of the churchly tradition, the Grace Thalia, above,
would suggest Eve in her state of purity; Euphrosyne, "Mirth,"
turned away from the god, her inclination to rebellion; Thalia below, Eve in exile, subject to the serpent and consequently to the
fears, hopes, and bereavements of time; and finally, the Grace
Aglaia, "Splendor," above, with her gaze turned toward the god,
the Virgin Mother Mary, "changing Eva's name"—Eva to Ave!—
and thus undoing the work of Euphrosyne, "Mirth," or, as a proper
Christian might say, of "Sinful Pleasure."

However, as a glance again at the picture of God the Father fishing (Figure 8) reminds us, according to the usual Christian reading of such symbols the serpent power is not an emanation earth-
ward of God's creative will, but a contrary force, opposed to it;
hence the Muses, placed in series by Gafurius along the length of
the serpent body, would in orthodox thought be associated rather

with the Fall than with a redemption, and the arts would be condemned: as they are, in fact, both in Christian Puritanism, and in
the biblical First Commandment against images (Exodus 20:4).

In a properly Christian art the forms do not seduce the senses to
this world, but are allegorical of spiritual themes and of the
legends of the Savior and his saints, by which the mind and spirit
are exalted beyond this world to God, who is transcendent and
apart. Whereas in Gafurius's design—as in general in classical art
—the Muses represent and are addressed to the spheres of their
respective stations, all of which pertain to the body and field of
power of the serpent itself. And the serpent, in turn, is not opposed
to the Lord of Life and Light, but a manifestation of his creative
force and harmony. To realize this, and to rise then along the
mounting scale from one glory to the next, one has only to face
and dare to enter the lion's mouth: the flaming sun door of the
present, absorbed totally in the living here-and-now, without hope,
without fear. Whereupon the rapture of the Muses—the arts—will
begin to be experienced in the body of this world itself, transport-
ing our spirit from glory to glory, to that summit of joy in consciousness where the world eye—beyond hope, beyond fear—
surveys the universe in its coming, going, and being. For, just as
the serpent is not opposed to the Lord, but the vehicle of his downgoing grace, so are the Muses—clothed in the garments of this
world—not opposed to the unclothed Graces, but in triple rhythm
(3 times 3) the earthly heralds of their paradisial dance. And they
are nine because (as Dante tells of his own Muse, Beatrice) their
root (the square root of nine being three) is in the trinity above.

Beyond the frightening visage of all-consuming time, the arts—
the Muses—initiate us to the enduring harmony of the universe,
the planes or aspects of which are controlled by the planets and
their spheres. Gafurius shows the signs and deities of these at the
right of his design, matching the Muses at the left. As Thalia, below, is of the earth, so Clio (lower left), the Muse of History, presides on the plane of the moon, controller of the tides of time,
while Calliope, Heroic Poetry, matches Mercury (Hermes), the
guide of souls beyond the temporal sphere. Next come Terpsi-
chore, Muse of the Dance and Choral Song, in the sphere of Venus
and Cupid; Melpomene, Tragedy, who purges and illuminates with
the fire and light of the Sun; and Erato, Lyric and Erotic Poetry,

on the plane of Mars, god of war. Beyond this central, tragic triad, then, we are released by the power of music from all visible forms whatsoever.* Euterpe, the Muse of Flute Music, elevates the mind to the plane of Jupiter, where the soul, as the child to its father in the confirmation scene at the right, is turned to the protecting aspect of the Lord. Polyhymnia, the Muse of Sacred Song, celebrates the aspect of the Father in Saturn, wielding the scythe that cuts us free from this world controlled by the planetary spheres, after which, in the sphere of the fixed stars, the Muse Urania, Astronomy, transports us from the body of the serpent altogether (the loop of whose tail suggests the sun door), to the very feet of the highest transformation of the Father, sheer light.

This ladder of the planetary shells, presented by a fifteenth-century Italian music master to demonstrate, as he declares, "that the Muses, Planets, Modes, and strings correspond with one another," [19] actually is an idea of the greatest age. It was known already to the Stoics and is developed in Cicero's "Dream of Scipio" (cited in *Occidental Mythology*),[20] where the spheres are named in this same order and said to produce a loud agreeable sound by the motion of their revolutions. But the earthly sphere, the ninth, "remains ever motionless and stationary in its position in the center of the universe": hence Gafurius's *surda Thalia*. "Learned men, by imitating this harmony on stringed instruments and in song," Cicero states, "have gained for themselves a return to the supernal heights." And Gafurius, in accord, has allotted to each step both a note of the scale and the title of a Greek musical mode.

The names of the notes are at the left; they are of the Classical conjoint Dorian-Phrygian tetrachord (our A-minor scale), as follows: Proslambanomenos (A), Hypate hypaton (B), Parhypate hypaton (C), Lichanos hypaton (D), Hypate meson (E), Parhypate meson (F), Lichanos meson (G), and Mese (the octave). At the right are the matching modes: Hypodorian, Hypophrygian, Hypolydian, Dorian, Phrygian, Lydian, Mixolydian, and Hypomixolydian. Assigned, furthermore, to each sphere is a metal whose symbol is that of its planet: to the moon silver, quicksilver to Mercury, copper to Venus, gold to the sun, iron to Mars, tin to Jupiter, and lead to Saturn. The soul, descending from its heavenly home, takes on the matter and weight of these metals and, ascend-

* Compare Schopenhauer, supra, p. 83.

ing, casts them off, to arrive naked again above. Hence the symbolism of nakedness—the naked soul—before God: the naked Graces before Apollo and the figures in the mystery-cult bowl. Hence, too, the "dance of the seven veils" performed by Salome before Herod, the earliest extant version of which symbolic "stripping of the self" is the Old Sumerian "Descent of Inanna to the Underworld" of about 2500 B.C.[21]

Now, according to Hesiod (eighth century B.C.), the nine Muses were the daughters of Mnemosyne, "Memory," and Zeus.[22] Born of Memory, they cause the soul to *remember* its forgotten higher estate, where, at the summit of this eightfold noble path of return, there is discovered the very god of light represented in the Pietroasa bowl (Figure 3) and addressed in the Orphic hymns of our second bowl (Figure 12). Moreover, the number of nude females within the holy of holies of this second bowl is nine, the number of the Muses; while the number of the men is seven, the number of the visible spheres. In Gafurius's design the draped Muses correspond to the guiding females of the first of these two bowls and the undraped dancing Graces to the naked initiates of the second. Euphrosyne, "Mirth," turned away from the Presence, represents the outward-going, descending movement of divine grace animating the world; Aglaia, "Splendor," facing the Lord, is the returning grace of the human spirit; and Thalia, "Abundance," who is one with the Muse of Nature, denotes the balance embracing the outward and returning modes.

The triadic round of these three is magnified in the world-animating triple rhythm of the Nine and far below reflected in the triad of the heads of Cerberus: future, present, and past. Furthermore, the ascending form of this serpent is the winged apparition of Figure 11, bearing instead of those animal heads at either side, the wings of the revealed spirit. And Thalia, the Muse of the Idyll of Life's Garden—who on the inferior stage was silent—here in the knowledge of eternity is at one with the movements both of Splendor and of Mirth. And all three, in turn, are unfoldments of the spirit of the goddess Venus, Love, whose special art below is the dance.

Thus in this Renaissance diagram the whole sense of the two bowls together is comprised. Silent Thalia at the base corresponds to the goddess in the center of the Pietroasa bowl, holding the cup of intoxicating yet elevating blood of the vine; and her restricting circle, earth, surrounded by the water of the abyss, having air and fire above, corresponds to the inner circle of the bowl, where the shepherd dreams the dream of life. The ladder of ascent with its guiding Muses corresponds to the circle of initiations, leading to the vision of the god; and as vines and fruit there appeared at the moment of arrival, so here there is a vase of flowers. The instrument in the god's hand has seven strings, the seven spheres; and these are matched on the second bowl (Figure 12) by the rings leading to the center, the sun door to illumination. Both the inside of this second bowl and the inside of the chalice of the Pietroasa goddess (Figure 4) thus correspond to the top of Gafurius's diagram, the cosmological lesson of which is written on the scroll above the god: *"Mentis Apollineae vis has movet undique Musas:* The energy of the Apollinian Mind sets these Muses everywhere in motion"—which, exactly, is the sense of the first of the Orphic hymns inscribed on the alabaster bowl:

> Hear, Thou who turnest forever the
> radiant sphere of distant motion. . . .*

And then finally, of course, the two music-makers at the upper corners correspond, in this two-dimensional design, to the four nude blowers of horns and conchs around the bowl.

Now, in the course of the long five centuries of the Roman occupation of Gaul and Britain (c. 50 B.C. to c. 450 A.D.), the myths and rituals of the Hellenistic mysteries were not only carried to those colonies but associated syncretically with appropriate local gods. For example, in the Gallo-Roman altar from Reims shown in *Oriental Mythology,* page 307, the Celtic god Cernunnos sits in the posture of Hades-Pluto, between Mercury and Apollo, as though uniting the powers of these two. Likewise, in *Occidental Mythology,* pages 306 and 307, two panels are shown from a Gallo-Roman altar unearthed near Notre Dame de Paris, in which a Gaulish divinity identified with the Irish hero Cuchulinn is shown chopping a tree beneath which a bull stands, upon whose back there perch *three* goddesses in the form of long-necked cranes. Cuchulinn was the prototype of the Round Table knight Sir

* Supra, p. 99.

Gawain.[23] His pagan legends were recorded during that period of Irish Christian civilization, between the sixth and eleventh centuries, when Greek and Latin learning still was cultivated by the Irish clergy as nowhere else in devastated Europe. The Abbot Aileran of Cloncard, writing c. 660 on the mystical meanings of the names in Christ's genealogy, for example, quoted familiarly from Origen, Jerome, Philo, and Augustine. The Abbot Sedulius of Kildare, c. 820, corrected his Latin New Testament from a Greek original and composed for Charlemagne's grandson a treatise on the art of government.[24] The Neoplatonist Scotus Erigena (c. 815–877),[25] whom Professor Adolph Harnack termed "the most learned and perhaps also the wisest man of his age," [26] is to be named *magna cum laude* in this context. And for a bit of direct visual evidence of a relationship between the Neoplatonic symbolism of both Alexandria and the Renaissance and the works and prayers of the Irish monkish scribes of Glendalough, Dingle, and Kells, a reconsideration of the Tunc-page of the ninth-century Book of Kells should suffice (reproduced and discussed in *Occidental Mythology*, pages 467–470 and 480). The invocation by Gottfried of the Muses nine before Apollo's throne acquires for us now a new force—particularly in relation to the enspelling power of Tristan's harp (Figure 2), which is a match for that of Orpheus, who in the earliest Christian tradition could even stand, as in the Domitilla fresco (Figure 1), for the Redeemer. Dante's entire *Divina Commedia,* moreover, is of a piece with this pagan vision of a spiritual dimension of the universe.

"In the middle of the road of our life, I found myself in a dark wood, where the right way was lost." So commences the mighty work.[27] And the poet states that he cannot well say how he came into that wood. "I was so full of sleep," he tells, "at the time that I left the true way.

"But when I came to the foot of a hill where that valley ended which had pierced my heart with fear, I looked upward and beheld its shoulders already clothed with the rays of the planet [the sun] that guides man aright, along no matter what road." [28]

A suspicion that Dante's dark wood of fear must be analogous to the circle of Silent Thalia, and the hill where the valley ended, clothed with "the rays of the planet that guides man aright," to Mount Helicon, with Apollo, is increased by the next event of the adventure. For immediately, as Dante tells, three dangerous beasts appeared: the first a she-leopard, "light and very nimble, covered with a spotted coat"; the second a lion, "coming at me with head high and with ravening hunger"; and the last a she-wolf, "which in her leaness seemed laden with all cravings, and ere now had made many folk to live forlorn." [29] The leopard, of fair and varied seeming, typified for Dante temptations of the flesh, that false allure of desire which in Gafurius's design is represented by the head of a dog. The lion symbolized pride, the fundamental sin by which man, self-bounded, is held from the vision of God. And the she-wolf symbolized avarice, striving for what time takes away. These are the forces—functions of the false allure of time—by which those who have lost the right way are held trapped in delusion.

However, as in Gafurius's design, so here. The grace of poetry, sent by the Muses, bore the voyager past the dangerous beasts. Falling back before them in fear, he beheld approaching the figure of Virgil.

"I will be your guide," said the pagan poet.[30]

"O Muses," Dante then prayed; "O lofty genius, now assist me!" [31]

And with this noble guide, casting fear away, the lost Christian moved along the deep and savage road into the mouth of Hell itself.[32]

Besides Virgil, furthermore, there were six other classical masters whom Dante encountered on his way and who, as Professor Curtius shows, were the chief intellectual authorities of the Middle Ages. They were, namely, Homer, Horace, Ovid, and Lucan, in Limbo, the first circle of Hell; Cato at the foot of Mount Purgatory; and Statius at its summit, the Earthly Paradise, where Dante at last found again his personal muse, Beatrice. In life she had opened his eyes to earthly beauty,* and now in death bore his spirit, in faith, beyond the natural virtues of the pagans, up the very scale of the planets of Gafurius's design, to the seat of that triune god of Christians, one substance in three divine persons, of whom (according to the Christian view) the merely natural light of Apollonian reason is but the earthly figuration.

This Christian devaluation of the pagan light of lights, Apollo, and along with Apollo the whole classical mystery tradition from

* Supra, p. 68.

which the Christian was in part derived, is an elegant instance of
the manner in which a later cult may supplant an earlier simply by
refusing to recognize the interpretation of its symbols given by its
own supreme initiates, reading them in a reductive way and then
setting its own symbol in the emptied higher place. Dante's termination of the guiding power of the pagans at the summit of Mount
Purgatory, the Earthly Paradise, accords with the formula of Aquinas, whereby reason may lead, as it led the ancients, to the summit
of earthly virtue, but only faith and supernatural grace (personified in Beatrice) can lead beyond reason to the seat of God.

However, as we regard with Dante the features of this god in the
aspect of a trinity, we are led to a further observation, to wit, that
in the Christian doctrine of *three divine persons* in *one divine substance* what we actually have is a transposition of the symbolism
of the *Graces three* and *Hyperborean Apollo* into a mythological
order of exclusively masculine masks of God—which accords well
enough with the patriarchal spirit of the Old Testament but unbal-
ances radically the symbolic, and therefore spiritual, connotations
not only of sex and the sexes, but also of all nature.

The Greek formula was of immeasurable age and represented,
furthermore, a symbolic system of astonishingly broad distribution. We may recall, for instance, the myths from West Ceram
(Indonesia) of Hainuwele and her two sisters, and the prominence
there not only of the number three but also of the number nine.[33]
Or consider again those cranes on the back of the Celtic bull. In
the patriarchal revision of the old heterosexual symbology, the Son
corresponds to the downgoing Grace; the Holy Ghost, to the returning; the Father, to the all-bounding Grace; and the One Substance, to the light of the Apollonian mind. Three persons, differentiated, would, according to classical thinking, have to be regarded as conditioned; i.e., comprised in a field of relationships,
within the matrix of the cosmic goddess Space-Time—as they do
in fact appear in the fifteenth-century French image of the mother
of God reproduced in *Occidental Mythology*, page 513, Figure
32. Though defined as male, they represent functions of *māyā*,*
and might as properly, therefore, have retained the female form.
Moreover, a certain almost ridiculous difficulty has followed upon
this exclusion of the female principle from its normal cosmic

* Supra, pp. 77 and 78–79, and *Oriental Mythology*, p. 335.

role. The mythological females of the Christian myth have had
to be interpreted historically: Mother Eve, before and after the
Fall, as a prehistoric character in a garden that never was; and
Mary, the "mother of God," as a virgin who conceived miraculously and was physically assumed into a place called "Heaven
above" that does not physically exist.

Throughout the history of the Christian cult, the liability of its
historicized symbols to reinterpretation in some general mythological sense has been a constant danger; and, reciprocally,
the susceptibility of the Greek—and even Buddhist, Hindu,
Navaho, and Aztec—mythologies to readings approximately
Christian has also been a threat, of which advantage has been
recently taken by T. S. Eliot in his *Four Quartets,* James Joyce
in *Finnegans Wake,* and Thomas Mann in *Joseph and His
Brothers.* Many artists of the Renaissance and Baroque periods, likewise, took advantage of these possibilities, and even
as early as the period of the catacombs there is that Domitilla ceiling (Figure 1). In fact, this possibility and the knowledge of it
are what I have termed the secret stream, below ground, of our
classical heritage of symbolic communication.

For a passing glance at the other stream, let me conclude this
brief memorandum of the wealth of our classical endowment with
a passage from Professor Curtius's summation of the meaning to
the Middle Ages of those six great names whom Dante met as he
was led along his way:

> Homer, the illustrious progenitor, was hardly more than a
> great name in the Middle Ages. For medieval Antiquity is Latin
> Antiquity. But the name had to be named. Without Homer,
> there would have been no *Aeneid;* without Odysseus's descent
> into Hades, no Virgilian journey through the other world; with-
> out the latter, no *Divina Commedia.* To the whole of late An-
> tiquity, as to the whole of the Middle Ages, Virgil is what he is
> for Dante: "l'altissimo poeta." Next to him stands Horace, as
> the representative of Roman satire. This the Middle Ages re-
> garded as wholesome sermonizing on manners and morals, and
> it found many imitators from the twelfth century onwards.
> Whatever else it may be, Dante's *Commedia* is also a denuncia-
> tion of his times. Ovid, however, wore a different face for the
> Middle Ages than he does for us. In the beginning of the *Meta-*

morphoses, the twelfth century found a cosmogony and cosmology which were in harmony with contemporary Platonism. But the *Metamorphoses* were also a repertory of mythology as exciting as a romance. Who was Phaeton? Lycaon? Procne? Arachne? Ovid was the *Who's Who* for a thousand such questions. One had to know the *Metamorphoses;* otherwise one could not understand Latin poetry. Furthermore, all these mythological stories had an allegorical meaning. So Ovid was also a treasury of morality. Dante embellishes episodes of the *Inferno* with transformations intended to outdo Ovid, as he outdoes Lucan's *terribilita.* Lucan was the virtuoso of horror and a turgid pathos, but he was also versed in the underworld and its witchcraft. In addition he was the source book for the Roman Civil War, the panegyrist of the austere Cato of Utica whom Dante places as guardian at the foot of the Mount of Purgatory. Statius, finally, was the bard of the Fratricidal Theban War, and his epic closes with homage to the divine *Aeneid.* The "Tale of Thebes" was a favorite book in the Middle Ages, as popular as the Arthurian romances. It contained dramatic episodes, arresting characters. Oedipus, Amphiaraus, Capaneus, Hypsipyle, the infant Archemorus—the dramatis personae of the *Thebais* are constantly referred to in the *Commedia.*

Dante's meeting with the *bella scuola* seals the reception of the Latin epic into the Christian cosmological poem. This embraces an ideal space, in which a niche is left free for Homer, but in which all the great figures of the West are likewise assembled (Augustus, Trajan, Justinian); the Church Fathers; the masters of the seven liberal arts; the luminaries of philosophy; the founders of monastic orders; the mystics. But the realm of these founders, organizers, teachers, and saints was to be found only in one historical complex of European culture: in the Latin Middle Ages. There lie the roots of the *Divine Comedy.* The Latin Middle Ages is the crumbling Roman road from the antique to the modern world.[34]

III. The Celto-Germanic Heritage

But let us now turn our thoughts to that fund of native North European lore which in the twelfth and thirteenth centuries became suddenly and with marvelous effect the chief inspiration of the golden age of courtly romance. Classical as well as Christian strains, together with Islamic, had already been threaded through the legends. In the Celtic sphere, the Gallo-Roman altars already noticed testify to the classical influence,* while for the Germans there is the old runic script, developed from the Greek, which in the first centuries A.D. passed from the Hellenized Gothic provinces northwest of the Black Sea, up the Danube and down the Elbe, to Scandinavia and England.[35] There is the figure, furthermore, of Othin (Woden, Wotan), self-crucified on the World Ash as an offering to himself, to gain the occult wisdom of those runes, which is clearly a Hellenistic motif (compare Figure 9).

Perhaps the most suggestive revelation yet disclosed, however, of what one authority has called the "highly cosmopolitan culture" of the old Germanic courts is to be seen in the astonishing Sutton Hoo ship-burial that in 1939 was unearthed in Suffolk, on the River Deben, six miles inland from the sea. The large buried hull with its rich grave hoard has been assigned to a date between 650 and 670, and the associated warrior-prince seems to have been either the pagan Anglian King Æthelhere (d. 655), whose wife, a Christian, had left him to enter a nunnery near Paris, or his younger brother, King Æthelwald (d. 663–664), a Christian. Among the objects found were silver dishes from Byzantium, Merovingian gold coins, what appears to be a Swedish sword, a beautiful little harp, and numerous elegantly fashioned jeweled ornaments of local Anglo-Saxon manufacture. Mr. R. L. S. Bruce-Mitford of the British Museum, where these objects now are displayed, remarks that in this treasure "there is the revelation of the wide contacts—Frankish, Scandinavian, Central European, Byzantine, and beyond—of a Saxon royal house of the early seventh century"; and he adds: "Already in all probability in the time of Redwald [c. 618] there had developed in East Anglia a highly cosmopolitan culture, one element of which was a direct knowledge of objects and patterns of the classical world." [36]

The first known name in the history of English literature belongs to the date of this ship-burial; namely of the gentle poet Caedmon, who flourished c. 657–680. According to his legend preserved by the Venerable Bede (whose dates are also of this time, 673–735), he was a cowherd in the employ of the Abbess Saint Hilda of Whitby, who because of his lack of education had been used to quit the banquet hall whenever the company began to sing and the

* Supra, p. 105.

harp came his way. Retiring to his stable, he would lie down dis-
consolately to sleep; but there one evening, as the legend tells:

> While he slept, someone stood by him in a dream, greeted,
> called him by name, and said to him, "Caedmon, sing me some-
> thing." He replied, "I know not how to sing; that is the reason I
> left the feast. I am here because I cannot sing." The personage
> insisted: "No matter, you must sing to me." "Well," he an-
> swered, "what shall I sing?" To which the other responded:
> "Sing the beginning of created things." And at that, straightway,
> Caedmon sang in praise of God the Creator verses he had never
> heard.[37]

The tale reminds one of the Chinese legend of the Zen patriarch
Hui-neng, whose dates, 638–713, coincide with those of Caedmon.[38] The two legends render the same doctrine of a wisdom beyond learning; yet no one, as far as I know, has yet worked out, or
even suggested, any relationship between the spiritual worlds of
the British cowherd and Chinese kitchen-boy. On the face of it, the
common idea involved is—in the Jungian sense—archetypal and
might be expected to arise independently in any number of traditions. However, it is a fact that in early medieval times there were
great movements of hardy peoples in the regions between Europe
and the Far East.

As early as the fifth century A.D. related tribes of Huns struck
simultaneously into Europe, India, and China. A dynasty of vigo-
rous Tibetan kings was expanding its inner Asian conquests and
influence from the period of Song-tsen Gam-po (c. 630) to the
death of Ral-pa-chen (838). Nestorian as well as Manichaean
monasteries were on the caravan ways to China and even flourished in China itself until the reign of the fanatic Emperor Wu-
tsung (r. 841–846).[39] And, as remarked in *Oriental Mythology,*
there is a more than incidental similarity between the myths
and legends of the Iron Age Celts and Iron Age Japan—the
dates of the earliest Japanese collections, the *Kojiki* and *Nihongi,* being 712 and 720 A.D.[40] The entire question is wide
open, fascinating, and, as far as I know, unexplored as yet by
scholar's eye.

According to our school textbooks, Hui-neng's contemporary
Caedmon is significant for literature in having applied the techniques of traditional Germanic bardic verse to the rendition of bib-

lical themes in Anglo-Saxon. He was followed, perhaps c. 730–750,[41] by the unknown *Beowulf* poet, who sang in the same Germanic style for an aristocratic, not monastic, audience, rendering for its lately converted Christian ears an old Germanic hero-legend of the monster- and dragon-killings of a Scandinavian king ancestral to the local Anglian line.[42]

Authoritative scholars have detected signs of the influence of Virgil in this Christianized pagan work,[43] and in the light of the learning of that time such an influence was almost inevitable. Bede, the "Father of English History," was writing his important *Historia Ecclesiastica Gentis Anglorum,* which at least one authority has termed "probably the best history written by an Englishman before the seventeenth century." [44] Bede was the author also of substantial works on theology, grammar, natural science, chronology, and the calendar. We have already mentioned the state of learning in Ireland in this period. The *Beowulf* poet, too, was erudite in both native and classical lore.

But in Bede there are signs also of at least a modicum of Oriental influence; for in his *Ecclesiastical History* there is an arresting vision of Hell, attributed to a certain Drihthelm of Cunningham, in which an unmistakable Eastern feature appears. "Radiant in face and look and in bright apparel was he who guided me . . . ," the passage begins.

> We arrived at the valley of great breadth and depth, and of infinite length. . . . One part was very dreadful, being full of boiling flames; the other not less intolerable through the chill of hail and snow. Both were full of men's souls, which seemed to be cast to either side in turn, as though by the overpowering violence of a great storm. When they could not endure the force of the excessive heat, they sprang away in their misery into the midst of excessive cold; and when they could find no rest there, they sprang back into the midst of the burning fire and the unquenchable flame.[45]

In *Oriental Mythology* it is seen that in the Indian Jain and Buddhist Hells torture by cold is as prominent as that by fire.[46] It is prominent also in Zoroastrian belief, whence it entered the lore of Islam. But, as Father Miguel Asín y Palacios states in his pioneering study of Moslem influence on Dante, "Biblical eschatology makes no mention of any torture of cold in hell." [47] The influence

of Islamic thought and imagery on Dante is now conceded, even
(though reluctantly) in Italy itself. And in fact, how could there
possibly have been none? Since the period of Charlemagne (r.
768–814), and with increasing force since the First Crusade
(1096–1099), the civilization of the Near East had been a major
contributor to Europe. Spain had fallen to the Moors in 711. Sicily, plundered as early as 655, remained a battleground of the two
religions throughout the ninth, tenth, and eleventh centuries. The
twelfth-century troubadours and thirteenth-century scholastic theologians were enormously indebted to Islam. Moreover, the Neapol-
itan court of Dante's most admired Emperor, Frederick II (r.
1220–1250), was even brazenly hospitable to Moslem learning.
Hence, though it is indeed a bit surprising to find a Buddhist-Zoro-
astrian motive in a Christian vision of Hell as early as 731, the date
of Bede's completion of his *History,* it is not impossible; and by
Dante's time it would have been impossible for there *not* to have
been such an influence.*

Thus *Beowulf* was the product of an age already of mixed traditions. It is the earliest extant work of length in the vernacular liter-
atures of Northern Europe and sounds in its sturdy verses a significant number of themes that were to be echoed, amplified, restated,
and interpreted through many centuries, even to our own. The
"aristocratic tone" of the poem, the "refinement and deep courtesy of the life in the dwellings of kingly warriors" which it depicts,
have been remarked by Professor C. L. Wrenn of Oxford in his
recently published commentary; "and this nobility of tone," as he
states, "accords well with the dignity of a style which freely uses
periphrases." [48] Or, as my own revered master, the late Professor
W. W. Lawrence of Columbia, states in his volume on *Beowulf
and the Epic Tradition,* "although derived to a large extent from
popular sources," the poem was "the product of an *ars poetica* of
settled principles and careful development." [49]

In the seventh century [Professor Lawrence continues] the
Irish monks were active in the north, and their preaching was
fortified by that of the celebrated [Roman] mission of Augus-

* That the works, or at least the reputation, of this Venerable Bede were
known to Dante is indicated by his appearance in the place reserved in the
Paradiso for the great Christian theologians, the sphere of the sun (*Paradiso*
X. 131).

tine [d. 604: the first Archbishop of Canterbury] which in the same century extended its efforts effectively from its headquarters in the south to the Anglian kingdom in the north. The Irish monks were scholars as well as missionaries; their schools were famous, and they taught their converts the best that had remained of classical letters. The Roman churchmen, too, brought with them a knowledge of Latin and Greek, a love of books and learning, not only establishing ecclesiastical foundations noted for scholarship, but keeping closely in touch with the best that the Continent had to give. The result was that England came to lead the world in humane letters. When Charlemagne [r. 768–814] looked about for a scholar to direct his palace school and combat heresy, he chose, not a Continental scholar, but the celebrated Alcuin [735–804], a product of the Cathedral school at York.[50]

Of course, by "the world" Professor Lawrence here can have meant only the little world of Europe. For in the *world* the actual leadership in letters at that time was in India and T'ang China, with Baghdad and Cordova soon to come: so that, in fact, Charlemagne's court was itself in many ways colonial to the Orient by way of Islam. Or, as Spengler states the case in his characteristic style:

In Charles the Great what we see is a compound of primitive spirituality on the point of its awakening mingled with a superimposed type of late intellectuality. Regarding certain features of his reign, one could speak of him as the Caliph of Frankistan, but he is, on the other hand, still the chieftain of a German tribe. And it is in the combination of these two strains that his symbolic value lies—as, likewise, that of the form of his palace-chapel at Aix-la-Chapelle, which is no longer a mosque but not yet a cathedral.[51]

And the *Beowulf* poet, approximately a contemporary of Charlemagne, born like him of a German race recently converted, combined, like him, in a manner abounding in contradictions, the two profoundly incompatible strains of Europe and the Levant. He was an Englishman writing of Swedes and Danes, a Christian writing of pagans; and one of his great points seems to have been that God, the Christian deity, had had care for those old warrior folk, far though they were from Jerusalem. "This truth," he wrote, "is well known, that God almighty has ever ruled the race of men." [52]

Figure 14. The Queller of Beasts; England, 650–670 A.D.

It has not yet been shown that the hero Beowulf, sailing the Kattegat c. 500 A.D., was an actual historical character, as Arthur, his British contemporary, seems to have been. However, King Hygelac, his uncle in the poem, was an actual king of the Geats, a Germanic folk of southern Sweden, killed by the Franks on the lower Rhine about the year 521; while Hygelac's friend, King Hrothgar of the Danes, to the rescue of whose mead-hall Beowulf came, seems also to have been historical: hardly historical, however, the adventure.

Figure 14, from a jeweled ornament on the lid of a purse from the Sutton Hoo ship-burial, almost certainly does *not* represent the monster-killer Beowulf between his two grisly victims, Grendel and Grendel's dam; yet its theme suggests the possibility. It illustrates a variant of the ancient mythic theme of the Queller of Wild Beasts. Figure 15 is from a Cretan seal, c. 1600 B.C., and Figure 16 from a Chinese bronze, roughly c. 1200 B.C.

In the case of Beowulf the adventure commenced when his noble uncle, Hygelac, received word that the mead-hall of the King of the Danes was being harried by a monster, Grendel. When

Figure 15. The Queller of Beasts; Crete, c. 1600 B.C.

darkness fell this baneful wight, emerging from his moors and fens, would spy about the high warrior hall, wherein all would be asleep, and, entering, take where they rested thirty thanes, bear them off to his keep, and there consume them, exulting. Hygelac sent Beowulf to quell this demon of the giant race of Cain. (For it was by Cain that all the elves and monsters were begotten that stray about as giants.) And Beowulf achieved his task.

In the dark of night the door of the mead-hall gave way, and the manlike walker in shadow, Grendel, laughing in his heart, took up and tore a sleeping thane, bit into his bone-frame, swallowed him piece by piece, and reached for another. But never had his arm met a mightier grief than at that moment laid hand to it. For the man that he touched was Beowulf, and the lordly hall became clamorous. Gold-ornamented mead-benches fell about the floor, and at Grendel's shoulder a wound began to show. The sinews sprang, the arm came off, the monster fled, and when morning came the marveling people tracked the trail of gore to a mere, of which the waters now were mingled red with blood.

We note that a Christian reading has been given to the monsters. They are sprung of the race of Cain. Thereby a sense of moral evil has been added to the old pagan one of natural terror. The lions on the Cretan seal of Figure 15 are quelled, not slain; and, even if slain, would not have been *morally* evil. Likewise in Figure 16,

Figure 16. Ink Rubbing from a Chinese Bronze; c. 1384–1111 B.C.

where the animals are tigers: in China the tiger is not evil but symbolic of the earth and in folklore a protecting spirit; for as one authority states, "he never needlessly attacks human beings, but destroys many pests to their fields." [53] And so the beasts of this early Chinese bronze must be guardians not antagonists; as may also be the pair from Sutton Hoo (Figure 14). It is thus even possible that originally in the *Beowulf* saga the monsters were conceived not as fiends but as the guardians of natural forces, to be not killed, but quelled and integrated. In fact, their residence in the Land below Waves suggests an association with those chthonic powers that have always been recognized as dangerous and frightening yet essential to all life. And in the subsequent adventure, of Beowulf against Grendel's dam, a sense pervades the scene rather of nature's terrible wonder than of moral evil and crime.

For, as the poet next tells, the monster-killer, after his victory, was given quarters with proper honors in a building apart; and that night it was Grendel's dam who entered the mead-hall for revenge.

Swords flashed, shields clashed; she seized an earl and made off. At dawn all followed to the haunted mere to which Grendel's gore had formerly led them, where all about in its waters were strange monsters of the sea—many a dragon kind making trial of the surge and on jutting rocks water-demons basking—all of which put out from shore when the company arrived. At one Beowulf shot an arrow, and when the men's spears brought it back to land there was marvel at the fearful thing.

The hero donned his armor, took up his shield and a sword that never had betrayed any man that grasped it, then strode into the mere. The water-wife saw his coming, seized him, dragged him below into her fire-glimmering roofed hall, where no water was within. His battle-blade there sang its greedy war-song on her skull, but failed and he flung it to the ground, seized her shoulders, and she tripped him. (However, God, the Wise Lord, Heaven's Ruler, was holding sway over that battle-victory.) Beowulf spied an old sword, the work of giants, greater in size than any man might bear, and, grasping its chain-bound hilt, despairing of his life, he smote so wrathfully that the ring-marked blade caught the she-fiend at the neck, broke the bone-rings, and went through. She fell, and the light of the roofed hall flared.

Discovering Grendel helpless on a bed, Beowulf cut off his head, after which the warriors above noticed blood in the waves and talked of their hero, dead. In his hand the sword blade, smeared with the monster's blood, was falling away in battle-icicles. A marvel to see, how it melted! And when he came to the surface, holding Grendel's head, four men bore it to the mead-hall, where the arm already hung above the door.

Like Theseus after his Minotaur deed, Perseus with the Gorgon's head, and Jason with the Golden Fleece, Beowulf, returning home, in due time succeeded to his throne, which he held for some fifty years; and when he was old, heavy with age, a last adventure challenged—to his doom.

Figure 17, from a Chinese scroll, is of a dragon appearing through mist and waves, clutching in his four-taloned claw a glowing sphere. A pearl? The sun? In either case, a great treasure. Chinese dragons are rain-producing, dangerous but benign. And

Figure 17. Dragon Treasure; China, 12th century A.D.

in India too the "serpent kings" guard both the waters of immortality and the treasures of the earth.

Not only jewels and wealth, but beautiful women also are of interest to dragons. The classical legend of Andromeda, saved from a sea monster by Perseus, surely will be recalled, and perhaps too the Japanese story of the storm-god Susano-O and the dragon he killed by a ruse, to save the eighth daughter of a couple whose first seven had already been eaten.[54]

In Beowulf's case, the dragon to be met kept guard of a hoard of gold. In a stone barrow, on a high heath above sea-waves, below which lay a path not known to men, a weeping prince of yore had stowed his battle gear and cups of gold, with a prayer to the protecting earth:

Hold these, thou Earth, this wealth of earls;
For in thee did good men first discover it.
None have I more, to wield sword or burnish gold.
Battle-death has taken every one of my folk.

And this evil, naked dragon, twilight-spoiler, which by night flew folded in fire, had one day found that joy-giving hoard, to which he had settled on watch. And he there remained three hundred years, no whit the better for it, until some man or other with his hand took from that hoard a golden cup. Waking, wrathful, the dragon snuffed along the rocks, finding his track, but not the man. And fearful then for the people of the land was that feud's beginning.

By night the angered barrow-warden flew: bright homesteads burned. He shot back before day to his hoard. And so again, night after night. Then Beowulf, now an old king, foreknew that death was next before him. He ordered a shield made marvelously of iron; the man who had taken the cup was forced to serve as guide. With eleven others, himself as twelfth, the guide thereto thirteen, the old king then sat him on the foreland and spoke his hearth-companions farewell.

> His heart was sad,
> uneasy and death-ready: *wyrd* immediately nigh.[55]

Now, this Anglo-Saxon word *wyrd* has about it a sense of haunting doom that is recaptured in Shakespeare's three Weird Sisters. These are transformations into witches of the Norns of old Germanic myth, who (as described in the Old Norse "Wise Woman's Prophecy," *Völuspó*) dwell by Urth's well, from which they water the roots of the World Ash. Shakespeare's trio, on a "desert heath," amid thunder, lightning, and rain, conjure from their witches' caldron prophecies that are heard *as though* from outside by Macbeth, yet are of deeds already maturing in his heart. In Old Norse the Norns' three names are given as Urth, Verthandi, and Skuld: [56] "Become, Becoming, and Shall Be," Past, Present, and Future, which appear to be a late invention, however, inspired perhaps (twelfth century A.D.?) by the model of the Greek three Graces. For there seems to have been originally but one Norn: called Urth in Old Norse, in Old High German Wurd, and in Anglo-Saxon Wyrd. The word may be related to the German *werden*, "to become,' to grow," which would suggest a sense of inward inherent destiny, comparable, essentially, to Schopenhauer's concept of "intelligible" character. Another association is with the Old High German *wirt, wirtel*, "spindle," by which the idea is suggested of a spinning and weaving of destiny. The classical triad of the Moirai may have contributed to this image; namely of Clotho, the "Spinner," who spins the life thread; Lachesis, "Disposer of Lots," determining its length; and Atropos, "Inflexible," who cuts it. And so the symbol of the spindle became significant of destiny, and the woven web, of life.

One recalls the fairytale of Little Briar Rose (Sleeping Beauty), who in her fifteenth year was pricked by the spindle of a cruel hag, whereupon she fell asleep for a century, until kissed by a king's son who found his way through briars to her slumbering castle.[57] And there is the comical tale of Three Spinners, "the first of whom had a broad flat foot, the second such a great underlip that it hung down to her chin, and the third a great broad thumb," respectively, from treading the wheel, wetting the thread, and twisting it.[58]

Returning, however, to the *Völuspó*—which Wagner took as inspiration for his *Götterdämmerung*—we find that there the universe itself unfolds from within, organically, to its day of doom, when Garm, the dog of Hel, howls before the "Cliff-Cave," Hel's gate, giants, dwarfs, and elves break free, and the gods (already knowing, as they do, the destiny before them) go to meet in mutual slaughter those monsters of the deep, at the close of the age.

And so too the old King Beowulf, and the dragon of his doom, at the close of his life:

"Not a foot's length," he said, "will I give back from the keeper of the barrow, but as Wyrd may grant, the ruler of all men, so shall it befall us in the fight." And rising, strong beneath his helm, he carried his battle sark to the stony steps, where beneath a wall and arch of stone, a stream, steaming with battle fires, was pouring from the barrow. The old king let sound his voice, and for the treasure warden within there was time no more for peace.

First the monster's breath, fuming hot, broke forth; the earth resounded; and the warrior, strong of heart, swung up his battle-shield for what was destined. The dragon coiled and came: at first slowly moving, then hastening, until, smitten by the sword, he cast forth a deadly fire and the blade gave up its strength. (No easy journey is it now to be for that old King of the Geats, who must leave this earth plain unwillingly to make his home in a dwelling somewhere else. And so must every man lay aside the days that pass.) Again the two became engaged.

And it was then that a young shield-warrior, Wiglaf, perceiving his lord hard laboring, moving into the slaughter-reek, bore his helmet to his lord's side. But his shield immediately melted, and the spoiler of people, with bitter fangs, took Beowulf's whole throat, whose blood gushed forth in waves. Wiglaf struck the dragon's neck; his sword sank in, the fire failed: the old king drew from his burnie a dagger, and those two together cut the worm in two.

But that was the last triumphant hour of that king in this world; for the poison within was rising in his breast. "Dear Wiglaf, quickly now," he said, "help me to see this old treasure of gold, the gladness of its bright jewels, curiously set, that I may yield my life the more easily and the lordship I have held so long." [59]

As a number of commentators have remarked, there was nothing of the Christian spirit in this noble death: no thought of sin, forgiveness, or Heaven, but the old Germanic virtues only of loyalty and courage, pride in the performances of duty, and, for a king, selfless, fatherly care for his people's good. Beowulf's joy, furthermore, in the sight of the earthly treasure is even decidedly *un*-Christian; [60] for the work is everywhere alive with love for the wonder of life in this world, with not a word of either anxiety or desire for the next.

The concluding scene is of the burning of the hero's body, then the building of the barrow. And as at Sutton Hoo, so here: in the barrow they placed all the rings, jewels, and trappings taken from the dragon hoard; whereupon, twelve sons of nobles, brave in battle rode about the mound, while they framed in sorrow words of praise.

The name Beowulf itself, "bee-wolf," apparently meaning *bear,* suggests affinities with a widely known folktale figure of prodigious strength, the Bear's Son (again see Figure 16), [61] the distribution of whose appearances, in North America as well as Eurasia, points to a background in that primordial cult of reverence for the bear discussed in *Primitive Mythology,* and which is still observed among the Ainus of Japan. [62]

A second mythologically empowered beast looming large in the Celto-Germanic legendary background of Europe is the pig, the boar, the same whose tusks brought death to Adonis and left the wound on Odysseus's thigh by which he was recognized when he returned (by way of his own swineherd's hut), after his visit to the underworld, to which he had been introduced by Circe, whose magic turned men into swine. [63] However, whereas the distribution of the bear's-son motif suggests an arctic, circumpolar range and a background—ultimately—in the cave-bear cults and sanctuaries of the paleolithic, those of the boar and the killed and resurrected god are of the later, planting and agricultural "Mediterranean" culture complex, which reached Ireland by the sea way of Gibraltar c. 2500 B.C., and in England is represented in the great circle of Stonehenge (c. 1900–1400 B.C.),[64] which in popular lore is attributed to the magic of the druid Merlin.

The Celts, like the Germans, were patriarchal Aryans; however, with their westward drive into Gaul and the British Isles in the first millennium B.C., they entered the old Bronze Age sphere of the Great Goddess and her killed and resurrected son, whose cults of the seasonal round and rebirth were soon combined with their own. Figure 18 is the image of a Gaulish god wearing the typical neck ornament of the Celtic noble and warrior caste, a golden torc, and holding before him a wild boar. It is a work in stone, ten inches high, of the first century B.C., about the time of Caesar's Gallic Wars.[65] Instead of arms, huge eyes are engraved on either side, exactly as long as the boar and disposed, like him, along the vertical axis. They are difficult to explain, unless by reference back to the pre-Celtic megalithic art of some two millenniums earlier, which had passed from Spain and Portugal north, through France, to the British Isles. For there an eye motif, associated with the Mother Goddess (the Eye Goddess),[66] is particularly prominent. In Figure 19 are three examples: a) on a piece of bone from Spain, b) a clay figurine from Syria, and c) a seal impression from Sumer, all of dates c. 2500 B.C. The stone-bound lines of the Gaulish figure with the boar suggest the pre-Celtic megalithic style, which was contemporary in the British Isles with Minoan Crete and Troy,[67] its creative center in the West being southern Spain, as a reflex of the Bronze Age of Mesopotamia, Egypt, and the pre-Homeric Aegean. And as there, so here, the chief divinity was the goddess of many forms and names, whose son and spouse was the ever-living, killed and resurrected lord of immortality: Tammuz, Adonis, Attis, et cetera, the god slain by the boar.

In central Spain and northern Portugal, there have been found in the neighborhood of Celtic forts a number of large stone sculptures of boars,[68] and in Orléans, France, there is in the historical museum an example in bronze more than 4 feet long, 2 feet, 3

Figure 18. Gaulish God with a Boar; France, 1st century B.C.

inches high.[69] Figure 20 shows a bronze 3 inches long, unearthed near London. Moreover, the boar appears on many such Gaulish coins as that of Figure 21, where on the obverse we see a squatting god with a torc in his right hand: the same as of Figure 18. He is here identifiable as the Celtic god whom the Romans equated with their own lord of the underworld, Pluto (Greek Hades), by whom Proserpina (Persephone) was abducted; and when the earth opened to receive her, it took down a herd of swine as well.[70]

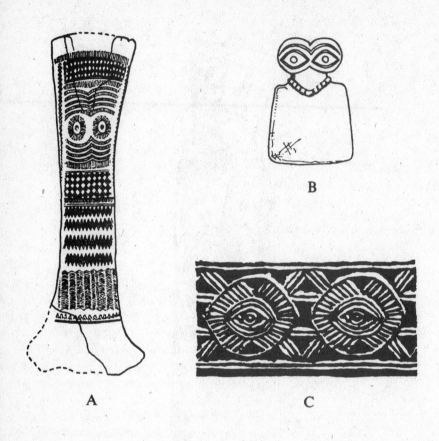

Figure 19. The "Eye Goddess"; three examples, c. 2500 B.C.: a) in bone, from Spain; b) in clay, from Syria; c) on a seal, from Sumer

The association of the pig with the underworld journey, laby-rinth motif and mysteries of immortality has been discussed at length in both the Primitive and the Oriental volumes of this work, and of especial interest in the present context is the Melanesian ceremony of the Maki,[71] where not only is the pig clearly a counterpart of the sacrificed Savior, opener of the way, and guide to eternal life—corresponding to the sacrificial bull and ram of the West (see Figure 1)—but the rites are conducted in association with a complex of megalithic shrines and chambered barrows that

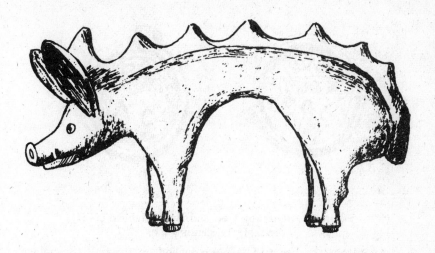

Figure 20. Sacred Boar; bronze, England, Roman Period

is almost certainly a remote extension of the Bronze Age complex of Western Europe.

In Irish legend, the daughter of the King of the Land of Youth was endowed with the head of a pig when she attached herself to Finn McCool's son Oisin.[72] Moreover, the Irish hero Diarmuid, who ran off with Finn McCool's bride, Grianne, and whose flight with her to the wilderness was the prototype of the "forest years" of Tristan and Isolt, was killed by a boar that he slew—as was Beowulf by his dragon. Tristan, like Odysseus, had the scar of a boar's tusk on his thigh; and, as though to insist upon the relationship of his love-death to the ancient theme of the god whose animal is the boar, there is an astonishing passage in Gottfried's version of the romance where King Mark's steward-in-chief, Marjadoc—who himself was harboring a passion for Isolt—dreamed of the love-mad Tristan as a rampaging boar violating the king's bed:

> As Marjadoc slept, he saw a boar, frightening and frightful, come running out of the wood. Foaming, sparkling, whetting his tusks and charging at everything in his path, he headed for the king's court. A crowd of palace attendants ran at him and many knights milled hither and thither, round about. Yet no one dared

Figure 21. Squatting God and Boar; Gaulish coin,
probably 1st century B.C.

to confront the beast. The boar dashed on through the palace
grunting, and when he came to Mark's chamber, crashed in
through the door. He tossed the king's appointed bed in all directions, befouling the royal bed and bed linen with his foam.
And though all of Mark's people witnessed this, not one of them
intervened.[73]

IV. The Legacy of Islam

1.

When the Roman Catholic priest Professor Miguel Asín y Palacios, in his pioneering work, published in Madrid in 1919, demonstrated with massive proof the great extent to which Dante and his
circle had been moved by Moslem inspiration, it came as a real
shock to the world of Dante scholarship.[74] "The analogies shown
by the author to exist between the Divine Comedy and Islam are
so numerous and of such a nature," wrote the reviewer in the *Analecta Bollandiana,* "as to be disquieting to the mind of the reader,
who is forced to picture to himself the great epic of Christianity as
enthroned in the world of Moslem mysticism, as if in a mosque
that were closed to Islam and consecrated to Christian worship." [75]
However, it is now completely certain that our poet Dante was
indeed significantly influenced not only by the philosophers but
also by the poets of Islam, and most particularly by a certain Spanish Sufi, Ibnu'l-'Arabi of Murcia (1165–1240), whose twelve-

volume production entitled *Meccan Revelations* anticipates many of the highest spiritual themes not only of the *Commedia* but of the *Vita Nuova* as well.

Asín points out that the famous Toledan school of translators under King Alfonso the Wise of León and Castile (r. 1252–1284) was in full career at the time of the visit to Spain of Dante's master, Brunetto Latini (1210–1294), whom the poet greets with the greatest respect in the seventh circle of Hell,[76] and that the legend of the *Mi'rāj* (the Hell and Heaven journeys of Mohammed), from the architecture and details of which the *Commedia* shows many imprints, had in the year 1256 been translated into Castilian—four years before Brunetto's visit.[77] Furthermore, as Father Asín states in conclusion:

> It is inconceivable that Dante, leading a life of such mental activity, should have been ignorant of Moslem culture, which at the time was all-pervading; that he should not have felt the attraction of a science that was drawing men of learning to the court of Toledo from every part of Christian Europe, and of a literature the influence of which was paramount in the Europe of that time, introducing there the novels, fables, and proverbs of the Orient as well as works of science and apologetics. The prestige enjoyed by Islam was largely due to the Moslem victories over the Crusaders. Roger Bacon, a contemporary of Dante, attributed the defeats of the Christians precisely to their ignorance of the Semitic languages and applied science, of which the Moslems were masters.[78] In another field of learning, Albertus Magnus, the founder of scholasticism, agreed with Bacon on the superiority of the Arab philosophers;[79] and Raimon Lull even recommended the imitation of Moslem methods in popular preaching.[80]

"Rarely," Father Asín concludes, "can public opinion have been so unanimous in admitting the mental superiority of an adversary." [81]

To summarize, then, very briefly, the outstanding correspondences between Dante's work and, specifically, the Sufi mystic Ibnu'l-'Arabi's, as remarked by Father Asín, let me simply quote from R. A. Nicholson's statement of his own concurrence in this view, in his essay on Moslem mysticism in *The Legacy of Islam:*

> The infernal regions, the astronomical heavens, the circles of the mystic rose, the choirs of angels around the focus of divine

light, the three circles symbolizing the Trinity—all are described
by Dante exactly as Ibnu'l-'Arabi described them. Dante tells us
how, as he mounted higher and higher in Paradise, his love was
made stronger and his spiritual vision more intense by seeing
Beatrice grow more and more beautiful. The same idea occurs
in a poem of Ibnu'l-'Arabi written about a century earlier.
. . . It may be added that Ibnu'l-'Arabi too had a Beatrice—
Nizām, the beautiful and accomplished daughter of Makinu'd-
din—and that owing to the scandal caused by the mystical odes
which he composed in her honor he wrote a commentary on
them in order to convince his critics that they were wrong. Similarly in the *Convito* Dante declares his intention to interpret the
esoteric meaning of fourteen love-songs which he had composed
at an earlier date, and the subject of which had led to the erroneous belief that they dealt with sensual rather than intellectual
love! In short, the parallelism, both general and particular,
reaches so far that only one conclusion is possible. Muslim religious legends, e.g. the Mi'rāj or Ascension of the Prophet, together with popular and philosophical conceptions of the after-
life—derived from Muslim traditionists and such writers as
Farabe, Avicenna, Ghazali, and Ibnu'l-'Arabi—must have
passed into the common stock of literary culture that was accessible to the best minds in Europe in the thirteenth century. The
Arab conquerors of Spain and Sicily repeated, though on a less
imposing scale, the same process of impregnation to which they
themselves had been subjected by the Hellenistic civilization of
Persia and Syria." [82]

But there is also an earlier phase to this story. Figure 22 is a
map showing the geographical extension of Islamic rule and commercial influence in the *tenth* century A.D. Of particular interest is
the evidence of a traffic from the Caspian Sea, up the valley of the
Volga, to the Baltic and on to Sweden, Denmark, and Norway—
homelands of the Vikings. "From the eighth to the eleventh centuries," Father Asín remarks, "an active trade was carried on between Moslem countries of the East and Russia and other countries of northern Europe. Expeditions left the Caspian regularly
and, ascending the Volga, reached the Gulf of Finland and so
through the Baltic to Denmark, Britain, and even as far as Iceland.
The quantities of Arabic coins found at various places in this ex-
tensive commercial zone bear witness to its importance. "In the

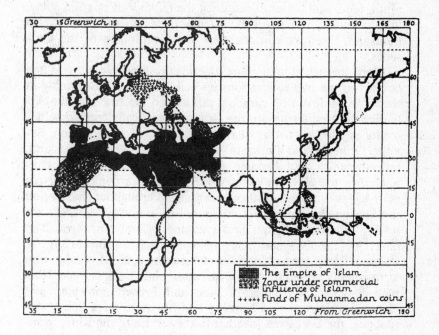

Figure 22. Extent of Islamic Rule and Influence,
10th century A.D.

eleventh century," Father Asín then continues, "trade was conducted by the easier sea route across the Mediterranean, chiefly by
means of Genoese, Venetian or Moslem vessels. Large colonies of
Italian traders settled in all the Moslem ports of the Mediterranean, and merchants, explorers, and adventurers sailed at will
across its waters."

But there is even more to this tale of interchange:

To the stimulus of trade must be added the impulse of the religious ideal. Pilgrimages to the Holy Land, which had been suspended owing to the early conquests of Islam, were renewed
and, with the establishment under Charlemagne [r. 768–814]
of the Frank Protectorate over the Christian churches of the
East, were assured by conventions and assisted by the establish-

ment of hostels and monasteries in Moslem lands. During the ninth, tenth and eleventh centuries the number of pilgrims grew, until some of the expeditions comprised as many as twelve thousand; these expeditions were the forerunners of the Crusades. . . .

More important and more interesting, however . . . is the contact of the two civilizations in Sicily and Spain. Beginning in the ninth century with piratical raids upon the coasts of the Atlantic and Mediterranean, the Normans gradually formed settlements in Moslem towns of the Peninsula (such as Lisbon, Seville, Orihuela and Barbasto) and in Sicily. The latter island, indeed, which had become permeated with Islam, was conquered in the eleventh century and ruled by a dynasty of Norman Kings until the thirteenth century. Throughout that period the Sicilian population was composed of a medley of races professing different religions and speaking several languages. The court of the Norman King, Roger II [r. 1130–1154], at Palermo, was formed of both Christians and Moslems, who were equally versed in Arabic literature and Greek science. Norman knights and soldiers, Italian and French noblemen and clergy, Moslem men of learning and literature from Spain, Africa, and the East lived together in the service of the King, forming a palatine organization that in all respects was a copy of the Moslem courts. The King himself spoke and read Arabic, kept a harem in the Moslem manner, and attired himself after the Oriental fashion. Even the Christian women of Palermo adopted the dress, veil, and speech of their Moslem sisters.

However, important as Norman Sicily was, Spain was of even greater moment in this interplay of cultures. "For Spain," as Father Asín points out, "was the first country in Christian Europe to enter into intimate contact with Islam." From 711 to 1492 the two populations lived side by side in war and peace. "As early as the ninth century the Christians of Cordova had adopted the Moslem style of living, some even to the extent of keeping harems and being circumcised. Their delight in Arabic poetry and fiction, and their enthusiasm for the study of the philosophical and theological doctrines of Islam, are lamented in his *Indiculus luminosus* by [the Bishop] Alvaro of Cordova [fl. 850 A.D.]." "Throughout the tenth century Arabicized monks and soldiers flocked to León, where their superior culture secured them high office at the court and in the ecclesiastical and civil administration of the kingdom." And finally: "King Alfonso VI [1065–1109], the conqueror of Toledo, married Zaida, the daughter of the Moorish King of Seville, and his capital resembled the seat of a Moslem court. The fashion quickly spread to private life; the Christians dressed in Moorish style, and the rising Romance language of Castile was enriched by a large number of Arabic words. In commerce, in the arts and trades, in municipal organization, as well as in agricultural pursuits, the influence of the Mudejars [Mohammedans living under Christian kings] was predominant, and thus the way was prepared for the literary invasion that was to reach its climax at the court of Alfonso X or the Wise." [83]

2.

Seven centuries before Alfonso's time the light of Hellenistic learning had been quenched for Europe when, in the year 529, the Byzantine Emperor Justinian ordered the schools of pagan philosophy closed in Athens. The only remaining repositories of Greek philosophy and science then were Sassanian Persia, Gupta India,[84] and Ireland, the one flickering candle in the West.* However, the Arabs who in the name of Mohammed conquered Persia in 641 cared nothing for either philosophy or science. Their Prophet had died in 632. His immediate successors, the "orthodox" caliphs, retained control of the spreading empire until 661, when a rival Meccan house, the Ummayads, usurped the caliphate.[85] These ruled until 750, when their fourteenth caliph was murdered, and the victors now—to the good fortune of mankind—were Persians, the Abbasids, who, in contrast to the Arab fanatics of the earlier two caliphates, were such discriminating patrons of philosophy, science, and the arts that Baghdad, their young capital (750–1258), became within a few decades the most important seat of classical learning in the world.

According to its own poets, Baghdad then was an earthly paradise of learning, ease, and grace, where, to use their own expressions, the ground was irrigated with rose water and the dust of the roads was musk, flowers and verdure overhung the ways and the air was perpetually sweet with the many-voiced song of birds; while the chirp of lutes, the dulcet warble of flutes, and the silver

* Supra, p. 106.

sound of singing houris rose and fell in harmonious cadence from every window of the streets of palaces that stood in vast succession amid gardens and orchards gifted with eternal verdure. The works of Aristotle, Hippocrates, Galen, Euclid, Archimedes, Ptolemy, and Plotinus were translated here into Arabic. Poets and musicians, mathematicians, astronomers, geographers, jurisprudents, philosophers, and historians carried forward the labors of a civilized humanity, to which contributions were coming, as well, from India and China. For these were the golden years of the Great East: the centuries of T'ang and Sung in China (618–1279); Nara, Heian, and Kamakura in Japan (710–1392); Angkor in Cambodia (c. 800–1250); and in India the timeless temple art of the Chalukya and Rashtrakuta, Pala, Sena and Ganga, Pallava, Chola, Hoyshala, and Pandya kings (550–1350).[86]

In all the world of Europe and Asia there were then but four essential languages of learning, science, and religion: in the Levant, Arabic; Latin in Europe; Sanskrit in the Indian sphere; and Chinese in the Far East. And as Arabic was the dominant of the two tongues of the West, so was Sanskrit in the Orient. From the yak trails of Tibet to the village markets of Bali, its syllables rose everywhere on the pluming smoke of incense to that void beyond non-being and being that is the destination, ultimately, of all Oriental prayer. And its echoes floated westward too. The influence of Indian thought on the Sufis cannot be doubted, and there is the case, furthermore, of the Buddha, converted into no less than two Christian saints: the Abbots Barlaam and Josaphat, the legend of whose labors in India, first recorded by John of Damascus (c. 676–770), rests immortalized in the chapter for their feast day, November 27, in Voragine's thirteenth-century *Golden Legend*.[87]

The most illuminating summary prospect of the paths, bypaths, and transformations through which a body of Oriental lore might pass from Sanskrit into Latin and thence into European life is provided by an Indian book of fables, the *Panchatantra*. Translated about 550 A.D. into Persian for the Sassanian King Khosru Anushirvan (531–579), it was turned into Arabic about 760 with a new title: *Kalilah and Dimnah, The Fables of Pilpay;* and this then was translated into Syriac, c. 1000; Greek, c. 1080; Hebrew, c. 1250; and old Spanish, 1251. About 1270 a Latin translation of the Hebrew appeared, *Directorum humanae vitae,* which in turn became, in 1481, *Das Buch der Byspel der alten Wysen,* and, in 1552, A. F. Doni's *La moral filosophia,* which in 1570 Sir Thomas North rendered as *The Morall Philosophie of Doni:* after all of which we have, finally, the elegant seventeenth-century *Fables* of La Fontaine, who in 1678 wrote in his introduction to the second volume: *"Seulement je diray par reconnoissance que j'en dois la plus grande partie à Pilpay, sage indien. Son livre a esté traduit en toutes les langues."* [88]

But it was not until the early twelfth century that European men of learning themselves undertook seriously, in a really significant way, to bring back to Europe from the gardens of Baghdad the bounty that in Justinian's day had been forfeited to Asia. We have already mentioned Toledo. In the year 1143 Peter the Venerable, Abbot of Cluny, on a visit to his order's Spanish monasteries, met the bishop of that city, Ramon of Sauvetat (1126–1151), whose scholars were at work translating from Arabic not only the writings of the Greeks but also both the commentaries on those writings and the independent works of the Arabs through whose hands the legacy had passed. To Gerard of Cremona (c. 1114–1187), for example, the most famous of the scholars in Toledo at that time, there are credited no less than seventy substantial titles, many of vast extent, including, besides a number of the most important books of Aristotle, Plotinus, Proclus, Euclid, Ptolemy, and Galen, the Arab Avicenna's medical *Canon,* which for a time replaced Galen's writings even in the West. Peter of Cluny, impressed, suggested to his host that a Latin version of the Koran would be an aid in the refutation of Islam, and when the work, undertaken by Robert of Kelene, was finished that same year, the Abbot composed his celebrated refutation: *Libri II adversus nefarium sectam saracenorum.*

Also to be mentioned is the interesting hermetic text, anonymously translated, of *The Book of the Twenty-four Philosophers* (*Liber XXIV philosophorum*), from which the sentence came that has already been more than once quoted in these pages: *Deus est sphaera infinita, cujus centrum est ubique, circumferentia nusquam.* *

Shall we be surprised to find, then, on the levels of folklore and

* Supra, pp. 31 and 36.

romance, that in turning from the popular *One Thousand Nights and One Night* of Islam to the legends of King Arthur, we have moved only from one room to another of the same enchanted palace? As remarked in my introduction to *The Portable Arabian Nights:* "The battle scenes might comfortably appear in the *Morte D'Arthur;* the tales of enchanted castles, miraculous swords, talismanic trophies, and quest in the realms of the Jinn, are reminiscent, in numerous features, of the favorites of Arthurian romance; the pattern of romantic love is in essence identical with that of twelfth-century Provence; the pious tales breathe the same odor of spiritual childhood and the misogynist exempla the same monastic rancor as those of Christian Europe; the animal fables are the same; and the convention of the frame story (represented in the West by the *Decameron* and Chaucer's *Canterbury Tales*) is here a basic device. Nor is it possible to miss the Lady Godiva, Peeping Tom motive in tale 167, 'Kemerezzeman and the Jeweler's Wife.' Parallels exist even to early Irish and Germanic literature." [89] Furthermore: "Precisely as Celtic gods became the fairies of Christian Irish folklore, so did Persian, Egyptian, Babylonian, and Indian become the Jinn of Moslem popular belief." [90] And of the greatest interest is the prominence in both these neighboring traditions of a type of tale of enchantment and disenchantment that on the European side is represented by the legends of the Grail.

In these the hero is generally one, set apart by disposition or accident, who comes by chance upon a situation of enchantment. There is always someone present familiar with the rules of this enchantment, yet nothing can be done without the help of an innocent youth, whose arrival is helplessly awaited. He is to be a sort of *puer aeternus,* virtuous and fearless, whose nature itself will be the key to the undoing of a spell that no *intentional* program of courage or virtue could dissolve.

And so it was that, whether in the cloisters of the great monasteries, in the halls and ladies' chambers of the castles, or in the rushlit humble cottages of the toiling illiterate folk, the legacy of neighboring Islam, and, as part of that, the whole Orient, was contributing largely to that twelfth- and thirteenth-century wakening and nourishing of the European imagination which was to lead in the next three centuries to the dawn of a new and spectacular age, not for the West alone, but for the world.

3.

It is of the essence of our study to recognize, however, that, no matter how great the force of the Oriental contribution to the twelfth- and thirteenth-century flowering of the European imagination may have been, the inward life and spirit of that European epoch was in every aspect different from anything the Orient ever had known or would be likely to achieve. For, as every serious study of intercultural exchange has shown, it is simply a fact—a basic law of history, applicable to every department of life—that materials carried from any time past to a time present, or from one culture to another, shed their values at the culture portal and thereafter either become mere curiosities, or undergo a sea change through a process of creative misunderstanding. We have already remarked the transformation of the cult of Amor as it passed from the Moorish *"tarab*-adors" to the troubadours of Provence.* In the chapter in *Oriental Mythology* on the massive influence of Rome on the Gupta flowering of India, the words of Dr. Hermann Goetz were cited to the point: "Though so many novel ideas, techniques and types were absorbed that practically a quite new and most important chapter of Indian art was opened, they were never taken over *en bloc*. . . . Everything was broken up, translated into Indian concepts and reconstructed on Indian principles." [91] And with reference, now, particularly to the manifold transmission of the precious Hellenistic, humanistic heritage from Europe to the Levant and back to a later Europe, the important third chapter of Volume II of Spengler's *Decline of the West* must be cited, in which he contrasts the axioms and suppositions of Roman, Byzantine, and modern European jurisprudence: "three histories of law," as he writes, "connected only by elements of linguistic and syntactical form, taken over by one from the other, voluntarily or perforce, without the receiver ever coming face to face with the alien nature that underlay them." [92]

For the shaping force of a civilization is *lived experience* and, as Spengler has demonstrated, the manner of this inwardness differs not only in differing civilizations, but also in the differing periods of a single civilization. It is not a function of any "influence" from without, no matter how great or inspiring. Consequently, when his-

* Supra, p. 62.

torians confine their attention to the tracing and mapping of such "influences," without due regard to the inward assimilating and reshaping force of the local, destiny-making readiness for life, their works inevitably founder in secondary details. "What a wealth there is of psychology," writes Spengler,

> in all the seeking, resisting, choosing and reinterpreting, misunderstanding, penetrating and revering—not only as between cultures in immediate contact with each other, whether in mutual admiration or in strife, but also as between a living culture and the world of forms of one dead, whose remains still stand visible on the landscape! And how poor and thin are the conceptions, then, that historians bring to all this with such verbal formulae as "influence," "continuity," and "effect"!
>
> Such labeling is pure nineteenth century. What is sought is merely a chain of causes and effects. Everything "follows," nothing is prime. Because elements of form from the surfaces of earlier cultures can be discovered everywhere in later, they must be supposed to have "produced effects"; and where a set of such "influences" can be exhibited together, the authority believes he has done a proper job.

On the contrary—and here is Spengler's critical point—"it is not products that 'influence,' but creators that 'absorb.' " [93]

The point is elementary and, once made, one would think, self-demonstrative. However, when such a torrent of "influences" can be classified and described as came pouring, throughout the Middle Ages, from the Near East into Europe, it is easy for a bookman to ignore the active force of creative interpretation by which all is recomposed and made again alive as it passes from one center of experience, expression, and communication to another. Furthermore, the man of learning, but little living, can be readily misled by the purely cerebral discourse of philosophy to assume that because the *words* of two traditions are matched in bilingual dictionaries, the *experiences* to which they refer must be the same: those, for example, implied in the nouns *fate, kismet,* and *wyrd.* Actually, a people's way of experiencing "fate" as life and their philosophers' way of discussing "fate" as a metaphysical problem, in terms of cause and effect, need bear no significant relationship to each other, since the latter is an abstract word game, played according to classic rules, while the other is an inward realization of existence.

Philosophically, the enigma of fate is impossible to resolve, unless by some such formula as that of Schopenhauer, according to which, when viewed from outside, logically or scientifically, the world's events can be recognized as governed to such a degree by the laws of cause and effect as to be inexorably determined; whereas, when experienced from within, from the standpoint of an acting subject, living yields an experience of choice. And since these contradictory views are but the functions of mankind's alternate modes of conditioned knowledge (the world as "idea" and the world as "will"), both fail of the ultimate question as to the ground of a man's becoming and being.

Alike in Islam and Christendom, theologians and philosophers, in their efforts to abide by the ground rules of all biblically based mythologizing, give credit simultaneously to God's foreknowledge and to man's free will as the ultimate *cause* of fate, and have thus tied themselves into knots as picturesque as any in a mariner's handbook, which can be studied—classified—in the manuals.[94] However, in the more popular romances of the two associated culture worlds, a distinct contrast is evident between the differing orders of experience epitomized in the terms *kismet,* on one hand, and, on the other, *wyrd.*

The key to the sense of the Moslem term is in the Koranic formula of submission, "There is no power and no virtue but in God, the Most High, the Supreme!"—pronouncing which, the Prophet promised, no believer could be confounded. The Arabic word *islām* itself means, literally, "surrender [to the Will of God]," and on the level of popular feeling and belief, this supports such a passive idea as *kismet,* "lot, distribution, fate." "Your augury," states the Koran, "is in God's hands." [95] The notion, essentially, is of *an outside determinant*—God's omnipotent will—by which one's destiny is ineluctably decreed. And although in official Christian doctrine a like sentiment is recommended (often along with an explanation of how God's supernatural grace affects, but does not effect, man's choice, which is free), throughout the literature of Europe's hero-deeds the experience communicated is on the side rather of *wyrd* than of *kismet:* not surrender to the invincible

force of an outside determinant, but the sense of an inward potentiality in the process of becoming, with, however, an approaching
inevitable end.

4.

I have said that in the cogitations of philosophers the ground
rules of their word games may have little, if anything, to do with
the native sense of life creatively operative in their culture. It has
been their custom, in fact, to look afield for their terms and themes
of discourse to thinkers of earlier times and alien traditions; so that
what in general passes for the formal schoolbook history of
thought is largely a sort of theater of Sir Imponderables elabo-
rately refuting their own misinterpretations of each other. So it was
when Aristophanes wrote his comedy *The Clouds*. So it is today.
And so it was in that great period, as well, of the reception by the
master minds of Europe of the legacy of Islam.

The *pièce de résistance* of this ponderously served up medieval
comedy of confusion was a duel of balloons on the splintery stage
of the Sorbonne by the matched champions, respectively, of the
"double" and the "single truth": the double truth being a doctrine
attributed in error to the great imam and philosopher of Cordova,
Averroes (ibn-Rushd, 1126–1198), which held that what is true
according to reason may be untrue according to faith, and vice
versa; while the single doctrine charged that the truths of reason and
religion were to be reconciled philosophically as one.

The leading spokesman for the former view at the University
of Paris was the brilliant Swedish Averroist, Siger of Brabant (fl.
1260), allied with whom, as contemporaries and followers, were
chiefly Boethius of Sweden (fl. 1270), Martin of Denmark (d.
1304), John of Jandun (d. 1328), and Marsilius of Padua (d.
1336 or 1343). The mightiest champion of the doctrine of the
single truth, on the other hand, was the Italian Dominican Thomas
Aquinas (1225?–1274), who, while contending directly with Siger,
was at the same time salting his paragraphs with syllogistic refuta-
tions of those same Arabs—Alfarabi, Avicenna, and Averroes—
from whose hands he had received not only his knowledge of Aristotle but also his leading idea and method of reconciling, in a
Summa Theologica, reason with revelation and philosophy with
faith. Siger, who supposed he was following Averroes, was saying

just the opposite, while Aquinas, who thought he was contending with the Moor, was saying the same, and at times even to the life. In the century of the battle itself there were so many shadows in play about the stage that the verbal strokes were falling as frequently on air as upon heads, and then as frequently on the wrong as on the right; so that in retrospect the whole controversy has much the air of an *opéra bouffe*.

Wrote the Averroist, Siger of Brabant:

Desiring to live worthily in the study and contemplation of truth as far as can be done in this life, we are undertaking to treat of natural, moral and divine things following the doctrine and order of Aristotle, but we are not making any attempt upon the rights of the orthodox faith made manifest to us in the light of the divine revelation by which the philosophers themselves were not enlightened; for, considering the ordinary and habitual course of nature and not divine miracles, they have explained things according to the light of reason, without, by doing so, contradicting the theological truth whose cognition derives from a loftier light. When a philosopher concludes that a certain thing is either impossible or necessary from the point of view of the inferior causes accessible to reason, he is not contradicting faith, which affirms that things can be otherwise thanks to the supreme cause whose causal power can be grasped by no creature. This is so true that the holy prophets themselves, imbued with the spirit of prophecy but taking account of the order of inferior causes, have predicted certain events which did not take place because the Prime Cause disposed otherwise.[96]

What had been actually said by Averroes was that, although philosophy and revelation (in his case, of course, the Koran) may on certain points *appear* to differ, they can and must be reconciled. As stated in his fundamental treatise on *What There Is of Connection between Religion and Philosophy:*

We, the Muslim community, know definitely that demonstrative study [i.e., philosophy] does not lead to conclusions conflicting with what Scripture has given us; for truth does not oppose truth, but accords with it and bears witness to it. This being so, whenever demonstrative study leads to any manner of knowledge about any being, that being is inevitably either unmentioned or mentioned in Scripture. If it is unmentioned there is no contradiction, and it is in the same case as an act whose category is unmentioned, so that the lawyer has to infer it by reasoning from Scripture.* If Scripture speaks about it, the apparent meaning of the words inevitably either accords or conflicts with the conclusions of demonstration about it. If this apparent meaning accords there is no argument. If it conflicts there is a call for allegorical interpretation. The meaning of "allegorical interpretation" is: extension of the significance of an expression from real to metaphorical significance, without forsaking therein the standard metaphorical practices of Arabic speech, such as calling a thing by the name of something resembling it, or a cause, consequence, or accompaniment of it, or such other things as those enumerated in accounts of the kinds of metaphorical speech. . . . The reason we have received a Scripture with both an apparent and an inner meaning lies in the diversity of people's natural capacities and the difference of their innate dispositions with regard to assent.[97]

Averroes classified people as of three categories: *1. the demonstrative class,* which is capable of strict reasoning and demonstration according to Aristotle's laws of logic; *2. the dialectical class,* which is satisfied with the plausible opinions general to thoughtful people; and *3. the rhetorical class,* who are persuaded simply by what they are told and whose views cannot stand up to criticism. It is to the last and second, according to his view, that the *apparent* readings of Scripture are addressed, and not so much for their enlightenment as for their moral control and improvement. For such folk cannot grasp philosophical demonstrations and, if unsettled in their minds, would be morally undone. The miracle of the Koran, he held, is that it serves all types simultaneously, and the proper function of philosophy is therefore to extract by demonstration for persons of the highest class the abstruse innermost meaning of God's Word. Or, as he formulates the proposition:

> With regard to things which by reason of their recondite character are knowable only by demonstration, God has been gracious to those of His servants who have no access to demonstration, on acount of their natures, habits, or lack of facilities for education: He has coined for them images and likenesses of these things, and summoned them to assent to those images, since it is possible for assent to those images to come about

* For this method of the Moslem legalists, see *Occidental Mythology,* pp. 430–40.

through the indications common to all men, i.e. the dialectical and rhetorical indications. This is the reason why Scripture is divided into apparent and inner meanings: the apparent meaning consists of those images which are coined to stand for those ideas, while the inner meaning is those ideas themselves, which are clear only to the demonstrative class.[98]

And that, in so many words, is the *actual* Averroist doctrine of the double truth. Ironically, it is the same, essentially, as the view of Saint Thomas Aquinas, not of Siger of Brabant. And indeed, as the same Father Miguel Asín y Palacios who disclosed Dante's debt to Islam has demonstrated in a richly documented publication entitled "The Averroist Theology of Saint Thomas of Aquino":

> Averroes' religious thinking, studied in itself, in contrast with that of the Latin Averroists and compared with that of Saint Thomas, appears on the whole to be analogous rather to the latter: analogous in its attitude, its general point of view, in its ideas and illustrations, and at times even in its words. That is the conclusion forced upon one after an attentive examination of the parallel passages that I have here assembled and discussed.
>
> But how shall we account for such a constellation of analogies? . . . The hypothesis of purely accidental coincidence will be the most appropriate if what we want is to leave the problem unresolved; and this would accord well enough with our current habits of intellectual indolence, as well as with the proclivity of popular theorists always to see in a work of scholastic synthesis the spontaneous fruit and idiosyncrasy of the genius of its authors, uninfluenced by anything alien to the Christian tradition. However, it has now long been axiomatic for the history of ideas, as it is likewise in biology, that the notion of spontaneous generation is absurd. . . . In a word: the hypothesis of accidental coincidence can be counted acceptable (and then only provisionally) only when the distance separating the authors of analogous systems is such, in space and time, that any communication between the two would be impossible to explain.* However, the case that we have at present under view does not fulfill these conditions. The development and perfection of the scholastic synthesis of the thirteenth century is fully explained by the introduction of the Musulman encyclopedia into Europe and, above all, by Aver-

* Compare *Primitive Mythology*, pp. 183–215.

roes' commentaries on the works of the Stagirite. Contacts between the patterns of Islam and scholasticism, therefore, far from being unlikely, are concretely and historically demonstrable. We have to reject therefore the hypothesis of coincidence. . . .[99]

Whence, however, could Saint Thomas have come to know of this doctrine of Averroes? . . . I believe I have found the leading thread that carried the reconciling doctrine that is occupying us here into the Thomistic synthesis—or, at least, its fundamental point: that is to say, its doctrine of the moral necessity of divine revelation. In dealing with the question, *Utrum necessarium sit homini habere fidem* (Whether it is necessary for man to have faith),[100] Saint Thomas founds the necessity on five motives which he declares explicitly he copied from Maimonides; and since that philosopher was a disciple, indirectly, of Averroes, it follows in all probability that his works can have been the channel through which the doctrine of the philosopher of Cordova was communicated to Saint Thomas.* Neither in the *Summa contra Gentiles* nor in the *Summa Theologica* does the Angelic Doctor allow himself to cite again this reference, and it soon came to pass that he was credited with a doctrine of which he was not himself the author.

Here, then, is the first likely channel of communication: the works of Maimonides, whose influence on those of Saint Thomas, in relation chiefly to philosophy, has already been studied by Guttmann.[101]

But I do not think that we have to fall back upon the sole intervention of Maimonides, when it is evident that the principal books of Averroes were in Saint Thomas's hands. Since the year 1217 the *Commentaries* [on Aristotle] of the Cordovan philosopher had been passed around in the schools, translated by Michael Scot in Toledo; and although the philosophical character of such works might make it appear little likely that Averroes would have discussed in them any problems of theology, the intimate relationship of these two disciplines in the Middle Ages, both for Christians and for Musulmans, is well known. *A priori* then, one might suppose that a close analysis of the *Com-*

---

* "Besides," Asín adds in a footnote, "we can find in the pages of Maimonides's *Guide for the Perplexed* practically all the ideas of Averroes and Saint Thomas touching this theme of the analogies between faith and reason." The dates of these three theologians are as follows: Averroes, 1126–1198; Maimonides, 1135–1204; Aquinas, 1225–1274.

mentaries of Averroes and those of Saint Thomas would show traces of flagrant imitation, even in matters theological.[102]

And indeed, the good Father Asín then proceeds to demonstrate at least one instance of such plagiarism by comparing the two great authors on the proposition, *Scientia Dei est causa rerum,* "God's knowledge is the cause of things." [103]

It is most amazing. The doctrine of the dual truth of Siger of Brabant, the Swedish Averroist, was by the Church officially condemned and Siger himself perhaps put to death. Thomas Aquinas refuted both Siger and Averroes, in his *Summa contra Gentiles* as well as in a special treatise *On the Unity of the Intellect against the Averroists.* Yet in Dante's *Paradiso,* at the station of the sun—the place of those learned in theology—whom do we find, luminously at peace and as comfortably at home as the great Saint Thomas himself, but Siger of Brabant, who, in the words of Dante's guide, had "syllogized invidious truths"! [104] Averroes, meanwhile, sits in Limbo, in the idyllic first circle of Hell, with his fellow Musulman Avicenna, chatting with their idol Aristotle, and with Socrates and Plato, Democritus, Diogenes, Anaxagoras and Thales, Empedocles and Heraclitus, Zeno, Dioscorides, Orpheus, Tully and Linus, Seneca, Euclid, Ptolemy and Galen.[105] But one searches in vain for the name of Dante's own Islamic precursor and poetic model, Ibnu'l-'Arabi, while both Mohammed and his cousin Ali, hideously mangled, are in the eighth circle of Hell.[106]

v. The Gnostics

1.

As the classical heritage of symbolic forms reached the poets and artists of later Europe in two associated streams, one above ground, the other below,* so also the Levantine—by way of the orthodox Church above and the various Gnostic sects below. The waters of the two subterranean streams, the classical and the Gnostic, became mixed at certain points, but, though mixed, never really fused; for in the Gnostic view, as in the authorized Christian, the world of nature is seen as corrupt, whereas in the pagan mysteries it was known as divine. Nor did the authorized Christian stream and its underground Gnostic complement ever really fuse;

* Supra, p. 95.

for in the orthodox the corruption of nature was attributed to man's Fall, but in Gnosticism to the Creator, so that whereas according to the former redemption was to be gained through an act of repentance and thereafter obedience to what were taken to be God's laws, the Gnostics strove for release from corruption through a systematic *dis*obedience of those laws in either of two ways, through asceticism or its opposite, the orgy.

Essentially, the reasoning and practices of the Gnostic ascetics were like those of the Jains of India; [107] for here too a strict dualism was posited of spirit and non-spirit, and a graded regimen undertaken of renunciative vows to clear the spiritual element of contamination by the material—life in this world, and this world itself, being conceived as a mixture of the two. As among the Jains, so here, there were laymen beginning the work, which might continue through many lifetimes; teachers, devoted both to instructing others and to disciplining themselves; and solitaries in the final stages of psychic dissolution. It may be recalled that already in Alexander's time the ascetic feats and theories of India's yogis became known to the marveling Greeks.[108] Later the Buddhist monarch Ashoka (r. 268–232) sent monkish missionaries to the West, to the courts of Syria, Egypt, Cyrene, Macedonia, and Epirus; [109] so that in the interchanges of ideas and goods that followed Alexander's "marriage of East and West" we have to reckon with tides of Indian lore flowing westward as well as classical flowing east. More than a few competent scholars have remarked that the Neoplatonism of such a mystic as Plotinus shares practically all of its essential points with the Sankhya of Kapila.[110] And like the forests of India with their hermit groves, so the Levantine deserts of the second, third, and fourth centuries A.D. were infested with spiritual athletes, striving to separate their souls from the glories and riches of this world. Some perched on the branches of trees or atop the columns of temple ruins; others chained themselves to rocks or enclosed themselves in cells; more bore on their shoulders heavy yokes; others browsed on grass.[111] The indestructible Saint Anthony (251–356!?!) is the model of the approved version of that life-negating mentality, and through the monks of the Middle Ages, on into modern times, there has been a continuation of its course—referred back to the words and example of Christ: "If you would be perfect, go sell what you possess and give to the poor . . . and come, follow me." "Follow me, and let the dead bury their dead." [112] Moreover, the Gnostics had their own version of the words of Jesus too, as in the "Gospel According to Thomas": "Whoever has known the world has found a corpse, and whoever has found a corpse, of him the world is not worthy." [113]

With the victories of Constantine in the early fourth century, however, and the subsequent enforcement of an imperial Christianity, the lead in the renunciatory movement passed from the Gnostics of the Near East to the new Manichaean religion of Persia, which—as noted in the Occidental volume [114]—had been founded by the prophet Mani a century earlier (216?–276? A.D.), under the patronage and protection of the liberal-minded Sassanian King Shapur I (r. 241–272). Mani had preached a syncretic doctrine combining Buddhist, Zoroastrian, and Christian ideas, wherein the Old Testament Creator was identified with the Zoroastrian power of darkness and deception, Angra Mainyu, and these two, in turn, with the Buddhist principle of delusion (*māyā*), by which the mind is turned from the pure light of unconditioned consciousness and made captive by the fascination of those things, mixed of light and darkness, that are the passing phenomena of this spatially and temporally conditioned universe of names and forms. He correlated both the Christian and the Zoroastrian prophecies of a literal end of the world with the purely psychological Buddhist doctrine of illumination (*bodhi*) as the end of delusion (*māyā*), declaring that the former, the literal end, would result when the latter, a total realization of illumination, had been achieved. And he associated the world-abandoning doctrine of social disengagement preached by Jesus and illustrated by his forty days in the desert with the Great Departure and world-abandonment of the Buddha.[115] Mani's protector, Shapur I, died in the year 272, and the orthodox Magian clergy thereupon contrived to have the prophet martyred: according to one account, left to die in his prison chains; according to another, crucified; but according to a third, flayed alive, and his skin, then stuffed with straw, hung at the city gate of Gundi-Shapur, known thereafter as the Mani Gate.

In spite of all persecution, however, Mani's doctrine of the fall of light into darkness and of the way of its return from bondage to its source and true being in purity, spread both eastward into China (where it survived until the years of the anti-Buddhist, anti-foreign purges of the Emperor Wu-tsung, 842–844) [116] and westward into the now Christian Roman Empire, where it again met persecution. Saint Augustine (354–430) was a Manichaean for nine critical years before accepting the Christian faith of his mother, Saint Monica, and composing then his dualistic master-work, *The City of God*. Every bit of his enormously influential theology is shot through with a Gnostic-Manichaean revulsion from the flesh, his principal change, ontologically, having been simply from the Manichaean doctrine of the immanence of divine light as the life within all beings to the Christian doctrine of the ab-solute transcendence of divinity—which, nevertheless, is the life that animates the life within all beings. "Thou art not the bodies; nay, nor yet the soul, which is the life of the bodies," he wrote to God in his *Confessions*. "But Thou art the life of souls." [117] A rather fine distinction, yet it meant a great deal to Augustine; and in line with this distinction, while maintaining with Saint Paul (whom the Gnostics also took as authority) that "the desires of the flesh are against the Spirit, and the desires of the Spirit are against the flesh," [118] he spurned the dualism of his Manichaean associates, who, as he declared in his great book, "detest our present bodies as an evil nature." [119] The Christian saint's own detestation of the body was based on the idea not of an evil nature but of a good nature, as created by God, corrupted, however, by its own evil act in disobedience of God, as a consequence of which man's will, though free, is unable to will anything but evil unless redeemed from its corruption by the grace of the sacraments of the Church.

As soon as our first parents had transgressed the command-ment [he wrote in explanation of this view], divine grace for-sook them, and they were confounded at their own wicked-ness; and therefore they took fig-leaves (which were possibly the first that came to hand in their troubled state of mind) and covered their shame; for though their members remained the same, they had shame now where they had none before. They experienced a new motion of their flesh, which had be-come disobedient to them, in strict retribution of their own dis-obedience to God. For the soul, reveling in its own liberty, and scorning to serve God, was itself deprived of the command it had formerly maintained over the body. And because it had willfully deserted its superior Lord, it no longer held its own inferior servant; neither could it hold the flesh subject, as it would always have been able to do had it remained itself subject to God. Then began the flesh to lust against the Spirit, in which strife we are born, deriving from the first transgression a seed of death, and bearing in our members, and in our vitiated nature, the contest or even victory of the flesh.[120]

What I have just quoted is the great theologian Saint Augustine's authoritative exposition of the fundamental Christian doctrine of Original Sin, from the mortal effects of which only the incarnation and crucifixion of the Son of God himself were effective to redeem us. The Manichaeans, on the other hand, blamed what both they and the Christians took to be the parlous state of the universe on the act of creation itself, and in this they were in accord with those earliest Christian Gnostics who had also identified the god of the Old Testament with the Zoroastrian devil, Angra Mainyu.

2.

As already mentioned, however, ascetic release from the world delusion was not the only method practiced by the Gnostics; for there was an orgiastic way as well. And the chief occasion for this exercise—which presently earned for the Christians an unsavory name in the pagan Roman world [121]—was the early church festival of the *agape* or Love Feast (ἀγάπη, "love," in the sense usually of "charity" or "brotherly love"), which so varied from one congregation to the next that, whereas the ritual "kiss of love" was in some exchanged with modest decorum, in others it became a rite in itself. Saint Paul himself had written, "Christ redeemed us from the curse of the law"; [122] but apparently without anticipating the reach to which the sense of that remark might be extended.

Originally, it would seem, the early Christian Love Feast was celebrated either in connection with or separately from the Eucharist, as a church supper with the wealthy providing most of the fare for rich and poor alike. In not a few communities these feasts settled down into mere banquets for the poor; however, already in the first century there is evidence in Paul's First Epistle to the Corinthians (c. 54–58) of an altogether different trend.

"When you meet together," wrote the Apostle, "it is not the Lord's Supper that you eat. For in eating each one goes ahead with his own meal, and one is hungry and another is drunk. What! Do you not have houses to eat and drink in? Or do you despise the Church of God and humiliate those who have nothing?" [123]

Forty years later (c. 93–96), in the Book of Revelation, the voice of the resurrected Christ himself was to be heard chastising the congregation of Thyatira in Asia Minor:

> I know your works, your love and faith and service and patient endurance, and that your latter works exceed the first. But I have this against you, that you tolerate the woman Jezebel, who calls herself a prophetess and is teaching and beguiling my servants to practice immorality and to eat food sacrificed to idols. I gave her time to repent, but she refuses to repent of her immorality. Behold, I will throw her on a sickbed, and those who commit adultery with her I will throw into great tribulation, unless they repent of their doings; and I will strike her children dead. . . . But to the rest of you in Thyatira, who do not hold this teaching, who have not learned what some call the deep things of Satan, to you I say, I do not lay upon you any other burden; only hold fast what you have, until I come.[124]

In the same holy text, the congregation in Pergamum is accused of harboring those who "hold the teaching of Balaam. . . . that they might eat food sacrificed to idols and practice immorality." [125] And by the opening of the second century the entire address of the Epistle of Jude (c. 100–120) was directed, as we read there, against those "ungodly persons who pervert the grace of our God into licentiousness. . . . They are blemishes on our love feasts, as they boldly carouse together." [126] At the opening of the next century the Church Father Tertullian wrote with infinite scorn (c. 217 A.D.) of those "whose Agape boils in the cooking pot, faith glows in the kitchen, and hope lies on a dish: and the greatest of all is that 'charity' of theirs, by virtue of which the men sleep with their sisters." [127]

Let us glance again, therefore, at the alabaster serpent bowl of Figures 11 and 12. As said, it was the vessel probably of a Dionysian-Orphic sect of the early centuries A.D. Were it not for its inscription to Apollo, however, it might have been taken for the vessel of some Gnostic Christian sect, and its scene accordingly interpreted as of the sanctuary of the Love Feast; for both nakedness and serpent-worship were associated in many of the early Christian cults with a restoration of Paradise, and release thereby from the bondages of time.

In the words of the Gnostic "Gospel According to Thomas": "Mary said to Jesus: 'Whom are thy disciples like?' He said: 'They are like little children who have installed themselves in a field that is not theirs. When the owners of the field come, they will say: "Release to us our field." They take off their clothes before them to release it to them and to give back their field to them.' " [128] And again: "His disciples said: 'When wilt Thou be revealed to us and when shall we see Thee?' Jesus said: 'When you take off your clothing without being ashamed, and take your clothes and put them under your feet as the little children and tread on them, then shall you behold the Son of the Living One and you shall not fear.' " [129]

Saint Epiphanius (c. 315–402)—who for thirty-five years was the bishop of Constantia, on Cyprus, where Aphrodite and her serpent spouse had been for millenniums the chief divinities, and whose lifetime spanned that critical century from the reign of Constantine (324–337) to Theodosius I, "the Great" (379–395), when the Roman Empire was being converted from pagan to Christian worship [130]—described in a denunciatory tract the eucharistic service of one of the Christian Ophitic ('ὄφις, "serpent") sects of his time:

They have a snake, which they keep in a certain chest—the *cista mystica*—and which at the hour of their mysteries they bring forth from its cave. They heap loaves upon the table and summon the serpent. Since the cave is open it comes out. It is a cunning beast, and knowing their foolish ways, it crawls up on the table and rolls in the loaves; this, they say, is the perfect sacrifice. Wherefore, as I have been told, they not only break the bread in which the snake has rolled and administer it to those present, but each one kisses the snake on the mouth, for the snake has been tamed by a spell, or has been made gentle for their fraud by some other diabolical method. And they fall down before it and call this the Eucharist, consummated by the beast rolling in the loaves. And through it, as they say, they send forth a hymn to the Father on high, thus concluding their mysteries.[131]

Professor Leisegang, from whose discussions of both the alabaster bowl of Figures 11 and 12 and the golden of Figures 3 and 4 we have already quoted, states in comment on this Ophitic sacrament described by Epiphanius, that for the rites of many pagan mysteries too, and those particularly of Dionysian type, a snake was kept in a chest. Then he adds: "We also know that the living snake was sometimes replaced by a golden one, which served in the performance of the initiate's mystical marriage rite with the godhead.* And it further seems possible," he concludes, "that an artificial snake could replace the real in the liturgy of the Ophites. . . . Might not the alabaster bowl," he then asks, "have served for the offering of consecrated wafers in a eucharistic ritual like that described by Epiphanius?" [132]

The question opens a large prospect. For if it is possible to argue in this way from the Christian sect to a pagan and from a pagan to the Christian, it must also be asked how far the Gnostic versions of the *agape* moved toward the Dionysian orgy, and how—of all beasts!—the serpent, which in normal Christian thought is the figure of Satan himself, could have been assigned the focal role in a Christian version of the mystic marriage.

Figure 23 is from a German sixteenth-century golden thaler struck by a celebrated goldsmith of the town of Annaberg in Saxony, Hieronymus Magdeburger by name. It is of approximately the date of Gafurius's "Music of the Spheres" (Figure 13), and can likewise have been influenced by Renaissance Neoplatonic thought. At first glance one might suppose it to refer to the upward turning of Gafurius's downgoing Orphic serpent; and a consideration of the crucified Orpheus-Bacchus (Figure 9) might seem to support this interpretation, since Bacchus and the winged upward-turned serpent of the alabaster mystery bowl are the same.

However, there is also a perfectly orthodox way to interpret its symbolism, based on a sentence of the fourth Gospel: "And as Moses lifted up the serpent in the wilderness, even so must the Son of Man be lifted up." [133] The reference is to that episode in the Book of Numbers where, the Hebrews in the desert having com-

* Compare *Occidental Mythology*, p. 184.

Figure 23. The Serpent Lifted Up; golden Thaler, Germany,
16th century A.D.

plained against both God and Moses (since there was no food or
water), "Yahweh," as we read, "sent fiery serpents among the
people and they bit the people, so that many people of Israel died.
And the people came to Moses, and said, 'We have sinned, for we
have spoken against Yahweh and against you; pray to Yahweh,
that he may take away the serpents from us.' So Moses prayed for
the people. And Yahweh said to Moses, 'Make a fiery serpent, and
set it on a pole; and every one who is bitten, when he sees it, shall
live.' So Moses made a bronze serpent, and set it on a pole; and if
a serpent bit any man, he would look at the bronze serpent and
live." [134]

The incompatibility of this command with that supposed to have
been previously delivered on Sinai, to make no "graven image, or
any likeness of anything that is in heaven above, or that is in the
earth beneath, or that is in the water under the earth" (Exodus
20:4), we may leave to the science of theology to resolve. Viewed
historically merely, the tale was derived from the so-called Elohim
(E) text of c. 750 B.C.,[135] and was apparently the origin legend
designed to account for the serpent-god of bronze that was in those
days worshiped in the Temple of Jerusalem, together with certain

images of his Canaanite goddess-spouse, Asherah. King Hezekiah, c. 725 B.C., as we are told in the Book of Kings, "cut down the Asherah: and he broke in pieces the bronze serpent that Moses had made, for until those days the people of Israel had burned incense to it; it was called Nehushtan." [136] The approved Christian allegory is simply that, as the serpent of bronze lifted up by Moses on a staff counteracted the poison of a plague of serpents, so the lifting up of Jesus on the cross countervailed the poison of the serpent of the Garden. Both events are accepted as historical, and the earlier is read as a *prefigurement* of the later. We are not to think of Christ crucified as in any way another form of the serpent. The two sides of Hieronymus's golden thaler, in other words, are not to be reckoned as of equal value; nor is the higher value on the serpent's side. Or, at least, that is what a proper Christian would like to think the goldsmith intended us to understand.

Could it be, however, that he actually intended the reverse, namely, that Christ is a reference to the serpent, or even that the two are alternative manifestations of a power transcending both?

Throughout the material in the Primitive, Oriental, and Occidental volumes of this work, myths and rites of the serpent frequently appear, and in a remarkably consistent symbolic sense. Wherever nature is revered as self-moving, and so inherently divine, the serpent is revered as symbolic of its divine life. And accordingly, in the Book of Genesis, where the serpent is cursed, all nature is devaluated and its power of life regarded as nothing in itself: nature is here self-moving indeed, self-willed, but only by virtue of the life given it by a superior being, its creator.

In Christian mythology, supplementing the Old Testament, the serpent is normally identified with Satan, and the words addressed by Yahweh to the serpent in the Garden ("I will put enmity between you and the woman, and between your seed and her seed; he shall bruise your head, and you shall bruise his heel") [137] are taken to refer to the crucified son of Mary, by whose wounds Satan's force was to be broken. As pointed out in *Occidental Mythology*,[138] the resemblance of the Christian legend of the killed and resurrected redeemer to the old myths of the killed and resurrected gods, Tammuz, Adonis, Dionysus, and Osiris, presented a certain advantage to the preachers of the new gospel, but on the other hand, also a danger. For whereas on one hand the resem-

blances made it possible for them to claim that in the historical reality of Christ's crucifixion the merely mythic promises of the earlier religions had been surpassed,* on the other hand the obvious
resemblances also made it possible for converted pagans to regard
the new revelation as simply one more transformation of Hellenistic mystery lore; and in fact, many sects of the first five or six
centuries can best be understood in just that way.

Saint Hippolytus (d. c. 230), writing about a century and a half
before the date of Epiphanius, opens a vista into the hidden sense,
or "higher wisdom" (γνῶσις), of serpent veneration through his
account of the cosmology of an Ophitic Christian sect of his day
called the Perates:

> Their cosmos consists of Father, Son, and Matter, each of
> which three principles contains infinitely many forces. Midway
> between the Father and Matter, the Son, the Logos, has his
> place, the Serpent that moves eternally toward the unmoved Fa-
> ther and moved Matter; now it turns to the Father and gathers
> up forces in its countenance; and now, after receiving the forces,
> it turns toward Matter, and upon Matter, which is without attri-
> bute and form, the Son imprints the ideas that had previously
> been imprinted upon the Son by the Father.
>
> Moreover, no one can be saved and rise up again without the
> Son, who is the serpent. For it was he who brought the paternal
> models down from aloft, and it is he who carries back up again
> those who have been awakened from sleep and have reassumed
> the features of the Father.[139]

The serpent of Gafurius's diagram, dramatically descending,
and the serpent circling the border of the Tunc-page of the Book
of Kells [140] are both suggested strongly by this unforgettable image.
Furthermore, the question now arises as to whether in the mind of
the goldsmith Hieronymus the relationship of the two sides of his
coin may not, after all, have been the opposite to that suggested by
the biblical reading: not the serpent as prefiguring Christ, but
Christ as an incarnation of the serpent. And if this were the case,
then there might have been a still further, deeper heresy dissem-
bled in his innocent design. For, according to the view of most of

* As, for instance, in the Second Epistle of Peter (c. 120 A.D.): "We did
not follow cleverly devised myths when we made known to you the power
and coming of our Lord Jesus Christ, but we were eye-witnesses of his majesty" (II Peter 1:16).

the early Ophitic sects, the "Father" named in the cosmological figure of the Perates would have been not Yahweh of the Old Testament but a higher, more serene divinity, infinitely above him; and the first descent of the serpent from that infinitude would have been not voluntary but a fall; moreover, this fall would have been brought about precisely by the machinations of Yahweh, the Old Testament creator of this fallen world, which is mixed of divine light and foulest darkness.

Briefly summarized: The basic idea of all these systems was that the origin of evil coincided with the act of creation itself. The god of the Old Testament, this secondary god—the Demiurge, as he is termed—created the world not from nothing but by engulfing a quantity of the light of the infinite true Father. This light, the Spirit, he lured, conjured, or ravished downward into Matter, where it now is entrapped. That was the first descent of the serpent, the Son, bearing the paternal models (or, as others might say, "the image of God") from the kingdom of the Father into Matter. And these spiritual forces, images, models, or ideas are now held entrapped in the created universe by the Demiurge's lieutenants, the Archons ('άρχων, "ruler") of the planets, who both control the laws of nature and enforce the commandments of the Old Testament—which are not of the true Father but of the Demiurge.

And so the second descent of the serpent was a voluntary downcoming, to release the entrapped spiritual forces; and the Bible story of the serpent in the garden is an account of this appearance. For the serpent there caused the male and female, Adam and Eve, to violate the commandment of the Demiurge, and so commenced the work of redemption. Yahweh struck back by delivering to Moses an impossible set of moral laws, to which the serpent then replied by coming down as the redeemer and taking up residence in a mortal, Jesus—who was not himself the redeemer, but the vehicle of the redeemer and as such taught the breaking of the laws, both of nature, through asceticism, and of the Old Testament, through his new gospel. As Paul had said: "Christ redeemed us from the curse of the law." Therefore the various Gnostic sects, following this teaching of the serpent, do indeed break those laws in various ways: on one hand, in the ascetic sects, the laws of nature through severe asceticism; and on the other hand, in the orgiastic sects, the laws of the moral code.

Now, matter of itself is inert and formless. Given life and form by the entrapped spirit of the Father, however, it is the living, beautiful universe of man's suffering and fear. The nature of this universe, therefore, is mixed. It is a compound of spirit and matter. Hence, although the usual Gnostic attitude was strictly dualistic, striving—like the Jains of India—to separate spirit from matter, with a strong sense of repugnance for the world, it is also possible to find in certain other Gnostic remains passages of inspiring affirmation; as, for instance, the words attributed to Jesus in the Gnostic Gospel "According to Thomas": "The Kingdom of the Father is spread upon the earth and men do not see it"; or again: "The Kingdom is within you and is without you. If you will know yourselves, then you will be known and you will know that you are the sons of the Living Father." [141]

Given such a positive attitude, however, there would be no need to suppose that the Son, the serpent, was originally brought down against his will. He would have descended voluntarily, to bring forth from formless matter the glory of this universe; and in fact this seems to have been the sense of the cosmological image of the Perates, who (if our informant, Saint Hippolytus, describes their myth correctly) had nothing to say of any secondary creator. Their serpent continuously descends and ascends of itself, imprinting and releasing in a fluent round. Furthermore, by the members of the sect themselves, the name Perates was interpreted as derived from the Greek πέρατος, "on the opposite side," which is exactly equivalent to the Sanskrit pāramitā, "the yonder shore." And, as we have learned from numerous Mahayana Buddhist texts of exactly the period of these Gnostic Perates, there is a "Wisdom of the Yonder Shore" (prajñā-pāramitā), which is, in fact, the ultimate wisdom of Buddhist realization; [142] namely, a knowledge beyond all such dualistic conceptions as matter and spirit, bondage and release, sorrow and bliss. Indeed, to think in such terms is to remain bound to the categories of this shore, the hither shore: the shore of those who have remained on the outside of the bowl of Figures 11 and 12. Whereas for those within the bowl, who have crossed beyond the round of the twenty-four columns of the hours of time and horizon of the four winds, there are no dualities at all. Those who have crossed to that Yonder behold in one immortal vision the serpent symbol of temporal change united with the wing symbol of release; or, to use the Peratean image: in one immortal instant the whole round of the serpent cycling ever in its play between Matter and the Father.

The Greek word *gnosis* (whence "Gnosticism") and the Sanskrit *bodhi* (whence "Buddhism") have exactly the same meaning, "knowledge"—referring to a knowledge, however, transcending that derived either empirically from the senses or rationally by way of the categories of thought. Such ineffable knowledge transcends, as well, the terms and images by which it is metaphorically suggested; as, for instance, that of a serpent cycling between the kingdom of the Father and Matter.

Our usual Christian way has been to take the mythological metaphors of the Credo literally, maintaining that there *is* a Father in a Heaven that *does* exist; there *is* a Trinity, there *was* an Incarnation, there *will be* a Second Coming, and each of us *does* have an eternal soul to be saved.

The Gnostic-Buddhist schools, on the other hand, make use of their images and words, myths, rituals, and philosophies, as "convenient means or approaches" (Sanskrit *upāya,* from the root *i*, "to go," plus *upa-,* "toward"),[143] by and through which their ineffable gnosis or bodhi is suggested. Such means are not ends in themselves but ports of departure, so to say, for ships setting sail to the shore that is no shore; and a great number of such ports exist. In the Mahayana Buddhist tradition they are known as Buddha Realms.[144] To modern scholarship they are known as sects. And they range from those appropriate for the simplest, least developed aspirants (ports planned, so to say, to handle companies of tourists requiring guides, pamphlets, tipping information, conversation dictionaries, and the rest) to those equipped for the maintenance and refreshment of the masters of the sea. The Perates seem to have been spiritual masters of this latter kind, like the Mahayana Buddhist illuminati, by whom the dualistic notions of matter and spirit, bondage and release, being and non-being have been left behind as illusory. However, many other Gnostic sects—in contrast to the Perates—were of the "hither shore" variety, not only recognizing a distinction between bondage and freedom of the spirit, but also working diligently to bring about literally the mythological end of days, when the last scintilla of enfolded light will have been released from its material coil. And they attended to this incongruous task in the two contrary yet affiliated ways already indicated; on the one hand, extreme asceticism, and, on the other, the orgiastic feast.

And so now, at last, for a dependable eyewitness account of what was actually going on at those by now notorious church suppers, the earliest Christian Love Feasts, the best authority is that same Saint Epiphanius from whose writings we have already drawn the report of the Christian serpent sacrament. For in his youth, in his quest for the road that leads to the place all wish to find, he had allowed himself to be seduced into a Syrian Gnostic congregation known as the Phibionites by certain women who were, as he later confessed, "in the forms of their appearance, very beautiful of feature," but "in the spirit of their corruption, such as had earned for themselves all the hideousness of the Devil." Not yet the saint that he was ultimately to become, Epiphanius remained among those women and their corruptions long enough to acquire a complete knowledge of their liturgy; and only after that did he embark on his better-known career by denouncing some eighty of his former associates to the local orthodox bishop, who saw to it, in the manner of the time, that the city was promptly purified of their filth.

Their women, they share in common [Epiphanius reported]; and when anyone arrives who might be alien to their doctrine, the men and women have a sign by which they make themselves known to each other. When they extend their hands, apparently in greeting, they tickle the other's palm in a certain way and so discover whether the new arrival belongs to their cult. When they have so assured themselves, they address themselves immediately to the feast, serving up a lavish bounty of meats and wines, even though they may be poor. And when they have thus banqueted, filling their veins, so to say, to saturation, they proceed to the work of mutual incitement. Husbands separate from their wives, and a man will say to his own spouse: "Arise and celebrate the 'love feast' (*agape*) with thy brother." And the wretches mingle with each other, and although I am verily mortified to tell of the infamies they perpetrate, I shall not hesitate to name what they do not hesitate to do, so that I may rouse in those who hear of the obscenities to which they make bold, a shudder of horror.

For after they have consorted together in a passionate debauch, they do not stop there in their blasphemy of Heaven. The woman and the man take the man's ejaculation into their hands, stand up, throw back their heads in self-denial toward Heaven —and even with that impurity on their palms, pretend to pray as so-called Soldiers of God and Gnostics, offering to the Father, the Primal Being of All Nature, what is on their hands, with the words: "We bring to Thee this oblation, which is the very Body of Christ." Whereupon, without further ado, they consume it, take housel of their own shame and say: "This is the Body of Christ, the Paschal Sacrifice through which our bodies suffer and are forced to confess to the sufferings of Christ." And when the woman is in her period, they do likewise with her menstruation. The unclean flow of blood, which they garner, they take up in the same way and eat together. And that, they say, is Christ's Blood. For when they read in Revelation, "I saw the tree of life with its twelve kinds of fruit, yielding its fruit each month" (Rev. 22:2), they interpret this as an allusion to the monthly incidence of the female period.

Yet, in their intercourse with each other they nevertheless prohibit conception. For the goal of their corruption is not the begetting of children but the mere gratification of lust, the Devil playing his own game with them and so ridiculing the imagery derived of God.

They gratify their lust to the limit, but appropriate the seed of their impurity to themselves, not letting it pour in for the procreation of a child, but themselves eating of the fruit of their shame. And if it should occur in the case of any one of them that the implanting of the natural effusion should take effect and the woman become pregnant—now listen to what still more horrible thing they dare: they tear out the embryo as soon as it can be reached, take the misborn unborn fruit of the body and pound it in a mortar with a pestle, after which they mix with it pepper, honey, and certain other balsams and herbs, so that it should not nauseate them: and then that entire congregation of pigs and dogs gathers round, and each dips up with his finger a morsel of the immolated child. And when they have thus consummated their cannibal act, they pray, as follows to God: "We have not let ourselves be tricked by the Archon of Desire but have harvested our brother's error." And they believe this to be the perfect Mass.

And they perpetrate many other horrors more. For when they have again goaded themselves to madness, they drench their hands with the shame of their effusions and elevate the polluted hands and pray, completely naked, as though, through any such antic, free and open discourse before God might be achieved.

They preen their bodies, night and day, both the women and the men, with ointments, bathing and self-indulgence; they take it easy, lolling and drinking. They execrate those who fast, and say, "One should not fast. Fasting is the work of the Archon by whom this present world-age was produced. One should take nourishment, so that bodies may be strong and able to render their fruits in their time." [145]

Now the underlying idea of all these sensational religious works was that, since Christ, the Son of the Father, is entrapped in the field of Matter, the whole universe is the cross on which the Son is crucified. Thus entrapped, suffusing all, he it is that gives life to all (Figure 9). But there was, furthermore, an extremely archaic biological theory involved in the offices of this cult, one that is in fact largely held to this day among Oriental and primitive peoples: namely, that the miracle of reproduction is effected in the womb through a conjunction of semen and menstrual blood. The interruption of the woman's periods during pregnancy conduced to the assumption that the blood withheld was being formed into the body of the child by virtue of the influence upon it of the sperm. Both the menstrual blood and the semen were at once feared and revered, therefore, as the very vehicles of life— apart as male and female, yet in substance one. And since the life force within each was thus the substance of that crucified Son—who suffers within all things—the urgencies and substances of sex, by which the life that is the Son was passed along, were, as these Gnostics stated in their prayers: "the very Body of Christ." Increasing in themselves the force of this life without allowing it to produce new bodies of bondage, they were accomplishing, as they believed, that divine work of redemption, disengagement of the light. And when by accident the life was passed on, it was solemnly taken back in the rite described as "the perfect Mass."

3.

At the climax of the European Middle Ages—the very century of the great Crusades, the Troubadours, Arthurian romance, and the burgeoning of cathedrals that Henry Adams called the moment of the apogee of European Christian unity, when "the movement from unity into multiplicity," began [146]—there was such an outbreak of Manichaean, Gnostic, and other heresies throughout Europe, though most conspicuously in southern France, that finally Pope Innocent III (r. 1198–1216), to protect the hegemony of Rome, let loose a version of the scourge of God, in his Albigensian Crusade, that left not only the south of France a desert, but the Gothic Church a cracked shell.[147] The revolts were largely—though not all—of a strongly reformatory trend; for the vices of the higher clergy had become to such an extent notorious that Innocent himself, in a letter to his legate in Narbonne, described those administering the sacraments there as "dumb dogs who had forgotten how to bark, simoniacs who sold justice, absolving the rich and condemning the poor, themselves regardless of the laws of the Church, accumulators of benefices in their own hands, conferring dignities on unworthy priests or illiterate lads. . . . And hence, the insolence of the heretics and the prevailing contempt both of the seigneurs and of the people for God and for his Church." "Nothing," he went on to say, "is more common than for even monks and regular canons to cast aside their attire, take to gambling and hunting, consort with concubines, and turn jugglers or medical quacks." [148]

The two leading reformatory movements were of the Waldensians and the Albigensians. The former were Christians, but strongly anti-papal, rejecting all clerical practices that lacked New Testament authority; and their most popular appeal was to that principle of the early fourth-century Donatist heresy which had been attacked by Augustine as of the greatest danger to the Church,[149] namely the contention that sacraments administered by priests of unworthy character cannot be efficacious. The Albigensians, on the other hand, were not Christians at all but Manichaeans. The geographical center from which their teachings had come into Western Europe, and from which they then received continuing support, was not the great Moslem world of the Levant,

Sicily, or Spain—where the Manichaean doctrines had already been absorbed and transformed by the Sufis and the Shi'a—but the European Southeast: Bulgaria, Rumania, and Dalmatia; the very zone, that is to say, in which the golden Orphic-Dionysian Pietroasa bowl of Figures 3 and 4 was found.

In Figure 24 we now see another sacramental bowl of essentially the same artistic tradition as that of Figures 3 and 4; but the religious symbols are of a Christian kind. This, in fact, is an Orthodox eucharistic bowl from the Greek monastery of Mount Athos, thirteenth century A.D., the date of the Albigensian Crusade. And, like the two already treated, it was intended as a vessel for sacramental breads. We count again a circle of exactly sixteen radiating figures; but in the center, instead of either a winged serpent or the earlier goddess with the grail-like vessel in her hands, we have the Virgin Mother with the Christ Child in her womb: the True Vine, the serpent to be lifted up as in Figure 23. The radiating presences now are adoring angels, the congregation of the mystai in Paradise, with a saint above each, a new initiate, in prayer. And in the sixteenth section is a tabernacle: the sanctuary of the presence of God in his Church, corresponding to Station 16 of the Pietroasa bowl (Figure 3).

For, as Professor Leisegang tells—from whose superb discussion of these three eucharistic vessels I have developed my argument:

In the Eastern European territories dominated by the Greek Orthodox church, both the forms and the spirit of the ancient mysteries have been preserved down to our own day. In the Russian sect of the Men of God, to which, according to Fülöp-Miller,[150] Rasputin belonged, we find the same secrecy, the hymns, the round dances in the direction of the sun's course and in the contrary direction, in imitation of the dances of the heavenly angels; the initiates cast off their clothes to don white shirts used solely for this purpose; they sing and dance to induce a state of ecstasy in which the Holy Ghost speaks through his prophets and prophetesses, and which culminates in a general sexual orgy, resulting in children begotten by the Holy Ghost. Rasputin himself danced before his faithful and threw off his clothes at the climax. A well-known picture, reproduced by Fülöp-Miller, shows him in the very attitude assumed by the mystai

Figure 24. Eucharistic Bowl; Mt. Athos, 13th century A.D.

on our alabaster bowl: one hand upon his breast, the other raised to the level of his head in blessing and adjuration.[151]

One need not be amazed, then, to learn that in twelfth- and thirteenth-century Europe the orgiastic as well as monastic forms of religious devotion flourished. The Albigensians were of the ascetic line; so also (at least officially) were the clergy of the Roman Church. However, as we know from many sources, wherever in the world the fostering powers of life are denied as gods, they reappear in malignant forms as devils. And there was a great deal more religious lore being carried to Europe in those centuries from the relic-fertile East than is represented merely in the arrival of such holy marvels as the bones, arms, and legs of apostles, splinters of the true cross, little vials of the Virgin's milk, Saint Joseph's breath, and the Lord's tears, several prepuces of Jesus, parts of the burning bush, feathers from the angel Gabriel's wings, and the cornerstone rejected by the builders.[152] There is, for example, the following description—marvelously familiar by now—of the rites alleged to have been practiced by a community of supposed Christians discovered in the city of Orléans, France, in the year 1022 and, when discovered, burned alive:

Before we proceed [states our informant, a contemporary hand], I shall describe at some length, for those ignorant of the method, how the "Food from Heaven," as they call it, is produced. On certain nights of the year, they come together in a designated house, each bearing in hand a lantern; and there they chant the names of the demons in the manner of a litany, until suddenly they see that the Devil has arrived among them in the likeness of some beast. And he having been seen somehow by them all, they put out the lanterns and immediately every man grabs whatever woman comes to hand, even though she may be his own mother, his sister, or a nun, without thought of sin; for such tumbling is regarded by them as holiness and religion. And when a child is begotten in this utterly filthy way, they reassemble on the eighth day and, kindling a large fire in their midst, pass it, like the old heathens, through that fire, and thus cremate it. The ashes then are collected and kept with as much reverence as Christians reserve for the blessed Body of Christ; and to those on the point of death they administer a portion of these ashes as a viaticum. Moreover, there is such power in those ashes, infused by the Devil's deceit, that when anyone tainted by that heresy happens to have tasted even the smallest quantity, his mind can hardly ever thereafter be turned from that heresy to the way of truth.[153]

One is put in mind, through all this, of the audaciously obscene religious rites and temple arts that were unfolding during those same centuries in India; in the sculptured temples, for instance, of Belur, Khajuraho, Bhuvaneshvara, and Kanarak.[154] And as the Gnostic Christians sought release from the deluding toils of this world by violating ritually the moral codes of their culture, so in India the followers of the "left-hand path" practiced the antinomian rites of the Five Forbidden Things—the "Five Ms," as they are called—consisting of wine (madya), meat (mamsa), fish (matsya), yogic postures involving women (mudrā), and sexual union (maithunā).[155] Moreover, there is an unmistakable resemblance to be remarked particularly between the rites of the South Indian "bodice (kanculi) cult," described in Oriental Mythology,[156] and a certain gallant custom of the fashionable gentry of southern twelfth-century France. In the Indian rites, it may be recalled, the female votaries, on entering the sanctuary, deposit their upper vests in a box in charge of the guru, and at the close of the preliminary ceremonies each of the men takes a vest from the box, whereupon the woman to whom it belongs—"be she ever so nearly kin to him"—becomes his partner for the consummation. The European version of this unconventional ceremony—turned to the taste, however, of a more playful, secular spirit, and where the female, not the male, is given the lead—retains the vestiges of its obscure religious background only in its manner of a carnival masque and its association thereby with both a mock Mass and the name of a third-century martyr, Saint Valentine (d. Feb. 14, c. 270 A.D.), on the day of whose decapitation, it is said, the birds begin to mate. The rites of these so-called "Valentine Clubs" may, in fact, have originated in some sort of spiritual marriage of the Valentinian Gnostics of second- to fourth-century Alexandria (Valentinus, the founder, fl. 137–166 A.D.) and have arrived in southern France along with the other Gnostic features of the time. They are described in the following amusing passage from the pages of John Rutherford's choice little book, The Troubadours.

Every year, on the 14th of February, these Valentines assembled on horseback in some convenient place, usually the center of the nearest town. Here they formed files, each consisting of a lady and a gentleman; and hence they departed to make the circuit of the neighborhood. They were led by two files got up to represent Cupid, Mercy, Loyalty and Chastity, and they were duly attended by trumpeters and banner-bearers, to say nothing of the inevitable rabble. The procession closed at the Hotel de Ville, whose principal apartment was gaily decorated for the occasion. Here the Valentines worshiped Love, in a neat parody on the Mass. Then each pair kissed and parted, for a new engagement was about to be formed. There was now produced a silver casket, containing the names of all the gentlemen present written on separate slips of parchment. One by one, each of the ladies drew a slip, until no more remained in the casket. Afterwards, the president, bedizened as Cupid, read out the names written on the slips, and the gentlemen who bore these names became the Valentines of the respective ladies who had drawn them for the ensuing year. When all the Valentines were thus recoupled, the laws of the institution were read over by the president. These specified that each gentlemen was to be faithful to his lady for the term of twelve months; to keep her well supplied with flowers, according to the season, and to make her presents at stated periods; to escort her whithersoever she wished to go for purposes of piety or pleasure; to make her songs, if a poet, and to break lances in her honor, if skilled in arms; and to resent to the utmost every insult leveled at her. The laws further specified that, should the gentleman happen to be convicted of willful failure in any item, he was to be expelled with ignominy from the society. In this case the Valentines were to assemble, as on the 14th of February, and march to his house. In front thereof his crime and sentence were to be proclaimed, and a bundle of straw was to be burned on his doorsill, in token of his excommunication. Finally, the marriage of a pair of Valentines was strictly prohibited, under the like penalty. The president having finished his recitation of the statutes, another parody of the Church services of the day was perpetrated, and the party broke up.[157]

Nor is it only in the cults of the left-hand path that resemblances between the Indian and European religions of the Middle Ages are to be found. The cathedral and temple forms that arose in both areas from the tenth to thirteenth centuries were themselves comparable in many fundamental features.

Ornamented without, as well as within, by the sculptured figures of enraptured beings—in the cathedrals, angelic and saintly, in the temples, often obscene—both were designed to suggest the precinct of a divine, supranormal presence, comparable on a vast scale to the interior of the alabaster bowl of Figures 11 and 12. One enters through a symbolic portal and proceeds through a long nave or mandapa to a sanctuary (Sanskrit, *garbha-gṛha*, "embryo house" or "womb") where the actual presence of the deity is to be worshiped in profound, indrawn meditation. In Europe the presence is of Jesus Christ himself, in the consecrated host; in India it might be the Goddess, in her consecrated image or yoni symbol; her spouse, Shiva, as the lingam; Vishnu, or some other god in symbol or image. In the Rajrani temple in Bhuvaneshvara, near Puri,[158] there is no symbol whatsoever in the lightless holy of holies. This beautiful little temple was built about 1100 A.D. by a wealthy courtesan for her king; and local legend has it that when he entered the sanctuary the presence there found was the consecrated courtesan herself. Whether true or false, the legend is certainly kindred, on one hand, to that of the love grotto of Tristan and Isolt, and on the other to the puranic fables of the loves of Krishna and Radha among the Gopis that were coming to flower at that time in India and culminated c. 1170 in the rapturous *Gītā Govinda* of Jayadeva—which in *Oriental Mythology* I have compared to the Tristan romances of the same date.[159]

To be remarked further is the astonishing point-for-point correspondence of the forms and paraphernalia of the rites performed in temple and cathedral. As Sir John Woodroffe has pointed out in his fundamental work on *The Principles of Tantra*, the following statement from the Roman Catholic Council of Trent (1545–1563) can be readily annotated in Sanskrit to indicate the Indian parallels; viz.: "The Catholic Church, rich with the experience of the ages and clothed with their splendor, has introduced mystic benediction (*mantra*), incense (*dhūpa*), water (*ācamana, padya,* etc.), lights (*dīpa*), bells (*ghaṇṭā*), flowers (*puṣpa*), vestments and all the magnificence of its ceremonies in order to excite the spirit of religion to the contemplation of the profound mysteries which they reveal. As are its faithful, the Church is composed of both body (*deha*) and soul (*ātman*). It therefore renders to the Lord (*īśvara*) a double worship, exterior (*vāhya-pūjā*) and interior (*mānasa-pūjā*), the latter being the prayer (*vadana*) of the faithful, the breviary of its priest, and the voice of Him ever interceding in our favor, and the former the outward motions of the liturgy." [160] The use of the rosary, too, might be mentioned, which entered Europe in the course of the late Middle Ages. Further, both the form and the sense of the main service in both religious precincts is the same. A priest conducts the rite, opening with preliminary prayers and, on high occasions, intoned chants. An offering—bread and wine in the West; in India, milk or butter, fruits, an animal or a human being—is consecrated, symbolically or actually immolated, and in part consumed in communion; after which, prayers of thanksgiving are offered and the company is dismissed.

The earliest appearances of this style of religious art and architecture in India date—significantly—from the Gupta Period, the reign of Chandragupta II (r. 378–414), whose dates include—as pointed out in my Oriental and Occidental volumes [161]—those of the Byzantine Emperor Theodosius the Great (r. 379–395), whose anti-pagan edicts initiated an exodus of intellectuals on all levels—priests, philosophers, scientists, and artists—eastward into Persia and to India. The demonstrations by Hermann Goetz of literally hundreds of correspondences between the Roman-Syrian art and culture forms and those that abruptly appeared in India at this time bear ample witness to what occurred. A golden age of Hindu and Buddhist art, literature, and temple architecture dawned, which from the fifth to mid-thirteenth centuries displayed many of those forms of mythology and worship that were being suppressed during the same centuries in the West.

It is a pity that no further cross-cultural studies have yet been undertaken of the consequences of the great Theodosian crisis, tracing, on one hand in Gupta India and subsequently T'ang China, and on the other hand in the underground heretical movements and witchcraft epidemics of semi-Christianized Europe, the two branches of the one vastly outspread mystery tradition, the most ancient stem and roots of which are to be recognized in Hellenistic Egypt, Syria and Asia Minor. There is here a capital op-

portunity for a broadly based science of comparative mythology to
register the whole constellation of both causes and effects—
geographical, psychological, sociological, philosophical, religious,
and aesthetic—of a major instance of historic transformation
through diffusion, noting, on one hand, the continuity through centuries of a single mighty context of mythic and ritual lore and, on
the other, its division into a confrontation of reciprocally incomprehensible opposites, contrary in every strain and feature, vice,
virtue, and ideal. Much as the characters of two sisters, one dark,
the other fair, may in comparison illuminate each other, so do
these two kindred worlds of the medieval Orient and Europe. And
particularly in relation to the interpretation of their shared symbols, the value of a glance from Europe to India can be considerable. For whereas in Europe only one, very literal, precisely defined orthodox reading has been officially allowed, in India every
possible symbolic inflection of meaning and application has been
applied both to worship and to art. Any scholarship that confines
itself, therefore, to a single province of this study is bound to be
baffled by phenomena that a knowledge from across the line would
illuminate in a trice. And in the cause, today, of that ecumenical
understanding which is the ultimate aim and necessity of all the
global works now in progress in this world, lacing East and West
together, it would seem that a seriously systematic full-scale examination of exactly this material should be an appropriate focus of
concern.

So let us return our own gaze, now, to the great creative masters
of the West, bearing in mind, as a basic principle of our study, that
the symbols put to use by them have come from afar. Their
sources are far deeper, broader, and more ancient, far more intimately associated with the primary faculties of the human spirit,
than the limits of any single religious, secular, moral, or antinomian tradition can allow. Hence, no matter what the medium that
carries them to view, they speak from beyond that medium itself
—like the serpent of the Garden of Eden, who had been known to
the peoples of the ancient Near East long before the advent of
Yahweh. The Orphics heard him speak a very different tongue
from that heard by the rabbis and Church Fathers; the Ophites,
otherwise again. And to us he has even more to say. So, too, the
symbols of the love life, the love death, of the man and woman,

woman and man, Tristan Isolt, Isolt Tristan: to read their life, to read their death, and to judge the power of their very great poet, one has to read through and beyond the various local mythologies (ethnic ideas) of Gottfried's day and our own, to the undertones and overtones, the new tones and the old as well, of the elementary song immortal of his art.

Part Two

THE WASTE LAND

THE LOVE-DEATH

✦✦

I. *Eros, Agape,* and *Amor*

I find it impossible to understand how anyone who had really read both the literature of Gnosticism and the poetry of Gottfried could suggest—as does a recent student of the psychology of *amor*—that not only Gottfried but also the other Tristan poets, and the troubadours as well, were Manichaeans.[1] The period of their flowering, it is true, was that of the Albigensian heresy. It is also true that the cult of *amor,* with its guiding light, the "Fair Lady of Thought," was in principle both adulterous and not directed to reproduction. Moreover, the consecration of this love was not an ecclesiastical affair of bell, book, and clergy, but a matter, purely, of the character and sentiments of the couple involved. And finally, the mad disciplines to which a lover might, in the name of love, subject himself, sometimes approached the lunacies of a penitential grove.

There is an account of one who bought a leper's gown, bowl, and clapper from some afflicted wretch and, having mutilated a finger, sat amidst a company of the sick and maimed before his lady's door, to await her alms. The poet Peire Vidal (c. 1150–c. 1210?), in honor of a lady named La Loba, "The She-Wolf," had himself sewn into the skin of a wolf, and then, provoking a shepherd's dogs, ran before them until pulled down, nearly dead—after which the countess and her husband, laughing together, had him doctored until well.[2] Sir Lancelot leapt from Guinevere's high window and ran lunatic in the woods for months, clad only in his shirt.[3] Tristan too went mad. Such lovers, known as Gallois, seem

175

to have been, if not common, at least not rare, in the days when knighthood was in flower. There were some who undertook the discipline called in India the "reversed seasons," where the penitent, as the year became warmer, piled on more and more clothing until by midsummer he was an Eskimo, and, as the season cooled, peeled away, until in midwinter he was, like Lancelot, in his shirt.[4] One is reminded of the childlike contemporary of these poets, Saint Francis (1182–1226), who, conceiving of himself as the troubadour of Dame Poverty, begged alms with the lepers, wandered in hair shirt through the winter woods, wrote poems to the elements, and preached sermons to the birds.

However, the first point to be remarked in connection with the Albigensian charge is that, whereas according to the Gnostic-Manichaean view nature is corrupt and the lure of the senses to be repudiated, in the poetry of the troubadours, in the Tristan story, and in Gottfried's work above all, nature in its noblest moment— the realization of love—is an end and glory in itself; and the senses, ennobled and refined by courtesy and art, temperance, loyalty and courage, are the guides to this realization. Like a flower potential in its seed, the blossom of the realization of love is potential in every heart (or, at least, every noble heart) and requires only proper cultivation to be fostered to maturity. Hence, if the courtly cult of *amor* is to be catalogued according to its heresy, it should be indexed rather as Pelagian than as Gnostic or Manichaean, for, as noticed in *Occidental Mythology*,[5] Pelagius and his followers absolutely rejected the doctrine of our inheritance of the sin of Adam and Eve, and taught that we have finally no need of supernatural grace, since our nature itself is full of grace; no need of a miraculous redemption, but only of awakening and maturation; and that, though the Christian is advantaged by the model and teaching of Christ, every man is finally (and must be) the author and means of his own fulfillment. In the lyrics of the troubadours we hear little or nothing of the fall and corruption either of the senses or of the world.

Moreover, in contrast to the spirit of the indiscriminate Love Feast, whether of the orgiastic Phibionite variety or the charitable church-supper type, the address of *amor* is personal. It follows the lead and allure, as we have said, of the senses, and in particular of the noblest sense, that of sight; whereas the whole point of the

Love Feast, and the very virtue of communal love, is that its aim is
indiscriminate. "Love thy neighbor as thyself." [6] Selectivity, the
prime function of the eye and heart, is in the *agape* methodically
abjured. The lights go out, so to say, and whatever is at hand, one
loves—either in the angelic way of charity or in the orgiastic, de-
monic way of a Dionysian orgy; but in either case, religiously: in
renunciation of ego, ego judgment, and ego choice.

It is amazing, but our theologians still are writing of *agape* and
eros and their radical opposition, as though these two were the
final terms of the principle of "love": the former, "charity," godly
and spiritual, being "of men toward each other in a community,"
and the latter, "lust," natural and fleshly, being "the urge, desire
and delight of sex." [7] Nobody in a pulpit seems ever to have heard
of *amor* as a third, selective, discriminating principle in contrast
to the other two. For *amor* is neither of the right-hand path (the
sublimating spirit, the mind and the community of man), nor of
the indiscriminate left (the spontaneity of nature, the mutual incitement of the phallus and the womb), but is the path directly before one, of the eyes and their message to the heart.

There is a poem to this point by a great troubadour (perhaps
the greatest of all), Guiraut de Borneilh (c. 1138–1200?):

So, through the eyes love attains the heart:
For the eyes are the scouts of the heart,
And the eyes go reconnoitering
For what it would please the heart to possess.
And when they are in full accord
And firm, all three, in the one resolve,
At that time, perfect love is born
From what the eyes have made welcome to the heart.
Not otherwise can love either be born or have commencement
Than by this birth and commencement moved by inclination.

By the grace and by command
Of these three, and from their pleasure,
Love is born, who with fair hope
Goes comforting her friends.
For as all true lovers
Know, love is perfect kindness,
Which is born—there is no doubt—from the heart and eyes.

The eyes make it blossom; the heart matures it:
Love, which is the fruit of their very seed.[8]

We have here attained, I would say, new ground: such ground
as in the whole course of our long survey of the world's primitive,
Oriental, and Occidental traditions has not been encountered before. It is the ground, unique and new, on which stands the modern
self-reliant individual—in so far, at least, as he has yet been able
to mature, to show himself, and to hold his gained ground against
the panic weight in opposition of the old and new mass and tribal
thinkers. In the nineteen lines of this troubadour poem, in fact,
there already comes to view a prospect of that world of Renaissance man which in art was presently to be typified in the rules, the
objectively discovered principles, of Renaissance (linear) per-
spective: the organization of a selected or imagined field from an
individual point of view, along lines going out toward a vanishing
point from the locus of a living pair of eyes—according to the impulse, moreover, of the individual's private heart. The world is
now showing itself in its own sweet light and form, at last, to men
and women of sense, who are daring to look, to see, and to respond. The system of problems of the controlling religious tradition is in principle disregarded, and the individual standpoint becomes decisive. And so, although it is true that in the century of
the troubadours there was rampant throughout Europe a general
Manichaean heresy, and that many of the ladies celebrated in the
poems are known to have been heretics—just as others were practicing Christians, and the poets themselves communicants of one
tradition or the other—in their character as artists and in their
poetry and song the troubadours stood apart from both traditions.
The whole meaning of their stanzas lay in the celebration of a love
the aim of which was neither marriage nor the dissolution of the
world. Nor was it even carnal intercourse; nor, again—as among
the Sufis—the enjoyment, by analogy, of the "wine" of a divine
love and the quenching of the soul in God. The aim, rather, was
life directly in the experience of love as a refining, sublimating,
mystagogic force, of itself opening the pierced heart to the sad,
sweet, bittersweet, poignant melody of being, through love's own
anguish and love's joy.

One thinks here of the Japanese courtly gallants and their loves
in Lady Murasaki's *Tale of Genji,* and there is indeed a common

sentiment in the Mahayana Buddhist "awareness of the pity of things" (Japanese: *mono no awaré wo shiru*);[9] however, as remarked in *Oriental Mythology*, the ambience of religion hangs there over all, whereas in the love lyrics of the troubadours, even where analogies to certain religious motifs would seem to be obvious, mythological references are ignored and the poem remains frankly and wholly secular, with the poet as the devotee of his lady, who is radiant and potent not by analogy, but with a brilliance and grace of her own that is sufficient for life in this world.

Let me cite, for example, three stanzas from a celebrated poem known as "The Joy of Being in Love," by another of the greatest of the Provençal masters of this art, Bernart de Ventadorn (fl. c. 1150–1200?):

It is no marvel, that I should sing
Better than any other singer;
For my heart more draws me toward Love,
And I am likelier made to her command.
Heart and body, wisdom and wits,
Strength and power, have I wagered:
The bridle so draws me toward Love
That I attend to nothing else.

*   *   *

This love smites me so gently
At heart and with such sweet savor!
Of grief do I die one hundred times a day,
And of joy revive, again a hundred.
My malady, indeed, is of excellent kind;
More worth, this malady, than any other good:
And since my malady is so good for me,
Good, after the malady, will be its cure.

*   *   *

Noble Lady, nothing do I ask of thee
But that thou shouldst take me for thy servant.
I would serve as one serves a good lord,
Whatever reward I might gain.
Behold, I am at thy command:
Sincere and humble, gay and courteous.
Neither bear nor lion art thou,
To kill me, as I here to thee surrender.[10]

From the courts of Provence this poetry passed to Germany, where it was reattuned to the language and spirit of the Minnesingers, the singers of *minne* (*amor*); and among these the leading master, wandering from court to court, was Walther von der Vogelweide (c. 1170–c. 1230), who brought to his lyrics a typically German tone of moral depth and fervor, threaded with a new strain of sympathy for the rustic and the natural against the artificialities of fashion. The morality of this Christian poet was of a type, however, not preached in church; for, as Henry Osborn Taylor has remarked of his blithe little "Under the Linden": "Marvelously, it gives the mood of love's joy remembered—and anticipated too. The immorality is complete . . . and rendered most alluring by the utter gladness of the girl's song—no repentance, no regret; only joy and roguish laughter." [11]

The pretty runs of rhyme and the charming sense of innocence of the medieval language I find impossible to rerender, but the sense of fresh young delight, I think, comes through:

> Under the linden,
> On the heath,
> There was our bed for two;
> There you will find,
> Gently arranged,
> Broken flowers and grass.
> Beside the woods in a dale,
>   Tandaraday!
>   Gently sang the nightingale.
>
> I came a-walking
> Toward the stream,
> My lover had come before.
> There was I greeted:
> "My lady fair!"
> So am happy now for evermore.
> Did he kiss me? Full a thousand clips.
>   Tandaraday!
>   See how red now are my lips.
>
> There he'd prepared,
> Luxuriously,
> A bedding place of flowers:
> It would still bring a smile

> Inwardly,
> If one chanced along that way.
> For by the roses one can see,
>   Tandaraday!
> The pillow where my head would be.
>
> That he lay beside me,
> If anyone knew
> (God forbid!), I'd be mortified.
> But whatever he did with me,
> No one shall ever
> Know anything of that: only he and I
> And a tiny little bird,
>   Tandaraday!
> Who will never let fall a word.[12]

The morality here is of Heloise in the first fair days of her love, and her courageous gospel can be heard again through many of Walther's lines:

> Whoever says that love is sin,
> Let him consider first and well:
> Right many virtues lodge therein
> With which we all, by rights, should dwell.[13]

"Woman will be ever woman's noblest name, greater in worth than Lady!" Walther wrote.[14] "It took a German," states Professor Taylor, "to say this." [15] And again, it took a German to recognize in the world-transfiguring sentiment of love as *minne, amor,* an experience of that same transcendent, immanent ground of being, beyond duality, which Schopenhauer six centuries later was to celebrate in his philosophy. We have already taken note of Gottfried of Strassburg's celebration of this mystery in his symbology of the love grotto with its crystalline bed in the place of the altar of the sacrament. A number of Walther's poems, also, extend the revelation of the goddess Minne to a metaphysical depth beyond anything suggested either in the Provençal or in the Old French love poetry of his day:

> Minne is neither male nor female,
> She has neither a soul nor a body,
> She resembles nothing imaginable.
> Her name is known; her self, however, ungrasped.

Yet nobody from her apart
Merits the blessing of God's grace.

She comes never to a false heart.[16]

Now it is a matter of no small moment that in the period of this
idyllic poetry the world of harsh reality should have been about as
dangerous and unlikely a domicile for *amor* as the nightmare of
history has ever produced. We have mentioned the devastation of
southern France. The whole of Central Europe likewise was in a
state of hideous turmoil. For with the death in the year 1197 of the
Hohenstaufen Emperor Henry VI, surnamed the Cruel, the crown
of the Holy Roman Empire had fallen to the ground and was rolling like a fumbled football for anyone to retrieve. And the armies
battling to possess it—on one hand, of the allied English, papal,
and Guelph contenders, and, on the other, of the German princes
and incumbent Philip of Swabia—were everywhere pillaging towns
and villages, devastating whole provinces, perpetrating the most
brutal and revolting crimes; [17] which wanton work continued until
about 1220, when the brilliant young nephew of the murdered
Philip, Frederick II (1194–1250), was finally crowned Emperor
in Saint Peter's by a reluctant and uneasy Pope. Walther had been
a witness to these horrors, and he wrote of them with unmitigated
scorn:

I saw with my own eyes hidden things about men and women,
heard and saw all they did and said. How Rome lied and betrayed two kings, I heard. And when the popes and laity had
formed their contending parties, there took place the most terrible war that ever was or will ever be: the worst, because both
the body and the soul were thereby slain. . . .[18]

Ironic, is it not? In the name of love and of peace on earth to
men of good will, treachery, arson, pillage, and massacre everywhere; and in such an age the elevation of the most glorious visions in radiant glass and carved stone of that peace and love fulfilled! Fulfilled, however, not on earth, but in a realm away from
this vale of tears, to which the most blessed opener of the gate is
that woman shining as the sun, to whom the cathedral itself is ded-
icate, earthly, yet the Mother of God—the Virgin Mary, Notre
Dame. In the words of the long-cherished hymn *"Salve Regina,"*
composed by Abelard's elder contemporary Adhemar de Monteil,

Bishop of Le Puy (d. 1098), which is to this day engraved, with love, in the heart of every kneeling Catholic:

> Hail, holy Queen, Mother of Mercy,
> Our life, our sweetness, and our hope,
> All hail!
> To thee we cry, poor banished children of Eve;
> To thee we sigh, weeping and mourning in this vale of tears.
> Therefore, O our Advocate,
> Turn thou on us those merciful eyes of thine;
> And after this our exile,
> Show unto us Jesus, the blessed fruit of thy womb.
> O merciful, O kind, O sweet Virgin Mary! [19]

The last three aspirations, "O merciful, O kind, O sweet Virgin Mary!" were added by Abelard's exact contemporary and dangerous challenger in debate, the mighty Saint Bernard of Clairvaux (1091–1153), to whom Dante, in the *Commedia*, assigns the loftiest possible station, at the very feet of God. Throughout his lifetime this passionate preacher of transcendental euphoria strained every metaphor in the book of love to elevate the eyes of men from the visible women of this earth to the glorified form of that crowned Virgin Mother above, who is the Queen of Angels and of Saints—and Dante, in due time, followed suit. However, the troubadours, minnesingers, and epic poets of the century, in their celebration of *amor,* remained in Nietzsche's sense "true to this earth," this vale of tears where the devil roams for the ruin of souls. For in their view, not heaven but this blossoming earth was to be recognized as the true domain of love, as it is of life, and the corruption ruinous of love was not of nature (of which love is the very heart) but of society, both lay and ecclesiastical: the public order and, most immediately, its sacramentalized loveless marriages.

Among the verse forms of the troubadours, the song of the parting of lovers at dawn, at the warning of the watchman (the *Alba,* "Dawn Song," or *Aubade,* which became the *Tagelied* of the minnesingers) rendered simply yet dramatically the sense of discontinuity between the two worlds, on one hand of love's rapture, and on the other of the social order epitomized in the lady's dangerous spouse, "the jealous one," *lo gilos.* Here is a frequently quoted anonymous example:

In an orchard, under a hawthorn tree,
By her side the Lady clasps her lover,
Till the watchman calls that dawn has appeared.
O God! O God! this dawn! how quickly it comes!

"Would to God the night never had ended,
That my love might never depart from me,
Nor ever the watchman sight day or dawn.
O God! O God! this dawn! how quickly it comes!

"Sweet love, let us start anew our dear game
In the garden where the birds are warbling,
Till the watch sounds again his flageolet."
O God! O God! this dawn! how quickly it comes! [20]

In the Tristan romance King Mark is of course in the role of the jealous spouse; and his royal estate, Tintagel, with its elegant princely court, stands for the values of the day world—history, society, knightly honor, deeds, career and fame, chivalry and friendship—in absolute opposition to the grotto of the timeless goddess Minne, which is of the order of enduring nature, in the forest where the birds still sing. Set apart from all spheres of historic change, the Venus Mountain with its crystalline bed has been entered by lovers through all ages, from every order of life. Its seat is in the heart of nature—nature without and within—which two are the same. And its virtue, so, is of the species, not of this particular culture, nor of that: Veda, Bible, or Koran; but of man pristine in the universe—which is something, however, that in this vale of tears is never to be seen, since we are each brought up (are we not?) in the ethnic sphere of this or that particular culture.

The immanent yet lost—but not forgotten—realm within us all is in Celtic mythology and folklore allegorized variously as the Land below Waves, the Land of Youth, the Fairy Hills, and, in Arthurian romance, that Never Never Land of the Lady of the Lake where Lancelot du Lac was fostered and from which Arthur received his sword Excalibur. In the earliest of the old chronicles of King Arthur—the Welsh monk Geoffrey of Monmouth's *Historia Regum Britanniae* (A.D. 1136)—it is told that at the time of his great last battle with his traitorous son Mordred, "Arthur himself was wounded mortally and borne away, for the healing of his wounds, to the island Avalon." [21] And in a later work, the *Vita Merlini* (c. 1145?), the same chronicler adds that the boat was steered by an old Irish abbot, Barinthus, and that in Avalon the wounded king was tended by Morgan la Fée and her sisters. The next we hear is from an old French verse chronicle by a Norman poet named Wace, the *Roman de Brut* (A.D. 1155), where it is added that "Arthur is still in Avalon and awaited by the Britons; for, as they say and believe, he will return from that place to which he passed and will again be alive." [22] And then finally (c. 1200), an English country priest named Layamon not only transformed the old Irish abbot into something more romantic but let the wounded king himself announce the prophecy of his second coming. Arthur, we here read, had been wounded with no less than fifteen dreadful wounds, into the least of which one might have thrust two gloves, and to a young kinsman, dear to him, who stood by where he lay on the ground, he said these words with sorrowful heart:

> "Constantine, thou wert Cador's son: I here give to thee my kingdom. Defend my Britons ever in thy life; maintain for them all the laws of my days and all the good laws of the days of Uther. And I myself will go to Avalon, to the most beauteous of all women, to the queen Argante, an elf marvelously fair, and she will make my wounds all sound, make me whole with a healing drink. And anon I shall come again to my kingdom and dwell among the Britons in great joy."
>
> And even while he was speaking thus there approached from the sea a little boat, borne by the waves. There were therein two women of marvelous form, and they took Arthur and bore him quickly and laid him softly in the boat and sailed away. [23]

We recall the telling line from Tennyson's "Passing of Arthur," in his *Idylls of the King:*

> From the great deep to the great deep he goes,

when the wounded king in a dusky barge, wherein were three dark queens, passed to Avalon, "to be king among the dead."

The name, Avalon, of that timeless land beyond the setting sun,

> Where falls not hail, or rain, or any snow,
> Nor ever wind blows loudly,

is cognate with the Welsh *afallen*, "apple tree" (from *afal*,
"apple"), and so reveals the affinity of this Celtic Land below
Waves with the Isle of the Golden Apples of the classical Hes-
perides [24]—and thereby with the entire complex of that garden of
immortality of the Great Goddess of the two worlds of death and
life to which so many pages of this study of the mythologies of
mankind have been devoted. An echo of the same theme of the
paradisial garden of the goddess, with its tree of immortal life, is to
be recognized even in the first stanza of the *alba* quoted earlier,
where the lady, under a hawthorn tree, clasps her lover to her side.
The Christian figure of the *pietà*, the dead Savior on his mother's
knees, who will presently return alive, is also of this complex. Can
it be accidental, then, that the king had fifteen wounds—the fifteenth day of the moon being that of the culmination of its waxing
and beginning of its waning, toward death and, after three days'
dark, rebirth? Moreover, the mortally wounded Tristan's first melancholy voyage to Isolt's Dublin Bay, in a self-propelled coracle
that bore him infallibly to her castle, is certainly but another variant and example of this same Land-below-Waves motif: so that
Isolt, the Lady of the Lake, and the Goddess Mother of the
pietà in their final sense are at one: opposed in every measure to
the judgments of this day world of ours, of the Sons of Light.

II. The Noble Heart

As in the poetry of the troubadours, so in Gottfried's *Tristan*, love
is born of the eyes, in the world of day, in a moment of aesthetic
arrest, but opens within to a mystery of night. The point is first
made in his version of the love tale of Tristan's parents, Blancheflor and Rivalin. For there was in their case no potion at work,
inspiring magically a premonition *a priori* of the course along which
they were to be drawn through sensuous allure, from love's
meeting of the eyes, to love's pain, love's rapture, and on to death.

Beautiful, innocent Blancheflor, the sister of King Mark, was
simply sitting among the ladies, watching the sort of tournament called a bohort, in which knights, jousting without armor, contend with only shields and blunt lances, when she began
to hear those around her murmuring: "Look! What a heavenly
man. How he rides!" And her eyes, searching, discovered Rivalin.
"How well he handles that shield and lance!" they were all saying.

"What a noble head! What hair! Happy the woman who gets *him!*"

He was a youth who had arrived lately from his own estates in Brittany, drawn to her brother's court by its fame. And when the game had broken up, this joy-giving knight came cantering Blancheflor's way to salute courteously his host's sister, in the kingdom of whose heart he had already won the crown. His eyes met hers. "May God bless you, beautiful lady!"

"*Merci!*" she answered kindly; and, though discomposed by his gaze, pressed on: "May the Blessed God, who makes all hearts blessed, give blessing to your heart and mind! I congratulate you heartily; yet I have a certain small complaint to plead."

"Ah?" said he. "Sweet lady, what have I done?"

She answered: "Through a friend of mine, the best I ever had" —and she meant by that her heart.

"Good Lord!" he thought. "What tale is this?" [25]

Gottfried's analysis, from this point on, of the brooding of the stricken couple opens poignantly, through a tale of young romance, to the ominous love-death theme announced already in his Prologue * and to be developed, ever mounting, through his handling of the legend of their son. As in the poem of the troubadour Borneilh, so in Gottfried's work, love is born of the eyes and heart.

However, here there is a new interest brought to the stricken heart itself: what happens there, and to what end; for not every heart opens to love. Gottfried's term is "the noble heart" (*das edele herze*); and as the most learned and discerning of his recent interpreters, Gottfried Weber, shows in a thoroughgoing two-volume total study of the romance,[26] this crucial concept is, in fact, the nuclear theme of the poet's entire work. It opens inward toward the mystery of character, destiny, and worth, and at the same time outward, toward the world and the wonder of beauty, where it sets the lover at odds, however, with the moral order. The poet in his Prologue had already dedicated himself, his life and work, to those alone who could bear together in one heart "dear pain" as well as "bitter sweetness"; and, as Professor Weber observes, it is just this readiness to embrace love's pain along with its rapture that makes the noble heart exceptional. "Nor is the pain

---

* Supra, pp. 37–38 and 42–43.

that is so endured," he writes, "merely adventitious, overlaid from without upon a pleasure in love that is alone essential. The pain is implicit, rather, in the very delight by which it is complemented—to such a degree that the pleasure and pain are indissolubly interlaced, as commensurate components of one experience of existence. And in fact," this perceptive critic concludes, "the poet's intention to give verbal force to this idea is what justifies, both poetically and philosophically, his repeated use—already anticipatively in the Prologue—of the rhetorical device of the oxymoron." [27]

Now this classical rhetorical term, "oxymoron," is defined in *Webster's Dictionary* as "a combination for epigrammatic effect of contradictory or incongruous words (*cruel kindness, laborious idleness*)." [28] It is a term derived from the Greek ὀξύ-μωρος "pointedly foolish," and denotes a mode of speech commonly found in Oriental religious texts, where it is used as a device to point past those pairs of opposites by which all logical thought is limited, to a "sphere that is no sphere," beyond "names and forms"; as when in the Upanishads we read of "the Manifest-Hidden, called 'Moving-in-secret,' which is known as 'Being and Non-being' ": [29]

> There the eye goes not;
> Speech goes not, nor the mind: [30]

or when we open a Zen Buddhist work called *The Gateless Gate* and there read of "the endless moment" and "the full void":

> Before the first step is taken the goal is reached.
> Before the tongue is moved the speech is finished.[31]

Compare the language of the Buddhist texts of "The Wisdom of the Yonder Shore" (*prajñā-pāramitā*), discussed in *Oriental Mythology*:

> The Enlightened One sets forth in the Great Ferryboat, but there is nothing from which he sets forth. He starts from the universe; but in truth he starts from nowhere. His boat is manned with all perfections; and is manned by no one. It will find its support on nothing whatsoever and will find its support on the state of all-knowing, which will serve as a non-support.[32]

We term such speech "anagogical" (from the Greek verb ἀν-άγω, "to lead upward") because it points beyond itself, beyond speech. William Blake in the same wisdom of the yonder shore wrote of *The Marriage of Heaven and Hell*. Nicholas Cusanus (1401–1464) wrote in his *Apologia doctae ignorantiae* ("Apology for Learned Unknowing") that "God is the simultaneous mutual implication of all things, even the contradictory ones," and in this sense protested against what he called "the present predominance of the Aristotelian sect, which considers the coincidence of opposites a heresy, whereas its admission is the starting point of the ascension to mystical theology." [33] Even Saint Thomas Aquinas states, in a sentence of mystical insight, that "then alone do we know God truly, when we believe that he is far above all that man can possibly think of God." [34] And accordingly, in Gottfried, for whom the mode of divine manifestation in human life is love, the "pointedly foolish" oxymoron is the most appropriate stylistic signal of the mystery of which his work is the text.

In the progress of his legend the steadily mounting tension of the polarities of joy and sorrow, love against honor, death-life, light and darkness, can be read as a gradually deepening and expanding realization of the nature of that mighty goddess beyond the male-female polarity who was celebrated by the Minnesinger Walther: * the same represented in the center of the Orphic Pietroasa bowl (Figure 3), between the two lords of the light and the great dark, the eye and heart, Apollo and the god of the abyss; or again, of whom the Graces and the Muses are the manifest allure (Figure 13)—dancing in tripody before the eye of heaven, while yet, with silent Thalia, immobile in the earth.

One cannot help thinking also, in this connection, of the modern finding in the realm of atomic physics of the "principle of indeterminacy, or complementarity," according to which, in the words of Dr. Werner Heisenberg, "the knowledge of the position of a particle is complementary to the knowledge of its velocity or momentum. If we know the one with high accuracy we cannot know the other with high accuracy; still we must know both for determining the behavior of the system. The space-time description of the atomic events is complementary to their deterministic description." [35]

* Supra, pp. 181–82.

Apparently in every sphere of human search and experience the mystery of the ultimate nature of being breaks into oxymoronic paradox, and the best that can be said of it has to be taken simply as metaphor—whether as particles and waves or as Apollo and Dionysus, pleasure and pain. Both in science and in poetry, the principle of the anagogical metaphor is thus recognized today: it is only from the pulpit and the press that one hears of truths and virtues definable in fixed terms. In Gottfried's world there was no tolerance of "the Ass Festival" (as Nietzsche named it) of those who would make thinkable the unthinkableness of being. "Life itself," wrote Nietzsche, "confided to me this secret: 'Behold,' it said, 'I am what must always overcome itself.' " [36] And in Gottfried's world as well, the self-surpassing power of life, which is experienced in love when it wakes in the noble heart, brings pain to the entire system of fixed concepts, judgments, virtues, and ideals of the mortal being assaulted.

Rivalin's spiritual plight, after his first brief exchange, eye to eye, with the beauty of Blancheflor, the poet likens to the agony of a bird that has come down on a limed twig: "When it becomes aware of the lime, it lifts to fly, still held by its feet, and spreading wings, makes to go; but then wherever it brushes the twig, however lightly, it is caught the more, and made fast." [37] The noble youth presently realized that he was trapped. "And yet," as the poet warns,

> even now that sweet Love had brought his heart and mind to her will, it was still unknown to him what a keen torment love was to be. Not until he had pondered in all detail, from end to end, the destiny [*aventiure*] * that was now his in his Blancheflor —her hair, her brow, her temples, cheeks, mouth and chin, the joyful Easter Day that couched laughing in her eyes—did True Love [*diu rehte minne*] come, that infallible fire lighter, who set going a fever of desire. And the flame that then fired his heart and incinerated his body let him know in full force what piercing pain and yearning anguish are. . . . Silence and a mien of melancholy were the best he could show the world, and what

---

* *Aventiure* (Middle High German, from Old French *aventure*, Latin *adventura*), "event, occurrence," or more usually "a marvel, an accident, a bold beginning of uncertain outcome," and especially, "a fortunate occurrence; a destiny." Matthias Lexer, *Mittelhochdeutsches Taschenwörterbuch* (Leipzig: Verlag von S. Hirzel, 17th edition, 1926), p. 9.

had formerly been his gaiety now turned to a yearning need.

Nor did the languishing Blancheflor escape a like history of pining. She was laden, through him, with the same weight of sorrow as he, through her; for Love, the Tyrant [*diu gewaltae-rinne Minne*], had invaded her senses too, somewhat too tempestuously and taken from her by force the best part of her composure. In her demeanor she was no longer at one—as she had used to be—with herself and with the world. Whatever pleasures she had been accustomed to, whatever pastimes she had enjoyed, they all displeased her now. Her life took shape as the very image of the need so close to her heart; and of nought that she was suffering from this yearning had she any understanding whatsoever. Never had she experienced such heaviness and heart's need. "O Lord God," she said to herself, time and time again, "what a life I lead!" [38]

The power of free choice, and even of conceiving of any end or joy beyond the destiny to which the tyrant-goddess Love (*diu gewaltaerinne Minne*) had consigned them, had been taken from this helpless couple. On a tide beyond their knowledge or control they were to be carried to the work—the destiny of surpassing themselves—to which they were assigned; and the occasion occurred as though arranged for them—and yet apparently only by accident—when the brave young earl, doing battle for his host in a war begun by a neighboring king, was run through by a lance and carried from the battlefield on the very point of death.

As Gottfried tells:

Many a noble woman wept for him, many a lady mourned for his life; indeed, all who had seen him lamented the misfortune. But no matter how sorrowful they, for his wounding, it was alone his Blancheflor—the pure maid, gentle and gracious— who with unrelenting fervor, moaned and wept with eyes and heart for the dear pain of her heart.[39]

Her old nurse, therefore, made anxious for the young thing's life, took thought and, reasoning, "What harm can it be with the man already half dead?" contrived to admit her delicate charge, alone, to the quiet chamber where the young earl lay wounded on a couch. And the anxious girl, beholding him there, approached gingerly in fright and, perceiving how close he lay to death, fairly swooned. She bent to study him, tenderly brought her cheek to his, and then swooned indeed. So that now the two lay together on that couch, unconscious and quite still, her cheek to his cheek, as though both were dead. And they remained so for some time.

Whereafter [as we next learn] Blancheflor, reviving a little, took her darling in both arms and, placing her mouth to his, in a very short space of time had kissed him one hundred thousand times; which activity so fired his senses and informed his zeal for love that [as Gottfried further relates] he strained that glorious woman to his half-dead body, ardently and closely, until, before long, their mutual desire was realized and from his body that sweet woman received a child. The man was nearly dead —both from the woman and from love; and never would have recovered had God not stayed him in his need. But he did recover, since so it was to be. . . . .

And thus Blancheflor was healed of her heart's anguish; but what she carried thence was death. She had been freed of her need when love came, but it was death she conceived with her child. Of the child and death within her, she knew not, but of love and the man, she knew well. For he was hers and she was his; she was he and he was she: there were they—and there was true love.[40]

The rest can be shortly told.

News arrived of an invasion of Rivalin's own estates and, with his Blancheflor, he sailed to Brittany, to be slain there in a battle. And when the girl, now big with child, received that grievous news, her tongue froze and her heart became stone; she uttered neither "Oh!" nor "Alas!" but sank to the earth and, four days later, in pain, gave birth and died.

"But look! The little son lives!" [41]

To protect the name of the dead parents of this little nephew of King Mark, his father's loyal marshal, Rual li Foitenant, with his wife raised him as their own son, letting no one—even the boy himself—know the story of his birth. They named him Tristan, as they said, because *triste* means "sorrow," and in sorrow Tristan had been born. When he was seven, they sent him off with a tutor named Curvenal (Wagner's Kurvenal) to learn languages abroad; and he mastered in short course more books than any youngster since or before. He learned, too, to hunt, to ride with shield and lance, to play every known stringed instrument, and at fourteen, still with Curvenal, returned home.

However, he then was kidnaped to sea by merchantmen, who, when struck by a storm that tossed their ship for eight days, set him ashore alone in Cornwall, where the waif, arriving at Tintagel, so impressed the good King Mark with his skills that he became his unrecognized uncle's chief huntsman, harpist, and companion. So it chanced—or rather, seemed to have chanced—that, as Gottfried, our poet, concludes this portion of his tale, "Tristan, without knowing it, arrived home yet thought himself astray; and noble, splendid Mark, the unsuspected 'father,' behaved to him right nobly. . . . Mark held him dear to his heart." [42]

III. Anamorphosis

The universally popular mythological theme known to folklore scholarship as *infant exile and return* carries in the legend of Tristan's boyhood, as wherever it occurs, the inherent suggestion of a destiny unfolding—like a seed into flower—ineluctably, in the incidents of a life. In the love story of Tristan's parents, on the other hand, there is no such evident mythic strain. Events are there presented in the manner of a naturalistic novel, as though determined only by chance. The unfoldment of the destinies *follows*—or at least *appears* to follow—upon the fall of outer circumstance. Yet we know that there, as here, all was predetermined in the author's mind, and that what was read as substantial event was actually but a veil, a tissue of circumstance, conjured forth for the realization of a plot already formed.

Might the same be said of the circumstances of our lives?

As Schopenhauer cautions in his wonderful paper "On an Apparent Intention in the Fate of the Individual": "Everything about such thoughts is questionable: the problem itself is questionable—let alone its resolution."

Yet, as he then goes on to remark:

Everyone, during the course of his lifetime, becomes aware of certain events that, on the one hand, bear the mark of a moral or inner necessity, because of their especially decisive importance to him, and yet, on the other hand, have clearly the character of outward, wholly accidental chance. The frequent occurrence of such events may lead gradually to the notion, which often becomes a conviction, that the life course of the individual, confused as it may seem, is an essential whole, having within itself a certain self-consistent, definite direction, and a certain instructive meaning—no less than the best thought-out of epics.[43]

On the naturalistic plane of Gottfried's romance of Blancheflor and Rivalin, the self-consistent plot of the two lives that in their fate and meaning were at one became known, both to the reader and to the characters themselves, only *a posteriori*—through what appeared to be chance event; whereas in such a romance as that of Tristan and Isolt, resting frankly on symbolic, mythological forms, which emerge with increasing force as the narrative proceeds, the sense communicated is rather of the force of destiny in the shaping of a life, or, to use the old Germanic term, of *wyrd*.*

Rationally, as Schopenhauer suggests,

The apparent plan of the course of a life might be explained, to some extent, as founded on the unchangeability and continuity of inborn character,† as a consequence of which the individual is being continually brought back to the one track. For each recognizes so certainly and immediately whatever is appropriate to his own character that, as a rule, he hardly even brings it into reflective consciousness, but acts directly and, as it were, on instinct. . . .

However, if we now consider the mighty influence and immense power of outer circumstance, our explanation in terms of inner character will seem hardly strong enough. Furthermore, that the weightiest thing in the world—which is to say, the life course of the individual, won at the cost of so much effort, torment and pain—should receive its outer complement and aspect wholly from the hand of blind Chance—Chance without significance or regulation—is scarcely believable. Rather, one is moved to believe that—just as in the cases of those pictures called anamorphoses, which to the naked eye are only broken, fragmentary deformities but when reflected in a conic mirror show normal human forms—so the purely empirical interpretation of the course of the world resembles the seeing of those pictures with naked eyes, while the recognition of the intention of Fate resembles the reflection in the conic mirror, which binds together and organizes the disjointed, scattered fragments.[44]

* Supra, pp. 121–22 and 138–40.
† Supra, p. 35.

I should like to fix in mind here this analogy of the anamorphosis (the word is from the Greek μορφόω, "to form," plus ἀνα
"again": ἀναμορφόω, "to form anew"). For it is a thought that
will clarify much in the fields of modern literature and art—as, for
example, James Joyce's title *Ulysses* for a novel about the wander-
ings of a Jewish advertising broker round and about Dublin. The
casual, chance, fragmentary events of an apparently undistinguished life disclose the form and dimension of a classic epic of
destiny when the conic mirror is applied, and our own scattered
lives today, as well, are then seen, also, as anamorphoses. Like
Shakespeare's mirror held up to nature, the symbols of myth bring
forward into view that informing Form of forms which, through
apparent discontinuity, is "manifest," as the Upanishads declare,
"yet hidden: called 'Moving-in-secret.' " * Primitive and Oriental
thought is full of presentiments of this kind: on the crudest level, in
the sentiment of magic and its force; more subtly, in the recognition of the force of dream and vision in the shaping of a life;
and, most majestically, in such intuitions of a support not alone of
the individual life, but of all things together, as in the following
from the Mundaka Upanishad:

> That on which heaven, earth, and the space between are woven;
> The mind, also, with the breath of life:
> That alone know as the one spirit. All other
> Talk dismiss. That is the bridge to immortality.[45]

And in the Occident too we find such thoughts; as, for instance, in
the romantic poet William Wordsworth's celebrated "Lines Composed a Few Miles above Tintern Abbey, on Revisiting the Banks
of the Wye During a Tour. July 13, 1798":

> For I have learned
> To look on nature, not as in the hour
> Of thoughtless youth; but hearing oftentimes
> The still, sad music of humanity,
> Nor harsh nor grating, though of ample power
> To chasten and subdue. And I have felt
> A presence that disturbs me with the joy
> Of elevated thoughts; a sense sublime
> Of something far more deeply interfused,
> Whose dwelling is the light of setting suns,

* Supra, p. 89.

And the round ocean and the living air,
And the blue sky, and in the mind of man:
A motion and a spirit, that impels
All thinking things, all objects of all thought,
And rolls through all things.[46]

The sense experienced by lovers, already at the first meeting of the eyes, of having discovered in the world without the perfect complement of their own truth, and so of a marvelous coincidence thereby of destiny and chance, inner and external worlds, may, in the course of a lifetime flowering from such love, conduce to the poetic conviction of an accord universal of the seen and the unseen.

But of course, on the other hand, to those upon whom neither love, nature, nor symbol has ever bestowed any conic mirror, such romanticism is moonshine. Furthermore, as Schopenhauer states in his ruminating paper: "The view of an ordering Fate can always be countered by comparing the orderly design that we may imagine ourselves to have recognized in the scattered facts of our lives to the mere unconscious work of our own organizing and schematizing fantasy when we look at a spotted wall and see there, clearly and distinctly, human figures and groups—ourselves introducing the orderly connections into a field of spots scattered by blind chance." [47]

The modern reader will think of the Rorschach Test, with its ink-blots in which different people see different forms, symptomatic of the psychology of their own fantasizing minds. And the world itself, it is said by some, is such an ink-blot, into which people read their own minds: the ordered universe, the great course of history and evolution, the norms of human life. There is a passage to this effect in *Ulysses,* in the scene where Stephen, in the library, is arguing a point with John Eglinton. "We walk," Stephen states, "through ourselves, meeting robbers, ghosts, giants, old men, young men, wives, widows, brothers-in-love. But always meeting ourselves."

Stephen Dedalus, in this conversation, has just quoted a line from Maeterlinck: " '*If Socrates leave his house today he will find the sage seated on his doorstep. If Judas go forth tonight it is to Judas his steps will tend.' "* And he has applied the lesson of this solipsism to an interpretation of Shakespeare's art, suggesting in

turn that such creativity by projection is analogous to God's creation of the world: "He found in the world without as actual what
was in his world within as possible." [48] In the micro-macrocosmic
dream-novel *Finnegans Wake,* Joyce drops the plane of vision
from the level of individuated consciousness to the unconscious
—of the race: an interior "Land below Waves," such as in one
transformation or another, according to local influence, is common
to mankind. However, in *Ulysses,* up to the moment, at least, of the
great spell-dispelling thunderclap that occurs just halfway through
the book [49] (after which the two apparently distinct universes of
Leopold Bloom and Stephen Dedalus gradually open to each other
and display their common strains), the plane and point of view is
strictly that of our common twentieth-century day-world of separate, self-preserving, self-assertive individuals; each the fragment
of a general anamorphosis, to which none has found the conic mirror.

For, in fact, do we not have among us in abundance today a
species even of philosophers who (maintaining in their own way
the biblical notion of nature as corrupt) cannot discover in the nature either of man or of the universe any sign of inherent order?—
to say nothing of a congruence of the two worlds, inside and out!
Consider, for instance, Jean-Paul Sartre's complaint that he "finds
it extremely embarrassing that God does not exist; for there disappears with Him all possibility of finding values in an intelligible
heaven. . . . Everything is indeed permitted if God does not
exist, and man is in consequence forlorn; for he cannot find anything to depend upon either within or outside himself. . . . We
are left alone, without excuse. That is what I mean when I say that
man is condemned to be free." [50]

But on the other hand, at the opposite pole, there are those who
believe that they know, can act upon, and can even teach—absolutely—the order in the mind of God for all mankind. They have
learned it from the Bible or Koran or, more passionately, through
some hysterical "leap of faith" and pentecostal "decision" of their
own. So, for example, in the journal of Søren Kierkegaard
(1813–1855), just a century before Sartre:

> The most tremendous thing that has been granted to man is:
> the choice, freedom. And if you desire to save it and preserve it
> there is only one way: in the very same second unconditionally

and in complete resignation to give it back to God, and yourself with it. . . . You have freedom of choice, you say, and still you have not chosen God. Then you will grow ill, freedom of choice will become your *idée fixe,* till at last you will be like the rich man who imagines that he is poor, and will die of want: you sigh that you have lost your freedom of choice—and your fault is only that you do not grieve deeply enough or you would find it again. . . .

There is a God; his will is made known to me in Holy Scripture and in my conscience. This God wishes to intervene in the world. But how is he to do so except with the help of, *i.e. per,* man? [51]

Between these two contending camps of uncompromising guessers, with their leaps and acts of faith in one direction or the other, there are those of a less dogmatic cast who are willing—like Schopenhauer and Wordsworth—to concede that, though one may indeed, in the contemplation of nature and one's life, be filled, like Wordsworth, with "a sense sublime of something far more deeply interfused," it is well and proper to remember that "everything in such thoughts is questionable," and, as Schopenhauer states further: "decisive answers, consequently, are [in such matters] the last things to be expressed."

Is a complete misadjustment possible [he asks], between the character and the fate of an individual? Or is every destiny on the whole appropriate to the character that bears it? Or, finally, is there some inexplicable, secret determinator, comparable to the author of a drama, that always joins the two appropriately, one to the other?

But this [he then goes on to reply] is exactly the point at which we are in the dark. And in the meantime we go on imagining ourselves to be, at every moment, the masters of our own deeds. It is only when we look back over the completed portions of our lives and review the unluckier steps together with their consequences that we marvel at how we could have done this, or have failed to do that; and it then may seem to us that an alien power must have guided our steps. As Shakespeare says:

> Fate, show thy force; ourselves we do not owe;
> What is decreed must be, and be this so! [52]

Or as Goethe says in *Götz von Berlichingen* (Act V): "We men do not guide ourselves; wicked spirits are given power over us,

to work their naughtiness to our destruction." And again, in
Egmont (Act V, last scene): "Man imagines himself to be conducting his own life; and irresistibly his inmost being is drawn to
its fate."—Yes, and it was said already by the prophet Jere-
miah: "A man's deeds do not rest in his power; it rests in no
man's power, how he moves or directs his way" (10:23). Compare Herodotus I. 91 ["It is impossible even for a god to escape
the decree of destiny"] and IX. 16 ["It is not possible for man
to avert what God has decreed shall occur"]; see also Lucian's
Dialogues of the Dead XIX and XXX.

Indeed, the ancients never tire of insisting, in verse and in
prose, on the power of fate and the comparative impotence of
man. One can see everywhere that this was their overpowering
conviction, and that they suspected a more secret, deep continuity in things than is evident on the clearly empirical surface.
Hence the great variety of terms, in Greek, for this idea:
πότμος ["that which befalls one"], ἀισα ["the divine dispensation
of one's lot"], εἱμαρμένη ["what is allotted"], πεπρωμένη ["what is
foredoomed"], μοῖρα ["one's portion"], Ἀδράστεια [a name of the
goddess Nemesis, goddess of divine retribution], and perhaps,
also, many more. The word πρόνοια ["foresight, foreknowledge"],
on the other hand, displaces our understanding of the matter:
for it is derived from νοῦς ["mind, a thought, an act of mind"],
which is the secondary factor, and though it makes everything
clear and comprehensible, is superficial and false.—And this
whole enigmatic circumstance is a consequence of the fact that
our deeds are inevitably the product of two factors: one, our
intelligible character, which stands unchangeably established,
yet becomes known to us only gradually, *a posteriori;* * and
two, our motivations, which come to us from without, are supplied inevitably from the tides of world event, and with almost
machinelike determinacy work upon our given character in terms
of the limits and possibilities of its permanent constitution.—
But then, finally, our ego judges the resultant event. In its role
as the mere subject of knowledge, however, it is distinct from
both character and motivation and so is no more than the critical
observer of their effects. No wonder if it sometimes marvels!

However, once one has grasped the idea of a transcendent
fatality and has learned to contemplate the individual life from
this point of view, one can have the sense, at times, of attending
the most marvelous of all theatrical productions—in the con-

* Supra, p. 35.

trast between the obvious, physical, accidental aspect of a situation and its moral-metaphysical necessity: the latter, however, never demonstrable and perhaps even, only imagined.[53]

IV. The Music of the Land below Waves

In the context of the Tristan legend, the symbolic forms and motifs through which the intimation is communicated of a moving destiny and alien power (which, paradoxically, is a function of the character of the motivated individual) were derived—as we have seen —from the pagan Celtic lore of Ireland, Cornwall, and Wales. Inherent in them, consequently, was the old, generally pagan message of the immanent divinity of all things, and of the manifestation of this hidden Being of beings particularly in certain heroic individuals, who thus stand as epiphanies of that "manifest-hidden" which moves and lives within us all and is the secret of the harmony of nature. Such a figure was the Christ of the Gnostics. Such a figure was Orpheus with his lyre (Figure 1). The Celtic myths and legends are full of tales of the singers and harpers of the fairy hills whose music has the power to enchant and to move the world: to make men weep, to make men sleep, and to make men laugh. They appear mysteriously from the Land of Eternal Youth, the Land within the Fairy Hills, the Land below Waves; and though taken to be human beings—odd and exceptional, indeed, yet as self-contained, after all, as you or I (or, at least, as we suppose ourselves to be)—they are not actually so, but open out behind, so to say, toward the universe.

The Irish mythological trickster Manannan Mac Lir was a figure of this kind. Actually a sea-god—after whom the Isle of Man is named—it was he, we are told, who through his magic concealed from human eyes those fairy hills, the Síd (pronounced "shee"), within which the Celtic gods of old, the Tuatha Dé Danann, are feasting to this day on the inexhaustible flesh of his divine swine, washed down with his ale of immortality. Like the classical water-god Proteus, Manannan was an adroit shape-shifter; and he is recorded to have appeared in various deluding forms even as late as the sixteenth century, as, for instance, at a famous feast in Ballyshannon, where the host was the historical Black Hugh O'Donnell (d. 1537).

From nowhere, as it were, the wild old sea-god appeared at that feast in the semblance of a kern, or churl, wearing narrow stripes: "the puddle-water plashing in his brogues and a moiety of his sword's length naked sticking out behind his stern, while in his right hand he bore three limber javelins of hollywood with fire-hardened tips." The javelins three suggest the trident of Poseidon and the puddle-water in his brogues is another significant sign. Having challenged each of the four cunning harpers at the feast (who played, each and all, we are told, such harmonious, delectable, smooth-flowing airs that with the fairy spell of their minstrelsy men might well have been lulled to sleep), this kern cried out that, by Heaven's graces three, such dissonance he had never heard this side the smoke-wrapped ground-tier of Hell, where the Devil's artists, and Albiron's, with their sledgehammers ding the iron. "And with that," our document continues, "taking up an instrument, he made symphony so gently sweet, and in such wise wakened the dulcet pulses of the harp, that in the whole world all women laboring of child, all wounded warriors, mangled soldiers, and gallant men gashed about—with all in general that suffered sore sickness and distemper—might with the witching charm of this his modulation have been lapped in stupor of slumber and of soundest sleep. 'By Heaven's grace,' exclaimed O'Donnell, 'since first I heard the fame of them that within the hills and under the earth beneath us make the fairy music, that at one and the same time make some to sleep, and some to weep, and others again to laugh, music sweeter than thy strains I never have heard: thou art in sooth a most melodious rogue!' 'One day I'm sweet another I'm bitter,' replied the kern." And thereafter, presently, once again taking the instrument, he made melody of such kind and so befuddled the company, that all in fury arose in wrath and began to do battle with each other—when he disappeared.[54]

Figure 25 is another of the series of tiles from Chertsey Abbey, of a date about 1270. It is of the young Tristan teaching the maid Isolt to harp on the occasion of his first visit to Ireland: with the same harp and same music by which he had spellbound his uncle (Figure 2).

"Tristan, listen!" King Mark had said. "You have all the talents I yearn for. You do everything I wish I could do: hunt, speak languages, harp. Let us be companions: you, mine; I, yours. We shall ride hunting by day and by night enjoy courtly

Figure 25. Isolt Taught by Tristan to Harp

diversions—harping, singing, fiddling—here at home. You do all these things so well! Do them now for me. And for you I shall play the tune *I* know, for which perhaps your heart already yearns: magnificent clothes and horses. All that you want I shall give you, and with these serenade you well. See, my comrade, to you I confide my sword, my spurs, my crossbow and my golden drinking horn." [55]

Born of a widow, beyond the sea, who expired on giving him birth, Tristan had come, as it were, from nowhere. Tossed ashore from the storming waters, he had been born as from the womb of nature itself: the boy brought ashore by the dolphin, the pig of the sea. Miraculously, as it were, he had appeared with the power and glory of a god, yet in the character of a boy. Furthermore, the vessel in which he had been abducted from his birthplace beyond the waters (the yonder shore) had been a merchantman (*ein kaufschif*). Hermes, the guide of souls to rebirth, was the lord and patron of merchants—also of thievery and cunning.

The tale is to be recalled at this point of Hermes' fashioning of the lyre when but an infant a couple of hours old. Conceived of Zeus, he had been born of a night-sky nymph named Maia (meaning "old mother, grandmother, foster-mother, old nurse, or midwife"; but also a certain large kind of crab). In a cave he had been born, at dawn; and toddling forth from his cradle before noon, he had chanced—or had seemed to chance—at the entrance of the cave upon a tortoise (an early animal symbol of the universe), which he broke up and fashioned into a lyre, to which at noon he beautifully sang. That evening he stole Apollo's cattle, and to appease the god gave him the lyre, which Apollo passed to his own son Orpheus (Figures 1 and 9). And, as the whole world knows, the sound of that lyre in Orpheus's hands stilled the animals of the wilderness, moved trees and rocks, and even charmed the lord of the netherworld when the lover descended alive to the abyss to recover Eurydice, his lost bride.

Now, as already remarked in relation to the old Celtic god of the boar of Figures 18, 20, and 21, the ultimate roots of the tree of Celtic folklore and mythology rest deep in that megalithic culture stratum of Western Europe that was contemporary and in trade contact with the pre-Hellenic seafaring civilizations of Crete and Mycenae of which Poseidon was a mighty god, and from which the basically non-Homeric, Dionysian-Orphic strains of classical myth and ritual derived.[56] There is therefore an actual, archaeologically documented, family relationship to be recognized between the mythic harpists of the Celtic otherworld and those of the Orphic and Gnostic mysteries. Furthermore, as remarked in *Primitive Mythology*,[57] there is evidence as well of a generic kinship of the classical mystery cults not only with the grandiose Egyptian mythic complex of that dying god Osiris and the Mesopotamian of Tammuz, but also with those widely distributed primitive myths and rites of the sacrificed youth or maiden (or, more vividly, the young couple ritually killed embracing in a sacramental love-death),[58] whose flesh, consumed in cannibal communion, typifies the mystery of that Being beyond duality that lives partitioned in us all. The same idea is expressed mythologically in the Indian account, quoted in *Oriental Mythology*, of the first being, the Self, which, in the beginning, swelled, split into male and female, and so, begetting on itself all the creatures of this world, became this world.[59]

The Indian god who is equivalent to Poseidon, and so to the Irish sea-god Manannan, is Shiva, who, as already seen, bears in his right hand the trident and in the Christian version of the netherworld is the Devil. He is known as the "Lord of Beasts" (*paśupati*),[60] also as the "Player of the Lyre" (*viṇa-dhara*); is, moreover, a phallic god and, as lord of the lingam-yoni symbol, often shown united in one body with his goddess, she the left side, he the right. Gottfried's metaphor of Tristan-Isolt as the two whose being is one is thus in India a familiar icon of the mystery of non-duality. Hermes, too, is both lord of the phallus and male and female at once. The word "hermaphrodite" (Hermes-Aphrodite) points to this secret of his nature. And with the goddess Aphrodite, of course, the inevitable associate is her child, the winged huntsman with his very dangerous bow: Roman Cupid, Greek Eros—the boy on the dolphin. Aphrodite too was born of the sea. And she is the consort, furthermore, of the ever-dying, ever-reborn god gored by the boar, whose celestial sign is the waning and waxing moon: the lord of the magic of night. So that Tristan, master of the arts of the hunt, as well as of music and all tongues, carried with him to Cornwall the powers of these gods.

To Mark he was to be as the young year to the old, or as David to Saul (Figure 2). He was the young god destined to supplant the old in possession of the queen, who in the ritual lore of the old Bronze Age tradition was symbolic of the land, the realm, the universe itself, and in the language of the later Hellenistic mystery cults became the guide and symbol of the interior kingdom of the soul: that realm of the spirit which can be found and fertilized only through death, humiliation, and a submission of the solar principle of rational self-reliant consciousness to the song, the sleep-song, of the interior abyss where the two—the male and female—become one (Figure 3, at Station 11). We may think also of those bull-bodied harps that were found in the royal tombs of Ur, the music they sang of the harmony of the universe, and the love-death there celebrated of the goddess and god of the deep: Inanna and Dumuzi-absu, Ishtar and Tammuz.[61]

There is the fragment of an episode from a lost, early version of the Tristan legend preserved in a Welsh triad, which opens a fresh prospect into the mythological background of Tristan in relation to Isolt, as follows:

> Trystan son of Tallwch, disguised as a swineherd,
> Tended the pigs of Marc son of Meirchyon
> While the [true] swineherd went with a message to Esyllt.[62]

One discovers here, first, that the father of the hero is named not Rivalin but Tallwch. Tracing the history of the legend back through its Breton, Cornish, Welsh, and Irish phases, the leading Celtic scholar of the last century, Dr. H. Zimmer,* discovered that in the Pictish marshlands of southern Scotland, from the sixth to ninth centuries A.D., there had actually been a reigning series of kings named Drustan alternating with a series named Talorc, of which the member reigning from 780 to 785 was the Drustan son of Talorc of the earliest—and now forever lost—version of our legend.[63] Drustan son of Talorc became, in Wales, Trystan son of Tallwch, and the name Rivalin was substituted only when the romance reached Brittany after c. 1000, where it received its final form.

The episode of the lover, masquerading as Mark's swineherd, sending his message by the real swineherd to Mark's queen, which is otherwise unknown to the Tristan cycle, suggests very strongly the legend, registered in *Primitive Mythology,* of the abduction of Persephone to the netherworld by Hades, where it is told that a herd of swine went down too, when the earth opened to receive her.[64] Significantly, the name of the swineherd of that lost herd was Ebouleus, "Giver of Good Counsel," an appellation of Hades himself; and, as Frazer in *The Golden Bough* points out, Persephone, in her animal aspect, was a pig.[65] Or again: in the *Odyssey* there is that episode of the magic isle of Circe, who, when she re-

---

* As noted in *Occidental Mythology,* p. 38, H. Zimmer (1851–1910) is not to be confused with his son of the same name, the distinguished Sanskritist, Heinrich Zimmer (1890–1943), whom I have cited in *Oriental Mythology.* To prevent confusion, I designate the elder as H. Zimmer and the younger as Heinrich Zimmer.

turned Odysseus's men to their former shapes (and they were younger and fairer than before), took Odysseus to her bed, after which she led him to the netherworld, where he met and talked with—among others of the living dead—the male-female sage Tiresias (once again Figure 3, Station 11). In the general body of Celtic folklore the classical legend of the pig-goddess-guide to the mysteries beyond the plane of death is matched by the Irish folktale, retold in *Primitive Mythology* and noted a few pages back, of the Daughter of the King of the Land of Youth whose head was the head of a pig. When she appeared on earth and attached herself to Finn McCool's son Ossian, he kissed the pig's head away and became the King of the Land of Youth.[66]

Gottfried's vision of Tristan as a wild boar ravaging King Mark's bed, the Welsh triad of his role as Mark's pretended swineherd, and the legend of the scar on his thigh all point in the same direction: to his derivation ultimately from the Celtic-megalithic god of the boar with the eyes of the Great Mother engraved along either side (Figure 18), who, as lord of the wilderness, the underworld, and the vital force of nature, was also king of the Land below Waves and the music-master of its spell.

But, on the other hand, King Mark appears to have been associated with a totally different mythic context, as contrary as the day to night, or as the world of fine clothes and horses to that of harping, fiddling, singing, and the lore of love and the moon. For whereas Tristan, as we have just seen, was originally a Pictish, pre-Celtic king of a Bronze Age matrilineal folk—possibly with memories of ritual regicide not distant in its past—and whereas Queen Isolt, as a legendary daughter of pre-Celtic Ireland, of the breed somewhat of Queen Meave,[67] was likewise of a matriarchal line; King Mark—known also, in Wales, as Eochaid—seems to have been a Celtic king of Cornwall of about the period of Drustan/Tristan (c. 780–785 A.D.), whose legend, on entering Wales some time before the year 1000, became combined with that of the other two—in a relation generally comparable to that of the Celtic warrior-prince Ailill to Queen Meave.

His name, Marc, is understood usually as an abridgment of the Latin Marcus, from the name of the war-god Mars. It may also bear some relation, however, to the Middle High German *marc,* meaning "war-horse," Welsh *march,* old Irish *morc* or *margg,* "stallion or steed"; and this alternative is supported by his other Celtic name, *Eochaid*, which is related to the old Irish *ech*, Latin *equus*, meaning "horse." Moreover, in one old French version of the romance (by the continental Norman poet Béroul, c. 1195–1205 A.D.) we find the following startling statement:

Marc a orelles de cheval,

"Mark has horses' ears." [68] And with this we are suddenly dropped into an extremely suggestive vortex of both mythological and high historical associations.

v. Moon Bull and Sun Steed

We think first of the classical legend of King Midas, who had ass's ears and whose touch turned everything, including his daughter, into gold, the metal of the sun; recall, too, that the leaders of the Anglo-Saxon invasion of Britain (c. 450 A.D.) were Hengest and Horsa, both of which names are from Germanic nouns meaning "horse." Figure 26 is a bronze solar disk ornamented with a gold

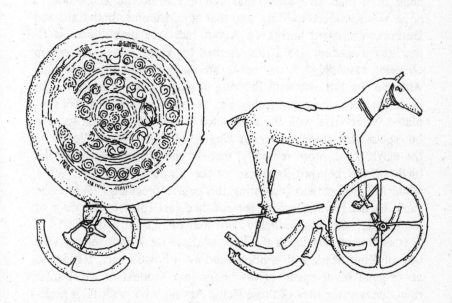

Figure 26. Bronze Solar Horse and Car; Denmark, c. 1000 B.C.

Figure 27. Sun Steed and Eagle; France, Gallo-Roman Period

design of spirals, set on wheels of bronze, and with a bronze steed before it, found at Trundholm, Nordseeland, Denmark (whence Hengest and Horsa came), and usually dated c. 1000 B.C.; while in Figure 27 are a couple of late Gaulish coins showing horses, each with an eagle (sun-bird) on its back, and in one the horse has the head of a man. We know that annually in Rome in October a horse was sacrificed to Mars, and that at midsummer both Celts and Germans sacrificed horses. In Aryan India the high "horse sacrifice" (*aśva-medha*) was a rite reserved for kings, where, as seen in *Oriental Mythology*,[69] the noble animal was identified not only with the sun but also with the king in whose name the rite was to be celebrated; whose queen then had to enact in a pit a ritual of simulated intercourse with the immolated horse: all of which gave to her spouse the status of a solar king whose light should illuminate the earth. And, more remotely, there is the kindred legend of the birth of the beloved Japanese prince Shotoku (573–621 A.D.) while his mother was inspecting the palace precincts. "When she came to the Horse Department and had just come to the door of the stables, she was suddenly delivered of him without effort." [70]

It is almost certain, in the light of these facts, that the association of King Mark with a horse, and even horse's ears, testifies to an original involvement of his image in a context of royal solar rites, the warrior rites of those Celtic Aryans who, with their male-oriented patriarchal order, overran in the course of the first millennium B.C. the old Bronze Age world of the Mother Goddess and

mother-right. The composition of the coin of Figure 27 in which a
human-headed horse leaps over a bull as the sun leaps over the
earth suggests the relationship of the two orders of the conquerors
and conquered in that early Celtic heroic age; and when these figures are compared with those of Pablo Picasso's "Guernica" (Figure 28), where a horse and its rider lie shattered and a bull stands
mighty and whole, the beginning and end are seen illustrated, in a
remarkably consistent way, of the long majestic day in Europe of
the conquering cavalier and his mount.

Oswald Spengler, in his final published work, *Years of the Decision* (published 1933), delineated in two bold paragraphs the
whole reach of this great day, of which we are now in the twilight
hour:

In the course of world history, there have been two great revolutions in the manner of waging war produced by sudden increases in mobility. The first occurred in the early centuries of
the first millennium B.C., when, somewhere on the broad plains
between the Danube and Amur rivers, the riding horse appeared. Mounted hosts were vastly superior to men afoot.* The
riders could appear and disappear before a defense or pursuit
could be assembled. It was in vain that populations, from the
Atlantic to the Pacific, supplemented their foot forces with
mounted contingents of their own: the latter were hindered in
maneuvers by the footmen. Nor were the Chinese and Roman
empires saved by the building of walls and moats: such a wall
as can be seen to this day cutting half across Asia; or such as
the Roman *limes* recently discovered in the Syro-Arabian desert.
It was impossible to send an assembled army out from behind
such barriers quickly enough to break up a surprise attack. The
settled agrarian, peasant populations of the Chinese, Indian,
Roman, Arabian, and West European spheres were, time and
again, overwhelmed, in helpless terror, by swarms of Parthians,

* "And to war-chariots as well, which could be employed only in battle
and were of no use on the march. Chariots first appeared about a thousand
years earlier than the mounted horse, in the same area, and, wherever employed, were invincible on contemporary battlefields: in China and India,
shortly after 1500 B.C.; in the Near East somewhat earlier, and in the Hellenic sphere shortly after 1600. Soon they were in service everywhere, but
disappeared when mounted troops came into general use—even when the
latter were employed only as special auxiliaries to forces afoot." (Spengler's
note.)

Figure 28. Adapted from Pablo Picasso: *Guernica:* 1937

Huns, Scythians, Mongols, and Turks. Cavalry and peasantry, it is apparent, are in spirit irreconcilable. It was in this way, to their superior speed, that the hosts of Jenghis Khan owed their victories.

The second decisive transformation, we are witnessing at this very hour in the displacement of the horse by the "horse power" of our Faustian technology. As late as through the [First] World War there hung about the famous old West European cavalry regiments an atmosphere of knightly pride, daring adventure and heroism, which greatly surpassed that of any other military arm. These had been, for centuries, true Vikings of the land. They came to represent more and more—much more than the infantries of the general armies—the true sense of vocation of the dedicated soldier's life and military career. In the future all this will change. Indeed, the airplane and tank corps have already taken their place, and mobility has been carried with these beyond the limits of organic possibility to the inorganic range of the machine: of (so to say) *personal* machines, however, which, in contrast to the impersonality of the machine-gun fire of the trenches of the [First] World War, now will again challenge the spirit of personal heroism to great tasks.[71]

In Picasso's "Guernica," the glaring electric bulb is the only sign of the new order of power and life by which the old is being destroyed: the old, of the barnyard bull and the warhorse, peasantry and cavalry. The shattered steed, the once conquering vehicle of the day of history now ending, appears to have been pierced by the lance of its own rider, as well as gored by the bull. The lance wound is a reference, obviously, to civil war: the Spanish Civil War of 1936–1939, during the course of which, in April 1937, the Basque town of Guernica was bombed. But the Basque race and language are pre-Aryan. They represent, thus, like Drustan's Picts, a period of history antecedent to the day and people of the horse. They typify and represent even to this present hour the patient spirit of those long, toiling millenniums of the entry into Europe and establishment there of its basic peasant population: when the myths and rites of the sacrificial bull—symbolic of the everdying, self-resurrecting lord of the tides of life, whose celestial sign is the moon—were the life-supporting forms of faith and prayer. In the bull ring, from which Picasso took his imagery, the old worn-out picador-horse is gored by the bull, but the bull itself is then slain by a solar weapon—the sword of the matador, who is clothed in a garment called "the garment of light." In Picasso's work there is no such avenger: the enigmatic bull still stands. The day of the cavalier is ended; and tracing back now through the centuries, to identify the symbolic moments of its beginning, culmination, climacteric, and dissolution, we may number the stages of this culture period as follows:

1. The long, general period represented by the coins of Figure 27, of the pagan Aryan beginnings of what today is Occidental civilization: the centuries, first, of the Celtic (Hallstatt and La Tène) expansions, raids, and invasions, c. 900–15 B.C., and then, of the rise and world empire of pagan Rome, c. 400 B.C.—400 A.D.[72]

2. The very dark, at first, but then brightening years of the Christian Middle Ages: first of the forceful conversion and immediate collapse of the Roman Empire in Europe (Theodosius the Great, 379–395 A.D.); next of the saints of Christian Ireland, maintaining a dim yet steady light while on the Continent the ravages of the pagan Germanic wars and plunderings were augmented by the works of riding Asiatic Huns and African Moors (the dark ordeals of this stage endured from the sixth to the ninth centuries);[73] the beginnings of improvement, then, among the Franks, Lombards, and Saxons, emanating largely from the palace school (but also the weaponry) of Charlemagne (Holy Roman Emperor, 800–814 A.D.); and then—at last!—with the fall of Moorish Toledo in the year 1085 and the preaching ten years later of the First Crusade, the sudden flowering of the golden age of European courtesy and *amor,* theology, cathedrals, and knighthood on adventure: that age *par excellence* of chivalry and the mounted steed, of which the paragons for all time must be the knights and ladies fair of King Mark's and Arthur's courts.

But now, passing the noon of that day of the mounted steed, and moving onward toward a later time when gunpowder and cannons will have given the advantage to men afoot, we ask:

3. who that strange silhouette against the setting sun might be, riding tall and lean, picador-like, on a tall, lean, knobby-kneed horse, with a short, round second figure trotting now beside, now after, on a donkey. Why none other, indeed, than Don Quixote, in his patched armor, on Rozinante, his "Horse of Yore": the Knight of the Rueful Countenance, about 1605 A.D., riding to adventure

on the dusty plane of La Mancha with his portly squire Sancho
Panza, "poor in purse and poor in brains," loyally behind! As Ortega y Gasset has remarked in his *Meditations on Quixote:* "Don
Quixote, in a certain way, is the sad parody of a more divine and
serene Christ: he is a Gothic Christ, torn by the modern anguish; a
ridiculous Christ of our own neighborhood, created by a sorrowful
imagination, which has lost its innocence and its will and is striving to replace them. . . ."[74]

"Don Quixote stands at the intersection where two worlds meet,
forming a beveled edge," he writes again: the two worlds, on the
one hand, of poetic aspiration and spiritual adventure, and, on the
other, empirical reality, "the anti-poetic *per se.*" [75]

"Cervantes looks at the world," Ortega states, "from the height
of the Renaissance. The Renaissance has tightened things. . . .
With his physics Galileo lays down the stern laws that govern the
universe. A new system has begun; everything is confined within
stricter forms. Adventures are impossible in this new order of
things. . . ."[76]

"Another characteristic of the Renaissance," Ortega then adds,
however,

is the predominance acquired by the psychological. . . . The
Renaissance discovers the inner world in all its vast extension,
the *me ipsum,* the consciousness, the subjective. The novel *Don
Quixote* is the flower of this great new turn that culture takes. In
it the epic comes to an end forever, along with its aspiration to
support a mythical world bordering on that of material phenomena but different from it. . . . The reality of the adventure is
reduced to the psychological, perhaps even to a biological humor. It is real insofar as it is a vapor from a brain, so that its
reality is that of its opposite, the material. . . .

Regarded for itself, in a direct way, reality, the actual, would
never be poetic: that is the privilege of the mythical. But we can
consider it obliquely, as destructive of the myth, as criticism of
the myth. In this manner reality, which is of an inert and meaningless nature, quiet and mute, acquires movement, is changed
into an active power of aggression against the crystal orb of the
ideal. The enchantment of the latter broken, it falls into fine,
iridescent dust, which loses gradually its colors until it becomes
an earthy brown.[77]

And with this we are brought to our terminal stage, namely:
4. The present, of Picasso's shattered horse and the broken,
hollow rider: T. S. Eliot's *The Waste Land* and "The Hollow
Men." For by the middle of the nineteenth century, three centuries
after Galileo, Quixote, and Shakespeare's Hamlet ("To be, or not
to be . . ."), not only had the motions of life become reduced to
mechanistic formulas, but even those of the mind and will were on
the point of being so interpreted. In Ortega's words, once again:

> The natural sciences based on determinism conquered the field
> of biology during the first decades of the nineteenth century.
> Darwin believed he had succeeded in imprisoning life—our last
> hope—within physical necessity. Life is reduced to mere matter,
> physiology to mechanics. The human organism, which seemed
> an independent unit, capable of acting by itself, is placed in its
> physical environment like a figure in a tapestry. It is no longer
> the organism that moves but the environment that is moving
> through it. Our actions are no more than reactions. There is no
> freedom, no originality. To live is to adapt oneself; to adapt
> oneself is to allow the material environment to penetrate into us,
> to drive us out of ourselves. Adaptation is submission and re-
> nunciation. Darwin sweeps heroes off the face of the earth.[78]

And so it is that, in this dismal scene of mechanized cities of
"adjusted" automatons, the age arrives, as Ortega states, of the
roman expérimental of Zola and the rest.

> The subject matter is still man, but since man is no longer the
> agent of his acts but is moved by the environment in which he
> lives, the novel will look to the representation of the environ-
> ment. The environment is the only protagonist. People speak of
> evoking the "atmosphere." Art submits to one rule: verisimil-
> itude . . . : the beautiful is what is probable and the true lies
> only in physics. The aim of the novel is physiology.[79]

With the conditioned-reflex experiments on dogs of the Russian
physiologist Ivan Petrovich Pavlov (1848–1936) [80] and the application of his methods to the study and control of human thinking and behavior,[81] psychology itself became a department of
mechanics. The last dark cavern of retreat of Schopenhauer's "intelligible character" of the individual was about to become wholly
illuminated by a laboratory lamp, and the old Germanic sense of

destiny as *wyrd,* an irreversible process of becoming from within,* reduced to an electrician's diagram of afferent and efferent nerves; so that what romantics still were attributing to some vague force, felt to be divine, within, was actually to be analyzed as a property of matter, no less and no more mysterious or divine than what goes on within the carburetor and cylinders of one's car. In the words of an American master of this ultimate field of nineteenth-century science:

> There are common factors running through all forms of human acts. In each adjustment there is always both a *response or act* and a *stimulus or situation* which calls out that response. Without going too far beyond our facts, it seems possible to say that the stimulus is always provided by the environment, external to the body, or by the movements of man's own muscles and the secretions of his glands; finally, that the responses always follow relatively immediately upon the presentation of the stimulus. These are really assumptions, but they seem to be basal ones for psychology. . . . If we provisionally accept them we may say that the goal of psychological study is *the ascertaining of such data and laws that, given the stimulus, psychology can predict what the response will be; or, on the other hand, given the response, it can specify the nature of the effective stimulus."* [82]

Little wonder, then, if in Picasso's apocalyptic "Guernica" the fallen broken hero is revealed as a hollow statue and his pierced Rozinante a strange thing of papier-mâché. The dead child of the pietà at the left is a doll, and the entire canvas, for all its great size (11 feet, 6 inches, by 28 feet, 8 inches), suggests a puppet stage: the only centers of possible life being the heads and mouths, with their flashing tongues, of the bull, the mother, and the screaming horse, plus the tails of the two beasts, the mother's hair, and the modest flower at the fallen hero's right hand. The other mouths are without tongue. Even the flames are unreal of the ecstatic (falling or rising?) woman at the right. The figures are two-dimensional cut-outs, without depth, as we all are now supposed to be in this self-moving machine world: mere masks of nothing beyond.

This seems to many to be an exclusively modern way of conceiving of the universe and mankind. However, in the long per-

* Supra, pp. 121–22 and 138–40; also, p. 194.

spective that has been opened to our view by the scholarship of comparative world mythology, it must be recognized that it actually was anticipated, together with its moral implications, in the absolutely impersonal, mathematical space-time cosmology and associated social order of those priestly watchers of the skies of the old Sumerian temple cities (fourth millennium B.C.), from whose heaven-oriented gaze and related cerebrations the world has received all the basic elements of archaic high civilization: calendric astronomy, mathematics, writing, and monumental symbolic architecture; the idea of a moral order of the universe, made known by way of the features of the night sky, with the waning and waxing moon its focal sign (the rhythmically dying and reappearing lunar bull, whose light is for three nights dark), and, subordinate to this, the moral order and symbolic rites of the hieratic priestly state, with its symbolic king and court enacting, as well as enforcing, here on earth the order of death in life and life in death made known aloft. We have discussed all this at length in the earlier volumes of this series: in *Primitive Mythology,* pages 144–69 and 404–60; in *Oriental Mythology,* throughout; and in *Occidental Mythology,* pages 9–92. There can now be nothing new to us about it, or surprising.

However, what I do find surprising, and cannot help pausing a moment to remark, is the fact that in the tortured figures of Picasso's masterpiece (and he surely knew what he was doing—as will appear on a later page) what we are contemplating is a constellation of perfectly traditional mythological symbols, arranged in such a way as to bear to us in their silent speech (whether intended or not by the artist) a message still in perfect concord with the spirit and lore of the old Sumerian lunar bull: "That One," as we read in the Indian Shatapatha Brahmana, "who is the Death on whom our life depends. . . . He is one as he is there, but many as he is in his children here." [83]

In *Occidental Mythology* there is an illustration (Figure 16, page 55) in which the old Sumerian bearded moon bull is shown with the sun bird perched on his back biting into his flank. The bull is unconcerned, as here in Picasso's piece. Moreover, the flames emanating from the knee joints of the earlier symbolic beast have their counterpart in the flamelike spike pointing backward from the right foreknee of the "Guernica" bull. And further, since the mountain peak above which the old Sumerian lunar bull stands represents the mountain body of the Mother Goddess Earth, whose child is that ever-dying, self-resurrecting god that is in substance one with his father (and so, is "the bull," as they say, "of his own mother"),[84] symbolically, in traditional terms of which Picasso surely was aware, the bull and pietà of his "Guernica" correspond precisely to the moon bull and world-mountain of the old Sumerian icon. The dead child is the living god in the oxymoron of his death: the Christ of the sacrifice, who in the Gnostic view (as we have seen) is the living substance of us all. And the scene, then, of the gored horse in the central, triangular field—illuminated by the hand-held lamp, which intervenes below the higher light—is the scene of this dear death that is our bitter life, where, as we read in the Bhagavad Gītā: "Even as a person casts off worn-out clothes and puts on others that are new, what is embodied casts off worn-out bodies and enters into others that are new." [85]

The hollow hero of Picasso's vision and the torn body of his paper horse contrast calamitously with the young, naïve, life-willing and -daring hero-symbols of the early European pagan coins. The bird of prey, the sun bird riding on the back of the prancing steed, has become, in the late work, a broken, screaming pigeon. The most obvious thing to say is that the initiative in shaping history and the destiny of man has passed from the cavalier and his civilization; and that a great, a very great culture cycle has therewith terminated—whether we like it or not.

Picasso's enigmatic bull, unharmed, has eyes of two perspectives. The eye in the center of the brow is at that point at which in Indian art the eye of time-transcending vision opens, to recognize in the passing forms of this world the mere shadow-play of that inevitable, bitter yet bitter-sweet round that James Joyce, in Finnegans Wake, has dubbed "the Here-we-are-again Gaieties":[86] the bull-god Shiva's cruel, ecstatic, unremitting, everlastingly repetitive Dance of the Burning Ground. And the other eye, beneath the pricked ear, is apparently regarding—as the ear is heeding—the catastrophe of the day: the day, that is to say, of the witness of the picture; for its focus, certainly, is on us. Worth noticing also is the fact that the nostrils of both this bull and the sacrificial horse, as well as the eyes of both the wailing mother and the flaming figure at the right, suggest the well-known *yang* and *yin* elements of the Chinese symbol of the ineluctable, ever-revolving light-and-dark

Way and law of nature, the Tao: .[87] The rays from

the glaring bulb are dark as well as light. So too is the body of the dove—which, in contrast to the solar eagle riding the backs of the conquering steeds of the Gallo-Roman coins, suggests the suffering, complaining, as opposed to the active, aggressive, energetic, side of the yin-yang polarity. Meanwhile the Graces three—those three women at the right, participating with surprise and anguish in the scene, as though it were not an already well-known passage of their own oft-repeated choreography—are without tongues. They are in the place here of Silent Thalia at the base of Gafurius's scale of the Music of the Spheres (Figure 13), at the top of which—above that blazing bulb, as the mystai of Figure 11 are above the blazing sun door—they would have been revealed in their supernal aspect, in that dance before the lord of light of which this scene below is but a reflex in Plato's shadow cave.

Picasso's bull, like the serpent of Gafurius's design, is thus the vehicle of the appearance of an eternal present in the field of passing time: future, present, past. Standing in the posture of the world-father bull of the old Sumerian archetype, beyond the triangle of the lesser light, within which the tragedy of the pierced horse appears, he elevates us, through his two eyes, to that higher sphere, where his horns suggest the balanced crescents of the waning, but then waxing, moon. And finally, we note that the floral element of Gafurius's design, represented blooming in the vase of the immortal water above, has here its counterpart in the modest flower blooming by the clenched hand of the broken hollow hero and bent right foreknee of his steed.

Of Picasso's treatment of traditional symbolic forms there will be more to say in our last chapter. Already obvious here, however, is the power of his art to capture and inflect anew the multifarious ambiguities of their silent speech. His choice of black and white for this masterwork, and its setting, at once indoors and out, suggest immediately the shadow play of Plato's cave. The door at the extreme right is ajar; a wall is omitted at the left; the window at the upper right opens to a void, a light void, whereas the void within the steed is black; so also, that within the hollow man. . . .

In Schopenhauer's paper "On an Apparent Intention in the Fate of the Individual" it has been asked whether in such an overwhelming event, for example, as that here depicted by Picasso there could be any possibility whatsoever of detecting an accord between the outer circumstance and inward character of the individuals involved. Picasso's figure of the *hollow* man suggests strongly that there might. Moreover, since all the other elements of his scene are well-known classical symbols of the play of a secret will in the general course of temporal event—death itself, however it may come, being of the essence, part and parcel, of each man's life, to which he must be reconciled if he is to penetrate beyond the monstrous show of things to what the poet Robinson Jeffers termed the "Tower beyond Tragedy"—it is evident that here, as in all truly tragic art (as opposed to critical caricature), there is implied an affirmation in depth of this world in being, either exactly as it is or as it might be taught to become.

The latter is the way of the historic hero, hero of a day: the knight riding on crusade, the bombardier in his plane. The whole history of a culture—briefly told—is a function of its incidence of heroes of this kind, tried and true; as in this European cycle of the four stages of a day fulfilled which we have identified schematically as: 1. the dawn—in the Celtic Aryan pagan coin, with its steed overleaping the bull, representing the young and barbarous beginning; 2. the forenoon, of the courtly world of King Mark (or, alternately, Arthur), at that supreme period of flowering of the European creative imagination when, as Henry Adams saw, the moment of the apogee of spirituality was attained (1150–1250); then 3. the post meridian of Don Quixote (1605), when the will to the ideal, though still there, was no longer a match for the force of matter; and finally 4. the Angelus hour of Picasso's "Guernica" and Wagner's *Twilight of the Gods*.

But there is another type of heroism as well; namely, of the son of the abyss, Dumuzi-absu: not the warhorse, but the ever-dying, self-resurrecting son, who is "the bull of his own mother," and whose sign is the orb not of day but of night, whose world is not of history but of nature and its mystery—nature without and nature within: as in Wagner's music of the all-resuming waters at the end

of his cycle of *The Ring,* or that of the soaring second act of his
Tristan, where the lovers together—"Heart to heart and lip to
lip"—curse the day with its deceits:

> Daylight phantoms!
> Morning visions!
> Empty and vain!
> Away! Begone!

VI. The Legend of the Fair Isolt

THE POISONED WOUND

Figure 29 is another of the Chertsey tiles. At the left Prince
Morold the Mighty, maternal uncle of Isolt, has come from Ire-

Figure 29. Morold Wounds Tristan

land to claim from the nobles of Mark's court sixty of their sons. There is here an echo of the legend of the youths and maidens required of Athens to feed the Cretan Minotaur. Morold has arrived as the emissary of King Gurmun the Gay of Dublin, scion of a northwest African house, who, having conquered Ireland many years before and there married Morold's sister, turned upon Cornwall and imposed this cruel tax. Gurmun is the Minos of this legend. His daughter, Isolt, bearing the same name as her mother, is to be its Ariadne, and Tristan (at the right), its hero Theseus. At the time of the previous tribute collection, Tristan had not yet appeared from the sea. But he is now a knight without peer. Having challenged to single combat the seasoned fighting man from Ireland, he is receiving on his left thigh a stroke from the enemy's poisoned sword.

"How now?" yelled Morold. "Will you give up?" He wheeled his charger and, on guard, continued shouting through his helm. "Think fast! No doctor now can save you, but only my sister Isolt. That wound, unless I help, will be your death." [88]

Figure 30 shows Tristan's answer. "He delivered a buffet on the helm" states Gottfried, "and went so deeply through that when he pulled the weapon out, his tug left a piece of blade in the skull, —which in due time would bring him into the greatest jeopardy and distress." [89]

In the earlier Norman French version of the legend by Thomas of Britain, Gottfried's source, the two champions met on a jousting field; in Gottfried, however, they battled on an islet off the Cornish coast, to which they and their mounts were conveyed in skiffs. Morold stepped into one, leading with him his charger, took up the oar, and ferried himself across. "And when he came," we read, "to the islet, he beached the boat and made it fast, quickly mounted, gripped his lance in hand, and across the isle went galloping most elegantly. His charges were as easy and playful as for a game." [90] And the young Tristan, eighteen, also unbeaten up to then, was standing at the bow of his own skiff, bidding God's grace to his uncle. "Be not anxious for me and my life. Let us leave it all in God's hands," he said and, pushing off, paddled, likewise with his mount aboard, to the isle.

It is amusing to remark that in the figures on the Chertsey tiles, where Tristan is attacking, the lion of his shield rears forward,

Figure 30. Tristan Slays Morold

but when attacked, its back is turned. This animal is the Lion of
Anjou, emblem of the royal house of England at the time of the
Norman poet Thomas. Gottfried, on the other hand, gives Tristan's emblem as a black boar. "The shield," he states, "having
been burnished to a splendid gloss, enough for a new mirror,
there was a boar inlaid upon it, masterly and well, as sable-black
as coal." [91] But the boar, as we have amply seen, was the sacrificial beast proper to such mysteries of the netherworld as those
to which Tristan now was to be consigned, whereas the lion, the
kingly solar beast, was of the sphere, rather, of Mark. Though
closely following Thomas for the main lines of his story, Gottfried
apparently recognized the preferability of the boar; and he added,

furthermore, the sign of an arrow engraved on Tristan's helm: "Love's prophecy," as he tells us, "which, however long he might be spared, was to be well verified by what Love, in time, would do to him." [92]

The lamentations in Ireland, when the carved-up beheaded body and head of the champion Morold arrived, were great;

> but the grief [states Gottfried] of his sister, Queen Isolt, surpassed all: her anguish and her weeping. She and her daughter (as women will, you know), completely abandoned themselves to every kind of torment, seizing upon this dead man as an occasion purely for keening, that the grief in their hearts should be increased. They kissed his head, and they kissed those hands by which peoples and lands had been conquered. The gash in his skull they scrutinized this way and that, closely, disconsolately, until presently the wise, discerning queen became aware of the piece of metal. She sent for a little pair of tweezers, and with these reached in, drew the piece of metal out. Then she and her daughter studied this, with sobbing and with anguish, and at last, together, took it up and laid it by in a casket—where, in due time, it was to bring Tristan to real trouble. [93]

So that again, as by chance, the course of destiny has been set by incidents of an external, unlikely kind: an exchange of tokens of death, yet heralding love and the opening of its way.

Richard Wagner's theme of the death potion was developed from this base. In his radically abridged version of the romance —commencing at the much later scene of the love potion aboard ship—the earlier adventures, meetings, and preparations, which in the twelfth and thirteenth centuries had occupied nearly half the plot, were dramatically reduced to a dozen or so passionately sung lines in the first act: as where Kurvenal, in a taunting ballad, insults Isolde with an account of Morold's death—who, according to Wagner's reconstruction, had been her betrothed, not her uncle.

For on Wagner's stage there was neither time nor place for the gradual unfoldment of a subtle psychological epic. By transposing Isolde's relationship to the man Tristan had killed, the composer contrived to intensify and to motivate convincingly the ambivalence of her dangerously irritable sentiments, and so to compress into a single ardent scene the whole force of that mounting agony of hate-against-love which was to culminate in her baffled, desperate resolve to implicate the object of her passion in a covenant neither of love nor of a lifelong renunciation of love in the fellowship and service of King Mark, but of death—right there, on the surging sea. And lo! The drink they had thought was to be their death, was of love.

In contrast, in all the earlier versions the potion was drunk by accident, not as a death potion, but as wine. For the symbolic passage through death's door had already been taken care of in a series of adventures treating of the cure of Tristan's wound, and Isolt's resentment over the murder had already been so assuaged that she and Tristan could chat about it lightly during their voyage to King Mark. Indeed, the sentiments of the gifted, beautiful young couple were of unawakened virginal innocence; whereas Wagner filled his art with the magic of his own hardly innocent rapture in the wife, Mathilde, of his friend and benefactor Otto Wesendonck. In her arms he wished to die.

Furthermore, in Wagner's mind the philosophies of Schopenhauer and the Buddha were at work; so that his art too had lost its innocence. Already the first strains of his Prelude release an atmosphere of longing, irresolution, loneliness, and lust; and when the curtain then rising reveals Isolde and her maid Brangaene on the broad opera-deck of Tristan's ship (which has more the look, by the way, of a sixteenth-century galleon of Spain than of anything on the Irish Sea in the early or late Middle Ages), the opening sung lines floating down from the lone sailor's chantey in the rigging sound immediately the mystic night-sea-voyage theme of loss and passage toward a culmination unknown:

> Westward strain the eyes,
> Eastward the ship flies:

telling of a loss not only of home, but of mastery, and an irreversible passage into what Wagner himself termed "that most beautiful of all dreams," compulsive, passionate love—already anticipatory of the end of the work and that great parting song of the love-death, drowning and dissolving, at last, in the unconscious sea of night—to the world-sigh of all things:

> *In dem wogenden Schwall,*
> *in dem tönenden Schall,*

in des Welt Athems wehendem All—
—ertrinken,
versinken,
unbewusst,
höchste Lust!

The curtain falls on the last chord. And in the course of three timeless hours everything that in the earlier master versions had been presented lightly, at leisure, at length, and at a certain remove from reality (like the scenes and figures of a tapestry) has been delivered, full force, in a triptych of swelling frames, wherein—as Nietzsche declared of his great friend—Wagner indeed proved himself to be "the Orpheus of life's secret pain."

"He creates most successfully," Nietzsche wrote, "out of the deepest depths of human delight, as it were from its already emptied chalice, where the bitterest, most unappetizing drops have run together with the sweet—for good and for ill." [94]

THE RUDDERLESS BOAT

The bitter-sweet draft that Wagner pours as music through the porches of our ears, Gottfried and the other poets of his day delivered silently to an inward sense, on the wings of mythic symbols to which the windows of that period still were open. Figure 31, again from the Chertsey tiles, shows the wounded Tristan magically voyaging in a rudderless boat, without oars, to the Ireland of Queen Isolt.

The place where the blow had struck [states Gottfried] emitted such a fearful stench that his life now was a burden, his own body repulsive to him; and he appreciated more and more the import of Morold's words. Further, he had often heard, in days gone by, of the beauty and cunning of Morold's sister; for in all the neighboring lands in which her name was known, there was a popular saying about her:

Isolt the Beautiful, Isolt the Wise:
She is radiant as dawn! [95]

In Thomas of Britain's version the rotting, reeking hero begged his friends to place him in a coracle, equipped only with his harp, and in this floated wonderfully to Ireland; so that the same marvelous child who had been carried by storm to Cornwall, now, as a

Figure 31. Tristan Afloat to Ireland

youth, was again borne by the tides. I would compare with this
the representation of Dionysus (Figure 32) from a sixth-century
B.C. Greek kylix, illustrating a myth known from a Homeric
hymn:

The god, we are told, was standing on a promontory in the
form of a youth in his first bloom, when Etruscan pirates put to
shore and, pouncing on the lad, bound and bore him off. But at
sea the bonds fell from his limbs, wine began pouring through the
ship, a grapevine burgeoned up the mast, and ivy curled about the
oarlocks. The youth, becoming a lion, roaring, tore the captain
apart, while the rest, leaping overboard, became dolphins.[96]

We shall have more of Dionysus anon. Meanwhile, his twelfth-
century avatar, Tristan, resting trustfully on the bosom of those

Figure 32. Dionysus in the Ship; 6th century B.C.

cosmic powers by which the movements of the heavens and all
things on earth are controlled, has been carried on the concord of
his Orphic-Irish harp, resounding to the music of the sea and
spheres, to that very Dublin Bay where Joyce's hero Dedalus was
to go walking centuries later, questioning his heart as to whether
he would ever have the courage to entrust himself to life.
In Gottfried's shaping of the legend, the altogether magical
theme of the unguided skiff has been discarded. Rejecting the lit-

tle miracle, the poet tells more rationally of the miserable Tristan's friends taking him in a seaworthy craft to the mouth of Dublin Bay and there, at night, setting him adrift in his skiff, a short way off Sandymount Shore. And when morning dawned, as he writes:

When the folk of Dublin spied that rudderless little boat upon the waves, orders were given to speed to it. An expedition went out. And as they approached, unable still to see anybody within, they all, to their hearts' delight, heard a lovely harp, sweetly sounding; and to that harp the voice of a man so pleasantly at song that every one of them deemed this the most marvelous greeting and adventure. And as long as he harped and sang they never stirred.[97]

The sight and the stench of what they found within, garbed as a minstrel, appalled them; yet for his song they bade him welcome. He declared he was from Spain. Having set to sea in a merchant ship, according to his tale, he had been attacked by pirates, wounded, and committed to this skiff, in which he had drifted now some forty days and nights—the period of Christ's ordeal and fast in the desert.

THE PRETENDER

Tristan gave his name as Tantris and, when towed ashore, so filled the city with the sweet strains of his song that all pressed around to hear. A physician among them took him to his home, where a priest of the palace, marveling at the talents of the youth in music, languages, and courtesy as well, took pity and brought him to the queen, who when she beheld him was overcome with compassion.

"Oh!" she exclaimed, examining his leg. "You poor poor minstrel! You are poisoned."

The invalid feigned amazement.

"Now Tantris, have confidence that I am really going to mend you. I shall be your doctor, myself," she said; then asked if he was strong enough to let her hear him play, and he replied that nothing whatsoever could prevent him from doing—and doing right well—anything she asked. The harp was sent for, and her daughter as well, that she too might enjoy this prodigy.

"Love's signet, she was," states Gottfried, "by which his heart was to be sealed away and impounded from all the world, save herself alone: beautiful Isolt. She entered. She paid very studious attention to the one there harping away. And he played better than he had ever played in his life." [98]

However, that ugly slash on his thigh was emitting such an insupportable stench that in spite of the rapture of his music it was more than anyone present could stand to remain as much as an hour in his vicinity. The queen presently spoke.

"Tantris, just as soon as we can bring it to the point that this foul odor of yours is quenched and people can bear to be near you, let me confide this young lady to your teaching."—Shades of Abelard and Heloise!—"She has always worked diligently at her books and music, and considering the time and opportunity she has had for it, does rather well. I shall repay you with your life and with your body in good health and of comely mien. Both to give and to withhold are in my hand." [99]

One thinks of the Greek Medusa, the blood from whose left side brought death, and from her right side, life.[100] For this Queen Isolt was indeed of the number of those mighty goddess queens of the Celtic past who controlled the destinies and powers even of the gods. In Ireland, their reign has continued to the present. "Have you ever seen a fairy or such like?" the poet Yeats asked an old man in County Sligo. "Amn't I annoyed with them?" was the answer. "Do the fishermen along here know anything of the mermaids?" he asked a woman in a village in County Dublin. "Indeed, they don't like to see them at all," she answered, "for they always bring bad weather." [101] There's little cause, then, for wonder in the magic of the beautiful Dublin queen Isolt of the medieval Tristan legend: far more in the way she let compassion veil her eyes to the identity of the trickster in her hands.

"The cunning queen," states Gottfried, "turned all her thoughts and every skill to the task of healing a man whom she would gladly have given her life and reputation to have destroyed. She hated him more than she loved herself, yet thought of nothing but to ease and advance him, and to bring about his cure—to which end she strove and labored, day and night." [102] And with such effect that in twenty days people could bear to approach him, and the princess was entrusted to his care. The young lady worked diligently and found that what she already knew greatly helped;

for she could speak French, Latin, and Irish, play the fiddle in
the Welsh style, besides the lyre and harp, and sweetly sing. Tristan's teaching improved her in all these, and he instructed her,
besides, in the valuable discipline called *moraliteit, w*hich, according to Gottfried's definition, is "the art that teaches beautiful
manners."

"All women," Gottfried urges, "should apply themselves to this
art diligently when young; for its delightful teaching, pure and
wholesome, accords with the world and with God, showing
through its precepts how to please both. And to all noble hearts it
is given as their nurse, that in its lore they may seek their living
and their life. For unless *moraliteit* directs them, they will enjoy
neither well-being nor good name." [103]

In not one word of all of which is there any hint, nuance, or
possibility of discovering so much as a trace of that Gnostic-
Manichaean philosophy of world-rejection of which Gottfried has
been, by some of his critics, accused. Indeed, it would be difficult
to coin a formula that would have less about it of the Manichaean. Professor August Closs of the University of Bristol, in the
introduction to his edition of the Middle High German text, compares Gottfried's concept of *moraliteit* to the classical ideal of
καλοκάγαΘία, the character and conduct of a perfect man, which
is an ideal, as he points out, that can be attained only "in the
most sacred moments in the life of men or nations." [104] And
Gottfried himself points in this direction—not the Manichaean—when he states of his love grotto that its fashioners had
been the giants of heathen times, and calls upon the Muses and
Apollo to inspire his work.

The gentle, beautiful, fateful Isolt, whom Tristan unwittingly
was training for his own destruction, learned to play her lyre and
harp with such grace that in six months all Ireland was talking.
"And to what," the poet asks, "might I compare that beautiful,
gifted girl but to the Sirens with their lodestone, who draw to
themselves stray ships? . . . It was to the agitation of many a
heart that she sang, both openly and secretly, by way of both ear
and eye. The song openly sung to her tutor and elsewhere was of
her own sweet singing and soft sounding of strings, which openly
and clearly traveled through the kingdom of the ears down deep
into the heart: but the secret song was of her beauty, which

meanwhile slipped covertly and silently through the windows of the eyes into many a noble heart, where it spread a magic that made those hearts instantaneously captive and bound them with yearning and yearning stress." [105]

Thus it was specifically and explicitly from the sensuous beauty of this virginal maid that the arrow of love passed through the eyes to the heart—as in the poem of the troubadour Borneilh. And it was these unintentional effects that were shaping Isolt's destiny. She was in a sense, thus, the unwilling victim of her own beauty. However, if Schopenhauer's proposal that one's body is an "objectification" of one's "intelligible character" * be taken seriously, it will appear that although her conscious mind may not have been the fashioner of her destiny, her actuality surely was; and that this in a profound sense was more truly she—an expression of her most essential "will"—than were all her drifting maiden thoughts and dreams. Moreover, reciprocally, the response of Tristan's noble heart to her beauty was a function of *his* character and will, as well: he had never played better in his life! So that, through a kind of valency beyond their conscious willing, the wills of these two were already co-authoring the romance that was to become, through apparent chance, the one realization in time and space of their only possible destiny.

When the wound of the Tantris who was Tristan had been healed by the unwitting queen, who would have wished rather to have slain him, both the wise yet deceived mother and her innocent, provocative daughter begged the honorable deceiver to remain with them in Ireland. He, however, prudently pleaded with such fervor to return to his nonexistent wife in Spain that, with thanks, great courtesy and honor, in God's name, he was let go.

THE INCITEMENT OF KING MARK

Tristan returned to Cornwall. And when he recounted his adventure, he was questioned particularly of the maid Isolt, and replied with such a paean of praise that neither Mark nor anyone else could put her image thereafter out of mind. "She is a maid," he said, "so lovely that everything the world has ever told of beauty is in comparison mere wind." And he went on: "Radiant Isolt is a princess of such superlative enchantment, both in man-

---

* Supra, p. 34.

ner and in person, that no peer of her ever was born, or will ever be. Luminous, effulgent Isolt: she glows like Arabian gold." [106]

In the Eilhart-Béroul version of the romance,* a fairytale motive is invoked to inspire Tristan's second voyage to Ireland. A swallow, building its nest outside the window of King Mark, had let fall a golden hair, which came floating, long and fair, into the room, shining like a beam of light; and the king, whose people had been urging him to marry, agreed to accommodate them only if his barons could find the maid to whom that hair belonged. The spirit of this fairytale motive accorded with a troubadour theme of the time, of the "Princess Far Away." The great troubadour Jaufre Rudel (fl. 1130–1150) was said to have fallen immediately in love on hearing the name of the Princess of Tripoli. "Sad and joyous shall I be," he sang, "When I meet my distant love." [107] Gottfried, however, in a side remark, makes mock of Eilhart's fairytale device. "Did ever any swallow ever build its nest," he asks, "in such a roundabout way that, with so much in its own land, it went searching for nesting material abroad, over sea?" [108] In his own version, following Thomas, there was no need for any such swallow, since Tristan's own mouth had carried golden tidings enough.

"I had believed," the infatuated innocent said, "from the books I had read in praise of Aurora's daughter Helen, that in her alone the beauties of all womankind were laid together in a single flower; but I have now escaped that illusion. Isolt has cured me of the notion, which I never again shall credit, that the sun rose in Mycenae. Beauty supreme never dawned upon Greece; beauty supreme has dawned only here. Let all thought and all mankind turn now to Ireland. Let the eyes there take delight and see how the new sun, succeeding to the light of its dawn—Isolt after Isolt— from Dublin shines into all hearts!" [109]

Clearly, Gottfried's Tristan is already head-over-heels in love, and the potion, consequently, will simply break open the gates to a tide already pressing to burst through: not consciously suppressed, as in Wagner's nineteenth-century moderns, but absolutely unrecognized, through innocence blinded by an ego-ideal of loyalty and some notion of the general good. The young man's glowing description of a golden female shining like the sun per-

* Cf. supra, p. 70.

fectly accords with C. G. Jung's definition of an archetypal *anima*-projection: the attribution to a living female of the male's unconscious image of the Woman of his soul.[110] And little wonder, meanwhile, if the entire nation of Cornwall is importuning King Mark, who has sworn to remain a bachelor and pass his throne on to his nephew, to take that Irish paragon, advertised by that same besotted nephew, for his queen.

"Gurmun the King and Isolt the Queen have but one sole heir," said the courtiers. "With Isolt comes Ireland itself."

And Mark, in a quandary, answered ruefully, "Tristan has brought her deeply into my thought." [111]

Which in Gottfried's book was a telling point against Mark: for he had not seen Isolt himself, the magic of her beauty had not passed through his eyes to his heart, but only her report, through his ears to his brain. It was not love, *amor,* that would join him to Isolt, therefore, but prudence, matters of state, importuning counselors, and a certain weakness of resolve. In the end, an expedition was equipped wherein, with a company of twenty knights, twenty barons, and three times twenty men, Tristan, again as Tantris, but pretending now to be a merchant, set sail, once again, for Dublin Bay.

BRIDE QUEST

From the point of view of a student of folklore, this second voyage is but a modified duplication of the first, culminating not in abandonment but in capture of the bride. And as Tristan, in the first, before meeting Isolt, had had to encounter Morold, who infected him with death, so in this a like threshold-guardian was to be encountered. In Thomas of Britain's version, Morold's shield had been emblazoned with the figure of a dragon.[112] He was a manifestation in human form of the same dark guarding power that Tristan now was to face on its home ground in its primal, animal shape (Figures 33 and 34).

For the tale speaks of a serpent in the country [Gottfried tells], which evil monster had laden the people and land with harmful harm so harmfully, that Gurmun the Gay, the Irish king, had sworn by his kingly honor that he would give his daughter Isolt to any knight of noble birth that would undo him. The report throughout the land and the ravishing beauty of the

Figure 33. Tristan and . . .

maid had sufficed to entail the deaths of thousands, who arrived
to give battle and meet their end. Ireland was full of the tale
—and Tristan knew it well: which, in fact, is what had heartened him to undertake the voyage; for no other hope did he
have, on which to rely to gain his end.[113]

Tristan galloped at the flaming open jaws of the lizard, and his
lance drove deep into its throat; but when the jaws snapped, the
entire front portion of his mount, as far as to the saddle, was
chopped off and consumed. The dragon turned and made for its
den, spreading fire to both sides, with Tristan after, afoot; then
turned at bay, and a terrible fiery battle ensued, until, with the
lance still in its throat, the devil's brat began to fail, and, sinking

34. The Dragon

to the ground, expired when Tristan thrust his sword into its heart.

A very different dragon battle from that of Beowulf, five centuries before!

The victor cut out the dead thing's tongue and thrust it into his bosom—which, however, sent such a burning poison through his body that, to cool himself, he dove into a nearby pond and remained there with only mouth and nose to the surface.

But now in the Irish court there was a very cowardly steward who had for years been zealous to follow every battle with this dragon, so that if ever the beast were killed he might claim to have shared in the work. And this fool, hearing from afar the dragon thunder of Tristan's combat, hastily mounted and came riding, saw the remaining rear of the mutilated horse, drew an optimistic conclusion, and, following the burned trail, suddenly, with a mighty shock, beheld the dead beast right before him. He drew back on the reins so hard that both he and his mount collapsed in a thrashing heap, then looked at the monster and fled. But he returned and presently, cautiously, guaranteed the situation, and with a mighty flashing, cutting, and stabbing of his trusty blade, made at the monstrous corpse, shouting meanwhile, as he lashed about, *"Ma blunde Isot ma bele."* And in the end contriving to cut off the prodigious head, he sent to court for a wagon, and so transported his trophy to the king.

The queen, however, realizing that the claim could not be sound, proceeded with her daughter, intuitively, directly to the pond, where they found Tristan, nearly dead. They found the dragon's tongue also and knew immediately what had happened; bore the knight secretly to their chambers, healed him, and when, before the nation, the steward proposed his arrant claim, the two cunning as well as beautiful Isolts released, to the astonishment of all, their knight—who, standing, simply required that the jaws of the trophy be opened, exhibited the missing tongue, and so won both the day and the girl—not for himself, but for his country and his king.[114]

THE BATHTUB SCENE

The name Isolt has not been explained. However, as the mythological associations of the dragon attach to Morold, and the pig and horse respectively to Tristan and to Mark, so to Isolt the sun bird, the lion-bird of the Magna Mater.[115] In a passage of great charm Gottfried describes her as the falcon of the goddess.

> So came the Queen Isolt, the glad Dawn; and by her hand led the Sun, the wonder of Ireland, the brilliant maid Isolt . . . shaped in her attire as if Love had formed her to be her own falcon. She was in her posture as erect and forthright as a sparrow hawk, as well preened as a parrot. Like a falcon on a bough she let rove her two eyes, which together sought their prey, neither gently nor yet too intently: so smoothly flying, silently and sweetly hunting, that there were there many eyes to whom her flashing mirrors were a wonder and field of delight.[116]

There can be no doubt: Gottfried knew what mythological figures he was using. He took care, however, to subordinate them to
a playfully pretended rational concern for naturalism and factual
truth, as Ovid had pretended in his *Metamorphoses,* a mythological work that in the twelfth and thirteenth centuries, though rejected from all ecclesiastical lists of approved "curriculum authors," [117] nevertheless decisively influenced the whole narrative
art of the secular tradition. And Gottfried played his game
most aptly in his handling of the celebrated bathtub scene, which
occurred in the period of Tristan's convalescence, between the
dragon fight and his victory in court.

The scene is pivotal. First, on the mythological plane, it reveals
the terrible aspect of the goddess—the goddess of the lion and the
double ax—through whom the sacrifice of our divine wild boar
was all but consummated in a household version of the watery
abyss. Secondly, on the psychological plane, the scene represents
a total reversal of the sentiments of the two Isolts in relation to
their guest, and as such was used by Wagner as a base for
the motivation of his heroine's wrath in his opening act. And
finally, on the purely narrative plane, certain separated themes of
the First and Second Voyages to Ireland are here dramatically
brought together, and the whole emotional coloration of the romance thereby transformed.

The scene occurs shortly after the two Isolts, mother and maid,
have drawn their potential savior from the pond in which he had
sought to quench the fire of the dragon poison—all but dead,
once again, of a dragon wound. The duplication is obvious. The
women once again are ministering in their apartments to one
whose name is known to them only in reverse; but this time he
has come clad not as a minstrel, but in armor, with sword and
shield. And it was while he was soaking in a bathtub—in water
once again, as in the pond in which he had been found; or the
waters, so to say, to which he had given himself, alone with his
harp, in the little boat without oars; or again, the waters, finally, of
the Land below Waves, Avalon, the Isle beyond the Sunset Sky, of
which Ireland is the symbol—that the younger Isolt, in the other
room, examining his armor, *chanced* to draw his sword—and lo!
her falcon eyes pounced on the notch in the blade.

Appalled, she put the weapon down, turned to the reliquary

casket, took the fragment out, brought it to the notch in the blade; and they matched. Then it dawned on her that the names, Tantris-Tristan, also matched, as a negative to a positive. Stunned, then mortified, then seething at the deception by one to whom she had given love, she picked up the mighty blade in her suddenly strengthened hand and strode to the man now helpless in her tub. One thinks of Clytemnestra and her returned spouse, Agamemnon; one thinks today, retroactively, of Charlotte Corday's murder of Marat.

"So it is Tristan!" she said as she approached him with his own sword "So *that* is who you are!"

He answered from his disadvantage, "No, my lady! Tantris!"

"Yes," she said, "Tantris and Tristan, and the two are now one dead man."

But the elder Isolt, in the nick of time, entered and stopped her hand. The hero pleaded mercy from his tub, and the maid Brangaene, who had also appeared, pleaded reason—noticing, namely, that if the steward were to be proved false, this champion, notch or no notch, would have to be kept alive. And so it was that, after a moment of hesitation, with the sword meanwhile getting heavier in Isolt's hand, the danger passed and the Graces Three withdrew, to allow the necessary man to ascend, renamed, reborn as it were, from the ladies' bath.

THE LOVE DRINK

Therewith, the poison of hate, which had entered the minds of the two Isolts from the metal in Morold's skull, and the poison of the queen's magic, which from the blade of the same slain Morold had entered Tristan's wound, were brought dramatically together, to be transformed, in time, into the no less lethal daemonic aspect of *amor*. The innocent love in Isolt's heart became eclipsed by a violent surge of hate and, as Wagner recognized in his reconstruction, the psychological sense of the entire first portion of the legend is epitomized in this moment of peripety. On the broad deck of his opera stage, Isolde, swelling with mixed emotion, sings to his Tristan, who throughout the voyage has been avoiding her neighborhood aboard, "Blood-guilt hangs between us!"

"That," sings Wagner's tenor, "was absolved."

"Not between *us!*" she answers: and to the mixed strains of the leitmotifs of Spiritual Excitement, Longing, Sailors' Calls, and Death, Isolde rehearses the episodes of his cure at her hands, her recognition of the notch, and her failure there to slay him.

"Yet what I with hand and lips there had vowed, I swore to hold to, in secret."

"What, woman, had you vowed?"

"Revenge!" she responds. "For Morold!"

Figure 35 is another of the Chertsey Abbey tiles. It shows, in its twelfth-century style, the young Tristan passing the goblet to

Figure 35. Tristan Hands the Goblet to Isolt

Isolt, which the two suppose to be of wine. For there had been throughout the voyage, in these earlier versions, no such strained situation of longing with avoidance as Wagner contrived for his first act. Tristan frequently, in fact, to give comfort to Isolt in the anxiety and loneliness of her sea voyage to King Mark, had visited her cabin—where, as Gottfried tells,

> every time he came and found her in tears, he took her very gently and sweetly in his arms, but only in such a way as might a liege man his lady. What he loyally wished was only to be of solace in her pain. However, no sooner would his arm go round than the lovely girl would think of her uncle's death and say: "Now stop, sir, move back! Take your arm away! You are just too tiresome! Why do you keep touching me?"
>
> "Am I doing something wrong, my lady?"
>
> "Indeed you are—for I hate you."
>
> "But why, my dear lady?"
>
> "Because you killed my uncle."
>
> "I have made amends for all that."
>
> "Even so, I find you intolerable; for if it weren't for you I should be without worry or care. . . ." [118]

And it was on one of those intimate occasions that the potion was drunk by accident: but it really is remarkable how difficult many modern scholars have found the interpretation of that drink. Some, as already remarked (supra, p. 70), have argued that in Gottfried's view the potion was the *cause* of the love. Professor A. T. Hatto, for example, in the introduction to his translation, declares in so many words that the poet "adheres closely to the tradition of his story, namely that it was a philtre which made his lovers fall in love." [119] Professor August Closs, on the other hand, states that "Gottfried's love-potion does not cause love, but symbolizes it," [120] which surely is better. However, if there is one point completely clear in Gottfried's own version of his tale, it is that the potion cannot possibly have marked the birth of love, either as symbol or as cause, since love had already been animating this perfectly matched young couple for some time.

One would have thought that even if our scholars had themselves been deprived, through diligence in philology, of experiencing in the days of their youth the mystery of love's transformation, through the magic of a catalyst, from its personal-aesthetic to its compulsive-daemonic mode, they might at least have recalled, from the scene of Dante's *Inferno,* the words of the fire-ridden, Hell-bound Francesca da Rimini: that famous, oft-quoted passage describing the circumstance of her fall into what Dante and his God of Love condemned as carnal sin. Tristan also was in that Dantean circle of Hell, whirled along, with the other sorry lovers—Dido, Semiramis, Cleopatra, Paris, Helen, and the rest—on the tide of a blazing wind.

As Paolo and Francesca passed, embracing still, in torment, Dante, like a sociologist, asked what had brought them to that pass.

"At the time of the sweet sighs," he asked, "by what and how did love concede to you to know of your dubious desires?"

The question clearly anticipates our modern theory of the unconscious by a good six hundred years. And the suffering Francesca generously replied:

"For pleasure, we two, one day, were reading of Lancelot, how love constrained him. We were alone and without any suspicion. Many times that reading urged our eyes, and took the color from our faces, but only one point was it that overcame us. When we read of the longed-for smile being kissed by such a lover, this one, who never shall be divided from me, kissed my mouth all trembling. Galehaut was the book, and he who wrote it: that day we read no more." [121] *

Professor Gottfried Weber of Cologne, from whose formidable Tristan study we have already quoted, interprets the potion, it seems to me, correctly when he reads it as "a metaphor for that psychological moment in love when two people of strongly sensual disposition lose control of the human faculty of free choice, under the influence of an already vehement, unsuspected, inward approach to each other, and the tides of passion that have been stored in the unconscious flood together, submerging them, who have lost all power of will." Further, he goes on to state: "This psychological process—and here is the important point—is ele-

---

* Galehaut (also Galehos) is the name of a king opposed to Arthur in the prose text know as the *Vulgate Lancelot,* composed some time between 1215 and 1230 (see infra, p. 532), which became the most popular redaction of the romance in the late Middle Ages. In some manuscripts the title "Galehaut" is given to the first large section of this version of the romance.

vated by the poet into an objective experience of an existential
absolute and described as an independent force, more than human, opening out to the transcendent." [122]

In the magic potion's effect [he continues], the poet has thus
given aesthetic form to the idea that Tristan and Isolt have come
under the spell of an extra-mundane power, which is at work in
them irresistibly, with no possibility of a restraining act of will;
and it is this commanding power, within them and above them,
that is pressing them together, to the physical act of love's
union. Thus in the magic potion the belief and experience of the
poet is formulated of the lack of freedom of the will and the
compulsive force of circumstance. The lovers are incapable of
resisting each other. Moreover, they do not want to; but rather,
on the contrary, they affirm their lack of freedom—which is a
bondage, furthermore, that is not confined to the sphere of the
phenomenology of their love and urge to love's physical union,
but takes hold of them in the most comprehensive sense, forging
for them a common destiny unto death. . . . And this magical
force has been experienced and rendered by the poet as divine:
the very being and operation of the goddess Minne . . . [which
is to say, in opposition to the orthodox ecclesiastical imagery
and dogma of supernatural grace], in the way of an *analogia
antithetica,* even *analogia antithetica daemoniaca.* . . . For the
pain of love [which, in its extreme state, is of Hell] follows directly and inevitably both from the irresistible zeal of its experience as sensual delight, and from the further fact that its self-
moving overpowering consummation mounts to the spiritual
state of a willing affirmation.[123]

In Gottfried's poem the transformation from innocence to realization does not occur instantaneously, as in Wagner's dramatic
scene—or as in the case of Paolo and Francesca. The sense of the
need now to be near each other, a zeal, a new sense of pain, and
the dawn of a realization that this, indeed, was love, required a
day or two, until, when the couple again were together and Tristan asked innocently—but not quite—why the fair Isolt now
looked distressed, she answered: " 'Everything I think about torments me; everything I look upon gives pain. The sky, the sea,
they oppress me. My body and life are a burden.' She leaned, resting her elbow against him—and that was the beginning for them

both." [124] He took her, to comfort her, gently in his arms and asked again what ailed her.

"*Lameir!*" she answered; of which word he then strove to learn the sense. " '*L'ameir,* the bitterness?' he asked. '*La meir,* the sea?'

" 'No, my lord, no!' she replied. 'Neither of those: not the air, not the sea, but *l'ameir.*' "

And so he came to the heart of the word: *l'ameir, l'amour*—to which he answered: " 'Oh my lovely one, so it is, also, with me: *l'ameir* and you: you are my torment. Isolt dear, queen of my heart, you alone and my love for you have undone and robbed me of my wits. I have gone so completely astray that I shall never again be restored. There is in this entire world nothing dear to my heart but you.'

"Isolt replied: 'Sire, and so you are to me.'

"And since the lovers," we read, "now realized that there was between them just one mind, one heart, and one will, their pain began at the same time to subside and to come to light. Each regarded and addressed the other more boldly: the man, the maid; the maid, the man: the sense of a difference between them was gone. He kissed her and she kissed him, lovingly, sweetly; and that, for Love's cure, was a delightful start." [125]

LOVE'S CONSUMMATION

Brangaene was the only one aboard who knew that a love potion was in question; for Isolt's mother had confided the flask to her in secret, to be served as wine to Isolt and King Mark: "a love drink," Gottfried explains, "so cunningly produced and devised, with such power to its purpose and aim, that with whomsoever anyone shared the drink, that one, willy-nilly, he would love above all things, and she, him: there would be given them one death and one life, one sorrow and one joy." [126]

Brangaene, the good woman, had been out of the cabin when the philter had been served, and, returning, nearly fainted when she perceived what her negligence had brought to pass. She flung the flask into the sea and kept the secret to herself, but now, recognizing the philter's work, begged the tortured couple to tell her why they were sighing, moping, fretting, and complaining all the time.

"Poor me and poor Isolt!" Tristan responded. "What has happened to us, I do not know. In the briefest time, we have both gone mad with a singular affliction. We are expiring of love, but can find neither time nor place for it, since you, night and day, are so diligently watchful. And I can tell you, surely, if we die— there will be no one to blame but you." Isolt concurred, and "May God have pity," Brangaene said, "that the Devil has made mock of us this way! I now see, there is nothing for it, but I must henceforth for your two sakes work to my own sorrow and your shame." [127]

She withdrew, swearing secrecy. "And that night," the poet tells,

> when the lovely maid Isolt lay suffering, yearning for her dar-ling, there came stealing into her cabin, softly, her lover together with her doctor, Tristan with the goddess Love. The doctor held her patient, Tristan, by his hand, and there found the other patient, Isolt; she took hold of the two, directly, and gave to him, her, to her, him, to become each other's cure. For what else could have healed those two of the pain they shared when separated, but the joining of them together and entangling of their senses? Love, the Entangler, wove those two hearts together with the weaving of her sweetness, so skillfully and with such marvelous force that the bond, in all their days, was never undone. [128]

ETERNAL DEATH

The problem then arose, however, of presenting Mark with a vir-gin on the wedding night, and the answer found was to beg Brangaene to serve—who, on hearing the petition, turned red and pale a number of times, "for, after all," says Gottfried, "it was an odd request." Yet finally, uncomfortably, she consented; for she felt strongly that the guilt here was her own.

"My dear lady," she said to Isolt, "your mother, my lady the blessed Queen, entrusted you to my care. I should have protected you on this voyage, but instead, you are now in sorrow and pain, all because of my carelessness."

In amazement Isolt asked how that could be.

"The other day," Brangaene replied, "I threw a flask overboard."

"So you did."

"That flask and what it contained will be the death of you both," she said, and she told the two the whole tale.

Said Tristan: "So then, God's will be done, whether death it be or life! For that drink has sweetly poisoned me. What the death of which you tell is to be, I do not know; but *this* death suits me well. And if delightful Isolt is to go on being my death this way, then I shall gladly court an eternal death." [129]

And that, in sum, is the love-death theme, as understood by Gottfried, as by all true lovers in the Gothic Middle Ages. Dante, we have seen, consigned Paolo and Francesca to Hell; and for Gottfried too the meaning of the term "eternal death" was "Hell." That was the love-death sought by Heloise, but feared by Abelard—who, though from Brittany and a singer of love, was, finally, no Tristan. Three orders of "death" are referred to in this passage:

1. That of which Brangaene spoke, physical death.

2. That to which Tristan referred in his celebration of *"this"* death, namely his ecstasy in Isolt—which, as Professor Weber has shown, is the main mystical theme developed throughout the poem in antithetic analogy to the Christian idea of love. The crystalline bed in the grotto is, of course, the ultimate symbol of this analogy. The reference, unmistakably, is to the sacrament of the altar in its dual sense of love and death: Christ's love-death, celebrated in the eloquent passage of Philippians 2:6–8, which is enacted mystically every day—indeed every hour of the day—on the altars innumerable of Christ's Church.

The passionate Saint Bernard, in the very period of Heloise and Abelard, in a celebrated series of sermons on the biblical Song of Songs, had coined for ecclesiastical use a rich vocabulary of erotic terms based on the allegory of the soul—or, alternately, Holy Mother Church—as the bride of Christ, responding with yearning in their marriage bed to the provocation of God's zeal; and Gottfried threaded echoes of the celibate saint's seraphic rapture through many verses of his own inspired work:

"Love speaks throughout this nuptial song," the monk had declared in celebration of his text; "and if any one of those who read it desires to attain to a knowledge of it, let him love. . . .

"O love precipitate, passionate, impetuous, who suffer yourself to think of nothing but yourself, who loathe all else, who despise everything not yourself, content with yourself alone! You throw

order into confusion, you disregard custom, you know no restraint. Everything that seems a matter of propriety, a matter of
prudence or judgment, you triumph over in your own name and
bring into subjection." [130]

Now the Song of Songs, which the saint was here interpreting,
is not, as traditionally claimed, a poem composed, tenth century
B.C., by the king of a thousand wives and concubines, but a
composite of erotic pieces, mostly incomplete, all later than the
fifth century B.C. The book had required reinterpretation before
being read into the canon. However, its attribution to Solomon
had made it seem desirable, and the problem was solved by treating it "as a picture of love existing between Yahweh and the ideal
Israel." [131] But the Christian monk now was reading it in still
another sense, with the bride of the Lord played by an institution
of which the alleged author never heard. And in the name of this
second bride he cried to his congregation, as if in a paroxysm of
mad, illicit pain:

"By desire, not by reason, am I impelled. . . .

"A sense of modesty protests, it is true; love, however, con-
quers. . . .

"I am not unmindful of the fact that *the king's honor loveth
judgment*. But intense love does not wait upon judgment. It is not
restrained by counsel; it is not checked by a sense of false modesty; it is not subject to reason. I ask, I implore, I entreat with all
my heart: *Let him kiss me with the kiss of his mouth*." [132]

In India there was likewise a doctrine of divine love flourishing
in Bernard's time; * however its metaphors of rapture were not
confined to sermons but displayed in temple sculpture and translated into rites of the kind of our Gnostic friends, the Phibionites.† Jayadeva's "Song of the Cowherd," celebrating in volup-
tuous detail the love—illicit and divine—of the man-god Krishna
for the earthly matron Radha, goes considerably beyond Bernard
in its intimacies of the bed; [133] yet its spiritual aim is the same:
to offer a base for meditation whereby the heart may be elevated
from the earthly to the supernatural sphere, through what in psychological jargon might be termed "a supernormal image." [134]

Figure 36, from N. Tinbergen's *Study of Instinct*, shows a po-

* Supra, pp. 166 and 168.
† Supra, pp. 159–61.

Figure 36. Oystercatcher Responding to a "Supernormal Stimulus"

tentially saintly bird, an oystercatcher, spiritually responding to a
giant egg, a "supernormal sign stimulus," immensely greater than
her own; her own being the little thing in the foreground. The
middle-sized egg is of a herring gull. States Professor Tinbergen:
"If presented with an egg of normal oystercatcher size, one of
herring gull's size, and one of double the (linear) size of a herring
gull's egg, the majority of choices fall upon the largest egg." [135]
And Saint Bernard now continues the lesson of this bird:

> Thus, therefore, even in this body of ours the joy of the Bride-
> groom's presence is frequently felt, but not the fullness of it; for
> although His visitation gladdens the heart, the alternation of His
> absence makes it sad. And this the beloved must of necessity
> endure until she has once laid down the burden of the body of
> the flesh, when she too will fly aloft, borne on the wings of her
> desires, freely making her way through the realms of contem-

plation and with unimpeded mind following her Beloved *whithersoever He goeth.*[136]

Gottfried is recalling that spiritual bird back to earth, the oyster-catcher to her nest, in accord, prophetically, with the gospel of Nietzsche, "to remain true to this earth." And he thereby reverses the yonder-worldling's prospect: not abandoning the little for the big, but realizing in the little the rapture of the big. For there is no such thing as a love that is either purely spiritual or merely sensual. Man is composed of body and spirit (if we still may use such terms) and is thus an essential mystery in himself; and the deepest heart of this mystery (in Gottfried's view) is the very point touched and wakened by—and in—the mystery of love, the sacramental purity of which has nothing whatsoever to do with a suspension or suppression of the sensuous and the senses, but includes and even rests upon the physical realization.

Gottfried's version of the purity of love comprises thus two factors: *a*) uniqueness, singularity, unconditioned loyalty in the love experience, and *b*) a boundless readiness for the suffering of this love—which brings us, finally, to the ultimate and third order of "death" in his reading of the love-death:

3. An "eternal death" in Hell.

But this, actually, is only an affirmation absolute of the "purity" of love against the supernormal terrors of the Christian myth; or even in willing affirmation of the fire as merely the bitter aspect of the rapture, bitter-sweet, that would there endure forever. How seriously did Heloise fear that fire? She believed in it, as did Abelard. How seriously did Paolo and Francesca suffer in the flames in which Dante thought he heard them wailing? There is a "memorable fancy" of the poet Blake that may clear this matter up. "As I was walking," he wrote, "among the fires of Hell, delighted with the enjoyments of Genius, which to Angels look like torment and insanity, I collected some of their Proverbs. . . ." And among the number of these was the following: "Dip him in the river who loves water." [137]

For Dante, when he paused to interrogate Francesca, was at the start of a long dream-journey that was to bring him in its last canto to the auditorium of a lecture by Saint Bernard on the pop-

ulation of Heaven, together with a vision of the same, whereas for
Gottfried and his Tristan, as for Heloise (though not for Abelard), not the big egg but the little was the real, and the suffering
of the crucified, symbolized as of God and so eternal, is the rapture of love on this earth where all things die.

However again, as Gottfried tells, though love is the very being
of life, it is everywhere brutalized.

> I pity Love [he writes] with all my heart; for though almost all
> today hold and cleave to her, no one concedes to her her due.
> We all want our pleasure of her, and to consort with her. But
> no! Love is not what we, with our deceptions, are now making
> of her for each other. We are going at things the wrong way. We
> sow black henbane, then expect to reap lilies and roses. But, be-
> lieve me, that cannot be. . . .
>
> It is really true, what they say, "Love is harried and hounded
> to the ends of the earth." All that we possess of her is the word,
> the name alone remains to us; and that, too, we have so bandied
> about, misused and vulgarized, that the poor thing is ashamed of
> her name, disgusted with the very sound of it. She is cringing
> and flinching everywhere at her own existence. Misused and dis-
> honored, she sneaks begging from house to house, lugging
> shamefully a sack all of patches, crammed with her swag and
> booty, which she denies to her own mouth, and offers for sale in
> the streets. Alas! It is we who have created that market. We
> traffic with her in this amazing way and claim then to be in-
> nocent. Love, the queen of all hearts, the free-born, the one and
> only, is put up for public sale! What a shameful tribute is this
> that our mastery has required of her! [138]

And so *incipit tragoedia!*

For not love alone, but honor as well, was the motivating interest of both Tristan and Isolt: not love alone, but their reputations
in the fashionable courtly world, and commitments there in the
field of history and of day. And by striving to pay honor its due
while at the same time honoring love, they sacrificed both, and so
came finally to that death of which Brangaene had told.

"We cultivate love," states Gottfried, "with embittered minds,
with lies, and with deceit, and then expect from her joy of body
and heart: but instead, she bears only pain, corruption, evil fruit,
and blight—as her soil was sown." [139]

THE MARRIAGE OF KING MARK

The brideship arrived in Cornwall and was greeted there with royal splendor. The eyes of all at the wedding were addressed to the sunlike, miserable bride. When bedtime arrived, the king retired, the women swiftly exchanged garments, Tristan led Brangaene to her altar of sacrifice, and Isolt put out the lights.

"I do not know," Gottfried confesses, "how Brangaene felt when the affair began; she bore it so discreetly it went without a sound. Whatever her partner required of her, she rendered and fulfilled with brass and with gold, as fully as he wished." Isolt, however, was anxious. "Lord God," she prayed, "guard and help me, lest my cousin prove unfaithful. I fear that if she carries on too long with this bed-game, or too ardently, she may come to like it and lie there until dawn, when we shall all become the laugh and talk of the world."

But no! Brangaene was loyal and true. When she had fully paid her due, she quietly quit the bed, and Isolt came and sat there in her stead. The king called for wine; for it was the custom of those days that when a man had lain with a virgin the two should drink together; and this, in fact, was the moment for which the potion had been prepared. Tristan arrived with a light and the wine; the King drank, so too the Queen. The two lay down, the light was quenched again, and Isolt then paid her own dues, no less nobly than the maid Brangaene, while the King remarked no difference, whether of brass or of gold, in the coin. One woman, to him, was as another.[140] And that was the tragic fault through which Mark too became entangled, along with the ensnared couple, in the toils of the magic net of the goddess Love.

Indifferent to the individuality of his queen, he had become infatuated with her beauty, unmarried heart to heart. "And alas!" the poet exclaims. "How many Marks and Isolts one sees today —if one may speak of such a thing—who are as blind or even blinder in their hearts and eyes! Desire is the force that, throughout the world and through all time, has deluded the clearest eyes. For whatever may be said of blindness, no blindness blinds as dangerously and frighteningly as desire and appetite. Deny it though we may, the old saying remains true: 'Of beauty, beware!' " [141]

And so it came to pass that when the actual personality of the female he had contracted for began to be talked about in court and his chief steward, Marjadoc (who had had that dream of the wild boar),* reported rumors and gossip, the noble and good King Mark, altogether committed to his social role and the associated courtly concepts of honor and a royal marriage, became deeply troubled, concerned, suspicious, and finally a very pattern of the enemy, lo gilos.—("O God! O God! This dawn, how quickly it comes!")—He began to set guards and traps, which, however, only sharpened the wits and occasions of the lovers.

And that [comments Gottfried] is the point against surveillance. Surveillance, so long as it is practiced, nourishes and produces nothing but briars and thorns. That is the maddening aggravation that ruins honor and reputation and has filched from many a woman the honor she would gladly have held on to, had she only been properly treated. But when she is badly treated, honor and her spirits equally deteriorate, so that surveillance actually reverses their condition. And after all, no matter what one may do, surveillance is wasted on a woman. For no man can keep watch on a wicked one, whereas a good one should not be watched: she will keep watch on herself, as they say. And if, for all that, a man sets watch upon her, what he will earn will be her hate. He will be the ruin of his wife, in both her life and her reputation; and most likely to such a degree that she will never recover sufficiently not to have clinging to her, ever after, something of what her hedge of thorns will have borne. . . . Accordingly, the wise man, or whoever would grant to woman her honor, should turn no other watch upon her virtue, in lieu of her own good will, beyond counsel, instruction, tenderness, and kindness. With these he shall be her guard—and, moreover, let him know this for the truth: he will never keep better guard.[142]

In the case of poor Mark, as things went on, his eyes, on watch, finally told him all. His traps had all been outwitted; his spies and informers too. But his own eyes, ever watchful, read the truth many times in the meetings of the lovers' eyes, and the pain to his heart was great. In this blinding sorrow, tortured and at wits' end, he sent for the two before the court and, exposing his heart completely before all, sent them off. "My nephew Tristan,

* Supra, pp. 127–28.

my wife Isolt," he said to them, "you two are too dear to me
(loth as I am to admit it) for me to have you put to death, or to
do you any other hurt. However, since I now can see it in you
both, that, despite my every wish, you love and have always loved
each other more than me, then go, remain together as you will:
have no further fear of me. Since your love is so great, I shall not,
from this time forth, trouble or oppress you in any of your affairs.
Take each other by the hand and depart from this court and land.
For if I am to be wronged by you, I prefer not to see or hear of
it. . . . For a king to collaborate knowingly in such a love intrigue would be degrading. So go, both of you, in God's care! Go
love and live as you please! Our fellowship is ended, here and
now." [143]

OF HONOR AND LOVE

There followed the "forest years" in the lovers' cave, *la fossiure a
la gent amant:* the sanctuary of that crystalline bed where the
truth beyond the laws of this world is consummated in eternity. In
time, however, time caught up on them. For on a day when there
was heard a sound of horns and hounds floating distant through
the wilderness (we have come to the end of Wagner's Act II; with,
however, a notable difference), the lovers suspected the echos to
be of a party from the palace, and that night, lest they should be
chanced upon, slept apart on the crystalline bed with Tristan's
sword between—which was a violation of love's law, in the name of
honor, that marked the beginning of their end. For the hounds and
horns were indeed of Mark. He was riding with his chief
huntsman, pursuing a strange beast, a white hart with a mane like
that of a horse, strong and big, its antlers but recently shed, and
with the mere pedicles in their place. The quarry had disappeared.
Mark and his huntsman were astray. And by singular chance they
reached the lovers' cave, its secure bronze door, and, above, those
tiny windows, through one of which the king peered and
with a shock recognized his nephew and wife asleep, wide apart,
with Tristan's sword between.

"Merciful Lord of Hosts, what can this mean?" he thought;
and his doubts again assailed him: "Are they guilty?" "Assuredly,
yes!" "Are they guilty?" "Clearly, no!" And as he gazed down on
the loveliness of his lost wife's radiant face, over which love's

deception had spread her best cosmetic, golden denial, Love the Reconciler crept into his heart. Her beauty had never seemed to him more desirable. A beam fell through the window on her features; the one sunlight and the other were an ecstasy to see. To protect her from the rays, Mark gathered leaves, flowers, and grass, and with these tenderly blocked the window, then, committing her to God, turned away in tears.

Convinced and reconciled, he presently recalled the pair to court, where, however, he soon discovered them in bed together, and Tristan had to flee in fear to Brittany, alone. "To whatever regions of the earth you may fare," Isolt said to him when they parted, "take care of yourself: you are my body. If I, your body, am orphaned of you, I shall have perished. And I shall watchfully take care of myself, your body, for your sake, not mine. For you and your life—well I know—reside in me: we are one body and one life." [144]

THE SECOND ISOLT

In Brittany, as the world knows, Tristan married a second Isolt, Isolt of the White Hands, for the love, purely and merely, of her name; and at this point Gottfried's text breaks off. There is some question as to why. In the year 1212 there took place in Strassburg the first trial of heretics in that city, and that is approximately the year of our poet's death. Was he condemned? If so, there would almost surely have been some record of the execution. Did he take his own life, in despair of his world or in fear? Unlikely. He may have broken, however, psychologically, of the tensions, evident throughout his work, between the values of his two worlds, of his goddess Love and the Christian God.[145] In any case, for the terminal episodes of the legend we must turn to Gottfried's source, Thomas of Britain.

Briefly: In his homeland, Brittany, assisting a knight named (significantly) Dwarf Tristan to recover his abducted wife, Tristan was wounded by a poisoned spear thrust through his loins: and with that we are taken back to Part I; for, as in a symphony, all the early motives are to return now, transfigured and transposed. The wielder of the poisoned spear, Estult l'Orgillus of Castle Fer, was a dragon-knight with seven heads so to say, for he had six brothers. All seven were slain; but so, too, was Dwarf Tristan. And the great Tristan could be healed by none save Queen Isolt the

Fair, of King Mark—to fetch whom, the brother of Tristan's second Isolt set sail. And it was agreed that if Isolt responded to the call he would return with a white sail; if not, a black.

THE LOVE-DEATH

Figure 37 is of Isolt on her way. But, as in the classical legend of the return of Theseus to Athens after his battle with the Mino-

Figure 37. The Voyage of Isolt to Tristan

taur, there was a mix-up in the matter of the sails. The second Isolt was jealous, for, though married, she was still a virgin. She loved no one in the world but Tristan, whose heart was with Isolt of Ireland; while Mark had the body of that Isolt and delight of her as he liked, whose heart, however, was with Tristan. As the poet Thomas observes: "Between these four is a love strange indeed." [146]

Tristan's wife, no wife, was sitting at his bedside, gazing out to sea.

"My love," she said, "I see your ship. God grant it brings you comfort of heart."

"My love," he answered, "are you sure it is ours? Now tell me, what is the sail?"

"The sail," she answered, "is black."

He turned to the wall and sighed. "Isolt, my love, God save us." Three times he repeated, "Isolt, my love," and died.

The ship came to port and the sail was white.

And so there came to pass that death of both, of which Brangaene had foretold: Tristan of love; Isolt of pity. She stretched her body to his, laid her mouth to his, yielded her spirit, and expired. Which is the death that Wagner rendered as the love-death— with an Oriental turn, however, borrowed from Schopenhauer, of the transcendence of duality in extinction.

In the opera the entire theme of the marriage with the second Isolt is omitted, the mortal wound being delivered at the end of the second act by a traitorous friend at court, Melot, who in the older texts was but a malicious dwarf, tale-bearer to the King. With Mark, Melot rushes in upon the lovers, Tristan is wounded, and the act ends.

Act III, then, is in Brittany, without the second Isolt. Tristan's loyal servant, Kurvenal, has transported him for safety to his own land, his birthplace, where Isolde's arrival is expected; and the wounded lover, stirring from deep coma, sings of his longing for the kingdom of night, from which only his yearning to behold once again his sun, Isolde, has returned him to this world. The pipe of Tristan's shepherd sounds the "Sad Shepherd's Tune," *Oed' und leer das Meer,* "Waste and empty the sea"; but suddenly changes to the "Happy Shepherd's Tune": for the ship has appeared, its flag joyous at the masthead. There is no switching here of sails. "She is aboard!" sings out Kurvenal. "She is waving!" "She lives!" cries Tristan. "Life holds me still in its web!" And when his guardian, Kurvenal, has left the stage to welcome the queen, the lover, deliriously rising from his couch, shouting, tears off his bandages to greet life, and, when Isolde enters, dies in her embrace—as Wagner himself had wished to die in Mathilde's arms.

Forthwith Melot, Mark, and Brangaene appear, the maid having told the King at last the secret of the potion. He has come to forgive—too late. There emerge from the orchestra the strains of Isolde's "Death for Love Motive," and the sweetly tortured final aria begins, of love's transfiguration, parting, and exultation in the sounding sea of an eternal night.

PHOENIX FIRE

✦✦✦

I. O Truly Blessed Night!

James Joyce develops the Tristan theme anew, with all its "equals of opposites," throughout the ever-revolving labyrinth of his dream-book, *Finnegans Wake*. His first paragraph opens with the words, "Sir Tristram, violer d'amores. . . ," and Chapelizod, the legendary birthplace of Isolt, on the bank of the river Liffey, beside Dublin's Phoenix Park, is the chief scene of its dream events. The guilt-laden sleeper, through whose whiskey-soaked interior landscape we are following the lead and lectures of an erudite tourist guide, "of the every-tale-a-treat-in-itself variety" [1] (as Dante followed the lead and lectures of Virgil through his own sin-laden, visionary Purgatory), is a late-middle-aged burly Chapelizod tavern-keeper named Humphrey Chimpden Earwicker, about whom an embarrassing Peeping Tom scandal has recently been bruited, published abroad, and even balladized within the walls of his own hospitable premises. The incident—if there really was one, for we are never made quite sure—was rumored to have occurred in Phoenix Park (or was it Eden? was it Calvary?), possibly at night, and to have involved, besides the dreamer, two servant girls in the bushes and three drunken British-soldier witnesses. Four old tavern cronies, who are confused with the four Evangelists, four quarters of the world, and four posts of the bed, rehearse the legend variously, while a zodiac of inebriate customers toss it about, refreshed by more and more of their own confused elucidations. In his anguished, self-vindicatory yet -incriminating nightmare, the dreamer is identified with (among numerous other characters,

including all Three-in-One of the Trinity) Sir Tristram, but at the
same time King Mark. His wife, sleeping at his side, is the first
Isolt; his daughter, upstairs, the second; each confused with the
other, and the two with the maids in the park. His pair of incompatible sons, who appear respectively as the popular and unpop-
ular sides of his own uncertain image, bear his Tristan-dream into
the future by pressing himself, as Mark, into the past, and running
off with both Isolts, while his raucous tavern population are the
gossip-mongers in King Mark's troubled castle of Tintagel, or, as
the name here appears, "Tintangle." [2] In the murky midst of all
of which, an unidentified harsh voice rasps out the following rude
rann:

—*Three quarks for Muster Mark!*
Sure he hasn't got much of a bark
And sure any he has it's all beside the mark.
But O, Wreneagle Almighty, wouldn't un be a sky of a lark
To see that old buzzard whooping about for uns shirt in the dark
And he hunting round for uns speckled trousers around by
   Palmerstown Park?
Hohoho, moulty Mark!
You're the rummest old rooster ever flopped out of a Noah's ark
And you think you're cock of the wark.
Fowls, up! Tristy's the spry young spark
That'll tread her and wed her and bed her and red her
Without ever winking the tail of a feather
And that's how that chap's going to make his money and mark! [3]

The nightmare-language of this intentionally irritating, infinitely
fascinating, wise yet imbecile Book of the Opening of the Eyes to
Night—or, as we read, "Of the Two Ways of Opening the
Mouth" [4]—where every character is its own opposite and all together make one, is as difficult to reduce to wake-a-day sense as is
the phantasmagoria of dream; for as to meaning it is enigmatic,
yet of many meanings at once. "The proteiform graph itself," we
are truly told, "is a polyhedron of scripture." And yet, "under
closed eyes," we are advised, "the traits featuring the *chiaroscuro*
coalesce, their contrarities eliminated, in one stable somebody." [5]
And that One is, of course, the troubled dreamer himself, whose
initials, H. C. E., are to be read allegorically as "Here Comes
Everybody"; [6] that is to say, as archetypal of us all: inasmuch as

at the root of his anguish, as of our own, there lurks that dual
image of the god in whose form mankind (according to the
the Good Book) was created. For "God created man," we
are instructed, "in his own image, in the image of God he created
him; male and female he created them." [7] So that neither he
alone, "this upright one," the dreamer in his bed of tares, nor that
other alone, beside him in the bed, "that noughty besighed him
zeroine," [8] can be taken to represent the All in all of us; but the
two are that All together: H. C. E. and his nightmare A. L. P., or,
as Gottfried told:

> A man, a woman; a woman, a man:
> Tristan Isolt; Isolt Tristan.

"We read their life, we read their death, and to us it is sweet as
bread." *

The moral of it all is signaled by Joyce in a tantalizing number
clue that keeps turning up, throughout his work, in all sorts of
transformations: as a date, 1132 A.D.; a paragraph in a legal code,
"Subsec. 32, section 11"; an interval of time, "from eleven thirty
to two in the afternoon"; a musical composition, "Opus Elf,
Thortytoe"; an address, 32 West 11 Street; the number of a patent, 1132; [9] and so forth. But now, 32 (as Leopold Bloom was
given to musing in the course of his ramblings through *Ulysses*) is
the number of feet things fall "per sec. per sec.," the number,
therefore, of the Fall; whereas 11 is the number of the renewal of
the decade, and so, of Restoration. [10] Decoded thus, the number
implies a mythic theme of the conjoined Tree of Eden and Tree
of Calvary, Fall-Redemption, Death-Resurrection, Wake of the
Dead and Wake of Awakening, which is the leading theme of the
nightmare *Finnegans Wake*.

However, to find a clear and concise, unobfuscated verbaliza-
tion of the moral theology of this number-theme, the reader must
chance upon it in an Easter-egg cache outside the book altogether, namely in Paul's Epistle to the Romans, Chapter 11,
Verse 32, which reads: *"For God has consigned all men to dis-*
obedience that he may have mercy upon all." And this, furthermore, is the good news proclaimed in Saint Augustine's
famous oxymoron, which is also echoed throughout the *Wake:*

* Supra, p. 42.

O felix culpa! "O happy fault!"—the phrase of hope that is annually repeated by the priestly celebrant of the Roman Catholic ritual of the blessing of the Paschal candle on Holy Saturday: the dark, dark night of Christ's body lying in the tomb, between Good Friday and Easter Sunday.

The tabernacle of the church is open—empty—to symbolize the awesome mystery of God's death and descent into Hell. "This," prays the priestly celebrant, "is the night which at this time throughout the world restores to grace and unites in sanctity those that believe in Christ, and are separated from the vices of the world and the darkness of sinners. *This is the night in which, destroying the bonds of death, Christ arose victorious from the grave.* For it would have profited us nothing to have been born, unless redemption had also been bestowed upon us. O wonderful condescension of Thy mercy toward us! O inestimable affection of charity: that Thou mightest redeem a slave, Thou didst deliver up Thy Son! O truly needful sin of Adam, which was blotted out by the death of Christ! O happy fault [*O felix culpa*], which deserved to possess such and so great a Redeemer! *O truly blessed night, which alone deserved to know the time and hour in which Christ rose again from the grave!* This is the night of which it is written: And the night shall be as light as the day; and the night is my light in my enjoyments." [11]

"Poor Felix Culapert!" comments a disembodied voice on one of the airwaves of the nightmare of the sinner of Phoenix Park.[12] As the First Adam he falls and takes the world with him, but as the Second wakes with us all, and the two Adams are the same. They are the one multicolored soul-bird, namely, the Phoenix of "Felix Park" (Eden-Calvary), which resurrects of itself—"when the fiery bird disembers" [13]—from the ash of its self-immolation.

But between Joyce's and the Roman Catholic clergy's ways of interpreting Christian symbols there is a world of difference. The artist reads them in the universally known old Greco-Roman, Celto-Germanic, Hindu-Buddhist-Taoist, Neoplatonic way, as referring to an experience of the mystery beyond theology that is immanent in all things, including gods, demons, and flies. The priests, on the other hand, are insisting on the absolute finality of their Old Testament concept of a personal creator God "out there," who, though omnipresent, omniscient, and omni-everything-else, is ontologically distinct from the living substance of his world—and a ponderously humorless, revengefully self-centered, cruel old Nobodaddy, to boot. When, in *Ulysses,* toward the end of the Walpurgis Night of the brothel scene (*O felix culpa!*), THE END OF THE WORLD arrives with a Scotch accent and THE VOICE OF ELIJAH with an American, the latter, in the manner of a hell-and-damnation revivalist, calls upon the trio of prostitutes (Three Graces in the Abyss) * and their trinity of companions, naming them "Florry Christ, Stephen Christ, Zoe Christ, Bloom Christ, Kitty Christ, Lynch Christ," and then hollers apocalyptically: "It's up to you to sense that cosmic force. . . . You have something within, the higher self. . . . Are you all in this vibration? I say you are. You once nobble that, congregation, and a buck joy ride becomes a back number." [14]

Let us recall at this point the words reported of Jesus in the Gnostic Thomas Gospel: "I am the All, the All came forth from Me and the All attained to Me. Cleave a piece of wood, I am there; lift up the stone and you will find Me there"; [15] and add to these the words of Krishna in the Indian *Bhagavad Gītā:* "I am the origin of all; from me all things proceed. . . . I am the Self, established in the hearts of all beings, their beginning, middle, and end. . . . I am the gambling of cheats. I am the vigor of the strong. I am victory. I am effort. I am the principle of harmony in the good." [16]

In the brothel scene of *Ulysses,* after ELIJAH has delivered his message and confessions have been heard, there appears in the cone of a searchlight the bearded figure of the old Irish sea-god Manannan Mac Lir—enjoyer of a good laugh †—slowly rising, chin on knees, from behind a coalscuttle. A cold seawind blows from his druid mantle. About his head writhe eels and elvers. He is encrusted with weeds and shells. His right hand holds a bicycle pump. (Think of *pneuma, spiritus,* air, the breath of life.) His left hand grasps a hugh crayfish by its two talons. (Cancer, "the Crab," sign of the summer solstice, decline, disintegration, death.)

MANANAUN MAC LIR
(*With a voice of waves.*) Aum! Hek! Wal! Ak! Lub! Mor! Ma! White Yoghin of the gods. Occult pimander of Hermes Tris-

---

* Compare supra, Figure 13 (p. 100): Surda Thalia.
† Compare supra, pp. 200–201, "O'Donnell's kern."

megistos. (*With a voice of whistling seawind.*) Punarjanam pat-sypunjaub! I won't have my leg pulled. It has been said by one: beware the left, the cult of Shakti. (*With a cry of stormbirds.*) Shakti, Shiva! Dark hidden Father! (*He smites with his bicycle pump the crayfish in his left hand. On its cooperative dial glow the twelve signs of the zodiac. He wails with the vehemence of the ocean.*) Aum! Baum! Pyjaum! I am the light of the homestead. I am the dreamery creamery butter.[17] *

We are on the way here, full steam, to the vision of *Finnegans Wake,* where the dark hidden Father and his Shakti are indeed to come alive again by virtue of the magic of the left-hand way. We are on the dangerous path, that is to say, to the inward dark-forest sanctuary of the bed, *la fossiure a la gent amant,* the marriage and dream bed, which is in every home, every heart, and which Joyce, like Gottfried, represents as the altar and cross of the consummate initiation.

II. The Left-Hand Way

Figure 38 is from an early sixteenth-century alchemical text, the *Rosarium philosophorum,* "Rose Garden of the Philosophers," in which the art of distilling spirit from nature is taught in metaphorical terms that are intentionally misleading. For, as the text be-

---

* The name of the sea-god Manannan Mac Lir is here transformed to suggest both the Sanskrit holy syllable AUM and the Irish word *aun,* meaning "one." The seven exclamations imitate the mystic mantra syllables of Indo-Buddhist Tantric meditation. *Aum* is the holy sound supreme. *Hek* appears in *Finnegans Wake* (e.g. p. 420, lines 17 and 18) as a designation of H.C.E. *Wal* suggests the "Wall" of the Fall in *Finnegans Wake* and *Ak* the sound of its crash, God's voice in thunder, the end of the show, and the beginning of rumor (ibid., p. 44, line 20; p. 65, line 34). *Lub* in *Finnegans Wake* is associated with "love, libido," also, "lubber," "lubricity," etc. *Mor,* the Irish word meaning "old," suggesting French *mort* and English "more," is played upon throughout the *Wake* in numerous senses; and finally, *Ma* (Sanskrit *mā,* "to measure forth") suggesting Ma, "Mother," is the verbal root of the word *māyā,* which signifies the force that creates the world illusion. *Punarjanam:* Sanskrit *punar-janman,* means "rebirth, regeneration." *Shakti:* Sanskrit *śakti,* is the active spiritual power of a god or person, personified in his consort. For Shakti and for the "left-hand path," see *Oriental Mythology,* pp. 343–64. For the sense of the last two sentences, i.e., "I am the fire of the altar and the oblation sacrificed in the fire," see *Bhagavad Gītā* 9:16: "I am the ritual, I am the act of worship, I am the food to be offered, I am the sacred herbs, I am the chanted hymn, I am the melted butter, I am the fire, I am the pouring of the oblation."

PHILOSOPHORVM.

Nota bene: In arte noſtri magiſterij nihil eſt *Secretum* celatū à Philoſophis excepto ſecreto artis, quod *artis* non licet cuiquam reuelare, quod ſi fieret ille ma ledicerctur , & indignationem domini incur- reret, & apoplexia moreretur. ✠ Quare om- nis error in arte exiſtit , ex eo, quod debitam
C ij

Figure 38. Solar King and Lunar Queen

neath the picture states, "Mark well: in the art of our magiste- rium nothing is concealed by the philosophers except the secret of the art, which may not be revealed to all and sundry. For were that to happen, that man would be accursed; he would incur the wrath of God and perish of the apoplexy. Wherefore all error in the art arises, namely, because men do not begin with the proper substance." And on a later page: "So I have not declared all that appears and is necessary in this work, because there are things of

which a man may not speak. . . . Such matters must be trans-
mitted in mystical terms, like poetry employing fables and para-
bles." [18]

Now Christ himself, it can be recalled, issued a like warning to
those who would speak of spiritual things: "Do not give dogs
what is holy; and do not throw your pearls before swine, lest they
trample them underfoot and turn to attack you." [19] And again:
"To you," he said to his disciples, "it has been given to know the
secrets of the kindgom of God; but for others they are in para-
bles, so that seeing they may not see, and hearing they may not
understand." [20]

James Joyce's way of covering while uncovering his tracks
may not then, after all, have been, as many critics have held,
symptomatic of some bizarre psychological malfunction; for
he too, "forging in the smithy of his soul the uncreated conscience
of his race" (*A Portrait of the Artist as a Young Man,* last
lines), was at work in a zone to which tracks do not lead,
only a spiritual leap. The old Arabian master alchemist Muham-
mad ibn Umail at-Tamimi (c. 900–960)—who was known in
Europe as "Senior" and whose "Book of the Silvery Water
and Starry Earth" was translated into Latin in the poet Gottfried's
lifetime—describes the end product of his mystic art as "that stone,
which he that knoweth layeth upon his eyes, and he that knoweth
it not, casteth upon a dunghill." [21] Accordingly, in *Finnegans
Wake,* it was from a dunghill that a certain "lookmelittle likeme-
long hen," named Belinda of the Dorans, scratched up "a
goodishsized sheet of letterpaper," which on "exagmination"
proved to be something, indeed, to lay upon the eyes. And the
sixteenth-century Flemish alchemist Theobald de Hoghelande
might have been describing Joyce's handling of this arcanum
when he wrote: "This science transmits its work by mixing the
false with the true and the true with the false, sometimes very briefly,
at other times in a most prolix manner, without order and
quite often in the reverse order; and it endeavors to transmit the
work obscurely, and to hide it as much as possible." [22] For, as
stated by another late sixteenth-century master, "secrets that are
published become cheap." [23]

And so, with sharpened eyes returning to our picture, we now
note that the solar king and lunar queen have joined not their right

hands but their left. The rose garden of the philosophers, then, is
to be entered by the left-hand path.

"For this work," the text to the figure explains, "you should
employ venerable Nature, because from her and through her and
in her is our art born and in naught else: and so our magisterium
is the work of Nature and not of the worker."

Now it was exactly this idea of an approach to spirit through
nature that was the capital heresy of that bold young Dominican
monk (contemporary approximately with the author of the *Rosarium*) whose name, in various transformations, appears, disappears, and reappears through every episode of *Finnegans
Wake:* the same who, on the morning of February 16, 1600 A.D.,
in the Campo di Fiori in Rome, was burned alive at the stake, at
the age of fifty-two, for having cast his pearls before Clement
VIII and the learned doctors of the Roman Holy Office of the Inquisition.

"All of God is in all things (although not totally, but in some
more abundantly and in others less)," Giordano Bruno of Nola
had written, too clearly, in his reprobated work, *The Expulsion of
the Triumphant Beast.* "Because just as Divinity descends, in a
certain manner, to the extent that one communicates with Nature,
so one ascends to Divinity through Nature, as by means of a life
resplendent in natural things one rises to the life that presides
over them." [24]

An ordained Dominican, yet to the root of his being an incorrigible heretic, in flight from city to city before the various packs of
God's hounds—Naples, Rome, Venice, Padua, Brescia, Bergamo,
Milan, Chambéry, Geneva, Toulouse, Paris, Oxford, London,
Paris again, then Marburg, Wittenberg, Prague, Helmstadt, Frankfurt-am-Main, Zurich, and (alas!) Venice again (Office of the Inquisition), on to Rome (dungeons of the Inquisition for eight
years and finally, infallibly, the stake)—now in clerical, now in
secular garb, now here, more often there, unwittingly insulting his
friends, intentionally challenging his persecutors, believed by
some to have become a Calvinist, yet driven by that pack from
Geneva, he was himself an incarnation of that "coincidence of
opposites" of which he eloquently wrote, and, in a truly Joycean
way, his own worst enemy. "A Daedalus," he called himself, "as
regards the habits of the intellect." [25] And when his condemna-

tion was read to him, rising before the Triumphant Beast, "You pronounce sentence upon me perhaps with a greater fear," he said, "than that with which I receive it." [26] He was incinerated, and his books as well, but has reappeared in the *Wake:* as Bruno, Bruin, Mr. Brown, the Nolan, Nayman of Noland, the Dublin booksellers Browne and Nolan, Nolans Brumans, et cetera; and, as Professor William Tindall of Columbia University seems to have been the first to have recognized, the names Tristopher and Hilary, which are attributed to the Chapelizod tavernkeeper's two incompatible sons in one of the episodes of his dream,[27] derive from Giordano Bruno's motto on the title page of his play *Il Candelaio* ("The Candle-Maker"), to wit: *In tristitia hilaris hilaritate tristis,* "In sorrow, cheer, in cheer, sorrow," which is a perfect match to Gottfried's designation of the noble heart.

The left-hand path is the way, then, of a passage by way of the senses—the eyes, the heart and spontaneity of the body—to a realization and manifestation "at the still point of the turning world," in act and experience on earth, of the radiance, harmony, bounty, and joy of nature at the summit of Mount Helicon, where the lyre of Apollo sounds, the Graces dance in tripody, and the golden rose unfolds. In T. S. Eliot's words in "Burnt Norton":

> . . . . Neither flesh nor fleshless;
> Neither from nor towards; at the still point, there the dance is,
> But neither arrest nor movement. And do not call it fixity,
> Where past and future are gathered. Neither movement from nor
>   towards,
> Neither ascent nor decline. Except for the point, the still point,
> There would be no dance, there is only the dance.
> I can only say, *there* we have been: but I cannot say where.
> And I cannot say, how long, for that is to place it in time.[28]

The way of nature to the garden is not, as followers of the god divorced from nature have supposed, of an incline ever downward, of a mere crude physicality. The right hands, we note, of the solar king and lunar queen tender flowers, at the crossing of the stems of which a third flower intersects, carried by a dove descending from a star. The star is of six points, joined by three intersecting lines: three pairs of opposites. So also is the order of the flower stems, joining south and north, west and east, below and above, all together at the center: "the still point," here below in man's and woman's hands, as there above, celestially: as above, so below; as below, so above. Moreover, each flower stem has two blossoms: the one becomes two, and the two are one. We note, as well, that the entire composition is ordered to this theme: a line descending from the star bifurcates and continues in balanced parallels terminating at the sun and moon; the form as a whole suggests the seventh sign of the zodiac, Libra, which is entered by the sun at the autumnal equinox, the time of its downgoing into winter night. Astrologically defined, Libra is a masculine diurnal sign, movable, sanguine, equinoctial, cardinal, hot, and moist; western, of the airy triplicity, and the chief mansion of Venus. The dove is the symbolic bird of Venus-Aphrodite-Ishtar-Astarte-Isis-Minne-Amor; and we note that the artist, even with his clumsy hand, has contrived to suggest "the meeting of the eyes."

The left-hand path, as here conceived, is obviously *not* of the type of the early Christian Agape orgy or the Indian "bodice cult," * nor of the Valentine Clubs of fashionable twelfth-century Provence. For the work of the alchemist was intimately personal, and where it involved the cooperation of an actual woman in the mythic role of *regina, soror, filia mystica,* the relationship was necessarily, because of its psychological dimension, deeply personal and exclusive. Dr. C. G. Jung, who devoted some forty-odd years to a study of alchemical symbology, has demonstrated beyond question that in all its authentic practitioners, whether in Europe and the Near East or in the Far East, alchemy was as much an unconsciously psychological as consciously physical proto- or pseudo-science. In a manner broadly comparable to the relationship of a painter to the colors and materials of his palette and studio, the alchemist projected psychological associations, of which he was neither fully conscious nor in full control, into the metals, retorts, and other materials of his laboratory. The empty retort, like an empty stretch of canvas, was a vacuum for the reception of whatever demon within was pressing for manifestation without, and the work progressed through an interaction of impulse (spontaneity) and judgment (consideration) in relation to

* Supra, p. 166 and *Oriental Mythology,* p. 361.

the physical acts of mixing, heating, adding, subtracting, cooling, and observing metals. States Dr. Jung:

> The alchemical *opus* deals in the main, not just with alchemical experiments as such, but with something resembling psychic processes expressed in pseudo-chemical language. The ancients knew more or less what chemical processes were; therefore they must have known that the thing they practiced was, to say the least of it, no ordinary chemistry. That they realized the difference is shown even in the title of a treatise by (Pseudo-) Democritus, ascribed to the first century: τὰ φυσικὰ καὶ τὰ μυστικά (The Physical and the 'Philosophical'). And soon afterwards a wealth of evidence accumulates to show that in alchemy there are two—in our eyes—heterogeneous currents flowing side by side, which we simply cannot conceive as being compatible. Alchemy's *"tam ethice quam physice"* (ethical—i.e. psychological—as well as physical) is impenetrable to our logic. If the alchemist is admittedly using the chemical process only symbolically, then why does he work in a laboratory with crucibles and alembics? And if, as he constantly asserts, he is describing chemical processes, why distort them past recognition with his mythological symbolisms? [29]

In answering these questions, Dr. Jung quotes a number of texts describing in detail the actual work and meditations of seriously practicing alchemists, of which the latest in date is the following, from the *Abtala Jurain*, published 1732.

THE CREATION

Take of common rainwater a good quantity, at least ten quarts; preserve it well sealed in glass vessels for at least ten days, then it will deposit matter and feces on the bottom. Pour off the clear liquid and place in a wooden vessel that is fashioned round like a ball; cut it in the middle and fill the vessel a third full, and set it in the sun about midday in a secret or secluded spot.

When this has been done, take a drop of the consecrated red wine and let it fall into the water, and you will instantly perceive a fog and thick darkness on top of the water, such as also was at the first creation. Then put in two drops, and you will see the light coming forth from the darkness; whereupon little by little put in every half of each quarter hour first three, then four, then five, then six, drops, and no more, and you will see with your own eyes one thing after another appearing by and by on top of the water, how God created all things in six days, and how it all came to pass, and such secrets as are not to be spoken aloud and I also have not power to reveal. Fall on your knees before you undertake this operation. Let your eyes judge of it; for thus was the world created. Let all stand as it is, and in half an hour after it began it will disappear.

By this you will see clearly the secrets of God, that are at present hidden from you as from a child. You will understand what Moses has written concerning the creation; you will see what manner of body Adam and Eve had before and after the Fall, what the serpent was, what the tree, and what manner of fruits they ate; where and what Paradise is, and in what bodies the righteous shall be resurrected; not in this body that we have received from Adam, but in that which we attain through the Holy Ghost, namely in such a body as our Savior brought from Heaven.

A second experiment by the same anonymous author, no less remarkable, is reported in the following terms:

THE HEAVENS

You shall take seven pieces of metal, of each and every metal as they are named after the planets,* and shall stamp on each the character of the planet in the house of the same planet, and every piece shall be as large and thick as a rose noble.† But of Mercury only the fourth part of an ounce by weight and nothing stamped upon it.

Then put them after the order in which they stand in the heavens into a crucible, and make all windows fast in the chamber that it may be quite dark within; then melt them all together in the midst of the chamber and drop in seven drops of the blessed Stone; and forthwith a flame of fire will come out of the crucible and spread itself over the whole chamber (fear no harm), and will light up the whole chamber more brightly than sun and moon, and over your heads you shall behold the whole firmament as it is in the starry heavens above, and the planets shall hold to their appointed courses, as in the sky. Let it cease of itself, in a quarter of an hour everything will be in its own place.[30]

* These are, Mercury (Mercury), Copper (Venus), Silver (Moon), Gold (Sun), Iron (Mars), Tin (Jupiter), and Lead (Saturn). Supra, p. 103.
† An English coin of the fifteenth and sixteenth centuries.

And now, one more example: from the sixteenth-century Flemish master Theobald de Hoghelande.

They say also that different names are given to the Stone on account of the wonderful variety of figures that appear in the course of the work, inasmuch as colors often come forth at the same time, just as we sometimes imagine in the clouds or in the fire strange shapes of animals, reptiles, or trees. I found similar things in a fragment of a book ascribed to Moses: when the body is dissolved, it is there written, then will appear sometimes two branches, sometimes three or more, sometimes also the shapes of reptiles; on occasion it also seems as if a man with a head and all his limbs were seated upon a cathedra.[31]

"Hoghelande's remarks prove," comments Dr. Jung, "as do the two preceding texts, that during the practical work certain events of an hallucinatory or visionary nature were perceived, which cannot be anything but projections of unconscious contents. Hoghelande quotes Senior as saying that the 'vision' of the Hermetic vessel 'is more to be sought' than the 'scripture,'" where again, however, "it is not clear whether by 'scripture' is meant the traditional description of the vessel in the treatises of the masters, or the Holy Scripture."[32]

Figure 39 shows a pair of alchemists kneeling by their furnace

Figure 39. Alchemists at Their Furnace

and praying for God's blessing.[33] They are a man and a woman, and obviously actual persons, whereas the couple of Figure 38 are as obviously mythological. Between the two alchemists are the furnace, the vessels, and other materials of their ambiguous art, wherein the various transformations will occur to which the mythological names and interpretations are to be attached. That is to say, it will be in those vessels and materials that the solar king and lunar queen will be known to be reaching their left hands to each other, and the dove to be descending, as the metals and other materials—mercury, salt, sulphur, consecrated wine, rainwater, and what not—work upon each other, combine, separate, change color, et cetera. But, as we have seen, the alchemists will have to accompany these effects with appropriate sentiments and fantasizing meditations of their own, if the desired results are to be achieved. The fermentation, putrefaction, and sublimation of the metals will have to be matched by analogous motions in the conjoined, harmoniously cooperating hearts of the *artifex* and his *soror mystica,* the fundamental idea being that divinity is entrapped, as it were, in the gross physical matter of the bodies of men and women as well as in the elements of nature, and that in the laboratory of the alchemist the energies of this immanent spiritual presence are to be released. As Jung restates this basic idea:

> For the alchemist the one primarily in need of redemption is not man, but the deity who is lost and sleeping in matter. Only as a secondary consideration does he hope that some benefit may accrue to himself from the transformed substance as the panacea, the *medicina catholica,* just as it may to the imperfect bodies, the base or "sick" metals, etc. His attention is not directed to his own salvation through God's grace, but to the liberation of God from the darkness of matter. By applying himself to this miraculous work he benefits from its salutary effect, but only incidentally. He may approach the work as one in need of salvation, but he knows that his salvation depends on the success of the work, on whether he can free the divine soul. To this end he needs meditation, fasting, and prayer; more, he needs the help of the Holy Ghost as his πάρεδρος [ministering spirit]. Since it is not man but matter that must be redeemed, the spirit that manifests itself in the transformation is not the "Son of Man" but as Khunrath very properly puts it,[34] the *filius macrocosmi.* Therefore, what comes out of the transformation is not

Christ but an ineffable material being named the "stone," which displays the most paradoxical qualities apart from possessing *corpus, anima, spiritus,* and supernatural powers. One might be tempted to explain the symbolism of alchemical transformation as a parody of the Mass were it not pagan in origin and much older than the latter.

The substance that harbors the divine secret is everywhere, including the human body. It can be had for the asking and can be found anywhere, even in the most loathsome filth.[35]

Essentially, the idea is the same as that by which the obscene Love Feasts of the Phibionites and other deviant early Christian sects were inspired, against whom Paul, Tertullian, and numerous other preachers of the gospel were compelled to take corrective steps. There, however, the method by which the energy of the incarnate divine substance was to be released from its dual, male and female entrapment was as crassly physical as could be imagined, whereas here the main emphasis was to be—for the *human* participants—psychological. The *physical* aspect of the distillation and union of the male and female energies—the *coniugium, matrimonium, coitus,* or *coniunctio oppositorum,* as it was variously named—took place within the *vas Hermeticum,* the sealed hermetic retort, and whatever acts on the part of the *artifex* and his *soror* might have accompanied these developments were as between two intimately associated, emotionally interlocked, mutually respectful personalities—not comparable at all to the indiscriminate, anonymous Agape-in-the-dark of the earlier Christian redeemers of the Redeemer.

Yet there is enough theology in common between the two religious orders to make it perfectly evident that they are basically related. In the later, alchemical context the counterpart to the "divine child" that was occasionally born to practitioners of the Agape, and then ritually consumed,* was the mysterious hermaphroditic *lapis, rebis,* or "philosophers' stone," also known as tincture, elixir, vinegar, water, urine, dragon, serpent, *filius, puer,* and a multitude of other names. The mystic vessel, *vas Hermeticum,* represented in the various retorts within which the transmutations came to pass, was regarded with the utmost religious awe as a

---

* Supra, pp. 159–61 and 165–66.

virginal womb, fertilized by the spirit Mercurius, a veritable *vas mirabile,* and likened to (or even called) the Tree of the Fruit of Immortal Life and, in some of the later, fifteenth- and sixteenth-century texts, the Cross of Christ, or Mary's womb. As summarized in the words of Dr. Jung:

> It must be completely round, in imitation of the spherical cosmos, so that the influence of the stars may contribute to the success of the operation. It is a kind of matrix or uterus from which the *filius philosophorum,* the miraculous stone, is to be born. Hence it is required that the vessel be not only round but egg-shaped. One naturally thinks of this vessel as a sort of retort or flask; but one soon learns that this is an inadequate conception since the vessel is more a mystical idea, a true symbol like all the main ideas of alchemy. Thus we hear that the *vas* is the water or *aqua permanens,* which is none other than the Mercurius of the philosophers. But not only is it the water, it is also its opposite: fire.[36]

And finally, one complication more: since it is of the essence of this philosophy that divinity inheres in the lowliest as well as in the noblest things, one of the most striking traits of its literature is the frequent representation of its arcana in coarse and even revolting symbols. An eighth-century Arabic text of the Ommayad prince Kalid ibn Yazid, translated into Latin about the twelfth century as the *Liber secretorum alchemiae,* gives, for example, the following curious recipe: "Take a Corascene dog and an Armenian bitch, join them together, and they will beget a dog of celestial hue, and if ever he is thirsty, give him sea water to drink: for he will guard your friend, and he will guard you from your enemy, and he will help you wherever you may be, always being with you, in this world and the next." [37]

Now in the Tristan legend there is a little dog of this very kind that was sent by Tristan as a present to Isolt during one of their terms of separation, he having himself received it from a Welsh prince in gratitude for his killing of a giant, and the prince, in turn, having been given it as a token of love by a goddess of the fairy isle of Avalon. In our poet Gottfried's version:

> On a table before Tristan a purple cloth, noble, rich, rare, and wonderful, was spread and a little dog set upon it: a fairy thing,

as I have been told. . . . And its color was of such an amazingly cunning mixture that no one could rightly tell what the dog's color actually was. Its hair was of so many hues that when you looked at its chest you would have said it was whiter than snow; yet its flanks were greener than clover, one side redder than scarlet and the other more yellow than saffron; beneath it was like azure, while above there was such a beautiful blend that none of the colors stood out: it was neither green nor red, white nor black, neither yellow nor blue, and yet all these played a part in a silky opalescent brown. And when this marvelous little product of the isle of Avalon was viewed against the grain, no one, no matter how clever, could possibly tell its hue; for it was then of so many colors, and all in such bewilderment, that it seemed to be of none at all.

And around its little neck there went a chain of gold, on which there hung a bell, so sweet and clear that when it began to tinkle, Tristan, sorrowful as he was, sat there emptied and relieved of all the cares and anguish of his destiny, forgetful even of the suffering he was enduring for Isolt. . . . He reached carefully and stroked the tiny dog with his palms, and when he was fondling it so, he seemed to be touching the finest silk, it was everywhere so smooth. It neither growled nor barked; nor did it show any sign of viciousness, no matter what tricks one played with it. Moreover, it neither ate nor drank—or so, at least, the tale declares. But when it was carried off again, Tristan's sorrow and pain were back, as keen as ever.[38]

In *Ulysses,* Stephen Dedalus claps eyes on some such dog—or at least so it appears for a time, to his imagination. He is seated on a rock on Sandymount shore, at about the point where Tristan must have first touched foot to land; and he is gazing out beyond the white lines of the breakers to where a boat is rocking, waiting there for the body of a drowned man to rise. "Five fathoms out there," Stephen broods. "Full fathom five thy father lies." The problem he is bebrooding is the consubstantiality of the Father and the Son, whereby the Father is identified in his mind with the mystery of substance; the All in all of us: the same ubiquitous presence that in alchemical terms may be represented as the "pearl" or "treasure in the sea," or as the solar king (the Father) in the dark depths of the sea, as though dead, who yet lives and calls from the deep: "Whosoever will free me from the waters and lead me to dry land, him will I prosper with everlasting riches." [39]

"A corpse rising saltwhite from the undertow," Stephen broods, "bobbing landward. . . . Bag of corpsegas sopping in foul brine. A quiver of minnows, fat of a spongy titbit, flash through the slits of his unbuttoned trouser-fly. God becomes man becomes fish becomes barnacle goose becomes featherbed mountain. Dead breaths I living breathe, tread dead dust, devour a urinous offal from all dead. Hauled stark over the gunwale he breathes upward the stench of his green grave, his leprous nosehole snoring to the sun." [40]

Thus sitting, watching the boat out there, brooding on death, disintegration, life living on death, and the one substance in all, Stephen next remarks, way down the beach, a point, a live dog, approaching, running. "Lord," he thinks, "is he going to attack me?" Farther away, two figures, a man and woman, cocklepickers, are trudging with their wet bags.

Their dog [we read] ambled about a bank of dwindling sand, trotting, sniffing on all sides. Looking for something lost in a past life. Suddenly he made off like a bounding hare, ears flung back, chasing the shadow of a lowskimming gull. The man's shrieked whistle struck his limp ears. He turned, bounded back, came nearer, trotted on twinkling shanks. On a field tenney a buck, trippant, proper, unattired. At the lacefringe of the tide he halted with stiff forehoofs, seawardpointed ears. His snout lifted to bark at the wavenoise, herds of seamorse. They serpented toward his feet, curling, unfurling many crests, every ninth, breaking, plashing, from far, from farther out, waves and waves.

Cocklepickers. They waded a little way in the water and, stooping, soused their bags, and, lifting them again, waded out. The dog yelped running to them, reared up and pawed them, dropping on all fours, again reared up at them with mute bearish fawning. Unheeded he kept by them as they came towards the drier sand, a rag of wolf's tongue redpanting from his jaws. His speckled body ambled ahead of them and then loped off at a calf's gallop. The carcass [of a drowned dog] lay on his path. He stopped, sniffed, stalked round it, brother, nosing closer, went round it, sniffing rapidly like a dog all over the dead dog's bedraggled fell. Dogskull, dogsniff, eyes on the ground, moves to one great goal. Ah, poor dogsbody. Here lies poor dogsbody's body.*

—Tatters! Out of that, you mongrel.

The cry brought him skulking back to his master and a blunt bootless kick sent him unscathed across a spit of sand, crouched in flight. He slunk back in a curve. Doesn't see me. Along by the edge of the mole he lolloped, dawdled, smelt a rock and from under a cocked hindleg pissed against it. He trotted forward and, lifting his hindleg, pissed quickly short at an unsmelt rock. The simple pleasures of the poor. His hindpaws then scattered sand: then his forepaws dabbled and delved. Something he buried there, his grandmother. He rooted in the sand, dabbled, delving and stopped to listen to the air, scraped up the sand again with a fury of his claws, soon ceasing, a pard, a panther, got in spousebreach, vulturing the dead.[41]

T. S. Eliot in *The Waste Land* asks:

"That corpse you planted last year in your garden,
"Has it begun to sprout? Will it bloom this year?
"Or has the sudden frost disturbed its bed?
"Oh keep the Dog far hence, that's friend to men,
"Or with his nails he'll dig it up again!" [42]

It is amazing with what consistency the images return. The fairy dog from Avalon beyond the waves, where the wounded king reposes who will appear again, may not immediately suggest Tatters racing along the edge of a tide wherein a drowned man rests among fish and a fishing boat floats beyond the surge, waiting (compare Figure 6); however, the shape-shifting of this mongrel—now a bounding hare, now a twinkling buck, bearish, fawning, with a speckled body, a wolf's tongue, at a calf's gallop, and so on—is as various as the coloration of the other. His approach frightens Stephen, whereas Tristan, at the sight of the dog, is relieved of all sorrow and pain. These are opposite effects. However, a glance again at the dog Cerberus of Figure 13 will explain them. Joyce, on a later page,[43] holding his devil's mirror to nature, reveals the word "Dog" in reverse to be "God"; and the

---

* "Dogsbody" is one of Stephen's names for himself, his own unhealthy body.

same secret is suggested in Eliot's capitalization of the word. The downcoming and the upgoing are of the same dogsbody, God's Body; and whereas Stephen, holding to his ego at the bottom, is confronted by the face of mortal terror, Tristan, lost in Isolt, the Muses' care, is carried to the top.

"Full fathom five thy father lies," Stephen thinks, quoting Ariel's song in *The Tempest;* and Eliot, in *The Waste Land,* continues the quotation, commencing with a line from the "Sad Shepherd's Tune" of the last act of Wagner's *Tristan:* *

> *Öd' und leer das Meer.*
> Madame Sosostris, famous clairvoyante,
> Had a bad cold, nevertheless
> Is known to be the wisest woman in Europe,
> With a wicked pack of cards. Here, said she,
> Is your card, the drowned Phoenician Sailor,
> (Those are pearls that were his eyes. Look!) [44]

The wisest woman in Europe is Wagner's Earth Spirit of *The Ring of the Nibelungs:* the Eddic prophetess of the *Völuspó.*† In Eliot's poem, she continues:

> Here is Belladonna, the Lady of the Rocks,
> The lady of situations.
> Here is the man with three staves, and here the Wheel,
> And here is the one-eyed merchant, and this card,
> Which is blank, is something he carries on his back,
> Which I am forbidden to see. I do not find
> The Hanged Man. Fear death by water.
> I see crowds of people, walking round in a ring. [45]

The man with three staves we have met in O'Donnell's kern. The one-eyed merchant is Wotan—Hermes—the lord of initiations, roads, and merchants; the god self-crucified on the Cosmic Tree (Figure 9), which is what he carries on his back. "The Man with Three Staves," writes Eliot in a footnote, "I associate, quite arbitrarily, with the Fisher King himself," [46] pointing thus to the legend of the Grail, where indeed we are to encounter all these figures, again transformed.

* Supra, p. 255.
† Supra, pp. 121–22.

III. Puer Aeternus

Figure 40, from an undated manuscript in the British Museum, the "Cabala mineralis" of Rabbi Simeon ben Cantara,[47] shows a

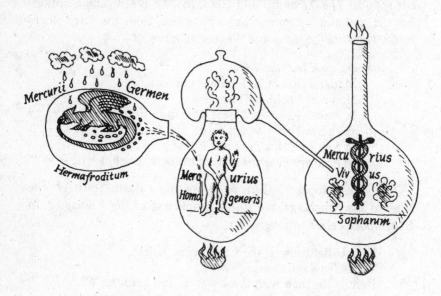

Figure 40. Homunculus in the Alchemical Vas

functioning assemblage of alchemical vessels. At the right is a perfectly spherical flask with a long phalloid neck, containing a substance labeled *Sophaium* (if I read aright), from which the fire beneath the flask is distilling a spiritual vapor called *Mercurius vivus*, symbolized by the caduceus of Mercury-Hermes. At the left is a womb-shaped vessel, containing a winged dragon labeled *Hermafroditum*, which is eating its own tail. It is bathed by a rain called Mercury's Sperm (*Mercurii Germen*), descending from three clouds, which as the name indicates, is a transformation into "living water" of the energy of the "living fire" flaming from the open mouth of the phalloid flask: three tongues of Mercurial fire there, three clouds of Mercurial water here. The biological reference, obviously, is to the fertilization of the womb.

The alchemical reference, however, is to a process known as *nigredo* (blackness) or *melanosis* (blackening), which is characterized by the decay or disintegration (*putrefactio, solutio*) of the materials in the retort and their reduction thus to the condition of elementary matter (*prima materia*); which is to say, the undifferentiated state of the primal energies or waters out of which the world first came into being.* For at the end of each cosmic aeon, the forms of all things must disintegrate and dissolve into this primal state before a new universe can arise; and analogously, when the womb is fertilized, the substance within it (which, according to archaic science, consists of undischarged menstrual blood) breaks down to be re-formed into the new life.

During the period between the end of one cycle and beginning of the next, this undifferentiated primal matter is a chaos, or *massa confusa*, in which the pairs of opposites—hot-cold, moist-dry, up-down, north-south, east-west, past-future, male-female, subject-object, et cetera—are not distinguished from each other. Hence the beast in the womb-shaped retort symbolic of this condition is a bird-serpent eating itself. "Before the sea was, and the lands, and the sky that hangs over all," states Ovid at the opening of the *Metamorphoses*, "the face of Nature showed alike in her whole round, which state have men called chaos: a rough, unordered mass of things, nothing at all save lifeless bulk and warring seeds of ill-matched elements heaped in one. . . . All objects were at odds, for within one body cold things strove with hot, and moist with dry, soft things with hard, things having weight with weightless things." [48] Presently, however, the rain of Mercurial Sperm starts in this *massa conjusa* a process of separating out (*divisio, separatio*) of the pairs of opposites. "God," as Ovid tells, "God—or kindlier Nature—composed this strife; for he rent asunder land from sky, and sea from land, and separated the ethereal heavens from the dense atmosphere. When thus he had released these elements and freed them from the blind heap of things, he set them each in its own place and bound them fast in harmony. The fiery weightless element that forms heaven's vault leaped up and made place for itself upon the topmost height. Next came the air in lightness and in place. The earth was heavier than these, and, drawing with it the grosser elements, sank to the bot-

---

* Compare, above, the rainwater experiment, pp. 268–69.

tom by its own weight. The streaming water took the last place of all, and held the solid land confined in its embrace." [49] *

In the *vas* at the left we see the beginning of this process. It is suggested by, on one hand, the black spots—"matter and feces" † —scattered around the dragon and, on the other hand, the vapor coursing rightward through the orifice of the *vas,* to play upon the eggshaped vertical vessel in the center. And within this central vessel is a boy, *Mercurius Homunculus,* in the attitude of the famous "Pissing Manikin" fountain of the city of Brussels.

For belief in the medicinal and other virtues of the urine, particularly of chaste boys, was an old, old story in archaic medicine. This wine is already recommended in the influential *Historia naturalis* of Pliny the Elder (23–79 A.D.).[50] A Byzantine physician, Alexander of Tralles, in the period of Justinian recommends it specifically against epilepsy and gout.[51] The Benedictine monk Theophilus (fl. 1100 A.D.), in his *Schedula diversarum artium,* suggests for the tempering of iron the use of the urine of a small redheaded boy,[52] while the Portuguese physician who became Pope John XXI (r. 1276–1277) asks, in a commentary on diet, why it is that human urine enriches vines.

Joyce, throughout both *Finnegans Wake* and *Ulysses,* plays repeatedly on this theme. We have had it already in the dog pissing on a rock. Together with his repeated references to dung, dungheaps, and the like, these allusions have won him the reputation, among clean-fingernailed Freudian critics, of having been afflicted with an infantile scatological fixation. However, his usage seems to me to accord perfectly with the alchemical inspiration and purpose of his art, which was to present—from the first page of *Portrait of the Artist as a Young Man,* through *Ulysses,* to *Finnegans Wake,* and on to the work that was never written—the process of a total transmutation of the whole world of human experience, from its earliest infant stage of "Once upon a time and a very good time it was there was a moocow coming down along the road and this moocow that was coming down along the road met a nicens little boy named baby tuckoo. . . ," [53] through the broadening and deepening, progressively clarified stages of a young male intellect in prime growth, until, in the episodes of the

---

* Compare Genesis 1.
† Cf. Supra, p. 268, beginning of the rainwater experiment.

first half of *Ulysses,* it has reached the impasse of one who "so loves his life" that he is in imminent danger of losing it.

Whereupon a prodigious crack of thunder resounds:—"A black crack of noise in the street, here, alack, bawled, back. Loud on left Thor thundered: in anger awful the hammerhurler" [54]—and the arrogant Stephen, who in spite of his flint-hard exterior is actually an interior jelly of phobias, sits frozen with unreasoned fear. "Came now the storm," we read, "that hist his heart." Immediately after which, the alchemical process commenced of a *nigredo* and *separatio* that was to culminate in the pandemonium of the night-scene of the brothel—beyond which the reader himself was to be sublimed in the *vas mirabile* of *Finnegans Wake,* to a state where all the foul "matter" of *Ulysses* would be seen undergoing transubstantiation, with Stephen's self-defensive ego reduced to the mere shadow of one of the two incompatible dreamsons of H.C.E.

In alchemy, not only were feces and urine commonly utilized in the *vas,* but the technical term *urina puerorum* was one of the usual appellations of the *aqua permanens,* the "water of life that ever endures." Here, in this vial, it is proceeding from the *puer aeternus* himself, who is an anthropomorphic counterpart of the *lapis* by which all things are turned into gold: however, as the old masters ever insisted, not the common gold, *aurum vulgi,* of the markets of this world, but the "gold of philosophy," *aurum philosophicum, aurum mercurialis, aurum nostrum, aurum volatile, aurum non vulgi:* gold, in other words, such as only art bestows on the mind through its transubstantiation of the matter of this world.

Beneath the vial containing Homunculus there is a flame by which the Mercurial urine is vaporized; and in a special retort above, this vapor is condensed and carried off to the flask at the right, from which our course began; so that there is a closed circuit here indicated, of the transformations of Mercurius: which again brings *Finnegans Wake* to mind; for there the last sentence of the book breaks off abruptly in a void—"A way a lone a last a loved a long the   "—leaving the reader the alternative either of resting there, with the ring broken, or of returning to the start of the book, where the rest of the sentence awaits, to pick us up and bear us on again, along the riverrun of this dream of Phoenix Park, for another round.

iv. Chaos

It is clear, then, that the solar king and lunar queen of Figure 38 are not the *artifex* and his *soror mystica,* but symbols of a process occurring (or supposed to be occurring) in the retorts. The alchemists themselves, meanwhile, as in Figure 39, are resting on the earth. Yet in their subtle spiritual parts they are indeed that royal pair, suspended celestially and precariously on the wings of a dove descending from a star. What star? Both of Venus and of Bethlehem. What dove? Mercurius Vivus and the Holy Ghost.

Figure 41 is again from the *Rosarium philosophorum,* continuing the left-hand-path adventure of the sulphur, salt, mercury, and other matters in the retort. This corresponds to a stage of the *nigredo,* the beginning of a dissolution, moving toward the primal state of chaos where all pairs of opposites coalesce; and in the human, psychological sphere it corresponds to the beginning of a regression—backward of civilization to the idyll of Paradise and, beyond that, the primal abyss.

In *Oriental Mythology* we have encountered a number of such disciplines of intentional regression; in India in Yoga and in China in the Taoist idea of a "return to the uncarved block":

> Blank as a piece of uncarved wood;
> Yet receptive as a hollow in the hills.
> Murky as a troubled stream—
> Which of you can assume such murkiness,
>   to become in the end still and clear?
> Which of you can make yourself inert, to
>   become in the end full of life and stir? [55]

We also recall the old Sumerian myth, and associated rites, of Inanna's descent to the netherworld to join her departed kingly brother-spouse: of how she passed the seven gates and at each was divested of a portion of her raiment, until

> Upon her entering the seventh gate,
> All the garments of her body were removed.

She was turned into a corpse:

> And the corpse was hung on a stake.

However:

> After three days and three nights had passed,
> Her messenger Ninshubur,
> Her messenger of favorable winds,
> Her carrier of supporting words,
> Filled the heaven with complaints for her,
> Cried for her in the assembly shrine,
> Rushed about for her in the house of the gods.

And Enki, the "Lord of the Waters of the Abyss," fashioned of dirt two sexless creatures, to one of which he gave the food of life, to the other the water of life; and to both he issued his commands:

> "Upon the corpse hung from a stake direct the fear of the rays of fire,
> Sixty times the food of life, sixty times the water of life, sprinkle upon it,
> Verily Inanna will arise."

And indeed Inanna ascended, alive again, from the netherworld.[56]

The Royal Tombs of Ur, with their impressive awesome evidences of entire courts following their kings and queens to the netherworld,[57] and in Egypt the terrible mansions of the dead, beneath desert sands, of literally hundreds who departed with their kings;[58] in China, the Shang tombs; the "death following" of Japan;[59] and finally the suttee rites of India and Vedic ritual of the queen's descent into the pit of the sacrificed solar stallion:[60] all these bear testimony to the antiquity of the idea of the two that in the pit of darkness become again one, for the renewal of the flow of the forms of time, which in their separateness hold fixed the life that in flow is the substance of all.

We have to this point the words of Christ: "Unless a grain of wheat falls into the earth and dies, it remains alone; but if it dies, it bears much fruit. He who loves his life loses it, and he who hates his life in this world will keep it for eternal life."[61]

Joyce, in the pages of *Ulysses,* depicts a world of rock-hard, separate men, moving dryly among and around each other. There is a drought in the land; the cattle are diseased; women are unable to give birth. Then, however, exactly in the middle of the book, that thunderclap resounds and a change begins. In Eliot's *Waste Land* the same thunder and promise of renewed life resounds in the last section: Part V, "What the Thunder Said." And remarkably, just as in *Ulysses* the Indian god and goddess Shiva and his Shakti, of the left, are announced, so here it is again from India the message comes:

> Ganga was sunken, and the limp leaves
> Waited for rain, while the black clouds
> Gathered far distant, over Himavant.
> The jungle crouched, humped in silence.
> Then spoke the thunder
> DA
> *Datta:* what have we given? [62]

The poet, in his interpretative notes, refers to a passage in the Brihadaranyaka Upanishad [63] where the god Prajapati, the "Father of Creatures," having been asked by his offspring, gods, men, and anti-gods, to communicate his ultimate word, spoke: "*Da.*" And in this sound the gods heard the word *damyata*, "restrain yourselves"; but the men heard *datta*, "give"; and the anti-gods, *dayadhvam*, "be compassionate." The passage of the Upanishad concludes: "And this same thing is repeated by the divine voice here, as thunder: *Da! Da! Da!* restrain yourselves, give, be compassionate. These three are what one should practice: self-control, giving, compassion."

And so, returning to the poem:

> DA
> *Datta:* what have we given?
> My friend, blood shaking my heart
> The awful daring of a moment's surrender
> Which an age of prudence can never retract
> By this, and this only, we have existed
> Which is not to be found in our obituaries
> Or in memories draped by the beneficent spider
> Or under seals broken by the lean solicitor
> In our empty rooms
> DA
> *Dayadhvam:* I have heard the key
> Turn in the door once and turn once only *

---

* Eliot gives as reference here, Dante's *Inferno* XXXIII. 46: the horrible story of the Guelph Count Ugolino della Gherardesca, who with his sons

> We think of the key, each in his prison
> Thinking of the key, each confirms a prison
> Only at nightfall, aethereal rumours
> Revive for a moment a broken Coriolanus
> DA
> *Damyata:* The boat responded
> Gaily, to the hand expert with sail and oar
> The sea was calm, your heart would have
>   responded
> Gaily, when invited, beating obedient
> To controlling hands.[64]

In the light of all these documents, the meaning of the narrative change from Figure 38 to 41 is manifest. The meeting of the eyes of Figure 38 having communicated its import to the noble, ready hearts (nobility being the import of the crowns), the left hands —of the heart side—reached spontaneously forward, and the right—of the spirit—crossed flowery tokens of the shared ideal to be realized: not the common, of desire, but the noble, of the self-loss of each in the identity that was theirs beyond space, beyond time, beyond what Joyce in *Ulysses* terms "the modality of the visible" and "modality of the audible," or again, "the diaphane." [65]

Having at first appeared to be separate from each other— strangers, "poles apart" (to continue with Joyce's terms) [66]—the two recognized their "consubstantiality" (again Joyce),[67] whereupon all artifice fell away. For as we have read in the *Rosarium:* in this art the substance to be employed is "not of the worker," i.e. of artifice, learning, civilization, but "venerable Nature: because from her and through her and in her is our art born and in naught else." †

In Figure 41 the protective, historically conditioned clothing of the couple has been removed. They have cast aside, that is to say, not only the social order of their time and place, but also all their personal, individually developed, self-protective artifices of decorum and disguise. And there is real danger here. For nature is not all beauty, nor all gentleness and goodness. Venus, the Moon, and

---

and grandsons was by his pretended friend, the Ghibelline Archbishop Ruggieri degli Ubaldini, treacherously locked in a tower and left there to starve to death: "And I heard the door of the horrible tower being locked." Eliot here adds the quotation from F. H. Bradley cited supra, pp. 89–90.

† Supra, p. 265.

ROSARIVM

corrũpitur, neço ex imperfecto penitus fecundũ
artem aliquid fieri poteſt. Ratio eſt quia ars prí
mas diſpoſitiones inducere non poteſt, ſed lapis
noſter eſt res media inter perfecta & imperfecta
corpora, & quod natura ipſa incepit hoc per ar
tem ad perfectionẽ deducitur. Si in ipſo Mercu
rio operari inceperis vbi natura reliquit imper
fectum, inuenies in eo perfectionẽ et gaudebis.

　　Perfectum non alteratur, ſed corrumpitur.
Sed imperfectum bene alteratur, ergo corrup
tio vnius eſt generatio alterius.

Speculum

Figure 41. The Mercurial Bath

Mercury, too, have their dark as well as luminous sides: so
have we all. Protection gone, each is vulnerable to the whole
dark, as well as to the luminous, aspect of the other. That is the
meaning of the appearance here of the abyssal, watery element.
"The earth-spirit Mercurius in his watery form," states Dr. Jung
in comment on this scene, "now begins to attack the royal pair
from *below,* just as he had previously descended from above in
the shape of the dove. The contact of the left hands in Figure 38
has evidently roused the spirit of the deep and called up a rush of
water." [68]

The scene suggests Tristan's perilous moment in the bath, when Isolt tore his disguise away and exposed him as he was: at which instant her own dangerous, murderous "other side" also came to view. Agamemnon, we have remembered, was murdered in his bath. The danger illustrated is of death by drowning ("Fear death by water," Eliot's seeress warned in *The Waste Land*): * drowning in the ocean storms of uncontrolled and uncontrollable crude emotion, or, in psychological terms, the engulfment of ego, the principle of individuality, in instinctual compulsions and associated fantasies welling from the couple's own unconscious share in "venerable Nature." For these can be aggressive, filthy, and cruel, as well as of love and erotic bliss. Jung compares the scene to the mythological "Night-Sea Journey" of the sun-god in the netherworld, where unknown powers are encountered and overcome.

All the adventures in the Tristan legend following its hero's infection with the poison of Queen Isolt, and culminating in his sharing of the potion with her daughter, match the symbolism of this scene: the foul and stinking wound (*putrefactio*), night-sea journey in the coracle, encounter with the dangerous yet healing mother and daughter in the Land below Waves, and the engagement there with a dragon; infection with its poison and then, through the magic of the Queen, the purgation of this putrefaction (*separatio, divisio elementorum*); the adventure of the bath; and finally, wonderfully, the potion. . . . If we compare, furthermore, the place and function of the harp represented in Figure 25, with the role and placement of the star, the dove, and the flowers in Figure 38, and equate the force of the love potion with that of the rising abyss of Figure 41, it will be evident enough that a significant relationship existed between the lines of symbolism of medieval alchemy and romance.

In the words of the *Rosarium,* "this stinking water contains everything required." [69] However, as the operations displayed in Figure 40 have already revealed, a clarification (*diviso* or *separatio*) must occur before the gold-producing *lapis* can be born; and this cannot be left to "venerable Nature," but is the work and virtue of this art. In the text above the picture it is stated that "art is unable to establish the primary arrangements." Art, that is to say, cannot begin its work *ab initio,* independently of nature.

* Supra, p. 277.

"Our stone is something," the text continues, "midway between perfected and unperfected bodies; and what Nature herself initiates, is by art carried to perfection. If you set to work on that state of Mercurius where Nature has left imperfection, you will arrive at its perfection and rejoice. What is perfect does not alter, but is destroyed. However, what is imperfect does indeed alter. Hence, the destruction of the one is the generation of the other."

We note in the picture that though the heavenly star has vanished, the dove and associated flowers still are present. However, the queen has passed her flower from her right hand to her left, thus breaking the circuit of the joined left palms; or rather, transforming it into a floral circuit. For the king is now, with his freed left hand, grasping the blossom of *her* stem, while she, conversely, with her freed right, is grasping the blossom of *his*. And each stem now bears but a single flower. That is to say, the queen herself has become the second flower on the king's stem and he the second on hers. Initially the floral signs of the one-that-is-two and two-that-are-one had represented no tangible realization; they were dreams in air, ideas: hence, properly of the right side only, spirit. However, with the meeting of the eyes and joining of the heart-side hands, the dreams began to come true. For each, the idea of the other blossom had found embodiment. And simultaneously the dove's second flower also vanished, to become the rising water of the abyss. The entire setting had dropped one degree: the star above was gone; the waters from beneath were in rising tide. The solar king and lunar queen were already on the left-hand path of descent, from the great above to the great below.

The left, the side of the heart, the shield side, has been symbolic, traditionally and everywhere, of feeling, mercy and love, vulnerability and defenselessness, the feminine virtues and dangers: mothering and seduction, the tidal powers of the moon and substances of the body, the rhythms of the seasons: gestation, birth, nourishment, and fosterage; yet equally malice and revenge, unreason, dark and terrible wrath, black magic, poisons, sorcery, and delusion; but also fair enchantment, beauty, rapture, and bliss. And the right, thereby, is of the male: action, weapons, hero-deeds, protection, brute force, and both cruel and benevolent justice; the masculine virtues and dangers: egoism and aggression, lucid luminous reason, sunlike creative power, but also cold unfeeling malice, abstract spirituality, blind courage, theoretical dedication, sober, unplayful moral force. "The body," states the *Rosarium,* "is Venus and feminine, the spirit is Mercurius and masculine." [70] But the soul is of the two: *Anima est Sol et Luna.* "The unrelated human being," states Jung, "lacks wholeness, for he can achieve wholeness only through the soul, and the soul cannot exist without its other side, which is always found in a 'You.' " [71]

The building of such a soul is what has here begun. From the queen's *left* hand, along her flower stem, the lunar current is passing to the left hand of the king, sublimated by the stem into a spiritual, not directly physical force, while reciprocally the spiritual solar current is passing from the king's *right* hand, along the stem of his flower, to the queen's right. Direct physical contact has been broken—at least above the water line, though apparently not below, where their feet seem to be touching—and the presence of the dove assures us still of the spiritual character of the relationship. The water presently will engulf the two, and the dove and flowers then will disappear; for they are indeed descending into the element of the left, the tides, the sea, and ultimately chaos. Yet for the present, and for a season of uncertain length, they are to remain, as here, in balanced "Platonic" interchange, each integrating reciprocally the spiritual force of the other.

And so it was too in the twelfth-century springtime of the châtelaines and their troubadours. *Merci* was not to be granted the *cavaliér servénte* until a sufficient season had prepared him for an experience of his lady's love, not as "vulgar" but as "noble gold." In relation to suitors of low degree, cultivated merely for their flattery, the ultimate boon granted, after a course even of some years, might be nothing more than the allowance of a kiss, once, upon the lady's neck; and there were also, as we have seen, stylish burlesques of the mysteries of *amor,* as well as cheatings, this way and that. When, however, the knight was of high degree, and his love, as represented in the paradigm of Lancelot and Guinevere, legitimate, full, and true, the quality of his lady's grace was in accord.

In Figure 42 the descent toward primal chaos has proceeded one stage further. Dove and flowers have disappeared. Even the manmade curbing of the well is gone. The scene suggests strongly

CONIVNCTIO SIVE
Coitus.

O Luna durch meyn vmbgeben/vnd ſuſſe mynne/
Wirſtu ſchön/ ſtarck/vnd gewaltig als ich byn·

O Sol/ du biſt vber alle liecht zu erkennen/
So bedarffſtu doch mein als der han der hennen·

ARISLEVS IN VISIONE.

Coniunge ergo filium tuum Gabricum dile-
ctiorem tibi in omnibus filijs tuis cum ſua ſorore
Beya

Figure 42. The Maternal Sea

the start of *Finnegans Wake:* "riverrun, past Eve and Adam's
. . ." where the word "riverrun" refers not only to Dublin's river
Anna Liffey, forever running through Phoenix Park to join her
father and lover, the sea, while she and her sinning spouse, the
city itself, support and feed the lives and dreams of their sinning
progeny; but also the river of the energy of life that is ever pouring through us all and all things, on into the void from which it
simultaneously rises: both of which streams are, in turn, identified
by Joyce with the Indian concept of the energy of the world

dream as Shakti-Maya, the great Goddess Mother of the universe, who is the ultimate life and substance of us all, and whose womb, wherein we dwell, is both unbounded space, out there, and the innermost, deepest ground of gently streaming peace, in here— where all her quarreling children come to rest in dreamless sleep. There is a passage in the Indian Brihadaranyaka Upanishad appropriate to this point:

> As a hawk, or other great bird, soaring in space, becomes weary and, bending its wings, glides down to its place of rest, even so does Purusha, the human spirit, glide to that state in sleep where no desire whatsoever stirs and no dream is seen. . . . And when it there feels itself to be a god as it were, a king as it were, thinking "I am this, I am all," that is its own best world. That, verily, is its form beyond desire, untroubled, and free of fear. As a man embraced fully by a loving woman knows no distinction of other and self, so too this human spirit, embraced fully by that wisdom of absolute being knows no distinction of other and self. That, verily, is its form wherein—desire attained, Self alone desired, desireless—sorrows end.[72]

> O Luna, folded in my sweet embrace/
> Be you as strong as I, as fair of face.
>
> O Sol, brightest of all lights, known to men/
> And yet you need me, as the cock the hen.

So, approximately, the little German poem beneath the scene of Figure 42.[73]

Dove, flowers, and the manmade curbing gone, enveloped in the ever-living waters of the timeless rapture of this wilderness, before heaven and earth were parted, and with the moon as well as sun shining full, the lunar queen, the solar king, and "venerable Nature" together have recomposed the image of the sixth day of Creation. However, the trend of their achievement is not forward in time, but back: they are riding the reversed stream, the leftward-running stream, and they have farther still to go. As the text of the *Rosarium* states in relation to this strange connubium: "Then Beya [the maternal sea] rose up over Gabricus and enclosed him in her womb, so that nothing more of him was to be seen. And she embraced Gabricus with so much love that she absorbed him completely into her own nature, and dissolved him into atoms." [74] There is a less gentle version of this event from another, and older alchemical text known as "The Tumult of Philosophers," the *Turba Philosophorum*,[75] as follows:

> The Philosophers have put to the death the woman who slays her husbands, for the body of that woman is full of weapons and poison. Let a grave be dug for that dragon, and let that woman be buried with him, he being chained fast to that woman; and the more he winds and coils himself about her, the more will he be cut to pieces by the female weapons which are fashioned in the body of the woman. And when he sees that he is mingled with the limbs of the woman, he will be certain of death, and will be changed wholly into blood. But when the Philosophers see him changed into blood, they leave him a few days in the sun, until his softness is consumed, and the blood dries, and they find that poison. What then appears is the hidden wind.[76]

Obviously, the reference here is to events like those of the *vas* at the left of our Figure 40. However, according to the notions of the alchemists themselves, those events in the *vas* recapitulated the processes by which the universe not only comes into being but repeatedly destroys itself and is renewed. They were as aware as Dr. Jung, though in a different way, of the psychological, theological, mystical, and biological, chemical, historical, and erotic implications of their operations.

In Figure 43, which is our last from this series, the two have indeed become one. Furthermore, that one is dead; the watery bed has become a sarcophagus.

> Here King and Queen are lying dead/
> In great distress the soul is sped.

So reads the first of a series of rhymes characterizing the stages of the *putrefactio* of this strange dual being in whom the shape first seen in the two-flowered stems of Figure 38 has become realized as of the king and queen themselves. The scene suggests the crystalline bed of the lovers' grotto in the wilderness of great danger, of the two whose heart was one; but also the androgyne at Station 11 of the classical mystery illustrated in the golden sacramental bowl of Figure 3—which series of initiations, viewed in the light of what we now have learned, shows how far we have come, and how far in this mystic round we have still to go.

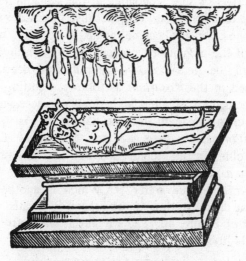

PHILOSOPHORVM

ABLVTIO VEL
Mundificatio

Hie felt der Tauw von Himmel herab/
Vnnd wascht den schwartzen leyb im grab ab-

K ij

Figure 43. Mercurial Rain

Biologically this dual form can be compared to that stage in the fertilization of an egg cell when the nuclear contents of the egg and sperm commingle to constitute the new life. As separate units of being, the egg and sperm cell no longer exist. And if the image now be extended to include the begetting parents, they, in a sense, no longer exist either as independent units; for their generation has been surpassed, the new is now the living center, in relation to which they are to function as a protective husk, to be in due time cast away. And so, likewise, when a psychological-spiritual fertilization has occurred: this predicament is described in a second rhyme:

> Here is the division of the four elements/
> As from the lifeless corpse the soul ascends.

"The decomposition of the elements," Jung comments to this text, "indicates dissociation and the collapse of the existing ego-consciousness. It is closely analogous to the schizophrenic state, and it should be taken very seriously because this is the moment when latent psychoses may become acute. . . . The 'torments' that form part of the alchemist's procedure," he continues, "belong to this stage of the *iterum mori*—the reiterated death." And these are described in the *Rosarium* as follows: "cutting up the limbs, dividing them into smaller and smaller pieces, mortifying the parts, and changing them into the nature that is in the stone." * The *Rosarium* passage then goes on: "You must guard the water and fire dwelling in the arcane substance and contain those waters with the *aqua permanens,* even though this be no water, but the fiery form of the true water." [77] Which is another way of describing that disintegration of the dragon illustrated in the womb-shaped *vas* of Figure 40. The Mercurial water from clouds falls here as well—to which there is another rhyme:

> Here falls the heavenly dew, to lave/
> The soiled black body in the grave.

"The falling dew," comments Dr. Jung, "is a portent of the divine birth now at hand. . . . The black or unconscious state that resulted from the union of opposites reaches the nadir and a change sets in. The falling dew signals resuscitation and a new light: the ever deeper descent into the unconscious suddenly becomes illumination from above." [78]

"Whiten the *lato* † and rend the books," the *Rosarium* advises, "lest your hearts be rent asunder. For this is the synthesis of the wise and the third part of the whole *opus*. Join, therefore, as is said in the *Turba,* the dry to the moist, the black earth with its water, and cook till it whitens. In this manner you will have the

---

* Compare the visions of dismemberment, etc., of the shaman-crisis described in *Primitive Mythology*, pp. 251–67.

† *Lato,* the "black substance," a mixture of copper, cadmium, and orichalcum. [Jung's note.]

essence of water and earth, having whitened the earth with water: but that whiteness we call air." [79]

Thus, the long way round, we have come back to the sense of Joyce's reference, Romans 11:32; and thereby also to a fresh appreciation of the sense of the coarseness of his imagery.

Again and again we note [states Jung] that the alchemist proceeds like the unconscious in the choice of his symbols: every idea finds both a positive and a negative expression. Sometimes he speaks of a royal pair, sometimes of dog and bitch; and the water symbolism is likewise expressed in violent contrasts. We read that the royal diadem appears "in menstruo meretricis (in the menstruum of a whore)," or the following instructions are given: "Take the foul deposit [foecem] that remains in the cooking-vessel and preserve it, for it is the crown of the heart." The deposit corresponds to the corpse in the sarcophagus, and the sarcophagus corresponds in turn to the mercurial fountain or the vas hermeticum.[80]

In the lewd brothels chapter of Ulysses, the length of which is approximately one-quarter of the book, the turbulent mixture, on one and the same plane, of hallucinated images and those of tangible life corresponds perfectly (as Joyce shows that he knew) to the condition of mind of the alchemist, who was himself undergoing a sort of transubstantiation along with the metals and filth in his retort. The nigredo and putrefactio of both Bloom and Stephen, "poles apart," throughout this chapter, and the breaking down particularly of Stephen's flint-hard defense system, led the latter, at the crisis of the book, to an experience that was for him absolutely new, namely, of sympathy, compassion, a moment of spontaneous identification—with Bloom, "poles apart." [81] And the sense by which he was touched thereby actually resolved for him a certain problem that had been nagging him all day, to wit, the consubstantiality of the Father and the Son: of Stephen sitting on the beach and the drowned man in the sea. And it was very soon thereafter that THE END OF THE WORLD overtook him, ELIJAH brayed his message of Christ the One Being of All, and the figure of MANANNAN appeared from a scuttle of black coal, after which there occurred the following apotheosis of the dog—"dog of my enemy"—in the midst of a hallucinated Black Mass:

FATHER MALACHI O'FLYNN

Introibo ad altare diaboli.

THE REVEREND MR. HAINES LOVE

To the devil which hath made glad my young days.

FATHER MALACHI O'FLYNN

(Takes from the chalice and elevates a blood dripping host.)
Corpus Meum.

THE REVEREND MR. HAINES LOVE

*(Raises high behind the celebrant's petticoats, revealing his grey
bare hairy buttocks between which a carrot is stuck.)* My body.

THE VOICE OF ALL THE DAMNED

Htengier Tnetopinmo Dog Drol eht rof, Aiulella!

(From on high the voice of Adonai calls.)
ADONAI

Dooooooooooog!

THE VOICE OF ALL THE BLESSED

Alleluia, for the Lord God Omnipotent reigneth!

(From on high the voice of Adonai calls.)
ADONAI

Goooooooooood!

*(In strident discord peasants and townsmen of the Orange and
Green factions sing* Kick the Pope *and* Daily, daily sing to
Mary.*)* [82]

In accord with which, "poles apart," there is the following lesson to be read in *The Vision of God* of Nicolaus Cusanus
(1401–1464):

For God, being the Absolute Ground of all formal natures,
embraceth in Himself all natures. Whence, although we attribute
to God sight, hearing, taste, smell, touch, sense, reason and intellect, and so forth, according to the divers significations of
each word, yet in Him sight is not other than hearing, or tasting,
or smelling, or touching, or feeling, or understanding. And so all
Theology is said to be stablished in a circle, because any one of
His attributes is affirmed of another, and to have is with God to
be, and to move is to stand, and to run is to rest, and so with the

other attributes. Thus, although in one sense we attribute to Him movement and in another rest, yet because He is Himself the Absolute Ground, in which all otherness is unity, and all diversity is identity, that diversity which is not identity proper, to wit, diversity as we understand it, cannot exist in God. . . .

Whence I begin, Lord, to behold Thee in the door of the coincidence of opposites, which the angel guardeth that is set over the entrance into Paradise.[83]

+++++++++++++++ *Chapter 6* +++++++++++++++

THE BALANCE

+++

I. Honor against Love

For the absolute lover, as for the saint, the world with its values of honor, justice, loyalty, and prudence is well lost in the realization of desire. For the knight and lady of the world, however, such a mystic end of all in ecstasy is not, and never has been, the ideal of a noble life; and in twelfth- and thirteenth-century France it was not even approximately the courtly ideal of *amor*. As one of the most sensitive recent critics of this literature, the late Mme. Myrrha Lot-Borodine, has pointed out: "It was not the French trouvères who conceived this type of ardent, blind, absolute passion: the disordering blast that blows from the Tristan poems hardly suggests the gentle fragrance of the sweet perfume of French courtesy." [1]

It would seem, therefore, no more than appropriate, after all the time we have given to the secondary Continental tale, to glance back to the old Irish of the "love-spot" of Diarmuid O'Duibhne. For it is there that the primary clues appear to the source not only of the love-magic and forest themes, but also of the boar's wound on Tristan's thigh and his relationship thereby to the boar-slain god and hero-king of the old megalithic pig-god complex: the ever-dying, ever-living son, consort, and lover of the goddess-queen of the universe: Dumuzi-Osiris-Adonis. The antiquity of this tale goes back far beyond Celtic times; and the contrast, furthermore, of its Celtic version with the Greek of Theseus, the Minotaur, and the signal of the black sails reveals some-

298

thing of considerable interest concerning the balance of the northern, "romantic" Celto-Germanic element in our heritage, and the southern, "classical" Greco-Roman.

So then, it was in the reign, as we are told, of the earliest clearly historical High King of Ireland, Cormac son of Airt son of Conn of the Hundred Battles, who ruled in Tara two hundred years before the advent of Saint Patrick and exactly one thousand before the passing on of his daughter's adventure to Isolt. Her name was Grianne. As daughter of the King, she had the privilege of being present on the field of champions at the time of a great goaling match. She was, moreover, the fairest of feature and form and speech of the women of the world. And it was then (as she later confessed) that she turned the light of her sight upon Diarmuid O'Duibhne, the man of most extraordinary beauty in the world; from which instant forward (as she averred) she never gave such love to any other: nor would she, forever.

Then, however, as it happened, immediately following that glance, Finn Mac Cumhaill (Finn McCool) arrived to sue for the princess's hand and was himself a man of extraordinary beauty. Diarmuid was Finn's sister's son, as Tristan was to Mark's. Further, Diarmuid had on his forehead a love spot that he kept covered with his abundant wild Irish hair, lest women, beholding it, should become infatuated; for such was the virtue of that spot. However, Grianne with that glance had seen it. And when all then sat at tables, she filled a golden, jewelled, chased goblet with a drink sufficient for nine times nine men, which she handed to her handmaid. "Take the goblet first to Finn," she said, "and tell him it is I that sent it."

Now this Finn Mac Cumhaill was the same who is fabled to have guarded Dublin Bay for some two or three hundred years, and is now believed to sleep, like Arthur, either in a hill or on an isle somewhere, whence he will appear again with his giant fighting men, the Fianna,[2] at some hour of Ireland's need. The title "Finn-again's Wake" can be read to refer to this second coming; and Joyce, in fact, is reported to have told a friend that his polymorphous work was " 'about' Finn lying dying by the river Liffey with the history of Ireland and the world cycling through his mind"[3]: an Irish fellow to William Blake's English vision of the fallen giant Albion. So this story is of threefold interest: in its own right, for its influence on Tristan, and for its place in *Finnegans Wake*.

But, to get on: Finn received the goblet; and no sooner had he drunk a draft than he fell into a stupor of deep sleep. King Cormac took the next; and so all the rest. But the cup was not passed to Diarmuid; and Grianne turned to him her face.

"Will you accept courtship from me, O son of O'Duibhne?" she asked.

"I will not."

"Then I put a *geis* on you," she answered. A *geis:* that is to say, a dare, magically enforced, that can be refused only at extreme peril. "I put you under bonds of danger and destruction, if you do not take me out of this household tonight, before Finn Mac Cumhaill and Cormac, King of all Erin, awake and rise from that sleep. And I shall not part from you until death part me."

"Then, O Grianne, go forward," he answered. And Diarmuid yoked two horses to a chariot.

However, beyond the ford of Athlone the couple fled afoot; and that night, already in Galway, Diarmuid cleared the brush from the midst of a grove, set seven doors of wattles around, and in the center of that wood settled beneath Grianne a bed of tender tips of the birch and of soft rush, but himself slept without.

Finn, Cormac, and the rest next morning woke to find Diarmuid and Grianne gone; and Finn, seized with a burning jealousy and rage, sent his trackers to follow the path. They lost it at the ford, then discovered it and followed. Flight and pursuit continued in this manner for some weeks with adventure, and Diarmuid all the while preparing his bed apart from Grianne. But they also sheltered in caves, and when forced by lack of space to bed beside her, he placed a large rock between, or, others say, his sword.

Then of a day it chanced, when she was striding at his side, that Grianne's foot plashed in a puddle and a jet of water scattered to her thigh. Softly, guardedly, she muttered to herself:

"A plague on thee, streaky splash!
Thou art bolder far than Diarmuid."

"What is that you just said?" he asked.
"Oh, nothing at all," she answered.

"Not so!" he said. "For I think I heard a part of it and won't rest till I hear all."

"O Diarmuid," she then said to him, very timidly and modestly, "great is your bravery in war; but for encounters of another kind, this splash has had more courage than yourself."

He was ashamed. And it was then he first took her to a thicket. And when they came that night into the forest, he made for them a hunting booth; and whereas formerly their fare had been salmon caught and broiled on a spit, that night Diarmuid slew a deer, and for the first time they enjoyed their fill together of clear water and fresh meat.

But now, there was another *geis* upon him, of which Finn Mac Cumhaill was aware; and it was, namely, never to hear the baying of hunting hounds without following the sound. Moreover, there was a boar of terrible strength then ravaging the country, and when Finn, one day out hunting, saw the whittlings of a stick floating down the waters of a brook, he recognized the whittling as of Diarmuid's knife: for the speal curled nine times, and there was no one other in Ireland could do the like.

Finn, that night, released his hunting hounds, and Diarmuid heard the voice of one of them in his sleep, out of which he started. Grianne caught him, threw her two arms about him, and asked what he had seen.

"It is the voice of a hound I have heard," he said; "and I marvel to hear it in the night."

"It is the fairy people that are doing this to you," she replied, and lulled him back to bed. Twice more he heard and started; and the last time, at dawn, went forth with his favorite hound.

Now when he came, in Sligo, to the table-topped Mount Benbulbin, up the face of it there came the wild boar at him and with all the Fianna after. His hound took flight. He cast his javelin, smote the beast in the fair middle of its face, without effect, then drew his sword and struck fully on its back, which heavy stroke cut not a bristle from the boar, but made two pieces of the sword. The animal tripped him and he fell astride its back, facing the rear of the beast that ran down the fall of the hill, turned about, ran up again, and, tossing Diarmuid, ripped him open with a tusk, so that his entrails fell about his feet. Nonetheless, with a triumphant cast of the hilt of his sword, he dashed out the brains of that boar and it fell beside him, without life. Whereupon Finn Mac Cumhaill appeared.

"Well, it pleases me, O Diarmuid," he said, "to see you in this plight, and it grieves me only that all the women of Erin are not now gazing upon you; for your extraordinary beauty is now ugliness, and your choice form a deformity."

"You might nevertheless heal me, O Finn, if you had a mind to it," said Diarmuid.

"In what way could I do that?"

"When as a lad you received the gift of knowledge," Diarmuid said, "from the salmon in the pool beneath the Tree of Knowledge, you received with it the gift that anyone to whom you would give a drink from the palms of your hands would be young and well again from any sickness."

"I know of no well on this hill," said Finn.

"That is not true," Diarmuid answered. "For not nine footsteps away from you is the well of the best fresh water in the world."

Finn went to the well. He took up the full of his two hands of water, and during the nine steps back let it trickle away through his fingers. Again he went, and again let it go. And so again; at the end of which third venture Diarmuid O'Duibhne was dead. And when Grianne, pregnant, standing on the wall of her fort, beheld the men of Finn's hunt approaching without Diarmuid, she fell from the wall and gave birth to three dead sons.

Finn with his eloquence, however, presently persuaded her to his own fort and bed in peace; and they remained with one another until death.[4]

Mme. Lot-Borodine was correct: *"Ce ne sont pas les trouvères français qui ont créé ce type de la passion brûlante, aveugle, absolue."* Professor Roger S. Loomis, the leading recent authority on this subject, held that it was in Wales that the Irish elopement tale of Diarmuid and Grianne was joined to the Pictish-Cornish composite of Tristan, Isolt, and King Mark; * whence the amplified composite, some time before the year 1000, passed to Brittany. And there it chanced that a certain Lord Rivalon named a son after its hero, with the curious effect that in later years this son was thought to have been the hero Tristan himself; so that in-

_____
* Cf. supra, p. 205.

stead of the Pictish Drustan son of Talorc, it was a Breton Tristan son of Rivalon that was sung by the Breton *conteurs*.[5]

The earliest versions of the resultant Pictish-Welsh-Cornish-Irish-Breton romance are forever lost. However, the best scholars now believe that a period of largely oral development must be assumed, c. 1066–1150, when both Welsh and Breton fabulators were made welcome in the French and Norman courts. Thomas of Britain credits his source, for instance, to a certain Welsh author, Bréri, whose name has been rendered by others, variously, as Bledri, Bleheris, and Blihis.[6] Thomas declares that this Bréri knew "all the feats and all the tales of all the kings and all the courts who had lived in Britain." [7] Another author states that he possessed the knowledge of the secret of the Grail.[8] A third declares not only that he was "born and begotten in Wales," but also that it was he who introduced the legend of Gawain to the court of the Count of Poitiers [9]—that Count having been either William IX of Aquitaine or his son William X, respectively the grandfather and the father of Queen Eleanor: and that Provençal court itself, at the very border of Spain, was precisely the first and foremost province in the West to be touched by the influence of the Moors. So that, no matter what the earlier relationship (if any) of the Celtic tradition to Islam may have been,* we have here, absolutely without question, a significant creative matrix, where Islamic, Celtic, and classical lore, both esoteric and popular, came together and combined in a highly sophisticated environment, to be carried then, in newly rendered forms, to all the courts of the Western world.

Among the primary Celtic themes derived specifically from the Diarmuid and Grianne romance, we may note the idea of a potion (sleep-producing in the Irish tale), love-magic of irresistible force (the love-spot), the flight and forest years, the sword between, and the nephew-uncle (i.e. matrilineal) relationship. The detail of the speal coming down the stream also is matched in the Tristan tale by an episode in which the lover sends whittlings down a stream to his lady, which arouse suspicions in Mark.† And fi-

---

* Cf. supra, pp. 62, 110–11, 130–36.

† It is interesting and puzzling to compare this Celtic complex with the Japanese legend of the chopsticks floating down the stream, seen by Susano-O, who ascends, to slay a dragon and win a wife. *Oriental Mythology*, pp. 471–72.

nally, the detail of the bold splash appears in relation to the second Isolt, who was riding beside her brother when her palfrey's hoof splashed in a puddle as she opened her legs to give spur; the cold water splashed the inside of her thigh and she gave a startled cry, but then, deep in her heart, thought of something, whereat she laughed so hard that if threatened with a penance of forty days she could not have stopped. When her brother asked the reason, she answered: "This splash has been more bold than ever was Tristan."

How soon or where the *classical* matter was brought into the legend is not clear at all. The parallels are many and so essential both structurally and symbolically that the contact cannot have been late. A case might even be made for direct derivation, somewhere, somehow, from the Minotaur and labyrinth legend, or some other closely related early Bronze Age mythic cycle; both the northern and the southern tales then being interpreted as local variants, reshaped by local manners, of a strain of ritual and mythic lore stemming ultimately from that ageless, widely disseminated, primitive planter complex defined and discussed in *Primitive Mythology* in the chapters on "The Ritual Love-Death" and "The Province of the Immolated Kings." [10]

The white-or-black-sail motive, which is, of course, the most striking indicator, opens to many more parallels. We have already remarked the periodic tributes. Equally noteworthy is the fact that in both legends the hero is the oppressed king's heir, his son (patrilineal tradition) or adopted nephew (matrilineal). Theseus, setting forth, was provided by his father, King Aegeus, with a black as well as a white set of sails, and, if the Minotaur were slain, was to return with the white unfurled, if not, the black. He was aided in Crete by Ariadne, daughter of King Minos and half-sister of the Minotaur: compare Isolt, daughter of King Gurmun the Gay and niece of the dragon-knight. Having slain the Minotaur, he took the princess with him, but on the island of Dia abandoned her—as Tristan, after killing the dragon, sailed away with Isolt, but then gave her to King Mark; at which point, however, the tales appear to go apart. According to one Greek version, the abandoned Ariadne hanged herself; according to a second, she had remained behind because pregnant; according to a third, however, the god Dionysus ravished her from Dia and carried her to Naxos, where first he, then she disappeared. In any case, Theseus had lost her, and there was such confusion aboard when his ship put out to sea again that the crew forgot the sails, and King Aegeus, watching from a coastal cliff, supposing the black to signify his son's failure, flung himself from the cliff into the sea that to this day bears his name. Thus the greeting of the hero when he stepped ashore in the city, of which he now was king, was equally mixed of jubilation and grief.[11]

In the Greek legend the woman is abandoned and a throne gained, as in the later Roman Virgilian legend of Dido and Aeneas; whereas in the Celtic, as a consequence of the fairy magic of the potion (which, as we have seen, was of Irish provenance), the results are reversed. Also, the tragedy is reversed: in the Greek legend the father dies when the wrong sail appears, in the Celtic legend, the son.

But to glance now at the beginnings of these two hero lives: Tristan as a child arrived unknown at the castle of his uncle; Theseus likewise at the palace of his father. For Aegeus had begotten him out of wedlock, on the daughter of the governor of a city in Argolis, and had left as tokens only a pair of shoes and a sword beneath an extremely heavy stone, giving the mother to understand that if the child she bore were a boy, he would be able, on coming to manhood, to lift the stone (as in later romance the young Arthur, also born out of wedlock, was to prove himself the son of a king by drawing the sword Excalibur from its stone). The youngster was fostered by his grandfather, Pittheus, here in the role played in the Tristan tale by Rivalin's loyal marshal. He was put to study under a tutor, Connidas, who is the counterpart of Curvenal. And in due time he did lift the stone, after which he came, unrecognized and unknown, to the palace of his father, who was then living with the sorceress Medea.

For after begetting his only son, Aegeus had been rendered sterile by a curse (a debility consistent with the bachelorhood of King Mark), from which Medea had promised to relieve him by her magic art: and her presence suggests a comparison of this palace rather with the perilous situation into which Tristan came at the Irish court of Gurmun the Gay and the sorceress Queen Isolt, than with his childhood arrival at Tintagel. For, according to Euripides, Medea had a chariot drawn by dragons. We have seen that

the guardian of the Irish house, the brother of Queen Isolt, not
only bore the emblem of a dragon, but fought with a poisoned
blade, and in the second Irish adventure was supplanted by an
actual dragon, whose tongue infected Tristan with its poison. The
young Theseus, on arrival, did not reveal his identity, but Medea
knew who he was and sought to kill him at a banquet with a poisoned
cup of wine. However, the father, in the nick of time, recognizing
the token of the sword, struck the poisoned goblet to the floor.
There followed the adventure of the Minotaur, where—according
to Plutarch's account—the protectress of the voyage was the goddess Aphrodite. On the Irish adventure, Tristan—in Gottfried's
account—bore the arrow of love emblazoned on his helm. But in
both legends the goddess of love was ill served; for the maid, her
agent, through whom death was overcome, was in both adventures abandoned. Whereupon the boon of Love was transformed,
became daemonic, diabolic, and the goddess took a terrible revenge.

She took revenge in Theseus' case, first and almost immediately, in the confusion aboard his ship, which eventuated in his
father's death; but then, years later, in his maturity, more terribly
and with devastation to his whole life, through the fatal passion of
his queen, Phaedra, for Hippolytus, his son—to the destruction of
both. Which is again, essentially, the Tristan theme, but from an
alien point of view, with Theseus now in the place of Mark,
Phaedra's nurse in that of Brangaene, and the moral, as chanted
by the chorus of Palace Women in the tragedy *Hippolytus* of Euripides, of love not as a boon but as a curse:

> I pray that Love may never come to me
> with murderous intent,
> in rhythms measureless and wild.
>
> Not fire nor stars have stronger bolts
> than those of Aphrodite, sent
> by the hand of Eros, Zeus's child.
>
> Love is like a flitting bee in the world's garden
> and for its flowers, destruction is in his breath.[12]

That is hardly as Heloise would have sung; or Isolt, Tristan, or
Gottfried. For the Greek, in contrast to the Celtic-medieval version of the shared theme and legend, has stressed the standpoint

of the world, society and achievement, ethical values and common day, against the abyss of inwardness, erotic-personal values, and the realization of rapture. As in Virgil's legend of Aeneas's desertion of Dido to assume manfully his epochal, hard historical role as founder of mighty Rome, so here: it is ROMA against AMOR, the task of the day against the mysteries of night; time and its call against eviternity; the one that is two against the two that are one.

Yet in both versions of the legend the irony of the choice is recognized as tragic: an illustration of the intrinsic dissonance that is the beginning and end of a properly human life, doomed in the end, either way, to reversal. Theseus denied Aphrodite in his desertion of Ariadne, and his son, Hippolytus, a lover only of horses, denied Aphrodite absolutely. As in Abelard's case, so in both of these, a world philosophy and associated ethical program, formulated previously to the opening and offering of a new dimension of experience, was held to, when the time had come to consider something else. And Tristan's case was much the same. He was so taken with the maid Isolt that when he returned from his first visit he could talk of nothing else; yet his concept of his place in the courtly world was such that he never thought of winning her for himself.

However, in his case, when the new dimension could no longer be denied, he gave in—with a will; and the old world of honor and chivalrous deeds fell away. Its heroic values lost force. And yet—and here was the circumstance of his tragedy—the rest of the world remained attached still to the old, and would have it that way, and in fact had to. Nor, finally, were the claims of the old completely wiped out of the lives and minds even of Isolt and Tristan. That was the sense of the sword between them. For mystic harmony, peace, and the idyll of the ideal realized, as in the forest refuge of the grotto, do not yield a properly *human* life at all. They are of the womb, before—and of the tomb, hereafter —and, as such, are for the meditations of what Nietzsche called "yonder-worldings."

Yet they are also—and here is Gottfried's point—of the ultimate depth and very ground of our existence here and now, where they can and must be found and affirmed *along with* the dissonance, while the latter is sounded with all power, *crescendo* to *fortissimo*. That is why Nietzsche wrote of man as "the sick ani-

mal," celebrating doubt, ill health, decay, and decadence—what
Thomas Mann in *The Magic Mountain,* writing in Nietzsche's
spirit, has called "temperature"—as the essential characteristics
of life in the process of alchemical transmutation, "surpassing itself," becoming golden. That is the earthly way to the knowledge
of the secret of the "door of the concidence of opposites" of
which Cusanus wrote, "which the angel guardeth that is set over
the entrance into Paradise." * And that is what Joyce is singing
about in every sentence of *Finnegans Wake,* where, as he states in
one of his key passages, joy and sorrow, violence and love, male
and female, the sword and the pen, profit and loss, day and night,
"cumjustle" with each other "as neatly . . ." (but here let us set
the sentence apart a bit, for contemplation, like a poem):

> as neatly . . . as were they *isce et ille* equals of opposites,
> evolved by a onesame power of nature or of spirit, *iste,*
> as the sole condition of its himunderher manifestation
> and polarized for reunion by the symphysis of their
> antipathies.[13] †

In short, the choral chant of the Palace Women in Euripides'
Hippolytus, and the sudden tragedy of the socially oriented, sunny-
side-up personalities of the Greek plot, stand for the values, dangers, and way of experiencing destiny of the people of this world
on the King Mark side of Gottfried's piece, for whom duty and
honor, social ties and service, are the measures of personal merit;
whereas in the Celtic and medieval "romantic" works of the
northern poets, whom the mists of Gothic forests and the fogs of
coastal seas had seasoned with the inwardness of sweet melancholy, there is another song: a lyric learned in silence, alone, by
one, or by two together, of the "noble heart," unafraid of the un-
marked way. "Lord," sings Joyce, "heap miseries upon us yet en-
twine our arts with laughters low." [14]

II. The Individual and the State

Among the most important of those authors of the first half of
the present century who, together with James Joyce, transformed

---

* *Supra,* p. 297.
  † *isce et ille* (Latin), "that there and that"; *iste,* "that (yonder)." *Symphysis* (Greek), "a growing together, a natural junction" (as of bones), as
  being not mere contact but continuity of substance.

the naturalistic nineteenth-century society novel into a secular vehicle of mythological wisdom and symbolic initiations, Thomas Mann (1875–1955) was perhaps the most ardently aware of the social and pedagogical relevance, and consequent responsibilities, of his profession. Contrary to the way of Joyce, whose point of conscience it was to remain from first to last the artist, with the absolutely impartial binocular vision of an Olympian—nonparticipant as partisan, omniparticipant as viewer and mover—Thomas Mann, throughout his long, productive career, was always seriously engaged, either covertly or explicitly, in delivering a sociological, political—and, in his later years, mystagogic—message.

Now I do not wish to compare him in this point to such a socialistic tub-thumper as Bernard Shaw, who himself declared that the very long prefaces to his plays were as much to his purpose as the plays themselves; however, it is a fact that as an essayist, elucidating the philosophical and sociological backgrounds and implications of his own creative achievements, Thomas Mann is hardly matched in the history of letters. The essays, which are numerous and as sedulously composed as the fictional works themselves, are among the most illuminating and important treatments we possess of the relationships of modern literature to those spheres of experience and symbolic communication that in the past were the province of myth alone. And in relation to the study of mythology itself—its sources, meanings, and moral implications for today—there have been no more sophisticated elucidations.

For it is simply a fact (as I have already remarked in my Prologue to the first volume of this tetralogy) that poets and artists, who are dealing every day of their lives with the feeling- as well as thought-values of their own imageries of communication, are endowed with a developed organ for the understanding of myth that is too often lacking in the merely learned; so that when the artist or poet is also learned, he may be a more dependable guide to the nuclear themes of a given mythic complex, and a much more profound interpreter of their relevance to life, than even the most respected of its specialized academic elucidators. And finally, since Mann, as I have just said, was concerned not simply with the universal psychological and metaphysical implications of his mythological symbols, but also with their practical, moral and

political application, he was compelled, during the long and stately course of his career in a period of catastrophic changes in the
character of European culture, to commit his art and sympathies
first to one extreme, then to the other, of the social-political spectrum, until in the end he found himself in such a whirlabout of
reversals that the magnificent ship of his art began to crack and to
leak Hermetic water at the seams. Thus the careful student of his
interpretations is provided not only with readings of equal perspi-
cacity from more than one point of view, but also with what my
grandmother would have called "a good object lesson" in the
mercurial nature of mythological universals. And in addition,
since Mann knew exactly what he was doing—shutting first one
eye, then the other—there is in that a further lesson for the student of morality, as well as a corollary, touching the discipline of
the parallax, for the student of binocular vision.

Mann's earliest schematic formulation of the contrasting terms
of the problem that he continued to revolve in his mind to the end
of his days was presented in a very early short story entitled
"Tristan" (1902), which, like his later masterpiece, *The Magic
Mountain* (1924), had for its setting a tuberculosis sanatorium,
and for its theme the counterplay and dialogue, in that setting, of
the will to freedom and peace against the will to life—twenty
years before Sigmund Freud's *Beyond the Pleasure Principle*.[15]
As its date reveals, at the time of the publication of this short
story, in which an astonishing number of those themes were announced that in the later novel were to be developed and ex-
panded to the magnitude of a symphony in honor of the Lord-and-
Lady Hermes-Aphrodite of the left-hand way to illumination, the
author was but twenty-seven years old. His novel *Buddenbrooks*
(1902) had already won renown; and two more short works,
"Tonio Kröger" (1903) and the play *Fiorenza* (1904), were
immediately to follow. Those were the critical years of his career,
during which his fundamental philosophical stance was being established on a base principally of Goethe, Schopenhauer, Wagner,
and Nietzsche, with a touch, as well, of Dostoevski and Tolstoi.
The principal texts around which his cogitations revolved, besides
Goethe's *Faust* and Wagner's operas, were Nietzsche's *Birth of
Tragedy* and Schopenhauer's speculative essay "On an Apparent
Intention in the Fate of the Individual." These works brought his

thinking to focus almost compulsively on the enigma of death and renewal, on the psychological factors contributing to both individual and social disintegration, and on those contrary factors that might be counted on to withstand, or even overcome, the processes of dissolution and death. In a letter "On Marriage," sent to Count Hermann Keyserling in the late nineteen-twenties, Mann declared: "For me the concepts of death and individualism have always coalesced. . . . and the concept of life, on the other hand, has united with those of duty, service, social ties, and even worth." [16] However, things were not really quite as simple as that in his mind. For in the course of his long career the various elements of these opposed combinations occasionally separated from their fellows and changed sides. The series of cultural shocks delivered by the cataclysms of his century (during the rapid sequence of which the nation and folk of his first concern, which in his earliest order of alignment had represented duty and service to life, became for him the symbol of ultimate evil) left him finally with no ground on earth on which to stand. In terms of the basic philosophic position that he had made his own by 1902, this should not have greatly surprised or unsettled him. However, he had also in those critical years given his heart, as he declared in his novella "Tonio Kröger," to the normal, usual, fair, and living, happy, and commonplace human beings of this world, and not even the power of his disengaged, sophisticated artist eye and mind could accept with equanimity what they had done.

"I stand between two worlds," his hero, Tonio, had written to a young Russian intellectual, Lisabeta, in that work.

I am at home in neither, and I suffer in consequence. You artists call me a *bourgeois,* and the *bourgeois* try to arrest me. . . . I don't know which makes me feel worse. The *bourgeois* are stupid; but you adorers of the beautiful, who call me phlegmatic and without aspirations, you ought to realize that there is a way of being an artist that goes so deep and is so much a matter of origins and destinies that no longing seems to it sweeter and more worth knowing than longing after the bliss of the commonplace.

I admire those proud, cold beings who adventure upon the paths of great and daemonic beauty and despise "mankind"; but I do not envy them. For if anything is capable of making a poet of a literary man, it is my bourgeois love of the human, the living and usual. It is the source of all warmth, goodness, and humor; I even almost think it is itself that love of which it stands written that one may speak with the tongues of men and of angels and yet having it not be as sounding brass and tinkling cymbals. . . .

Do not chide this love, Lisabeta; it is good and fruitful. There is longing in it, and a gentle envy; a touch of contempt and no little innocent bliss.[17]

In his earlier short story, "Tristan," the side of prosperous, buoyant life is represented by a lusty, rather peasant-like red-faced big-businessman, Herr Klöterjahn by name, of the firm A. C. Klöterjahn and Co., who arrived at the sanatorium Einfried only to deposit there—with care and tender concern—his exquisitely fragile young wife, who, since giving birth with extreme difficulty to their vigorously blooming baby boy, had been afflicted with a tracheal condition dangerously close to consumption. She had been ordered to Einfried by her doctor to find rest, repose from all agitation, release from duties for a while, and the very best medical attention. While on the other side, the cause of art, beauty, intellect, and the spirit was represented by an odd unsocial little person with very large feet, Detlev Spinell, in his early thirties, yet graying already at the temples, and known to the wits of the sanatorium as the moldy infant. He had once composed a short novel, now in print in a large volume, every single letter of the jacket of which had the look of a Gothic cathedral; and he kept this on a table in his room, where he spent the days writing letters. He was at Einfried, he would say, not for the cure, but because of the Empire style of the furniture; and on beholding any sudden sight of beauty—two matching colors, mountains tinged by a sunset—"How beautiful!" he would exclaim in a paroxysm of sensibility, pitching his head to one side, lifting his shoulders, spreading out his hands, and distending lips and nostrils. "God! just look! how beautiful!" he would cry and then fling his arms about the neck of any person, male or female, at hand.

Well, to make an elegant short story very short indeed: To everybody's amazement, for he had never sought company before, this gift of the spirit to Einfried became, as soon as he beheld her, the solicitous, humble servant of the lovely Frau Klöterjahn's exquisite beauty. Then he did two things: he flattered her refinement as too spiritual for this coarse world and for the husband whose coarse name ill befitted her; then he induced her to play again the piano, as she had played it in her childhood, when her father had played the violin. "But the doctors have expressly forbidden it," she said. "They are not here," he answered; "we are free. . . . Dear Madam, if you are afraid of doing yourself injury, then let the beauty be dead and still that might have come into being from the touch of your fingers. . . ."

She played. And it went from Chopin's Nocturnes to Wagner's *Tristan:* Oh, the boundless, inexhaustible joy of that union eternal beyond the bounds of time, et cetera. . . . Two days later there was blood on her handkerchief, and not long thereafter Klöterjahn was summoned to what proved to be her last hours. Spinell wrote him a letter: a personally insulting presentation of his hate-filled case against life; and the sturdy man of the world, in reply, simply walked into the author's room and told him to his face what he was: an impotent clown, a coward, and a sneak, scared sick of reality, and with beauty on his tongue that was nothing more than hypocrisy and a fool's grudge against life.

The radical opposition of the two hemispheres of experience and value represented in this story, on one hand by the man of business, healthy and socially at ease in his world of aggressive, unselfcritical, lusty life, and on the other by Spinell in his favorite sanatorium, with its pleasant grounds and garden, rambling walks, grottoes, bowers, and little rustic pavilions, is matched in the medieval legend by the contrast of the courtly world of King Mark, with its uncritically accepted and enforced customs of both courtesy and religious faith, and, on the other hand, the couple in the wilderness and its timeless grotto. There is an Oriental analogy also intended; one suggested by the works of Schopenhauer and their reflection in Wagner's theme: namely of the contrast recognized in India between the two worlds, on one hand of life in the context of society, bound to the wheel of ignorance, suffering, rebirth, old age, and death, and on the other of life in the forest, in the penitential groves, striving by all means to achieve release from the senseless round. However, in India, in neither of these situations does the problem of individuality arise. For in the social sphere one obeys—one is compelled to obey—the ritual laws and disciplines of one's caste, without resistance, without question, whereas in the penitential groves the aim is not to realize individuality but to erase it, to eliminate absolutely and forever whatever taint or trace of ego, personal will, and individuality may yet remain to one, even after a lifetime—yea, innumerable lifetimes—of the socially enforced, impersonal disciplines of caste.[18]

In our modern European West, on the other hand, largely as a result of the forthright intransigency of a sufficient number of actually great, courageous individuals, the principle of individuality and an appreciation of the worth of individuality have won through—at least for the present. So that, properly, the forest must have here an altogether different sense from that assigned to it in any Indian code. "I will not serve that in which I no longer believe," declared Joyce's hero, Stephen Dedalus, "whether it call itself my home, my fatherland or my church; and I will try to express myself in some mode of life or art as freely as I can and as wholly as I can, using for my defence the only arms I allow myself to use—silence, exile, and cunning." [19] That has a very different ring from self-erasure. And so there is a new problem to be faced here: one that for the West and for the coming history and character of civilization is to be decisive, either as solved and integrated socially in our institutions, or as lost—beneath the rising waves of Asia. For it has been in Europe and the European sphere alone (which includes, for now at least, North America), that this problem of the radical dissociation and collision of individual and group values has emerged as the critical challenge of a maturing humanistic civilization.

But the difficulties posed are great. Chiefly they derive from the fact that the values of *both* of the opposed hemispheres, the individual and the social, are positive; hence, by all the laws both of physics and of biology, mutually repellent. That is to say, the partisans of each banner view the values of the other side merely as negative to their own and therefore, in every attempt either to attack or to achieve concord, succeed only in dealing with their own negative projections, giving battle to their own shadows on the

walls of their own closed minds—which presents a fine circus of
clowns for the laughter of the gods, but for mankind, with increasing danger, a *turba philosophorum* that is being reflected not
in a sealed retort but in the carnage of exploded cities.

Somewhere about midway between the dates of his letter to
Count Keyserling on marriage and his youthful composition of
"Tristan," Thomas Mann, during the years of the First World
War, was revolving, from one viewpoint to another, his thoughts
on the counterplay of opposites that was at that time represented
to him by the contending ideals of Germany and the Western Al-
lies. And as he had already made things a little difficult for himself by associating individualism with death and submission to the
social order with life, so now he added to his philosophical stress
by linking radicalism with individualism and conservatism with
duty, associating the latter with German culture and the former
with the French Revolution, English economic materialism, international class socialism, and the ideals of a money-based luxury
civilization. He made a great many statements in this book that
he came later to regret, and retracted. However, it is the work out
of which *The Magic Mountain* came: a fearless, really extraordinary work of self-scrutiny and analysis, a night-book of lightning
flashes bursting from dark impenetrable clouds; and is to be read
as a diary of such confusion as anyone of good will, condemned
by destiny to settle his own mind with respect to the values at
stake in a modern war of mighty nations, of which his own was
one, might, if he had the courage to do so, force himself to write.
The work, first published 1919, and then, abridged, in 1922, bore
the title *Reflections of a Non-Political Man,* and the following
brief selection lets the reader know why.

Politics I hate, and the belief in politics, because it makes
people arrogant, doctrinaire, harsh, and inhuman. I do not believe in the formulae of the anthill, the human beehive; do not
believe in the *république démocratique, sociale et universelle;*
do not believe that mankind was made for what is being called
"happiness," or that it even *wants* this "happiness,"—do not believe in "belief," but rather in despair, because it is this that
clears the way to deliverance; I believe in humility and work—
work on oneself, and the highest, noblest, sternest, and most
joyous form of such work seems to me to be art.[20]

In those days Mann identified this kind of work on oneself, humility, and integrity, with what he termed at that time the "aristocratic principle," exemplified in Europe pre-eminently, in his view, by the culture ideal and discipline of the Germans, in contrast not only to the highly emotional class revolution of the French with its "Marseillaise" and guillotine, but also to the cold-blooded, utilitarian, economic materialism of the Anglo-Saxon Industrial Revolution, while Marxism he described as but "a fusion of French revolutionary thought and English political economy." [21] "You party politicians," he could at that time write, quoting Strindberg, "are like one-eyed cats. Some of you see only with the left eye, others only with the right, and for that reason you can never see stereoscopically, but only one-sidedly and flat." And again, still quoting the Swedish author: "As poet, one has a right *to play with ideas, to experiment with standpoints,* but not bind oneself to anything: for freedom is the life breath of the poet." [22] And the real good of humanity, as he then believed, was served in art, not in manifestos; for the curse of politics, mass politics, so-called democratic politics, derived from its reduction of all life, art itself, and religion as well, to politics, the marketplace, newspaper thinking. "No experience," he wrote, "is more likely to put politics out of mind, more thoroughly prove it irrelevant, and better teach how to forget it, than the experience, through art, of what is everlasting in man. And at a time when world political events of truly fearful force are involving all that is in us of individual human worth in sympathetic participation, overwhelming it and bearing it away—precisely at such a time it is fitting to stand firm against the megalomaniacs of politics, in defense, namely, of the truth that the essential thing in life, the true humanity of life, never is even touched by political means." [23] "Man is not only a social, but also a metaphysical being. In other words, he is not merely a social individual, but also a personality. Consequently, it is wrong to confuse what is above the individual in us with society, to translate it completely into sociology. Doing that, one leaves the metaphysical aspect of the person, what is truly above the individual, out of account; for it is in the personality, not the mass, that the actual superordinated principle is to be found." [24]

So far, so good. No one who has ever understood or experienced anything either of art or of life—anything, that is to say, beyond the sphere of sociology—would have much to say against all that. However, the author, in addition, had involved himself in this book (in spite of its nonpolitical title) in a political commitment to the idea and cause of German culture, against what he conceived to be the revolutionary internationalism of the bourgeois (French, English, and incidentally American) democracies. Moreover, by 1930, having made that first mistake, he had gone on to the logical second. He had abandoned his earlier distinction between the personal and social spheres and had aligned himself with the latter, in the currently fashionable way of Marxist socialism—even to the point of identifying Marxism, in a manner that was also fashionable at that time, with the progressive ideals of bourgeois liberalism and democracy. But this identification he had already made in his nonpolitical "Reflections"; so that he was now simply shifting allegiance from one pole of his own dichotomy to the other. And to make matters even more confusing, both for himself and for those still striving to admire him, he refused to concede that in turning from one side of his ledger to the other, he had left the values of the first behind. What he had been calling the "spiritual values" of the "aristocratic principle"—i.e. (as he understood them) the personally responsible, dutiful, form-conserving, humanistic ideals of a worthy people's national heritage—he now simply transferred to the workers' class revolution, reducing even the experience of God (in orthodox Levantine-Marxist style) to a social occasion:

"The human race dwells on earth in communities," he announced in a talk on "Culture and Socialism," published in the same volume, called *The Challenge of the Day* (1930), in which the letter to Count Keyserling "On Marriage" appears; "and there is no sort of individual realization or direct relationship to God, to which some form of association—of sociability—does not correspond. The religious 'I' becomes corporative in the parish." [That is the Judas kiss.] "The cultural 'I' celebrates its festival in the form and name of the community—which is a word that bears in Germany strong religious and aristocratic associations, setting the holiness of its idea of social life altogether apart from the concept of society of the democracies. . . . German socialism, the invention of a Jewish social theorist trained in Western Europe, has always been felt by German cultural piety to be alien to this land and contrary to the national heritage, indeed sheer devilry, and has been accordingly despised"—and now comes the crucial gambit and the timely transfer of values:

> and with full right; for it does indeed represent the dissolution of the idea of a national culture and community, in the name of an idea of social classes to which that of the nation and community is opposed. However, the fact of the situation is, that this process of dissolution has already progressed to such a degree that the complex of German cultural ideas signified by the terms "nation" and "community" can be today dismissed as mere romanticism; and life itself, with all its meaning for the present and for the future is now, without doubt, on the side of socialism. . . . For although the spiritual significance of individualistic idealism derived originally from its connection with the idea of a cultural heritage, whereas the socialistic class concept has never denied its purely economic origin, the latter nevertheless entertains today far friendlier relations with the sphere of the spirit than does its romantically nationalistic middle-class antagonist, the conservatism of which has clearly, for all to see, lost touch and sympathy with the living spirit and its present-day demands.

The author had spoken on other occasions of the discrepancy, which others have also remarked, between the nobility and wisdom of the greatest men of our times and the lag in the public domain of law and international affairs, and he recurs now to this theme, to advance and settle his argument.

> I have recently spoken elsewhere, of the unhealthy and dangerous tension that has developed in our world between the state of knowledge already attained and spiritually assimilated by those who represent the summits of our humanity and the material actualities of our present; pointing also to the dangers potential in this tension. The socialistic class, the working class, shows an unquestionably better and more vital will to overcome this shameful and dangerous discrepancy than does its cultural adversary, whether it be in matters of legislation, the rationalization of public affairs, the international conception of Europe, or what you will. It is indeed true that the socialistic class concept, in contrast to the idea of a national culture, is in its economic theory antagonistic to spiritual values; nevertheless in practice it

favors them, and that, as things stand today, is what really counts.[25]

Within a decade of the delivery of this talk, the world's supreme model of the economically based but spiritually disposed socialistic class-state joined hands with the nationally based, unspiritual socialistic state, to invade, dismember, and share Poland, and so began the Second World War. Thomas Mann, in due time, took flight, not to socialistic Russia but, by way of nonparticipant Switzerland, first to Princeton, then to Hollywood, whence, from the distant shores of the Pacific, a few hours before Pearl Harbor, he sent off the following radio broadcast to the German people:

German listeners, he who speaks to you today was fortunate enough to do something for the intellectual reputation of Germany in the course of his long life. I am grateful for this, but I have no right to pride myself for it, as it was destiny and did not lie in my hand.

No artist accomplishes his work in order to increase the glory of his country. The source of productivity is individual conscience. You Germans are not allowed to thank me for my work, even if you desired to do so. So be it. It was accomplished not for your sake but from innermost need.

But there is one thing which has been done really for your sake, which has developed from social and not private conscience. With every day I am more and more certain that the time will come, and, in fact, is already near at hand, when you will thank me for it and rate it higher than my stories and books. And this is, that I warned you, when it was not yet too late, against the depraved powers under whose yoke you are harnessed today and who lead you through innumerable misdeeds to incredible misery. I knew them. I knew that nothing but catastrophe and misery for Germany and for Europe would grow from their unspeakably base nature while the majority of you were seeing in them the forces of order, beauty, and national dignity—blinded as you were to a degree which today has unquestionably already become incredible to yourselves. . . .

Collapse is near. Your troops in Russia lack doctors, nurses, medical supplies. In German hospitals the severely wounded, the old and feeble are killed with poison gas—in one single institution, two to three thousand, a German doctor has said. . . . Comparable to the mass poisoning is the compulsory copulation where soldiers on leave are ordered to go like stud horses to the young German girls in order to produce sons of the State for the next war. Can a nation, can youth sink lower? Can there be a greater blasphemy of humanity? . . . Three hundred thousand Serbs were killed by you Germans at the order of the villainous men who govern you, not during the war, but after the war had ended in that country. Unspeakable are the deeds against the Jews and the Poles. But you do not want to acknowledge the ever-growing gigantic hatred which one day, when the forces of your people finally weaken, is bound to engulf you all.

Yes, it is right to feel the horror of this day. And your leaders know it. They who led you to commit all those horrible deeds tell you that you are chained to them through these deeds and that you must stand by them to the end; otherwise hell will come over you. If you break with them you will still be able to be saved, to gain freedom and peace.[26]

Thus, in the end as in the beginning, under pressure, heat, and horror sufficient to effect a *fermentatio,* the artist again became separate and rediscovered for himself in old age what both Schopenhauer and Nietzsche had taught him in his youth: that between the individual and the multitude, a man's integrity and his society, the inward and the outer, categorical and contingent worlds of experience and commitment, there is indeed an opposition, as deep as to the ground of being. I have italicized the paragraph that makes this point. It has the ring, a bit, of Detlev Spinell. But in the following sentence we learn of something of which Spinell seems not to have known, namely, a distinction between private and social conscience: and this we now must recognize as posing a profound problem—*the* problem, I should say— that from the period of the early Tristan poets, when it first seriously emerged in our literature in terms of the tragic tension between *minne* and *ere,* love and honor, has remained unresolved in the West to the present.

Mann's radio address was broadcast, we have said, but a few hours before the Japanese dawn raid on Pearl Harbor. Soon the prophesied fire and brimstone were purging to rubble the culture-cities of Central Europe: Munich, Dresden, Frankfurt, Marburg, Cologne, Hamburg, Berlin. The monstrous empire of Hitler dissolved and the armies of Stalin's no less monstrous slave state moved supreme across the European heartland, across half the European map. Within a decade another Asian monster, its Chinese counterpart, was standing back to back with it, also breathing fire—a fire furnished to both, ironically, by the sciences of the West—while the Dutch, Belgian, French, and British world empires meanwhile went to pieces; so that by 1950 a scientifically enforced Asiatization of world affairs was beginning to be evident, which, as far at least as the politics of the free individual are concerned, is the leading challenge of the present hour. The old Bronze Age world image of an absolutely inexorable, mathematical cosmology of which the social order is but an aspect (which, as we have seen, is at the base of both the Chinese and the Indian world views),[27] now supplemented by an equally inexorable Marxian notion of the logic of history, and implemented in its inhumanity by a modern mechanical technology of equivalent impersonality, in the name of what Nietzsche with disdain prophesied as "the new idol, the State," bodes well, largely with American aid, to represent the future of man of the next millennium. For as Aldous Huxley stated in the 1946 Foreword to his Utopian novel *Brave New World:* "Without economic security, the love of servitude cannot possibly come into existence." [28] And as Nicolas Berdiaeff states in the passage quoted by Huxley on the motto-page of that volume:

> *Les utopies apparaissent comme bien plus réalisables qu'on ne le croyait autrefois. Et nous nous trouvons actuellement devant une question bien autrement angoissante: Comment éviter leur réalisation définitive? . . . Les utopies sont réalisables. Le vie marche vers les utopies. Et peut-être un siècle nouveau commence-t-il, un siècle où les intellectuels et la classe cultivée rêveront aux moyens d'éviter les utopies et de retourner à une société non utopique, moins "parfaite" et plus libre.*

III. Erotic Irony

In *The Magic Mountain,* the novel composed by its author in a period of perfectly achieved balance at the noon of his career, there is a pair of now famous political chatterboxes, Settembrini and Naphta, whose amusingly counterpoised, ultimately self-defeating arguments form a substantial portion of the work. The setting is again, as in the author's youthful "Tristan," a mountain sanatorium, to which an undistinguished German civilian comes for a brief stay: in the present instance a young engineer, Hans Castorp, for a three-week holiday visit with his afflicted cousin, a youthful army officer, Joachim Ziemssen, who, in spite of the healthy look of his tan, is seriously ill. The steep train ride up the mountain is described as a thrilling passage from the flatland of our normal, banal duties in life to a sphere of timeless rest, above the range of deciduous trees, where silent peaks, everlasting snows, and evergreens speak of eternity; and, as the literary man Settembrini tells the young voyager days later, in that ascent he had passed from the land of the living to the land of the dead. He had gone not upward but actually downward, to the netherworld: he was in danger and, before tasting of its fruit, had better leave.

There is a passage in Mann's *Reflections of a Non-Political Man,* telling of the conception of this novel, which apparently had been incubating for years. "Before the war," it states,

> I had begun to write a brief novel, a sort of pedagogical fable, in which a young man, trapped in a morally dangerous resort, to which he had come for a brief stay, was to be placed between two equally ludicrous educators, an Italian littérateur, humanist, rhetorician and progressive, and on the other side a rather disreputable mystic, reactionary, and advocate of anti-reason: the innocent young man was to be forced to choose between the powers of virtue and seduction, the duties and service of life and the fascination of corruption—to which latter he was not to have been unsusceptible. And in this work an important thematic element of the composition was to have been the phrase: "Sympathy with Death." [29]

Not only in *The Magic Mountain,* but already in his "Tristan," as well as in the first of his novels, *Buddenbrooks,* that theme is fundamental; and in a volume of his essays published in 1925, in a paper "On the Spirit of Medicine," he has rendered an elucidation and moral as well as social evaluation of the force and import of that sentiment.

"My novel, *The Magic Mountain,* presents in its foreground a social-critical aspect," he there states;

> and since the foreground of this foreground is a medical environment, namely the setting of a de luxe Alpine sanatorium in

which the capitalistic society of pre-war Europe is mirrored, it was of course inevitable that certain professionally specialized critics, hypnotized by the foremost foreground, should have been able to see nothing in the book but a novel about a tuberculosis sanatorium, and that these then should have been afraid lest its effect should be that of a sensational exposé—a kind of medical counterpart of Upton Sinclair's Chicago stockyard exposure. That, however, was an ironic misunderstanding indeed. For social criticism—as the company of the literary critics well knows —is not one of my passions; nor is it one of my strong points. It enters my works only accidentally and incidentally, taken in only by the way. The real motivations of my authorship are of a sinfully individualistic, that is to say, metaphysical, moral, pedagogical, in short, innerworldly kind; and as in my other works, so too in *The Magic Mountain.* . . .

The book owes its success, in the first place, to what Dr. Margarethe Levy of Berlin has, without professional prejudice, called the lifelikeness and vitality of its characters. And it owes its success, in the second place, to its spiritual themes and problems, which are such that fifteen years ago in Germany would not have tempted a dog from the stove, but today, thanks to the uprooting experiences of our time, are at the tips of everyone's fingers. It does not owe its success to the thrills of any scandalous revelations of the "inside life" in Alpine sanatoriums.

Among these themes and problems there is what one critic has called the web of ideas about life and death, health and disease—and I am permitting myself to speak of this because a critic of mine in *The Munich Medical Weekly* has complained that I have painted an *Inferno,* which, in contrast to that of my great medieval predecessor, lacks all ethical pathos. Amazing! A number of my literary critics have impatiently advised me finally to get back to my art, instead of lashing around any longer with the ethical problems of mankind—and now this doctor can see nothing but cold-blooded artistic cruelty in the work. He accuses me of a lack of respect and sympathy for ailing life, a repulsive want of that "Christian reverence for suffering" of which [the book's heroine] Frau Chauchat speaks: and he is apparently completely unaware that the attitude he thus stigmatizes could not possibly have accommodated the actual (though admittedly not too obvious) "ethical pathos" of the work. Which again is strange! The whole educational process through which the young hero of my story passes, this medical reader has missed: he remains untouched. For it is a correcting process, the process of the progressive disillusionment of a pious, death-revering young man concerning sickness and death. My critic disapproves of this course of education and its means —and, finally, how could he not! Has it often happened in literature or in art—has it ever happened—that death has been turned into a comic figure? In any case, here it has. For this book, which has the ambition to be a European book, is a book of good will and decision, a book of ideal renunciation of much that is beloved, many dangerous sympathies, enchantments, and seductions to which the European soul has been and is disposed and which, all in all, has only *one* piously majestic name—a book of departure, I say, and pedagogical self-discipline; its service is to life, its will is to health, its goal is the future. And in that it is a work of healing. For to that variety of humanistic science known as medicine, no matter how profoundly its studies may pertain to sickness and death, the goal remains health and humanity; its goal remains the restoration of the human idea in its purity.

Death as a comical figure. . . . Does it play only this role in my novel? Does it not show in this role two faces, the one laughable, the other grave? Schopenhauer has said that without death on earth there could scarcely be philosophy. Also, there could hardly be any "education" on earth without it. Death and disease are not at all just romantic caricatures in my novel:—I have been unjustly accused. They are there also as great teachers, great leaders toward humanity, and the opinion of the contributor to *The Munich Medical Weekly* that my intention, my reprehensible, defamatory intention had obviously been "to show that in the environment of a tuberculosis sanatorium the character of a young, honorable, and well brought up young man must necessarily degenerate"—this opinion is refuted to the ground by the book itself. Did Hans Castorp degenerate? Did he go under? He in fact improved! This "environment" is actually the hermetic retort in which his simple primary material is forcibly sublimated and purified to an unsuspected ennoblement. In this "environment," which has been said to be defamed in the book, its modest hero is brought to think about things and matured to a sense of duty to his government in a way that in the "flatland" (and do we not have an ear for the ironic appraisal sounded in that word?) he would never have attained in his whole life.

"The Standard Dialogue of Disease," someone has called my book—not exactly in the way of praise, but I accept the judgment. The disreputable aspect of disease is brought out in relation to the ideal; but it is represented also as a mighty medium of knowledge and as the "genial" way to humanity and to love. Through disease and death, through the fervid study of the organic, through a medical experience, that is to say, I let my hero attain, as far as this was possible to his shrewd simplicity, to a premonition of a new humanity. And in doing this I am supposed to have maligned medicine and the medical profession? [30]

The novel is much too rich in life and in closely interwoven ideas to be summarized, or even adequately suggested; however, it is such an important and illuminating landmark in the field of mythological research, not only representing the passage of a modern man, stage by stage, through initiations in effect equivalent to those of the ancient mysteries, but also revealing the analogues of ancient mythic themes in the imageries of modern science, that an attempt to mark the main course of its hero's development from health, through sickness, to a higher health is not to be avoided.

The book appeared two years after *Ulysses.* The two masterworks were conceived and realized independently, yet were dealing with equivalent problems in equivalent—though contrasting —terms. For in both the novelistic foreground is so contrived that, throughout, mythological themes echo and appear, re-echo and reappear, in such a way as to suggest that in our lives today, largely unrecognized yet present, the archetypes of mythic revelation are manifest and operative still. Schopenhauer's figure of the anamorphoscope * can here be applied again. Chance occurrences scattered through a lifetime, when viewed reflected in a mythic form, come together and show an order in depth that is the order of man everlasting; and to effect such ideated epiphanies, where to the unassisted eye only disconnected fragments would appear, both Joyce and Mann have employed the rhetorical device of the *Leitmotiv,* the recurrent verbal constellation, to bring together apparently unrelated, widely separated occurrences, persons, settings, and experiences. Apparently independently, inspired each

* Supra, p. 194.

by the art of music—Mann admittedly by Wagner, Joyce possibly as well—these two authors of remarkably parallel courses and aims made use of recurrent verbal figures to lead the mind not only from point to point of the narrative, but also, and more significantly, backward, downward, into depths that in both cases proved (as in Wagner) to be of mythic mysteries: myth conceived as referring, not as in archaic times and orthodox religious life, directly to supernatural beings and miraculous occasions, but as in poetry and depth psychology, symbolically, to the root and seed potentials, structuring laws and forces, interior to the earthly being that is man.

The *Leitmotiv* appears already in Homer in an elementary way in the epic epithet: "wine-dark sea," "rosy-fingered dawn," and so forth. In Mann's first novel, *Buddenbrooks,* it is an immediately recognizable coordinating device, employed principally to maintain the sense of a continuity of character through all the acts, decisions, and appearances of each of the numerous personages of the work; but serving also to establish and develop certain thematic continuities and contrasts: for instance, the call and demands of duty represented to all true Buddenbrooks by the name of the family firm, and the opposition to this sobering family summons represented by the romantic call to the individual of the sea—romance—music—dream—and then sleep—metaphysics—death. In Joyce's *Portrait* (the first draft of which was finished in the year of Mann's short story "Tonio Kröger," 1903), a like building up of continuities and of counterpoised thematic aggregates through verbal echoes and refrains can be recognized; and in that case many of the motives announced were to be carried on systematically to *Ulysses* and *Finnegans Wake.* In his short story "Tonio Kröger," however, Mann developed his use of the *Leitmotiv* in a new, symphonic, musical way (a "prose ballad," he himself called the work);[31] for in contrast to the novel *Buddenbrooks,* where a comparatively simple, sequential, epic technique of repetition had been used (*the firm—the firm—the firm,* against a cumulative aggregation of counterthemes: *the sea—music—romance—dream and sleep—metaphysics—disengagement—death*), there is in this short story a musical development and unfolding of the range of associations of each of the motifs at each of its restatements. For example:

The title of the work and the hero's name, "Tonio Kröger," already suggests a dichotomy: from the father's side, northern blood, and from the mother's, Mediterranean. Among the blue-eyed blonds of his school, Tonio is dark-haired and dark-eyed, and the inward dissonance thus socially evident is again complemented inwardly by the love, yearning, and envy, mingled with a certain strain of contempt, that Tonio feels for his companions. For, inheriting his mother's emotional temperament, he is more complex than they, indrawn, moody, and susceptible: to the beauty of the walnut tree and the fountain, the comely blue-eyed girls and boys themselves, to music and the sea, to solitude, and to experiences and readings of his own—such as of Schiller's *Don Carlos*, where he finds a counterpart of his own complicated case. At parties he is inept, and the girls spontaneously drawn to him are those who fall down when they dance; the lovely, competent, blue-eyed blondes do not sense and respond to his deeper strain. And now the ranges of association of these announced motives expand. Tonio is neglecting assigned schoolwork in favor of his own findings, and his grades consequently are suffering. His blue-eyed father is angry, his dark mother, however, indifferent: she has a temperament for disorder, which Tonio recognizes in himself. "What is the matter with me?" he muses. "We are not gypsies in a green wagon, but decent folk." The gypsy-in-a-green-wagon motif, now joining those of dark eyes and hair, sensibility, and detachment, adds connotations of adventure, freedom, and disgrace, while the blue-eyed-blond theme acquires, in contrast, the dignity of responsible respectability, social engagement, and worth. Tonio departs to be a writer, and the final stand of the motifs is that of the letter, already cited, that he writes to Lisabeta Ivanovna: * of the world of art and letters against life and the simple heart, and with Tonio Kröger between.

"Whereas in *Buddenbrooks*," wrote the author himself in his wartime book of reflections,

> only the influence of Schopenhauer and Wagner, the pessimistic ethical vein, the musical and the epical, found expression, in 'Tonio Kröger' the Nietzschean, pedagogical, life-fostering factor broke through that was to remain predominant in my later works. In the experience and feeling that inspired this novelette,

* Supra, pp. 311–12.

the lyric philosopher Nietzsche's conservative dithyrambic conception of life, and his defense of this against the moralizing nihilistic spirit, became transformed into *erotic irony:* a loving affirmation of all that is *not* intellectuality and art, but is innocent, healthy, decently unproblematical and untouched by spirituality. The name of Life, yea of Beauty, is attributed in this work (sentimentally, it is true) to the world of burgher living (*Bürgerlichkeit*), normality recognized as blessed, the antithesis of intellectuality and art.

And no wonder this appealed to the younger generation! For if "life" came off well here, the "spirit" came off still better, since it was this that was the lover, and "the god" is in the one who loves, not the beloved—which is something the "spirit" in this case well knew. What it did not yet know, or for the time being was leaving aside, however, was the fact that not only does the spirit yearn toward life, but also life yearns toward the spirit, and that the requirement of life for salvation, its yearning, its sense of beauty (for beauty is nothing but yearning) is perhaps more serious, perhaps more "godly," perhaps less arrogant, less haughty, than that of the spirit.

But irony is always irony in both directions, something in the middle, a neither-nor and a both-and: as, indeed, Tonio Kröger pictured himself—as something ironically in the middle, between burgher life and life in art. In fact, his name itself is already a symbol for all kinds of problematical mixtures: not only that of Latin and German blood, but also those of the middle ground between health and sophistication, respectability and adventurousness, heart and temperament. The name thus suggests the pathos of a dual position, which again is obviously influenced by Nietzsche, who declared that the clarifying force of his philosophy resulted from the fact that he was at home in the *two* worlds, of the decadence and of health. He stood, as he declared, between the setting and the rising. The whole of my story was a mélange of elements apparently incompatible: melancholy and criticism, inwardness and skepticism, Theodor Storm and Nietzsche, mood and intellectuality. . . . No wonder, as I say, that the younger generation went for this and preferred these mere ninety pages to the two thick volumes of the *Buddenbrooks*.[32]

Erotic irony, then, or, as Mann also frequently termed it, plastic irony, is the key to the aesthetic posture of his scriptural revelation. It is the posture of an artist not afraid to see what is before him in its truth, its frailty, its inadequacy to the ideal, and whose heart then goes out to it in affirmation of this frailty, as of its life. For it is according to its imperfection that each existence moves, acts, and becomes, perfection being not of this earth. Consequently, it is in naming its imperfection that the artist gives to each its life, its possibility; and this, be it said, is a cruel act—though with ironic result.

The look that one directs at things, both outward and inward, as an artist [our author states], is not the same as that with which one would regard the same as a man, but at once colder and more passionate. As a man, you might be well-disposed, patient, loving, positive, and have a wholly uncritical inclination to look upon everything as all right: but as artist, your daemon constrains you to "observe": to take note, lightning fast and with hurtful malice, of every detail that in the literary sense would be characteristic, distinctive, significant, opening insights, typifying the race, the social or the psychological mode; recording all as mercilessly as though you had no human relationship to the observed object whatsoever—and in the "work," then, everything comes to light. . . .

But besides this split between the artist and the human being, which can lead to the most serious outer and inner conflicts, there is still another factor, it seems to me, on which the art of authorship rests: a painful sensibility, of which the expression and manifestation is a "critical force" or "cogency" in expression that I have found to be a source of misunderstanding. That is to say, it is not to be supposed that the refinement and alertness of the faculties of observation can be sharpened to an exceptional degree without having one's susceptibility to pain sharpened as well. And there is a degree in such susceptibility that turns every experience into an affliction. But the only weapon given to the artist, with which to react to such things and experiences, and to protect himself in his own fashion, is that of expression, his power of denoting; and this reaction to things by expressing himself about them with psychological destructiveness, which is the sublime *revenge* of the artist on his experiences, will be the more violent, the greater the sensibility of the center the experience has touched. This is the origin of that cold and merciless accuracy in description: this, the tensely drawn bow from which the *word* flies, the sharp, feathered

word, that whirs and hits and lodges quivering in its mark.
—And the stern bow: is it not, as well as the gentle lyre, an instrument of Apollo? [Figure 44, p. 360.]—Nothing would be
farther from the secret of art than the idea that coldness and passion exclude each other! Nothing more mistaken than to conclude
that critical force and cogency of expression are derived from
malice and animosity—in the human sense! . . . The accurate
expression always seems spiteful. The right word hurts.[33]

So far, so good; we have read, and we have heard: the artist,
always a little sorry for himself, has experiences with pain and replies with the arrow of a word, well made, well aimed. But to
what end? To kill?
The author has more to say:

The intellectual, the spiritual man has the choice (to *this* extent he can choose) to work either with ironic or with radical
effect: a third possibility is not decently possible. And what he
manages to make of himself in this regard depends on the final
point of his argument. It hangs on the question as to which of
the two arguments seems to him the final, decisive, absolute
one: that of Life, or that of the Spirit (the Spirit as Truth, or as
Righteousness, or as Purity). For the Radical, life is no argument. *Fiat justitia,* or *veritas* or *libertas, fiat spiritus—pereat
mundus et vita!* So speaks every form of radicalism. And on the
other hand: "Is then Truth an argument—when the question is
Life?" This question is the formula of irony.
Radicalism is nihilism. The ironic mood is conservative. A
conservatism is only then ironic, however, when it does not represent the voice of life speaking for itself, but the voice of the
spirit, speaking not for itself, but for life.
Here it is Eros that is in play. This love has been characterized as "the affirmation of an individual, regardless of his
worth." Now that surely is not a very spiritual, not a very moral
affirmation, and indeed, the affirmation of life by the spirit is not
moral either. It is ironic. Eros ever was ironic. And irony is
erotic. . .
And this is what makes art so worth our love and worth our
practice, this wonderful contradiction, that it is—or at least
can be—simultaneously a refreshment and a judgment, a celebration and reward of life through its delightful imitation, and at
the same time, a morally critical annihilation of life; that its

effect is in equal degree an awakening of delight and of conscience. The boon of art proceeds from the circumstance (to use
diplomatic terms) that it maintains equally good relationships
to life and to pure spirit, that it is simultaneously conservative
and radical; from the circumstance, that is to say, of its mediate
and mediating place between spirit and life. Which is the place
of the source of irony itself.[34]

Mann's first formulation of this ironic principle appeared, as
we have seen, in "Tonio Kröger" (1903), immediately after completion of his "Tristan" (1902), and thereby opened the way for
him to a mode of thought and feeling that should carry his craft
between the Scylla and Charybdis of the hard sheer rock of
"truth," on one hand, "perfection," "justice," "judgment," and
"release from the prison of this flesh," and on the other, the vortex
of involvement in the spirit-killing toils, banalities, lies, cheatings,
and blind passions of mere life for life: an answer, in other
words, to the basic Tristan problem, as he saw it, of exclusivism,
aesthetic snobbism, retreat from the fields of common life, and, as
he termed it, "sympathy with death." The medieval poet Gottfried's high disdain for those "who are unable to endure sorrow
and wish only to revel in bliss" * was here explicitly renounced,
and a mode of seeing and feeling proposed that should view with
equal eye and loving heart both the noble and the base, the wicked
and the just, transmuting all, through its art, its alchemy, into
"gold."

However, if we may be honest here for a moment—and not
again, immediately, ironic—this transmutation, to be realized,
must include all those whom we fear and hate, as well as those
whom we merely despise: the monsters, sadists, beasts, and de-
generates of our kind, in the all-embracing spirit of Christ's own
fundamental word, "You have heard that it was said, 'You shall
love your neighbor and hate your enemy,' but I say to you, Love
your enemies, and pray for those who persecute you." [35] And
again: "Judge not, that you may not be judged." [36] Or in the
spirit of the Buddhist axiom: "All things are buddha-things." [37]
And indeed, Mann himself has said of his undiscriminating *eros*
—which in his definition, finally, is indistinguishable from the in-

* Supra, p. 38.

discriminate *agape* of which we have already heard—that in its "affirmation of an individual, regardless of his worth," it is "not a very spiritual, not a very moral affirmation."

This presents us with a multileveled, many-headed problem.

First, there is that which Mann recognized when he distinguished between the writer as artist and the writer as mere human being. As an artist, the writer must be cruel and merciless in observation, even with pain to himself, and yet as a human being may be gentle, cordial and unassuming; or, as we now have also learned, as an artist he must be all-loving (in his own way), all-understanding, and yet, as a mere man, may still be capable of righteousness and even the use of brute force—as we hear, indeed, of Christ himself in that instance of the money-changers in the temple. Thomas Mann returned to his own secular mode in his self-exile from Hitler's Reich and his address, then, from the yonder shore—with the disembodied voice, as it were, of the ghost of one they once knew—to the German people still entrapped in the *māyā* of European history. And there is room here for irony all round.

For no one in the history of thought has yet proposed a formula sufficient to eradicate that "beveled edge" of phoenix fire where the spiritual and the earthly, metaphysical and moral planes intersect: the line or point of meeting symbolized in the bed (the sweet-bitter altar) of the Cross. *Not the voice of the spirit speaking for itself, but the voice of the spirit speaking for life:* that is the self-crucifixion of the spirit ("who, though he was in the form of God, did not count equality with God a thing to be grasped, but emptied himself, taking the form of a servant, being born in the likeness of men: and being found in human form he humbled himself and became obedient unto death, even death on a cross").[38] And on the other side: *"Not the voice of life speaking for life, but the yearning of life toward the spirit";* which is the self-crucifixion of life (as again in Paul: "I have been crucified with Christ; it is no longer I who live, but Christ who lives in me").[39] To all of which there is the corollary that *"irony is always irony in both directions, something in the middle, a neither-nor and a both-and"*—which last is a phrase that comes marvelously close to sounding like an aphorism of the Mahayana Buddhist teaching of the Middle Way, where compassion (*karuṇā*) is a function of the realization that all these suffering beings are no-beings, but spirit, which neither is nor is not.[40] "When it is seen that all form is no form, the Buddha is recognized." [41] "It cannot be called either void or not void, or both or neither." [42]

The artist lives thus in two worlds—as do we all; but he, in so far as he knows what he is doing, in a special state of consciousness of this micromacrocosmic crucifixion that is life on earth and is perhaps, also, the fire of the sun, stars, and galaxies beyond.

Which, however, is not all he has to endure. For in his special sphere of irony there is another confrontation of opposites to be resolved in the imbroglio of *eros, agape,* and *amor:* the first two, as we have seen, being religious in the Dionysian-Orphic, Gnostic-Christian ways of indiscriminate, all-embracing love, whereas *amor* is aristocratic, discriminatory, and aesthetic: as defined in the literature of the troubadours, by the Minnesingers, and by Gottfried, an experience of the "noble heart" and its scouts, the eyes. But if the truth is to be told here again, as it was, I believe, in "Tonio Kröger," it was actually Tonio's noble heart's commitment *aesthetically* to the pert little commonplace blue-eyed Ingeborg Holm (who did not fall down when she danced and so had no sense of his own soul's need) that had locked him in a sort of troubadour's lifetime of vassalage in poet's service to the *general* face of those simple folk (less simple, however, than he thought they were) of this fair world—whom it is even God's whole privilege and function to love, to forgive, and to woo.

See again both Romans 11:32 and Figure 8.*

IV. Identity and Relationship

In the art of Thomas Mann, the principle of rapture *(eros-agape)* is represented—following Nietzsche's designation of music, the dance, and lyric poetry as the arts specific to the Dionysian mode —through the author's craftsmanly concern for the musical effects of his prose, its rhythms, verbal tones, and spheres of emotional association, as well as through his masterly employment of the *Leitmotiv.* And on the other side, the side of the claims of the unique, ephemeral, induplicable moment, sentiment, or individual —the side of the principle of individuation (*principium individuationis*), which Nietzsche assigned to Apollo as the lord of light

* Supra, pp. 259 and 18.

and to the arts of sculpture and epic poetry—Mann served in the merciless accuracy of his almost incredibly alive, descriptive style. The work of Nietzsche that most profoundly influenced him in his fashioning of this style, and even came in *The Magic Mountain* to a sort of novelized restatement, was the philosopher's youthful manifesto, *The Birth of Tragedy* (1872).

"A great deal will have been won for the science of aesthetics," Nietzsche wrote in the opening, key passage of this work, "when we shall have succeeded in not merely recognizing intellectually, but directly and clearly seeing, that the development of art depends on the dual influence of Apollonian and Dionysian forces —as reproduction depends on the sexes, in their unrelenting conflict and only occasional—periodic—reconciliation."

That is the basic, germinal idea. We come now to its elucidation, the powers in question being those of Figure 3, at Stations 16 and 10.

> I have borrowed these two names [Nietzsche explains] from the Greeks, who interpreted the profound mysteries of their doctrines of art to those of adequate understanding, not in conceptual terms, but through the eloquently impressive figures of their pantheon. Hence it is through their two divinities of art, Apollo and Dionysus, that we are led to recognize that in the Greek world there existed a great division, with respect to both source and aim, between the art of the sculptor, Apollonian art, and the non-pictorial art, music, of Dionysus. The two impulses, different as they are, were carried along side by side, generally in open opposition, provoking each other to ever new, more mighty births through which to perpetuate the war of a pair of opposites that the shared word "art" only apparently over-bridges; until at last, through a metaphysical miracle of the Hellenic "will," the two were united, and in that pairing generated the art that was as Dionysian as Apollonian: Attic tragedy.[43]

Nietzsche describes next, in contrast, the opposed powers and features of these two divine domains.

> To familiarize ourselves more closely with these two forces, let us begin, [he suggests] by regarding them as the separate art worlds of *dream* and *intoxication*, between which physiological phenomena an opposition is to be remarked that is analogous to that between the Apollonian and Dionysian spheres. It was in

dream, according to Lucretius, that the forms of the gods appeared before the souls of men; in dream the great sculptor saw the enchanting bodily forms of supernatural beings; and if the Hellenic poet had been asked concerning the secret of poetic inspiration, he too would have referred to dream, and proposed a doctrine like that of Hans Sachs in *The Meistersinger:*

> My friend, this is the poet's task,
> His dreams to mark, their sense to ask.
> Man's truest rapture, so I teach,
> In dream is opened to his speech.
> All poetic inspiration
> Is but dream interpretation.

The fair illusion of the world of dream, in whose creation everyone is a finished artist, is the precondition of all visual art and, as we shall see, of an important half of poetry as well. We enjoy in dream a direct comprehension of form, every figure speaks to us, there is nothing indifferent or superfluous. And even in moments of the greatest vividness of this dream-reality, we have nevertheless the prevading sense of its *illusion:* or that, at least, has been my experience, for the frequency, indeed normality, of which I could offer considerable evidence, and the statements of the poets besides. Moreover, the philosophical mind even has a premonition that beneath this other reality, also, in which we live and have our being, a second, quite different, lies concealed; in other words, that this too is an illusion: and Schopenhauer even designates as the true sign of the philosophical talent, just this susceptibility to the impression, at times, of people and all things as an imagery of dream. And now, much as the philosopher relates himself to the reality of existence, so the artistically sensitive man to the reality of dream: he observes it closely and with pleasure, since it is from these images that he interprets life, and on these that he prepares for life. Nor is it only the pleasant and favorable images that he experiences this way, with ready understanding, but the austere, turbid, sorrowful, and dark, as well: abrupt frustrations, the taunts of chance, frightful expectations, in short, the entire "divine comedy"of life, along with its *inferno,* passes before him: not simply as a shadow play—for he lives and suffers in these scenes—yet not without that ineffable sense, either, of illusion. And there may be others who, like myself, in the very midst of the perils and terrors of a dream have reassured themselves by crying: "It is a dream! I want it to go on!" Also, I

have heard tell of those who have been able to keep the circumstances of one and the same dream going on through a course of
three or more successive nights. These are facts which clearly
testify that our innermost being, the common ground of us all,
experiences dream with deep delight and a joyous sense of its
necessity.

And this sense of joyous necessity in the experience of dream
is what the Greeks likewise expressed in their Apollo. Apollo is
the god of all visioning powers and at the same time the sooth-
saying god. He who at root is the "appearing" one, the divinity
of light, is the lord also of the fair "appearance" of the inward
world of fantasy. The higher sense of validity, the wholeness, of
these conditions, in contrast to the incompletely comprehensible
realities of day, taken together with the deep consciousness of
the healing and helping powers of Nature in sleep and dream, is
symbolically analogous to the prophetic faculty and in general
to the arts, through which life is made possible and worth living.
But then also, that thin line which the dream image must not
cross, if it is not to work pathologically, in which case the appearance would deceive us and be taken for crude reality: that
line of limitation, that freedom from the more uncontrolled
emotions, that wisdom-filled repose of the sculptor's god, the
image of Apollo itself must also honor. His eye must be "sunlike," in accord with his origin: even when its glance is wrathful
and incensed, there dwells in it the benison of the fair illusion.
Hence, of Apollo one can say, in an eccentric way, what Schopenhauer, in Book One of *The World as Will and Idea,* says of
mankind caught in the net of *māyā:* "As on a raging sea,
where, limitless in all directions, roaring mountains of water rise
and fall, a boatman sits in his skiff with trust in the fragile craft,
so in the midst of a world of torments, the individual calmly sits,
supported and trusting, upon the *principium individuationis.*"
Yes, it can be said of Apollo that in him the unshaken trust in
that *principium,* and the calm repose in it of the being entrapped
in it, have received their most sublime expression; and one
might even designate Apollo as the glorious divine image of the
principium individuationis itself, in whose gestures and glances
the whole delight and wisdom of the "world illusion" speaks to
us, together with its beauty.

But in the same passage Schopenhauer has pictured to us the
monstrous horror (*das ungeheure Grausen*) that takes hold of
the individual when he suddenly finds himself in error with re-

spect to his interpretation of the forms of appearance—which is what occurs when the logic of causality, in one or another of its laws, seems to have been fractured by an exception. And if we now add to this horror the rapturous transport that rises from the innermost ground of the individual, yea from the ground of Nature itself, at that shattering of the *principium individuationis,* we shall gain an insight into the essence of that *Dionysian* state, to which we are brought closest by the analogy of *intoxication.* Through the influence either of those narcotic potions to which all primitive men and peoples give praise in hymns, or of the mighty approach of spring, suffusing delightfully all of Nature, those Dionysian motions awake that, when heightened, erase all sense of individuality in self-forgetfulness. In the German Middle Ages, under the influence of just such a Dionysian force, ever-growing hordes, singing and dancing, were sent swarming from place to place. In these St. John's and St. Vitus' dancers we recognize again the Bacchic choruses of the Greeks, with their predecessors in Asia Minor and on back to Babylon, the orgiastic Scythians as well. There are those who, either from lack of experience or from dullness of wit, turn away from such phenomena with mockery or pity and a feeling of their own health, as from "endemic diseases": poor chaps! they have no idea how corpse-pale and ghostly this very "health" of theirs appears when the glowing life of the Dionysian revel swarms past them.

Under the magic of the Dionysian force, not only does the bond between man and man again close together, but alienated, hostile, or suppressed Nature celebrates her festival of reconciliation with her lost son, man. Freely, of herself, the earth bestows her boons, and, ready for peace, the beasts of prey, of the rocks and deserts, draw nigh. [Figure 1.] With flowers and garlands is the car all strewn of Dionysus: in its span stride panther and tiger. Turn Beethovan's "Paean to Joy" into a painting and fill it with everything you can imagine, where the millions, in awe, sink prostrate to the dust: that is the way to arrive at some notion of the Dionysian. Now the slave is a free man, now all those hard, hostile boundaries shatter that misery, willfulness, or "insolent custom" have set up between man and man. Now each, in the Gospel of World Harmony, feels himself to be not only united with his neighbor, reconciled and blended, but one—as though the veil of *maya* had been rent apart and now only fluttered in shreds around the mysterious primordial One.

Mankind, singing, dancing, professes itself to be a member of a higher commonalty. It has forgotten how to walk and speak, on the point of flying, in dance, into the air. Enchantment speaks through all its gestures. And as now the animals talk and the earth yields milk and honey, so there resounds through all of this, something supernatural. One feels oneself to be a god and now strides in the same enraptured and exalted way as the gods in dream were seen to stride. The man now is no longer an artist, but himself a work of art. The art power of all Nature here is manifesting itself in the thrill of intoxication, to the supremely rapturous satisfaction of the primordial One. The noblest clay, the most precious marble, namely man, is here kneaded and hewn; and to chisel blows of the Dionysian world-artist, the cry is heard sounding of the Eleusinian mysteries: "Are you prostrating yourselves, you millions? Do you not mark your creator, the World?" [44]

Taken for granted in this philosophy, as also in that of Schopenhauer and in the operatic world of the young Nietzsche's adored friend Wagner, is the Kantian concept of all phenomenality as conditioned, through and through, by the organs through which it is perceived—whether eyes be open, as by day, or shut, by night. (Compare, in Figure 3, the dreamer, at the goddess's feet.) Also accepted is the recognition, which Schopenhauer seems to have been the first to have realized, of this Kantian concept of the *a priori* forms of sensibility and categories of logic as practically identical with the Hindu-Buddhist philosophy of *māyā*.[45] And accordingly, as Vishnu is the lord of *māyā,* the god whose dream is the universe and in whom (as all figures in a dream are actually but functions of the energy of the dreamer) all things, all beings, of this *māyā*-world are but refractions of the one substance, so also, in Hellenic mythology, is Apollo. Comparatively viewed, both as to character and as to sense, the classical Apollo, as interpreted by Nietzsche, and the Indian god Vishnu as Narayana, floating on the Cosmic Sea, dreaming the lotus-dream of the universe, are the same. And James Joyce also, in *Ulysses,* takes this transcendental philosophy for his base; so that in the Sandymount chapter, where Stephen Dedalus strolls brooding by the sea, the very terms of Schopenhauer appear in designation of the conditioning *a priori* forms of sensibility; i.e.

the *Nebeneinander* (the field of things "beside each other"), namely Space; and the *Nacheinander* ("after each other"), Time: [46] following which, and still in Schopenhauer's vein, Joyce treats of the principle of causality, the chain of cause and effect, in the amusing image of a telephone line of navel cords linking all of us back to Edenville, each with his own navel as the phone mouthpiece by which he might communicate with his first cause: "The cords of all link back . . ." so we read: "strandentwining cable of all flesh. That is why mystic monks. Will you be as gods? Gaze in your omphalos. Hello. Kinch here. Put me on to Edenville. Aleph, alpha: nought, nought, one.—Spouse and helpmate of Adam Kadmon: Heva, naked Eve. She had no navel." [47] The aim of this brooding hero, as we have seen, was to penetrate that threefold veil of Space (the *Nebeneinander*), Time (the *Nacheinander*), and Cause-Effect (the *Satz vom Grunde*), and so to come to the "Father," "Drowned Man," "Finn-again" (the Irish word *fionn,* meaning "light"), who is lost to view in the deep, dark "adiaphane": beyond and within the "diaphane" of this limitless mothering sea of forms, rising, falling, roaring all around us, like waves.

Immanuel Kant (1724–1804), in his *Prolegomena to Every Future System of Metaphysics that May Ever Arise in the Way of a Science* (1783) supplies an extraordinarily simple formula for the metaphysical or mystical interpretation not only of mythic metaphors, but also of the phenomenal world itself from which such metaphors derive, the world of empirical fact, and the world of dream as well. What he offers is a four-term analogy, *a* is to *b* as *c* is to *x,* which is to be interpreted as pointing not to an incomplete resemblance of two things, but to a complete resemblance of two relationships between quite dissimilar things ("*nicht etwa, eine unvollkommene Ähnlichkeit zweier Dinge, sondern eine vollkommene Ähnlichkeit zweier Verhältnisse zwischen ganz unähnlichen Dingen*"): not "*a* somewhat resembles *b*," but "the relationship of *a* to *b* perfectly resembles that of *c* to *x*," where *x* represents *a quantity that is not only unknown but absolutely unknowable*—which is to say, metaphysical.

Kant demonstrates this formula in two examples:

1. As the promotion of the happiness of the children (*a*) is related to the parents' love (*b*), so is the welfare of the human race

(c) to that unknown in God (x) which we call God's love.

2. The causality of the highest cause (x) is precisely, in respect to the world (c), what human reason (b) is in respect to the work of human art (a).

He then discusses the implication of the second of these examples, as follows:

> Herewith the nature of the highest cause itself remains unknown to me, I only compare its known effect (namely, the constitution of the universe) and the rationality of this effect with the known effects of human reason, and therefore I call that highest cause a Reason, without thereby attributing to it as its proper quality, either the thing that I understand by this term in the case of man, or any other thing with which I am familiar.[48]

Mythological, theological, metaphysical analogies, in other words, do not point indirectly to an only partially understood "metaphysical" term (God, *brahman, ātman,* the Self, the Absolute, for example), but directly to a *relationship between two terms,* the one empirical, the other metaphysical; the latter being absolutely and forever and from every conceivable human standpoint, unknowable: unconditioned as it is by Time, Space, Causality, and the categories of logic—and to such a degree that even to speak of it as unconditioned is to represent, and so to misrepresent, it, which cannot be represented and is no *which.* It is evident that Kant's metaphysical *Ding-an-sich,* therefore, is equivalent (as far as it goes) to the *brahman* of the Upanishads, the Void (*śunyatā*) of the Buddhists, and the "Nameless" of the Tao Te Ching.

To which Schopenhauer added the complementary insight (which completed the Oriental equivalence) that that which is thus absolutely and forever and from every conceivable human standpoint unknowable as the metaphysical ground of all things is accordingly, inevitably, the ground of being of each one of us, and so our very self; and by analogy, as the figures of your dream (a) are to you (b), so are the forms and creatures of this world (c), to that unknown (x) who, as Apollo-Vishnu, is called the dreamer of the world illusion.

"Life," Schopenhauer wrote in his paper already cited, "On an Apparent Intention in the Fate of the Individual," "has long been recognized and often declared to resemble dream. And indeed, this comparison with dream permits us to perceive, even if only as at a misty distance, how the hidden power that directs and moves us toward its intended goals by means of the outward circumstances affecting us, might yet have its roots within the very depths of our own unfathomable being."

Schopenhauer is here continuing the argument, as the reader no doubt has surmised, concerning the problem announced in his title of this piece: of the curious sense that occasionally comes to one, of an intention behind those apparently chance events by which one's life has been shaped—and in certain lights even appears to have been shaped by highly conscious art, as by the plan of a creative author.

For in dreams too [he now goes on to suggest] the circumstances that motivate our acts seem to befall us from without, as independent, often repulsive, completely accidental occurrences, and yet there is a concealed, purposeful continuity throughout: for there is a hidden power, to which all those accidents of the dream conform, which is actually directing and coordinating its incidents—and always with exclusive reference to ourselves. But the most extraordinary thing is this: that this hidden power can finally be nothing other than our own will—operating from a standpoint, however, that is not embraced in the horizon of our dreaming consciousness. That is why it happens that the occurrences in our dreams so often go completely against the wishes of which we are aware in our dreams; surprise, depress, and even frighten us nearly to death; while the dream-fate that we ourselves are covertly directing sends us neither rescuer nor relief. Or, comparably: we inquire eagerly about something, and receive an answer that sets us in amazement. Or again: we ourselves are being questioned, as though in an examination, and are unable to find the reply, whereupon another, to our humiliation, answers perfectly. And in both of these cases the answer can have come only from our own resources.

To clarify this mysterious guidance of dream events by the dreamer himself, and to bring it a little closer to our understanding, there is still another available illustration; but it will be unavoidably obscene, and so I must presuppose that a reader worthy of my writing for him will neither take offence, nor consider merely the comical aspect of the matter. As is well known, certain dreams serve a material function, namely of emptying the overfilled seminal glands. Dreams of this kind, naturally enough, present indecent scenes; but other dreams, too, present indecent scenes without serving the same material function. Here, then, we find that in the first sort of dream opportunity and the desired object favor the dreamer and nature has its way, whereas in dreams of the other sort, on the contrary, all kinds of obstacles intervene between ourselves and the object so eagerly desired. We strive and strive again to overcome them, without success, and the goal is never attained.—But now, the power that is erecting these obstacles, rendering all our dearest wishes futile, is none other than our own individual will—however, working here from a zone far outside the range of the perceiving dream consciousness and hence experienced by the latter as pitiless, inexorable Fate.

May it not be, now, that the Fate that appears in the world of reality, the design that probably everyone has had occasion to observe in the development of his own life, may have something about it analogous to the relationship here observed in the dream?

Sometimes it happens that we draw up a plan and set our hearts upon its accomplishment, until later it becomes apparent that the plan was not for our true good at all. And in the meantime, trying our best to carry it out, we have found that Fate had somehow cursed it, setting all its machinery into motion against it; so that ultimately, entirely against our will, we find ourselves pressed back into what for us is the better path. In the face of such apparently intentional opposition, people are accustomed to saying: "It wasn't meant to be!" Some call it ominous, others a sign from God; but all share the opinion that when Fate with obvious determination thus sets itself against a project, we had better give it up. The project being one that does not befit our unconscious destiny, it will never be brought to fulfillment, and in sticking to it stubbornly with stiff-necked persistence, we are only inviting Fate to deal us stiffer and stiffer pokes in the ribs, until finally we are got back into our proper channel. Or if, on the other hand, we at last succeed in forcing the project through, it will only redound to our injury and distress. In this, the above quoted *ducunt volentem fata, nolentem trahunt* finds its adequate justification.

Often it becomes apparent, after the struggle is over, that the defeat was for our good. But is it not possible that the defeat may have been for our good even when its benefits never become apparent—particularly when we consider our true good from the metaphysical-moral point of view?

And if we look back now to the main conclusion of my entire philosophy; namely, that what the phenomenon of the world embodies and represents is the Will, the very same Will that lives and struggles in each separate individual; and if we consider the generally recognized similarity of life and dream; then, summarizing our entire discussion, we may permit ourselves to imagine that, just as each of us is the hidden director of his own dreams, so, in analogous fashion, may the fate that governs each of our lives proceed ultimately from that Will, which, though it is our own, yet works its influence from a region far beyond the horizon of our individual perceiving consciousness. Still, it is this limited perceiving consciousness that furnishes the motives to our empirically knowable, individual will. Naturally, then, this latter must frequently come into violent conflict with that other will of ours which appears to us as our Fate, as our guiding genius, as our "Spirit, dwelling outside of us, his throne the highest stars," whose vision, far outdistancing that of the individual consciousness, reveals itself as an inexorable outer coercion, preparing and controlling what, though it cannot be revealed to the individual, he must never get wrong.

To lessen the strangeness, yea, the exorbitance, of this bold proposition, let me quote a passage from Scotus Erigena. His "God," it must be kept in mind, is without knowledge. Neither time and space nor the ten Aristotelean categories can be predicated to him. He has, in fact, only one predicate, and that is— Will. Clearly then, he is nothing other than what I have been terming the Will to Life. In Erigena's words: "There is yet another kind of ignorance in God, inasmuch as he may be said not to know what things he foreknows and predestines until they have appeared experientially in the course of created events." And directly thereafter: "There is a third kind of divine ignorance, in that God may be said to be ignorant of things not yet made manifest in their effects through experience of their action and operation; of which, nevertheless, he holds the invisible causes in himself, by himself created, and to himself known." [49]

But now, if, in order to make our point a bit more comprehensible, we have called upon the well-known similarity of the individual life to dream, let it not be forgotten, on the other hand, that in dreams the relationship is one-sided; that is to say, that only *one* ego actually wills and experiences while the others are nothing but phantoms, whereas in the great dream of life there exists a reciprocal relationship: each not only appears in the other's dream precisely as there required, but also experiences the other in a similar way in his own dream; so that, by virtue of an actual *harmonia praestabilita,* each dreams only what is appropriate to his own metaphysical guidance, and yet all the life dreams are interwoven so artfully that, while each experiences only what redounds to his own increase, he performs what the others require. Hence, a vast world event conforms to the destiny-requirements of many thousands, befitting each in his own way.

Every event in every individual life must then be implicated in two fundamentally different orders of relationship: first, in the objective, causal order of the course of nature, and second, in a subjective order relevant only to the experiencing individual himself and as subjective, consequently, as his dreams—where the sequence and content of the occurrences are as predetermined as the scenes of a drama, and, indeed, in the same way, namely, by plan of the author. However, that these two sorts of relationship should exist together, and in such a way that every event must be a link simultaneously in two completely different chains with the two conjoining perfectly, the fate of each thus harmonizing with the fate of every other, each the hero of his own drama and yet an actor in all the rest: this is certainly something that surpasses our comprehension, and can be imagined as possible only in terms of the most miraculous *harmonia praestabilita.*

But, on the other hand, would it not be an act of narrow-minded cowardice to maintain that it would be impossible for the life paths of all mankind in their complex interrelationships to exhibit as much concert and harmony as a composer can bring into the many apparently disconnected and haphazardly turbulent voices of his symphony? Our timidity before this colossal prospect may be allayed if we remind ourselves that the Subject of this great dream of life is, in a certain sense, only one, namely the Will to Life itself; and furthermore, that all this multiplicity of the phenomena is conditioned by time and space. It is a vast dream, dreamed by a single being; but in such a way that all the dream characters dream too. Hence, everything interlocks and harmonizes with everything else.[50]

It would be difficult to find a more exact statement than this of the sense and plane of experience of *Finnegans Wake,* where the

plunge, so to say, has actually been taken into those waters of the
sea that Stephen, in *Ulysses,* was considering from the point of
view only of the shore: the shore of waking consciousness, where
the knower and the known, the slayer and the slain, begetter and
begotten, subject and object, are set apart and distinguished from
each other. In sleep, the dreamer and the dream are one, though
seeming to be two, and a clue to the mystery has thus here been
found of that "consubstantiality of the Father and Son" upon
which Stephen, throughout his day, was brooding. However,
with this image of the dreamer and analogy of sleep, a porten-
tous step has been taken away from the position assumed by
Kant toward all definitions of the metaphysical sphere.

Let us pause on this problem for a moment.

In the Kantian vein, it would not be suggested that God either
is or could *be* the sleeper—nor has Schopenhauer, indeed, said so
much, either. It is only "as if" (*als ob*) God were the sleeper: as a
dream (a) is to its dreamer (b), so is the manifold of this universe (c) to that unknown (x), which is called in our tradition
"God." One might also say, however, without preference or
prejudice for any one metaphor over another: as children (a^1)
from parents (b^1), or as the work of art (a^2) from the artist
(b^2), as sparks (a^3) from a fire (b^3), or as an idea (a^4) from
the mind (b^4), so is the manifold of this universe (c) derived
from that unknown (x) which is called in Buddhist texts "the
Void." The term x, it is to be insisted, remains, through all this,
absolutely unknown and unknowable; and this being so, oneness
can no more be a quality of x than can love or reason, wrath,
personality, goodness, justice, mercy, being, or non-being. Athe-
ism, as well as theism, is but an optional way of thinking beyond
thought. As Kant has shown, it is only by analogy that we speak
of love or reason as of God: x remaining unknown, the nature of
its relationship to c must likewise remain unknown. In fact—and
here, now, we come to our splitting of the ways—to speak in
terms of a *relationship* is itself entirely optional, since in the idea
of a relationship a duality is implied—a c and an x; whereas it is
also possible, as in Oriental thought, in Neoplatonic thought, and
as in this metaphor of dream, to speak of *identity*—and to mean it.

Let us use the simple sign R to signify *relationship,* a relationship of any kind whatsoever; then let c, as above, stand for the

manifold of the universe or any part of it, and x, as above, for the unknown that is called "God" in our part of the world both by those who think they know, and by those who know that they do not know, what they are talking about when they use that suggestive term. The popular, ecclesiastically authorized *Occidental* manner of thinking about c and x will then be represented by the formula:

$$cRx$$

which means: this manifold of the universe and everything in it (c) stands in some sort of relationship (R) to the unknown (x); whereas, according to the basic *Oriental* formula (first pronounced, as far as we know, by the Indian sage Aruni, while instructing his son Shvetaketu, some six or eight centuries B.C.): [51]

$$tat\ tvam\ asi,\ \text{"thou, }art\text{ that," }c = x.$$

It is made clear in the Oriental texts, however, that the term "thou" (c) here intended is *not* to be understood flat-footedly in the way "common to all men" of experiencing the universe and themselves. As we read in the Mandukya Upanishad, there are four planes, or modes, or "quarters" of being:

1. The first is that "common to all men." Its field is the waking state. Its consciousness is outward-turned. Here subject and object are separate from each other, A is not B ($A \neq B$), and the laws of Aristotelean logic prevail.

2. The second field or portion of being, called "the shining one," is of the dream state. Its consciousness is inward-turned. Here subject and object are one yet seem to be two: the laws of Aristotelean logic do not apply. This is the field of *Finnegans Wake*, into which that of *Ulysses* dissolved when Stephen disappeared into the night, Bloom fell asleep in Molly's bed, and Molly herself went off to sleep, musing "I said yes I will Yes." [52] In Nietzsche's *Birth of Tragedy*, it is the field called Apollonian. In Schopenhauer's *World as Will and Idea*, it is the field of Platonic ideas, and the visual arts.* It is the field of all mythic forms, the gods, the demons, heavens and hells, and since the seer and seen are here one and the same, all the gods, demons, heavens

---

* Supra, pp. 33–36 and 80–83.

and hells, whether of the Orient or of Dante, are to be recognized here as within us.

3. The third field and portion of being is of deep dreamless sleep, where the sleeper neither desires anything desirable nor is in fear of anything terrible. It is called the field of "the knower" (*prājñā*), who is here undivided, as an "undifferentiated continuum" * of unconscious consciousness, consisting of bliss and feeding on bliss, "its only mouth being spirit." "This," declares the text, "is the Generative Womb of All, the Beginning and End of Beings." It is, in Gottfried's *Tristan*, the state symbolized in the love grotto, where the two, conjoined, lived on love and fed on bliss; in alchemy, that symbolized in Figure 43 and by the dragon in the *vas*, Figure 40: Ovid's Chaos.†

4. What is known as "the Fourth," the fourth portion of the self, is silence unqualified: neither of any thing nor of no thing; neither inward- nor outward-turned, nor the two together; neither knowing nor unknowing—because invisible, ineffable, intangible, devoid of characteristics, inconceivable, undefinable, the coming to peaceful rest of all differentiated, relative existence: utterly quiet, peaceful-blissful, without a second. "This," we read, "is the Self to be realized." [53] A ground that is no ground: this, then, is the ultimate ground of being.

The totality of being, however, is all four of these states, not merely any one. Hence, while it is true that "thou art that" ($c = x$), nevertheless, if by "thou" you understand only the person and world of stage 1, then "thou art not that" ($c \neq x$). This point is made in meditation disciplines through an exercise of the realization *neti neti*, "not this, not this": thou art not thy body, but the witness, the consciousness, of the body; not any of thy thoughts or feelings, but the witness, the consciousness of thy thoughts," and so forth; after which comes the realization *iti iti*, "it is this, it is this": *śivo-'ham*, "I am myself the Blissful One." All of which yields the ultimate oxymoron:

$$c \neq \, = x.$$

In Schopenhauer's philosophy, as suggested by the title of his major work, *The World as Will and Idea*, both ways of conceiv-

* This is Professor F. S. C. Northrup's term for this field, translating the Sanskrit, *ghana*, "homogeneous lump."

† Supra, p. 279.

ing of the inconceivable mystery are represented: the way of the oxymoron $c \neq\, = x$ being that of "the world as will," and the way of relationship, cRx, that of "the world as idea"—which two, in Nietzsche's vocabulary, became respectively the Dionysian and Apollonian modes—with these, in turn, corresponding to the contrasting Indian types of religion associated respectively with Shiva and with Vishnu.

Glancing back, furthermore, to what we have learned of the archaic beginnings of these mythic forms, we recall the early Osirian cult of the first four dynasties of Egypt: an awesome, terribly dark affair of massive suttee burials, which, with the coming of the Fifth Dynasty (c. 2480–2350 B.C.), was supplanted by the religion of light, of the god Re. The antecedents of the Osirian cycle were developed, as we have seen in *Oriental Mythology*,[54] in the nuclear Near East, possibly as early as the eighth millennium B.C., during the critical epoch of the dawn of the arts and cults of agriculture, and the reference of its mysteries was not originally, as in later times, to the death and life immortal of individuals, but to the death and rebirth of that Being of beings, that Lord of life and death, who puts on individuals and puts them off as a man puts on and puts off clothes. The moon, ever waxing and waning, is the celestial sign of this power, and on earth its chief animal symbols are the serpent, the boar, and the bull (Figures 11 to 18), whereas the cult of Re was of the sun, the falcon, the lion, and, in later times, the horse (Figures 26 and 27). Moreover, as the blithe little legend of the birth of the first three Fifth Dynasty Pharaohs shows,[55] the solar, in contrast to the somber lunar cult, brought with it a spirit of just such delight and joyous grace as Nietzsche assigns to the Apollonian sphere.

And so we are dealing here, actually, with two mythological archetypes of immemorial age, going back, respectively (if my surmise holds), to the primitive plant-environment of the tropics, where from the death and rot of vegetation, life is seen to spring ever anew and the individual counts for no more than a fallen leaf; and, on the other hand, the primitive animal environment of the Great Hunt of the paleolithic animal plains, where the individual and his hunting skill counted for a great deal indeed.— But all this I have discussed already, at length.[56]

v. Beauty Way

In Schopenhauer's philosophy, which is generally taken to be pessimistic, the path followed is *neti neti,* "not this, not this," the first stage of its passage to wisdom being marked by a radical turn of interest from the crude struggle for existence to those arts that Nietzsche terms Apollonian. Here empirical objects are beheld not as things desirable or to be feared (i.e. in any biological, economic, political, or moral relationship [R] to the subject), but as objectifications of their own informing ideas,* objects in and for themselves. And the sentiment characteristic of this stage is that "enchantment of the heart" of which Joyce speaks in *A Portrait of the Artist as a Young Man,* where his hero, Stephen Dedalus, quotes Aquinas: *Ad pulcritudinem tria requiruntur integritas, consonantia, claritas:* "Three things are needed for beauty, wholeness, harmony and radiance"; and proceeds, then, to an exposition of the basic aesthetic theory of his author, James Joyce.

Stephen was walking with his coarser-grained college companion Lynch along a Dublin street, pointing to a basket that a passing butcher's boy had slung inverted on his head. The clipped style of his discourse carries a mixture of dead seriousness and banter, while Lynch cooperatively clowns the role of straight man:

—Look at that basket, Stephen said.
—I see it, said Lynch.
—In order to see that basket, said Stephen, your mind first of all separates the basket from the rest of the visible universe which is not the basket. The first phase of apprehension is a bounding line drawn about the object to be apprehended. An esthetic image is presented to us either in space or in time. What is audible is presented in time, what is visible is presented in space. But, temporal or spatial, the esthetic image is first luminously apprehended as selfbounded and selfcontained upon the immeasurable background of space or time which is not it. You apprehend it as *one* thing. You see it as one whole. You apprehend its wholeness. That is *integritas.*
—Bull's eye! said Lynch, laughing. Go on.
—Then, said Stephen, you pass from point to point, led by its

* Supra, pp. 33–36 and 80–83.

formal lines; you apprehend it as balanced part against part within its limits; you feel the rhythm of its structure. In other words, the synthesis of immediate perception is followed by the analysis of apprehension. Having first felt that it is *one* thing you feel now that it is a *thing*. You apprehend it as complex, multiple, divisible, separable, made up of its parts, the result of its parts and their sum, harmonious. That is *consonantia*.

—Bull's eye again! said Lynch wittily. Tell me now what is *claritas* and you win the cigar.

—The connotation of the word, Stephen said, is rather vague. Aquinas uses a term which seems to be inexact. It baffled me for a long time. It would lead you to believe that he had in mind symbolism or idealism, the supreme quality of beauty being a light from some other world, the idea of which the matter is but a shadow, the reality of which it is but a symbol. I thought he might mean that *claritas* is the artistic discovery and representation of the divine purpose in anything or a force of generalisation which would make the esthetic image a universal one, make it outshine its proper conditions. But that is literary talk. I understand it so. When you have apprehended that basket as one thing and have then analysed it according to its form and apprehended it as a thing you make the only synthesis which is logically and esthetically permissible. You see that it is that thing which it is and no other thing. The radiance of which he speaks is the scholastic *quidditas*, the *whatness* of a thing. This supreme quality is felt by the artist when the esthetic image is first conceived in his imagination. The mind in that mysterious instant Shelley likened beautifully to a fading coal. The instant wherein that supreme quality of beauty, the clear radiance of the esthetic image, is apprehended luminously by the mind which has been arrested by its wholeness and fascinated by its harmony is the luminous silent stasis of esthetic pleasure, a spiritual state very like to that cardiac condition which the Italian physiologist Luigi Galvani, using a phrase almost as beautiful as Shelley's, called the enchantment of the heart.[57]

Now the term "stasis," of which Stephen has here made use, is of the very essence of Joyce's thesis; for, as made clear at the opening of his argument: "proper" as opposed to "improper" art (art serving ends, that is to say, that are proper to art itself) is static—not kinetic.

"The feelings excited by improper art," Stephen said, "are kinetic, desire or loathing. Desire urges us to possess, to go to something; loathing urges us to abandon, to go from something. The arts which excite them, pornographical or didactic, are therefore improper arts. The esthetic emotion . . . is therefore static. The mind is arrested and raised above desire and loathing." [58]

Compare the state of the Buddha at the time of his awakening on the "Immovable (i.e. Static) Spot," moved neither by desire nor by fear.[59]

I call this parallel important.

Compare, also, the words of Schopenhauer on the mode of vision proper to art, where the "Platonic Idea" (his equivalent of Joyce's *quidditas*) or "Thing-in-Itselfness" of an object is perceived by an unselfconscious subject:

> The shift from the usual way of perceiving individual objects to their perception as Idea occurs abruptly [Schopenhauer declares], when the act of perception has become dissociated from the service of the will, because the seeing subject has ceased to be merely ego-oriented and is now a pure, will-less subject of knowledge, no longer attentive to relationships in a causal context, but resting and fulfilling itself in fixed contemplation of the presented object, out of all connection with any other. . . . When one is no longer concerned with the Where, the When, the Why and the What-for of things, but only and alone with the What, and lets go even of all abstract thoughts about them, intellectual concepts and consciousness, but instead of all that, gives over the whole force of one's spirit to the act of perceiving, becomes absorbed in it and lets every bit of one's consciousness be filled in the quiet contemplation of the natural object immediately present—be it a landscape, a tree, a rock, a building, or anything else at all; actually and fully, in the sense of a highly meaningful manner of speech, *losing oneself* in the object: forgetting one's own individuality, one's will, and remaining there only as a pure subject, a clear mirror to the object—so that it is as though the object alone were there, without anyone regarding it, and to such a degree that one might no longer distinguish the beholder from the act of beholding, the two having become *one,* with the entire field of consciousness filled and taken in by that single perceptible form; in sum: when the object has been to that extent removed from all relationship to anything but itself, and the subject out of all relation to the will, then what is beheld and recognized is no longer that thing as commonly known, but

the Idea, the timeless Form, an immediate, self-standing objectification of the will at this grade of being. And by the same token, the person absorbed in this mode of seeing is no longer an individual—the individual has lost himself in the perception —but is a pure, will-less, painless, timeless, Subject of Apprehension. . . . And it was just this that was running in Spinoza's mind when he wrote: *mens aeterna est, quatenus res sub aeternitatis specie concipit* ("Mind is eternal, in so far as it apprehends an object under the species of eternity").[60]

And there is, too, the poem "Natural Music" of our own Californian poet Robinson Jeffers:

The old voice of the ocean, the bird chatter of little rivers,
(Winter has given them gold for silver
To stain their water and bladed green for brown to line their banks)
From different throats intone one language.
So I believe if we were strong enough to listen without
Divisions of desire and terror
To the storm of the sick nations, the rage of the hunger-smitten
  cities,
Those voices also would be found
Clean as a child's; or like some girl's breathing who dances alone
By the ocean-shore, dreaming of lovers.[61]

The next stage or level in Schopenhauer's understanding of the order of depth experiences furnished by life itself is that of the awe, mystic dread, or terror described in his passage cited by Nietzsche: where the individual, feeling himself to be safe on the raging sea in his little floatable craft, "suddenly finds himself in error with respect to his interpretation of the forms of appearance." The transition then is from an aesthetic (Apollonian) to a properly religious dimension of experience (or, in Nietzsche's terminology, toward Dionysian rapture); and the sense of awe, dread, or terror that is then experienced is something different altogether from any "kinetic," natural loathing or terror before an odious or dangerous object. For the precipitating cause here is not an object. It is the sense, rather, of a break in the tissue of temporal-spatial-causal relationships by which objects are supported, by which the subject too is supported: a chilling, stilling, indubitable sense of the immediacy of something—there? here? where?—that is inconceivable: a void perhaps, a god perhaps, or a ghost.

Professor Rudolf Otto, in his work on *The Idea of the Holy,* cited to this point in *Oriental Mythology*,[62] has identified this experience of awe, of dread, as reciprocal to the Kantian x,* the source and prime ingredient of religion—all religion: an experience *sui generis,* which is lost, however, when identified with the Good, the True, Love, Mercy, the Law, this conceptualized deity or that. No one can be taught it; nor can it be explained to anyone who has not known it. Yet all religions, mythologies, and "proper" works of art both derive from and refer to it, and so must remain, for all those inaccessible to the experience, mere shells to be applied to other use: as, for instance, to magic, to pageantry, and to the maintenance of fools in the seats of the wise, to consolation (like the psalms), to the flattering of a race (like the Old Testament) or of an ecclesiastical social mission (like the New), to the disciplining of youth, decorating of blank walls, or blank hours, or to the preparation of old folk for approaching death.

> The feeling of it [Professor Otto writes] may at times come sweeping like a gentle tide, pervading the mind with a tranquil mood of deepest worship. It may pass over into a more set and lasting attitude of the soul, continuing, as it were, thrillingly vibrant and resonant, until at last it dies away and the soul resumes its "profane," non-religious mood of everyday experience. It may burst in sudden eruption up from the depths of the soul with spasms and convulsions, or lead to the strangest excitements, to intoxicated frenzy, to transport, and to ecstasy. It has its wild and demonic forms and can sink to an almost grisly horror and shuddering. It has its crude, barbaric antecedents and early manifestations, and again it may be developed into something beautiful and pure and glorious. It may become the hushed, trembling, and speechless humility of the creature in the presence of—whom or what? In the presence of that which is a *Mystery* inexpressible and above all creatures.[63]

Joyce, in his discussion of aesthetics, writes of the same as the "secret cause" of the arresting (static) tragic emotion of *terror,* the other face of which is tragic *pity:* so that here again, as in Nietzsche's view, the birth of tragedy as an art of the depth and species of a religion is interpreted in terms of a simultaneous revelation of the powers of the two gods, respectively, of the abyss and of individuation.

"Pity," Stephen said, "is the feeling which arrests the mind in

* See Kant's formula, supra, p. 339. $a:b::c:x.$

the presence of whatsoever is grave and constant in human sufferings and unites it with the human sufferer. Terror is the feeling which arrests the mind in the presence of whatsoever is grave and constant in human sufferings and unites it with the secret cause." [64]

A properly tragic art, that is to say, points to what is grave and constant in the lot of man: what cannot be done away by any alteration of social, political, or economic conditions, but, if life is to be affirmed, must be included in the affirmation. What is secondary and contingent, and so can perhaps be altered, is for the social critics and their kinetic—didactic—art. However, they mislead and poison to the root the very lives and life they conceive themselves to be improving if, in a zeal for social-political change, they attribute to the mere conditions of the century those pains and impulses that are actually of life itself and which, if life is to be affirmed, must also be affirmed. For when these are impugned, life is impugned and emptied—without, however, being honestly denied, nor yet existentially affirmed; and as Schopenhauer already saw, this internally blind, externally deluded way of work is one of the most dangerous, psychologically destructive forces of our time.

> Everywhere and in all ages [he wrote in the middle of the nineteenth century], there has been great dissatisfaction with governments, laws, and public institutions; mainly, however, because people are always ready to blame these for the misery that inheres in human existence and is the curse, so to say, that descended on Adam and his whole race. Never has there been a more lying and impudent exploitation of this false projection, however, than that of the demagogues of this "modern" day. These enemies of Christianity are optimists: the world, for them, is an end in itself and in terms of its own crude conditions available for conversion into a dwelling of perfect bliss. The howling, colossal evils of our century they ascribe entirely to the regimes, blame altogether and only on these; and without these, there would be heaven on earth, i.e. all of us, set free of toil and pain, would be able, to our hearts' content, to feed and swill, propagate and burst: for that is the paraphrase of this "end in itself" and the goal of the "endless progress of mankind," that they tirelessly preach with their overblown clichés.[65]

That is perhaps a bit strong. However, it makes the difficult point: that if the truth of life is not recognized and faced where it is and as it is, either to be denied as saints deny it, or else to be affirmed without shame in oneself, as in all, if life is to be affirmed, then the fruit of the tree of this world can be only a brain-maddening poison, causing each to ascribe to someone else—and to curse there and to battle there—the source of all pain, which is the monstrous thing that, in himself, is the very living of his life.

It is the function, the power and fascination of the tragic art, as indeed of all art when turned to art's proper task—which is namely *"de faire ressortir les grandes lignes de la nature"* (to quote again the words of the sculptor Antoine Bourdelle)—to render an experience in affirmation of life as it is, in form and in depth, in this vale of tears: over and above the terror, the pity, and the pain, communicating an exhilaration of the will's affirmation of life in its being and becoming, here and now.

In order for art to exist, or indeed for any aesthetic doing or seeing whatsoever to exist [Nietzsche wrote in one of his last works, *The Twilight of the Idols* (1888)], "there is a physiological prerequisite that is not to be avoided: intoxication. Intoxication must first have heightened the sensibility of the whole machine, before it can come to any art. And all kinds of special varieties of intoxication have the power to work in this way: above all, that of sexual excitement, which is the first and oldest form of intoxication. And then, too, the intoxication that comes with any great desire, any great emotion: the intoxication of the festival, of a combat, bravado, victory, or of any extreme movement; the intoxication of ferocity; the intoxication of destruction; intoxication under various sorts of meteorological influence, that of spring for example; or under the influence of narcotics; or finally the intoxication sheerly of the will, of an overcharged, inflated will.—The essential thing in all intoxication is the feeling of heightened power and a fullness. With this feeling one addresses oneself to things, *compels* them to receive what one has to give, one overpowers them: and this procedure is called *idealization*. But let us, right here, get rid of a prepossession: idealization does *not,* as is generally thought, consist in a leaving out, a subtraction of the insignificant, the incidental. What is decisive, rather, is a tremendous exaggeration of the main features, before which those others disappear.

In this condition, one enriches everything out of one's own abundance: whatever one sees or desires, one sees swelling, bursting, mighty, overladen with power. The individual in this condition changes things until they are mirrors of his own energy—reflections of his own perfection. And this compulsion to change things to perfection—is art. Everything, even what he is not, becomes for such a one a delighting in himself: in art man takes delight in himself as perfection.

The psychology of the orgiastic as of an overflowing feeling of life and power in which even pain has the effect of a *stimulant,* provided me with the key to the concept of the *tragic* feeling, which has been misunderstood as well by Aristotle as, particularly, by our modern pessimists. Tragedy is so far from proving anything about the pessimism of the Hellenes that it may, on the contrary, be taken as its definitive rejection and antithesis. Saying yes to life, even in its most inimical, hardest problems, the will to life delighting even in the *offering up* of its highest types to its own inexhaustibility—*that* is what I have called Dionysian, *that* is what I have divined to be the bridge to the psychology of the *tragic* poet. *Not* to be unladen through pity and terror, *not* to be purged by this vehement discharge of a dangerous emotion (as in Aristotle's view), but beyond terror and pity, to be *oneself* identified with the everlasting joy of becoming—that joy which includes in itself the. joy in destruction as well. . . .[66]

For Schopenhauer, on the other hand, all those were the faults, not the virtues, of art.

The enjoyment of the beautiful, the consolation that art affords [he declared from his own, more somber, tender, and more solemn point of view], the enthusiasm of the artist, which allows him to forget the pains of existence (such a faculty for enthusiasm being the only advantage of the genius over other men, by which he is compensated for the intensified sorrow that he will experience in proportion to the clarity of his consciousness, as well as for the desert loneliness he experiences among people of a different order of being), all this rests upon the fact that while the very being of life, the will, our sheer existence, is an unremitting agony, part pitiful, part terrible, nevertheless, when viewed purely as Idea (as Image), and when reproduced thus in art, free of its inherent torture, it affords a drama full of significance. This purely knowable side of the world and its reproduction in art, one art or another, is the artist's element. He is locked to the contemplation of the drama of the objectification of the will: with that he rests, and he never tires of regarding and reproducing it in pictures; and meanwhile, he himself bears the costs of the production of that play, for he is himself the will that is objectified that way, and so remains in constant pain. That pure, true, and deep knowledge of the inward nature of the world becomes for him an end in itself: he does not go past it. Hence, it does not become for him, as for the saint who attains to resignation, a quieter of the will; it does not release him from life permanently, but only momentarily, and so is not for him the way out of it but only an occasional consolation within it: until his powers, increased by this contemplation, finally, becoming tired of the play, grasp the seriousness of it all—for which transition we may take the painting of St. Cecilia by Raphael as our type.[67] *

For in Schopenhauer's view, the will, the will to life, which is the very Being of beings, is a blind, insatiable drive, motivating all and eventuating mainly in the sorrows and deaths of all—as anyone can see—yet willfully continued. The more strongly the will to life is affirmed, the more painful are its effects, not only in the willing subject, whose will for more is only enhanced by success, never quelled; but also, and even more hurtfully, in those round about him, whose equivalent wills he frustrates. For each of us in his own way, as Schopenhauer tells, is metaphysically and essentially the entire world as will, and consequently can be satisfied with nothing less than possession of the entire world as object, which, since everyone would have it so, is not possible to any. Recognizing this, and filled, like the Buddha, with compassion by the spectacle of universal pain (the First Noble Truth: "All life is sorrowful"), the undeluded, really honest individual—in Schopenhauer's view—can only conclude that life is the will's (or God's) mistake, something that never should have been, and, renouncing its dynamism in himself, achieve within—ironically—that absolute peace sought by all: assisting others then, through example and through teaching, to the same end—the only end possible (except the aggravation of pain) this side of death.

And as the philosopher tells in the last sentence of his major work, *The World as Will and Idea:* "What then remains, after the will has been extinguished utterly, is, in the view of all those still full of the will, nothing, to be sure. However, conversely, for those

---

* St. Cecilia, patroness of music, is there shown at the organ, gazing upward to a light descending from aloft.

in whom the will, turning, has denied itself, this our world, which is so real, with all its suns and Milky Ways is—nothing." And to this he adds in his last footnote: "This precisely is the Prājñā-pāramitā, the 'Yonderside of All Knowledge' of the Buddhists, where subject and object are no more."

VI. The Altar and the Pulpit

In *The Magic Mountain* the musical device of the *Leitmotiv* carries a Dionysian, oceanic sense of recurrences, ever returning like waves, the same again, yet not the same: expanding, breaking, throwing spray in all directions, interpenetrating in the way of the forms of life—which likewise arise, take shape, and, interpenetrating, dissolve into the substance of all. Schopenhauer had written of music as an art corresponding in principle to the world experienced as will, and this idea had excited Wagner.* The young Nietzsche, then, taking Wagner's music drama—and specifically his *Tristan*—as example, wrote in *The Birth of Tragedy* of music, on one hand, and stage characters, on the other, as representing respectively the spheres of the universal and particular, the *universalia ante rem* (the will) and the *principium individuationis* (the individual), with the myth, the Dionysian legend, joining the two: functioning in such a way that the music should not ravish us altogether from this world of separate lives, nor, on the other hand, our concern for the two individuals lead us to forget their immortal ground. The myth, Nietzsche thus saw, is the Apollonian display of what Joyce was to call the grave and constant in human sufferings: a vision of enduring forms midway between the passing figures of day and the night of dreamless sleep. And, as the world has ever known, it is exactly here, in this sphere of vision, that the individual nightly meets the gods, those personifications of the functioning of will by which his own destiny is controlled.

Thus mythology and the psychology of dream are recognized as related, even identical. And as Thomas Mann has pointed out in his anniversary essay on "The Sorrows and Grandeur of Richard Wagner" (February 10, 1933: fiftieth anniversary of Wagner's death), not only did that great master release opera from its merely historical-anecdotal limitations by expanding it to myth (and to such a degree that "as one listens to him," writes Mann,

* Supra, p. 83.

"one can almost believe that music was created for nothing else, and could never again submit to anything else, but to serve the myth"); but he also joined, to this synthesis of music and mythology, psychology.

A book could be written [wrote Mann] on Wagner's psychology, and it would deal with the psychological art of the musician as well as of the poet, in so far as these two powers in him can be separated. The technical device of the "recognition theme" (*Erinnerungsmotiv*), already suggested in earlier operas, became gradually developed in his work to a profoundly meaningful virtuosic system that converts music into an instrument of psychological associations, deepenings, and references, to a degree never known before. The transformation, for example, of the naïve, epic, magic theme of the "Love Potion" into a mere device for releasing a passion already present (actually, it could have been pure water the lovers drank, and believing they had drunk *death,* they would have been released psychologically from the moral laws of their day) is the poetic inspiration of a great psychologist. And consider how, even from the beginning, the poetic powers of Wagner transcended the scope of mere libretto. . . .

Mann points to the words of the Flying Dutchman, sung to Senta in their duet of Act II, where he asks whether love be really the name for the glow that he feels burning in his breast, and replies to himself, "Ah no! it is the yearning for release!" Release through her from the curse that binds him to the world. "May it—through such an angel as this—be mine!"

> *Die düstre Glut, die hier ich fühle brennen,*
> *Soll ich Unseliger sie Liebe nennen?*
> *Ach nein, die Sehnsucht ist es nach dem Heil.*
> *Würd' es durch solchen Engel mir zuteil!*

"Simple, singable lines," comments Mann, "but never before had any such complicated, psychologically intricate thought been sung, or even programmed to be sung." Pointing next to the case of the dawning love-yearning of the boy Siegfried, as rendered by Wagner in both words and music, as a complex of presentiments welling from the unconscious, glowing with mother-associations, sexual desire, and anxiety; and then again to the scene where the dwarf Mime is striving to teach fear to his young pupil, while in the orchestra the motive sounds, in a darkly distorted way, of Brünnhilde asleep in her ring of flame: "—that is Freud," states Mann, "that is Analysis, nothing else. And we also recall," he adds, "that in Freud too (whose psychological root-research and depth-science were anticipated in grand style by Nietzsche), the interest in mythology, in the primitive and pre-cultural aspects of humanity, was in the closest manner bound to his psychological interest." [68]

The figure of the lyre in Mann's own monogram (Figure 44) is

Figure 44. Monogram of Thomas Mann

the sign of his identification of himself with this tradition, wherein music, myth, and depth psychology are one and carried in the *Leitmotiv*—which is a device that Mann even compares at one point to a monstrance: the radiant golden receptacle in which, in the Roman Catholic benediction service, the consecrated Host is exposed to view and elevated by the priest for admiration, contemplation, and worship.[69] Wagner's music, as he points out, is no longer properly music, but literature.

It is psychology, symbol, mythology, accent—everything; but not music in the pure and full sense. . . . Nor are the texts around which it burgeons, fulfilling them as drama, properly literature—but music. Furthermore, even while gushing like a geyser from prehistoric depths of myth (and not only seemingly, but actually), this music is nevertheless thought up, calculated, highly intelligent, pointedly clever, and no less literary in conception than the texts are musical. Broken down to its prime components, music is turned to the service of mythic ideas of philosophical purport, forcing them into high relief. The disquiet chromatic scale of the "Liebestod" is a literary idea. The elemental flow of the Rhine; the seven primal blocks of accord that build Valhalla: these too are literature. . . . These sequences of symbolic motive-quotations, strewn about like fragments of rock in the streambed of an elementary musical torrent: to ask that these should be experienced as music in the sense of Bach, Mozart, and Beethoven, were to ask too much.[70]

As in *Ulysses,* then, so here: the *Leitmotiv* serves both in Wagner and in Mann to release in us recognitions of connection between moments, events, characters, and objects that are apparently separate from each other, yet in depth of a single form—in the manner, as we have already said, of the coming together of the scattered parts of an anamorphosis. And the memories recalled, furthermore, will meanwhile have become associated in our minds with related matters of our own unconscious. "Music," states Thomas Mann, "is the language of 'Once upon a time' in its double sense of 'As all once was' and 'As all is to be.' " [71] And so too, we know, is myth. So too is dream: so romance; so love: and so too is night. Alpha and Omega: Beginning and End.

"With yearning," Wagner wrote from Paris to Mathilde Wesendonck, March 3, 1860, "I frequently gaze toward the land Nirvana. But then, very soon, Nirvana becomes for me Tristan: you know the Buddhist theory of the beginning of the world. A breath disturbs heaven's clarity . . ." and here in his letter Wagner set down the four notes, chromatically ascending, that open his metaphysical score and bring it to its close (G sharp, A, A sharp, B); after which his sentence continues, but referring now simultaneously to the turbulence of the world's beginning, his score, and his own spirit: "this swells, condenses, and finally in impenetrable massiveness, the world again stands before me." [72]

"To link art and religion this way," comments Mann, "through a bold operatic treatment of sex, and to offer such a holy piece of unholy artistry as a Lourdes-theater and miracle-grotto, catering to the hankering for belief of a jaded *fin de siècle* public: that is sheer romanticism; something absolutely unthinkable in the classically humanistic, properly respectable sphere of art." [73] "Romanticism," he states (and here I want to place an accent), "is linked to all those mythic mother and lunar cults that have flourished since the earlier periods of the human race in opposition to solar worship, the religion of fatherly, masculine light: and it is under the spell of this general lunar world-view that Wagner's *Tristan* stands." [74]

But Mann's own work, for the most part, is under this spell as well; and he points this out himself, both repeatedly and clearly, throughout his mythological tetralogy of *Joseph and His Brothers* —I. *The Tales of Jacob* (1933), II. *Young Joseph* (1934), III. *Joseph in Egypt* (1936), and IV. *Joseph the Provider* (1943) —where Jacob and Joseph, his heroes, are explicitly associated with the ambiguous, neither-nor, both-and logic of what he calls, "lunar syntax," [75] in contrast to the uncomplicated, black-is-not-white and white-is-not-black, sunny-side-up mode of flatland thought of both Esau, the ruddy, hairy man, and the band of Joseph's warrior brothers. Moreover, the principle of erotic irony, defined in "Tonio Kröger" as balanced between the two worlds of light and of night, is itself already of the lunar, Aphroditic-Hermetic, musical mode of being, and nowhere is this balance of life, and of the whole created world, between the two opposed simplicities more amply and richly made manifest, in a veritable symphony of echoing associations, than in the great work of this author's apogee in mid-career, *The Magic Mountain*.

The main lines of this novel, as already remarked, are simple enough; namely, of a young man who fares to an Alpine sanatorium for a visit of three weeks, develops there a fever, and, instead of three weeks, spends an aeon of seven years, returning to his homeland only when the First World War breaks out, to serve voluntarily his country's flag. The adventure conforms, that is to say, in both structure and sense, to a traditional *rite de passage*, or mythological hero adventure, the archetypal course of which—as I have shown in my earlier work, *The Hero with a Thousand Faces* [76] —universally follows a pattern of three stages: *separation, initiation, return*, which I have called (using a term from *Finnegans Wake*), the nuclear unit of The Monomyth. [77] (Compare, for example, the cycle of the mystery-cult initiation illustrated in the bowl of Figure 3.)

In *The Magic Mountain* the absolutely indispensable break from the world of common day—from those duties, thoughts, feelings, and highest concerns "common to all men" which are dictated not by one's own experiences and discoveries but by others—is represented directly at the opening, in the steep climb of the narrow-gauge Alpine train to its almost inaccessible destination aloft. Mann compares the clear sky, the sight of timeless snow-capped peaks, and the heart-accelerating thin air up there to a potion, a magic drink, as of the river Lethe; and the mountaintop itself he compares to the summit of the Brocken, where the gods of pre-Christian Europe annually celebrate Walpurgisnacht—to which saturnalia of devils, witches, and the dead, Mephistopheles guided Faust. An equivalent association (already evident in the title) is with the legendary Venus Mountain, where the Minnesinger Tannhäuser, as celebrated by Wagner, was supposed to have dwelt in love with the Lady Venus. And still another is with the night-sea voyage of Odysseus to Circe's isle and to the underworld (to which she introduced him) of Persephone, Queen of the Dead. Mann compares the sealed-off situation of his hero in the sanatorium with that of the primal matter in the alchemist's *vas Hermeticum,* undergoing fermentation for sublimation into philosophical gold.

Thus in Mann's ostensibly naturalistic novel, as in Joyce's of approximately the same date (*Ulysses,* 1922; *The Magic Mountain,* 1924), there is an intended, scrupulously controlled opening downward of associations—largely through a skillful use of the *Leitmotiv*—to the timeless, "grave and constant" archetypes of myth; and in each instance, furthermore, the author's subsequent work (*Finnegans Wake,* 1939; *Joseph and His Brothers,* 1933–1943) dropped into the sphere of myth altogether. Essentially, the problem that both faced and resolved was the same on at least three levels: first, on the personal level of the artist dwelling in a world of people (as Schopenhauer phrased it) of another race, another order of experience and expression; next on the aesthetic level of twentieth-century novelists, who had inherited from their forebears an essentially rationalistic, naturalistic, anecdotal-historical narrative art, inadequate to their understanding of psychology in its universal, mythological, as well as individual, biographically conditioned aspects; and then, thirdly, on the religious level, the related problem of an inherited ecclesiastical tradition of publicly professed beliefs, altogether incongruent not only to the sciences but also to the actual moral order and humanistic conscience of the secularized "Christian" nations of this modern world.

James Joyce had been born a Catholic; Thomas Mann, a Protestant. Both had broken from their family spheres of belief in the ways fictionized in their first novels and short stories ("Stephen Hero," 1903, and *A Portrait of the Artist as a Young Man,* 1916; *Buddenbrooks,* 1902 and "Tonio Kröger," 1903); and each then cleared the way for himself—along parallel courses, at about the same pace, date for date—to an art of the most sophisticated psychologico-mythological ambiguities. Mann developed his position toward myth from Luther and Goethe, Schopenhauer, Wagner, and Nietzsche; Joyce, on the other hand, from the Middle Ages, Dante and Aquinas, Shakespeare, Blake, and then Ibsen. Consequently, although they were indeed on parallel courses, there were great differences between them in approach and aim as well as background, and with significant contrasts in result.

Joyce, for instance, as a Catholic, had been at home in the sphere of religious myth from infancy and, as he shows in *A Portrait of the Artist as a Young Man,* was already at a very tender age interpreting his experiences in mythological terms and his mythology in terms of what he saw, felt, and was able to think. As we read of the little schoolboy sitting brooding at his classroom desk:

He turned to the flyleaf of the geography and read what he had written: himself, his name and where he was.

Stephen Dedalus
Class of Elements
Clongowes Wood College
Sallins
County Kildare
Ireland
Europe
The World
The Universe

That was in his writing: and Fleming one night for a cod had written on the opposite page:

Stephen Dedalus is my name,
Ireland is my nation.

Clongowes is my dwellingplace
And heaven my expectation.

He read the verses backwards but then they were not poetry.
Then he read the flyleaf from the bottom to the top till he came
to his own name. That was he: and he read down the page
again. What was after the universe? Nothing. But was there anything round the universe to show where it stopped before the
nothing place began? It could not be a wall; * but there could
be a thin thin line there all round everything and everywhere.
Only God could do that. He tried to think what a big thought
that must be; but he could only think of God. God was God's
name just as his name was Stephen. *Dieu* was the French for
God and that was God's name too; and when any one prayed
to God and said *Dieu* then God knew at once that it was a
French person that was praying. But, though there were different
names for God in all the different languages in the world and
God understood what all the people who prayed said in their
different languages, still God remained always the same God
and God's real name was God.
It made him very tired to think that way.

A little later, another set of religious problems arose to occupy
his thought:

The protestants used to make fun of the litany of the Blessed
Virgin. *Tower of Ivory,* they used to say, *House of Gold!* How
could a woman be a tower of ivory or a house of gold? Who was
right then? . . .
Eileen had long white hands. One evening when playing tig
she had put her hands over her eyes: long and white and thin
and cold and soft. That was ivory: a cold white thing. That
was the meaning of *Tower of Ivory.* . . .
One day he had stood beside her looking into the hotel
grounds. A waiter was running up a trail of bunting on the flag-
staff and a fox terrier was scampering to and fro on the sunny
lawn. She had put her hand into his pocket where his hand was
and he had felt how cool and thin and soft her hand was. She
had said that pockets were funny things to have: and then all of
a sudden she had broken away and had run laughing down the
sloping curve of the path. Her fair hair had streamed out behind

* Here is the source of the "wall" theme in *Finnegans Wake.*

her like gold in the sun. *Tower of Ivory. House of Gold.* By
thinking of things you could understand them.[78] *

Moreover, Joyce to the end retained an essentially priestly attitude toward the practice and function of his art; whereas Mann,
the German Protestant, had the attitude, rather, of the preaching
parson. The priest, saying Mass with his back to the congregation,
is performing a miracle at his altar, much like that of the alchemist, bringing God himself into presence in the bread and wine, out
of the nowhere into the here: and it matters not, to either God, the
priest, the bread, or the wine, whether any congregation is present
or not. The miracle takes place, and that is what the Mass, the
opus, the act, is all about. Its effect is the salvation of the world.
Whereas the preacher in his pulpit is addressing himself to people,
to persuade them to some sort of life way, and if no one is present
there is no event. Mann, accordingly, is writing to persuade. He
explains, interprets, and evaluates discursively the symbols of his
art, whereas Joyce simply presents, without author's comment.
Furthermore, in his approach to symbols Mann comes to them
from the secular world, through literature and art, not by way of
the ingraining from childhood of the iconography of a seriously
accepted, ritually ordered religion. Not the altar but the pulpit is
the center of his *mysterium,* and where symbols are involved, they
are associated in his mind rather with a family cult of household
events and ancestral personages, leading back through time, than
with timeless visionary personifications of cosmological, metaphysical import: which, by the way, is perhaps one of the great reasons
why Protestant versions of the Christian faith tend to lean more
heavily than the Catholic on the family-cult theology of the Old
Testament, which when seriously considered as an appropriate
base for a proper world religion is constitutionally ineligible, since
it is finally but the overinterpreted parochial history and manufac-
tured genealogy of a single sub-race of a southwest Asian Semitic
strain, late to appear and, though of great and noble influence, by
no means what its own version of the history of the human race
sets it up to be. Nor was the ancestral line of the Buddenbrooks,
the Krögers, or the Castorps quite comparable in import or in

* There is an echo of this little moment too in *Finnegans Wake*, p. 327:
"playing house of ivary dower of gould. . . ."

force to the metaphysical mysteries symbolized in the Trinity, the Word Made Flesh, and the sacrament of the Mass.

Carl Jung has well described the contrast of the Catholic and Protestant psychological states in relation to their understanding of symbols:

> The history of Protestantism [he writes] has been one of chronic iconoclasm. One wall after another fell. And the work of destruction was not too difficult once the authority of the Church had been shattered. We all know how, in large things as in small, in general as well as in particular, piece after piece collapsed, and how the alarming poverty of symbols that is now the condition of our life came about. With that the power of the Church has vanished too—a fortress robbed of its bastions and casemates, a house whose walls have been plucked away, exposed to all the winds of the world and to all dangers.
>
> Although this is, properly speaking, a lamentable collapse that offends our sense of history, the disintegration of Protestantism into nearly four hundred denominations is yet a sure sign that the restlessness continues. The Protestant is cast out into a state of defenselessness that might well make the natural man shudder. His enlightened consciousness, of course, refuses to take cognizance of this fact, and is quietly looking elsewhere for what has been lost to Europe. We seek the effective images, the thought-forms that satisfy the restlessness of heart and mind, and we find the treasures of the East. . . .
>
> Shall we be able to put on, like a new suit of clothes, ready-made symbols grown on foreign soil, saturated with foreign blood, spoken in a foreign tongue, nourished by a foreign culture, interwoven with foreign history, and so resemble a beggar who wraps himself in kingly raiment, a king who disguises himself as a beggar? No doubt this is possible. Or is there something in ourselves that commands us to go in for no mummeries, but perhaps even to sew our garment ourselves?
>
> I am convinced [Jung continues] that the growing impoverishment of symbols has a meaning. It is a development that has an inner consistency. Everything that we have not thought about, and that has therefore been deprived of a meaningful connection with our developing consciousness, has got lost. If we now try to cover our nakedness with the gorgeous trappings of the East, as the theosophists do, we would be playing our

own history false. A man does not sink down to beggary only to pose afterwards as an Indian potentate. It seems to me that it would be far better stoutly to avow our spiritual poverty, our symbol-lessness, instead of feigning a legacy to which we are not the legitimate heirs at all. We are, surely, the rightful heirs of Christian symbolism, but somehow we have squandered this heritage. We have let the house our fathers built fall into decay, and now we try to break into Oriental palaces that our fathers never knew. Anyone who has lost the historical symbols and cannot be satisfied with substitutes is certainly in a very difficult position today: before him there yawns the void, and he turns away from it in horror. What is worse, the vacuum gets filled with absurd political and social ideas, which one and all are distinguished by their spiritual bleakness. But if he cannot get along with those pedantic dogmatisms, he sees himself forced to be serious for once with his alleged trust in God, though it usually turns out that his fear of things going wrong if he did so is even more persuasive. This fear is far from unjustified, for where God is closest the danger seems greatest. It is dangerous to avow spiritual poverty, for the poor man has desires, and whoever has desires calls down some fatality on himself. A Swiss proverb puts it drastically: "Behind every rich man stands a devil, and behind every poor man two."

Just as in Christianity the vow of worldly poverty turned the mind away from the riches of this earth, so spiritual poverty seeks to renounce the false riches of the spirit in order to withdraw not only from the sorry remnants—which today call themselves the Protestant church—of a great past, but also from all the allurements of the odorous East; in order, finally, to dwell with itself alone, where, in the cold light of consciousness, the blank barrenness of the world reaches to the very stars.

We have inherited this poverty from our fathers. . . .[79]

The plight of the Catholic, on the other hand, is today precisely the opposite. For he is not deprived; he is overladen with symbols which have been built into his very nerves but have no relevance to modern life; and his dangerous exposure, therefore, is not to a void within, but, as a kind of Rip van Winkle or perennial Don Quixote, to an alien world without, which in his heart is dogmatically denied and is yet, to his eyes, visibly before him. If he has luck (shall we call it luck?), he may live to the end encapsulated in his Nicene Creed (of the date 325 A.D.) and die, so to say, as yet unborn from the womb of Holy Mother Church. But if the walls of his Church break apart—as they had for many already in the middle of the Middle Ages—he has literally Hell to pay. His problem then is either to liquidate in himself the structuring mythology of his mythologically structured life, or else somehow to unbind its archetypal symbols from their provincial Christian, pseudo-historic references and restore to them their primary force and value as mythological-psychological universals—which in fact has been the typical effort of unorthodox Catholic thinkers in the West ever since the military victory of Constantine and the enforcement, then, by Theodosius the Great (r. 379–395 A.D.) of one incredible credo for the Western world.

Dogma [states Jung], takes the place of the collective unconscious by formulating its contents on a grand scale. The Catholic way of life is completely unaware of psychological problems in the Protestant sense. Almost the entire life of the collective unconscious has been channeled into the dogmatic archetypal ideas and flows along like a well-controlled stream in the symbolism of creed and ritual. It manifests itself in the inwardness of the Catholic psyche. The collective unconscious as we understand it today was never before a matter of "psychology"; for before the Christian Church existed there were the antique mysteries, and these reach back into the gray mists of neolithic prehistory. Mankind has never lacked powerful images to lend magical aid against all the uncanny things that live in the depths of the psyche. Always the figures of the unconscious were expressed in protecting and healing images and in this way were expelled from the psyche into cosmic space.

The iconoclasm of the Reformation, however, quite literally made a breach in the protective wall of sacred images, and since then one image after another has crumbled away. They became dubious, for they conflicted with awakening reason. Besides, people had long since forgotten what they meant. Or had they really forgotten? Could it be that men had never really known what they meant, and that only in recent times did it occur to the Protestant part of mankind that actually we haven't the remotest conception of what is meant by the Virgin Birth, the divinity of Christ, and the complexities of the Trinity? It almost seems as if these images had just lived, and as if their living existence had simply been accepted without question and without reflection, much as everyone decorates Christmas trees or hides

Easter eggs without ever knowing what these customs mean. The fact is that archetypal images are so packed with meaning in themselves that people never think of asking what they really do mean. That the gods die from time to time is due to man's sudden discovery that they do not mean anything, that they are made by human hands, useless idols of wood and stone. In reality, however, he has merely discovered that up till then he has never thought about his images at all. And when he starts thinking about them, he does so with the help of what he calls "reason"—which in point of fact is nothing more than the sum-total of all his prejudices and myopic views.[80]

James Joyce opened his *Portrait of the Artist as a Young Man* with a motto taken from Ovid's *Metamorphoses* (Book VIII, line 188), *"Et ignotas animum dimittit in artes:* And his mind he addresses to unknown arts." The verse refers to the artist-craftsman Daedalus in Crete, at the moment when he determined to escape and turned his mind to the task of inventing wings, wings of art, by which to fly to the mainland. In Joyce's mind the immediate reference of this image, allegorically, was to his own (his hero Stephen Dedalus's) decision to fly from the little world of Ireland to the larger of the European mainland. But there was also in his mind the idea of flying from the lesser horizon, the mythological province so to say, of the Roman Catholic version of Christianity, and even the Christian version of the mythological archetypes, to the larger—if possible, largest—human view: not by way of a conversion of any kind to some other communal order of so-called belief, but by way of art.

When his friend Cranly asked Stephen Dedalus whether he was thinking now of becoming a Protestant: "I said that I had lost the faith," Stephen answered, "but not that I had lost selfrespect. What kind of liberation would that be to forsake an absurdity which is logical and coherent and to embrace one which is illogical and incoherent?" [81]

The structure of any completely unfolded, well-considered mythological system—be it Byzantine or Gothic, Hindu, Buddhist, Polynesian, or Navaho—is harmoniously beautiful and of Apollonian clarity, and at the same time fully electrified with experienced (though not necessarily rationalized) life significance and radiance. The Roman Catholic linkage to myth, therefore, is not "romantic" in the yearning Protestant sense, as to a void of unknown purport, but is firm and solid and clear. For the Catholic it is rather the outside, non-Catholic, non-mythological world that has been handed over to the Devil and is chaotic, daemonic, and void. "History," states Stephen, in the course of his long hell-journey of *Ulysses* in a world of living man, "is a nightmare from which I am trying to awake." [82] And in the late afternoon of that same day the great thunderclap resounds, announcing rain—the break in the sterile Waste Land spell of dissociation between the inward, sense-giving structure and the outward context of his life; after which, in the *Walpurgisnacht* of the brothels chapter, there follows the regenerating interplay between the two undeniable worlds of inward symbolic imagery and outward literal fact, which is to lead directly to the purgatorial *dream* of *Finnegans Wake*. There the optically present but spiritually uninterpreted, unassimilated, hence alien, deracinated Waste Land of a world of merely waking consciousness, separately self-defensive personalities, separated religions, separate national histories, even separate scholar-specialists, gives way to the principle of the "consubstantiality" of myth in dream. The meaningless nightmare of history is disintegrated and significantly recomposed in the mythological image of the ever-revolving cycle of four world ages. All becomes radiant with the omnipresent, all-suffusing, polarized image of that "one-same power of nature or of spirit" that is simultaneously and everywhere at serious war and humorous peace with itself, "as the sole condition and means of its himundher manifestation." * And there resounds through all the outside world, thereby, the echo of that yea which is the undismayed, inward, world-asserting and -maintaining creative principle in all: as the Hindus say, "from the Being of beings to the blade of grass."

But in *The Magic Mountain,* also, something similar occurs. It is amazing, in fact, how many themes and symbols these two independently working contemporary novelists shared; in *Ulysses* and *The Magic Mountain,* for instance: the symbolism of a land of the dead, with a brooding, questing youth searching for an attitude to life; a naturalistic setting, structured in such a way as to include significantly, on one hand, a hospital and medical environment and, on the other, a library and atmosphere of study, affording

* Supra, p. 308.

pedagogical influences from the spheres both of literature and of science, all with bearing on the grave and constant themes of death and love; an emergent mythological underpainting, which assimilates the fields of modern life-experience to those of traditional humanity and is musically suggested through an echoing *Leitmotiv* technique; a sexual strain, culminating in a chapter conceived as a *Walpurgisnacht* adventure; and even, indeed, a thunderclap to mark the moment of transformation, when the hero's life in the land of the dead turns to life, and he is seriously confronted with the task of integrating substantially his two worlds. However, and here is the contrast, whereas in *Ulysses* the voice of thunder is heard *before* the *Walpurgisnacht* of hallucinatory inward-outward interplays, in *The Magic Mountain* the chapter entitled "The Thunderbolt" is the last of the novel and *follows* all the great revelatory scenes. Moreover, it leads the young hero not further into sleep, but back to the field of history. It is the news of the start of the First World War which bursts "like a thunderpeal" and brings Hans Castorp, "the Seven Sleeper," voluntarily, and even gratefully for his awakening to life, into the nightmare of the trenches —and not on the side of the political dream of his Mediterranean, Francophile, literary friend and mentor, Settembrini, but on the home side, "there where blood called," of his kindred.

Thus on the Irish–Catholic side the call of thunder had come from within, from the ingrained mythic world of timeless universals to which the particulars of the world without were now to be integrated, while on the German–Protestant side the call came, on the contrary, from without, from the field of specifically European history—homeland, parochial family history, and partisan commitment—which in fact, however, had been made interior to the soul of this particular German youth by the family-oriented Christianity of his reverent paternal home. Yet the two adventures, though historically opposite, were in depth equivalent, having to do alike with the one task of integrating the temporal and timeless aspects of existence.

A practical relationship to the temporal-historical order of his century had been well established in childhood in Hans Castorp, whereas with the timeless world of universals he became familiar only during those seven years of meditation (ages twenty-three to thirty) on the summit of the Magic Mountain. Stephen Dedalus, on the other hand, had been brought up not on family Bibles and heirlooms, but on the mystery of transubstantiation, and when the call of the temporal world came to him in the lovely form of that girl who stood before him in midstream, "like one whom magic had changed into the likeness of a strange and beautiful seabird," what he encountered when he went forth, in answer to her call, "to live, to err, to fall, to triumph, to recreate life out of life," * was a nightmare vision of Hell, which it required the whole mighty work of *Finnegans Wake* to sublimate into philosophical gold.

The same mythological themes, the same depths, are thus sounded in these two contrasting works by two very different artists: men, however, of equivalent profundity of experience, breadth of learning, and skill in communication. And they will serve, therefore, to make my point—or rather, Nietzsche's point—of the myth as the revelatory factor by which the incidents of the daylight world are discovered linked to that ground which is the ground of all and gives to everything its life. However, to be known as such, the myth cannot be thought of as fixed, once and for all, dogmatically defined. Rather it is to be rediscovered by the artist eye, fresh and alive, as the form of this event and that: as a pattern that is no pattern, but in each thing uniquely present as never before.

VII. Democracy and the Terror

What, then, is the Waste Land?

It is the land where the myth is patterned by authority, not emergent from life; where there is no poet's eye to see, no adventure to be lived, where all is set for all and forever: Utopia! Again, it is the land where poets languish and priestly spirits thrive, whose task it is only to repeat, enforce, and elucidate clichés. And this blight of the soul extends today from the cathedral close to the university campus. Nietzsche made the point almost a century ago.

Here and there I come in touch with German universities [he wrote in his *Twilight of the Idols,* 1888]: what an atmosphere prevails among the scholars, what a spiritual desert, how lukewarm and complacent! It would be a profound misunderstanding to bring up German science against me on this point —and a proof, besides, that not a single word I have written had been read. For I have been calling attention for the past

* Supra, p. 69.

seventeen years, untiringly, to the *despiritualizing* influence of
our present-day science industry. The hard helotism to which
the prodigious range of the contemporary sciences condemns
every individual scholar is the main reason why the fuller,
richer, more *profoundly* endowed of our students can no longer
find appropriate education or *educators*. There is nothing from
which this culture suffers more than from superabundance of
pretentious corner-watchers and fragments of humanity; and the
universities, *against* their will, are the real hothouses of this kind
of stunting of the spiritual instincts. All of Europe has already a
realization of this: no one is fooled by our high politics. . . .
Germany is regarded, more and more, as Europe's *Flatland*.[83]

The only correction I can find needed for a translation of this
murderous criticism to our own mid-twentieth century would be a
change of the word "against" to "with all." First, a religious
training in coined platitudes from a world as far from the modern
as any could possibly be; next, a so-called liberal-arts education,
by way of lecture courses, seminars and quizzes, week by week:
"great books" summarized and evaluated, stuffed into emptied
heads as authorized information, to be signaled back, for grades;
and then the sciences—at the outer reaches of thought!—all taught
by sterilized authorities who, in those unrecapturable years of their
own youth, when the ears, eyes, and heart of the spirit open to the
marvel of oneself and the universe, were condemned to that same
hard helotism of which Nietzsche writes. There is no time, no place,
no permission—let alone encouragement—for *experience*. And to
make things even worse, along now come those possessed socio-
political maniacs with their campus rallies, picket-line slogans,
journalistic ballyhoo, and summonses to action in the name of
causes of which their callow flocks had scarcely heard six months
before—and even those marginal hours that might have been left
from study for inward growth are invaded, wrecked, and strewn
with daily rubbish. It is hardly to be wondered if the young people
of the world today look a bit like rubbish-strewn rooms themselves
and in their Dionysiac "trips" and "happenings" promise to match
the *agapes* of the early Christian Church.

Thomas Mann in *The Magic Mountain* makes a good deal of
the term "hermetic pedagogy." The idea suggested is of a sealing-

off from historical time and an inward-turning to inward time: activation of the mind through appropriate influences from without, but then a response in terms of one's own readiness and pace of growth, not the needs, ideals, and expectations of anyone else, any group, or any so-called world. On the flatland life is reaction, whereas on the timeless mountaintop—as in the alchemist's *vas Hermeticum*—there can be fermentation, spontaneity, action as opposed to reaction: truly what is meant by the term "education" (*e-ducere,* "to lead or draw forth") as opposed to "inculcation" (*inculcare,* "to stamp in with the heel"). And absolutely indispensable for any such development is that *separation* from the demands of the day which all educators—until recently—understood to be the first requirement for anything approaching a spiritual life.

In *The Magic Mountain* the figure most strongly opposed to Hans Castorp's separation from history and surrender to the luxury of self- and world-discovery is the first of those two ludicrous pedagogues between whom the author placed his hero: the delicate, graceful, black-mustached Italian humanist and journalist, Settembrini, who reminds Hans not a little of an organ-grinder. Mann introduces him as Satana, Mephistopheles, a personification of the intellect striving to gain control over life: the pied piper of rhetorical progressivism, Mediterranean clarity, reason, and grace of form, whose name, however, suggests the ominous verb *septembriser,* "to massacre in cold blood" (from the noun *septembrisades,* referring to the massacre in Paris prisons of the royalists, September 2–6, 1792). Seedy yet elegant in his frayed jacket and black-and-white-checked trousers, which, though threadbare (like his ideas), were always neatly pressed, this mellifluous encyclopedist of the political school of Mazzini plays the role in relation to Hans of Mephistopheles to Faust: able to furnish advice and aid, with an aim to winning his charge's soul, but unable either to understand or to gain control over his will.

"When I want to read something to turn my insides upside down," wrote Mann in his volume of unpolitical reflections,

something at which every bit of me roils in opposition (and such reading can at times be useful), I open the volume of Mazzini that one day, without any merit or effort of my own, came, as though sent from heaven, into my hands, and to which I owe not only the beginnings of my bit of insight into the nature of political virtue, but also my understanding of the background from which the German *civilisation-littérateur* has derived the style, posture, intonation, and passion of his political manifesto. Here I have in hand the Latin Freemason, Democrat, literary revolutionary, and progressive rhetorician in pure culture and full bloom. Here I learn to think of the spirit as something between the spirit of the deep Orient and the spirit of the Jacobin Club, which indeed is how it has to be understood today, now that "virtue" [in the sense of Marat and Robespierre] has been rehabilitated. Here I can admire a spectacle of activism stopping at nothing, untouched by any blemish of doubt, one moment standing before its people, eyes lifted to heaven, declaiming with broadest gesture, and the next, fists clenched and with hissing breath, leaping about, inciting, agitating, goading to rebellion. Here the barricades are called "the people's throne." Here I hear a man who can say: "morality and technology!" "Christ and the Press!" [84]

This type of champion of the light of reason, in the sense of *liberté, egalité, fraternité—or death,* is a late stereotyped and vulgarized, so to say priestly, reduction of the great Renaissance type of the free spirit; and Mann has succeeded marvelously in communicating to his trite pedagogue an afterglow of the nobility of those great humanists in whose light he abides: Virgil himself, as well as Petrarch, Lorenzo and Politian, Machiavelli, and Castiglione, on to the French Enlightenment in Diderot and Voltaire. The purifying, consecrating influence of literature, the destruction of the passions through knowledge and the word; the idea of literature as the highway to understanding, to forgiveness, and to love; the saving power of speech; the literary spirit as the noblest manifestation of the human spirit altogether; the literary man as man fulfilled, as saint: it was to this luminous tune that Settembrini's *apologia* was ever sung.

But in Nietzsche's terminology, as announced in *The Birth of Tragedy,* this precisely was the character of Socrates, Socratic man, as prototype and protagonist of "the Decadence," in the sense of the intellect subduing, disorienting, and dissolving life, unloving of its imperfection, sterilized to its mystery; the type, in other words, that Schopenhauer had denounced in his paragraph, above cited, on those who attribute to local, temporal conditions the ills inherent in life itself, and, in their zeal to correct, discompose the life they would save.*

A key is offered to the character of Socrates [wrote Nietzsche] in that remarkable phenomenon known as "the daemon of Socrates." When in certain situations his prodigious intellect began to vacillate, he would recover assurance from a divine voice that addressed him only at such times. And whenever this voice was heard, it warned *against*. That is to say, in the case of this altogether abnormal character, instinctive wisdom asserted itself only occasionally, and then, in restraint of his conscious judgment. Whereas in all productive people it is precisely instinct that is the creative, urging force and the conscious mind that plays the critical, warning role, in the case of Socrates, instinct is the critic and consciousness the creator—which is truly a monstrosity *per defectum!* Moreover, what his case in fact represents is a monstrous occultation of the mystical faculty; so that Socrates must be viewed as the specific pattern of the *non-mystic,* in whom the logical faculty has become as exorbitantly developed by superfetation as instinctive wisdom in the mystic. Furthermore, for the logical talent of Socrates to turn against itself was altogether impossible. In that unbridled verbal torrent of his there is manifest such a power of nature as we otherwise encounter with awestruck amazement only in the most grandiose manifestations of instinct. Whoever, while reading the Platonic dialogues, has received any impression at all of the divine simplicity and assurance of Socrates' way of life, must also have gotten a sense of the way the prodigious driving wheel of logical Socratism is revolving, as it were, *behind* Socrates and is to be seen through Socrates as through a shadow. And that he himself had some suspicion of this is evident in the noble earnestness with which he everywhere avouched his divine calling, even before his final judges. To confute him in this was ultimately as impossible as to call his disintegrating influence on the instincts good.[85]

As the proclaimed antagonist of instinct and the self-appointed corrector of those unconsidered modes of life that are inspired not by intellect but by impulse (in Tonio Kröger's terms, not by "spirit" but by "nature") Socratic man appears and becomes dominant at the end, not the beginning, of a culture. Oswald Spengler, in *The Decline of the West* (1923), following Nietzsche in this observa-

* Supra, p. 354.

tion, compared the courses of eight high culture histories (Egyptian, Sumero-Babylonian, Greco-Roman, Indian, Chinese, Maya-Aztec, Levantine, and West European; with the Russian, in his view, at about the stage today of the West European in the period of Charlemagne), and demonstrated, with supporting evidence enough to persuade anyone who would take pains to check fully and carefully on his data, that in each of these great superindividual life courses a moment did indeed inevitably arise when the critical-intellectual faculties gained ascendancy over the lyric-instinctual, at which point a brief period of enlightened creativity unfolded that always ended, however, in exhaustion, sterility, and mechanical repetition. Goethe (who, with Nietzsche, was Spengler's leading inspiration, as he was also Thomas Mann's) in a brief study called "Epochs of the Spirit" had outlined, already at the opening of the nineteenth century (1817), a sequence of four stages normal to all culture cycles, whether of mankind in general, a civilization, or a nation, which he then summarized in the following diagram:

Beginnings

deeply experienced perceptions: aptly named

I	Poetry	Folk Belief	Hearty	Imagination
II	Theology	Idealizing Exaltation	Holy	Reason (*Vernunft*)
III	Philosophy	Clarifying Devaluation	Wise	Understanding (*Verstand*)
IV	Prose	Dissolution in Banality	Vulgar	Sensuality

Confusion, Resistance, Dissolution

It is in the passage from Stage II to Stage III that mentality gains the upper hand and reductive criticism begins to devaluate and, where possible, even eradicate the instinctual impulses to life. As Goethe states the problem:

The man of understanding tries to appropriate everything imaginable to his own sphere of clarity and even to interpret reasonably the most mysterious phenomena. Popular and ecclesiastical beliefs, consequently, are not rejected, but behind them a comprehensible, worthy, useful component is assumed, its meaning is sought, the particular is transformed into the general, and from everything national, regional, and even individual, something valid for mankind as a whole is extracted. We cannot deny to this epoch the credit of a noble, pure, and wise endeavor; however, its appeal is rather to the unique, highly talented individual than to an entire folk.

For, no sooner does this type of thought become general than the final epoch immediately follows, which we may term the prosaic, since it has no interest in humanizing the heritage from earlier periods, adapting it to a clarified human understanding and to general domestic usage, but drags even the most venerable out into the light of common day and in this way destroys completely all solemn feelings, popular and ecclesiastical beliefs, and even the beliefs of the enlightened understanding itself—which might yet suspect behind what is exceptional some respectable context of associations.

This epoch cannot last long. Human need, aggravated by the course of history, leaps backward over intelligent leadership, confuses priestly, folk, and primitive beliefs, grabs now here, now there, at traditions, submerges itself in mysteries, sets fairytales in the place of poetry, and elevates these to articles of belief. Instead of intelligently instructing and quietly influencing, people now strew seeds and weeds together indiscriminately on all sides; no central point is offered any more on which to concentrate, but every-odd individual steps forward as leader and teacher, and gives forth his perfect folly as a perfected whole.

And so, the force of every mystery is undone, the people's religion itself profaned; distinctions that formerly grew from each other in natural development now work against each other as contradictory elements, and thus we have the Tohu-wa-Bohu chaos again: but not the first, gravid, fruitful one; rather, a dying one running to decay, from which not even the spirit of God could create for itself a worthy world.[86]

Thomas Mann presents Settembrini as the paradigmatic master of Stage III, surviving, however, only as an invalid in a world that is at the opening of Stage IV, where an apparently new, but actually harshly medieval, reactionary type of self-appointed pedagogue is emerging as both teacher of youth and adviser to the leaders of state. In *The Magic Mountain* this second, altogether ambiguous type of spiritual mentor is represented by the small, haggard, clean-shaven, expensively tailored little figure of a man named Naphta, who comes into the novel just halfway through: an aggressive, well-rehearsed debater of almost corrosive ugliness, whose thin, pursed, disdainful lips are surmounted by a vast hooked nose, and this, in turn, by thick glasses framing a pair of pale gray eyes. Settembrini teasingly refers to him as *princeps scholasticorum;* he to Settembrini, in turn, as the Master Mason, "Master of the Lodge"; and with every phrase, every word, on every conceivable subject, the two clash blades in endless verbal combat, flashing and splitting definitions. One is defending the glory of man and the spirit as revealed in the faculty of reason; the other, God and the spirit transcendent, absolutely apart from and against fallen, natural man, his instincts, reason, pretensions to freedom, progress, science, rights, and all the rest. Naphta charges Settembrini with the heresy of monism; Settembrini, Naphta with dualism and world-splitting. Both pretend to stand for the individual; Naphta, however, for his eternal soul, not his rights or powers here on earth. Both stand for man's zeal for truth; however, truth, according to Naphta, is inaccessible to reason, its sole authority being revelation; nor is the formulation of laws and customs properly a function of human councils, since there is but one law eternal, that of God, the *ius divinum,* which is to be enforced— *enforced*—by those anointed in authority:

"That the Renaissance brought all those things into the world that are called liberalism, individualism, humanistic citizenship, I am well aware," said the acrid Naphta to his humanist antagonist; "but the striving, heroic age of your ideals already is long past. Those ideals are dead; or, at least, they lie today gasping their last, and the feet of those who will deal the finishing kicks are already at the door. If I am not mistaken, you call yourself a revolutionary. But if you think freedom is to be the issue of future revolutions, you are wrong. The principle of freedom has, in the past five hundred years, fulfilled its course and outlived itself. Any method of pedagogy that still considers itself to be a child of the Enlightenment and regards as proper aims for itself a development of the critical faculties, liberation and cultivation of the individual, and thereby the dissolution of modes of life eternally fixed—may still enjoy for a while an apparent rhetorical success: but to those who know, the reactionary character of such teaching is beyond question. All truly serious educational orders have known forever what the one and only possible principle of all pedagogy must be: namely the absolute command, the iron bond, in the name of discipline, sacrifice, denial of ego, subjugation of the personality. And finally, it is an unloving misunderstanding of youth to suppose that it finds its pleasure in freedom. Its deepest pleasure is obedience. . . .

"No!" he continued. "Not liberation and development of the individual are the secret and requirement of this age. What it needs, what it yearns for, and what it will create for itself is—the Terror."

The expensively tailored little talker had, for that final word, lowered his voice; he uttered it without move or gesture. Only his glasses briefly flashed. And the auditors, Hans and his military cousin, as well as Settembrini, were appalled. The eloquent humanist, recovering however, asked with assumed levity whence the Terror, then, was to arrive.

"Is your English economic liberalism unaware of the existence of a school of social thought," the other disdainfully replied, "which represents the human victory over economic thinking, and of which both the fundamentals and the aims correspond precisely to those of the Christian City of God? The Church Fathers called 'mine' and 'thine' pernicious words, and private property, theft and usurpation. They repudiated personal possessions because, according to the God-given Law of Nature, this earth is common to all men and brings forth its fruits for the general use. They taught that it is only avarice, a consequence of the Fall, which has put forward the rights of property and created private ownership. They were humane enough, anti-commercial enough, to call economic activity of any sort whatsoever a danger to the soul's salvation— which is to say: a danger to humanity. They hated money and finance, and called capitalistic wealth the burning point of the fire of Hell. . . . And now: after centuries of disregard, all these economic principles and criterions are being resurrected in the modern movement of Communism. The agreement is complete, even to the point of the claim to world dominion made by International Labor against international business and finance; the world proletariat is today opposing to the capitalistic corruption of the bourgeoisie the ideal of humanity and criterion of the City of God. The Dictatorship of the Proletariat, this politico-economic means to salvation proper to our age, does not intend to dominate for its own sake and for all time, but only in the

way of a temporary annulment of the opposition of Spirit and
Force in the Sign of the Cross: in the sense of overcoming the
World by the means of World Mastery, in the sense of transition,
transcendence, the Kingdom. The Proletariat has taken up again
the work of Gregory the Great, his zeal for God dwells in it, and
no less than he will it withhold its hand from blood. Its task is to
strike fear into hearts for the redemption of the world and the
gaining, at last, of the Redeemer's goal, the stateless, classless
condition of man as the child of God." [87]

The little vehicle of cynical hate giving utterance to this apocalyptic vision of the Day of God was an ordained Jesuit, born a Jew:
a full Judeo-Christian! but developing ideas just a bit ahead of
those conventional to either of his successive Testaments, and so,
running a temperature, residing on the Magic Mountain with a
touch of death in his lung. *"Ein joli jésuite,"* thought Hans, *"mit
einer petite tache humide."* "All his thoughts," said Settembrini,
"are lascivious: they are under the sign of Death." [88] And indeed,
in his luxurious, silk-upholstered apartment, a fourteenth-century
pietà proposed an ideal of ugly beauty that was altogether in contrast to that of Settembrini's Renaissance *bellezza*. It was a work
(as he explained to Hans) conceived in the ascetic spirit of a witty
piece of writing by Innocent III, bearing the title *De miseria
humanae conditionis:* not the prettified production of any Monsieur
This or Monsieur That, but anonymous, impersonal, a radical
revelation, *sub signo mortificationis,* of the knowledge of sorrow
and frailty of the flesh.[89]

The young engineer was able to recognize in this impressive
work, and in the arguments of Naphta, a depth of insight into the
woes of the world that went beyond that of his other mentor, Settembrini. However, the separation by Naphta of the values of the
spirit from those of living in this world with love for it as it is, left
him unconvinced. Pain, sickness, death and corruption, indeed:
but were these a refutation of life? Mann has managed to bring
to focus in Naphta, this little monster, the whole historic sweep
of Levantine spirituality, in irreconcilable opposition to the native humanistic individualism of Europe.

Behold, the Lord will lay waste the earth and make it deso-
late, and he will twist its surface and scatter its inhabitants. And
it shall be, as with the people, so with the priest; as with the

slave, so with his master; as with the maid, so with her mistress; as with the buyer, so with the seller; as with the lender, so with the borrower; as with the creditor, so with the debtor. The earth shall be utterly laid waste and utterly despoiled; for the Lord has spoken this word.

The earth mourns and withers, the world languishes and withers; the heavens languish together with the earth. The earth lies polluted under its inhabitants; for they have transgressed the laws, violated the statutes, broken the everlasting covenant. Therefore a curse devours the earth, and its inhabitants suffer for their guilt; therefore the inhabitants of the earth are scorched, and few men are left.[90]

There is no need to ask or to wonder what the new world is to be like; for we have read of it in the annals of the past and see its latter form before us, even now, in the People's Paradise of the U.S.S.R., China, Eastern Europe, and Tibet, leaking refugees at every unwalled, unwired, unmachine-gunned rathole.[91]

They found a man gathering sticks on the sabbath day. And those who found him gathering sticks brought him to Moses and Aaron, and to all the congregation. They put him in custody, because it had not been made plain what should be done to him. And the Lord said to Moses, "The man shall be put to death; all the congregation shall stone him with stones outside the camp." And all the congregation brought him outside the camp, and stoned him to death with stones, as the Lord commanded Moses.[92]

Society everywhere [states Emerson] is in conspiracy against the manhood of every one of its members. . . . It loves not realities and creators, but names and customs. . . . Nothing is at last sacred but the integrity of your own mind.[93]

And Goethe:

The Godhead is effective in the living and not in the dead, in the becoming and the changing, not in the become and the set-fast; and therefore, accordingly, reason (*Vernunft*) is concerned only to strive toward the divine through the becoming and the living, and the understanding (*Verstand*) only to make use of the become and set-fast.[94]

VIII. The Amfortas Wound

In *Primitive Mythology* it has been pointed out that there is no such thing as man *qua* man. The young of the species *Homo sapi-*

ens are born too soon, absolutely helpless, and acquire their specifically human faculties of speech, thought, and a symbolizing imagination, as well as erect posture and ability to use tools, under the tutelage of the particular social body into which they are adopted. They grow up to its style and world, imprinted with its signature, molded to its limitations; and the first function of the myths and rites of each group is simply to bring this specialized development to pass. The earliest social units, furthermore, were hardly greater than large families, of which every adult member was in possession of the entire cultural heritage. The myths embodied the substance of this heritage and the rites were the means by which it was both communicated to the young and maintained in force among the old. The myths and rites, that is to say, served a fostering, educative function, bearing the unfinished nature product to full, harmonious unfoldment as an adult specifically adapted for survival in a certain specific environment, as a fully participating member of a specific social group; and apart from that group he would neither have come to maturity nor have been able to survive.

In our present world we have such family rites as well, and as long as it is this psychological, educative function that they serve, as rites of passage, fostering the young to a maturity fit for *this* day and age, there can be little quarrel either with them or with those by whom they are administered. However, the world today is not as it was in the paleolithic ages, when the roving family hordes of mankind were rare and scattered companies on this earth, foraging as newcomers in a perilous environment of beasts. Nature was then very hard; society, therefore, too. Youngsters found to be intractable were simply wiped away. Conformity in the narrowest sense was an absolute necessity. And yet even then there was an allowance made for a certain type of deviant, the visionary, the shaman: the one who had died and come back to life, the one who had met and talked with spirit powers, the one whose great dreams and vivid hallucinations told effectively of forces deeper and more essential than the normally visible surface of things. And it was, in fact, from the insights of just these strangely gifted ones that the myths and rites of the primitive communities were in largest part derived.[95] They were the first finders and exposers of those inner realities that are recognized today as of the psyche. Hence the myths and rites, of which they were the masters, served not only the outward (supposed) function of influencing nature, causing game to appear, illness to abate, foes to fall, and friends to flourish, but also the inward (actual) work of touching and awakening the deep strata and springs of the human imagination; so that the practical needs of living in a certain specific geographical environment—in the arctic, tropics, desert, grassy plains, on a mountain peak or on a coral isle—should be fulfilled, as it were, in play: all the world and its features, and the deeds of man within it, being rendered luminous by participation in the plot and fabulous setting of a grandiose theater piece.

The animal slain for food, for example, which had been summoned by a rite, had appeared as a willing sacrifice, self-offered, with the understanding that through a second rite its life would be returned for rebirth to the source. And among planting folk, in the same way of make-believe, the work of gardening, tilling and harvesting, was likened to the mysteries of begetting and of birth. Very much like a boy galloping with all his might as a mustang down a street, where he would have gone bored and weary at a walk, so primitive man, from the first we know of him, through his myths and rites turned every aspect of his work into a festival. These gave to everything a meaning not there in any practical, economic sense, but only as play, enacted dream: a grave, yet joyous, tragicomic play, to the grave and constant roles of which the young were introduced and trained by the elders of their world. To say with Emerson that a society of this type was in conspiracy against the manhood of every one of its members would be absolutely incorrect.

However, as we have already amply seen in the earlier volumes of this survey, a totally new situation developed in the suddenly flowering village world of the nuclear Near East, immediately following the introduction there of the arts of grain agriculture and stock-breeding, c. 7500 B.C. No longer forced to forage for their food, people settled in established villages, the number and size of which grew; and when the richly fertile mudlands of the lower Tigris-Euphrates were entered c. 4000 B.C., the rate of increase accelerated. Villages became towns; towns, cities: the first cities in the history of the world. And no longer were the functioning social units simple groups, of the order of large families, but compound, complexly functioning organisms of variously specialized classes: tillers of the soil, tradespeople, governors and the governed, craftsmen of various kinds, and professional priests. And as we have seen,[96] it was precisely at this point of space and time, in the Near East, and specifically Sumer, c. 3500–3000 B.C., that the evidence first appears among the ruins of those earliest city-states—Kish, Uruk, Ur, Lagash, Larsa, and the rest—first, of a disciplined social order imposed from above by force, and next, of deliberate expeditions of military conquest against neighbors: not the mere annihilation raids of one tribe or village horde against another, in a spirit of plunder, malice, or revenge, but deliberately progressed campaigns of systematic conquest and subjugation.

In the words of a great Orientalist, the late Professor Hans Heinrich Schaeder (1896–1957) of the Universities of Königsberg, Berlin, and Göttingen, it was exactly here, with this epochal crisis in the history of mankind, that the world-historical process of which we ourselves are a part took its rise, its special theme, and its characteristic being: *the programmatic exercise of power by men over men.*

And this development took place [states Professor Schaeder], not in the way of a gradual evolution, but abruptly, in a brief span, with the coming into being of the earliest form of the state, or of anything eligible to such a name. It appears in the city-states and their rapid combinations into territorial states of the lower Tigris-Euphrates and Nile, after which, likewise, on the rivers Indus, third millennium B.C., and Hwang Ho, second millennium. All of which state foundings derived from one and the same historic process, namely, the overrunning and subjugation of earlier, locally settled tillers of the soil by conquering warrior herdsmen from Central Asia. . . .

Now the exercise of power is governed everywhere by the law of intensification, or as the Greeks would say, πλεονεξία, "greed for more than one's share." There is within it no principle of measure; measure is brought to it only from without, by counterforces that restrict it. So that history is the interaction of power, on one hand—its establishment, maintenance, and increase—and those counterforces, on the other. Various names have been given to the latter—of which the simplest and most inclusive is love. They are released when doubts arise (generally among the governed, but occasionally, also, in circles of the ruling class) conducing to a criticism of the power principle. And this criticism may develop to the radical point of an absolute renunciation of power, generating then the idea and realization of an order of life based on brotherly love and mutual aid. Self-confidence, and thereby the strength to influence others, accrues to those in this position from their belief that only in this, and not in power, which they reject, can the meaning of human existence be fulfilled. Meaning is then sought no longer in the organized powers of a state, the domination of the governed by their masters, but in individuals, giving and welcoming love.

When such an order prospers in its conversion of people, guiding them to a new life, it may bring into being a spiritual movement that nothing can stop. This is passed on, from one generation to the next, and spreads from the narrow circle of its origin over lands and continents. It succeeds, along the way, in persuading even the holders of worldly power to concede recognition—either actually or ostensibly—to its truth and obligations, and lays restraints on their will to power that are not an effect of that will itself. Twice in the history of the world, in Buddhism and in Christianity, such movements have acquired the character of world-historical powers; and in the course of their development they have themselves become infected by the will to power and mastery, which has at times even darkened them to the core. Yet both are such that they can be restored to their pristine character, in the sense of the life and teaching of their founders. Of all the spiritual movements in the history of Eurasia, it is these two that, even to our own day, offer the most abiding and dependable guarantees against that soul-destruction and degradation which the man beset by the Will to Power can render both to others and to himself.

The sequence of the periods of world-history was not produced, however, by love, but by an expansion of the power field, which in the course of a development of more than three millenniums finally brought the whole of Eurasia into its sphere, divided into separate states. This occurred by way of an interaction between the earlier city states and later conquering hordes, who either seized the mastery and extended it, or else set up new states of their own nearby on the pattern of the old. . . .[97]

As we have seen throughout the volumes of this study, it has been the chief concern of all these power groups, in their interpretation, formulation, and enforcement then of their rites, not so much to foster the growth of young individuals to maturity as to validate supernaturally, and to render religiously unchallengeable, their own otherwise questionable authority, whether as dynasty, as tribe, or as churchly sect. The timeless symbols, taken over and recombined, are applied systematically, and with full intent, to the aims of subjugation through indoctrination. A totally new order of state beliefs and rites, to the glory of some name or other, is superimposed upon the old life-fostering order of the family and spiritual rites of passage and initiation: a "faith," as it is called, is proposed for belief.

The Waste Land, let us say then, is any world in which (to state the problem pedagogically) force and not love, indoctrination, not education, authority, not experience, prevail in the ordering of lives, and where the myths and rites enforced and received are consequently unrelated to the actual inward realizations, needs, and potentialities of those upon whom they are impressed. It would be ridiculous to argue that such reigns of force never should have been. In the first place, here they are. In the second place, they have been the givers of everything good and great beyond the range of thought, vision, art, and civilization of Shakespeare's apeman Caliban. And in the third place, for those caught up in the creative labor and exhilaration of their development—whether as members themselves of the creative élite by whom the new forms are advanced, or as mere hands, willing contributors, whose lives are given meaning through association—the privilege of participating in the great creative moments of world history is hardly a grant of life to be despised.

However, as Spengler has well shown in his own creative masterwork, there are moments of climacteric when the culture forms thus brought into being attain and pass their apogee. Furthermore—but here is a point for which Spengler had little sympathy—there are those, as Schaeder has pointed out, generally among the governed, but occasionally also in circles of the ruling class itself, who begin to feel uneasy about, and so to criticize, the power experience and power task of the day as the proper, sole, and highest human experience and concern. Jean Jacques Rousseau (1712–1778) was such a critic at the moment of the height of glory of the eighteenth-century Enlightenment. And a like figure in the Middle Ages was the poet Jean de Meung (1240?–1305?), whose celebration of Dame Nature in his long concluding portion of the *Roman de la Rose* (c. 1277) corresponds curiously to the celebrated argument of Rousseau in his *Discours sur les arts et sciences* (1749), that the savage state (back to nature: the Noble Savage) is superior to that of civilized man. In Greece, at the time of the apogee of Athenian power and light, the cynic Diogenes (412?–323 B.C.) was such a rebel; in India the Buddha (563–483 B.C.), rejecting caste and the rules of Brahminical social life, as well as the authority of the Vedas, stands for an identical crisis; while in China we find the Tao Te Ching (fourth century B.C.), with its summons of the spirit to "return to the root." [98] There is in all these voices a common call—away from the fixed and the setfast to the as yet unformed potential, the "remainder" so to say, which the rites and myths and special aims of the local group, the "collective faith," have left unmet, untouched, and unconvinced. In the words again of Emerson:

> There is one mind common to all individual men. . . . Of the works of this mind history is the record. . . . Without hurry, without rest, the human spirit goes forth from the beginning to embody every faculty, every thought, every emotion which belongs to it, in appropriate events. But the thought is always prior to the fact; all the facts of history preëxist in the mind as laws. [99]

The wicked thing about both the little and the great "collective faiths," prehistoric and historic, is that they all, without exception, pretend to hold encompassed in their ritualized mythologies all of the truth ever to be known. They are therefore cursed, and they curse all who accept them, with what I shall call the "error of the found truth," or, in mythological language, the sin against the Holy Ghost. They set up against the revelations of the spirit the barriers of their own petrified belief, and therefore, within the ban of their control, mythology, as they shape it, serves the end only of binding potential individuals to whatever system of sentiments may have seemed to the shapers of the past (now sanctified as saints, sages, ancestors, or even gods) to be appropriate to their concept of a great society. Thus, even a period of civilization that from without, and in the historian's view, would appear to be a golden age, might be a waste when viewed from within. To quote Ortega y Gasset:

Every culture that has triumphed and succeeded turns into a topic and a phrase. A topic is an idea that is used, not because it is evident, but because *people* say it. A phrase is that which is not thought out every time, but is simply said, repeated. . . . The culture, which in its origin, in its own moment of genuineness was simple, becomes complicated. And this complicating of the inherited culture thickens the screen between each man's self and the things that surround him. Bit by bit his life becomes less his own and more the collective life. His individual, effective and always primitive "I" is replaced by the "I" which is "people," by the conventional, complicated, cultivated "I." The so-called cultivated man always appears in periods of a very advanced culture which are already made up of pure topics and phrases.

This is an inexorable process. Culture, the purest product of the live and the genuine, since it comes out of the fact that man feels with an awful anguish and a burning enthusiasm the relentless needs of which his life is made up, ends by becoming a falsification of that life. Man's genuine self is swallowed up by his cultured, conventional, social self. Every culture or every great phase of culture ends in man's socialization, and vice versa; socialization pulls man out of his life of solitude, which is his real and authentic life.[100]

There is no doubt that in the twelfth and thirteenth centuries a major threshold of cultural change had been attained. The aims of the Christian conquest of Europe had been accomplished—largely by force; the power of the papacy was at its height; the crusades were in full career; and yet from every side sounds and alarms of heresy were beginning to arise and to spread. The whole structure was cracking. For the cathedral of God's love, the Church, and the chalice of his divine blood—the *vas* of his self-giving on its altar —had been turned frankly and openly to sheer force: the Church was a power-state, a super power-state, and its Pope—as well as its image of God—was a Levantine King of Kings in the perfect style of an Achaemenian Darius.

But there was a new strong wine in ferment, which the golden chalice in the priestly hands, elevated at the altar, to the pungency of incense and the chime of altar bells, the bowed heads of multitudes and the silence of angelic choirs, could no longer hold. In a sense, that age, like our own, and like the great Hellenistic age, was one in which a cross-fertilization of cultures, Oriental and European, had unsettled all local dogmas and the claims thereby of power-élites to authority from aloft. Like cells released from an organism in decay, individuals, unbound, spontaneously trans- ferred allegiances to new, unforeseen combinations. And so it is that we find in all three of these periods of crisis analogous erup- tions of pathological social phenomena, symptomatic of what Jung (following Heraclitus) has called *enantiodromia:* i.e., a "conver- sion into opposite," a "crossing over," a compulsive "running the other way"; which is to say, a loss of control on the part of the conscious faculties, and exactly such an overpowering upsurge of instinctual impulse as occurred in the case of Tristan and Isolt when they drank the potion.

Certainly that was not the ideal of *moraliteit* that the poet Gott- fried, and Tristan himself, had celebrated.* It was an overwhelm- ing, irresistible, daemonic invasion, beyond control of the active will, and its force, finally, was as baneful in effect as any force ap- plied in the name of king, god, or civilization from above. This was the point that Wagner recognized even at the opening of his labors on the *Tristan,* when he had just been overwhelmed by his dis- covery of the philosophy of Schopenhauer. On the surge of that in- spiration, he was at work on the music of *Die Walküre,* in the fall of 1854, when the conception of a Tristan opera occurred to him, and, as he tells in his autobiography:

> Returning, one day, from a walk, I outlined for myself the contents of its three acts in a summary way, to serve as a base for the development of the material later on. And in the last act I introduced at that time an episode, which, finally, I did not in- clude: namely, a visit to Tristan's sickbed by the Grail-questing, wandering Parzival. For in my thoughts, I had identified Tris- tan, languishing from the wound he had received and yet not able to die of it, with Amfortas of the Grail romance.[101]

That was another of those brilliant psychological insights, such as Mann remarked in Wagner. For the wound of the Maimed King in the Castle of the Grail, as the reader perhaps recalls, was in a magical way associated with the waste and sorrow of his land. In the various versions of the legend his reception of the wound has been explained in various ways. According to the oldest extant text—the *Perceval,* or, as it is also called, *Li Contes del Graal,* of

* Supra, p. 230.

the French court poet Chrétien de Troyes (1140?–1191?)
—he had been wounded in a battle by a javelin thrust through
both thighs, and was still in such pain that he could not mount a
horse. Hence, when he desired distraction, he would have himself
carried to a boat, to be rowed fishing on a river; whence he was
known as the Fisher King.[102] Wagner's source, however, was not
this old French version of the romance, which remained unfinished
at the time of its author's death, but the Middle High German *Parzival* of Wolfram von Eschenbach (c. 1170–1230), where a
deeply perceived sociological and psychological significance is recognized both in the wound itself and in the circumstances of the
wounding of the king.

For it had been at a tender age that the Grail King Anfortas
had been appointed to his sacred office. The earlier king, his
father, had been slain; and he, the eldest son, a mere boy, had
been chosen to succeed. Thus he was king not by virtue of his
character and personal realization, but by inheritance, perforce: the role was to him (in Ortega's terms) a topic, a phrase:
unearned, unrelated to his nature. And so, as we read in Wolfram's
words:

> He reached the years when his beard began to grow, the age
> when Love turns her malice upon youth. She then urges her be-
> loved so compellingly that one can only say of her that she lacks
> honor. However, if a Lord of the Grail craves for love in a man-
> ner otherwise than prescribed, he will endure trials and most
> piteous anguish.[103]

The young Grail King, coming of age, rode forth therefore
on adventure, like any young knight of his day, and his battle-
cry was Amor.

> But that cry [we read] was not at all appropriate to the spirit
> [required of the Grail King] of gentleness and humility. The
> King fared forth alone that day (which was to prove a great sor-
> row to his people), riding in quest of adventure, steered along
> by his joy in love: for love's zeal so compelled him. And he was
> pierced, wounded in a joust, by a poisoned spear through his
> testicles, so severely he could not be healed.
> A heathen it was who had there engaged him and delivered
> that stroke: one born in the land Ethnise, where the river Tigris
> flows from Paradise: one who had been confident that his battle-
> courage would gain the Grail for him. Its name was engraved on

his heathen spear, and in quest of knightly deeds afar, he was wandering over land and sea, only for the power of the Grail.

That heathen was there slain by the King; and for him too we may somewhat lament. However, when the King returned to us so pale and empty of strength, a doctor's hand searched the wound, found the iron spearhead therein, a splinter of the shaft as well, and removed them. . . . Whereupon, he was immediately borne, through God's help, to the Grail: but when he looked upon it his torture only increased, for he now was unable to die.[104]

Note the irony here and compare Mann: The heathen child of nature, born near the Earthly Paradise, rides in quest of the supreme symbol of the spirit while the authorized guardian of that symbol goes the opposite way.* The young king's name, Anfortas, from the old French *Enfertez* (*Enfermetez*), means "Infirmity."[105] Its prophecy is fulfilled (as though by chance) when the two riders collide, to the ruin of both. Nature is then dispatched, and the guardian of the symbol of the spirit, though emptied of his virtue, is nevertheless retained by his sorrowing people in his spiritual role, ever in hope of healing, but without event.

The life-desolating effects of this separation of the reigns of nature (the Earthly Paradise) and the spirit (the Castle of the Grail) in such a way that neither touches the other but destructively, remains to this day an essential psychological problem of the Christianized Western world; and since it is at root a consequence of the basic biblical doctrine of an ontological distinction between God and his universe, creator and creature, spirit and matter,† it is a problem that has hardly altered since it first became intolerably evident at the climax of the Middle Ages. In briefest restatement: The Christian is taught that divinity is transcendent: not within himself and his world, but "out there." I call this *mythic dissociation*.[106] Turning inward, he would find not divinity within, but only his own created soul, which might or might not be in proper relationship to its supposed Creator. The Old Testament doctrine held that God (x) had concluded a Covenant (R) with a certain people (c). None other enjoyed this

* Supra, p. 332.
† Supra, figure 8 and pp. 18–21.

privilege; it was unique. A relationship (R) to God was possible, consequently, only through membership in this group, this people: cRx. To which the New Testament adds that in the fullness of time a child, Jesus, begotten of God, was born of that holy race, in whom humanity (c) and divinity (x) were miraculously joined. All of us in our humanity (c) are related to that of Jesus, who in his divinity relates us to God (x). However, participation in this relationship (R) can be only by way of the Church that he founded (once thought to be single, but now of a million differing sects, any one of which might be true or false). Consequently, just as in the Old Testament view a relationship to God could be achieved only through physical birth as a member of the Holy Race, so in the New, only through baptism (spiritual birth) into membership in Christ's Church; i.e., participation, in either case, in a specific social group. I call this the way of *social identification*. One equates the realm of value with one's social affiliation, and *extra ecclesiam nulla salus*.

Unhappily, however, in the light of what is now known, not only of the history of the Bible and the Church, but also of the universe and evolution of species, a suspicion has been confirmed that was already dawning in the Middle Ages; namely, that the biblical myth of Creation, Fall, and Redemption is historically untrue. Hence, there has now spread throughout the Christian world a desolating sense not only of no divinity within (*mythic dissociation*), but also of no participation in divinity without (*social identification dissolved*): and that, in short, is the mythological base of the Waste Land of the modern soul, or, as it is being called these days, our "alienation."

The sense of desolation is experienced on two levels: first the social, in a loss of identification with any spiritually compelling, structuring group; and, beyond that, the metaphysical, in a loss of any sense either of identity or of relationship with a dimension of experience, being, and rapture any more awesome than that provided by an empirically classifiable conglomerate of self-enclosed, separate, mutually irritating organisms held together only by lust (crude or sublimated) and fear (of pain and death or of boredom).

It has become fashionable to write of this broken image of a world as though it were a function of some new social construct, brought about by a combination of recent economic, scientific, and political developments: the industrial revolution, capitalism, colonialism, atom bombs, high or low taxes, or what not. In the broad prospect of our present, nearly concluded survey of the epochs of mankind, however, it can be seen that the actual nuclear problem was already present, and recognized by many, at the very peak of that great period of burgeoning French cathedrals (1150–1250) which Henry Adams characterized as representing the highest concentration of moral fervor in the history of the West. As the ravaged lives of Abelard and Heloise already had foretold as early as the first years of the twelfth century, neither human love nor human reason could much longer support the imposed irrational ordeals of an imported mythic order, out of touch with every movement of the native mind, as well as heart, and held in force only by a reign of terror. The cathedral-building passion itself, it would even seem, was but a compensatory, desperate screening effort to deny and nullify the increasingly obvious fact that the mighty image from Asia had begun to crack, disintegrate, and go asunder.

In the heart of Heloise the boon, the blessing from within— bitter-sweet—of nature's goddess Love, had rendered the mythic threat of the fires of Hell indifferent: her love was, for Heloise, the Real. And Gottfried's celebration, a century later, of Tristan's willing challenge even of "an eternal death" * gives further evidence of the trend in those years to accept the judgment of one's own experience against the authority of Scripture and the Church.

On the side of Heloise's beloved, Abelard, however—as of the young Grail King Anfortas—an altogether different order of mind was brought under pressure from the urge of the goddess within. For, as in the case of the unreadied youth whose beard had begun to grow, so in that of the middle-aged celibate theologian, the impulse to love had not been inspired by a message from the eyes to a readied "noble heart"; as his confessional letter itself declares: at the age of about thirty-six, "having hitherto lived continently," he was "casting his eyes about." And they lit upon a girl of eighteen, innocent, aware of his greatness, and available, as would the eyes of a wolf on a lamb.†

The real greatness of Abelard, where he stands in majesty un-

* Supra, pp. 244–45.
† Supra, pp. 53–54.

surpassed in his time, as Heloise in the courage of her heart, was in the kingdom, rather, of reason. For it is from the period of his sensational lectures in Paris, the first years of the twelfth century, that the beginning is dated of the end of the reign in Europe of that order of unreason, unreasoning submission to the dicta of authority, that is epitomized in the formula of the early Church Father Tertullian (160?–230?): *"Credo quia ineptum:* I believe because it is absurd." "The son of God died; it is by all means to be believed," Tertullian had written, "because it is absurd. And He was buried and rose again; the fact is certain, because it is impossible." [107] And before that Saint Paul himself had opened the door to such impudent idiocies when he had written: "For since, in the wisdom of God, the world did not know God through wisdom, it pleased God through the folly of what we preach to save those who believe." [108]

Abelard, in his early thirties, still a student under Anselm of Laon, had shocked his fellows by suggesting that one should be able to study scripture for oneself, and at their urging demonstrated his point by giving, without previous training, a series of lectures on Ezekiel that proved more popular than the master's— for which indiscretion he was expelled. In Paris he resumed the lectures, and the fame that there accrued to him as philosopher and theologian, poet and musician (a veritable Tristan of Brittany incarnate) gained for him—alas for both!—his Heloise and their destiny of calamity.

The most dangerous part of Abelard's message, both for the faith which he held sincerely, and for his own personal safety, lay in his conviction that a knowledge of God can be attained by reason—as it had been by the Greeks—and that such knowledge, consequently, is not confined to the Christian world. At the hour of his death he was at work on a *Dialogue between a Philosopher, a Jew, and a Christian* [109] wherein this point was to be made and Christianity represented not as a mythology of incredible tenets, but as "the total verity, which includes all others within it." [110] The approach to God by reason implied the reasonableness of God and that what reason cannot accept need not, and indeed cannot, be believed. "He that is hasty to trust," Abelard once had written, "is light-minded." Further: "The doctors of the Church should be read, not with the necessity to believe, but with liberty to judge." [111] And to drive this last point home, in his important work *Sic et Non* ("Yes and No"), he presented a series of contrary opinions, drawn from the Fathers, on all the leading disputes of the theology of his time. "By doubting we are led to inquire, by inquiry we perceive the truth," he wrote; and of those who argued that we are not to reason in matters of faith, he asked, with a cut that could not be answered:

> How, then, is the faith of any people, however false, to be refuted, though it may have arrived at such a pitch of blindness as to confess some idol to be the creator both of heaven and of earth? As, according to your own admission, you cannot reason upon matters of faith, you have no right to attack others upon a matter with regard to which you think you ought yourself to be unassailed. [112]

Abelard was harried from pillar to post for his views, driven throughout his mutilated life from one monastic haven to another. On one occasion he was compelled to burn his own book with his own hands ("So it was burnt," he wrote of this brutal event, "amid general silence"); and to read aloud then the Athanasian Creed ("the which I read amid sobs and tears as well as I might"). He was sent to a convent near Soissons, which had acquired the reputation of a penitentiary through the stern discipline of its abbot Geoffrey and his frequent use of the whip, from which he was presently released, only to fall into more trouble, and then more, until at one point he fled to a forest hermitage, to which, when it was found, students flocked, and it became itself a monastery; from which, however, he then took flight again for fear of the fierce power of that saintly lover of God's love and singer of the Song of Songs, Saint Bernard of Clairvaux. "God knows," he wrote of those terrible years, "that at times I fell into such despair that I proposed to myself to go off and live the life of a Christian among the enemies of Christ." [113] Abelard was indeed Tristan as the mutilated Grail King, and he stands symbolic for his time and for the sterilization of heart, body, and mind that the Waste Land theme represents.

And yet the schoolrooms in Paris in which he had lectured became, within a generation, largely through his influence, the leading university of Europe; and it was chiefly there that the great scholastic movement came into being, of which Aquinas was to be the culminating master. The Church today is rightly proud of the intellectual splendor of this movement, which, however, in its own time, as a flowering of free creative thought, was greatly feared and finally broken. So that actually the fate of its initiator, Abelard—the Waste Land theme of the agony of his life—had been the announcement, as in a symphony, of all the passages to follow, through which, in amplification, demonstration, variation, culmination, and dénouement, the same dreadful murder of light and life by grim power (the art of the systematic exercise of power by men over men) was to be rehearsed.

The optimistic aim of this movement had been to prove that Greek philosophy and biblical supernaturalism, reason and revelation, are not absolutely incompatible, but, as far as reason reaches, in accord; revelation extending, however, beyond. For example, in Aquinas's words, from his *Summa Theologica*:

> To know in a general and confused way that God exists is implanted in us by nature, inasmuch as God is man's beatitude. For man naturally desires happiness, and what is naturally desired by man is naturally known by him. This, however, is not to know absolutely that God exists; just as to know that someone is approaching is not the same as to know that Peter is approaching, even though it is Peter who is approaching; for there are many who imagine that man's perfect good, which is happiness, consists in riches, and others in pleasures, and others in something else.[114]

The Greek philosophers, most notably Aristotle, had gone, according to the schoolmen, as far as natural reason could in demonstrating questions of this kind; however, that God was a Trinity, of which Jesus Christ was the Second Person, who, furthermore, had been begotten by the Third, to be born then of a Virgin, crucified, and buried, only to rise again three days later and ascend to Heaven, where he sits now at the right hand of the First Person, no ignorant Greek, not even Aristotle, could ever have come to know—partly, of course, because nothing of the kind had yet occurred in the fourth century B.C.; but also because that is not the kind of truth to be arrived at by syllogism.

That which is proposed to be believed equally by all is equally unknown by all as an object of science [states Aquinas]. Such are the things that are of faith absolutely. Consequently, faith and science are not about the same things.

Unbelievers are in ignorance of things that are of faith, for neither do they see or know them in themselves, nor do they know them to be credible. The faithful, on the other hand, know them, not as by demonstration, but by the light of faith which makes them see that they ought to believe them.—The arguments employed by holy men to prove things that are of faith are not demonstrations; they are either persuasive arguments showing that what is proposed to our faith is not impossible, or else they are proofs drawn from the principles of faith, i.e., from the authority of Holy Scripture. Whatever is based on these principles is as well proved in the eyes of the faithful as a conclusion drawn from self-evident principles is in the eyes of all. Hence, theology is a science. . . .[115]

Dante in his *Divina Commedia,* half a century after Aquinas's *Summa,* represented the logic of this hierarchy of truths—natural and supernatural, reasonable and revealed—in his imagery of the two guides of his soul, Virgil and Beatrice. The first, the pagan poet, conducts the confused Christian out of the dangerous "dark wood," * safely past the pits of Hell and up the World Mountain of Purgatory, to the Earthly Paradise on its summit. There, however, Beatrice greets him, to become his guide aloft, in Christian charity and faith, to the beatific vision of God.

Not all, however, nor even a majority, of the creative spirits of those centuries, striving to bring Moses, Paul, and Aristotle to their knees together before the tabernacle of the consecrated Host, were found by the authorities to be facing in the right direction. Creativity, after all, is not conformity, and there was a lot going on in the young universities of those days that could not be brought into fellowship with the Athanasian Creed. For instance, the most celebrated Averroist of Aquinas's time, the Master Siger of Brabant—who had the luck to have left France before the French inquisitor Simon du Val arrived, November 23, 1277, to apprehend and question him—is reported to have put forward, if not actually to have held, such views (suggesting Asia) as the following: That the created world is eternal and that, since the world is eternal, the

* Supra, pp. 106–107.

same species of creatures are bound to reappear, so to speak in a circular way, succeeding each other in the same order as before, and so on indefinitely. Further, that the supreme felicity of man in this life formally consists in the intellectual act by which his intellect understands the essence of the intellect that is God; and moreover, that for the human intellect the intellection by which God is understood is God himself.[116]

On January 18, 1277, therefore, three years after Aquinas's death, Pope John XXI wrote to the Bishop of Paris, Etienne Tempier, to ascertain the number, nature, and sources of the reported "errors" then being circulated in his precinct; and on March 7 of the same fateful year the bishop, accordingly, issued a stunning condemnation of no less than two hundred and nineteen philosophical propositions, which delivered the *coup de grâce* to philosophy as an exercise within the sanctuary of the Church. A few days later the Archbishop of Canterbury endorsed this so-called *Condemnation of 1277,* and on April 28 a second letter of Pope John prescribed measures for its implementation. Among the propositions scored were the following (and what is most remarkable and significant here is the fact that we do not possess the books or even know the names of the authors of any of these thoughts; so that were it not for their mention in this condemnation, we should not have known that such thoughts arose and were taught in the Middle Ages):

That the Christian religion hinders education. That there are falsehoods and errors in the Christian religion as in all others. That one does not know more for knowing theology. That what the theologians say rests upon myths. That true wisdom is the wisdom of the philosophers, not of theologians, and that therefore there is no state superior to the practice of philosophy. That man's good is in the rational sciences, from which knowledge flow the natural moral virtues described by Aristotle, these making up all the happiness accessible to man in this life, after which there is no other. That there are no other virtues possible, none supernaturally infused; and that we should therefore return to those virtues that Aristotle reserves for an élite and which are not made for the poor. That if the world is eternal, it is because God cannot not produce it, and if the world is such as it is, it is because God cannot produce it other than it is. For from the first principle, which is one, there can come only a single effect, which is similar to it; God, therefore, cannot immediately and freely produce a plurality of effects, but the multiplicity of things presupposes a multiplicity of intermediary causes whose existence is necessarily required for their own.

This 28th condemned proposition is to be carefully noted [comments Professor Gilson], for it is of capital importance for the understanding of the subsequent history of medieval philosophy and theology: the Primary Principle can be the cause of different effects here below only through the medium of other causes, because nothing which transmutes can effect transmutations of several sorts, without itself being transmuted. To maintain this principle was radically to deny the liberty and omnipotence of the Christian God. The Jewish and Christian God was not only able to create at a single stroke the world with the multiplicity of beings it holds, he still could intervene in it freely at any instant, either directly to create in it human souls or to act miraculously and without the intervention of secondary causes; between Yahweh and the Greco-Arabian god * from whom effects proceed one by one and according to a necessary order no conciliation was possible. Before the condemnation, Philip the Chancellor, William of Auvergne, Bonaventure, and others had already perceived their incompatibility; from 1277 on, all the theologians knew it. The condemnation of 1277 is a landmark in the history of mediaeval philosophy and theology. . . . Instead of carrying on its effort to conquer philosophy by renovating it, scholasticism acted on the defensive. At that very moment, its golden age came to an end.[117]

And at that very moment, also, institutional Christianity was finished as a creative force in European life. For not only had its God dropped back once more into the Bible, but there were presently two popes, then three (the Great Schism 1377–1417); after which, two Christianities, then a hundred (Martin Luther, 1483–1546). And meanwhile the new theological tone had been set by the powerful chancellor of the still supreme University of Paris, John Gerson (d. 1429), the pious power-man chiefly responsible for the execution of John Huss,[118] the whole sense of whose influential work entitled *Against Vain Curiosity in Matters of Faith*

---

* N.B. The Greco-Arabian god here meant is not the god of the Koran, but the god described by the philosophers and already condemned by Moslem orthodoxy a century and a half before the blast from Paris.

(1402, 1403) he himself epitomized in the words from the Gospel according to Mark 1:15: "Repent and believe the gospel." That, for him, was the whole of Christianity. And from there to our contemporary great Protestant, Karl Barth, with his "leap of faith," or back the other way to Paul and Tertullian— *credo quia ineptum*—where (exactly where?) is *creative* thought?

THE WAY AND THE LIFE

Chapter 7

THE CRUCIFIED

I. The Turning Wheel of Terror-Joy

The origins of Arthurian romance were Celtic.[1] However, beneath and behind the Celtic stratum lay the widely disseminated neolithic and Bronze Age mythic and ritual heritage, which had originated in great stages, c. 7500–2500 B.C., in the earliest agricultural and city-state communities of the nuclear Near East and represents finally the fundamental spiritual heritage of all higher civilization whatsoever.[2] Its diffusion from the matrix—the mythogenetic zone, as I have termed it—where it first took form as a profoundly inspired intuition of an all-governing cosmic order, carried its heavily charged imagery to every quarter of the cultivated earth. Hence the Celtic myths of the Great Goddess and her consort dwelling in the fairy hills, Land under Waves, Land of Youth, or Isle of Women (Arthurian Avalon), participate in a world tradition, of which they represent the remotest northwestward extension.

Moreover, the later, Iron Age features of the popular Celtic legends of the chariot-warriors of King Conchobar and giant-men of Finn Mac Cumhaill likewise are of the widest distribution. Stemming from a second mythogenetic zone, the broad grasslands of Eastern Europe and Southwest Asia, the matrix of the Aryan races, they belong to the brilliant hunting-herding-fighting complex of male-oriented patriarchal legendry that was carried by tough, war-loving, widely ranging nomads—masters of the horse and inventors of the war chariot—westward as far as to Ireland, eastward even to China, and southward to Italy, Greece, Anatolia, India, and Egypt; so that the chariots, battle hymns, and battle-ready gods of the Vedas, Homer, and the Irish epics are akin, as variant developments of this single Aryan, Indo-Celtic, Indo-Germanic, or, as it is now commonly called, Indo-European complex.

Furthermore, the interactions of the conquering gods and heroes of this later, patriarchal mythology, on one hand, and the local, earth-bound, earth-fructifying goddesses and their consorts—guardians of the order of mother-right—on the other, exhibit analogous features wherever the two contrary systems came together, clashed, and finally, perforce, amalgamated. In some areas —India and Ireland, for example—the point of view and mythic order of the earlier Bronze Age civilization held its own, absorbed the other, and finally became dominant in the combination, whereas in others—most notably in Continental Europe, the classic land of the paleolithic hunt, to which the art of the great caves of Altamira, Lascaux, Trois Frères, Tuc d'Audoubert, and the rest, bears a testimony of some thirty thousand years—the moral and spiritual order represented by the Aryan battle-gods prevailed. Nevertheless, in the main, like features are evident everywhere, here stressing one, there the other side of the interaction. And as we have seen, it was out of one such arena of mythogenic superfetation—the well-named "fertile crescent," again, of the nuclear Near East—that the late classical, Hellenistic, and Roman mystery cults developed, of which the Christian sect was a popular, nonesoteric, politically manageable, state-supported variant, wherein symbols that in others were read in a mystic, anagogical way, proper to symbols, were reduced to a literal sense and referred to supposed or actual historical events. Together, official Christianity and a number of the mystic traditions (Orphic and Mithraic, Gnostic, Manichaean, and so forth) were carried by Roman arms and colonization to northern Europe, and there, following the victories of Constantine (324 A.D.) and promulgation of the Theodosian Code (438 A.D.)—which banned in the Roman Empire all beliefs and cults save the Christian—the mysteries, like a secret stream, went underground, while the same symbols that were there being employed in rites of initiation as anagogic metaphors were enforced officially, above ground, as reports of hard historic fact.

In that bold and learned study of the legend of the Grail to which T. S. Eliot refers in his footnotes to *The Waste Land,* Miss

Jessie L. Weston's *From Ritual to Romance* (published 1920), it is suggested that the rites of a mystery cult of this subterranean kind may lie at the root of the Grail tradition: some such esoteric sect as we have seen indicated in the sacramental bowls of Figures 3 and 4, 11 and 12.

> *C'est del Graal dont nus ne doit*
> *Le secret dire ne conter. . . .*

So states the so-called "Elucidation" attached by some unknown redactor to Chrétien de Troyes' unfinished *Perceval:* [3] "The tale is of the Grail, of which none may speak or recount the secret." But as Miss Weston reminds us, the rites of the Christian Church were never secret; nor are the fertility rites of the primitive nature cults. Taken together with the general atmosphere of wonder, mystery, quest, and initiation that pervades the Grail tradition, these two lines would therefore seem to indicate a relationship of some kind between the enigmatic symbols displayed in the Castle of the Grail and the rites of the late classical mystery sects. In these latter, we have seen, the earlier field-cult symbols of vegetal fertility were turned to the ends of inward spiritual fructification, wakening, and rebirth. Furthermore, as we have also seen, the native Celto-Germanic gods of northern Europe were identified in Roman times with their Greco-Roman counterparts, and so made available for service in local extensions of the classical mystery tradition. The Irish sea-god Manannan Mac Lir was the northern, Celtic analogue of Neptune (Greek Poseidon), who in turn—as disclosed at the culminating moment of the brothel scene of *Ulysses* *—was the Occidental counterpart of Shiva. In the Hellenistic age of Alexander's "Marriage of East and West," such Occidental-Oriental equivalencies were already recognized both in mythological and in philosophical contexts; so that with the later Roman carriage of the mysteries and philosophies of the Hellenized Near East to France and Britain, the secrets of the Orient came too. And a knowledge of their psychologically effective mysteries, in alchemy, the Grail tradition, Rosicrucianism, Masonry, and so on, has come down, even to the present hour.

Figure 45 is from an illuminated manuscript (c. 1300 A.D.) of a late prose version of the Grail romance known as the *Estoire del*

* Supra, pp. 261–62.

Figure 45. Bishop Josephe Confers the Grail on King Alain

Saint Graal (date c. 1215–1230), in which the Grail hero is no longer Perceval but the perfectly chaste Galahad, and the holy vessel itself is identified with that from which Christ, at the Last Supper, served the Apostles. This Grail, or dish, was supposed to have been brought to Britain most marvelously, together with the lance that pierced Christ's side, by the chaste son, Josephes, of that good man Joseph of Arimathea, in whose rock-cut tomb the Savior had been buried.[4] The illustration is of the scene, late in the romance, where Josephe confers the Grail upon the king who is to succeed him as its keeper,* and who will be known as THE RICH FISHER when he will have miraculously served a large company with a

_____
* Infra, p. 536.

single fish he is now to catch. Note the form of the vessel. A comparison with the bowls of Figures 3 and 4, 11 and 12, and then 24, which last is of the same date as this illumination, will of itself tell a story of the Grail—in silence—better than words.

Let us again regard, therefore, in Figure 3, at the opening of the round of initiation, the mystagogue Orpheus, the Fisherman, with his pole, his net, and caught fish. Miss Weston had already recognized a relationship of the figure of the Fisher King not only to the Christian "fisher of men" theme but also to the earlier pagan mystery-cult symbologies of the fish, the Friday fish meal, and the fisher god; [5] and Professor William A. Nitze of the University of California has carried her suggestion a step further by pointing to a sea-god of Celtic Britain whose name, Nodens, actually means "Fisher." In the Irish epics he appears as King Nuadu of the Silver Hand, of the people of the fairy hills, who, having lost an arm in combat, replaced it with an arm of silver, and so, like the Fisher of the Grail Castle, was a maimed king. [6]

Now silver is the metal of the moon, as gold, of the sun; and the reader has surely thought by now of the symbolic association, already frequently alluded to in these volumes, of the sea-god and the moon, that celestial cup of the liquor of immortality, which is ever emptied and refilled. When personified as the tide-controller himself, the moon is lame, lopsided; and accordingly, as noticed in Oriental Mythology, both the Chinese flood hero Yü and the biblical Noah became lame, according to folk legend, in the course of their water labors: the latter when struck by the paw of the lion (the sun beast) in his ark, and the former from a sickness that made him shrivel in half his body, like the moon. [7] This celestial orb, like the soul and destiny of man, is both light and dark, of both the spirit and the flesh, bound to the orbit of this earth and, like the serpent of Figures 11, 13, and 23, ever circling from the light of the empyrean to the dark of the abyss.

But as a cup the moon is the inexhaustible vessel of immortal food and drink of the lord of the tides of life—and such an inexhaustible vessel is also the Grail. Moreover, the moon may be viewed as a head ("the Man in the Moon"), and in the Welsh version of the Grail romance, Peredur, what the hero is shown at the Castle of the Grail is neither a cup nor a bowl but a man's head, carried on a large salver by two maidens. [8] And finally, as Miss

Weston remarks [9] and every Wagner devotee knows, there are in the Grail Castle not one but two disabled kings: the Maimed or Fisher King, in the foreground, suffering terribly from his wound, and another king, in extreme old age, in a room unseen, into which the Grail is carried and from which it again returns. These two, in lunar imagery, would correspond to the dark, the old moon, into which the light goes and from which in three days it returns, and the young or visible moon, which is successively young, full, and declining. In Wolfram's words:

> The king can neither ride nor walk, neither lie nor stand: he leans but cannot sit, and sighs, remembering why.* At the time of the change of the moon his pain is great. There is a lake by the name Brumbane: they bring him there for the fresh air for his painful open wound and he calls that his hunting day. But what he can catch there with his wound so painful would never provision his home. It is from this the legend came that he was a fisher. [10]

Figure 46 is a ritual bowl of silver, the metal of the moon. It was found at Gundestrupp, Jutland, in a bog. On the outside are a number of deities unidentified, and within, a series of strange scenes. Figure 47, one of these, shows the Celtic underworld god Cernunnos, whom the Romans identified with Pluto-Hades. Figures 18 and 21 have already been discussed in relation to this complex. Cernunnos, Manannan Mac Lir, Poseidon, Hades, Dumuzi-Tammuz, and Satan are alternate names of this same lord of the abyss, who is also the god in Figure 3 at Station 10.† In *Oriental Mythology*, Figure 20, page 307, is a horned image of this Celtic god, seated cross-legged on a low dais and holding on his left arm a cornucopia-like bag, from which grain pours as from an inexhaustible source. Before him stand a bull and stag, feeding on the downpouring grain (as here, a bull and stag at the god's right), while at either hand stands a classical divinity: Apollo at his right, Hermes-Mercury at his left, the lords respectively of the light world and the road to the abyss; while above is the emblem of a large rat, which in India is the animal of Ganesha, the

---

* Compare T. S. Eliot's line in *The Waste Land:* "Here one can neither lie nor stand nor sit" (supra, p. 6).

† Supra, pp. 10 and 17–21.

Figure 46. The Gundestrupp Bowl; Jutland

god of thresholds: and in my discussion of this altarpiece I have remarked its resemblance to the numerous images in India and the Far East of a seated Buddha between two standing Bodhisattvas; also, greatly earlier, from the Indus Valley period, c. 2500–1500 B.C., certain figures on stamp seals in seated yogic postures, among which there is one seated on a low dais flanked by worshiping serpent princes (*Oriental Mythology,* Figure 29, page 170), and another, again on a low dais, wearing a large headpiece of buffalo horns with a high crown between (*Oriental Mythology,* Figure 18, page 169), suggesting a trefoil or trident, the symbol of Shiva, Poseidon, Satan. Two gazelles stand before this dais in the place exactly of the beasts before Cernunnos; also, of the two deer that frequently appear in Buddhist art before the seat of the Buddha preaching his first sermon ("The First Turning of the Wheel of the Law") in the Deer Park of Benares. Around

Figure 47. The God Cernunnos; Gundestrupp Bowl detail

the Indus figure, furthermore, stand four assorted beasts, which again suggest Shiva in his character as "Lord of Beasts" (*paśu-pati*). Compare the Orpheus-Christ of Figure 1.

It is next to certain that all these figures are related, not only in form, but also in sense, deriving ultimately from a common background in the old Bronze Age culture matrix. The reader has perhaps already recalled in this connection our discussion in *Oriental Mythology* of Shiva and his Shakti in "The Isle of Gems" (*Oriental Mythology*, Figure 21, pages 334–35.), where the male divinity appears in two aspects simultaneously: one turned away from his goddess spouse in the aspect known as Shava, "The Corpse," *deus absconditus*, the inconceivable, unmanifest, transcendent aspect of the ground of being; and the other in connubium with her as Shiva-Shakti, the lord and lady of life. I there compared this dual view of the one mystery to the two aspects of Egyptian Pharaonic power symbolized as early as c. 2850 B.C. in (*a*) the dead Pharaoh in his tomb, identified with Osiris in the underworld, lord of the dead, and (*b*) the reigning Pharaoh on his throne, as Horus, son of the dead Osiris, lord of the living. Comparably, in Mahayana Buddhism the mystery of enlightenment is personified in two contrasting forms: (*a*) the Buddha, the departed one, represented as a monk, dead to the world, and (*b*) the Bodhisattva, a noble, princely being wearing a richly jeweled tiara, symbolic of the world-regarding, compassionate aspect of illuminated consciousness.[11]

When he teaches, the Bodhisattva assumes the form of his auditors. He is free of passion, free also of thought. He is benevolence without purpose; he is merit, put to the service of all beings. When shown with many arms, many hands, many heads, gazing and serving in all directions, he carries in his hands skulls filled with flowers (compare in Figure 1 the plants growing from the rams' heads), also tridents encircled with serpents (compare the symbols of Hermes and Poseidon). From his fingers flow rivers of ambrosia, which cool the hells and feed the hungry ghosts. In the palm of each hand is an eye—regarding the world and with sympathy participant in its pain: each eye a wound, pierced with sorrow, as the wounds in the palms of Christ the Savior on the Cross. He is called the "god of the present," "he who bears the world," and as such bears and absorbs in his infinite person the sorrows of the world.[12]

There is an astonishing fable in the Hindu *Panchatantra,* where an awesome reflection of the pain-bearing aspect of the Bodhisattva principle appears in a strange adventure that throws light on the meaning and background of the Maimed King of the Grail. It is of four friends, Brahmins, stricken with poverty, who determined to try to get rich. They set forth together and in the Avanti country met a magician named Terror-Joy, whom they asked for assistance. He gave to each a magic quill, with instructions to go north, to the northern slope of the Himalayas [i.e., to Buddhist Tibet]; and wherever a quill dropped, the owner would find treasure. The leader's quill dropped first, and they found the soil to be all copper. So he said, "Look here! Take all you want!" But the others decided to go on. The first took his copper and turned back. Next the second leader's quill dropped; he dug, found silver, and was the second to return. The next quill yielded gold. "Don't you see the point?" said the fourth. "First copper, then silver, then gold. Beyond, there will surely be gems." And he went on.

And so this other went on alone. His limbs were scorched by the rays of the summer sun and his thoughts were confused by thirst as he wandered to and fro over the trails in the land of the fairies. At last, on a whirling platform, he saw a man with blood dripping down his body; for a wheel was whirling on his head. Then he made haste and said: *"Sir, why do you stand thus with a wheel whirling on your head?* In any case, tell me if there is water anywhere. I am mad with thirst."

The moment the Brahmin said this, the wheel left the other's head and settled on his own. "My very dear sir," said he, "what is the meaning of this?" "In the very same way," replied the other, "it settled on my head." "But," said the Brahmin, "when will it go away? It hurts terribly."

And the fellow said: "When someone who holds in his hand a magic quill, such as you had, arrives and speaks as you did, then it will settle on his head." "Well," said the Brahmin, "how long have you been here?" The other asked: "Who is king in the world at present?" And on hearing the answer, "King Vina-batsa," he said: "When Rama was king, I was poverty-stricken, procured a magic quill, and came here, just like you. And I saw another man with a wheel on his head and put a question to him. The moment I asked a question (just like you) the wheel left his head and settled on mine. But I cannot reckon the centuries."

Then the wheel-bearer asked: "My dear sir, how, pray, did you get food while standing thus?" "My dear sir," said the fellow, "the god of wealth [Kubera = Hades–Pluto], fearful lest his treasures be stolen, prepared this terror, so that no magician might come so far. And if any should succeed in coming, he was to be freed from hunger and thirst, preserved from decrepitude and death, and was merely to endure this torture. So now permit me to say farewell. You have set me free from a sizable misery. Now I am going home." And he went.[13]

The fable, as here retold in this frankly worldly work, devoted not to sainthood but to the art of getting on, is presented as a warning to all of the danger of excessive greed; however, as Theodor Benfey was the first to show (already in 1859), this was originally a Mahayana Buddhist legend treating of the path to Bodhisattvahood.[14] The key to its hidden religious import—which is just the opposite to that of the secular fable—is betrayed in the name of the magician, Terror-Joy (*Bhairavānanda*), "the exhilaration or bliss (*ānanda*) of what is awesome or terrible (*bhairava*)"—which is an oxymoron fiercer than Gottfried's "bittersweet," yet of the same sense.

"Terror," Bhairava, is the cult-name of Shiva in his most terrific aspect, as the terrible destroyer of illusion, consort of the bloodcurdling, blood-consuming black goddess Kali. Divinities of this furious kind, representing the dark, brutal, implacable aspects of nature and of human nature, befit people who are themselves dark, brutal, and passionate of heart. They are, in fact, the only gods that people of such temperament can truly recognize, credit, and respect. Hence—since the Bodhisattva, as we have said, assumes the form of his auditors when he teaches—the harsh, brutal traits of these fierce Hindu divinities and their equally terrible rites were taken over by the later Mahayana as means for the conversion of passionate men through the medium of their own passions into sages of a truly terrible wisdom: knowers through an experience (by reflection of the force of their own life zeal) of the monstrous thing that is life, which lives, in each of its beings, on the death and pain of all the rest.

The magician of this paradoxical fable gave instruction to those who came to him in such a way that each should receive a reward appropriate to his nature. Hence, it was only the one whose greed was truly boundless who achieved the boon of *bhairavānanda*: that experience beyond the bounds of knowledge, purpose, and value, which is learned with a terrible joy "at the still point of this turning world"—in the way of William Blake's Proverb of Hell: "The road of excess leads to the palace of wisdom," [15] or in the way of Christ crucified; Atlas bearing the world on his back; Loki tortured by the venom of a serpent continually dropping on his head; or Prometheus pinned to a crag of Caucasus. One may think also of Job.

The wheel in Buddhist iconography is known as the "Wheel of the Law" (*dharma-cakra*). It is symbolic of the reign of the World Monarch, the so-called "Turner of the Wheel" (*cakra-vartin*), but also of the teaching of the Buddha, the World Savior, who in his first sermon, in the Deer Park of Benares, set the Wheel of the Law in motion. The World Monarch is to reign in the spirit of that law. And the wheel is to be known as of two sides: in its commonly manifest aspect, as the wheel of sorrows of this everlasting round of births and rebirths, disease, old age, and death (all life is sorrowful); but also in the deeper, darker, yet more luminous revelation of the Mahayana doctrine of the "Great Delight" *(Mahāsukha)*: the realization of this world, just as it is, as the Golden Lotus World; of *saṁsāra,* the painful wheel of rebirth, and *nirvāṇa,* the still state at the center of the wheel, as the same—for those with the courage and strength of will to endure the terrible cutting edge.*

And should the reader wish to know how such an experience of the cutting edge can be endured in this world, let him turn to the ambrosial book, *Man's Search for Meaning,* of Dr. Viktor E. Frankl (now of the University of Vienna), who, for endless days in the Nazi prison camps, bore on his head the whole weight of that wheel.[16]

II. The Maimed Fisher King

In the mythologies of the Celts, behind the Grail romance and figure of the Fisher King, the idea of a revolving wheel, platform, or castle is an essential feature. Figure 48 is of a Gallo-Roman statue found at Châtelet, Haute-Marne. It shows a bearded Celtic god with a wheel; and like the Buddhist "wheel of being," this also has six spokes.† The god has slung over his right shoulder his supply of thunderbolts and elevates in his right hand the cornucopia of ambrosia that he holds for his devotees. Figure 49 shows another of these early Gallic divinities, Sucellos, who as here depicted is a manifestation of the power of his own world-creating, world-annihilating hammer (Sanskrit *vajra,* "diamond bolt," the highest

---

* Compare in *Occidental Mythology,* p. 262, Figure 24, the Mithraic-Zoroastrian figure and mystery of Zervan Akarana, "Boundless Time."

† The six areas between the spokes of the Buddhist wheel represent the six realms of the "round of being" (*bhavacakra*). Commencing at the top and revolving clockwise, these are: of 1. the gods, 2. the titans, 3. ghosts, 4. hell-beings, 5. animals, 6. men. The felly is bound by the linked chain of the twelve causes of rebirth: ignorance, action, consciousness, name-and-form, the sense organs, contact, sensation, desire, intercourse, birth, life, and finally disease, old age, and death. Within the hub motion is communicated by three ever-circling beasts: a cock or dove, a serpent, and a pig, which represent desire, anger, and stupidity. (Compare, in Figure 13, the wolf, lion, and dog, and in Dante's "dark wood," the she-wolf, lion, and leopard.) For a discussion of the Buddhist wheel of being, see Marco Pallis, *Peaks and Lamas* (New York: Alfred A. Knopf, 1949), pp. 125–57.

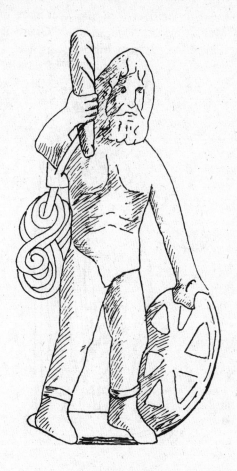

Figure 48. The God of the Wheel; France, Gallo-Roman Period

Hindu-Buddhist symbol of illumination, by which the world-illusion is destroyed and which itself is indestructible). The five hammers fixed to this large bolt suggest the energies of the five elements of which (in the Indian view) the world and its creatures are composed: ether, air, fire, water, and earth. The circles on the hammer suggest both the Buddhist Wheel of the Law and the symbolic cosmic circles on the Orphic serpent bowl (Figure 12). And in the right hand of this god—whom the Romans identified with Pluto—there is again the ambrosial cup.

Figure 49. The God Sucellos; France, Gallo-Roman Period

Now the Irish sea-god Manannan had a vessel of this kind, of
inexhaustible ambrosia; so also his Welsh counterpart, Bran the
Blessed, son of Llyr, known also as Manawyddan, whose dwelling
in the Land under Waves was called *Annwfn,* "the abyss," but also
Caer Sidi, "the revolving castle." [17] And all around that whirling
castle, difficult to enter, flow the ocean streams. At its festive
board the meat is served of immortal swine killed every day, which
come alive the next, and this delicious fare, washed down with an
immortal ale, gives immortality to all guests. Moreover there is in

that land an abundant well, sweeter than white wine: hazel trees of knowledge drop crimson nuts into its waters, which are eaten by the salmon there; and the flesh of those fish gives omniscience. Now that Elysium with its castle and hospitable host is coextensive with the world, only hidden in mist; hence may appear anywhere to voyagers and as strangely disappear—like the Castle of the Grail. But there have also been places where it has been found to be more present; as on the summit of Slieve Mish, County Kerry, where there would appear, from time to time, the whirling castle of a shape-shifter named Curoi, who possessed an ambrosial caldron, stolen from a king of the fairy hills along with the latter's daughter and three cows—all of which treasures he lost in turn, however, to the greatest trickster of all, Cuchullin.*

It is a moot question as to whether the obvious relationship of the Panchatantra fable, in motifs and general sense, to the Grail Castle adventure is to be attributed mainly to remote, very early connections—say in Gallo-Roman times—or, more closely, to the period of the crusades; for as Theodor Benfey's study of the *Panchatantra* showed, over a century ago,[18] the passage of literary matter in the Middle Ages from India to Europe was considerable. As already remarked,† an Arabic translation of the Sanskrit *Panchatantra*, made in the eighth century, was carried into Syriac in the tenth, Greek in the eleventh, old Spanish, Hebrew, and Latin in the middle and late thirteenth. Benfey himself remarked, furthermore, that an independent version of the fable of the four treasure-seekers itself appears in the Grimm collection (Tale Number 54),[19] and that variants have been discovered since in every language and even dialect of Europe.[20] However, the all-important Wheel and Question motifs were dropped from these European versions, where the fourth seeker, after long wandering, comes only to a tall tree (the *axis mundi*) under which he rests, and when he wishes for a meal, a table appears set with a feast—after which the tale goes on with episodes from a totally different source.

The image of a spoked wheel symbolic of the turning world is attested for India already c. 700 B.C. in the Chandogya and Brihadaranyaka Upanishads: "Even as the spokes of a wheel are held fast in the hub, so is all this on *prana*, the life-breath." [21] "As

* For Cuchullin, see *Occidental Mythology*, pp. 303–307; 470–71; 508.
† Supra, pp. 134–35.

spokes are held fast by the hub and felly of a wheel, so are all beings, all gods, all worlds, all breathing things, all of these selves, held fast in *ātman,* the Self." [22] And in the later Prashna Upanishad, where the immanent ground is personified as that mythic "Person" (*puruṣa*) of whose dismembered body the universe is made,* we read: "He in whom all these parts are well fixed, like spokes in the hub of a wheel: him, recognize as the Person to be known—that death may not afflict you." [23]

Clearly the authors of these passages were familiar with the spoked wheel of the Aryan war chariot, which first appeared in the world in the early second millennium B.C. The figure dates, therefore, from the Vedic age, and cannot have appeared before that, or among people to whom the chariot was unknown. A very much earlier form, however, long antedating the invention even of the old Sumerian solid wheel (c. 3500 B.C.), was the almost universally known swastika, of which we have at least one example from the late paleolithic period, as early, perhaps, as c. 18,000 B.C.[24] In the beautifully painted ceramic wares of the high neolithic of Iran (Samarra ware, c. 4500 B.C.), this same sign is a conspicuous, even dominant, motif; and, as shown in *Primitive Mythology,* it was apparently from there that it was diffused to well nigh every corner of the earth.[25]

From what we know of the temper of early cultures, it is safe to assume that the myths, rites, and philosophies first associated with these symbols were rather positive than negative in their address to the pains and pleasures of existence. However, in the period of Pythagoras in Greece (c. 582–500? B.C.) and the Buddha in India (563–483 B.C.), there occurred what I have called the Great Reversal.[26] Life became known as a fiery vortex of delusion, desire, violence, and death, a burning waste. "All things are on fire," taught the Buddha in his sermon at Gaya,[27] and in Greece the Orphic saying *"Soma sema:* The body is a tomb" gained currency at this time, while in both domains the doctrine of reincarnation, the binding of the soul forever to this meaningless round of pain, only added urgency to the quest for some means of release. In the Buddha's teaching, the image of the turning spoked wheel, which in the earlier period had been symbolic of the world's glory, thus became

---

* Compare, *Primitive Mythology,* pp. 170–225, *Oriental Mythology,* pp. 83–91; 211; *Occidental Mythology,* pp. 80–86.

a sign, on one hand, of the wheeling round of sorrow, and, on the other, release in the sunlike doctrine of illumination. And in the classical world the turning spoked wheel appeared also at this time as an emblem rather of life's defeat and pain than of victory and exhilaration in the image and myth of Ixion (Figure 50), bound by Zeus to a blazing wheel of eight spokes, to be sent whirling for all time through the air.

As the king of a late Bronze Age people of Thessaly, the Lapi-

Figure 50. Ixion; Etruscan bronze mirror, 4th century B.C.

thai, Ixion had been a god-king, symbolic thus of that cosmic Person who in the Prashna quotation is celebrated as that one in whom all parts of the world are made fast, like spokes in the hub of a wheel; and he is here being punished by Zeus for two crimes, the first, of violence (the murder of his father-in-law), and the second, of lust (an attempt to ravish the goddess Hera): i.e., the same two compulsions of desire and aggression recognized in Hindu and Buddhist thought (as well as in modern depth psychology) as the creative powers of the world illusion—which hold the world together and were overcome by the Buddha in his victory over the great lord of life named Lust and Death (*kāma-māra*), beneath the Bodhi-tree, at the hub of the wheel of the world (the *axis mundi*).[28]

The legend of Ixion is cited by Pindar (522–448? B.C.) in a victory ode to the winner of a chariot race.[29] Five centuries later Virgil (70–19 B.C.) refers to it in the *Aeneid*,[30] by which time, however, the scene of the suffering has been transferred from the air to the underworld, where it is placed also by Ovid (43 B.C.–17 A.D.) in the *Metamorphoses*.[31] And down there, together with Ixion, are a number of other tortured characters, all symbolic, one way or another, of the agony of life: Tityos, with his vitals being torn forever by a vulture; Tantalus, tortured with thirst, teased by a water he cannot reach; and Sisyphus, shoving his huge boulder up a hill, down which it is again to roll—each to be tortured thus forever.

In the classic, popular view of these pains, they are punishments for crimes; however, as the existentialist Albert Camus, in his "Essay on the Absurd," *The Myth of Sisyphus*, remarks: such figures are figures of life. The unilluminated common man lives normally in hope: the belief that his labor will lead to something, or at least the knowledge that in death his pains will end. Sisyphus knows, however, that the labor of getting his great rock up the hill is to end with its rolling down again; and, since he is immortal, the absurdity of this unexhilarating grim labor will last—forever.

> Sisyphus [writes Camus] watches while the stone, in a few minutes, rolls down to that lower field again, from which he is going to have to push it up, once more, to the top. And he goes down again to the plain.
>
> It is during his return, that pause, that Sisyphus interests me.

A face that toils so close to stone is itself already stone. I see that man going down again with heavy but steady tread, to the torment of which he will know no end. This hour, which is like a breath of relief and returns as surely as his woe, is the hour of consciousness. At each of these moments, when he leaves the heights and makes his way, step by step, toward the retreats of the gods, he is superior to his destiny, stronger than his rock.

If this myth, then, is tragic, it is because its hero is conscious. For where, in fact, would the agony be, if at each step he were sustained by hope of success? The laboring man of today works every day of his life at the same tasks, and that destiny is no less absurd. However, it is not tragic, save in those uncommon moments when it becomes conscious. Sisyphus, impotent and rebellious, the proletarian of the gods, knows the whole extent of his miserable condition. It is of this that he thinks at the time of his descent. And yet, this foreknowledge, which was to have been his torment, simultaneously crowns his victory: there is no destiny that is not overcome by disdain.

If on certain days the descent is made in sorrow, it can also be made in joy. The term is not too strong. I again imagine Sisyphus returning to his rock. The sorrow was only at the beginning. For it is when the scenes of earthly life weigh in the memory too strongly, when the call of happiness becomes too urgent, that sorrow surges to the human heart: that is the victory of the rock, that is the rock itself. The weight of sorrow is too heavy to be borne. Those are the nights of our Gethsemane. However, the crushing verities, when recognized, dissolve. It was thus that Oedipus obeyed his destiny, at first without knowing. And from the moment that he knew it, his tragedy commenced. Yet, at the same instant, blind and despairing, he realized that the only bond that held him to the world was the cool fresh hand of a young girl. And it was then that a remark resounded, immeasurably great: "In spite of all these trials, my advanced age and the grandeur of my soul lead me to conclude that all is well." [32]

"In a man's attachment to his life," this author concludes, "there is something stronger than all the miseries of the world." [33]

The sentiment is noble. There is, however, something wonderfully French—Cartesian, Socratic—in the declaration that, since life (or, as we are saying today, "existence") will not conform to reason, it can properly be termed absurd. "I think, therefore I am," has had to become, "I am, but I can't think why!" which can be embarrassing to one who thinks of himself professionally as a thinker. The Bodhisattva, on the other hand, is "without thought." The Buddha is called "the one who is thus come" (*tathāgata*). And as Dr. Frankl states to this point in his ambrosial book: "What is demanded of man is not, as some existential philosophies teach, to endure the meaninglessness of life; but rather to bear his incapacity to grasp its unconditional meaningfulness in rational terms. *Logos* is deeper than logic." [34]

The question as to meaning, to be asked by the young hero of the Grail quest when he beholds the rites of the Grail Castle, is the same, essentially, as that asked by the hero of the *Panchatantra* fable, and its effect also is the same: the release of the sufferer from his pain and the transfer of his role to the questioner. Moreover, these two questions are at root the same as Hamlet's "To be, or not to be," since their concern is to learn the *meaning* of a circumstance "thus come"—to which there is no answer. There is, however, an *experience* possible, for which the hero's arrival at the world axis and his readiness to learn (as demonstrated by his question) have proven him to be eligible. Will he be able to support it? Nietzsche, in *The Birth of Tragedy,* wrote of what he termed the "Hamlet condition" of the one whose realization of the primal precondition of life ("All life is sorrowful!") has undercut his will to live. The problem of the Grail hero will therefore be: to ask the question relieving the Maimed King in such a way as to inherit his role *without* the wound.

The Maimed King's wound and the agony of the revolving wheel are equivalent symbols of the knowledge of the anguish of existence as a function not merely of this or that contingency, but of being. The common man, in pain, believes that by altering his circumstances he might achieve a state free of pain: his world, in Gottfried's phrase, being of those who want only "to bathe in bliss." Socratic man too believes that life can be trimmed somehow to reason—his own Procrustean bed for it. Hamlet learned, however, that *his* world, at least, had something at the heart of it that was rotten and, like Oedipus, who read the riddle of the Sphinx ("What is man?"), became maimed. Oedipus, self-blinded, is equivalent to the Maimed King—and, as Freud has shown, all of us are Oedipus. For this there is no cure. However, as Camus points out, Oedipus, like Sisyphus, came through his experiences of his maimed life to the realization that all is well.

The wound in Christ's side, delivered by Longinus's spear, is a counterpart of that of the Maimed Fisher; also, the poisoned wound of Tristan. The crown of thorns is a counterpart of the Bodhisattva's turning wheel, and the Cross, of the wheel of Ixion (Figures 9 and 50). Christ's role as the Man of Sorrows, blood flowing from the nail wounds in his palms and feet, head dropped to one side, eyes closed, and blood streaming from that painful crown, corresponds to the Grail King in torture. In his other mode, however, as Christ the Logos, Triumphant (as True God), crucified yet without anguish, head erect, eyes open, outward gazing at the world of light, the nails there, but no sign of blood, he is the image of that immanent "radiance" (*claritas*), "thus come," which hangs everywhere, as the world's joy-to-be-known, behind its battered face of torment. In his being, as in the Bodhisattva, there is ambrosia. He too descended into Hell: and though the credo of his church returned him to the sky, in his Bodhisattvahood he is still there—as Satan.

"Look forward!" Virgil said to his follower, Dante, when, having descended through all the murk of Hell, the two were approaching on a plain the center of the earth—the center of the universe—the immovable spot! "See if thou discern him."

Dante peared ahead. And so we read:

As when a thick fog breathes, or when our hemisphere darkens to night, a mill that the wind is turning might look from afar, such a structure, it seemed to me that I then saw. Because of the wind proceeding from it, I drew me behind my Leader; there was no other shelter. For I was now (and with fear I put it into verse) there where the shades were wholly covered with ice and showed through like a straw in glass. Some are lying down; some are upright, this one with his head, and that with his soles uppermost; another, like a bow, bends his face to his feet. And when we had gone so far forward that it pleased my Master to show me the creature that once had had the fair semblance [i.e. Lucifer, now Satan], he took himself from before me and made me stop, saying: "Lo Dis! and lo the place where it is needful that thou arm thyself with fortitude!"

How frozen and faint I then became, ask it not, Reader, for I do not write it, because all speech would be little. I did not die and did not remain alive: think now for thyself, if thou hast a grain of wit, what I became, deprived alike of death and of life.

The emperor of the woeful realm stood forth from the ice from the middle of his breast; and I were better compared to a giant, than a giant to his arms. Imagine how great now must be the whole, proportionate to such a part. And if when he lifted his brows against his Maker he was as fair as he now is foul, well indeed should all tribulation proceed from him.

Oh, how great a marvel it seemed to me, when I saw three faces on his head! one in front, and that was crimson; the others were two, adjoined to this above the middle of each shoulder, and they were joined up to the place of the crest: and the right seemed between white and yellow, the left such as those who come from where the Nile descends. Beneath each came forth two great wings, of size befitting so great a bird; I never saw such sails on the sea. They had no feathers, but their fashion was of a bat; and he was flapping them so that three winds were proceeding from him, whereby the river of that part of Hell was all congealed. With six eyes he was weeping, and over three chins were trickling the tears and bloody drivel. At each mouth he was crushing a sinner with his teeth, in the manner of a hackle, so that he thus was making three of them woeful. To the one in front the biting was nothing to the clawing, whereby sometimes his back remained all stripped of the skin.

"That soul up there which has the greatest punishment," said the Master, "is Judas Iscariot, who has his head within, and plies his legs outside. Of the other two who have their heads downward, he who hangs from the black muzzle is Brutus; see how he writhes and says not a word; and the other is Cassius, who seems so large-limbed. But the night is rising again; and now we must depart, for we have seen the whole." [35]

And then, grotesquely, when the wings opened, the two moved in and caught hold of the shaggy flanks of the awesome, prodigious, suffering monster, and down through the ice in which he was fixed, between the matted hair and frozen crusts, crawling from shag to shag, down his side they descended, Virgil ahead, Dante after. And when they had come to where the haunch becomes thigh, the Leader, Virgil, with great effort and stress of breath, grappled hard and now was climbing; for he had just passed the center of the earth and was going up.

The meanings of the colors of the faces of the Angel of Eternal Sorrow they had seen were as follows: *impotence,* the red, scarlet with rage; *hate,* the white and yellow, pale with jealousy and envy; *ignorance,* the black, in its own darkness—exactly in negative to the attributes of the Trinity: Power, the Father; Love, the Son; and Wisdom, the Holy Ghost. So that God and Satan are here a pair of opposites—and we know, by now, what *that* means. Hell and Heaven too, Satan, Trinity, and all, are as meaningless —thus come—as being itself. The affirmation of one is the affirmation of all. They are separate in the field of space-time as appearances, or as concepts, whereas in truth—the Wisdom of the Yonder Shore, the *logos* deeper than logic, beyond opposites—they are the left and right of one being that is no being and neither is nor is not: as indeed Dante, when viewing that vision of the shadow of God, had himself been neither dead nor alive.

The Buddha at the world tree, the "immovable spot" around which all revolves, transcended sorrow in illumination: "There is release from sorrow—nirvana," he taught, and in the end he vanished from this world. The Bodhisattva, on the other hand—he whose "being" (*sattva*) is "illumination" (*bodhi*)—remains addressed to this vale of tears, testifying to *the non-duality of nirvana and the sorrows of this world:* the bitter-sweetness of the life that, in Gottfried's words, is bread to all noble hearts in its terrible joy. There is no escape to which the Bodhisattva on the revolving platform refers us, but only a source within ourselves of the competence to be and not to be, to move with the world and to be absolutely still within—at once.

Comparing the four orders of imagery, then, of Christ crucified, the suffering yet not suffering Bodhisattva, the sinner Ixion, lashed to his whirling flaming wheel, and the wounded Grail King of the Waste Land, it appears that though at root related—in a certain sense even the same—yet in import they differ, as representing four interpretations or modes of experience and judgment of the same reality.

The two Asian figures, the Bodhisattva and Christ, are of immaculate virtue and supernatural race, whereas the Europeans are both sinners who in their symbolic suffering achieved no such stature as either of the Asian saviors. Of the two Asians, the Bodhisattva is entirely of this world. There is no Heaven to which he refers us, no place or god "out there," whence or from whom he has come down. He is a reflex of the consciousness of being—of which not men alone, but beasts, trees, and even minerals are the organs, modifications, and degrees. And in reminding us of that in ourselves, he is our savior from the illusion of this, our ephemeral yet everlasting suffering.

Christ Jesus, on the other hand, has been traditionally interpreted altogether differently: in the way, for example, of Pope Gregory, as our "Agenbuyer" from the Devil (page 18, and Figure 8); or in the way of Saint Anselm, as our compensation to the Father for Adam and Eve's happy fault (pages 18–19); or still again, according to the view put forward first by Abelard, as a demonstration of God's love for man, to recall our hearts to himself from the false allures of this Devil's world (pages 19–20).[36] Only add to this last the Indian words *tat tvam asi,* "thou art that"—thou thyself, unknown to thyself, art that beloved lover (in the sense of the words of the Sufi mystic Bayazid: "Then I looked and I saw that lover, beloved, and love are one!")[37]—and behold! the two savior figures, along with even the Allah of Islam, and the Devil as well, have become one. "For in the world of unity," said Bayazid, "all can be one.—Glory to me!"[38]

In contrast, both of the European figures have been somehow made aware of themselves as sinners and are in need, consequently, of redemption. But what is their redemption to be? Well, since they were both originally redeemer figures, one might suggest that all they require is to be reminded of their own occluded divinity. That would accord with the final stanza of Wagner's opera when the wonderful youth Parsifal, "through compassion's supreme power [*karuṇā*] and the force of purest knowledge [*bodhi*]," has healed the suffering king of his wound and himself assumed the sacred role: *"Erlösung dem Erlöser!* Redemption to the Redeemer!" sings the chorus, and the curtain falls.

Parsifal, become the Grail King, did not inherit the wound. We must now learn why.

III. The Quest beyond Meaning

Chrétien de Troyes, whose version of the Grail Quest is the earliest we possess, declares that he derived the subject matter of his legend, the *matière,* from a certain book given him by the Count

Philip of Flanders [39]—who, it is known, was twice in the Levant: first in 1177 and again in 1190, when he died there. "And the best tale it is," states Chrétien, "that may be told in a royal court." Wolfram von Eschenbach, on the other hand, cites a Provençal author, otherwise unknown to us, named Kyot, whose existence many scholars doubt. Chrétien's unfinished version of the romance lay on the desk before Wolfram as he wrote. However, his own version, starting as it does with the career of Parzival's father in the Orient and following the young Grail quester himself through a series of trials not described in Chrétien's work—and, moreover, from a totally different point of view, Chrétien having been, apparently, a cleric concerned to reduce the Quest to Christian terms [40] —makes it certain that if there never was any such book as that of Kyot for him to follow, Wolfram must either have had before him the same—or somewhat the same—book as Chrétien, or else have been himself wholly responsible for everything that qualifies his work for consideration as the first great spiritual biography in the history of Occidental letters.

According to Wolfram's perhaps invented reference, the Provençal author Kyot discovered the legend of the Grail in Toledo, in the forgotten work of a heathen astrologer, Flegetanis by name, "who had with his own eyes seen hidden wonders in the stars. He tells of a thing," states Wolfram, "called the Grail, whose name he had read in the constellations. 'A host of angels left it on the earth,' Flegetanis tells, 'then flew off, high above the stars.' " [41]

Now the Holy Grail, even in Chrétien's text, was neither a bowl nor a cup, not the chalice of the Last Supper, nor the cup that received Christ's blood from the Cross, but, as Professor Loomis reminds us, "a dish of considerable size." The word grail is defined by a contemporary of Chrétien, the abbot Helinand of Froidmont, as "a wide and slightly deep dish, in which costly viands are customarily placed for rich people," and one of the continuators of Chrétien's unfinished romance mentions a hundred boars' heads on grails: "an impossibility," states Loomis, "if the grails were chalices." [42]

In Wolfram's text the Grail is a stone. "Its name," he declares, "is lapis exilis," which is one of the terms applied in alchemy to the philosophers' stone: "the uncomely stone, the small or paltry stone"; [43] so that Wagner's representation of Wolfram's intentionally nonecclesiastical, indeed even non-Christian, almost Islamic, symbol as a glowing super-chalice of Christ's blood brings to his production—as Nietzsche protested—a note of Christian sanctimoniousness that is inappropriate.

"By the power of that stone," we read in Wolfram, "the phoenix burns and becomes ashes, but the ashes restore it speedily to life." The stone, that is to say, will bring us not only to the *nigredo* and *putrefactio* of the alchemical love-death (Figure 43), but also back to the world—as gold. "So the phoenix," we continue with Wolfram, "molts and thereafter very brightly shines. Moreover, there never was a man so ill that, if he saw that stone, would not live, unable to die within a week of that day. Nor in complexion would he ever change: one's appearance, whether maid or man, remains the same as on the day that stone is seen, or as at the commencement of the years of one's prime. And should one look upon that stone for two hundred years, nought but one's hair would gray. Such virtue does it communicate to man that flesh and bones grow young at once. The stone is also known as the Grail." [44] *

Figure 51 is a fanciful portrait of Wolfram in his jousting armor: for he was a poet of knightly race, more proud of his feats in arms than of his literary gifts; yet he was honored in his day, and is honored now, even above Gottfried, as the most significant poet of the German Middle Ages, and on the European scale is to be ranked second not even to Dante. In contrast to the Tristan poet, who, we have seen, was a gracefully sophisticated, classically educated city man of letters, learned in Latin, philosophy, and theology, as well as in French and German poetry and romance, Wolfram claimed (perhaps ironically, to contrast himself with Gottfried; however, possibly also with that deep disdain of the aristocrat for the cleric smell of ink) not to know a single letter of

* Dr. Hermann Goetz, in an important article on "The Orient of the Crusades in Wolfram's Parzival" (*Archiv für Kulturforschung*, Bd. II, Heft 1, 1967), which appeared too late to be noticed in my pages, suggests for the name *Flegetanis*, two sources: 1. the Kabbalah of the Spanish-Arabian Jews, with its theory of the *Falak-ath-Thani* ("Second Heaven"); and 2. the name *Aflaton* (< Plato) of a great astrologer-magician of Islamic legend (confused possibly with *Phlegethon*, the fiery stream of Pluto's Hades). In the Grail, he sees, combined with the *Lapis exilis* of alchemy, the *Lapis exulis* of the Kabbalah, the materialized *Shĕkhīnāh* ("Divine Manifestation" or "Earthly Residence" of God). Another possible influence: legends of the Buddha's begging bowl.

Figure 51. Wolfram von Eschenbach

the alphabet.[45] In Gottfried's work battle scenes are described with sardonic wit, as from a distance; in Wolfram's, on the contrary, as by one who had himself engaged in chivalrous battle and experienced its moral worth. Gottfried's settings are largely domestic, urban; Wolfram's, all afield. And his aim for life was neither rapture aloft, quit of the flesh, nor rapture below, quit of the light, but—as the symbol on his shield and flag, horse and helm makes known—the way between. His own fanciful interpretation of his hero Parzival's name, *perce à val,* "pierce through the middle," [46] gives the first clue to his ideal, which is, namely, of a realization here on earth, through human, natural means (in the sinning and virtuous, black and white, yet nobly courageous self-determined development of a no more than human life) of the mystery of the Word Made Flesh: the *logos* deeper than logic, wherein dark and light, all pairs of opposites—yet not as opposites—take part. "A life so lived," as he wrote at the conclusion of his epic, "that God is not robbed of the soul through the body's guilt; yet can retain with honor the world's favor: that is a worthy work." [47] Or as in his opening stanza:

> If vacillation be neighbor to one's heart, this can become distressful to the soul. Blame and praise alike are inevitable for the man whose courage is undaunted, mixed of white and black as it must be, like a magpie's plumage. Such a one may nevertheless know blessedness, though both colors have a part in him: that of Heaven, that of Hell. Completely black-complexioned is the one uncertain of himself, who in his hue of darkness even increases; whereas he of steady purpose trends to the light. [48]

So let us trend now, through the middle, to the Castle of the Grail and its stone of wisdom, here on earth, which is called the Perfection of Paradise.*

---

* From the article of Dr. Goetz it appears that actual Oriental names and reports of historic events in current talk of the crusades contributed to Wolfram's epic; e.g., in the opening adventure: 1. Queen Belakane of Zazamanc: Belakāna, the "wife or widow of Balak," i.e., Nūr-uddīn *Balak* ben Bahram, conqueror of Aleppo (1123) and captor of the Christian King Baldwin II of Jerusalem; his wife and widow was a Seljuk princess. 2. Isenhart ("Hard as Iron"), translation of the Turkish name Tīmūrtāsh: Hasāmūid-dn *Tīmūrtāsh,* who, when Balak was killed by an arrow, succeeded him as lord of Aleppo. He released Baldwin, but then found his city besieged by the Christian king in alliance with a Seljuk prince, Sultan Shah: two armies, "a white and a black." When he fell in battle the city was defended by its people in the name of the Caliph of Baghdad. "Wolfram's story corresponds so closely to this rather complicated historical episode that he must have been acquainted with reports from participants in the Christian army" (Goetz, op. cit., p. 13).

THE PARACLETE

I. The Son of the Widow

BOOK I: THE BLACK QUEEN OF ZAZAMANC

"Brave, and slowly wise: thus I hail my hero." So the poet introduces Parzival.

His father, Gahmuret, brave too, had been a younger son of royalty, who, though invited to share his brother's kingdom, had preferred to prove himself on his own, and so, adventuring, came to Baghdad, where he served the caliph so valiantly that his reputation extended soon from Persia to Morocco. He left, however, to sail to Zazamanc, where the people are as black as night.

The black ladies leaned from their windows to watch the company descend from his ship into their port, Patelamunt: ten pack horses before, with twenty squires behind; also pages, cooks, and cooks' helpers; twelve noble cavaliers, a number of them Saracens; eight caparisoned steeds with a ninth bearing the knight's jousting saddle and a young shield-bearer striding saucily at its side; mounted trumpeters and a drummer that swung and struck his instrument over his head, flute-players and fiddlers three; after all of which came the great knight himself with his ship's captain riding beside him.

Gahmuret was greeted with delight by the black Queen Belakane; for her city was under siege, with a black army of Moors at the west, and eastward a white, of Christian knights. Her crown was an immense transparent ruby that encased her head like a bubble; through it her dark face could be seen. Courteously she received him. They looked upon each other and their two hearts were unlocked. And when he asked the reason for the siege, with sighs and tears she confessed she had been hesitant in love. Her chivalrous lover, Isenhart, driven to desperation, a princely youth, black like herself, had sought renown by riding without armor into battles and these armies were of his friends, come to avenge his death. Her whole kingdom was in mourning.

"I will serve you, my lady," said Gahmuret.

"Sir," she replied, "you have my trust."

And he overthrew, next day, the champions of both sides.

The rescued queen led him in triumph to her castle, where she removed his armor with her own black hands and bestowed on him her kingdom and herself. More dear to him than his life was then that black and heathen wife; not more, however, than the feats of arms from which she restrained him. As king, therefore, he languished, and one night, at last, sailed away; so that in grief she bore their son (Feirefiz Angevin, she named him), in whom God had wrought a miracle: he was piebald, white and black, like a magpie's plumage.

And his mother, when she saw him, kissed him over and over and over again, on the white spots.

BOOK II: THE WHITE QUEEN OF WALES

The maiden queen Herzeloyde of Wales proclaimed at Kanvoleis a tournament: herself and two countries, the prize. And as the kings and knights, arriving, set up tents and pavilions on the meadow, she with her ladies sat watching from the windows.

"What a pavilion *that* one is!" an impudent young page exclaimed. "Your country and crown aren't half its worth."

It was of the rich king of Zazamanc: its transport had required thirty horses.

The unofficial warming-up games commenced next morning gradually when the kings and knights from many lands, galloping up and down the great field, began maneuvering in companies, colliding in single charges, splintering spears, clashing swords, and running each other down. The old father of King Arthur was out there, and Gawain, still a mere lad; Gawain's father, King Lot of Norway; also Rivalin, who had yet to sire Tristan, and the mighty Morholt of Ireland, who was yet to be Tristan's foe.

The king of Zazamanc, resting in his tent, lured by the gradually increasing tumult, rose, became arrayed, put on his headgear (which, like the ruby crown of his queen, was an immense transparent diamond, fitting over his whole head), and mounting his caparisoned charger, rode out onto the field, where he unhorsed one man of might after another. Many spears became snow on that field, saddles flew, men in iron clothing ran about among the legs of horses, shattered shields and banners lay all about. And when darkness closed it was evident to all, from the general exhaustion, there could be no tournament the next day.

In his pavilion that night the infinitely rich king of Zazamanc was entertaining the kings, princes, and others who had fallen to him, when the noble Lady Herzeloyde arrived with joy in her eyes to embrace him; for the talk of all was that he had gained the field. He had just that evening learned, however, of the deaths, during his years of absence, of his brother and his mother, so that when the queen came into his tent he was in tears. Moreover, nostalgia for his distant wife had been coming upon him all that day. Further, an embassy had just brought a letter from an earlier lady with claims on him, the Queen of France. So that when Herzeloyde also claimed him, he demurred.

"I have a wife, my lady, who is more dear to me than myself."

"You must renounce that Moor," she answered; "renounce your heathendom and love me—by our own religious laws."

He put forward the claim of the Queen of France; after that, of his new sorrow; next, the cancellation of the tournament: at which last, however, appeal was made to a judge, who declared that, having donned his helm, he had officially competed and must now accept the award. She capitulated to his last demand: never, like his former wife, to prevent him from entering tournaments. And when that was done, she took his hand.

"And so now," she said, "you belong to me and must yield yourself to my charge."

She led him by a secret way to a place where he dismissed his sorrow and she her maidenhood. And he then did an admirable thing: he released those he had overthrown; to all poor knights gave Arabian gold; to the traveling minstrels, presents; and to the kings who were there, his gems. In delight and full of praise for that king all rode away to their homes.

However, the sword blade of Herzeloyde's joy soon snapped; for when Gahmuret learned that his former lord, the caliph, was being overridden by Babylon, he sailed to serve him and six months later the message returned of his death.

Queen Herzeloyde gave birth to a son so large she hardly survived. *Bon fils, cher fils, beau fils,* she called him, as she pressed into his tiny mouth the little pink buds of her breasts. "I am his mother and his wife," she thought; for she felt that she again held Gahmuret in her arms. And she mused: "The supreme Queen gave her breasts to Jesus, Who for our sake suffered death on the Cross, and thus to His faith in us remained loyal. But the soul of anyone who underestimates His wrath will be in trouble on Judgment Day. This fable I know to be true."

BOOK III: THE GREAT FOOL

Overwhelmed with grief, the widowed queen withdrew from her castle and world to a solitary waste, charging her people never to mention a word about chivalry to her son. He was thus raised ignorant of his heritage and even of his name. All he ever heard himself called was *fils: bon fils, cher fils, beau fils.* Yet with his own little hands he made himself a tiny bow with which to shoot at birds. The sweetness of their song transfixed his heart, and when he saw them dead, he wept.

His mother told him of God. "He is brighter than day, yet assumed the form of man. Pray to Him when in trouble; He is faithful and gives help. There is another, however, the Lord of Hell, dark he is and faithless. Turn your mind away from him, and from doubt."

In early youth strong and beautiful, the boy was one day rambling on a mountainside when he heard galloping hoofs and thought the noise must be of devils. Three knights then flashed into view, and, deciding that they were angels, he fell to his knees to pray. A fourth appeared with bells ringing from his stirrups and right arm, who pulled to a halt and asked the stupefied youth if he had seen two knights ride past with an abducted maid.

"O God of help!" the youth prayed to the knight. "Give me help!"

Gently the prince answered: "I am not God. We are four knights."

"What is a knight?" the lad asked; and he was told: told, also, of King Arthur, who made knights. And when they had shown him what a sword was and a lance, and passed on, he ran in rapture to his mother, who, when told what he had seen, collapsed.

Believing that if she made him look the fool, he might be forced to return, she procured the poorest horse she could find and clothed him in a clown's rig of hempen shirt and breeches in one piece, coming halfway down his legs, a monk's hood, and clumsy, untanned boots; then gave him the following advice: 1. to cross streams only where most shallow; 2. to greet people with the words, "God protect you!"; 3. to ask advice of those with gray hair; and 4. to strive to win a good lady's ring and then to kiss and embrace her. She also told of a knight, Lähelin, who had taken from her two countries. "I will avenge that," her son said as he mounted, with a quiver of darts on his back. She kissed him, stumbled after as he rode, and when he had disappeared, fell and was dead.

Simplicity's child came to a brook that a rooster could have crossed, rode along to a very shallow place, and forded to the meadow beyond, where a colorful tent was to be seen. Within, a young wife lay asleep with her coverlet to her hips (God himself had fashioned that body), and on her soft white hand there was a ring, to seize which the youth pounced upon the bed. During the lively tussle that ensued he acquired, besides the ring, a forced kiss and a brooch; then made a meal of her provisions, forced another kiss, and rode off.

"Aha!" the knight, her husband, exclaimed when he returned.

He was the brother of the knight Lähelin, Duke Orilus de Lalander, and in a paroxism of mortification, smashed her saddle, tore up her clothes, bade her ride behind him in shreds, and departed to find the youth by whom his honor had been undone—who, meanwhile, had come to a forest cliff, beneath which a lady sat with a dead knight on her knees, tearing her hair in grief. Simplicity approached.

"What is your name?" she asked.

"*Bon fils, cher fils, beau fils,*" he replied.

She was Sigune, his mother's sister's child, and she recognized the litany. "Your name," she said, "is Parzival. Its meaning is 'right through the middle'; for a false love cut its furrow through the middle of your mother's heart." Then she told him his parents' story and of how the knight on her lap, Prince Schianatulander, had been slain defending his heritage against Lähelin and Orilus.

"I shall avenge these things," he told her. But she, fearing for his life should he come to Arthur's court, sent him off in the wrong direction, along a broad, much-traveled road, where he greeted whomever he passed, "God protect you!" and when night came, turned to the large dwelling of an avaricious fisherman, who refused shelter until the brooch was offered, then became so hospitable that the next morning he brought his guest all the way to the towers of Arthur's court.

No Curvenal had trained this youth as Tristan had been trained. Trotting forward on his stumbling mount, he saw come galloping from the castle a knight in bright red armor with a goblet in his hand, who, when greeted, reined and called to him to tell the court, he would be waiting on the jousting field—with apologies to the queen for having splashed her gown with the wine. He was King Ither of Kukumerlant, who had seized the cup in token of his claim to a portion of Arthur's kingdom.

At the castle gate were sentries and a crowd; but God had been in good spirits when fashioning Parzival: his beauty and the kindness of a young page got him through to the Round Table, where Arthur himself heard his brash demand to be knighted on the spot and given the red suit of armor he had seen on the knight outside—whose message he briefly told. The court's rude seneschal, Keie, shouted to let him get the suit himself; but a lady, Cunneware by name, of whom it had been prophesied that she would never laugh in her life until she saw the flower of knighthood, laughed loudly as Parzival passed, going out, for which Keie beat her with his staff. And when the court fool Antanor cried that Keie would be sorry for that beating, he too tasted of that stick.

Parzival trotted to the field, challenged Ither for his suit, and the knight, indignantly reversing his bright red lance, struck him with its butt so hard that both he and his pony went sprawling among the flowers of that April day—who got quickly to his feet, however, and replied with a swift dart through the grill of the Red Knight's vizor to his eye, and he fell from his charger, dead. The powerful stallion whinnied loud. And the lout was rolling the knight about to remove his bright red armor, when the queen's page who had shown him to the court came running, helped with the suit and attired him over his mother's clothes, shoes and all (which he refused to remove), took away the darts (forbidden to knighthood), taught him briefly the use of shield and spear, and fastened upon him the knight's sword. Parzival then sprang onto the charger. "Return the goblet to the king," he said as the horse began to move, "and tell that beaten maid I will avenge her pain."

He rode the great Castilian at a gallop all day because he had not been taught how to check it, and that evening came to the towers of the aged Prince Gurnemanz de Graharz (Wagner's Gurnemanz, with whose words the opera starts, who is here the lord of a castle of his own, not, as in Wagner's work, a member of the company of the Grail). Reposing with his young falcon beneath a large tree outside his castle, the old knight rose to greet the red horseman, whose steed halted before him. "My mother told me," said the rider, "to ask advice from people whose hair is gray." To which the elder replied courteously, "If you have come for advice, young man, you must pledge to me your friendship." And he cast from his hand his hawk, which, wearing a little golden bell, flew as messenger to the castle, where the gates opened, a company appeared, and the visitor was made welcome. But when his armor was removed, his fool's costume came to view, and all were embarrassed and amazed. Yet his form was noble. Gurnemanz took him to his heart and for a season coached him in knighthood.

"You talk," said the old knight, "like a little child. Why not be quiet now about your mother and take thought of something else?" He gave the youth certain rules of conduct: never to lose the sense of shame; to be compassionate to the needy; neither to squander wealth nor to hoard it; not to ask too many questions; to reply to questions frankly; to be manly and of good cheer; not to kill a foe begging mercy; to be loyal in love, and to remember that a husband and wife are one: they blossom from a single seed.

Old Gurnemanz, who had lost three sons, hoped now to marry Parzival to his daughter. The youth had a feeling, however, that before experiencing a wife's arms he should prove himself in the field. In the poet's words: "He sensed in noble striving a lofty aim for both this life and beyond—and that is still no lie." [1] Compare in Goethe's *Faust* the famous line: "Whoever strives with unremitting effort, we can redeem"; [2] also, Goethe's words to Eckermann on the Godhead effective in the living.* When Parzival rode away, therefore, with his mentor's sad permission, the old man, riding beside him a short way, felt in his heart that he was giving to knighthood a fourth son, his fourth great loss.

BOOK IV: CONDWIRAMURS

Parzival, now a knight well schooled, let his stallion take him through the forest as it would, too melancholy to care; and riding into wild, high, wooded mountains came, before day was done, upon a roaring mountain stream that tumbled downward over cliffs to the city of Pelrapeire, where it was spanned by a wicker-work drawbridge, flimsy and without a rope, under which its waters coursed to the sea. Across the bridge some sixty armed knights were to be seen, who as Parzival approached warned him back. His stallion balked, so he dismounted, and as he led the beast across the rocking span, the knights withdrew and the city gates closed. A pretty maid leaning from a window asked if the knight were a friend or a foe, and when a portal was opened he found within the city walls the whole population armed. But they were frail, haggard with hunger, and there were everywhere towers, turrets, and armed keeps.

Admitted to the castle, relieved of his arms, and clothed in a mantle of sable with a fresh wild furry smell, he was conducted to the maiden queen, the beautiful Condwiramurs. He sat beside her for some time in silence, in obedience, he thought, to Gurnemanz's law, and the young queen wondered; but then deciding that, as hostess, she might start the talk herself, she asked whence he had come. He told of Gurnemanz and then learned from this queenly maiden that she was his niece. She was more radiant, like a rose both red and white, than the two Isolts together.

When her guest that night had retired and already slept, she came quietly to his bedside, not for such love as changes maids into women, but for aid and a friend's advice. Yet she wore the raiment of battle: a white silk nightgown, over which she had tossed a samite robe; and since all in the castle were asleep, she could talk now as she would.

She knelt beside his bed. He woke and discovered her.

* Supra, p. 383.

"Lady, are you mocking me?" he said. "One kneels that way only to God."

She replied, "If you will promise on your honor, to be temperate and not to wrestle with me, I shall lie then by your side."

Neither she nor he, states the poet, had any notion of joining in love. Parzival lacked all knowledge of the art, and she, desperate and ashamed, had come in misery of her life. In tears, Condwiramurs, the orphan queen, told him of her plight. A certain powerful king, Clamide by name, with an army led by his seneschal Kingrun, had taken every castle of her land, right up to that rickety bridge. He had slain the elder son of Gurnemanz and now wanted her for his wife. "But I am ready," she said, "to kill myself before surrendering my maidenhood and body to Clamide. You have seen the height of my palace. I would cast myself into the moat."

And there we have Wolfram's second point, the second term of an opposition right through the middle of which his hero and heroine were to pass: on one hand, the magic of the senses, sheer passion (the side of Isolt and Tristan), and on the other hand, the sacramentalized marriage of convenience, society, and custom, without love (Isolt and King Mark).

Said Parzival to the young queen weeping in bed beside him: "Lady, is there no way to console you?"

"Yes, my lord," she answered, "if I could be freed from the power of this king and his seneschal Kingrun."

"My lady, let Kingrun be a Frenchman, a Briton, or what-not, my hand here will defend you as far as my life can serve."

And that night ending, its day arrived, and with day the army of Kingrun, showing many a banner and Kingrun himself in the lead.

Riding forth to his first battle, Parzival galloped out the castle gate and against the charging seneschal with such force that the girths of both saddles broke. Their swords flashed, and presently Kingrun, whose fame in the world was great, lay on his back surrendering, with Parzival's knee on his chest. The fresh young knight, recalling his mentor's rules, bade him go submit to Gurnemanz.

"Gurnemanz," said the man, "would kill me: I slew his son."

"Then surrender here to the queen."

"They would hack me to bits in that town."

"Go to Britain, then, to King Arthur's court, and submit there to the maiden who was beaten for my sake."

So the battle ended, and Condwiramurs, when her knight returned, embraced him before all. Her citizens paid him homage, and she declared him to be her *ami,* her lord and theirs.

"I shall never be the wife," she said, "of any man on earth but the one I have just embraced." Then all looked to the sea, and behold! there were merchantmen arriving, ships bearing food and nothing but food, good meats and wine.*

After a jubilant feast and festival, the two were asked would they share one bed, and they answered together, yes. However, he lay with her so decently that not many a lady nowadays would have been satisfied with such a night. He left the young queen a maiden. Yet she thought of herself as his wife, and next day, in token of her love, did up her hair in the way of a matron; conferring on him, her beloved, all her castles and her land: this virgin bride. Two days and two nights more they were happy in this way—although now and then there came to him the idea which his mother had advised of embraces. Gurnemanz too had explained to him that husband and wife are one. And so—if I may tell you so—they enlaced legs and arms and he found the closeness sweet; and that old custom, ever new, was theirs thereafter: in which they were glad and nowise sad.[3]

"The ineffable, the mystical and transcendent quality of this love," comments Gottfried Weber on this critical passage, "is epitomized in the 'purity' of the first three nights, in the full sense of the Middle High German term, *kiusche.* The morning following the first night, the 'virgin bride' (*magetbaeriu brût*) felt herself to be a 'woman' (*wîp:* a 'wife'); for her soul had already absorbed an absolutely new, perfectly fulfilling, traumatic impression, experienced as completely unique: the virginality of her heart had been bestowed upon that other as her gift, he was now her spouse

---

* Note the way in which an old mythic formula has here been applied to the new ideal: 1. desolation, the Waste Land, as a function of the social order typified in Clamide; 2. a combat of the old king and the new, legitimized sensuality (Clamide) against noble personal love (Parzival); 3. the marriage of a goddess-queen and god-king, here two integral individuals; and finally 4. the renewal of life.

vor gote, 'before God.' . . . And it was only after this consummation of the marriage purely in soul and spirit that the bond, already
recognized as confirmed, was substantiated through extension to
the physical estate." [4]

In time, however, Clamide himself arrived, having heard report
of his seneschal's defeat at the hands (it was said) of the Red
Knight (King Ither of Kukumerlant, whose armor Parzival wore).
He appeared with a second army, and all the machines of war.
Greek fire, catapults, battering rams, and portable sheds, were
brought to bear, until, learning from his captives of the marriage of
the maid he had come to win, Clamide sent to the castle a challenge to single combat, and the Red Knight again broke from the
city at a gallop. The king charged to meet him and they fought till
their steeds collapsed, then went at it with their swords. Presently
Clamide weakened. Parzival tore his helm off, so that the blood
gushed from his nose and eyes, and was about to do him dead
when the once great king begged mercy and was sent—like his
seneschal—to Arthur's court, to be subject to the Lady Cunneware. And there was amazement there indeed when those two appeared; for that beaten king had been richer even than Arthur in
wealth of lands.

But at Pelrapeire, after fifteen months of love and jubilation, a
time came for departure. One morning Parzival said courteously
(as many there saw and heard), "If you will permit, my lady, I
should like, with your allowance, to see how things stand now with
my mother: I know not whether ill or well."

He was so dear to her, the young queen could not deny him, and
he rode forth from their castle and town, again alone.

BOOK V: THE CASTLE OF THE GRAIL

And again riding without reins, but now through autumn foli-
age, not spring, he arrived that evening at a lake where he saw two
fishermen floating at anchor in a boat, one so richly clad he might
have been king of the world. From his bonnet peacock feathers
plumed. The Red Knight called to know where lodging for the
night might be obtained, and the fisherman richly clad—he was
deeply sad of mien—replied that he knew of no habitation but
one within thirty miles. "There, at the head of the cliff," he called
back, "turn right, ascend the hill, and when you come to the moat,

call to let down the bridge. But have a care! The roads here lead astray; no one knows where. If you arrive, I shall be your host."

The perilous wilderness again: the "dark wood" of Dante's opening lines!

Without difficulty, at an easy trot, Parzival rode past the cliff, turned right, and ascended the wooded hill to the moat before a castle of many turrets, where a squire from within caught sight of him and cried to know what he wanted.

"The fisherman sent me," Parzival called, and the drawbridge descended. He crossed and passed into a spacious court, where the grass was unworn by jousting; for that castle was in sorrow: no banners flew. When his armor was removed and they beheld his beautiful young face, still boyish, beardless, they were joyful. A cloak of finest silk was cast around him, which, he was told, was of the queen, whom he was presently to see: Repanse de Schoye (*Repense de Joie*). He was conducted kindly to an immense hall with a full hundred chandeliers and as many couches, well apart, a carpet before each, and on each of which there sat four knights. In three great marble fireplaces fires blazed of aromatic aloewood, and the lord of castle, carried in on a stretcher, was set before the central of these: who bade Parzival sit beside him. And the sense of it all was of sorrow.

Through a door a squire then came rushing, bearing a lance; and by this rite the sorrow was increased. From its point gushed blood that ran down its length to the bearer's hand and on into his sleeve. The squire circled the hall and when he reached the door again, ran out.

A steel door opened at the end of the great room and two beautiful maidens entered, clothed in gowns of earth-brown wool, drawn tight by girdles at the waist. Wreaths of flowers crowned their long flowing fair hair, and each bore a lighted candle in a golden candlestick. They were followed by another two, each with a little ivory stool, which, when they bowed, all four, before the host, was set before him on the floor. The four stood back, and from the door there entered twice four again, clad, however, in gowns more green than grass, long, full, and gathered at the waist by long, narrow girdles, richly wrought. The first four of these bore candles, and the second four a precious tabletop carved of hyacinth-tawny translucent garnet, which they carefully set down on the two little ivory stools; after which the eight in green stepped back to the four in brown, and the number standing now was twelve.

Next appeared six: two bearing on cloths two very sharp white silver knives, which the candles of the other four made to gleam. Clothed in gowns of two manners of silk, one dark, the other shot with gold, these, approaching, courteously bowed. The two knives were placed upon the table, and all six stood back before the twelve. When see! from that door there entered six again in the same parti-colored gowns, bearing in tall glass vessels lights of costliest balsam; and they were followed by the queen, Repanse de Schoye: radiant as a dawn breaking, clothed in Arabian silk, and she bore on a deep green cloth of gold-threaded silk the Joy of Paradise, both root and branch.

That was the object called the Grail. It was beyond all earthly joy, and such that its bearer was required to preserve her purity, cultivate virtue, and spurn falsity [in contrast to that doctrine of the Church whereby the personal morals of its clergy—who, moreover, were exclusively male—were declared to bear no relation to the operation of the sacraments they dispensed]. The queen, together with her six maidens bearing lights, advanced and courteously bowed as she placed the Grail before the host—while Parzival, watching as she did so, thought only, "The robe I have on is hers." The seven drew back to the other eighteen and the queen, then standing in the center, had twelve at either hand.

A hundred tables, now carried in, were set before the couches. White cloths were spread upon them. The host washed his hands from a vessel and Parzival from the same. Four cars carried costly golden vessels to every knight in the hall, and a hundred squires, bearing white napkins, began gathering from before the Grail a feast which they served to the knights.

"And I have been told," states Wolfram, "and I pass it on to you (but on your responsibility, not mine, so that if I speak false, we do so together), that whatever one reached one's hand to take, it was found there before the Grail: food warm and cold, foods new and old, both cultivated and wild. . . . For the Grail was be-atitude's own fruit and provided such abundance of the world's sweetness that its delights were very like what we are told of the kingdom of Heaven. . . . And for whatever drink one held one's cup, that was the drink that flowed by the power of the Grail: white wine, mulberry, or red."

And Parzival marked all this, the richness and great wonder, but thought, remembering Gurnemanz: "He counseled me, in sincerity and truth, not to ask too many questions."

There appeared a squire, bearing a sword in a jeweled sheath, its hilt a ruby, its blade a source of wonder. Presenting this to Parzival, the melancholy host declared that before God had maimed him, he had worn this sword in battle. And still the guest never spoke.

"For that I pity him," declares Wolfram; "and I pity too his sweet host, whom divine displeasure does not spare, when a mere question would have set him free."

The queen and twenty-four maidens advanced, bowed courteously to both Parzival and his host, took up the Grail, and proceeded to their door, through which, before it closed behind them, he saw on a couch in a large room, where there was also a great fireplace, the most beautiful old man his eyes had ever seen: he was grayer even than mist. "Your bed," said his host politely, "I think, is ready," and the company dispersed.

The youth was shown to his room. Four fair maidens saw him to bed with wine and fruits of the sort that grow in Paradise. And he slept long, but with threatening, terrible dreams, and when he woke the morning was half gone. His armor and two swords were on the carpet, and he had to don them alone. His steed was tethered outside, at the foot of the main exit stair, with his shield and spear set up nearby; but not a soul did he see about. Nor did he hear anywhere a sound. He mounted. The great gate was open. Through it ran the tracks of many horses. And as he crossed the bridge, a squire, unseen, pulled the draw so hard that it nearly struck his steed as it sprang clear. Then somebody's voice was heard: "Ride on, you goose, and bear the hatred of the sun. If you had only moved your jaws and asked the question of your host! You've lost for yourself great praise!"

The knight called back for an explanation, but the castle again was all silence, and, turning, he followed the other tracks, which, however, gradually dispersed and were lost. . . .

Before him, in a linden tree, sat a maiden with a dead knight, embalmed, propped against her: again Sigune, his mother's sister's child. When she saw him, "This wilderness," she warned, "is dangerous; turn back!" Then she asked whence he had come, and he told her of the castle. "It is a mile or so from here," he said.

"Do not lie to me," she answered. "For thirty miles round about, no hand has touched here either tree or stone, save for a single rich castle that many seek but none has found. *For he who seeks will not find it.* The name is Munsalvaesche, and its kingdom, Terre de Salvaesche. It was bequeathed by the aged Titurel to his son, King Frimutel, who was killed in a joust for love. One of his sons, who can neither ride nor walk nor lie nor stand, is its present lord, Anfortas. Another son, Trevrizent, has retired as a hermit from the world."

"I beheld great marvels there," declared Parzival; and it was then that she recognized his voice. "I am the same," she told him, "who revealed to you your name."

"But your long brown wavy hair," he asked, "what has become of it?" For she was bald. "And let us bury that dead man," he suggested, "whose company you keep."

For response, she only wept. Then, noticing his sword, she disclosed its danger. On the second blow it would break. However, if dipped in the waters of a certain spring beneath a rock it would come together and be stronger than before. "It requires a magic spell," she said, "which perhaps you failed to learn. Did you ask the question?"

"No," he answered.

"Oh, alas," she cried, "that I must look upon you!" And she stared with loathing. "You should have felt pity for your host and have asked concerning his pain."

"Dear cousin, show me a friendlier mien," Parzival protested. "For whatever wrong I have done, I shall make amendment."

"You are cursed," she cried. "At Munsalvaesche you forfeited both your honor and your fame. I will say no more."

She turned away. And he too turned away. He wheeled his charger and, riding off, came remarkably soon upon two fresh tracks: one of a charger well shod, the other of an unshod mount —which latter he soon overtook. It was a beast in miserable case, with a lady on its back clad in shreds, who, when she turned and saw him, gave a start.

"I have seen you before," she said. "And may God give you more honor and joy than, from your treatment of me, you deserve!"

She was the lady of the tent. No part of her gown was untorn, yet in her purity she was clothed. And when Parzival's stallion, bending its head to her mare, neighed, the knight riding far ahead turned back and on seeing a knight beside his dame, immediately couched his spear for the charge. He was elegantly armed. On his shield was a dragon, as though alive; another was on his helm; and there were many more, in gold, rare stones, and rubies, on his gambeson; more still on the trappings of his steed. The two collided, and the lady, watching, wrung her hands, wishing neither any harm. The dragons, one by one, received blows and serious wounds. The two champions fought with swords from their mounts, but finally, seizing each other, tumbled to the ground with Parzival on top; and the other, forced to surrender, was compelled next to forgive his all-but-naked wife and to report, then, to Arthur's court and the Lady Cunneware.

Afraid of what her husband now would do to her, the lady held apart; but at last, "Lady," said he, "since I am beaten for your sake—well, come here: you shall be kissed." She leaped down and ran to him, kissing as commanded, careless of the blood about his face. On a sacred relic, which they presently discovered in an empty hermitage, Parzival swore that in the episode of the tent the lady had been all innocence, and he no man, but a fool. Orilus thereupon was reconciled, and the couple rode off to Arthur's court in joy. "For, as all the world knows," comments the author, "eyes that weep have a mouth that is sweet. Great love is born of joy and sorrow, both."

BOOK VI: THE LOATHLY DAMSEL

"Would you not like to hear," the poet asks, "how Arthur with his court set forth from Karidoel, his castle and land?" He set forth to add to his Round Table company the champion (of whom no one knew the name) responsible for those three impressive arrivals submitting to Cunneware: Kingrun, Clamide, and now, with his lovely wife Jeschute, the Lady Cunneware's own brother, proud and fierce Orilus.

The company had been out some eight days with its tents, ban-

ners, and pavilions, when a party of the king's falconers, hawking
of an evening, lost their best bird. It disappeared into the woods.
But the night being chill and the forest unfamiliar, it flew to the
neighborhood of a campfire, which chanced to be of Parzival, who
was also in that wood. Next morning the world lay covered with
the winter's first light snow; and when the Red Knight mounted,
to ride on, the falcon followed.

Before them, with a great roar of wings and cackling, a thousand wild geese went up, and the hawk, darting, struck at one so
fiercely that its blood fell on the snow in three large drops—bright
red on purest white—the sight of which brought Parzival to a stop.
And he was sitting on his mount, in recollection of his wife's complexion (the bright red of her cheeks and chin on the pure white
of her skin), when a squire of the Lady Cunneware, riding with
a message to her brother, spied him in the distance, like a statue on
his steed, and galloped back to camp, setting up a din.

"Fie! You cowards! Wake up! The Round Table is disgraced!
There is a knight here trampling your tent ropes!"

The whole camp became a-clatter, and a young knight, Sir Segramors, dashed into Arthur's tent, where the king lay sweetly
sleeping with his queen, snatched away their sable coverlet, and
cried at them to be the first to go—to which, laughing, they consented. And he rode at the unknown knight still lost in absorbed
arrest—whose steed, however, to meet the charge, wheeled of itself, and when its rider's view of his idol was broken, his knightly
honor was saved; for he lowered his spear in such a way that the
oncoming Sir Segramors soon learned what it meant to fly. Without a word or sign, the stranger knight then returned to his contemplation of the snow.

Sir Keie came next, and the Lady Cunneware was avenged; for
he ended wedged between a rock and his shattered saddle, with a
broken arm and leg, and his horse beside him, dead, while the
knight, again without word or sign, wheeled back to his dream.

Third to come was the courteous knight, Sir Gawain, with neither spur, sword, shield, nor lance. "What if it be love that holds
that man enthralled," he thought, "as, at times, it has held me!"
Remarking the focus of the knight's gaze, he flung a yellow scarf
across the red drops; and when Parzival murmured to the vanished presence, "Who has taken you from me?" and more loud-

ly, "But what has become of my lance?" Gawain courteously answered, "You just broke it in a joust, my lord." He mollified skillfully the other's irritation at the interruption, told his name, offered his service, and in peace led the knight to Arthur's camp, where the two were greeted by a joyous crowd, from which the Lady Cunneware emerged to welcome her champion with a kiss.

The precious guest, brought to Gawain's pavilion, was relieved there of his armor and clothed in a mantle of silk, provided by Cunneware. It was fastened with an emerald at the neck, and at the waist with a girdle of rare stones; so that he looked like an angel come to flower on this earth when Arthur and his knights arrived.

"You have brought me pain as well as joy," said the king; "yet more honor than I have ever received from any man before." And he ordered spread on a flowery field a great circular cloth of Orient silk, large enough for every knight to be seated by his lady, and there, when all had made the guest welcome, they awaited an adventure: "For," as the poet tells, "it was a firm custom of the king that none should eat with him on a day when adventure failed to visit his court." And it was then that she appeared of whom we have now to speak, whose tidings brought grief to many.

On a mule the maiden rode, as tall as a Castilian steed, yellow-red, with nostrils slit and sides terribly branded. The rich bridle was excellently wrought. She was Cundrie [Wagner's Kundry], the sorceress, eloquent in many tongues, Latin, Arabic, and French. She wore a cape more blue than lapis lazuli, tailored in the French style, with a fine new hat from London hanging down her back, over which there fell and swung a switch of long black hair, as coarse as the bristles of a pig. She had a great nose, like a dog; two protruding boar's tusks, and eyebrows braided to the ribbon of her hair, bear's ears, a hairy face, and in her hand a whip with ruby grip, but fingernails like a lion's claws and hands charming as a monkey's. She rode directly to Arthur.

"O son of King Utpandragun," she said to him in French, "what you have here done today has brought shame both to yourself and to many a Briton. The Round Table is destroyed: dishonor has been joined to it. Parzival here has the look of a knight. The Red Knight, you call him, after that noble one he slew; yet none could less resemble that noble knight than this." She turned and rode directly to the Welshman. "Cursed be the beauty of your face! I am less a monster than you," she said. "Parzival, speak up! Tell why, when the sorrowful Fisherman sat there, you did not relieve him of his sighs. May your tongue now become as empty as your heart is empty of right feeling. By Heaven you are condemned to Hell, as you will be by all the noble of this earth when people come to their senses. I think of your father, Gahmuret; of your mother, Herzeloyde: alas that I have had to learn now of the dishonor of their child!

"Your noble brother Feirefiz, son of the queen of Zazamanc, is black and white, yet in him the manhood of your father never has failed. He has won through chivalrous service the queen of the city of Thabronit, where all earthly desires are fulfilled; yet had the question been asked at Munsalvaesche, riches far beyond his would here and now have been yours."

She broke into great tears, wrung her hands, and changing the subject, turned to the company. "Is there here no noble knight yearning to win both fame and noble love? I know four queens and four hundred maidens, all in the Castle of Wonders; and all adventure is wind compared to what might there be gained through noble love. The road is difficult, yet I shall be in that place this night." And she rode abruptly off with the words: "O Munsalvaesche, sorrow's home! To comfort you, alas, there now is none!"

But to Parzival of what help were now his brave heart, true breeding, and manhood? Yet there was one great virtue more in him, namely shame. He had not been guilty of real falsity. Shame brings honor. Shame is the crown of the soul and a sense of shame the highest virtue.

The first to begin to weep for the shamed knight in whose welcome this circle had been gathered was the lady Cunneware; many another lady followed. And they were all thus sitting in sorrow and tears when there came riding a knight, richly armed, holding a sword aloft, still sheathed, who cried, "Where is Arthur? Where Gawain?" He gave greeting to all save Gawain, whom he then challenged to a duel of hate. "He slew my lord while giving greeting," he said; "and I here challenge him to meet me forty days from this day before the King of Ascalun [Avalon], in the city of Schanpfanzun." When he gave his name he was recognized as a knight of the greatest wisdom, honor, and fame, Prince King-rimursel; and when he rode away the entire astonished company rose and broke into a tumult of talk.

"I am resolved to enjoy no joy," said Parzival to a dark heathen lady from Janfuse, who had approached to tell him of his brother. "The man whom Cundrie named may well be your brother," she had told him. "He is a noble king, both black and white, worshiped as a god. I am the daughter of his mother's sister, and perceive that you too have nobility and strength."

"I am resolved to enjoy no joy until I shall have seen again the Grail," Parzival declared. "If I am to suffer the scorn of the world for having obeyed a rule of courtesy, the counsel of Gurnemanz may perhaps not have been quite wise. A sharp judgment has here been passed upon me."

The manly Gawain came and kissed him. "God give you good fortune in battle," said Gawain. "And may God's power help me to serve you one day as I would like!"

"Alas," replied Parzival, "what is God? Were He great, He would not have heaped undeserved disgrace on us both. I was in His service, expecting His grace. But I now renounce Him and His service. If He hates me, I shall bear that. Good friend, when your own time comes for battle, let a woman be your shield. May a woman's love be your guard! When I am to see you again I do not know. My good wishes go with you."

The Lady Cunneware, sorrowing, led her knight to her pavilion, with her soft, lovely hands there to arm him. King Clamide, whom he had sent to her in service, had lately asked her to marry him, and for that she thanked her knight. He kissed her and rode away, clad in shining steel. And many more of Arthur's knights that day rode away for the Castle of Wonders; but Gawain left for his war in Schanpfanzun.

II. First Intermezzo: The Restitution of Symbols

Parzival's denunciation of God—or of what he took to be God: that Universal King, "up there," reported to him by his mother —marks a deep break in the spiritual life not only of this Christian hero, as a necessary prelude to his healing of the Maimed King and assumption of the role without inheriting the wound, but also of the Gothic age itself and thereby Western man. In Joyce's

Portrait of the Artist as a Young Man the same break is represented in essentially the same terms; for in each of these Catholic
biographies (eight centuries apart), the hero's self-realization required a rejection first of his mother's mythology of God, the
authorized, contemporary ecclesiastical mask, and a confrontation then, directly, with the void wherein, as Nietzsche tells,
the dragon "Thou Shalt" is to be slain: [5] the void of Parzival's
exit to the wilderness and of Stephen's alienation from home, and
his brooding, in *Ulysses,* on the mystery deeper than the sea.

In each of these works it was through "a struggle for the existential possibilities of faith" (to use a phrase coined by the philosopher Karl Jaspers) [6] that the redemptive symbols of the hero's inheritance of myth were transformed and effectively integrated as
guides for the unfolding of his life. The local, provincial Roman
Catholic inflections of what are actually archetypal, universal
mythic images of spiritual transformation are, in both works,
opened outward, to combine with their non-Christian, pagan, primitive, and Oriental counterparts; and they become thereby transformed into nonsectarian, nonecclesiastical, psychologically (as
opposed to theologically) significant symbols. I have already remarked the relevance of the Waste Land theme to the state of the
European Church under its authorized yet inauthentic spiritual
guides (wolves in shepherd's clothing, as they were called by their
contemporaries) in the period of Innocent III.[7] In Joyce's work
the hero, Stephen Dedalus, though grateful to his Jesuit masters—"intelligent and serious priests, athletic and highspirited pre-
fects, who had taught him Christian doctrine and urged him to live
a good life and, when he had fallen into grievous sin, had led him
back to grace"—yet began to realize at an early age that "some of
their judgments sounded a little childish in his ears," and that "the
chill and order of their life repelled him." [8] "He was destined," he
mused, "to learn his own wisdom apart from others or to learn the
wisdom of others himself wandering among the snares of the
world. The snares of the world were its ways of sin. He would fall.
He had not yet fallen but he would fall silently, in an instant. Not
to fall was too hard, too hard; and he felt the silent lapse of his
soul, as it would be at some instant to come, falling, falling, but
not yet fallen, still unfallen, but about to fall." [9] And then, in the
brothel scene of *Ulysses,* at the nadir of this young man's plunge to

the abyss, in the context of a Black Mass and at a stage of his adventure roughly comparable to Station 10 of the round of Figure 3, that vision of the Irish sea-god appeared, amalgamated with Shiva, which was to him the sign of a power deeper than the sea, in which all beings, all things, are consubstantial: [10] and he then was able to recognize in his sympathy for Bloom's suffering a shared life, as of one power in two reflections, poles apart.[11]

Comparably, in Wolfram's Castle of the Grail, where Celtic, Oriental, alchemical, and Christian features are combined in a communion ritual of unorthodox form and sense, the young hero's spiritual test is to forget himself, his ego and its goals, and to participate with sympathy (*caritas, karuṇā*) in the anguish of another life.

However, Parzival's mind on that occasion was on himself and his social reputation. The Round Table stands in Wolfram's work for the social order of the period of which it was the summit and consummation. The young knight's concern for his reputation as one worthy of that circle was his motive for holding his tongue when his own better nature was actually pressing him to speak; and in the light of his conscious notion of himself as a knight worthy of the name, just hailed as the greatest in the world, one can understand his shock and resentment at the sharp judgments of the Loathly Damsel and Sigune. However, those two were the messengers of a deeper sphere of values and possibilities than was yet known, or even sensed, by his socially conscious mind; they were of the sphere not of the Round Table but of the Castle of the Grail, which had not been a feature of the normal daylight world, visible to all, but dreamlike, visionary, mythic—and yet to the questing knight not an unsubstantial mirage. It had appeared to him as the first sign and challenge of a kingdom yet to be earned, beyond the sphere of the world's flattery, proper to his own unfolding life: a kingdom hidden from the known world and screened from even himself by his fascination with the glamour of knighthood; a kingdom the vision of which had opened to him—significantly—only *after* his series of great victories, not as a retreat from failure but as his guerdon of fulfillment. His decision to act in that intelligible sphere, not according to the dictates of his nature but in terms of what people would think, broke the line of his integrity, and the result to his soul was first shown to him alone by

the baldness of his cousin, but then to all the world, and to his utmost shock and shame, by that Loathly Damsel, richly arrayed, as
ugly as a hog.

This figure of the Loathly Damsel is comparable, and perhaps
related, to that Zoroastrian "Spirit of the Way" who meets the
soul at death on the Chinvat Bridge to the Persian yonder world.
Those of wicked life see her ugly; those of unsullied virtue, most
fair.[12] The Loathly Damsel or Ugly Bride is a well-known figure,
moreover, in Celtic fairytale and legend. We have met with one
of her manifestations in the Irish folktale of the daughter of the
King of the Land of Youth, who was cursed with the head of a
pig (as here, a pig's bristles and boar's snout), but when boldly
kissed became beautiful and bestowed on her savior the kingship
of her timeless realm. The Kingdom of the Grail is such a land:
to be achieved only by one capable of transcending the painted
wall of space-time with its foul and fair, good and evil, true and
false display of the names and forms of merely phenomenal pairs
of opposites. Geoffrey Chaucer (1340?–1400) provides an
elegant example of the resolution of the Loathly Bride motif in his
"Tale of the Wife of Bath"; John Gower (1325?–1408) another, in his "Tale of Florent." There is also the fifteenth-century
poem "The Weddynge of Sir Gawen and Dame Ragnall," as well
as a mid-seventeenth-century ballad, "The Marriage of Sir
Gawain." The transformation of the fairy bride and the sovereignty that she bestows are, finally, of one's own heart in fulfillment.

The knightly rules of Gurnemanz had prepared Parzival well for
his ambition in the world, but left his own unfolding interior life,
his "intelligible character" (to use Schopenhauer's term), not only
unguided but unrecognized and completely out of account. And
yet, when the old knight offered him his daughter, the youth discreetly departed, not because she was unlovely, unworthy of him,
or unkind, but because an inward knowledge already told him that
a life—a life with substance—has to be earned and fashioned from
within, not received from the world as a gift, as the Maimed Grail
King had received his castle and throne. And it was precisely this
integrity of heart that marked Parzival for a destiny beyond the
bounds and gifts of any settled social order, proved him eligible to
approach the Grail, and brought him in the next adventure directly
to his counterpart, a young woman resisting to the death the suit of

a powerful, highly respected king who, though offering her the world, had not awakened love. In contrast to her cousin Liaze, the compliant daughter of Gurnemanz, submissive to her father's will, Condwiramurs, like Parzival, stood for a new ideal, a new possibility in love and life: namely, of love (*amor*) as the sole motive for marriage and an indissoluble marriage as the sacrament of love—whereas in the normal manner of that period the sacrament was held as far as possible apart from the influence of *amor,* to be governed by the concerns only of security and reputation, politics and economics: while love, known only as *eros,* was to be sublimated as *agape,* and if any such physical contact occurred as would not become either a monk or a nun, it was to be undertaken dutifully, as far as possible without pleasure, for God's purpose of repopulating those vacant seats in Heaven which had been emptied when the wicked angels fell.

But now, it is rather curious and of considerable interest to remark that in Wagner's operatic transformation of the *Parzival* there is no mention either of Condwiramurs or of the new Grail King as a married man, whereas in Wolfram's work it was precisely because of this love-marriage and through his loyalty to its sacrament that Parzival was to achieve at last the healing of Anfortas and succeed to his throne *without* inheriting his wound. Furthermore, whereas in Wolfram's Castle of the Grail all members of the procession except the startling bearer of the bleeding lance were female—young, stately, and lovely—those of Wagner's chorus and procession are exclusively male. And still further, Gurnemanz, whose calls to the guardians of the Grail Forest sound the opening words of Wagner's opera, serves there not as a teacher of the laws of chivalry but as a guide directly to the Grail Temple. He has no daughter to offer, nor respect for marriage, but is himself a member of the Temple order, and in the spirit rather of a monk than of a knight cries out at Parsifal, when the "Guileless Fool" has failed to ask the question: "Go find yourself a goose, you gander!" After which, the first curtain falls.

The leading theme of Wolfram's writing is thus in Wagner's work dismissed: the lesson of loyalty in true love, joined with heroism in action, as the *human* way to perfection, passing in freedom between the two impersonal compulsions, on one hand of mere nature, the daemonic species-lust (*eros*) of the body, and on the other of sheer spirit, the celestial charity (*agape*) of saints. Accordingly, in Wagner's work the Grail is represented, as in Tennyson's sentimental *Idylls of the King,* as the holy chalice of the Last Supper; and when the vessel is uncovered before the suffering Amfortas a ray of light pours upon it from aloft, while a chorus of boys' voices, floating down from high in the dome, echoes angelically the words of Christ in consecration of the sacrament of the altar:

> Take and drink my blood,
> In recollection of our love!
> Take and eat my body,
> And in doing so, think of me.

But there is absolutely nothing of this kind either in Wolfram or in Chrétien's work.

Jessie Weston was the first to suggest, I believe, that the symbols of the Bleeding Lance borne by a squire and the Grail carried by a maiden must have been originally sexual emblems in some classical mystery rite.[13] The Greek vase painting of Figure 52, from the fifth century B.C., attests to the antiquity of such symbols in the context of initiation rites. The flaming staff and empty pitcher in the hands of the young girl are matched by the sprouting thyrsus, running with living sap, and the proffered wine cup of the god.

Figure 52. Dionysian Scene; mid-5th century B.C.

Figure 53. The Fisher among Bacchic Satyrs; c. 500 B.C.

And in Figure 53, from another vase of about the same date, showing the Fisher among Bacchic satyrs, we have a most striking confirmation of Miss Weston's thesis. In the early Christian communities Christ became associated with the imagery of such rites: with the Singer and Good Shepherd Orpheus (Figures 1 and 9); the bread and wine of Dionysus, in which the god himself is consumed; the death and resurrection of Tammuz, Adonis, Attis, and Osiris; and the sexual imagery (in certain Gnostic sects) of the god in menstrual blood and semen, suffering in both the woman and the man, made whole through sexual union. The original reference of such pagan symbols, however, had not been forward to the birth, death, and resurrection of Jesus Christ (i.e. to Roman Catholic theology), but inward to the powers of nature operative in the universe and in man; and the function accordingly of the Hellenistic initiation rites had not been to refer the mind to Christ or even, finally, to Apollo, but to effect in the individual certain psychological transformations, adjustments, and illuminations. The lance that pierced Christ's side is, by analogy, the boar that slew Adonis and, like the boar, a counterpart of the slain divinity himself, in whom opposites are transcended: death and birth, time and eternity, the slayer and the slain; also, male and female. Accordingly, the lance in Christ's wound is comparable to the *lingam* in the *yoni* (or as the Buddhists say, "the jewel in the lotus"), and the blood pouring from the wound (the *yoni*) is equally pouring from the lance (the *lingam*), as the one life-substance of the god: for the two, though apparently separate, are the same. And that is the lesson of the bleeding lance symbolically borne about the great hall, with the blood running down the length of its shaft and over the bearer's hand into his sleeve. It tells of the lance by which the Maimed Fisher was wounded: Anfortas on his bed of pain, Christ upon the Cross; announcing the sense of the mystery to come, of the Grail, the Perfection of Paradise, in which opposites are at one. For such signs to be effective in life, however, they must move the human heart to recognition and response in *human* terms, until which moment their mere presence, *supernaturally* interpreted, though perhaps of comfort and of promise, do not quite convince.

The Castle of the Grail, like the bowl of a baptismal font or the sanctuary of the winged serpent (Figure 11), is the place—the *vas* the *temenos*—of regeneration and, as such, a sanctuary in which sexual symbolism is both appropriate and inevitable. The great virtue of Wolfram lay in his translation of the magically interpreted symbols back into the language of human heterosexual experience, illustrating in his narrative, through many modes and on many levels, the influence of the sexes on each other as guiding, inspiriting, and illuminating forces—with the symbols there to inform us of the grades of realization achieved: as in the instance of Parzival. When crude and raw, seeking only his own good (kneeling in prayer to what he took to be a god of help, indifferent to his mother's sorrow, violently taking what he wanted from the lady of the tent), he met an avaricious fisherman who pointed him to the castle of worldly fame; but when he had risked death for another and experienced with her the initiation of love (Condwiramurs: Old French, *conduire-amours*, "to conduct, to serve, to

guide love"), the fisherman met was the Fisher King, pointing to
the Castle of the Grail, for the attainment of which he was now eligible to strive. And in this dreamlike epic of earthly spiritual
quest the heroes and heroines are many, though the destinies of all
—as in Schopenhauer's cosmic vision of the most miraculous *har-
monic praestabilita*—* interlace.

III. The Ladies' Knight

BOOK VII: THE LITTLE LADY OBILOT

Parzival, now at large, alone, in the Waste Land of his own
disoriented life, is to wander for a span of five years. He may be
thought of as the Stephen Dedalus of this medieval work, an intro-
verted, essentially solitary youth, deeply moved by a supreme sense
of purpose; while Gawain, his elder by some sixteen years, can
be compared in a way to Bloom, the extrovert, moving in a casual
course from one adventure to the next, largely with ladies on his
mind.

Gawain had been riding, we know not how many days, when he
left the forest and beheld before him on a hillside many banners
and a mighty host on the move in his direction. And where their
road joined his, he drew aside to watch many costly helmets go
past and multitudes of new white spears, flying pennons. Mules
bearing armor followed, and numerous loaded wagons; tradesmen
laden with exotic wares, and ladies in large number: no queens,
these last, but soldier girls, some wearing their twelfth love-token.
A rabble of young and old besides, footsore and bedraggled, of
whom some would have been appropriately garnished with a rope
around the neck.

Gawain asked a young squire whose multitude this was, and
learned that its lord was King Poydiconjunz of Gors, the father of
that rude Prince Meljacanz who had once abducted Arthur's
queen. Poydiconjunz and his son, with the powerful Duke Astor of
Lanverunz, were here in the van of the still larger force of the
king's young nephew, King Meljanz of Liz, who, having been
spurned by the daughter of his loyal vassal, Duke Lyppaut of
Bearosche, was here coming to gain his suit by force. The duke had
raised Meljanz from boyhood and was now in the deepest distress.

* Supra, p. 344.

Gawain's interest was greatly excited by this tale, and, not knowing that Parzival was in the army of Meljanz, he pressed on to the fortified town, before which a large defending army was encamped; and although one tent rope crowded the next, he and his equipage rode through, until he came below the castle walls. Above, from a window, leaned the difficult daughter, Obie, who had brought this all about, together with her mother and little sister, Obilot.

"Who is that fine young knight just arrived?" the mother asked.

"O Mother!" answered the daughter. "That is no knight. That is just a merchant!"

"But they have brought along his shields."

"Many merchants have that custom," said the girl.

The little sister, however, was admiring the knight. "Shame on you!" she scolded. "He is no merchant. He is handsome. I want him for *my* knight."

Gawain's squires had meanwhile settled him beneath a large linden tree, and presently the old Duke Lyppaut himself came out to request him to assist in the coming battle.

"I would do so, gladly," said Gawain, "but must avoid battle, my lord, until an appointed time. For I am on the way to redeem my honor in combat, or else to die on the field."

The old man, disheartened, rose and returned to his city gate, but within found his little Obilot.

"Father," she said, "I think the knight will do it for me: I want to pledge him to my service." And her father, with hope, having released her, out she ran to Sir Gawain, who, when she arrived, stood to receive the little guest.

"Sir," she said, "God is my witness: you are the first man I have spoken to alone. My governess tells me that speech is the garment of the mind; I hope mine will show me to be modest and of good breeding. It is only the greatest distress that brings me to this. I hope you will let me tell you what it is.

"You are really I and I am you, though our names are different. I shall give you now my name, and that will make you both maid and man, so that I shall be speaking both to you and to myself. Sir, if you wish it, I will give you my love with all my heart; and if you have a manly heart, you will serve us both well for my reward alone."

Gawain thought of how Parzival had said it was better to trust a woman than God, and gave the little lady his word.

"Into your hands I give my sword," he said. "When I am challenged, it will be you who ride for me. Others will think they see me, but I shall know they see you."

"That will not be too much for me to do," she said. "I shall be your protection and shield."

"Lady!" said he, and her little hands now lay clasped between his own. "Now I live at your command, and by the gift of your comfort and love."

"Sir," she said, "I must now leave you; for there is something more I must do. I must arrange my token. If you wear it, no knight will be greater in fame." And with her playmate, the burgrave's little daughter Clauditte, she ran off.

"What a gallant and good man!" the Duchess said when the story had been told. They made the child a new dress of golden silk, of which they took one sleeve and gave it to her playmate to carry to Gawain, who immediately, in delight, nailed it to one of his three shields.

Next day, like splitting thunder, with a sound of cracking spears, the great voice of battle rose, and Gawain rode to the attack, overthrowing swiftly two young lords. When, however, he heard the Duke Astor of Lanverunz shout the battle cry, "Nantes," of the knights of the Round Table and saw on a shield among his men the coat of arms of Arthur's son, he wheeled away and left that army, riding to attack the other, of King Meljanz, whom he unhorsed and bound to the service of Obilot. Parzival was elsewhere on the battlefield, clashing with the champions of Duke Lyppaut's brother, while the duke himself was engaged with Poydiconjunz: and Gawain, returning to assist him, struck down the rude Meljacanz, whom Astor, however, rescued. So that the day of battle ended with King Meljanz a captive and the best deeds of the day having been performed in the name of Obilot.

Nor did Gawain fail to receive a kiss when they asked him to take his lady in his arms. He pressed the pretty child like a doll to his breast and, summoning King Meljanz, bound him to her service. Whereafter Lady Love, with her powerful art, old yet ever young, waked love anew—and as to how the wedding of that humbled king with Obilot's elder sister went, ask those who there received gifts. Gawain himself departed. His little lady wept bitterly. Her mother could scarcely get her away from him, and he rode into the forest with a heavy heart.

BOOK VIII: THE WILLING QUEEN OF ASCALUN

"Now help me lament Gawain's woes!" the poet writes. High ranges and many moors he crossed, then saw approaching, before a mighty castle, an army of some five hundred knights out hawking. On a tall Arabian steed from Spain, their king, Vergulaht of Ascalun of the race of the fairy hills,* shone like day in the midst of night. However, when he wheeled to pursue and rescue a falcon that with its prey had dropped into a pond, his Arabian stumbled and he was hurled into the wet—at which moment, up rode Gawain, to ask the way to Schanpfanzun.

"You see it before you," said the king. "My sister is there, but if you will permit, I shall continue here a while longer. She will care for you till I come, and you will not be sorry if I tarry."

The reader familiar with the fourteenth-century *Sir Gawaine and the Green Knight* will have guessed that we are approaching here a variant of its temptation scene,[14] at the opposite range of Gawain's spectrum from his affair with tiny Obilot.

The castle was immense; the lady, beautiful. "Since my brother has so highly recommended you," she said, "I shall kiss you if you like. But you must let me know what I am to do, according to your own rules." She was standing there with all charm.

"Lady, your mouth," Gawain said, "looks to me so kissable, I will have that kiss of greeting."

The mouth was hot, plump, and red. Upon it Gawain affixed his own, and there took place a kiss that was not of the sort recommended for greeting guests. She and her well-born guest sat down. Sweet talk, quite frank, ensued, which advanced rapidly to a point where she could only repeat a refusal and he an unchanging plea.

"Sir," she said, at last, "if you know what you are doing, you will realize that I have already gone far enough. Besides, I don't even know who you are."

"I am my aunt's brother's son," he answered, "of a line high

---

* Ascalun, Avalon: Gawain's adventures generally are transformations of Celtic visits to the fairy hills.

enough to match yours; so that if you'd like to grant that favor, don't let our ancestors prevent you."

The waiting maid who had been pouring their drink disappeared, and some other ladies who had been sitting there did not forget they had things elsewhere to attend to. The knight who had escorted Gawain also was out of the way. And he, then reflecting that even a badly wounded eagle may catch a big fat ostrich, reached his hand beneath her mantle, "and I think," states the poet, "touched her hip"—which only increased his anguish. They were in such distress of love that something very nearly happened. Both the man and the maid were ready for it, when alas! their hearts' sorrow arrived! A white-haired knight came to the door and, on perceiving Gawain, set up a loud halloo of war, "Alas and hey hey for my master," he cried, "my master, whom you murdered! And now you would rape his daughter!"

People usually answer a call to arms, and so it happened now. Here a knight appeared; there, a merchant. They heard the rabble coming from the city.

"Lady," said Gawain, "let me now know your advice! If I only had my sword!"

"Let us fly into that tower," she said. "It's the one next to my chamber." And the two made for the door.

Gawain yanked from the wall the bar to lock the tower, and, wielding this, held the door while his lady ran upstairs. Above, she rushed about for a weapon of some sort, found a beautifully inlaid chessboard with its pieces, and brought these down to Gawain, who used that square board for a shield while the queen, behind him, flung the kings and rooks, and (as our story tells) they were heavy, so that those whom they hit went down. Like a knight that mighty lady fought, and no market woman at carnival time ever offered battle more warlike. A female soiled with armor-rust soon forgets what is seemly. And all the while, giving battle, she was in tears.

But Gawain? Every chance he got, he turned to have another look at his queen. You never saw on a spitted hare a better shape than hers. Between hips and breast, where the belt went round, no ant had ever slimmer waist. Every time Gawain had a fresh sight of her, more attackers lost their lives.

Then the king arrived, Vergulaht. He saw that battle, how it

stood; "and I am afraid," interjects the poet, "that I am now going to have to let you hear that a king there disgraced himself
in his handling of a guest." Gawain had to stand waiting until
Vergulaht donned his armor, then he fell back, retreating up the
stairs.

However, at this juncture the noble Prince Kingrimursel appeared, who at the field banquet of Arthur had challenged Gawain
to this journey. And when he saw what was going on, he tore his
hair in distress, for he had guaranteed on his honor that Gawain
should come in peace until met in single combat on the field. He
beat the rabble back from the tower, cried to Gawain to let him
come fight by his side, and the two escaped to the open.

The king's counselors persuaded him first to proclaim an armis-
tice, and then to make up his mind how his father was to be
avenged. The battlefield became still. The lady appeared from her
tower, kissed her cousin, Kingrimursel, on the lips for having rescued Gawain, and turned upon the king, her brother:

"Modesty and good manners were the only shield I had," she
said, "to protect myself and the knight you sent to me. You have
done me a grievous wrong. Furthermore, I had always heard that
when a man turns for protection to a lady his opponent should give
up the combat. The flight of your guest to me, King Vergulaht,
is going to do your reputation no good."

The prince accused him too. "I gave Gawain guarantee. You
betrayed him, and I too, therefore, have suffered affront. My fellow
princes all will look into this. If you cannot honor princes, we shall
not respect your crown."

There were some further verbal exchanges, but the upshot of it
all was that while the lady—her name was Antikonie—that evening
entertained Gawain and Kingrimursel with a dinner of wines,
pheasant, partridge, fish, and white bread, served by beautiful
maidens—all slim-waisted as ants—the king, meeting with his
counselors, told of a battle he had lately fought with a powerful
knight in the forest who had sent him flying from his steed and
made him swear to procure for him the Grail within a year. "And
if I fail I must go to Queen Condwiramurs and pronounce an
oath to her of submission."

The counselors then agreed that since Gawain was in Vergulaht's grasp, flapping his wings in his trap, the king should turn the

Grail task over to him. "Let him rest for the night," they suggested, "and let him hear of this in the morning."

So when Mass had been said, and the lady with her two knights appeared, a wreath of flowers in her hair of which no rose was redder than her lips, King Vergulaht begged his guest to help persuade his sister to forgive him. "And I will then forgive you my heart's sorrow for my father—provided," he added, "that you swear to me without delay you will seek for me the Grail."

Thus all were reconciled, and, breakfast having ended, Gawain's time came for departure. The queen approached without guile, spoke *adieu,* and her mouth again kissed his. "I think," states the poet, "they were both very sad." Then his pages brought his steeds, and he mounted Gringuljete (his white fairy horse with shining red ears) and in quest of the Grail for King Vergulaht of Ascalun rode away.

IV. Illuminations

BOOK IX: THE GOSPEL OF TREVRIZENT

"Open up, now, my heart," writes the poet, "to the knock of Lady Adventure! Let us hear how fares that noble knight whom Cundrie, with her harshest words, sent questing for the Grail. Has he yet seen Munsalvaesche?"

The book of his adventure tells that as he rode one day in the forest—"I know not at what hour"—God took thought for his guidance, and he spied among the trees a hermit's hut. Within was a hermitess, kneeling over a coffin, and the knight, hoping for direction, called, "Is anybody in?" She responded, and when he heard a woman's voice he quickly turned his mount away and, while she was rising, left his horse, shield, and sword by a tree.

She wore a hair shirt beneath a gray gown, but wore also a garnet ring. "May God reward you for your greeting, as He rewards all courtesy," she said as she came to sit beside him on a bench, where he asked concerning her life. "My food is from the Grail," she said. "Cundrie brings it, the sorceress, on Saturdays, for the week." And that seeming to him an unlikely tale, he indicated the ring.

"I wear this," she explained, "for a man beloved, whose love, in the way of human love, I never knew. And I have worn it since the day the lance of the Duke Orilus struck him dead. I am unmarried and a maid; yet in God's sight he is my husband, and this ring is to go with me before God."

Then he realized that the woman was Sigune.

Grief pressed his heart; he removed his helm and she looked hard into his face. "Parzival! It is *you!*" Her manner became very hard. "How do you stand now with the Grail? Have you learned its meaning yet?"

"It is cruel of you, my cousin, to bear me such ill will," he replied. "I have lost in these years all joy because of the Grail. We are kin, dear cousin. I behaved there as one bound to be a loser. Give me counsel."

She answered more kindly. "May the hand of Him now help you, to Whom all sorrow is known. You may succeed yet in finding a track that will take you to Munsalvaesche, for Cundrie has just now gone that way. Her mule stands over there when she comes, where the spring flows from the rock.* I suggest you follow Cundrie; she may not be far ahead."

He thanked her and mounted; but the fresh track soon was lost, and there came riding at him instead a bareheaded knight in shining mail and rich surcoat, shouting at him to get out. "Munsalvaesche allows no one this close who is not prepared either for battle," he cried, "or else for that transformation that in the world outside this forest is called death." The knight donned his helmet, which he carried in his hand, and Parzival, charging, struck him just above the shield and sent him rolling down a ravine. Parzival's steed went over too, but himself quickly catching a cedar branch, he dangled there until, groping with his feet, he found a rock. Below, his great Castilian lay dead, but the Temple Knight was scrambling up the other slope, and his mount, not far from Parzival, was standing with its feet tangled in the reins.

Mounting and now missing nothing but his spear, Parzival again was riding without aim, and so for weeks on end, until one morning when a light snow had fallen—just enough to be chill—he chanced upon a file of pilgrims, barefoot, all in rough gray cloaks. In the lead were a white-haired nobleman, his wife, and their two daughters, the ladies with little dogs trotting at their sides; and

* Compare again Eliot, *The Waste Land:* "If there were rock/And also water/And water/A spring/A pool among the rock" (lines 348–52).

these were followed by a troupe of squires and knights, also in pilgrim garb. Said the leader as he passed, to the armored horseman, who had turned his steed out of their path: "I am shocked to see you mounted on this day, and not barefoot, like ourselves." To which the mounted Parzival answered, "Sir, I do not know what day this year began, how many weeks have passed, nor what day this is of the week. I used to serve someone named God, until His mercy condemned me to shame."

"Do you mean God, Whom the Virgin bore?" the elder asked. "He died for us on this day, Good Friday, when all the world, though rejoicing, sighs with grief. Sir, if you are not a heathen, think upon this day and follow in our track. There is a holy man ahead who, if you confess to him with contrite heart, will absolve you of your sin."

The daughters interrupted. "Father, why torment him so? In that armor he must be freezing. We have tents nearby, lots of pilgrim cloaks: if Arthur himself were to visit us, we'd have food enough for a feast. Now be a decent host and take this knight to a place where he can get warm."

The old man, abashed, relenting, confessed that every year he took this walk with his household and would gladly share his provisions. The daughters begged the knight to join them and they did not seem at all sad. But he thought: "He whom they love, I hate."

"May good fortune bring you well-being," he said, and with courtesies took his leave—but with repentance already stirring in his heart. He thought of his Creator. "What if God should give me help?" he thought, and let the reins fall on his mount's neck. "Let Him show this steed the road that for me is best." And so he came to the place where Trevrizent, the brother of the Grail King, dwelt in fasting, prayer, and struggle with the Devil.

"Sir, give me counsel," Parzival begged, when asked why he rode that day in armor. "I am one who has sinned." And when the hermit asked who had sent him, he told of the pilgrims on the path, then asked, "When I rode at you that way, were you not afraid?"

"Stag and bear have frightened me," said the hermit, "but there is nothing human I fear. I once, like you, was a knight, and I strove for noble love. But I have now forgotten all that. Give me your reins!"

He led the steed to a protected ledge, and the knight himself to his cave. There were some books there, and an altar of stone with a casket on it of relics: the same, Parzival realized, on which he had once sworn to the beaten Duke Orilus that he had not ravished his wife.* Thus he had passed that way before—four and a half years and three days before. He sighed when he was told the date.

"How long! Unguided and in grief! Toward God I hold great hatred," he said. "He is the Lord, they say, of all help. Why, then, did He not help me?"

The holy man was quietly regarding him. "May God help us both!" he prayed. "So now tell me, calmly and soberly, how this wrath of God came about, by which He gained your hate. But before you begin accusing Him to me, let me tell you of His innocence. He is loyalty. Be loyal! He is called truth. Whatever is false, He abhors. Anyone seeing you defy Him with hate would take you for insane. With such anger you get nowhere. Think of Lucifer and his host."

Then he told the old tale of Adam and Eve, the Fall, and the sin of Cain, the blood of whose brother fell upon the earth, whence hatred first arose. The virgin earth, from which Adam had been born, was desecrated by that blood. But then God Himself became the Virgin's child, so that there have now been two men born of virgins: from the first, Adam, came sorrow; from the second, joy.

"Hear these ancient tales as new," said Trevrizent. "Let them teach you how to speak truth. The prophet Plato taught in this manner in his day; the sibyl, too, the prophetess. Many years ago they assured us that for even the greatest debt of sin, redemption might be ours.

"With Divine Love, the Highest Hand delivered us from Hell: the unclean alone He left there. For God shares with man His love and His hate, and between them all the world can choose. But if you wish God only ill—Who is ready for either your love or your wrath—it will be you alone who are lost. So now turn to Him your heart and let Him answer your good will. Listen well to the sweet tale of this Lover True."

"My greatest grief," said Parzival, "is for the Grail; my second grief for my wife. I yearn for them both."

"As for your marriage, that is well," said Trevrizent. "Re-

* Supra, p. 448.

main true in that, and though you may suffer in Hell, the agony will end, and with God's grace you will be freed. But you tell me also of the Grail, and in that you are a fool: for no man ever achieved the Grail who was not named to it in Heaven. This I tell you, for I know and have seen for myself."

"You have been there?"

"Yes, sir, I have."

And Trevrizent then told Parzival of the king, his injury, the marvel of the stone, and of how, moreover, on a day there had been one who came to the castle unbidden. "A foolish man," said Trevrizent, "who bore sin away with him for not having spoken one word to the king concerning the anguish that he saw."

And each now looked the other full in the face.

"There is a horse now standing in my stable," said the elder, "with the sign of Munsalvaesche on its saddle, the sign of the dove. Furthermore, you bear a certain resemblance to the late Grail King Frimutel. Now tell me, sir, where you come from and of what family born." And when told of Parzival's birth and of his trip to Arthur's court, "Alas, O world!" he exclaimed. "You have slain your own flesh and blood. The Red Knight, Ither, was your relative; and your mother, my sister Herzeloyde, because of you, died of grief!"

The youth had not heard this last before. "Oh no! No!" he exclaimed. "What are you telling me, good sir!"

It was, however, some time before he could bring himself to confess that it was he, misfortune's child, who had failed to ask the question of the Grail.

BOOK X: THE BEAUTY OF THE LADY ORGELUSE

Wild tales are now in store; for Gawain, as we have heard, was on the way to adventures of great peril. Whoever seeks the Grail must do so with his sword. And so he rode, one morning, onto a meadow, where he saw a horse tethered to a linden. There was a shield beside it that a spear had pierced, yet the bridle and saddle were for a woman's use; and our knight, therefore imagining that he might now have to wrestle with someone to whose throw he would gladly fall, peered around the tree and found sitting there a lady on whose lap lay a knight, pierced through.

"Sir," she said, "he is alive, but not for long."

The man's blood was pouring inward. So Gawain—no fool in the matter of wounds—plucked a branch of the tree, slipped the bark off like a tube, and inserting this in the wound, bade the woman suck until the blood flowed outward. And when the knight, reviving, saw Gawain there bending over him, he warned against the road ahead.

"I shall ever regret this adventure," he said, "and you will too, if you continue. Lischoys Gwelljus unhorsed me with a perfect thrust through my shield."

The trail Gawain found all bloody, as though a stag had been shot there, and this brought him soon within sight of the magician Clinschor's towered castle.* (The road winds around the hill on which it stands, so that ignorant people declare it spins like a top.) † And he came, as he continued upward, to a spring that welled from a rock, where he saw a lady whose beauty brought him to a stop. She was Orgeluse de Logroys.

"By your leave, may I dismount?" he asked. "Let me die if ever I have seen a woman of greater beauty."

"I too know that very well," she said. "Little honor is it, however, to be praised by all and sundry: the praise I want is of the wise. It is time you were riding on. You will be closest to my heart when far away. And if adventure brings you questing for love, the only reward you will get from me will be disgrace."

He replied, enchanted, "My lady, you are right. My eyes do imperil my heart: they have seen you and I am in your keep. Loose or bind me: I shall like it either way."

She replied indifferently: "Oh well, then take me along! You will regret it. If honor is what you want, you had better give this up."

"Who wants love unearned?" he answered, and she pointed down the road. "Dismount! Walk down that footpath, over the lit-

---

* Clinschor is Wagner's Klingsor. His magic castle, according to Wagner, was the Garden of Delights where Amfortas received his wound. In the opera, Kundry is Klingsor's slave; the lance is still in his possession. Moreover, Parsifal, not Gawain, is Wagner's knight of this adventure. A very different Parsifal from the Parzival of Wolfram (more like Tennyson's Galahad), he resists seduction in the garden (Act II) and comes away with Klingsor's lance, which, when applied to the wound, heals the king.

† Thus Wolfram's rationalization of the Celtic "Whirling Castle" motif. Curoi has become Clinschor; Cuchullin, Gawain. Cf. supra, pp. 418–19.

tle bridge and on into the orchard. People are there, dancing, beating tambourines, playing flutes. Walk on, right through, you will see my horse. Untie it; it will follow you back."

Confiding his own horse to her charge, he did as told; and as he passed among the folk a number of men and women came to him, lamenting his misfortune. He saw the horse tethered to an olive tree with a gray-beard knight leaning on a crutch nearby, who warned him: "If you will take advice, you will not lay hand on that horse." But Gawain untied the beast, and it followed him back to the mistress of his heart.

"Welcome, you goose," she said.

He offered to help her mount. "I didn't ask for your help!" she retorted and mounted by herself. "Now follow me, and may God throw you from that steed."

He followed, and they rode to a flowery heath, where, noticing a plant that was good for healing wounds, Gawain got down to dig it up. "I see my friend is both doctor and knight," was the lady's comment. "He will earn for us a good living if he knows how to sell ointment jars."

He explained that he had lately passed a knight to whom this plant would be of benefit. "Oh good!" she said. "I am going to learn something!" And rode on.

Following, Gawain saw approaching a strange squire, a sort of monster, Malcreatiure his name: he was Cundrie's brother and had a face like hers, but male, with a wild boar's tusk at either side and hair like the bristles of a hog. In the land Tribalibot, by the Ganges, people grow that way. Our father Adam, who named all things according to their nature, and knew, moreover, the movements of the stars and seven spheres, knew also the virtues of herbs. And when any of his daughters came of childbearing age he would warn her against eating certain things that would spoil the human fruit. But some—as women will—did exactly as they pleased, and with this perverse result. And there were a number of such people in the land now ruled by Feirefiz and his noble Queen Secundille. The queen had heard reports of the Grail and of its guardian King Anfortas. In her own realm there were flowing streams of gems and mountains all of gold. And when she thought, "How can I learn more about this king to whom the Grail is subject?" she sent to him the most valuable gems, along with two of these monsters,

Cundrie and her brother—the latter of which sweet Anfortas then generously bestowed upon the Lady Orgeluse.*

And this Malcreatiure, kinsman of the plants and stars, riding on a runt of a nag that was lame in all four quarters, now came shouting insults at Gawain. "You fool! You are going to get such a beating for your service to this lady, you will wish you had done something else!"

Gawain grabbed him by his bristling hair and flung him from the nag, and when the bristles cut his hands, the Lady Orgeluse laughed. "I love to see you two in such a pet," she said. Malcreatiure remounted, and turning, they all rode back until they reached again the wounded knight, to whose hurt Gawain applied the plant.

"You have brought with you the lady through whose fault I lie here in pain," the man said. Then he asked Gawain to lift his lady to her horse, and while that was being done, leapt up and onto Gawain's own steed, and with a laugh the couple spurred away.

Orgeluse laughed too. "I took you first for a knight, then a doctor, and now I see a page. If you ever have to live by your wits, you have a lot to fall back on. You are still eager for my love?"

"Yes, my lady," came the answer. "If I could know your noble love, there is nothing I would hold dearer. Call me knight, squire, page, or villain—anything you like. Hurting me, you are damaging your own property, but since I am your vassal, that is your right."

The fellow who had ridden off meanwhile had returned for a parting gibe. "Gawain, I have now paid you for that beating you gave me when you took me to your uncle's house, and he kept me four weeks eating with the dogs!"

"Urians!" Gawain cried. "It is you! But I *saved* your life!"

The other laughed. "Have you never heard the old saying about saving someone's life? He will be your enemy forever!" And with that he wheeled and was gone.

Gawain turned to his lady. "It happened," he explained, "like this. A lady had been ravished of her maidenhood, and I, riding after this doer of the deed, overthrew him. He is the Prince of

---

* Dr. Goetz calls attention to Indian images of tusked gods and goddesses as probable sources of the idea that such creatures lived by the Ganges. For a Celtic parallel of this encounter of. Gawain with Orgeluse and the Malcreatiure, cf. *Occidental Mythology*, pp. 303–305.

Punturtoys. To save his life he surrendered and I brought him before the king, who condemned him to be hung: whereupon he appealed to me, who had guaranteed his life, and I begged both the king and the injured lady for clemency, which they granted—but only on the king's condition he should eat for a month from the trough with the palace dogs."

Then said the lady Orgeluse: "I shall see that he gets his deserts —not for what he has here done to you, but for what he did there to that lady.

> *"Wickedness must be repaid*
> *With blows of a knightly blade."*

She sent Malcreatiure off walking, and Gawain turned to the nag.

"Is my knight now going to ride on that?"

"I shall follow your orders," he replied.

"They may be slow in coming."

"I shall serve you, even so."

"Well, in that case, you seem to me stupid," she said. "You will soon quit the world of the glad and be joined to that of the sad."

"In joy or in sorrow, either way," he replied, "whether riding or afoot," and he turned to inspect his mount. The stirrup straps were of bark, and the saddle so frail he was afraid he might pull it to pieces: the animal, too, might break apart. So he led it, and himself carried both his shield and one of his spears.

The lady taunted: "Do you now bring merchandise to my land? First a medical man, now a tradesman! Watch out for tolls on the way!"

Her remarks he adored: it was such a pleasure just to watch her lovely mouth. And since loss and gain were the same in her, he was equally bound and made free.

"O love!" here exclaims the poet, "I should have thought you too old to play tricks of this childish sort! I should like to get Gawain out of this fix, but to save him would be to end his joy."

The two thus arrived before a castle that lay beyond a broad, swift, navigable stream; a castle full, Gawain could see, of ladies. He was now astride the lame nag and saw a knight approaching at a gallop.

Said his lady, "You see? Just as I promised! You will have chance enough now for disgrace. That chap is going to finish you, and if your breeches split when you tumble from your beast, will it not be a sight for those ladies?"

A ferryman had come at her beck, and she, on her steed, rode aboard, leaving Gawain to make out as he might.

It would be wrong to say that Lischoys Gwelljus was flying; but he was coming pretty fast, and Gawain thought: "How shall I receive him?" His decision was to let him come full tilt and stumble over the nag, then deal with him afoot, which is exactly how it worked. And the battle afoot was great, until at last Gawain—who was marvelous at wrestling—seized and flung the other to the ground, who when charged to surrender, refused.

"Better for me to be dead," he said, "than to live conquered."

And Gawain, thinking, "But why should I kill this man?" let him up, without guarantee.

They sat apart among the flowers until Gawain presently became aware that the other's horse was Gringuljete, his own, which had been ridden away only a while ago by Urians. He got up, mounted, rode about and, again dismounting, noticed that the animal's hock was now branded with a turtle dove, the emblem of the Grail. But Lischoys Gwelljus, having recovered his sword, was coming at him for another round, and the ladies watched while he again was thrown, again refused surrender, and again was let up by Gawain.

By this time the ferryman had returned. It was the custom of that place, he told Gawain, that the mount of the knight defeated should be given to him as ferry toll.

"*He* defeated *me*," answered Gawain, "when he first ran down my horse. You can have the nag. It's over there. But if you value a man as highly, you can have the knight himself who rode my own steed against me. I'll bring him to your door with my own hand."

The ferryman laughed. "In that case, you will surely be welcome," he said. And they fared thus all three to the farther shore, where the boatman said to Gawain, "You are now yourself the master of my house."

The good man's son attended Gawain's mount, and his daughter, Bene, Gawain. She conducted him to his room, where there were strewn on the floor fresh rushes, scattered with pretty flowers, and she helped to remove his armor. The son then brought in cushions, the father and mother entered, and all sat courteously to eat. When done, the table was removed and a bed was prepared by the daughter of snow-white sheets, a head pillow and a coverlet, over cushions.

v. Second Intermezzo: The Secularization of Myth

Gawain had now passed from the sphere of earthly adventure to a transcendental yonder shore, which his poet Wolfram was to associate with the magic of the mystic East; and as Heinrich Zimmer has made evident in his important, as well as delightful, comparative study of a series of Oriental and Occidental tales, *The King and the Corpse*,[15] there is indeed a correspondence both in incident and in sense, between the adventures of Arthur's knights and those of the great and little heroes of the Orient, even of the Buddha himself; and, by analogy, the Gnostic and other heretical versions of the miracles of Christ.

One of the most remarkable things about Wolfram is that in his development of the Grail romance he was already aware of these unorthodox analogies and could make use of them; as in his unprecedented assimilation of the Grail to both the philosophers' stone and the Ka'aba. Moreover, he applied his interpretations consciously to an altogether *secular* mythology, of men and women living for *this* world, not "that," pursuing earthly, human, and humane (i.e., in Wolfram's terms, "courtly") purposes, and supported in their spiritual tasks not by a supernatural grace dispensed by way of sacraments but by the *natural* grace of individual endowment and the worldly virtue of loyalty in love. That is what gives to his work its epochal significance as the first example in the history of world literature of a *consciously developed secular Christian myth*. As the great modern poet (perhaps the greatest of our century) William Butler Yeats pointed out in his strangely inspired revelation of an orderly destiny, fate, or *wyrd* made manifest in history, *A Vision:*

Throughout the German *Parsifal* there is no ceremony of the Church, neither Marriage nor Mass nor Baptism, but instead we discover that strangest creation of romance or of life, "the love trance." Parsifal in such a trance, seeing nothing before his eyes but the image of his absent love, overcame knight after knight, and awakening at last looked amazed upon his dinted sword and shield; and it is to his lady and not to God or the Virgin that Parsifal prayed upon the day of battle, and it was his lady's soul, separated from her entranced or sleeping body, that went beside him and gave him victory.[16]

In that parody of spiritual effort represented in the Good Friday excursion of the old aristocrat and his family—barefoot, yet with their pet dogs trotting at their side and entire household behind— there is a delicious strain of irony; yet the poet allows this shallow domestic comedy to affect profoundly the sentiments of his *actual* spiritual pilgrim: the knight in armor, not as pilgrim clad, who, cut off from the world for nigh onto five years, had been riding on a really significant spiritual adventure.

"And when you fast, do not look dismal, like the hypocrites, for they disfigure their faces that their fasting may be seen by men. Truly, I say to you, they have their reward. But when you fast, anoint your head and wash your face, that your fasting may not be seen by men but by your Father who is in secret; and your Father who sees in secret will reward you" (Matthew 6:16–18).

The pious pilgrim for a day told the actual knightly saint to seek absolution for his sins from the hermit down the road; yet Trevrizent was a layman, not a priest. He had never been ordained. In his forest retreat, in fact, he was not even attending Mass or otherwise partaking of the sacraments. Nor was that strange neurotic lover of a corpse, Sigune: "She heard no Mass," Wolfram declares, "yet her whole life was a kneeling." [17] She was fed in her abstracted state from the bounty of the Grail,[18] which itself received its power from a dove that on Good Friday annually flew from heaven with a wafer, which it placed upon the stone: [19] a sign substantial of God's love, not derived from the sacrament of the altar, but directly from the sphere of grace itself. And Trevrizent defined that sphere in terms rather of a psychological than of a sacramental order, as corresponding—and responding reciprocally—to the human sentiments of hate, love, and loyalty, in the mysteries of Hell, Heaven, and the Crucifixion. The Crucifixion he interpreted, furthermore, in accord with Abelard, as the freely rendered signal of God's love, to move our hearts, so that He might fill, and thus redeem, our lives.* And accordingly, the knight Parzival's conversion (not reconversion to his mother's image of God, for that, in his heart, was dead) † occurred on the festival of the Crucifixion, Good Friday; but there was no churchly sacrament, no Mass, no proper confession or eucharistic communion; only a turning of Parzival's heart from hate and mistrust, inspired first by the mock pilgrims, and confirmed by the unordained hermit Trevrizent's psychologically pointed retelling of the old tales "as new."

To quote again from the commentary of Gottfried Weber:

It is not true, as Parzival had supposed before his encounter with Trevrizent, that God can be understood in courtly terms, measured by courtly standards, and conceived of as a kind of supreme knight, who can be expected to render assistance to those of his own social set, according to the rules of courtly life. . . . Parzival's thought that he might somehow alleviate the sufferings of the Grail Castle through a performance of external knightly deeds was thus shown by Trevrizent to have been a cruelly naïve mistake.[21]

It is to be recalled that during Wolfram's lifetime the Abbot Joachim of Floris (c. 1145–1202) was publishing those prophecies over which James Joyce's hero Stephen Dedalus pored as a boy "in the stagnant bay of Marsh's library," [22] according to which there were to be, in all, three ages of humanity (Figure 54): the first, following a dark preludium from the time of Adam to Moses, the "Age of the Father" (of the Mosaic Law and Israel); the second, the "Age of the Son" (the Gospel and the Church); and the last (to commence about the year 1260), the "Age of the Holy Spirit," when the authority of Rome was to dissolve and the world become an earthly Paradise of saints communing directly with God.[23] Saint Francis too was a prominent figure of this time (1186–1226), and, as noticed in *Occidental Mythology*, was thought by many to have marked the start of Joachim's final period through the founding of his order of friars. In Wolfram's work Trevrizent and Sigune represent this almost Indian ideal of the for-

* Supra, pp. 19–20.
† Compare the problem of Stephen Dedalus in *A Portrait of the Artist as a Young Man* and *Ulysses,* culminating in the latter.[20]

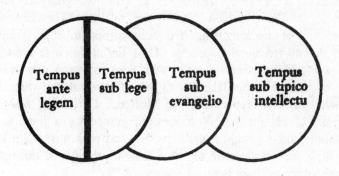

Figure 54. The Ages of the World (Joachim of Floris); c. 1200 A.D.

est saint, which Parzival is to surpass, however, as Christ surpassed the Baptist [24] and the Buddha his teachers, Arada and Udraka.[25]

For, though wakened by Trevrizent to a new understanding of spirituality, Parzival was not content to rest bound by the rules that up to that time had prevailed (according to his teacher) in relation to the Grail quest, namely: 1. that no one who had failed the adventure would be given a second chance; and 2. that no one consciously striving for it could ever achieve the Grail. As he had once departed from his worldly teacher, Gurnemanz, so would he now from Trevrizent. And as the Old Law was transcended—"the veil of the temple was rent" [26]—through Christ's passion, so through Parzival's, a new age, of neither a chosen people nor an authorized church, but of authentic individuals, fulfilled right here on earth in truth, loyalty, and love, was to be gospeled in the winning of the Grail. Trevrizent's Joachimite hermitage, on one hand, and the love grotto of Tristan (no less removed from the world), on the other, stand exactly for the two poles between which Wolfram's Parzival was to pass "through the middle." And his counterplayer in this passage was to be the worldly, sterling character Gawain, supporting him throughout through a series of parallel, though less exalted, exploits of his own.

Both knights were engaged in adventures announced by the self-same Loathly Damsel: adventures of enchantment and disenchantment, of a type well known to fairy lore. For example, as Professor William A. Nitze has recognized in his Grail study already cited,[27] there is in *The Arabian Nights* the tale of "The Ensorceled Prince": a young king who had been turned to stone from the waist downward by the sorcery of his unfaithful wife consorting with a black magician. His city with its population also was enchanted, turned into a lake full of fish of four colors: white, blue, yellow, and red (respectively the Moslems, Christians, Jews, and Magians of his realm). A fisherman, guided by a jinni to that spellbound lake, caught four of its fish and presented them to his own king, who undertook to solve their mystery, and through his adventure the enchantment was dissolved.[28]

In *The Hero with a Thousand Faces* I have shown that myths and wonder tales of this kind belong to a general type, which I have called "The Adventure of the Hero," that has not changed in essential form throughout the documented history of mankind: 1. A hero ventures forth from the world of common day into a region of supernatural wonder (in the present instances, regions under enchantment); 2. fabulous forces are there encountered and a decisive victory is won (the enchantments are dispelled); 3. the hero comes back from this mysterious adventure with the power to bestow boons on his fellow man.[29] In Wolfram's *Parzival* the boon is to be the inauguration of a new age of the human spirit: of *secular* spirituality, sustained by self-responsible individuals acting not in terms of general laws supposed to represent the will or way of some personal god or impersonal eternity, but each in terms of his own developing realization of worth. Such an idea is distinctly— and uniquely—European. It is the idea represented in Schopenhauer's "intelligible" character; * the old Germanic *wyrd,*† a life responsible to itself, to its own supreme experiences and expectations of value, realized through trials in truth, loyalty, and love, and by example redounding, then, to the inspiration of others to like achievement.

In the long course of our survey of the mythologies of mankind we have encountered nothing quite like this. The Indian notion of *sva-dharma,* "one's own duty," suggests comparison: "Better is one's own dharma, imperfectly performed, than the dharma of an-

* Supra, p. 35.
† Supra, pp. 121–22 and 139–40.

other, performed to perfection," states the *Bhagavad Gītā*.[30]
However, the idea of duty there is of the duties of one's caste, as
defined by the timeless (supposed to be timeless) Indian social
order. The Westerner reading such a text might think of duties self-
imposed, self-discovered, self-assumed: a vocation elected and realized. That is not the Oriental idea. Nor is the Oriental "person"
the same as ours. "Even as a person casts off worn-out clothes and
puts on others that are new, so the indwelling being casts off worn-
out bodies and enters into others that are new." [31] The "indwelling being" is the reincarnating monad; and the aim of a well-lived
lifetime is not to realize the unique possibilities of its temporal embodiment, but on the contrary, to achieve such indifference to this
body and its limitations, potentialities, and vicissitudes, that,
"completely devoid of the sense of 'I' and 'mine,' one attains
peace." [32] One attains "release," from the destiny of this body
and its deluding attachments to this world; and the reincarnating
monad then dissolves, as Ramakrishna says, "like a salt doll that
has walked into the ocean": [33] the ocean of the Cosmic Self
(*brahmātman*), which is at once the nothing and the all. Likewise
in Buddhism—even in the Mahayana of Japan—it will be long and
in vain that one seeks for anything like the European sense of
wyrd. Carl Jung has made the point in his distinction between the
"Self" as understood in Eastern thought and the "self" in his own
science of individuation. "In Eastern texts," he writes, "the 'Self'
represents a purely spiritual idea, but in Western psychology the
'self' stands for a totality which comprises instincts, physiological
and semi-physiological phenomena": [34] exactly the "garment," in
other words, that the "reincarnating monad" puts on and casts off.
Schopenhauer's "intelligible character" might be likened to this
"indweller of the body," and since he too sees the ultimate aim of
life in a denial of the will, there is much in his philosphy that can
be compared with Hindu-Buddhist thought. However, when he
states in so many words that "every human being represents an altogether unique Platonic Idea," he writes as a Western man.

The arts devoted to the representation of the idea of humanity [he continues] have as their concern, therefore, besides
the rendition of beauty as a quality of the species "Man,"
equally that of rendering the character of the individual, which
is what, properly, we call *character*. And this must be rendered,

furthermore, not as something merely accidental, altogether particular to the individual in his uniqueness, but as an especially stressed aspect of the idea of humanity, so appearing just in this individual, and to the revelation of which his portrayal is to serve. . . . Neglect of the character of the species for that of the individual yields a caricature, and of the individual for the species, insignificance.[35]

As expressed in our Western arts of portraiture, in a Rembrandt, in a Titian, this experience of the metaphysical dimension of the individual as a value is set forth in a manner unmatched in this world history of art; and in Dante's work as well, the souls disposed in Hell, Purgatory, and Paradise retain for eternity their characters exhibited on earth. For here the individuality is not (as in the Orient) a mere figment of illusion, to be analyzed away and dissolved at last, but a substantial entity in itself, to be realized, brought to flower. And the adventure of each, so interpreted, will consist in the following of a summons *away* from "the fixed and the set fast" (Goethe's phase) * of the world conceived as law, to a "becoming," the Purgatory, of an individual life moving toward its own proper end, its *wyrd,* or, in Dante's terms, its own appropriate place among the petals of the Paradisal golden rose.

Thus in the *Parzival* of Wolfram it is precisely in the general, authorized, socially ordered life-ways of his time that the obstacles are recognized to that solitary journey to fulfillment, that lonely, dangerous quest, which is the only way to an individual life. And in Thomas Mann's *The Magic Mountain,* as well, the call to adventure is to a land of no return, like Gawain's, that is absolutely removed from every law and notion of value of the "flatland" (as Mann calls it): the business-land, the newspaper-and-ledger-land, of the hero's native city.

In the first chapter of *Ulysses,* the initiating "call to adventure" is served by a little old Irishwoman who comes at breakfast time to bring the milk to the triad of the book's young heroes—Buck Mulligan, Stephen Dedalus, and their English companion, Haines—who are sitting at table in their symbolic (and now world-famous) Martello Tower on the shore of Dublin Bay. She was unaware of her symbolic role as she entered the circular, ill-lighted room.

* Supra, p. 383.

—How much, sir? asked the old woman.

—A quart, Stephen said.

He watched her pour into the measure and thence into the jug rich white milk, not hers. Old shrunken paps. She poured again a measureful and a tilly. Old and secret she had entered from a morning world, maybe a messenger.[36]

She could not speak her own language, Gaelic, but the Britisher, Haines, could. He had deprived her of her speech as well as land, and has come now to collect her folklore for an English publication. Stephen's sense, at that moment, as he watched, of the poverty of his land and people, corresponds, according to one layer of Joyce's multilayered allegory, to the call, in Homer's *Odyssey,* brought by the goddess Athene to Odysseus's son, Telemachus, to go forth in search of his father and clear his heritage of the usurpers, the suitors, who were blithely consuming his goods and even threatening his life.

In *The Magic Mountain,* on the other hand, Hans Castorp's summons to adventure emerges from the heart of the hero himself, or rather, his lungs, his failing body, by way of the orders of his family physician. He had begun to come home from his shipping firm, Tunder and Wilms, "looking rather paler than a man of his blond, rosy type should," and his family doctor, Heidekind, finally advised a change of air, a few weeks in the high mountains. His cousin, Joachim Ziemssen, was already in Switzerland, at Davos. Why not, then, visit Joachim? And so, hardly recking to what whirling mountain of Klingsor his destiny had summoned him, he left his home on the Baltic for a season—three weeks, he thought—in the Land of No Return.[37]

At the opening of the *Parzival,* the summons to adventure was conveyed by the flashing armor of the knights whom the rustic mistook naively for angels. Traditionally all the fabulous powers encountered by heroes in their spiritual adventures were personified as such supernaturals. In tales told for amusement, of course, the personifications were not meant to be taken seriously. The ensorceled prince never lived. In the bibles of the world, on the other hand, such fantasies are advanced, generally, as "facts": in the legend of Moses' talk with God, for example, or Christ's harrowing of Hell. The important thing about Wolfram's Grail is that, though his tale is for amusement and its characters and episodes are frankly fantasies, they are nevertheless understood to be true in a timeless, trans-historic dimension. As in esoteric rites the mythic forms are displayed not in the crude sense of supernatural "facts," but as signs revelatory of insights, so here: the adventures, once of Celtic gods, are presented as paradigms of secular human experiences in a depth dimension. They are represented, however —in contrast to the older, esoteric, ritualized approach to initiation—as inherent in the episodes of men's normal daily lives, displayed for those with eyes to see in the sights of common day. As in the words of the Gnostic Thomas Gospel: "The Kingdom of the Father is spread upon the earth and men do not see it." [38] Poets see it. That is the faculty of poets. And great biographers and novelists have always recognized that, in the lives of people growing up, initiations transpire through the revelations of chance, according to the readiness of the psyche. Beneath the accidental surface effects of this world sit—as of yore—the gods. Their ageless order of the archetypes of myth, "the grave and constant in human sufferings," can be discerned through all time and tide. The entire course of a lifetime is thus a rite of initiation and can be experienced as such. And in the works of both Joyce and Mann, as well as of Chrétien de Troyes and Wolfram, this inherent relevance of myth to biography is indicated by just such juxtapositions of fantasy and fact as those of the young Parzival's thought of angels when he saw the shining knights, Stephen's thought of Mother Ireland while watching the little old woman with the milk, and Mann's comparison of Castorp's mountain journey with a visit to the world of King Death.

In the legend of Parzival, when the boy's imagination had been roused by the message of his angels, he left everything of his childhood—his mother and his play—behind him and through a dreamlike cycle of adventures, among which the most important were his marriage to Condwiramurs and his first, unwitting visit to the Castle of the Grail, he developed gradually to young manhood as the paramount knight of his day and was linked then by Gawain, the gentle, most noble knight of the world, to King Arthur's company and court, his worldly goal. But then, immediately, a second, more mysterious adventure was announced: what Jung has termed the task of life's second half.[39] The aim of the first half, properly, is to reach maturity as an adult functioning responsibly in the context of a society, and in Parzival's case society was represented by Arthur's court. At the moment of fulfillment there, however, the claims begin to be heard of what Joyce terms "the uncreated conscience" of one's race,[40] an inward world of potentials unrealized in the visible order of one's time; and accordingly, the messenger, the summoner to this more inward quest is not, like the angel of the first task, a normal figure of the light world: in the case of Parzival, not a shining knight but an apparition with the muzzle of a boar, the boar of the wound of Adonis, the same pigfaced Daughter of the King of the Land of Youth who in the fairytale appeared to Oisin.* And the adventure itself, in accord with the character of its announcer, required a passage beyond the known bounds and forms of time, space, and causality to a domain of vision, where time and eternity were at one: in Parzival's case, the Grail Castle, and in Gawain's—announced at the same weird hour by the same weird sister of night—the Château Merveil.

In the brothel scene of *Ulysses*, Bloom, the elder of the two heroes of that work (he is thirty-eight, Stephen, twenty-two),[41] is in his own imagination transformed into a pig by the massive whoremistress Bella Cohen.

> (*Her eyes are deeply carboned. She has a sprouting moustache. Her olive face is heavy, slightly sweated and fullnosed, with orangetainted nostrils. She has large pendant beryl eardrops. . . . She glances around her at the couples. Then her eyes rest on Bloom with hard insistence. Her large fan winnows wind toward her heated face, neck and embonpoint. Her falcon eyes glitter.*)
>
> THE FAN
> (*Flirting quickly, then slowly.*) Married, I see.
> BLOOM
> Yes. . . . Partly, I have mislaid . . .
> THE FAN
> (*Half opening, then closing*) And the missus is master. Petticoat government.
> BLOOM
> (*Looks down with a sheepish grin.*) That is so.
> THE FAN
> (*Folding together, rests against her eardrop.*) Have you forgotten me?

* Supra, p. 127 and *Primitive Mythology*, pp. 432–34.

BLOOM

Nes. Yo.

THE FAN

(*Folded akimbo against her waist.*) Is me her was you
dreamed before? Was then she him you us since knew? Am all
them and the same now we?
(*Bella approaches, gently tapping with the fan.*)

Presently she is transformed before him, becoming in his sight a
male; he is beginning to feel female. The sexes are reversed. Bella
has become Bello, and Bloom is now called "she":

BELLO

Down! (*He taps her on the shoulder with his fan.*) Incline
feet forward! Slide left foot one pace back. You will fall. You
are falling. On the hands down!

BLOOM

(*Her eyes upturned in the sign of admiration, closing.*)
Truffles!
(*With a piercing epileptic cry she sinks on all fours, grunting,
snuffling, rooting at his feet, then lies, shamming dead with eyes
shut tight, trembling eyelids, bowed upon the ground in the attitude of most excellent master. . . . Bloom creeps under the
sofa and peers out through the fringe.*) [42]

This whole unsavory adventure of the night had been foretold at
Bloom's breakfast time, at the hour, exactly, of the coming of the
little old woman with the milk to the younger hero, Stephen.
Bloom had decided to eat for his breakfast that morning a *pork
kidney*—and he a Jew!—to the purchase of which, he then went
out to the shop of a Jewish pork-butcher, where he found on the
counter a pile of cut sheets, announcing the project of a Zion-
ist center in Jerusalem. He read the advertisement. "A barren
land," he mused, "bare waste. Volcanic lake, dead sea: no fish,
weedless, sunk deep in the earth. . . . A dead sea in a dead land,
grey and old. . . ." [43] And as Stephen's heart, that same hour,
was being awakened to a sense of a land become waste, so Leopold's. The two were to wander that day separately, in separate, un-
defined quests, like Parzival and Gawain, to come together at last in
a brothel. Bloom folded the page into his pocket, feeling old. Cold
oils slid along his veins, chilling his blood. "Well, I am here now,"
he thought. "Morning mouth, bad images. Got up the wrong side

of the bed. Must begin again those Sandow's exercises. On the hands down." [44]

Like Bloom, the noble ladies' knight Gawain, Parzival's elder by some sixteen years,* was defenseless, absolutely, against women. We have seen him ensnared with equal ease by the innocence of Obilot and seductiveness of the sister of King Vergulaht. Both those adventures were of the normal daylight world. However, when he went on past the mock pietà at the tree of the wounded knight Urians, he entered the field of a stronger, very different spiritual force. Urians had warned him not to go on—as Settembrini in *The Magic Mountain* was to warn Hans Castorp (a type altogether different from Gawain, as well as from Bloom, yet embarked in his own phlegmatic way on the same adventurous path). Like Castorp to the Magic Mountain and Leopold Bloom into Nighttown, Sir Gawain pressed on; and he had not ridden far up the magic mountain of Logroys when there, by a spring, sat absolutely, unquestionably, the woman of his life.

So too in the mountain adventure of Hans Castorp:

The young marine engineer was sitting at table in the large institutional dining room, when a most irritating event occurred, an event such as had occurred before, and always onward into the meal: the slamming of a glass door. It occurred this time during the fish course (and the fish being the animal of Venus and Good Friday, this coincidence, like many in the book, is of more than accidental force).

Hans Castorp [we now read] gave an exasperated shrug and angrily resolved that this time he really must find out who was doing that. . . . He turned his whole upper body to the left [the side of the heart, the female, and the perilous "left-hand path"] and opened wide his bloodshot eyes.

It was a lady there passing through the room, a woman, or rather, a young woman of middle stature, in a white sweater and colorful skirt, with red-blond hair, simply wound in braids around her head. Hans Castorp caught no more than a glimpse of her profile, practically nothing. She moved without a sound, in wonderful contrast to the noisiness of her entrance, and with a peculiar gliding step, her head a little thrust forward, proceeded to the last table on the left, at right angles to the veranda door, the "good" Russian table, namely; and as she

* See supra, p. 460.

walked she had one hand in the pocket of her close-fitting wool sweater, while the other she raised to the back of her head, supporting and ordering her hair. . . .[45]

We need not go on: the novel is readily available and certainly to be read, one of the five or six greatest of the century. My only remark at this point is that in the *Odyssey* both Circe and Calypso are described with braided tresses,[46] and that the engineer Hans Castorp's declaration of love to this Eurasian nymph with her Kirghiz eyes, Madame Clavdia Chauchat by name, is to be found in the chapter entitled "Walpurgisnacht," where a lively game takes place to see who can draw blindfolded the best outline of a pig. Madame Chauchat of the braided locks is Castorp's "Lady of Destiny," as is the Lady Orgeluse Gawain's. Each—literally—is an invitation to death and corresponds exactly to those guiding, shining nymphs in the cycle of the sacramental bowl of Figure 3, by which the eligible neophyte without fear is initiated into the knowledge (*gnosis, bodhi*) beyond death.

In C. G. Jung's terminology, such women, shining with the light of the sun, are *anima* figures, the *anima* being for the male, he states, *the archetype of life itself*,[47] life's promise and allure. In Sanskrit, the term is *śakti* ("power"): the wife is her husband's *śakti;* the sweetheart the lover's; and the goddess the god's.[48] "The *anima* lives," writes Jung, "beyond all categories, and can therefore dispense with blame as well as with praise." [49] "This image," he writes again, "is 'My Lady Soul.' " [50] And as the great archetypes of myth are personified variously in differing local traditions (the resurrected god as Dumuzi, Osiris, Christ, or the Aztec Quetzalcoatl), so in the province of individual psychology the *anima* embodiments of Mr. B. cannot be those of Mr. A. "Every mother and every beloved is forced to become the carrier and embodiment of this omnipresent and ageless image," states Jung, "which corresponds to the deepest reality in a man." [51]

As in Dante's moment of "aesthetic arrest" on first beholding Beatrice,* so in the case of Gawain: when he beheld, with a shock of recognition, the reflection of the moving principle of his life mirrored as by magic in the form of a woman sitting by a spring—not simply *any* woman but exactly and fully this only *one* —the order and sense of his lifelong service to love was irreversibly

* Supra, p. 68.

transformed. A moment of psychological readiness must be presumed to have been attained, and at the critical instant, lo!—the indelible imprint was impressed and the life thereafter committed.[52] No longer in quest, for his object now was found, Gawain abruptly passed from the sphere of female forms merely "there," in the field of space and time, to a depth experience of this only one as "forever"; and his spiritual effort thenceforth was to be to hold to that experience of his own whole meaning as "out there": to hold to it in loyalty and love, beyond both fear and all desire for distraction—as strongly confirmed in that outward reference of his being, that "immovable point," as the Buddha inward, beyond fear and desire, beneath the Bo-tree. For psychologically, as well as mythologically, the sense of such a female by a spring is of an apparition of the abyss: psychologically, the unconscious; mythologically, the Land below Waves, Hell, Purgatory, or Heaven. She is a portion of oneself, one's destiny, or, as Schopenhauer states in his meditation on Fate,* one's secret intention for oneself. Rachel at the well, in the legend of Jacob; Zipporah with her sisters at the well, in the legend of the young Moses; [53] in the world of Stephen Dedalus, the girl wading in the stream played such a part,† and in that of Bloom, Molly, his ample spouse, the sum of all the nymphs and matrons, memories and prospects, of his life.

"She is the man's solace for all the bitterness of life," states Jung in discussion of the *anima,* this perilous image of Woman. "And, at the same time, she is the great illusionist, the seductress, who draws him into life with her Maya—and not only into life's reasonable and useful aspects, but into its frightful paradoxes and ambivalences where good and evil, success and ruin, hope and despair, counterbalance one another. Because she is his greatest danger she demands from a man his greatest, and if he has it in him she will receive it." [54]

In a rather amazing speech, delivered in Vienna on the occasion of Freud's eightieth birthday, May 6, 1936, Thomas Mann discoursed on both the psychology and the mystery of such personifications of fate. He was then at work on *Joseph and His Brothers,* of which he had just completed Volume III, *Joseph in Egypt*:

* Supra, pp. 341–43.
† Supra, pp. 68–69.

In Volume I, *The Tales of Jacob,* he had introduced Rachel, his
heroine, standing by a desert well, and described her, both before
and after marriage, as her husband's *śakti-anima.* In Volume II,
Young Joseph, the focus of the adolescent *anima* fixation of Rachel's very handsome son was the beauty of his own body, reminiscent of that of his departed mother; and on a fateful day when he
was flaunting his father's special gift to him, his mother's wedding
veil (his "coat of many colors"), he was tossed by his indignant
brothers into a second well—through which he passed, in Volume
III, into Egypt, to encounter there, in Potiphar's wife, an *anima*
figure of such scope that he was unable to meet its challenge and
ended in the Pharaoh's jail: once again in the pit of his own (and
as Mann tells the tale, also Israel's) unconscious.

Now one could have thought that this mighty novelist, on the
eightieth birthday of the most influential psychologist of his time,
might have seized upon the occasion—with the old man there before him—to acknowledge Freud's influence on his own creative
life. But no! The leading theme of his eulogy was that, though he
recognized strains of relationship between his own ideas and those
of the great psychologist—deriving, as he believed, from their
common spiritual descent from the masters of German romanticism (Goethe, Novalis, Schopenhauer, Nietzsche, and the rest)—
he had discovered the works of Freud only after his own ideas had
been placed before the world in his earliest novel and short stories,
Buddenbrooks, "Tristan," "Tonio Kröger," and so on; while in his
writing of the Joseph novels the ideas by which he was being most
fruitfully inspired were of C. G. Jung ("an able but somewhat un-
grateful scion of the Freudian school," as he termed him); particularly Jung's application of analytical evidence (as Mann expressed
the idea) "to construct a bridge between Occidental thought and
Oriental esoteric," reuniting Freudian clinical psychology with its
antecedents, not only in Schopenhauer and Nietzsche, but also in
Oriental wisdom and that *philosophia perennis* which had been for
millenniums and forever both implicit and explicit in the universal
pictorial script of myth. And the master novelist brought forward
in evidence to this point, the "pregnant and mysterious idea" (as
he called it) developed by Schopenhauer in his paper "On an Apparent Intention in the Fate of the Individual" as representing (to
use Mann's words again) "the most profound and mysterious

point of contact between Freud's natural-scientific world and Schopenhauer's philosophic one."

"Precisely," said Mann in summation of this theme, "as in a dream it is our own will which unconsciously appears as inexorable objective destiny, everything in it proceeding out of ourselves and each of us being the secret theater-manager of his own dream; so also in reality, the great dream which a single essence, the will itself, dreams with us all, our fate, may be the product of our inmost selves, of our wills, and we are actually ourselves bringing about what seems to be happening to us." [55]

Mann then quoted the words of Jung in his "significant introduction" to *The Tibetan Book of the Dead* (to which astounding work Jung himself had declared he owed "not only many stimulating ideas and discoveries, but also many fundamental insights"): [56] "It is so much more straightforward, more dramatic, impressive, and therefore more convincing, to see how things happen to me, than to observe how I make them happen." [57]

"The giver of all given conditions resides in ourselves," declared Mann, again quoting Jung.[58] "All phenomena merely arise from false notions in the mind," the Buddhist sage Ashvaghosha had said two thousand years before; [59] and Schopenhauer: "Life accompanies the will as inseparably as the shadow accompanies the body; and if will exists, so will life, the world, exist." [60]

It is possible, even probable—indeed, I would say, it is evident —that our poet Wolfram von Eschenbach also had such an idea in mind: at least in relation to the apparition of the Grail Castle in Parzival's way and the Lady Orgeluse in Gawain's. These events are clearly functions of the states of readiness of the knights. But all the other episodes are too. In fact, this correlation between will and appearance, readiness and experience, subjectivity and object —as in dream—is exactly what gives to mythic tales their quality of revelation. And one of the most amazing things about modern thought is the way in which it is coming back—by one route or another—to this deeply mysterious primordial sense of life in this world as (in Schopenhauer's words) "a vast dream, dreamed by a single being." *

The dreamer Gawain, however, seems not to have been as aware as his poet that it was he himself who had made the fas-

* Supra, p. 344.

cinating Lady Orgeluse appear beside that spring on the whirling mountain, as the mirrored shape, in the form of a woman, of the moving principle of his life. It was so much more dramatic and impressive to see her as one who had just happened to be sitting waiting for him in that place! But he now was hers and she his; though there were still to be trials, many trials, and of increasing force, to test his willingness to let go of himself. She had withdrawn him in service to her love from the world of those who were merely of this world. As we have seen, when he had met his first mortifying tests, he was ferried to the yonder shore, to which his lady had already passed, and there, in the ferryman's home, within sight of her Marvelous Castle itself, he slept.

In the imagery of alchemy, the elementary substance to be sublimated has been now placed in the *vas*, the retort, for the fires of great trials, and hermetically sealed.

VI. The Castle of Marvels

BOOK XI: THE PERILOUS BED

When, at the first light of day, he woke, Gawain noticed that the wall of his room had many windows, and, rising to enjoy the birdsong of dawn, was amazed to remark that the ladies over in the castle were all still moving about, awake. He had entered the realm of those tireless forces that operate without thought of fatigue in nature and the psyche; the same to which Goethe's Faust descended with a magic key in hand to release the shade of Helen of Troy: "The Realm of the Mothers." There as Goethe tells:

> *Göttinnen thronen hehr in Einsamkeit,*
> *Um sie kein Ort, noch weniger eine Zeit;*
> *Von ihnen sprechen ist Verlegenheit.*
> *Die Mütter sind es!* [61]

Gawain was to find here his mother, grandmother, and two sisters, none of whom, however, would recognize him; for they and all about them were under an enchantment, bound, like the figures of a dream, by laws of a strange twilight compulsion, the force of which Gawain was to break. The same Loathly Damsel had announced the Grail adventure and this: the two enchantments were reciprocal. Parzival's task it would be to release the Grail King and people of his realm; Gawain's, the Lady Orgeluse and the bound folk of her Castle of Marvels: Gawain, therefore, was on the female side, as Parzival on the male, of the same Waste Land spell of life in death. And as Christ, crucified, descended into Hell to break the law of Hell and release the souls of the just from that same eternal death to which Dante thirteen centuries later condemned Paolo and Francesca, Tristan and Isolt, Lancelot and Guinevere, so these two supreme knights of the gospel of loyalty in love were to renew for their day (at least in Wolfram's view) the life-releasing redemptive lesson—*O felix culpa!*—of Paul's message in Romans 11:32. *

"O certe necessarium Adae peccatum," we read in the prayers to be recited Holy Saturday at the blessing of the Paschal candle: "O truly needful sin of Adam, which was blotted out by the death of Christ! O happy fault, which deserved to possess such and so great a Redeemer! This is the night of which it is written: And the night shall be as light as the day; and the night is my light in my enjoyments." [62]

Gawain, gazing from the window—between night and day, as it were—into Hamlet's "undiscovered country from whose bourn no traveler returns," [63] was at precisely that point in the archetypal ordeal of death and transformation where Christ at Gethsemane prayed that the ordeal before him might be withdrawn; and his disciples slept, for in them "the spirit indeed was willing, but the flesh was weak." [64] In Gawain the flesh too would have to be willing; for it was himself alone who was about to endure the ordeal. He gazed long at those ladies, wondering, then thought, "I shall honor them by going back to sleep"; and when again he woke, he found the daughter of the ferryman sitting by his bedside on the carpet.

"God keep you, little lady," he said, and she answered that both she and her family wished he might stay and be their lord. But when he asked why all those ladies were in the castle, with a look of horror she burst into tears. "Oh, don't ask me that!" she cried. "Ask anything else!" At which point her father came in, who, when he saw his daughter in that horrified state and his night's guest still abed, supposing that something else had happened,

* Supra, p. 259.

reassured her. "Bene, don't cry. When this sort of thing happens in play, it may at first make you angry, but soon it will be all right."

Gawain assured him nothing had occurred ("though," as Wolfram states, "if it had, the father would not have been angry"), then asked again about the ladies, and he too, with a cry of anguish, pleaded with his guest not to insist. Gawain, however, did insist and finally was answered: "You are in the Land of Marvels, at the Castle of Marvels, about to enter the Bed of Marvels, where your end is going to be death."

"Then," said Gawain, undaunted, "you must give me your advice."

"If God lets it appear that you are not doomed," the ferryman told him, "you will become the lord of this land and all those ladies, with many a knight besides, who are held here by enchantment. However, should you turn at this point and depart, you would suffer no dishonor: for fame is already abundantly yours from your defeat of Lischoys Gwelljus, who arrived here questing for the Grail." [65]

Gawain stood firm, and his host then offered him his own shield. "My shield," he said, "is sound." Then he told Gawain that on arriving at the castle he would see a merchant at the gate with a bounty of marvelous wares. He was to buy something, leave his horse with the man, and proceed to the Bed of Marvels. "And never let go of this shield or of your sword; for though you have known adventures before, they will have been child's play to this. When you think your troubles over, they will have just begun."

The brave knight mounted; the boatman's daughter wept; and at the gate Gawain did as told. The merchant's booth was high and spacious, and not all the gold of Baghdad would have paid the worth of its wares. "Sir, if you live," the merchant said to him, "everything here, I and all that I own, will be yours." He took charge of Gringuljete, and Gawain, going on, entered a great hall with a ceiling of many hues, like a peacock's tail. Many couches stood about, where the ladies had been sitting, all of whom, however, had withdrawn. He passed through and on into a chamber where he saw, in the middle of the floor, the Marvel Bed.

It stood on four wheels made of rubies on a floor of jasper, chrysolite, and sard, so smooth that he could scarcely keep his feet; and every time he tried to touch it, the bed darted from his reach—as Heinrich Zimmer has humorously said, "like a reluctant bride in rebellion against the embrace being forced upon her." [66] In desperation, heavy shield and all, the knight gave a great leap and landed directly in the bed's middle, whereupon, with the greatest speed anyone has ever seen, that irritating article of furniture began dashing, bumping back and forth, slamming into all four walls with such force the entire castle shook. Getting little rest in that bed, though lying on his back, Gawain covered himself with his shield and gave himself up to God. The noise subsided and the bed stood quiet in the middle of the floor. But Gawain remembered the warning.

Abruptly five hundred bolts from as many slings flew at him from all sides; next, arrows from as many crossbows struck and quivered in the shield. A hideous burly churl, garbed in a surcoat, bonnet, and pair of pantaloons, all of fishskin, rushed at him with a prodigious club—who, however, when the knight sat up, backed out with a curse and a great lion dashed into the chamber in his stead.* Gawain sprang to the floor with his shield, at which the lion struck so fiercely its talons stuck, and the knight sliced off that leg, which remained hanging there while the animal ran about on three, the floor becoming so wet with its blood Gawain could scarcely stand. Finally, with a prodigious pounce, the beast flew at Gawain, whose sword went through its chest, and it fell dead, with the warrior, dazed and bleeding from its blows, unconscious on its back.

Presently a maiden peered into the quiet room and her cry apprised the ladies of the condition of their knight. She tore a bit of sable from his gambeson, held it to his nose, and the hair a little stirred: he was alive. When water was brought, she forced her ring between his teeth and poured very slowly, watching. He revived and, giving thanks, begged her forgiveness for the unseemly state in which he had been found. "If you would not mention it to anyone," he said, "I would be grateful."

He had fifty wounds or more. The four hundred ladies of the castle were able, however, to restore him, chief among them being

---

* Like the fish, so is the lion a symbol of the power of the Goddess. See, for example, *Occidental Mythology*, p. 45, Figure 12.

his own grandmother, Queen Arnive, the mother of King Arthur, who had no idea who he was. She ordered a bed to be set for him by the fire, applied salves brought by the sorceress Cundrie from Munsalvaesche of the Grail, gave him an herb to make him sleep, and at nightfall brought him food. Noble ladies stood all about; he had never known such attendance. Yet, as he regarded them, every one of loveliest form, the only yearning in his heart was for his Orgeluse.

BOOK XII: THE KING OF THE WOOD

1.

The knight woke next morning in the greatest pain, not so much from his wounds as from the yearning in his heart; and he rose, donned the rich clothes set out for him, strolled from his room across the sumptuous hall, and climbed a winding stair at the end of it into a circular tower rising high above the roof, where he found an amazing pillar, wrought by sorcery. The whole tower had been brought from the lands of Feirefiz by the necromancer Clinschor. Its windows were of various gems; so too its roof and columns. And to Gawain it seemed that he could see in that marvelous central pillar all the lands round about, and the people there riding and walking, running or standing still. He sat down to watch, and had scarcely done so when the old queen, his grandmother, entered, accompanied by his mother, Sangive, and his two sisters, Itonje and sweet Cundrie,* none of whom, however, yet realized who he was.

"Sir," the old queen said, "you should be sleeping." She bade him kiss the ladies, which he did, and then he asked about the pillar. "No hammer can destroy it," he was told; "and its light shines for six miles around. It was stolen from Feirefiz's queen, Secundille, by the necromancer Clinschor."

As he gazed, he saw two riders approaching on the meadows where he had jousted with Lischoys the day before: a lady leading a knight. And when he realized who she was, her image passed through his eyes to his heart as swiftly and keenly as hellebore (the sneezing herb) into a nose.

"That is the Duchess of Logroys," the old queen said. "I won-

---

* Not the sorceress Cundrie of Munsalvaesche.

der who it is she has snared now! Why, it's Florant the Turkoyte! He's a valiant man, too strong for you now, with all your wounds unhealed."

Gawain got up, calling for his fighting gear, went below, and while fair eyes wept, mounted Gringuljete, scarcely holding his shield for the pain. He was ferried across by his friend, and when the Turkoyte came at him galloping, Gawain's well-aimed point met his visor and he fell, a colorful flower of knighthood spread upon the flowers of the earth. He pledged security, the ferryman took his horse, and the victor then turned gladly to his lady.

"That lion's paw in your shield is quite a sight," she said. "All those holes in it make you pretty proud, and those ladies up there think you wonderful. Well, go back to them! You would never dare what I have in store for you now—if you still have heart for my love."

This was to be her final test. She was about to reveal who she was. And to the modern reader, its accord with the Bronze Age rite discussed by Frazer in *The Golden Bough* will perhaps be a surprise; though (God knows!) after all that we have been through together in the way of exhibits of the archetypes of myth, it should be, rather, an expected satisfaction.

"You must bring me a wreath," the lady said, "from the branch of a certain tree. By that deed you will earn my praise, and if you then ask for my love, it will be yours."

Frazer in *The Golden Bough,* asked and resolved two questions; first: "Why had Diana's priest at Nemi, the King of the Wood, to slay his predecessor?" and second: "Why before doing so had he to pluck the branch of a certain tree which the public opinion of the ancients identified with Virgil's Golden Bough?" [67]

The priest at Nemi who had had to slay his predecessor was in the service of Diana as the Goddess Mother of Life. Her sanctuary was a grove about a lake where the object of veneration was an oak, of which the priest, the King of the Wood, was the consort and protector. The bough to be plucked was of the mistletoe (according to Frazer's view); a plant that grows aloft, on the limbs of trees, whence it was culled by the Druids for ritual use. It is green throughout the year and when plucked and dried turns golden, hence typifying the ever-living force personified in the priest himself. The man who plucked it came into possession of this force and, if he then could slay the one before him, became an eligible consort of the goddess. That the knight in the service of the Duchess of Logroys had to prove himself in this adventure speaks volumes for the authenticity of Wolfram's understanding of his symbols.

When the ladies of the Castle of Marvels saw their knight turn his steed to follow the duchess into the wood, they wept. "Alas!" the old queen sighed. "The Ford Perilous won't be healthy for those wounds." The couple, disappearing from view, rode along a road that was wide and straight into the beautiful grove known as Clinschor's wood, a stand of tamarisk trees, through which they continued to a great ravine filled with the roar of a mightily rushing torrent, beyond which the tree could be seen from which the wreath was to be culled.

"Sir, that tree," said the lady, "is guarded by the man who robbed me of my joy. Bring me a branch of it and never will knight have gained a greater reward than yours in the service of love. But you will have to force your mount to a mighty leap to clear the Perilous Ford."

Gawain galloped on, heard the terrible roar of water through its wide and deep ravine, dug his spurs into his horse's flanks, and with a vast spring nearly made it. The beast touched the farther bank with its front two feet, and the lady broke into tears when she saw the horse and rider fall. Gawain, though encumbered by his armor, yet contrived to pull himself ashore, then ran downstream to where Gringuljete was being whirled close to the bank and, catching the bridle, drew his mount to land, where the animal stood and shook itself dry. The knight mounted, rode to the tree, plucked the bough, and, when he had wreathed his helmet, saw a splendid knight riding toward him unarmed, wearing a bonnet of peacock plumes and a cloak of grass-green samite trimmed with ermine, so long it trailed the ground on both sides.

"Sir, I have not yielded my claim to that wreath," said the knight. He was King Gramoflanz of Rosche Sabins, who had sworn never to fight fewer than two knights at a time. "By the state of your shield I perceive that you have survived the Bed of Marvels. Were I not so friendly with Clinschor, I should have had to endure that too. He and I are the enemies of the Lady Orgeluse, whose noble husband, Cidegast, the Duke of Logroys, I killed; and I made her my captive, offering my lands, held her for a whole year; but she repaid my service with hate.* I tell you this, for I know that she has promised you her love, since you are here to seek my death."

The king told Gawain he would not battle him alone but asked instead a service. "I have here a token, a ring," he said; "for I have turned my thoughts from the duchess to a lady in the castle of which you are now the lord, and I would have you bring her this ring." He named Gawain's own sister Itonje, and when Gawain had given his word then said, "There is but one man in the world I would fight alone, and that man is Gawain; for his father treacherously killed mine."

To which the knight now bearing both the ring and the wreath responded: "Sir, it seems to me strange indeed that you should hope to gain a maid's love whose father you charge with treachery and brother you would slay. My name is Gawain."

"I am both glad and sad that he whom I hate with a hate unappeased is so noble a knight," the other answered; "pleased, though, that we shall fight. And since our fame will be increased if ladies are invited, I shall bring along fifteen hundred. You have those of the Castle of Marvels. Arthur's whole court, too, should be invited. Sir, we shall meet the sixteenth day from this, on the jousting field of Joflanz."

Gawain, with a great bound across the water, rode to Orgeluse with the bough, and she cast herself at his feet. "Sir," she said, "my love, I am not worthy of the risks I have asked."

He had won, but now became stern. "The shield of knighthood deserves respect and you have sinned against it. Here, lady, is the wreath, accept it. Never use your beauty again to bring disgrace to any knight. And if I am still to be mocked, I can do without your love."

She was in tears. "Sir, when I tell you of the sorrows of my heart, you will, I hope, forgive. Cidegast, my noble husband, was a unicorn of good faith.† He was my life; I, his heart—I lost him: slain by Gramoflanz. Sir, I beg you. How could I have given myself to anyone less the knight than he? These have been my tests, and you are gallant, you are gold."

Appeased, Gawain glanced about. "I have just pledged myself to

---

* Compare the case of Condwiramurs, supra, pp. 440–41.

† The unicorn was symbolic of purity in love and, as such, a figure of Christ.

meet your enemy. Unless death do me in, I shall put an end to his works. And now, my lady, my advice would be that you should here and now behave honorably. There is no one about. Grant your favor."

"In iron arms?" she answered. "I should hardly be moved to warmth. At the castle I shall not resist."

She was embraced in his iron arms. She wept, he lifted her to her mount, and as they rode she continued to weep. He asked her why.

"You are not the first," she answered, "through whom I have sought to kill Gramoflanz. There was a king once offered me his service, a young king named Anfortas. Though young, he was the lord of what all men most desire, and it was he who gave me that booth full of wares that stands before the castle gate. But in my service, striving like you for my love, all that he gained was sorrow; and my grief for his misfortune is even greater than for Cidegast."

The two legends—dramatically, suddenly—have come together as one: of the Castle of Marvels and the Castle of the Grail: the wound of the Maimed King had been acquired in the service of Orgeluse. Like the wounded knight Urians, like Lischoys Gwelljus and Gawain himself, he had been sent against the King of the Wood to regain, in the service of love, the office usurped by one who, refusing that service, had thought to prevail by force. I cannot find that Wolfram has made clear the relationship of Gramoflanz and Clinschor, his ally, to the young heathen knight from the precincts of the earthly Paradise whose lance, engraved with the name of the Grail, dealt the fearful wound to Anfortas. However, a general formula is evident, of which the sense is clear enough. As Orgeluse had been outraged by Gramoflanz's murder of her spouse and usurpation of her grove, so had Feirefiz's queen, Secundille, by Clinschor's theft of her magic tower. Queen Secundille, who had heard reports of the Grail, sent gifts to its guardian, King Anfortas: the monsters Cundrie and her brother Malcreatiure, along with those gems that were now in the booth before the Castle of Marvels. Anfortas had presented both the gems and Malcreatiure to his lady, Orgeluse, and then, one day riding forth with the cry "Amor!" had been wounded by a heathen spear from the realm of Secundille. Putting all of which together, we learn that the realm of nature, represented in the West by Orgeluse and her Diana grove, and in the East by Secondille, Feirefiz, and the young heathen quester for the Grail, is spontaneously moved (as in Mann's view) with yearning for the kingdom of the spirit. However, in that kingdom—namely Christendom—the just relationship of nature to spirit in mutual love has been violated and two ineligible kings now reign: Anfortas in the spiritual Castle of the Grail, and Gramoflanz in the nature-grove of the goddess Diana-Orgeluse. And that Wolfram intended to represent these two offices as complementary counterparts is clearly evident in the fact that the bonnets of the two kings, Anfortas and Gramoflanz, are alike of peacock plumes.

In early Christian art the peacock, like the phoenix, was symbolic of the Resurrection. Its flesh, it was believed, would not decay; in the words of Augustine: "Who was it but God that made the flesh of a dead peacock to remain always sweet, and without any putrefaction?" [68] Moreover, the peacock annually molts and puts on its bright feathers anew, like the universe each year. As we read in a late text:

The serene and starry sky and the shining sun are peacocks. The deep blue firmament shining with a thousand brilliant eyes, and the sun rich with the colors of the rainbow, present the appearance of a peacock in all the splendor of its eye-bespangled feathers. When the sky of the thousand-rayed sun is hidden by clouds, or veiled by autumnal mists, it again resembles the peacock, which, in the dark part of the year, like a great number of vividly colored birds, sheds its beautiful plumage and becomes drab and unadorned; the crow which had put on the peacock's feathers then caws with the other crows in funereal concert. [Compare the Raven theme in the cycle of Figure 3.] In winter the peacock-crow has nothing left to it except its shrill disagreeable cry, which is not dissimilar to that of the crow. It is commonly said of the peacock that it has an angel's feathers, a devil's voice, and a thief's walk." [69]

In alchemy the technical term "peacock's tail," *cauda pavonis* (Figure 55), referred to a stage of the process immediately following the *mortificatio* and *ablutio* (Figure 43), when in the *vas* there appeared, or seemed to appear, "many colors" (*omnes colores*). "In the gentle heat," states a late alchemical work, "the mixture will liquefy and begin to swell up, and at God's command will be

Figure 55. The Peacock's Tail (Cauda Pavonis)

endowed with spirit, which will soar upward bearing the stone and produce new colors." The first color will be "the green of Venus." "Green," comments Dr. Jung, "is the color of the Holy Ghost, of life, procreation and resurrection." [70] The green phase terminates when the color becomes a livid purple symbolic of the Lord's passion, at which moment the "philosophical tree" puts forth its blossoms and the phase known as the Regimen of Mars begins, showing "the ephemeral colors of the rainbow and the peacock at their most glorious"; and "in these days," the text then tells, "the hyacinthine color appears" [71]—which is the very color of the garnet-hyacinth table-stone that was set before the Fisher King by the maidens clothed in garments "greener than grass," on which the Grail-stone was to be placed.*

---

* The ceiling of the Castle of Marvels, also, was "like a peacock's tail" (supra, p. 494). Dr. Goetz sees in Wolfram's description of this fairy castle on a Celtic "Isle of Women" the influence of reports of the fabulous Baghdad palace of the Abbasid caliphs: *Qasr-at-Tāj*, on the Tigris, with its cupola and observation platform (destroyed 1154, rebuilt 1178). The mirror-pillar stolen from the Indian queen Secundille suggests the polished steel column *Qutb-Minār*, now standing in the Quwwat-ul-Islām mosque in Delhi, taken from the Hindu capital Ajmer. The very young Hindu queen of Ajmer when it fell (1195) was named Samyogita, celebrated in Old Hindi bardic song. *Somyogitā* > Somgita >Sogunda > Secunda, plus -illa (Italian diminutive) >*Secundille*. She ruled under protection of the Muslim viceroy (who was later the first Sultan of Delhi),

The eyes in the tail plumes of the peacock suggest the opening from within of the eyes of the ground of being, to view the universe of its own body. They are the eyes (stars) of the night sky; the eyes of the immanent Eye Goddess (Figure 19); those eyes in the extended palms of the offered hands of the merciful Bodhisattva which may be likened to the wounds of Christ.*

Or the eye of the peacock feather is that in the middle of the forehead, which opens in man to the vision of eternity. Again, it is the fiery sun door (the lion mouth of Figure 13): the eye of the Cyclops in the *Odyssey*, through which Odysseus passed.[72] In this sense, as the bird of the eye of danger, the peacock serves in Hindu iconography as the mount of the war-god Kartikeya (compare above: "the Regimen of Mars"), the young and fair, but fierce divinity who stands guard before the gate of the lofty mountain paradise of his father Shiva; in which role he is comparable to the cherub that Yahweh stationed with a flaming sword before the gate of Paradise [73]—from which very gate, as we have heard, the young heathen prince came forth from whose lance the unworthy Grail King, Anfortas, received his wound.†

There can be no doubt that Wolfram knew exactly what he was doing when he put peacock plumes in the bonnets of both King Gramoflanz, the guardian of the tree—the World Tree, the philosophical tree, the tree of the Garden, the tree of Christ's Cross, the Bo-tree of Buddhahood—and the wounded Fisher King, whose fishline from the Great Above to the Great Below is equally the *axis mundi:* awaiting everywhere, with its baited hook, in the waters of this world, to haul us up to the lotus boat of the radiant Fisher of Men with the peacock feathers pluming from his cap.

2.

Nor was Gawain, who had now been accepted by the lady of the Tree, the only member of his uncle's Round Table wearing on his helm at this time the wreath of victory. For, as the lady confessed, still weeping, as they rode back from the Perilous Ford: "Every

Qutb ud-dīn *Aibak:* the *Beg* ("Bey," a Turkish title of nobility) as handsome as *Ai*, "the moon." But the moon is mottled: compare *Feirefiz* (Old French, *vair,* "dappled," *fils* "son"). The lunar image links Feirefiz to the mythic moon-hero context of Osiris, Tammuz, etc.

* Supra, p. 413.
† Supra, pp. 392–93.

day of the week, every week of the year, I have sent out companies against Gramoflanz. Knights too rich to serve me for pay served, as you did, for love. And there was never one but I could have his service; none, that is, save one, whose name was Parzival. He came riding to the meadow and when my knights attacked him, he felled five. I offered him both my land and myself, but he replied that he already had a wife; and the Grail, he declared, caused him grief enough. He wanted no grief more."

We are to hear nothing more from Wolfram of this encounter of Parzival and Orgeluse. Wagner, however, devotes to it his entire second act. Act I is at the Temple of the Grail; Act III is to be there again. In Act II, however, the curtain rises upon Klingsor, sitting high in the magic tower of his Castle of Marvels, watching in his necromantic mirror (Wagner's adaptation of the radiant radar-pillar) the unwitting approach of Parsifal, who here is still the Great Fool. Klingsor's castle and Titurel's Temple of the Grail are in Wagner's legend opposed, as evil and good, dark and light, in a truly Manichaean dichotomy. They are not, as in the earlier work, equally enspelled by a power alien to both.

Moreover, Kundry, in whom Wagner has fused the chief female roles and characters of the legend (Orgeluse, Cundrie, and Sigune, together with something of the Valkyrie, a touch of Goethe's Ewig-Weibliches, and great deal of the Gnostic Sophia *) is herself enspelled by Klingsor and, against her will, his creature, yearning to be free. It was she, as his creature and agent—not, as in Wolfram's work, in her own interest, against his—who seduced the Grail King, Amfortas. And it had been when he was lying heedless in her toils, like Samson seduced by Delilah, that Klingsor, stealing his unguarded lance—the same that had pierced Christ's side—delivered a wound that would never heal until a savior—the prophesied "guileless fool"—should appear and touch it with the selfsame point.

Such a wound suggests, obviously, the wound of the arrow of love, which can be healed only by a touch of the one from whom the arrow came. In Wagner's work, however, the allegory is of lust and violence transformed by innocence to compassion (eros and

---

* Divine Wisdom, fallen (or enspelled) through ignorance; entrapped in the toils of this world illusion, of which—ironically—her own captured energy is the creative force.

thanatos to *agape*). In Malory's *Morte Darthur,* Book II ("The Tale of Balin"),* there is an evil knight named Garlon who is killed (Chapter XIV) when his head is split by the blow of a sword, and the broken truncheon of his own spear shoved into the wound. In Wolfram's epic, Trevrizent states that when the planets are in certain courses, or the moon at a certain phase, the king's wound pains terribly and the poison on the point of the spear becomes hot. "Then," he declares, "they lay that point on the wound and it draws the chill from the king's body, which hardens to glass all about the spear, like ice." [74]

There is the Greek legend, furthermore, of the hero Telephos, wounded by Achilles in the upper thigh with a wound that will not heal. An oracle declares, "He that wounded shall also heal!" and after a long and painful quest Telephos finds Achilles and is healed. Or, according to another reading, the cure is effected by the weapon: the remedy being scraped off the point and sprinkled on the wound. [75]

It is an old old mythic theme related to that of Medusa, whose blood from the left side brought death, but from the right, healing. [76] Or we may think of the elder Isolt and the poison of Morold's sword. In Wolfram's *Parzival* it plays but a minor part: is only once mentioned by Trevrizent. And the lance, moreover, is there in the Castle of the Grail, not Clinschor's palace. Wagner, in contrast, has elevated the lance theme to the leading role in his opus, in his own mind equating its poison with that of Tristan's wound. And in fact, he had been still at work on his *Tristan* when the idea of a *Parsifal* first occurred to him; still at the height, moreover, of his own Tristan affair with Mathilde Wesendonck, and indeed, even living, together with his tortured wife, Minne, in a house named the "Asyl," that had been provided by Mathilde and her patient spouse, Otto, adjacent to their home.

The year, as we read in Wagner's own story of his life, was 1857; the month, April; and the day—Good Friday. Richard and Minne had arrived the previous September in Zurich, and it was there, in the "Asyl," as he tells, that he finished, that winter, Act I of *Siegfried* and commenced work seriously on *Tristan.*

---

* Thomas Malory flourished c. 1470. His *Morte Darthur* is derived largely from much earlier Old French texts, Book II being from a version of the Prose Merlin (c. 1215) preserved in a single manuscript of a date c. 1300. An Old Spanish and an Old Portuguese translation also exist.

Now came [he states] beautiful spring weather, and on Good Friday, for the first time in this house, I woke to sunshine. The garden had turned green, the birds were singing, and at last I could sit up on the roof-tower of the cottage to enjoy a promising bit of long-desired quiet. Full of all this, suddenly I realized that today was, yes! Good Friday, and recalled how deeply a sense of the admonition of this day had once before struck me in Wolfram's *Parzival*. I had not occupied myself at all with this legend since that time of my stay in Marienbad [1845],[77] when I conceived the *Meistersinger* and *Lohengrin;* but now its ideal essentials came back to me in overpowering form, and from that Good Friday's inspiration I suddenly conceived an entire drama which with a few strokes I sketched out rapidly in three acts.[78]

Already in *Tannhäuser*, 1842–1844, the main lines of Wagner's interpretation of the Grail themes had been anticipated. The "Venusberg Bacchanal" is there a prelude to Klingsor's Garden of Enchantment, and the song of the poet Tannhäuser in celebration of the love grotto, altogether in the spirit of a Tristan:

> So that my yearning may forever burn,
> I quicken myself forever at that spring.[79]

However, the song there assigned to Wolfram as the rival singer in the song contest is (ironically) a paean to love as a *heavenly* gift— not at all "right through the middle," between black and white, sky and earth:

> Thou comest as though from God,
> And I follow at respectful distance.

Two years after his Good Friday morning inspiration in the roof tower of the "Asyl," Wagner was at work in Lucerne, in May 1859, on the last act of his *Tristan*, when the analogy of Tristan's wound with the wound of Amfortas in the opera yet to be written filled him with an appalled realization of the task he had assigned himself. "What a devilish business!" he wrote at that time in a letter to Mathilde. "Imagine, in Heaven's name, what has happened! Suddenly it has become hideously clear to me: Amfortas is my Tristan of Act III in a state of inconceivable intensification." [80]

"This 'intensification,' " comments Thomas Mann to this note,

was the involuntary law of life and growth of Wagner's productivity, and it derived from his own self-indulgence. He had been laboring all of his life, in fact, on the pain- and sin-laden accents of Amfortas. They are already heard in the cry of Tannhäuser: "Alas, the weight of sin overwhelms me!" In *Tristan* they attained to what then seemed to be the ultimate of lacerated anguish. But now, as he had realized with a shock, that would have to be surpassed in *Parsifal* and raised to an inconceivable intensity. Actually, what he was doing was simply pressing to the limit a statement for which he had always been unconsciously seeking stronger and profounder situations and occasions. The materials of his several works represent but stages— self-transcending inflections—of a unity, a life work self-enclosed, fully rounded, which "unfolds itself," yet in a certain manner was already there from the start. Which explains the box-within-box, one-inside-another, of his creative conceptions: and tells us also that an artist of this kind, a genius of this spiritual order, is never at work simply on the task, the opus, in hand. Everything else weighs upon him at the same time and adds its burden to the creative moment. Something apparently (but only half apparently) mapped out, like a life plan, comes to view: so that in the year 1862, while he was still composing *The Meistersinger,* Wagner foretold with complete certainty, in a letter written to von Bülow from Bieberich, that *Parsifal* was going to be his final work—fully twenty years before it was presented. For before that there would be *Siegfried,* in the midst of which both *Tristan* and *The Meistersinger* were going to be put forth; and there was, furthermore, the whole of *The Twilight of the Gods* to be composed: all to fill out spaces in the work program. He had to carry the weight of *The Ring* throughout his labors on *Tristan,* into which latter work, from the outset, the whisper of *Parsifal* was intruding. And that voice was present still while he was at work on his healthy Lutheran *Meistersinger.* Indeed, ever since the year, 1845, of the first Dresden production of *Tannhäuser,* that same voice had been awaiting him. In the year 1848 there came the prose sketch of the Nibelungen myth as a drama, as well as the writing of *Siegfried's Death,* from which *The Twilight of the Gods* was to evolve. In between, from 1846 to '47, *Lohengrin* took shape and the action of *The Meistersinger* was sketched out—both of which works belong, actually, as satyr-play and humorous counterpart, in the *Tannhäuser* context.

These years of the eighteen-forties, in the midst of which he reached the age of thirty-two, hold together and define the entire work plan of his life, from *The Flying Dutchman* to *Parsifal* which plan then was executed in the course of the following four decades, until 1881, by an inward labor on all of its boxed-together elements simultaneously. Thus in the strictest sense, Wagner's work is without chronology. It arose in time, it is true; yet was all suddenly there from the start, and all at once.[81]

In short: in Wagner's recognition of the wound of the Grail King as the same as that of Tristan—with his Parsifal then standing for an idealized, released, and releasing state of sunlike, boyish innocence—there is a reflex of his own entangled life, with loyalty to anyone or anything but himself the last thought in his mind or strain of truth in his heart. His Parsifal of Act II is still the nature boy of Act I, has gone through no ordeal of theological disillusionment or entry into knighthood, is unmarried, in fact knows nothing yet of either love or life, and is simply—to put it in so many words—a two-hundred-pound *bambino* with a tenor voice. The baritone Klingsor, gazing into his mirror, sees the innocent approaching, *"jung und dumm,"* and like the Indian god of love and death, tempter of the Buddha, conjures up, to undo the saving hero, a spectacle of damsels in a garden of enchantment, rushing about, all in disarray, as though suddenly startled from sleep. But, like the Buddha on the immovable spot, sitting beneath the Bo-tree, indifferent to both the allure of sex and the violence of weapons (unlike the Lord Buddha, however, in that he is not full, but empty, of knowledge), Parsifal, the guileless fool, simply has no idea of what these simpering women might be. "How sweet your scent!" he sings to them. "Are you flowers?"

Kundry tells him of his father's fame and mother's death; of how she knew his father and mother and has known himself since childhood (another Brünnhilde to a Siegfried); tells him it was she who named him Parsi-fal, the "Pure Fool," * and, inviting him to her mothering arms, plants a kiss full on his boy's mouth with a fervor that fills him first with intense terror, but then . . . with an appalled realization of the sense of Amfortas's wound: not, that is to say, with passion for the female, but with compassion for the male!

* Contrast the meaning of the name in Wolfram's version: Per-ce-val, "right through the middle." (Supra, p. 437.)

> Amfortas [he cries]! The wound! The wound!
> It is burning, now, in my heart.
>
> The wound I beheld bleeding:
> It is bleeding, now, within me.

Well, that is hardly Wolfram von Eschenbach!

Klingsor, like the tempter of the Buddha, now changing from his character as lord of desire to his other as lord of death,[82] appears with the precious lance in hand, which with a curse he flings. But again as in the legend of the Buddha, where the weapons of the lord of death, though flung at the savior, never strike him, when the great spear reaches Parsifal it hangs floating overhead; he simply makes the sign of the Cross, reaches up, takes hold of it, and will bear it now to Amfortas (Act III) to heal the sorrowful wound; and as from an earthquake the Castle and Garden of Enchantment disappear, the damsels collapse to the ground like faded flowers (see the Buddha's "Graveyard Vision"),[83] and the curtain falls.

"Richard Wagner," wrote his utterly disillusioned worshiper Nietzsche, "apparently the greatest victor, actually a now decayed and confused *décadent*, sank suddenly down, helpless and in pieces, before the Christian Cross." [84]

> One could have wished [he wrote again] that the Wagnerian *Parsifal* had been meant in a spirit of fun, as a kind of terminal piece and satyr-play with which the great tragic master—in a manner proper to and worthy of himself—might have taken his leave as well from himself as from us, and above all, from Tragedy: i.e., with an extravaganza of the most sublimely mischievous parody of the tragic art itself, and of all that ghastly, ponderous seriousness and agony of yore: that stupidest form of existence, now at last overcome, the un-nature of the ascetic ideal. Parsifal is actually operatic material *par excellence*. But is Wagner's *Parsifal*, then, his secretly superior laugh at himself? his final triumph in supreme artistic freedom and transcendence?. Do we have here a Wagner who knows how to *laugh* at himself?
>
> As I say, one could wish that that were so; for what, if earnestly meant, could this Parsifal be? Must we actually recognize in this (as people have sometimes said of me), the product of "a hatred of knowledge, intellect, and sensuality, gone mad"? a

curse, in one breath of hate, upon both the senses and the mind? an apostasy and reversion to sickly Christian, obscurantist ideals? And even, finally, a work of self-denial, self-cancellation, on the part of an artist, who, up to this, had been dedicated, with all the might of his will, to just the opposite, in the superlative spirituality and sensuality of his art? and not only his art, but also his life?

One recalls how enthusiastically Wagner walked, in his time, in the footsteps of the philosopher Feuerbach [1804–1872]. Feuerbach's theme of "healthy sensuality"! In the thirties and forties of this century, that had sounded to Wagner, as to many Germans—they called themselves the *young* Germans—like the Gospel of Redemption. Has he now finally unlearned that song? For, it looks, at least, as though he had made up his mind to unteach it!

Can it be that a hatred of life has got the better of him, as it got the better of Flaubert? For *Parsifal* is a work of malice and revenge, a secret poison against the preconditions of life, a *wicked* work. The sermon of chastity is an incitement to pathology, and I would despise anyone who did not feel in *Parsifal* an attack upon morality itself.[85]

When Gawain, then, wearing the wreath he had taken from the tree, rode with his lady Orgeluse onto the meadow before the Castle of Marvels, the ferryman pushed out from the other bank with Bene, his daughter, in his craft, and they welcomed the couple aboard. From the castle walls and windows the multitude of ladies joyously watched them ferried across, while the four hundred knights of the castle, whom Gawain had not before seen, colorfully jousted in their honor on the lawns.

BOOK XIII: THE LEGEND OF CLINSCHOR'S WOUND

There was in the castle that evening a festival at which the knights and ladies danced. They had been kept apart by Clinschor's arts, even unaware of each other, but that enchantment now was undone. Lischoys Gwelljus and the Turkoyte, set free without condition, were brought to the hall by Bene, who turned next to attend her lord Gawain, still in great pain from his wounds. And she was sitting beside him, chatting, when he asked softly to be shown which of the ladies was Itonje, then went to his sister, and after courteous preliminaries presented her with the ring of the man who had challenged him to the death. She blushed. "In my thoughts," she confessed, "I have already granted him all he desires of me and would have fled to him long since, had I been able to quit this horrid castle."

In the great hall the knights and ladies, that evening, moved freely among each other. Gawain had sent for good fiddlers. All they knew, however, were the old-style tunes, none of the new from Thuringia; yet many a lovely lady danced and many a handsome knight, pairing now with one, now another; one knight often with two ladies, one at either hand: and if any had wished that evening to offer his service for love, there were chances enough.

Gawain sat watching with his mother, Sangive; Arnive, his grandmother; and the duchess holding his hand. "You had better go to bed now," said the old queen to him at last. "Will the duchess keep you company tonight and see that you are kept covered?" "He shall be in my care," the lady answered. Gawain called for the drink to be brought that gave to all the sign of departure, and as she rose to go, the old queen turned to Orgeluse. "Now, you take good care of our knight." Faithful Bene bore the light before them and continued on with the others, while Gawain, alone with his lady at last, closed tight and made fast the door.

At Arthur's court, meanwhile, a messenger had arrived, bearing the message of the coming joust of Gawain with Gramoflanz. "Oh, blessed be the hand that wrote you!" the queen exclaimed when the letter came into her hand. "It is now four years and a half, and six weeks, since Gawain and Parzival rode away." Arthur read the letter through. "Gramoflanz," said he with angry mien, "must think my nephew another Cidegast. He had troubles enough in *that* bout! I shall add to his troubles in this." And when the messenger returned with Arthur's promise to attend, he told Gawain of the joy of the Round Table at the news of him, alive.

Then his grandmother told him something else. At a window apart, facing the river, he had taken a seat beside her. "Dear lady," he asked, "can you tell me something of Clinschor?"

"Sir," she answered willingly, "his magic is beyond measure. These marvels here are little, compared with those he holds in many lands. He was once a great noble of Capua. But he offered himself in service to the wife, Queen Iblis,* of the King of Sicily. And I now have a secret to tell. Forgive me, it is impolite to mention such things; but when the king discovered him in his wife's arms, one cut of a knife made him a capon."

Gawain burst into a loud, long laugh, and before he had finished, she was again talking.

"Magic," she was saying, "was first invented in a city called Persidia; not Persia, as many people think. Clinschor went there and returned with this magic art. Because of the shame he had suffered, he was so filled with hatred for all, that his greatest pleasure now lies in robbing those who are happiest of their joy, especially those most honored and respected.

"But now, in Rosche Sabins there dwelt a king, Irot, the father of Gramoflanz, who, frightened by Clinschor's magic, thought to buy his good will by offering him this impregnable mountain with the lands eight miles about, and Clinschor wrought here then this curious work. If the castle were besieged, there would be food for thirty years. When, next, Gramoflanz killed the Duke of Logroys, the duchess, in great fear of both him and his protector, presented Clinschor with the treasure booth that stands before this castle gate, which she had just received as a love-gift from the young Anfortas of Munsalvaesche; and it was then agreed between all that whoever survived the adventure of this castle would be left in peace by Clinschor and have gained both the castle and herself. However, in the meantime every noble knight and lady on Christian soil upon whom Clinschor laid eyes, he bound here in enchantment; and all now have become yours. Release us!"

Need we ask or tell what, or whom, the poet Wolfram might have had in mind when, about the year 1210, he was writing thus of a sterilizing magic brought upon Europe from the Near East by a life-despising castrate holding power over all spirits, good and bad? The King of Sicily at that moment was the infant Frederick II (1194–1250), crowned at Palermo 1198, who on the death of his mother six months later had become the ward of Innocent III (r. 1198–1216), the mightiest pope of all time.[86] † The medieval poet Wolfram's reading of the Waste Land theme was in any case dia-

---

* Iblis, Arabic name of Satan, here bestowed upon a heathen queen.

† *Clinschor*, derivation uncertain; possibly Provençal, *clergier*, "clergyman" (Goetz, op. cit., p. 37).

metrically opposite to that of Richard Wagner: For not the passion of love, but a castrate's revenge against it, was for him the source of the pall of death over both the palace of life (the Castle of Marvels) and the palace of awe (the Castle of the Grail). Nor would any such magical sign of the Cross as Wagner's "guileless fool" employs at the climax of Act II have broken the spell of Wolfram's necromancer. The necromancer himself, Innocent, was employing that very sign to enforce the magic spell of his interdicts, by which kings were undone, cowed, and brought to heel. Such magic allied with duress (Clinschor with Gramoflanz, religion with secular power) was, in Wolfram's day and age, precisely the force to be undone.

Anfortas, who, like Abelard, was unworthy of his ordination— hence split in two, a pretender—riding forth in quest of integrity, an experience of his own, had immediately entered the field of the allied king and eunuch, the field of his own limitations; and thus, like Joyce's Bloom and Dedalus, he had "found in the world without as actual what was in his world within as possible." * He had found his soul, his Lady Soul, whom he was seeking: the Lady Orgeluse. She was not, however, as she seemed. She had been bereaved of her lover in truth; there was a pretender in his stead. Superstition (magic) and violence had usurped the seats of truth and justice. Fear, hate, and deception were in the groves and gardens of desire, and she had been to such a degree dissociated from the spontaneities of innocent life that anyone who would release her to love would have first to undo the spell by which she was enthralled. Anfortas in her service—like Abelard, and for the same reason, by exactly the same enemy—was undone.

Gawain, on the other hand, was one who had spent his life not posing in a role unearned, conferred upon him by anointment, but in quest, sincerely, for his object of desire, and when he found her—after years, not days—he was transfixed, established in his own true center, and knew exactly where he stood. She was, again, the bereaved Orgeluse. But he was no toy king. There was no threat, no fear, either of man or of spirit, that could put him off his course or freeze him to a halt. His trials were proper to his own life and he was consequently their match: hence, at one with his Lady Soul; at peace with her; and in the fair castle of love, the master of his world.

* Supra, p. 197.

It remained only to make peace as well with the world beyond the broad stream. . . .

Sitting chatting with his grandmother at the window, Gawain with a start of joy espied on the meadow on the other shore the first of Arthur's host arriving with banners, colors, spears, and immediately setting up pavilions. With love in his heart, tears in his eyes, he watched, then ordered all his own castle company—knights and ladies, squires and pages—to make ready with their own banners and tents to cross and welcome his uncle's court. Arthur and his queen were introduced to Arnive, the king's mother, Sangive, his sister, and the sisters of Gawain. All kissed and laughed, wept and laughed and kissed again. Moreover, many a knight who had been mourning Gawain's death came smiling into his tent. But the seneschal Keie only murmured, "God surely does work wonders! Where did Gawain get all these queens?"

Next day a third host, that of Gramoflanz, arrived, and Gawain then rode forth onto a broad plain, alone, for exercise, where he saw a lone knight galloping his way, wearing armor redder than rubies. . . .

But we have heard of that man before and our tale here returns to its main stem.

VII. Third Intermezzo: Mythogenesis

Gawain is the basic Arthurian knight, in both his character and his adventures the closest to the Celtic sphere. Gringuljete, his horse, like many another fairy beast, was white with shining red ears,* and his sword Excalibur (which had been conferred on him when Arthur dubbed him knight) flashed, when drawn from its sheath, like lightning. The knight himself increased in strength every day until noon, like the sun, after which his fighting powers declined; whence it was customary at Arthur's court, in deference to Gawain, to hold tournaments in the morning hours. "Apparently," as Heinrich Zimmer has remarked, "the knight was a solar god, masquerading under medieval armament, doomed, as ever, to expire every twilight and pass into the 'Land of No Return.' Like Osiris, he there became the king, the sun, of the netherworld, but,

---

* Compare the words of the Goddess Morrigan quoted in *Occidental Mythology*, p. 305, from "The Golden Book of Lecan": "I will become a white red-eared cow, with a hundred white red-eared cows behind me."

like the rolling solar disk, traversed and broke free from the 'great below,' to reappear reborn in the east as the orb of the new day." [87] And in the words of Professor Loomis: "That Gawain is a counterpart of Cuchulinn is one of the commonplaces of Arthurian scholarship." [88]

In the oral, creative period of Arthurian romance—from, say, the time of the Norman Conquest to that of the *Tristan* of Thomas of Britain (1066–c.1160)—Sir Gawain was almost certainly the champion of that basic adventure later assigned to practically every hero of the century, the rescue of a harassed chatelaine from either an assault upon her own castle (Gahmuret and the Black Queen of Zazamanc, Parzival and Condwiramurs) or abduction to another (Lancelot's rescue of Guinevere from the castle of Meleagant). The other great Celtic hero deed (also assigned to Lancelot) of running off with another man's wife came into Arthurian romance through Tristan, whose own court, however, was of his uncle Mark, who had horse's ears—possibly red.

Arthur and his nephew Gawain, Mark and his nephew Tristan, stand for separate strains of invention, adapting related Celtic mythic themes to the modes of the French, Provençal and Norman, twelfth-century courts.* As already noted, the earliest versions of these adaptations are lost to us. So too is all record of the lives of the Welsh and Breton fabulators who brought them into being. However, there is that one master, apparently a great master, of whom the name, at least, is known, written variously as Bréri, Bleheris, and Blihis,[89] and of whom Thomas of Britain wrote that he knew "all the feats and all the tales of all the kings and all the courts who had ever lived in Britain," [90] while a second author, anonymous, states that he possessed the knowledge of the secret of the Grail.[91] A third, likewise anonymous, tells that he was "born and begotten in Wales" and was, moreover, the man who introduced the legend of Gawain to the court of the Count of Poitiers.[92] † So that in one sensational package, opened to view at the crucial court of Poitiers, c. 1120–1137, one Celtic bard could disclose in seed the whole magical world to come of Arthurian romance: the

---

* Supra, p. 303.

† This count, as already remarked, would have been either William IX of Aquitaine (1071–1127) or William X (d. 1137), respectively the grandfather and father of Queen Eleanor (1122–1204).

youthful dream, holding all the symbols of destiny, of the waking modern Occidental soul.

The earliest years of formation of this dream of youth belong to that period mixed of resurgent barbarism and disintegrating civilization when the Roman Empire in Europe was being sacked and turned to rubble: [93] a period of regeneration comparable in many ways to that of the fall of Crete and Troy at the opening of the Homeric age. In our inquiry here into the history and conditions of the coming-to-manifestation of the mythic forms specific to modern man, we may term it:

1. THE MYTHOGENETIC MOMENT: C.450–950 A.D.

Freud, in his *Moses and Monotheism,* finds a like moment in the background of the desert years of the Jews, when (as he believed he had shown) they slew their Egyptian master, Moses, an event which, according to his view, occurred some time between 1350 and 1310 B.C.[94] The catastrophe was followed by a period of forgetting, "latency," or incubation, of which the counterpart in the classical development would have fallen between the time of the Dorian attacks upon Pylos, Thebes, and Troy (c. 1250–1150 B.C.), and their literary transformation in the epics (c. 850–650 B.C.). Freud compared such moments in the histories of peoples to those earliest years of childhood when the crucial imprintings occur that determine the imagery and structuring themes of our dreams: the imagery, as Jung would say, of the *personal* unconscious, based on one's *personal* biography, through which the "grave and constant" themes of the inevitable common human destiny of growth, spiritual conflict, initiations, maturation, failure of powers, and passing, will in the individual case be inflected, interpreted, and expressed.

Specifically, in relation to Arthurian romance, the precipitating catastrophe was the conquest of Christian Britain by the pagan Angles, Jutes, and Saxons, c. 450–550 A.D. The Romans, after an occupation of four centuries, had just withdrawn. The undefended population was being harried from the north by the untamed Picts and Scots. King Vortigern of the Britons sent a cry for help to the Saxons, who, arriving under Hengest and Horsa, received a grant of land in Kent, and thence, in due time, launched their own campaign of conquest.

Arthur apparently was a native Briton who distinguished himself in a series of battles in the early sixth century and for a time represented the last hope of the Celtic Christian cause. The chronicle of a Welsh cleric of that time, Gildas (516?–570), *De exidio et conquestu Britanniae,* mentions a great battle at Mount Badon (in Dorset) on the day of the chronicler's birth; and in a later work, *Historia Britonum,* by another Welsh cleric, Nennius (fl. 796), the name of Arthur is celebrated in connection with the same event. Arthur, according to this text, was not a king but a professional military man (*dux bellorum*), who "fought in company with the kings of the Britons" in a series of twelve battles, in the eighth of which, at the castle Guinnon, he "carried on his shoulders [possibly meaning 'on his shield'] the image of the Holy Virgin Mary: the pagans that day were put to flight, and there was great slaughter among them through the favor of our Lord Jesus Christ and His Holy Mother, Saint Mary," while in the twelfth engagement, on Mount Badon, "there fell 960 men in one day at a single onset of Arthur: no one overthrew them but he alone, and in all battles he came out victorious." [95] Recorded also in this work is the legend of Ambrosius, later identified with Merlin: a marvelous "child without a father" who revealed to King Vortigern the secret of the insecure foundation of a tower he was building, namely, the presence in the earth beneath it of two battling dragons, a red and a white (allegorically the pagan Saxons and the Christian Celts).[96] And in still another chronicle of the time, the anonymous *Annales Cambriae,* written shortly after 956,[97] Arthur is again named in connection with the battle of Mount Badon, here dated 516, with the further notice of his death, together with that of Medraut (Mordred), at the battle of Camlann, 537.*

---

* The origins of the mainland Nibelungen legend date from this period as well; specifically, the early fifth century, when the Burgundians, an East German tribe, migrating from the Baltic southward, settled on the Rhine, near Worms, and in the year 435 rose against the Roman governor Aetius. Two years later these people were all but annihilated by a troop of Huns acting as agents of the Empire, and their remnants retreated to the Rhone. The Franks about Cologne, their former neighbors on the Rhine, preserved a memory of their disaster and developed it in the legend known to us from the following sources: a) from Iceland, in 1. *The Poetic Edda* (c. 1200), 2.

2. THE FIRST ORAL PERIOD OF DEVELOP-
MENT: C. 550-1066

Already in Nennius's chronicle there is evidence of an oral folk tradition rising throughout the Celtic "mythogenetic zone" (Brittany, Cornwall, Wales, Scotland, and Ireland), having as a leading theme the so-called "hope of the Britons" for a second coming of Arthur. And this tradition embraced a multitude of such scattered local sagas as that of a cairn in northern Breconshire (Wales) upon one stone of which Arthur's hound Caval had left a footprint while hunting the boar Troynt: you might carry off that stone as often as you liked; next day it would be back there on the cairn. Or again in Wales: a burial mound, said to be of Anir, Arthur's son, whom the *dux bellorum* had himself killed and buried there: when measured, that mound was sometimes six, sometimes nine feet long, or as much as fifteen, but never twice the same. Nennius had himself measured it and found this saying to be true.[98] "Originally," states Professor Loomis of King Arthur, "he was the historic champion of the Britons in their desperate struggle with the Saxons. Popular tradition came to associate his name with cairns and cromlechs, Roman ruins and crumbling castles. He survived in the isle of Avalon or in the deep recesses of Mount Etna or in the caverns of the Welsh hills. He became king of the pigmy people of the Antipodes, or he led the Wild Hunt by moonlight on the forested slopes of the Mont du Chat.* The Cornish and Breton folk regarded him as a Messiah and awaited the day when he would return to recover their ancestral home from the Saxons." [99] †

The Prose Edda, by Snorri Sturleson (c. 1179–1241), and 3. *The Völsunga Saga* (c. 1250); *b*) from South Germany, in the *Nibelungenlied* (c. 1250); and; *c*) from Denmark and Norway, in the *Vilkina Saga* (c. 1250). There is also a passage in *Beowulf* (c. 675–725, lines 875–913) in which an early version of the legend is briefly cited.

* Compare the "Wild Hunt" theme throughout *Finnegans Wake,* and in Wagner's *Tristan* the hunting horn motifs of Act II. Compare, also, in Mann's *Magic Mountain* the name of Castorp's Lady Soul, Mme. Chau*chat*.

† Similarly, in the kindred Germanic "mythogenetic zone," which extended from Iceland to the Alps and eastward to the Caspian Sea, elements of local history and saga became attached to the growing legend of the fall of the Burgundians. Attila, the king of the Huns (406?–453), who was not present at the massacre, was added to the tale, along with a popular interpretation of his death as from a hemorrhage in his throat the very night of his marriage to Ildico, or Hildico, a German princess. The rumor ran that

Both the oral tales and the Latin chronicles of this first stage of development of the reputation of Arthur were largely unselfconscious; not so, however, those of the next.

3. THE SECOND ORAL PERIOD OF DEVELOPMENT
c. 1066–1140

With the Norman Conquest of England, a new era dawned for Celtic bards. The Anglo-Saxon kings and courts were displaced, and a French-speaking aristocracy with strong Continental connections offered new stages and new audiences to the bards and fabulators of the older natives of the British Isles. These were disciplined creative and performing artists, trained in the mythopoetic craftsmanship of the old Druidic Filid, which included, besides a knowledge by memory of all the basic Celtic myths, practice and facility in the arts of improvisation. And it was these consciously creative master entertainers (of whom the Welshman Bréri, Blihis, Bleheris, was apparently an outstanding representative) who, in the brief span of years between the Norman Conquest of England and Bréri's appearance in the southern court of Count William of Poitiers, established along traditionally Celtic mythic lines the new European secular mythology of King Arthur and his questing knights—of whom chivalrous Gawain was, throughout this period, the chief inheritor of such roles of fame as in the elder Celtic sphere had been assigned to the chariot-fighter Cuchullin.*

---

she had killed him in revenge for the slaughter of her relatives (though in fact she was not a Burgundian).

In the *Nibelungenlied*, Attila became Etzel and Hildico, Kriemhild (*Hilda*, "Warrior Maid," *Hildico*, "Little Warrior Maid"; *Kriem-hild*, "Helmed Warrior Maid"). In the *Völsunga Saga*, Attila is Atli and Hildico, Gudrun.

Brunhilda ("Armored Warrior Maid") was actually a Visigothic queen of Austrasia, c. 543–613. In 567 she abjured Arianism and accepted orthodox Christianity, to marry King Sigebert of the Eastern Franks, whose brother, Chilperic of the Western Franks, married and then murdered her sister (having been urged to this deed by Fredegond, his mistress), whereupon war broke out between the brothers. In 575 Sigebert was murdered and Brunhilda, his widow, made captive; however, she married her captor's son, and so escaped; whereafter she flourished for some thirty years in a great career of political intrigue until, in 613, the Frankish nobles, in revenge for her murder of ten of their royal dynasty, seized and led her about in shame on a camel, tortured her for three days, and had her torn apart by wild horses, then burned her remains on a pyre.

* And meanwhile, as in the Celtic "mythogenetic zone," so too—though under totally different circumstances—in the recently Christianized Ger-

Mythological creativity of this kind is not to be explained romantically as a kind of spontaneous poetry of the "folk soul," in the sense, for example, of Jacob Grimm's *das Volk dichtet.*" Nor can we here go all the way with Freud and interpret the productions of these poets simply as symptoms of the traumata of what I have termed the Mythogenetic Moment. Something of the kind might perhaps be suggested of Period 2, the first oral stage of development. However, the fabulators of this *second* oral stage were traditionally trained master craftsmen, composing and manipulating the new pseudo-historical materials according to the inherited mythopoetic principles of a tradition long anteceding the cuts and blows of c. 450 A.D. This was an age, furthermore, of a number of considerable traumatic moments of its own: not only 1066, the Norman conquest of England, but also 1085, the Spanish conquest of Toledo, and 1097, the preaching of the First Crusade. New philosophical and theological concepts had to be mastered and assimilated. Translations from the Arabic, silks and fashions of the Orient, Manichaean heretics, Jewish Cabbalists and merchants: all were opening to the European mind a world of new horizons, a new

---

manic: the amalgamation of local, spontaneously generated folklore and saga with the larger heritage of Aryan (here specifically Germanic) myth must be attributed to a traditionally trained, highly appreciated generation of consciously creative poets. For it was at this time that the aristocratic art of old Germanic alliterative poetry matured, of which *Beowulf* (supra, pp. 114–23) is a prime example. Furthermore, among the Vikings the still more sophisticated poetry of the skalds came into being at about the turn from the eighth to ninth century. Passing from Norway to Iceland at the turn from the tenth to eleventh, skaldic verse continued to be composed there until about the close of the fourteenth. The Norwegian Bragi Boddason the Old (early ninth century) may be named among the first of these skaldic masters. Christianity reached the Norse about the year 1000, and the bulk of their written matter dates from c. 1100–1250. Snorri Sturleson (1179–1241), author of the *Prose Edda,* flourished at the culminating moment of the art.

To be recalled at this point also is the fact that the Pietroasa Bowl (Figure 3) was discovered in Germanic territory. Germanic mythology in the early Middle Ages was anything but "primitive." Zoroastrian, Hellenistic, Roman, and Byzantine influences can be recognized throughout. Hence the mythic themes of the twelfth- and thirteenth-century *Nibelungenlied, Völsunga Saga,* and Icelandic *Eddas,* which appealed so greatly to Wagner and give the works their epic force, show unmistakable affinities with all the great high mythologies to which we have been devoting the greater part of this four-volume work.

world that had to be entered, and with which the mind as well as heart had to be brought into accord. In *Primitive Mythology* I have used the term *land-náma,* "land naming," or "land taking," to designate the process by which the features of a newly entered land are assimilated by an immigrant folk to its heritage of myth.[100] The mythopoetic creativity of the Celtic bards and fabulators of the period of the great European awakening from 1066 to c. 1140 was in essence equivalent to that mythogenetic process: an appropriation and mastery, not of space, however, but of time, not of the raw facts of a geography, but of the novelties, possibilities, raw facts, dangers, pains, and wonders of a new age: a "mythological updating."

But the oral literature of the bards was not the only carrier of Arthurian lore in this second oral period; for, as in the first, there were now also written chronicles, and of these, principally two. The first was the *Gesta Regum Anglorum* of the most respected and respectable English historian of the age, the learned monk William of Malmesbury (c. 1080–c. 1143), whose book appeared about 1120; and here not only was Arthur again connected with the battle of Mount Badon, but a strong objection was registered, in the name of accurate history, to the body of irresponsible fable growing up around the great man's name.

"He is the Arthur," we read, "about whom the Britons rave in empty words, but who, in truth, is worthy to be the subject, not of deceitful tales and dreams, but of true history; for he was long the prop of his tottering fatherland, and spurred the broken spirits of his countrymen on to war; and finally at the siege of Mount Badon, trusting in the image of the Mother of God, which he had fastened on his armor, he alone routed nine hundred of the enemy with incredible bloodshed." [101]

We learn also from this "true history" that the name of a certain Walwen (Gawain) had already become attached to the legendry of the all but deified Arthur, leader of battles.

However, by far the most voluminous and important Arthurian document of this time was Geoffrey of Monmouth's really wonderful *History of the Kings of Britain* (*Historia Regum Britanniae*), which appeared in 1136 and of which one learned churchman, Giraldus Cambrensis, declared that, whereas if the Gospel of St.

John were placed on the chest of a dying man angels would flock
around him, if this chronicle of lies were placed there devils would
arrive.[102] For, whereas on the face of it the work was another
chronicle by a monkish hand purporting to be a "true history,"
namely, of the reigns of the Celtic kings of Britain, from the time
of the supposed first settlement of the island by refugees from Troy
(led by an eponymous hero, Brut, from whom the name Britain
was derived) to the years of the coming of the Anglo-Saxons, actually it was a great and wonderfully rich compendium of Celtic
legends up to then unrecorded; and, though known to be such by
the learned, was yet preferred by all the courtly world of that day
to any book of truth ever written. It became *à la mode* immediately and supplied for a time the fashionable talk of Europe—as,
centuries later, James Macpherson's *Poems of Ossian* (1760,
1762), which enspelled the mind even of Goethe. Geoffrey, like
Macpherson, pretended to have taken his text from an ancient Celtic book; in Macpherson's case, of the Gaelic tongue, in Geoffrey's, of the British. The two were scorned equally as liars by
the soberheads of their centuries: Macpherson by Samuel Johnson,
Geoffrey by Giraldus Cambrensis and many more. However, if the
opening through a single book of the freshets of a grandiose river
of tradition that is running in force to this day counts for anything
at all, then Geoffrey, like Macpherson, merits laurel. For in the
Latin of his pages there appear, for the first time in literature, not
only the figure of Arthur as a *king* and the whole story of his birth,
the names of his favorite knights, Gawain, Bedivere, and Kay, the
treachery of Mordred (here as Arthur's nephew, not his son), the
faithlessness of Guinevere (in adultery with Mordred), the last battle of Arthur with Mordred and the mortal wounding of the king, his
queen Guinevere's refuge in a convent, and the passage of himself
to Avalon in the year of Our Lord 542; but also the legend of King
Lear and his daughters, Goneril, Regan, and Cordelia, the name of
King Cymbeline, and the entire legend of Merlin's life, including
his magical transportation of the "Dance of the Giants" (Stonehenge) from Ireland to the Salisbury plain.

But with this we have been carried fully from the oral stages to
the great culminating century of Arthurian invention in:

4. THE LITERARY STAGES OF DEVELOPMENT:
c. 1136–1230

This is represented in documents roughly of four categories:

A. Anglo-Norman patriotic epics: 1137–1205
B. French courtly romances: c. 1160–1230
C. Religious legends of the Grail: c. 1180–1230
D. German biographical epics: c. 1200–1215

A. The Anglo-Norman patriotic epics, 1136–1205. There is reason to believe that Geoffrey of Monmouth was aware of the political value of his epoch-inaugurating *Historia;* for as Dr. Sebastian Evans states in the Epilogue to his translation of the work, it was indeed "a true national epos." The question arises, however, as to what the nation could have been that the book was written to serve; for it is not English, Norman, Breton, or Welsh. Dr. Evans answers:

> In a word, it was the national empire of Geoffrey's time, and his "time" was that of Henry I, Stephen, and the first year of Henry II.* The actual empire of Henry I consisted mainly in England, Normandy, Wales, and Brittany. The actual empire of Henry II extended from the Orkneys to the Pyrenees. The dominant idea of the first two Henries, the son and great-grandson of the Conqueror of England, was gradually to extend the frontiers of the Anglo-Welsh-Norman-Breton empire until, in the fulness of time, the descendants of the mighty William should be the emperors of Christendom.[103]

The poet Virgil, as Evans observes, had made the Roman Empire glorious and commended it to the intellect and imagination of the world by claiming for its founders the blood of the heroes of Troy, transforming an exiled Trojan prince into a national Roman hero. Why, therefore, should not Geoffrey do as much for the Anglo-Welsh-Norman-Breton empire of the Henrys?

> Geoffrey's book [Evans concludes] is an epic that failed, for it was to have been the national epic of an empire that failed. . . . King Arthur, Geoffrey's creation as Aeneas was the creation of Virgil, the king who was to have been the traditional hero of the Anglo-Welsh-Norman-Breton nucleus of empire and all the dominions which that empire might thereafter annex to

* Henry I, r. 1100–1135; Stephen, r. 1135–1154; Henry II, r. 1154–1189.

its own, was left without any empire to hail him as the founder of its glories. He became a national hero unattached, a literary wonder and enigma to ages which had forgotten the existence of the composite and short-lived empire which was the justification of his own existence.[104]

But in addition, as remarked by Professor Loomis, "Geoffrey was not unmindful of the parallel which his Arthur presented in a vague fashion to Charlemagne" [105]—Charlemagne, that is to say, of the French *Chansons de Geste,* and particularly the *Song of Roland,* the dating of which, sometime between c. 1098 and 1120, was two or three decades earlier than Geoffrey's work.*

---

* As the Arthurian legends developed in the mythogenetic zone of the Celts, and the legends of Sigurd and Brunhilda in that of the German tribes, so in France, *la douce France,* the *Chansons de Geste.* However, as the late Professor Joseph Bédier of the University of Paris demonstrated in a formidable four-volume study of the origins of these Gallic "songs of deeds"—*Les Légendes épiques: recherches sur la formation des Chansons de Geste* (Paris: Edouard Champion, 1907, 2nd ed., 1921, 3rd ed., 1926)— their sources are not to be sought for, either in the folk imagination or in the traditionally grounded mythopoetic creativity of bards, but specifically and precisely in Latin chronicles preserved in monasteries along and near the popular eleventh- and twelfth-century pilgrim routes from France to: *a*) the shrine in Spain of Saint James of Compostela, *b*) Rome, and *c*) Jerusalem. These monasteries served as inns, and, in order to advertise their neighborhoods, the monks furnished jongleurs and fabulators with stories of local deeds of fame from the precious parchments on their shelves.

Specifically, at the narrow pass of Ronceval in the Pyrenees, some rocks had been hurled upon the rear guard of Charlemagne's army in the year 791 or 792 as it was returning from an expedition, not against the Moors, but in alliance with the Moors against the Basques, who were Christians. The rocks hurled by the Basques from an ambuscade did little damage and the hillmen disappeared. However, some three centuries later, when the Moors were being pressed back (fall of Toledo, 1085), the name of Charlemagne was being recalled by the French as of an earlier great king—and theirs!—who had also fought the Moors. "I believe, actually," states Bédier in his commentary on *La Chanson de Roland* (Paris: L'Edition d'art, 1927, p. 14), "that the first inventions relative to the battle of Ronceval were composed in the eleventh century in the sanctuaries along the road from Blaye and Bordeaux to Ronceval." And he concludes: "The texts emanating from the churches, toward the close of the eleventh century, celebrating Charlemagne's tireless propagation of the faith were innumerable. 'Pious Charles,' we read in the *Translation of Saint Servais,* 'was not afraid to die for his country, to die for the Church; moreover, he traveled the whole earth; those whom he found in rebellion against God, he subdued with the sword.' That is why the preachers of the Crusade represented him as a model for all; that is why Godefroy de Bouillon and Baudoin de Flandre took pride in representing themselves as his descendants; and that is why, in the year 1101, on

But finally, no matter what Geoffrey himself may have intended, the value of his fabled king to the actual Norman throne was recognized, if not by the first Henry, then certainly by the second. The entire epic-as-chronicle was turned into Norman French octosyllabic couplets by a *clerc lisant* named Wace (1100–1175), educated in Abelard's Paris, whose *Geste des Bretons,* as he called his work—which is better known, however, as *Brut*—gained for him from Henry II advancement to the post of canon at Bayeux. And then, just half a century later, in the reign, however, of John, under whom the empire was disintegrating, an English country pastor in Worcestershire named Layamon turned the Norman poem, with many additions of his own, into a Middle English alliterative epic (1205): not to flatter any king, as he declares in his charming preface, but "to tell the noble deeds of the English; what they were named and whence they came who first possessed this English land after the flood that came from the Lord, which destroyed here all that it found alive except Noah and Shem, Japheth and Ham, and their four wives, who were with them in the ark." [106]

It was in Wace's work that the first literary mention of the Round Table appeared, and in Layamon's that its shape was explained as designed to avoid such disputes for precedence as were common at Celtic feasts.[107] Also in Wace, for the first time, clear mention was made of the "hope of Britain" for Arthur's return, while from Layamon's *Brut* we learn that the mortally wounded king was taken by fairies to Avalon, whence, after his healing by

---

the evidence of Ekkehard d'Aura, word went around among the crusaders that he had just revived and was about to put himself in their lead.

"It was in the course of this period, under influences partly secular, partly ecclesiastical, that the traditions up to that time dispersed among the various sanctuaries, up to that time kept apart, were gradually brought together, linked by the lines of the pilgrim routes and by the mystic line of an idea: the idea of the mission of France, which Charlemagne and his worthies had once represented, and which it was now incumbent on all to reassume. In the eyes of the clerics of the eleventh century, Charlemagne was still what he had been in the earlier age, the priestly king; and he became besides, in the course of the century, little by little, the crusading king. He remained the emperor of all Christendom, and became most especially king of the fairest kingdom this side of heaven: '*Par cels de France vuet il del tut errer.*' His Frenchmen conquered, not for themselves, but for God, to '*eshalcier sainte crestienté.*' This was wholly the spirit of the Crusades, wholly the spirit of the *chansons de geste,* and of the most beautiful of these, the *Chanson de Roland*" (p. 63).

Et voilà!—the mythology of France to this day, already full born.

the fairy queen Argante (a variant of the name Morgant or Morgan), he would return one day to this earth.[108] *

These three, then—of Geoffrey, Wace, and Layamon, in Latin, French, and English—are the basic texts of the first order of Arthurian literary legend, the Anglo-Norman epic texts of "the whole history of the king." There is little of love, nothing of the gentle heart, and much of the clash of armies in their pages; much about the king himself and little of his individual knights; nearly nothing of his queen, who is hardly more than a name (and, at that, a very bad one), now at his side, now in treasonous league with his nephew, and at last in flight to a convent from her noble husband's wrath. It was from this tradition of the "whole history of Arthur" that the concluding scenes of Malory's *Le Morte Darthur* were derived and of Tennyson's *Idylls of the King*.

Very different were both the ideals and flavor of the works of the following category.

B. *The French Courtly Romances, c. 1160–1230.* For in France, where the figure of Charlemagne had already inspired a beloved national epos, Arthur as king held small appeal. Interest shifted to his knights. And it was the court poet, Chrétien de Troyes (fl. c. 1160–1190?), of Queen Eleanor's daughter, the Countess Marie de Champagne, who first invented—or at least committed to writing in fluent octosyllabic couplets—the image of Arthur's court with its Round Table, as merely a base from which his model knights set forth, and back to which they returned when all was done. Chrétien's major works were as follows:

1. A *Tristan:* lost, date unknown
2. *Erec and Enid:* c. 1170
3. *Cligés:* c. 1176
4. *Lancelot, or The Knight of the Cart:* after 1176
5. *Yvain, or The Knight of the Lion:* c. 1180
6. *Perceval, or The Legend of the Grail:* after 1181

The poets of the Middle Ages employed the terms *matière* and *san* to refer, respectively, to their source materials and their own imaginative interpretations. What version of the Tristan *matière* Chrétien followed and what *san* he gave to it, are unknown. It is clear, however, that he cannot in any sense have been the inventor

* Cf. supra, pp. 184–86.

of the tale; nor was he of any of the rest—the first three of which, *Erec, Cligés,* and *Lancelot,* were attempts to counteract the influence of the powerful Tristan theme with what have been appropriately termed anti-Tristan works. The *Lancelot,* not quite finished, was terminated by a certain Godefroy de Lagny, and the *Perceval,* also unfinished, by four separate continuators: the first two anonymous (both before 1200), the next Manessier (between 1214 and 1227), and the fourth Gerbert (c. 1130).

Erec and Enid, a tale of wifely constancy resembling that (in the *Parzival*) of the lady of the tent and her spouse,* Chrétien declares to have been a story "which those who desire to earn their livelihood by telling tales are wont to dismember and spoil in the presence of kings and counts." A Welsh version of the same, *Geraint,* corresponds, not only in outline but in many precise details, and is of about the same date as Chrétien's piece.

Cligés, on the other hand, is a composite, based on several scattered models, Oriental and Celtic, deliberately put together as a direct negative to the *Tristan.* "Virtually every incident of the poem," declares Professor Bruce in his formidable work on *The Evolution of Arthurian Romance,* "can be traced to its source. It approaches, however, close to invention—certainly as near to invention as we can expect of a poet of the Middle Ages or of most of modern times—that is to say, Chrétien had taken widely separated details and brought them into a new combination, so as to produce the effect of originality." [109]

It is a crass, very cruel tale of a doting husband so befooled by his wife and her lover that he is finally shamed to death, after which the woman, who has been tantalizingly putting the lover off, "so as not to be like Iseult," accepts him in marriage. "A highly complicated but perfectly definite statement of the ideal relations of the sexes," states one amazing modern critic; [110] and apparently Chrétien thought so too.

Both the *matière* and the *san* of the *Lancelot,* Chrétien tells, were supplied to him by the Countess Marie, and in verse 468 (*car si con li contes afiche,* "for as the story testifies") he refers to a *conte,* an oral tale, as his authority. [111] But apparently in this case neither *san* nor *matière* quite appealed to him, since he left the

* Supra, pp. 437 and 447-48.

work to be finished by another. It is the famous tale of the abduction of Guinevere by the rude dark prince Meleagant and her rescue from his dangerous isle by Lancelot.

Yvain, a truly wonderful adventure tale, is by all odds Chrétien's best. It is perfectly duplicated, however, in the Welsh legend of *Owain and the Countess of the Fountain.*

But there is a Welsh counterpart also of Chrétien's *Perceval, Peredur.* Hence, since *Erec* is matched by *Geraint,* and *Yvain* by *Owain,* the question has been earnestly asked as to which came first, Chrétien's versions of these tales or the Welsh; the answer to which is now that Chrétien came first. However, it is not clear that Chrétien was the source, or at least the sole source, of the Welsh tales *Geraint, Owain,* and *Peredur.* Professor Loomis's answer is the best: namely, that in each of the first two cases the French and the Welsh authors worked independently from "what was substantially a common original, written in the French language"; and in relation, then, to *Peredur* and *Perceval,* the sources again were French, but apparently of variant forms. "For," as Loomis states, "it has been pointed out by a succession of scholars that again and again *Peredur* agrees with Wolfram's *Parzival* or the Middle English *Sir Percevelle* or the Italian *Carduino* against Chrétien. No one would suspect the Welsh author of reading the German, English, or Italian poems, especially since the last two were composed a hundred years or so after his time, and it is inconceivable that the English and Continental authors could read Welsh. Only French sources, other than Chrétien, can explain the numerous agreements. Even Wolfram, who knew and used *Le Conte del Graal* [Chrétien's *Perceval*], nevertheless repudiates Chrétien's authority and reveals a· large debt to sources which, though sometimes close to Chrétien, must have been independent branches of the widespread tradition of Perceval and the Grail." [112]

In sum: by Chrétien's time, c. 1160–1190, there was a floating body of Celtic lore available in French, both in oral and in written form, from which the poets of the age were deriving the *matière* of those masterworks of poetic romance that stand at the headwaters of our modern creative tradition. Back of all lay Celtic myth. Next, as a consequence of historic crises, new names and personalities—Arthur, Gawain, Tristan, Mark, et cetera—became the focal centers around which a new folk tradition developed, renewing the timeless archetypes of old: the well-known Celtic mythic and legendary patterns of hero birth and death, tragic loves and magical deeds. The composition of these folk materials into masterful oral epics followed, as the work of professional fabulators—some, no doubt, in the cottages of the peasantry, others, we know, in the palace halls of kings. Presently, c. 1150, written versions began appearing and what is known as the "history of literature" began —almost chemically, on every hand simultaneously, with inspired authors at work on identical themes: everywhere the same *matière*, but in each case, under each hand, a different *san*.

And as for Chrétien's *san*, let me quote Professor Bruce:

Taken altogether, Chrétien is undoubtedly the best of the French authors of metrical romances that deal with the *matière de Bretagne*. In saying this, however, we are making an ac-knowledgment of the limitations of what was achieved in this *genre*—at least, in France; for in the works of this writer there is no question of the higher imagination, of philosophical insight into the riddles of existence, of "the dower of spanning wisdom," with regard to either character or the conduct of life, or of the magic of diction and phrase, which have distinguished the representative poets of many other ages. His imagery is confined to a few similes—the majority of which are of a purely conventional kind—and to a restricted, though somewhat richer, store of metaphor. His "criticism of life" is merely that of a shrewd, alert, man of the world of his time. He was quite contented with the feudal society in which he moved and he delighted in the bustle and splendor if its festivities, its pageantry, and its tournaments. Within the bounds of this society, apart from the externals just mentioned, the code of chivalry and the problems of the relations of the sexes—the latter especially in the new form which these problems had assumed under the system of the *amour courtois*—were the things that most attracted him. Moreover, living in a naïve age, when in the elementary interests and emotions the grown man was nearer to the child than at present, he was keenly susceptible to the spell of the marvellous, as were his contemporaries generally. Consequently, the setting which he gives to the life of chivalry and to his solution of the above-mentioned problems is taken largely from the folk-tales of Celtic regions and of the Orient, where such fancies most abounded, with occasional admixture of classical *motifs*. In the case of *Perceval*, perhaps, he did not understand the full significance of the materials that he drew from his sources, but, in general, the combination of the various elements of content and setting in his poems produces on the reader an effect of harmonious unity, and the creation of this new world in which mediaeval barons and ladies jostle fairies and even stranger Otherworld figures is no mean achievement.

Since love is the dominant theme of Chrétien's romances, it is natural that he should display most knowledge of the human heart in his characterizations of women. We are wearied occasionally, it is true, with the hair-splitting analyses of amorous emotions in the lovers' soliloquies of his romances and with the conceits which such analyses engender, but the patient loyalty of Enid, the sovereign haughtiness of Guinevere, and the piquant fickleness of Laudine [Yvain's Countess of the Fountain] in their relations with their lovers or husbands are depicted with much truth to nature and with no little charm, and, in the last-named case, also, with an effective touch of *malice*.

It is particularly, however, as a born *conteur* that Chrétien can claim a notable place among the poets of the Middle Ages. In telling a story his sparkling vivacity never fails him, and, as a German critic has happily said, he makes the impression of a juggler who can shake couplets out of his sleeve as long as he pleases. . . .

However, his most memorable services to the great cause of poetry, perhaps, were in stimulating immeasurably the imagination of his contemporaries—for the vast forest of mediaeval Arthurian romance sprang mainly from the seeds of his sowing —and in enriching the whole poetic tradition of Europe with new and beautiful themes on which greater men than himself have exercised their genius, from the age immediately succeeding his own down to that of Tennyson and Wagner.[113]

And so let us turn now to the next great phase of development of this magical world of inspiration, wherein the Grail became the vessel of the Last Supper. For over what formerly had been but Celtic magic the baptismal waters of the Church were poured, and caldrons became chalices: where Manannan Mac Lir had served the ale of immortality and the flesh of swine that, killed today, were alive again tomorrow, Christ arrived to serve the wine of his blood and the meat of his immortal flesh.

C. *The religious legends of the Grail, c. 1180–1230.* The main works of this abundant, enormously influential tradition are four:

1. *Joseph d'Arimathie,* composed between 1180 and 1199 by a Burgundian poet, Robert de Boron, who claims for his source a mysterious "great book" (*grant livre*). It is here that the Grail is first represented as a chalice, the vessel of the Last Supper, which had been carried to Britain toward the end of the first century by Joseph of Arimathea.

2. *L'Estoire del Saint Graal,* the first member of a huge, rambling, heterogeneous quintet of prose romances in Old French known to scholarship as the Vulgate Cycle: their various authorships are anonymous, their dates c. 1215–1230, and the order of their composition is a matter of dispute.* The *Estoire,* the first member of this extremely popular treasury, duplicates the legend of Robert de Boron's *Joseph d'Arimathie,* but amplifies the tale considerably and, if Professor Loomis is correct, must have been drawn from the same *grant livre.* "Not Robert," Loomis states, "but the author of the 'grant livre' was the bold and clever man who linked certain authentic, originally Celtic traditions of the Grail with the early Christian legend of Joseph of Arimathea." [114] The *grant livre* has, of course, disappeared. Its author is unknown. But if it ever existed it must have antedated Robert's work and so may have influenced Chrétien's concept of the Grail as well.

However, in the *Estoire,* and throughout the Vulgate Cycle, the Grail, as in Chrétien, is an *escuele,* a "dish" or "bowl" (page 408, Figure 45), not, as in Robert's work, a chalice, or, as in Wolfram's, the philosphers' stone, while the Grail hero to whose coming the *Estoire* looks forward—whose career is described in the *Queste,* and whose begetting by the sinful lover of Queen Guinevere is the culminating episode of the *Lancelot*—is the absolutely chaste youth Galahad, who is unknown outside of the Vulgate Cycle.

Galahad is unknown even to Robert de Boron. He was ap-

---

* The members of the Vulgate Cycle are as follows: 1. *L'Estoire del Saint Graal,* 2. *L'Estoire de Merlin* (the *Prose Merlin*), 3. *Li Livres de Lancelot* (the *Prose Lancelot*), 4. *La Queste del Saint Graal,* and 5. *La Mort Artu.* "The whole vast corpus," states Professor Loomis, "was probably composed between 1215 and 1230, perhaps in the same county of Champagne which gave us our first Lancelot romance and our first quest of the Grail, the poems of Chrétien de Troyes" (Loomis, *The Grail,* p. 146). The popular attribution of the last three parts of this anthology to a learned clerk of Henry II's court named Walter Map, who died in 1209, has not been explained.

parently conceived and first put forward by the author of the *Queste*, a Cistercian monk, the immediate inspiration of whose highly symbolic, eminently Gothic work was the authoritative definition in 1215 by the Fourth Lateran Council, of the doctrine of the actual presence of the Savior in the bread and wine of the eucharist. Galahad's name, it has been shown, was derived from the Old Testament name Galaad (Gilead), which at times refers to a place, but at times also to a person. According to Genesis 31:47–52, the word *Galaad* means "heap of testimony." The Venerable Bede, Isidore of Seville, and numerous others in the Middle Ages construed it as a reference to Christ. Hence, Galaad (the Old French form of Galahad), who was conceived of by his author as himself a "heap of testimony" to our redemption in Christ, bears the appellation appropriately, and, as Professor Loomis comments: "Nothing better illustrates the ingenuity of the author of the Queste than the selection of this name." [115] The author of the *Estoire* almost certainly derived the name from the *Queste:* and he too was a monk, a Cistercian. The authors, on the other hand, of the bulky work that in the order of the cycle falls between the *Estoire* and the *Queste* were of a considerably more secular cast of mind; namely those of the infinitely influential, popular compendium:

3. *Li Livres de Lancelot* (*the Vulgate or Prose Lancelot*) *
This interminable terminal moraine of Arthurian bits and pieces is the product of many hands. It is in many passages wonderful, in many, simply banal. Commencing with the birth of Lancelot, whose baptismal name, significantly, is declared to have been Galahad, we pass to his fosterage in the Land below Waves of the Lady of the Lake, come then to the waking of his manhood by the beauty of Arthur's queen (at the first touch of whose hand, the text tells, he woke as it were from sleep), after which the rambling narrative moves through many adventures to the Grail Castle of King Pelles, Corbenic, where prophecies have announced that the Waste Land is to be redeemed by a son begotten by Lancelot on the king's virgin daughter. By sorcery the great knight is led to believe that he is lying with his love, Queen Guinevere, and so, the necessary work is accomplished, which is to lead to the birth and marvelous works of the "Desired Knight," as told in one of the

* See footnote, supra, p. 241.

major creative works of the Middle Ages; namely, the following member of the cycle:

4. *La Queste del Saint Graal.* The composition of this richly symbolic work almost certainly preceded the *Estoire*, which obviously was conceived as an introduction to its vision (a century before Dante's) of the journey of the Christian soul from temporal life to eternal being and bliss in the vision of God.

Let us review, as briefly as possible, the main lines of the common legend of these four interlacing works: the first by the poet Robert and the rest from the anonymous Vulgate Cycle, with two of the latter, *Estoire* and *Queste,* from the quills of cloistered monks.

1. When Joseph of Arimathea received from Pontius Pilate the vessel of the Last Supper, he was joined by Nicodemus, and the two, with Pilate's permission, removed Christ's body from the cross. They bore it to the tomb, and when the body was washed, blood flowed, which Joseph caught in the Grail.

The Jews, terrified by the Resurrection, believing that Joseph had hidden Christ's body, condemned him to a dungeon, where the resurrected Savior appeared and, again presenting the Grail, instructed him to entrust it to none save his brother-in-law Bron and the son who would be born to Bron. All who ever beheld the Grail, Christ declared, would be of his own true company and dwell in eternal joy.

And so Joseph remained with the Grail until it came to pass, in Rome, that the emperor's son Vespasian was cured of leprosy by the sight of the veil with which Veronica had wiped the face of Christ. In gratitude he went to Judea and, discovering Joseph in his dungeon, released him and slew many of the Jews.[116]

Joseph, together with his sister Enygeus and her saintly spouse Bron, then set off with a large company of converted Jews on an indeterminate journey, during the course of which, because of the sins of certain members, the crops failed and all were on the point of death. Joseph prayed before the Grail and the voice of the Holy Ghost declared that, in the name of the table at which Christ last sat, he was to build another table, at which one seat was to be left vacant because Judas, when he withdrew from the first, had left a vacant seat. Moreover, Bron was to catch a fish, and that, with the

Grail, was to be placed on the table. Joseph was to sit where Christ had sat, Bron at his right, and the vacant seat between, which should remain empty until occupied by the son of Enygeus's son.

Joseph did as told, and bade his people sit. Those who remained standing were the sinners and, so proven, were ordered to leave. However, one of them, named Moyses, presuming to sit in the vacant seat, the earth opened and he disapeared.

Now there were born to Enygeus and Bron twelve sons, of whom one, Alain, was not to marry but to be the keeper of the vessel and to voyage with his brethren westward to the farthest point, preaching Christ.* "The Lord," declared an angelic voice, "knows Bron to be a worthy man; that is why the Lord willed him to go fishing. He is now to receive the vessel from Joseph, who will instruct him in those holy words that God spoke to him in the dungeon—which are sweet and precious, merciful, and properly called the Secrets of the Grail." Bron was to be called THE RICH FISHER, because of the fish he had caught, at which time the period of grace began. And when his son's son arrived, he would pass the vessel on, whereupon the meaning of the Trinity would have been fulfilled. Joseph obediently consigned the Grail to Bron and, when the company, weeping, departed for the farthest West, returned alone to the land of his birth.

2. The author of the *Estoire* pretends that on Good Friday, 717 A.D., Christ, appearing in a dream, presented him with a book composed by the Savior *after* the resurrection. The recipient, reading, swooned and was transported to Heaven, to a vision of the Trinity. When he returned to earth, he put the book away and it disappeared, but reappeared on the altar of a mysterious forest chapel, where, following Christ's command, he transcribed from it "The Early History of the Grail."

In the main, the first portion of this untidy composition parallels Robert de Boron's *Joseph,* except that the keeper of the Grail is now not Joseph, who is married, but his celibate son Josephe. (The author, we have said, was a monk.) Moreover, the Grail company, before heading west, goes east to the city of Sarras, where

---

* The reader is not to worry about inconsistencies. First we hear that Bron's son is to be the last keeper of the Grail. Next we learn that it will be Bron's grandson. Now we hear that Bron's son is to remain chaste. These are not the only inconsistencies of this poet, who must have been drawing from different sources, which he simply failed to collate.

the heathen monarch and his brother, when converted, take the names Mordrain and Nascien. Christ, appearing, makes Josephe a bishop, the first in Christendom, and Nascien, uncovering the Grail, goes blind, but is healed with the blood pouring from a lance, which, as Josephe prophesies, will not again bleed until the Adventures of the Grail take place. At that time the unveiled marvels of the Grail would be disclosed to the last scion of Nascien's line.

A series of adventures follows around an extraordinary ship, which Solomon built on his wife's advice when he had had a vision of that same last scion of his own and Nascien's line. Within it on a rich bed in a sumptuous chamber lay David's sword and a crown—the sword, however, embellished with coarse trappings of tow and hemp put there by Solomon's wife, which were to be changed for better by a virgin at the time of the Adventures of the Grail. And on that bed there were three spindles, a red, a white, and a green, fashioned from sprouts of the Tree of Life that Eve carried from the Garden: the allegory of that ship being Holy Mother Church; of the bed, the altar of the sacrifice; and of the spindles, the red, the passion of Christ, the white, purity, and the green, hope. (Or, as interpreted in the *Queste:* the white, Eve's virginity; the green, her motherhood; and the red, the blood of her son Abel, whose death, the first in the world, prefigured that of Mary's son.) The ship moved marvelously of itself on the sea and came to a turning isle to which Nascien had already been spirited; but when his unworthy hand touched the sword it broke. His brother, Mordrain, touched it and it healed. Then Nascien dreamed that the last scion of his line was to return to Sarras in that ship.

All arrived miraculously in Britain, which they proceeded to convert. And there Mordrain, presuming to unveil the Grail, was blinded and paralyzed. He would be cured, a voice proclaimed, only when the blood of the lance again flowed and the good knight came to visit him. He retired, maimed, to a hermitage, which he made into an abbey and endowed.

And now Bron (who has not appeared before in this work) is told by Joseph's son Josephe that the vacant seat at the table of the Grail was of Jesus (not, as in Robert's work, of Judas) and was to remain empty until filled either by Christ or by someone sent by Christ (namely, Galahad). Moys (Moyses), daring to occupy it, is snatched away by fiery hands, after which Josephe consecrates Bron's son Alain as Keeper of the Grail (Figure 45), and Alain feeds the company with a single fish he has caught, for which miracle he and those to follow him are to be known as THE RICH FISHER.

After further marvels the company reaches Scotland, where an adventure like that of Tristan befalls the son of Bron who is to become the ancestor of Gawain. His name, as here given, is Peter. Wounded by a poisoned weapon while battling a sinful heathen, he has himself sent to sea in a boat, is discovered by the daughter of an island king, and, when cured, slays the King of Ireland; whereupon he is offered the hand of the island princess by her father.[117]

Joseph and Josephe die in Scotland, after which Alain, proceeding to *la Terre Foraine,* "the Foreign Land," cures its king, Alphasem, of leprosy: who in gratitude builds a castle for the Grail which he names Corbenic; but for daring to spend a night in it he is wounded by a lance through both thighs.[118] Joseph, before him, had been wounded, battling a heathen, by a sword thrust through both thighs;[119] Peter, we have just seen, was also wounded; and before that, early in the legend, Josephe himself had been wounded by an angel who thrust a lance through his right thigh.[120] Alain presently dies, then Alphasem; and in due time the seventh Rich Fisher, Lambor, is slain by a Saracen, who, with the sword from Solomon's ship, cleaves both him and his horse to the ground, whereupon *la Terre Foraine,* "the Foreign Land," becomes *la Terre Gaste,* "the Waste Land." Pelleam, next, is maimed in battle by a lance thrust through both thighs and is known, thereafter, as the Maimed King: but his son, Pelles, becomes father of the maid who is to give birth to Galahad.[121]

3. And so now, for the delicate scene of the begetting of that perfect knight, we may turn to Malory's translation of the episode in *Le Morte Darthur* (1485), from the Old French *Prose Vulgate Lancelot:*

> The king knew well that Sir Launcelot should get a child upon his daughter, the which should be named Sir Galahad the good knight, by whom all the foreign country should be brought out of danger, and by him the Holy Greal should be achieved. Then came forth a lady that hight Dame Brisen, and she said unto the king: Sir, wit ye well Sir Launcelot loveth no lady in

the world but all only Queen Guenever. O fair lady, Dame Brisen, said the king, hope ye to bring this about? Sir, said she, upon pain of my life let me deal; for this Brisen was one of the greatest enchantresses that was at that time in the world living.

Then anon by Dame Brisen's wit she made one to come to Sir Launcelot that he knew well. And this man brought him a ring from Queen Guenever like as it had come from her, and such one as she was wont for the most part to wear; and when Sir Launcelot saw that token wit ye well he was never so fain. Where is my Lady? said Sir Launcelot. In the castle of Case, said the messenger, but five mile hence. Then Sir Launcelot thought to be there the same night. And then this Brisen by the commandment of King Pelles let send Elaine to this castle with twenty-five knights unto the castle of Case.

Then Sir Launcelot against night rode unto that castle, and there anon he was received worshipfully with such people to his seeming as were about Queen Guenever secret. So when Sir Launcelot was alit, he asked where the queen was. So Dame Brisen said she was in her bed; and then the people were avoided, and Sir Launcelot was led unto his chamber. And then Dame Brisen brought Sir Launcelot a cupful of wine; and anon as he had drunken the wine he was so assotted and mad that he might make no delay, but withouten any let he went to bed; and he weened that maiden Elaine had been Queen Guenever. Wit you well that Sir Launcelot was glad, and so was that lady Elaine that she had gotten Sir Launcelot in her arms. For well she knew that same night should be gotten upon her Galahad that should prove the best knight of the world; and so they lay together until underne of the morn; and all the windows and holes of that chamber were stopped that no manner of day might be seen. And then Sir Launcelot remembered him, and he arose up and went to the window.

And anon as he had unshut the window the enchantment was gone; then he knew himself that he had done amiss. Alas, he said, that I have lived so long; now I am shamed. So then he got his sword in his hand and said: Thou traitoress, what art thou that I have lain by all this night? thou shalt die right here of my hands.

Then this fair lady Elaine skipped out of her bed all naked, and kneeled down afore Sir Launcelot, and said: Fair courteous knight, come of king's blood, I require you have mercy upon me, and as thou art renowned the most noble knight of the world, slay me not, for I have in my womb him by thee that shall be the most noblest knight of the world.

Ah, false traitoress, said Sir Launcelot, why hast thou betrayed me? anon tell me what thou art.

Sir, she said, I am Elaine, the daughter of King Pelles.

Well, said Sir Launcelot, I will forgive you this deed; and therewith he took her up in his arms, and kissed her, for she was as fair a lady, and thereto lusty and young, and as wise, as any was that time living. So God me help, said Sir Launcelot, I may not wyte this to you; but her that made this enchantment upon me as between you and me, an I may find her, that same Lady Brisen, she shall lose her head for witchcrafts, for there was never knight deceived so as I am this night.

Then she said: My lord Sir Launcelot, I beseech you see me as soon as ye may, for I have obeyed me unto the prophecy that my father told me. And by his commandment to fulfil this prophecy I have given the greatest riches and the fairest flower that ever I had, and that is my maidenhood that I shall never have again; and therefore, gentle knight, owe me your goodwill.

And so Sir Launcelot arrayed him and was armed, and took his leave mildly at that young Elaine; and so he departed, and rode till he came to the castle of Corbin, where her father was. And as fast as her time came she was delivered of a fair child, and they christened him Galahad; and wit ye well that child was well kept and well nourished, and he was named Galahad by cause Sir Launcelot was so named at the fountain stone; and after that the Lady of the Lake confirmed him Sir Launcelot du Lake.[122]

4. It was on the vigil of the feast of Pentecost, as we read in *La Queste del Saint Graal,* that a beautiful damsel rode into the dining hall of Camelot, and in the name of the Rich Fisher, King Pelles, summoning Lancelot to follow to the forest, conducted him to a nunnery where Galahad was being raised. There he found the knights Bors and Lionel, his cousins, and the next morning dubbed his son, not knowing who he was; then returned with the knights to Camelot, leaving Galahad with the nuns. But when they entered the dining hall, behold, an inscription had appeared on the Perilous Seat: FOUR HUNDRED YEARS AND FIFTY-FOUR HAVE PASSED SINCE THE PASSION OF JESUS CHRIST: AND ON THE FEAST OF PENTECOST THIS SEAT IS TO FIND ITS MASTER. A servant entered. "Sire," he cried to the king, "I bring most marvelous news." He

had seen a beautiful sword, fixed in a red stone, floating on the river, which all hastened to view; and on the pommel they read in letters of gold: NO ONE EVER WILL DRAW ME HENCE BUT HIM AT WHOSE SIDE I AM TO HANG: AND HE WILL BE THE BEST KNIGHT IN THE WORLD. Arthur bade Lancelot assay the adventure, but he refused. Gawain failed in it; also, Perceval. Whereat, marveling, all returned to Arthur's hall.

And when they were seated, the doors and windows suddenly closed of themselves, yet the room remained light, and there entered an old man clothed in white, conducting a knight arrayed in red, with neither sword nor shield. "King Arthur," said the old man "I bring to you the Desired Knight, sprung from the high lineage of King David and the line of Joseph of Arimathea, by whom the marvels of this country and the foreign lands are to be ended. Regard him!"

He departed, and the young knight, coming forward, occupied the Perilous Seat, where his name had appeared in gold: THIS IS GALAHAD'S SEAT. And Guinevere, the queen, then realized whose son this was.

Galahad rose, left the hall, and, with all watching, drew the sword from the stone, whereupon a tournament of joyous welcome was arranged, during which—though as yet without a shield—he unhorsed every knight except Perceval and Lancelot, his father. All heard vespers and returned to their evening meal.

And so they were sitting at table when a great crack of thunder was heard,* an intense light filled the hall, and the radiant Holy Grail appeared, covered with a white samite cloth and borne by hands invisible. There poured from it a marvelous fragrance. And it satisfied every knight that was there with the food that pleased him best; then disappeared.

Arthur, greatly marveling, spoke to those about him of the joy and thanks to the Lord that all should feel for the love and grace bestowed on them by this sign on the day of Pentecost. But Gawain, pointing out that the vessel had been veiled, proposed to all a vow: to depart for a year and a day, setting forth the very next morning, to find and see the Grail unveiled. All present following suit, the king became disconsolate; for he feared the loss of his knights. And the ladies too were distressed when they learned of

* Compare *Ulysses*, supra, p. 281.

this terrible vow: they cried in their dining room most tenderly and declared when they rejoined their knights that they were going too. At which point, however, an old hermit, entering, announced that it would be a mortal sin for any woman to go on that quest; nor should there go any knight who had not confessed his sins.

"For this quest," said he, "is not of earthly things. It is the search for the highest secrets and hidden things of Our Lord, those high mysteries which the Highest Teacher will disclose only to that blessed knight among the knights of this earth whom He has elected to His Service. To him will He uncover the great marvels of the Holy Grail, causing him to behold what no mortal heart can devise, nor terrestrial tongue describe." [123]

All retired with thoughts on the morrow, and the king unable to sleep. They had decided to ride forth, each in his own direction, because to start out in a group would have been shameful. And in the morning, at first light, the fellowship rose. When all had assumed their arms, they attended Mass and, when that was done, mounting, commended their good king to God, thanked him for the honors he had done them, and, issuing from his castle, "entered into the forest, at one point and another, there where they saw it to be thickest, *all in those places where they found no way or path.* . . ." [124]

Now Dante, in the *Convito,* and again when writing to Can Grande, his patron, was to make the point that spiritual writings "may be taken and should be expounded chiefly in four senses": the literal, the allegorical, the moral, and the anagogical. The literal of his own *Commedia* is the passage of himself out of the "dark wood" in which he had been lost on the vigil of Good Friday, 1300 A.D., midway along the road of his life; and his transit then beyond the spheres of Hell, Purgatory, and Heaven, to a vision of the Trinity in the rose of Paradise: and at every stage along the way there were those to be seen who had arrived only that far. So likewise in the *Queste:* the literal story is of the several adventuring knights, going their several ways in the wood "where they found no way or path," and of their various grades of achievement: Galahad alone, like Dante, arriving at the ultimate vision, beyond speech.

The allegorical senses are in both works announced by references to the calendar: in Dante, the vigil of Good Friday; in the

Queste, that of Pentecost. Thus each in its own way is an *imitatio Christi:* the first, of Christ in his death and resurrection; the second, of Christ resurrected, as he appeared in that upper room— "the doors being shut" [125]—where, on the day of Pentecost, his disciples were gathered together.[126]

The moral meanings of the two works are rendered in their definitions of character: their analyses of the sins and virtues of the personages variously met and left along the way between the "dark wood" and the Beatific Vision: the moral in both being of the turning of the heart from sensual to spiritual concerns. In the *Queste,* the precipitating event—the general vision of the covered yet radiant Holy Grail in Arthur's hall—corresponds, for all who beheld it, to that moment of "aesthetic arrest" described in Dante's *Vita Nuova* (and in Joyce's *Portrait of the Artist as a Young Man*),* when the first sight of Beatrice at the age of nine (the girl wading in the stream) transferred the appetite of the poet's noble heart from the forms of mortal sense to those of reason moving toward divine intelligence.† And as in Dante's Hell, Purgatory, and Paradise, so again here: there have been many called, but the impediments of sin leave all but the gifted few strewn variously in defeat or partial victory along the way.

In both works, furthermore, the anagogical sense—the "upward pointing," the "upward lead," to mysteries beyond the reach of sight, sound, word, or symbol ‡—is again the same: the Beatific Vision, beheld by Dante in the radiant celestial bowl of the rose of Paradise, and to be seen, finally, by Galahad within the mystic vessel of the Grail. (Compare again Figures 4, 11, and 45.) Thus the Grail in this work is equivalent to the celestial rose in Dante and, in Buddhist imagery, to the lotus of the saying "OM MANI PADME HUM: the jewel in the lotus." [127]

However, between the anagogical sense of the Buddhist lotus of the universe and the vessel of the Grail as viewed by the author of the *Queste*—though not of the Grail as viewed by Wolfram—there is a world of difference. It is certain that the Cistercian monk who was the author of the *Queste* had been greatly inspired by the confirmation at the Fourth Lateran Council, in the year 1215, of the

---

* Supra, pp. 68–69.
† Compare Goethe, supra, p. 383.
‡ Compare Kant, supra, pp. 339–40: $a:b = c:x$.

Catholic dogma of the Real Presence of Christ's body in the sacrament of the altar (the Host in the ciborium). As stated for all time in the Latin of that Council: *"Una vero est fidelium universalis ecclesia, extra quam nullus omnino salvatur. In qua idem ipse sacerdos, et sacrificium Jesus Christus; cujus corpus et sanguis in sacramento altaris sub speciebus panis et vini veraciter contenentur; transubstantiata pane in corpus et vino in sanguinem, potestate divina, ut ad perficiendum mysterium unitatis accipimus ipsi de suo quod accepit ipse de nostro:* There is, verily, one true, universal church, outside of which no one whosoever is saved. In which one and the same Jesus Christ is himself both priest and sacrifice, whose body and blood are truly contained in the sacrament of the altar under the species of bread and wine; * the bread being transubstantiated into the body and the wine into the blood, by the power of God, so that through the accomplishment of this mystery of unity, we receive him unto ourselves, that he unto himself may receive us." [128]

Part and parcel of the *literal* sense of the Cistercian *Queste del Saint Graal,* therefore, is its representation of the influence of the sacraments. Their effects upon those who receive or reject them are to be read literally and morally, as well as allegorically and anagogically. Those who reject them are lost and will end, literally, in Hell. Those who receive them properly will be saved, each according to his own life and faith. That is the aspect of the moral of this work which sets it (together with its Church) apart from the natural order of mankind, in a sacerdotal fairyland of nuns, angelic voices, forest chapels, and consecrations; along with false allures and temptresses dispelled (like Wagner's palace of Klingsor) by a gestured sign of the Cross.

Galahad, the fifth day out, came to an abbey of Cistercians, where there was kept a marvelous white shield emblazoned with a large red cross. A knight that was there, King Baudemagus, attempting to carry this away, a white knight (Christ) appeared, unhorsed him, and sent the shield to Galahad by a squire. Then Gawain, some little time later, came to that same Cistercian abbey and, learning of Galahad's passage before him, rode hard along the

---

* Compare in the *Bhagavad Gītā:* "Brahman is the process of the offering, brahman the oblation; by brahman the offering is made in the fire that is brahman. Verily, brahman is realized by anyone who in all action beholds brahman" (*Bhagavad Gītā* 4:24).

same way, hoping to follow his lead, but went soon astray and came to a forest hermitage where a saintly man, learning his name, urged him to confession, chiding him for his sins. "Gawain, Gawain," the old hermit pleaded, "if only you would renounce the life you have been leading all these years, you could still make peace with Our Lord." The knight remained at heart unrepentant, however, and so failed in his quest entirely: as did Hector, the pattern of knightly pride; and Lionel, of anger. Perceval, however, Gawain's dear friend, opened his heart to God's grace and consequently fared well—very well indeed.

Perceval in this work is not married but the beautiful chaste youth again of the first years of his knighthood; and, riding his way in the pathless wood, he came into the "Waste Forest," where he chanced on a little chapel, out the window of which a hermit female thrust her head to ask the knight his name. She proved to be his aunt, known now as the Queen of the Waste Land, *La Reine de la Terre Gaste,* though she had once been, as she told him, the richest woman in the world. She informed him of his mother's death; taught him, also, the history of the Grail and of tnree tables, the chief tables of this world, namely: 1. that of the Last Supper; 2. that of Joseph and Josephe; and 3. that of the Perilous Seat, which Merlin established for King Arthur. She warned him earnestly, moreover, to remain chaste.

And riding forth, thus spiritually armed, the young knight survived a series of perils, not the least of which was of a seductress who one moonlight night, when he stirred and woke from sleep, was there, inviting him to follow on adventure. He made the sign of the Cross and with a cry she vanished in a burst of flame. Then (thanks be to God!) he arrived at Solomon's ship, where he found Galahad and Bors; and together with these there was a pure virgin, his own sister, who explained to them the symbols of the ship and, as prophesied, removed the old coarse trappings from King David's sword, replacing them with those she had made from her own golden hair woven with jewels. Whereupon she died in a most saintly way—and her body was placed on a second ship, which, like the first, sailed the seas of itself.

Lancelot also, at the outset of his adventure, encountered hermits in the wood. And he strove manfully to reform his noble heart—which, however, was Guinevere's. Urged and persuaded to confess, even to wear a hair shirt, he went his way and arrived at the seashore, where before him he found the ship bearing the body of Perceval's sister, which he boarded; and it sailed with him by moonlight to a great and marvelous castle: Castle Corbenic, of the Grail, where at midnight he heard a voice. "Lancelot! Go from this ship into that castle! There you will find in great measure what you seek."

Two lions watched the gate, and Lancelot put his hand to his sword. "Shame!" the voice cried. "Why trust you more to your hand than to your Creator?" He made the sign of the Cross, breathing a prayer of thanks, and passed within.

There was no sound but of himself in those halls until he heard somewhere a voice so sweetly singing that it seemed to him scarcely human. "To Thee, O Father in Heaven, glory, praise, and honor!" it sang. He approached and fell upon his knees. The door of a chamber opened and he saw within a great brightness. A voice warned: "Do not enter!" And he beheld the Grail there on a table of silver, covered with a cloth of red samite. Angels were all about it, and before it stood an old priest celebrating Mass.

It was the moment of the elevation of the Host, and above the priest's lifted hands Lancelot distinctly saw two aged men supporting a youth, whom they placed in the hands of the priest, who seemed about to fall from the weight. Lancelot sprang to his aid, with a prayer for Christ's forgiveness, but as he approached felt on his face a blast like fire. . . . And the folk of the castle, next morning, found him lying before the chamber in a trance that lasted twenty-four days.

"I have seen so great marvels," were Lancelot's words when he revived, "that my tongue may not describe them, nor my own heart think upon them, they are so great. That was no earthly thing, but spiritual: and were it not for my great sins, I should have seen more."

King Pelles of the castle then informed him of the death of Elaine, who had died of sorrow for himself; and in grief, wearing still his hair shirt, the knight rode away.

Bors, Perceval, and Galahad next arrived at the same castle and were joined there by three knights from Ireland, three from Gaul, three from Wales, King Pelles also, his son Eliezar, and his niece: and at vesper time the Maimed King, Pelles' father, was carried in on a couch by four maidens, who, when they had set it down, withdrew. A voice ordered all to leave the room that were not of the fellowship of the quest, and all save Bors, Perceval, Galahad, and the Maimed King departed.

"And therewithal," we read in Malory's translation of this episode,

beseemed them that there came a man, and four angels from heaven, clothed in likeness of a bishop, and had a cross in his hand; and these four angels bare him in a chair, and set him down before the table of silver whereupon the Sangreal was; and it seemed that he had in the middest of his forehead letters the which said: SEE HERE JOSEPHE THE FIRST BISHOP OF CHRISTEN-DOM THE SAME WHICH OUR LORD SUCCOURED IN THE CITY OF SARRAS IN THE SPIRITUAL PLACE. Then the knights marvelled, for that bishop was dead more than three hundred year tofore. O knights, said he, marvel not, for I was sometime an earthly man.

With that they heard the chamber door open, and there they saw angels; and two bare candles of wax, and the third a towel, and the fourth a spear which bled marvellously, that three drops fell within a box which he held in his other hand. And they set the candles upon the table, and the third the towel upon the vessel, and the fourth the holy spear even upright upon the vessel. And then the bishop made semblant as though he would have gone to the sacring of the mass.

And then he took an ubblye which was made in the likeness of bread. And at the lifting up there came a figure in the likeness of a child, and the visage was as red and as bright as any fire, and smote himself into the bread, so that they all saw it that the bread was formed of a fleshly man; and then he [Josephe] put it into the holy vessel again, and then he did that longed to a priest to do to a mass. And then he went to Galahad and kissed him, and bade him go and kiss his fellows: and so he did anon.

Now, said he, servants of Jesu Christ, ye shall be fed afore this table with sweetmeats that never knights tasted. And when he had said, he vanished away. And they set them at the table in great dread, and made their prayers. Then looked they and saw a man come out of the holy vessel that had all the signs of the passion of Jesu Christ, bleeding all openly, and said: My knights, and my servants, and my true children, which be come out of deadly life into spiritual life, I will now no longer hide me from you, but ye shall see now a part of my secrets and of my hidden things: now hold and receive the high meat which ye have so much desired. Then took he himself the holy vessel and came to Galahad; and he kneeled down, and there received his Saviour, and after him so received all his fellows; and they thought it so sweet that it was marvellous to tell. Then said he to Galahad: Son, wotest thou what I hold betwixt my hands? Nay, said he, but if ye will tell me. This is, said he, the holy dish wherein I ate the lamb on Sher-Thursday. And now hast thou seen that thou most desired to see, but yet hast thou not seen it so openly as thou shalt see it in the city of Sarras in the spiritual place. Therefore thou must go hence and bear with thee this holy vessel; for this night it shall depart from the realm of Logris, that it shale never be seen more here. And wotest thou wherefore? For he is not served nor worshipped to his right by them of this land, for they be turned to evil living; therefore I shall disherit them of the honour which I have done them. And therefore go ye three tomorrow unto the sea, where ye shall find your ship ready, and with you take the sword with the strange girdles, and no more with you but Sir Percivale and Sir Bors. Also I will that ye take with you of the blood of this spear for to anoint the maimed king, both his legs and all his body, and he shall have his health.

Sir, said Galahad, why shall not these other fellows go with us?

For this cause: for right as I departed my apostles one here and another there, so will I that ye depart; and two of you shall die in my service, but one of you shall come again and tell tidings. Then he gave them his blessings and vanished away.[129]

Galahad healed the Maimed King with the blood flowing from the lance, and the old man immediately retired to an abbey of Cistercians. The knights then rode to the shore, where they found and again boarded Solomon's ship. It backed away, set to sea, and sailed with Bors, Perceval, Galahad, and the Grail aboard toward the distant city of Sarras, whence all this holiness originally came. On the way, Galahad prayed that he might die; for at Corbenic he had experienced such spiritual joy that his body was now an encumbrance. Perceval bade him lie upon the bed, the rich bed in the ship's holy chamber where the Grail on its silver table reposed; and night and day the ship sailed, none knowing to what port, while Galahad slept.

He woke when they reached Sarras. In port lay the other ship, bearing the body of Perceval's sister. "Truly," said Perceval, "in God's name! Well has my sister kept us covenant!" And they disembarked, bearing the table of the Grail, with Bors and Perceval before and Galahad behind. They bade an old cripple who had not walked for ten years to lend Galahad a hand; he rose and joined them: and when the king learned of that miracle, he thrust all three into a dungeon, where they were fed by the Grail until the king himself, falling ill of his deed, sent for them, prayed mercy, and, when forgiven, died. Then Galahad became king.

One year thereafter, entering the room of the palace where the Grail stood on its table, they beheld there kneeling a beautiful man in the likeness of a bishop, with about him a fellowship of angels. He rose and began a Mass in honor of Our Lady; and after the consecration, turned. "Come forward," he said to Galahad, "thou servant of Jesus Christ: now shalt thou see what thou hast long desired to behold."

And the knight arose. He went forward, gazed full into the bowl of the uncovered Grail, and as soon as he had done so began to tremble terribly, as when mortal flesh begins to regard spiritual things. He lifted his arms. "Lord," he prayed, "I adore and thank Thee; for Thou hast accomplished here my desire. Now I see all openly what tongue cannot speak, neither heart conceive: the beginning and end of the great adventure: marvels of all marvels. And my dear sweet Lord, since it is thus that Thou hast accomplished in me my wish, letting me see what I have all my days desired, so now I pray that in this great joy Thou mayest suffer me to pass on from this terrestrial to celestial life." [130]

The bishop took in his hands the very body of Christ, the consecrated Host, and proffered it to Galahad, who received it gladly and meekly.

"Do you know now who I am?" the bishop asked. "I am Joseph of Arimathea. And Our Lord sent me to bear you fellowship, for you have resembled me in two things: in that you have seen the marvels of the Holy Grail, and in that you have been a clean maiden, as I have been and am."

And when the bishop had said these words, Galahad went to Perceval and kissed him, commending him to God, and likewise to Sir Bors, to whom, however, he said: "Fair Lord, salute me to my lord, Sir Lancelot, my father, and as soon as you shall see him, bid him remember this unstable world."

"And therewith," Malory translates, "he kneeled down tofore the table and made his prayers, and then suddenly his soul departed to Jesus Christ, and a great multitude of angels bare his soul up to heaven, that the two fellows might well behold it. Also the two fellows saw come from heaven a hand but they saw no body. And then it came right to the Vessel, and took it and the spear, and so bare it up to heaven. Sithen was there never man so hardy to say that he had seen the Sangreal." [131]

Perceval expired also, but Sir Bors returned to Camelot, to recount there the adventure. However, in Arthur's court, as told in *La Mort Artu,* the last portion of the Old French Vulgate Cycle (Malory, Books XVIII–XXI, and Tennyson's terminal *Idylls of the King:* "The Last Tournament," "Guinevere," and "The Passing of Arthur"), pride, treachery, and the increasingly brazen conduct of a relapsed Lancelot and the queen, brought about an ugly *Götterdämmerung,* which today can be read as a prophecy of the end of the Gothic world itself, which, in fact, immediately followed. For the removal of the symbol of value, the Grail, from earth to Heaven in Solomon's ship had left life on earth without a spiritual center, and the City of Man, the kingdom of Arthur, went apart.

As in the crystalline bed of the love grotto, so here in Galahad's bed of rapture in the hold of Solomon's ship (which, like the rudderless boat of Tristan, sails of itself to its voyager's goal: a Celtic ship to Avalon, heading now the other way) all thought of service to life through knightly deeds is abandoned for an ecstasy: in Galahad's case, by the right-hand path, to the Father and the light; in Tristan's the left-hand way, to the Mothers.* The bed in the chamber of Solomon's ship is compared to the altar of the Mass; likewise, the bed in the grotto. Allegorically, the altar is the Cross of Christ, the place of sacrifice. But the Cross also is a bed. "A sweet bed is the wood of Thy Cross," we read, for example, in a sermon on Solomon's Song of Songs by a twelfth-century Cistercian abbot, Gilbert of Holland (d. 1172).[132] Galahad in the bed in the ship is, by analogy, Christ in his Church: the Church as inheritor of the Temple, but now departing from this world.

---

* Compare the two ways of the Gnostics, supra, pp. 145–61.

We recall Joachim of Floris (c. 1145–1202, Figure 54) and his doctrine of the Ages of the Trinity in history: of the Father and the Son (Temple and Church, i.e. Solomon's ship), to be followed by that of the Holy Ghost (the passage to Sarras). In Robert de Boron's poem (c. 1180–1199), when Joseph in his dungeon received the Grail and heard "those holy words that are properly called the Secrets of the Grail," it was the resurrected Christ who spoke to him: a later, higher, more mystic form—not visible to all—than that of the earthly Christ who had founded the visible Church. Further, when Joseph subsequently knelt before the Grail, the voice heard was of the Holy Ghost. And finally, when the last keeper of the Grail was born, the "meaning of the Trinity" would be fulfilled.

Likewise in the *Queste,* the entire order of symbols stands beyond the exoteric order of the Church. Joseph and Josephe are *not* of the line of the historical papal throne, established by the historical Christ on the rock of historical Peter, but of a line established by Christ Resurrected. And the way to Corbenic, their hidden palace-church, is *not* by any public path, but through an inwardly governed individual quest, commencing there where the forest is thickest and most dark. When the Grail, the summoning angel of this hermetic quest, appeared in Arthur's banquet hall, the time of historic deeds and aims had abruptly ended. The moment was apocalyptic. The Age of the Holy Spirit had begun. And, as by an irresistible magnet, the entire courtly fellowship was drawn away from their spheres of earthly service. Arthur, with reason, was distressed; and the ladies, too, with reason: for, like Eve, they were the antithesis of all that the Grail (in this version) represented.

Professor Loomis, in his authoritative work, *The Grail,* makes it evident beyond question that the *matière* of the *Queste* was derived in the main from Celtic myths, largely of Manannan Mac Lir and his Welsh counterpart, Bran the Blessed: the "Rich Fisher," Bron, with his "blessed horn of plenty," *cors-benoiz* (Corbenic); his boat, the moon that rides celestial seas; and his whirling castle of mist and dream from the fairyland "below waves." However, as another student of the *Queste del Saint Graal,* Professor Frederick Locke of Stanford University, points out, "It is first and foremost a Christian book, and nothing in it suggests a conscious use of any pagan mythology, ritual, or folklore in their primitive forms. . . . Once the pre-Christian elements had been appropriated, they became thoroughly Christianized and entered completely into the symbolic structure of the new religion. They had, in fact, been chosen for their insight value and as a means of illuminating the context of the new gnosis." [133]

"In the *Queste*," Professor Locke declares, "the progressive stages of illumination are symbolized by the revelation of the Grail as a movement from what is perceived by the eyes to what is absorbed by the spirit." [134] But that precisely is the sense of all myths and rites of illumination whatsoever. Compare again the round of Figure 3. The first idiosyncrasy of the Cistercian *Queste*, therefore, is not that it points a way to illumination, but that its view is so narrowly Christian: no other way of the spirit but that of the Roman Catholic sacramental system is admitted to exist. And the second idiosyncrasy is the extreme asceticism of its concept of that way. All the symbols and values of the Celtic world are consequently reversed in this work—and not only of the Celtic world. As Professor Albert Pauphilet of the University of Paris states in the introduction to his edition of the text:

> The author of the *Queste* shows in numerous passages that what he intended was to set his work in opposition to the literature in vogue in his time. He despised bravery, purely knightly exploit, and disparaged love, choosing to confound its "courtly" form with the "vile sin of lust." From the Round Table romances, and especially the *Lancelot,* he borrowed some of the most brilliant heroes—Gawain, Yvain, Lancelot, Hector—but only to assign them to pitiful roles. And by these means, with various others, he produced the impression, from the very start of his work, that in the precincts of the Grail the world assumes an aspect totally new, where the accepted values of men and things are reversed. [135]

The women in this inverted world are of two types: those who are not, and those who are, virgins. Those who are not, of course, once were, as Lancelot once had been Galahad: at the moment of his perfection—not exactly at his birth, that is to say, for then he had been merely fallen nature, but at the moment of baptism, when his eternal soul had been magically cleansed and restored to the state of Adam before his fall to Eve's allure. "A perilous thing

is the company of the female," we read in the rules of the order of
the Knights Templar, whose shield—exactly Galahad's—showed a
pure white ground emblazoned with a large red cross; "for the old
devil (*le deable ancien*) has lured many, through the company of
women, from the straight path to Paradise. . . . We believe it to
be a danger to all religion to regard too long a woman's face. None
of you, therefore, should presume to kiss any female: whether a
widow, child, mother, sister, aunt, or any other. The Knights of
Jesus Christ, for this reason, must eschew by all means that kissing
of women by which men have so frequently put it in jeopardy that
they should ever live and rest, in purity of conscience and surety
of life, before the face of God forever." [136] The ladies of Arthur's
court, accordingly, could neither participate in nor contribute to
the adventure of the *Queste*: only Perceval's sister, a virgin, in a
role like that of Dante's inviolate Beatrice. And yet even she arrived in the holy city of Sarras, the New Jerusalem, dead.

Sir Galahad as the Grail Hero, then, is entirely a monkish innovation. Originally, as we have seen, the model knight was Sir
Gawain, who in the *Queste* is in the place, virtually, of Paolo and
Francesca in the *Inferno*. In the courtly world, on the other hand,
even where his roles were taken over by Lancelot or Perceval, he
was not condemned, but was ever the noble, gracious elder of the
new heroes, aiding them in their adventures, much like a father to
his sons. In fact, as Miss Jessie Weston has shown, there was the
legend of a young knight fathered by Gawain, known as Guinglain
or *Le Bel Inconnu* in French, Wigalois in German, Libeaus
Desconus in English, and Carduino in Italian, whose life is in all essential points so close to that of the youthful "Great Fool" Perceval
that (in her words), "if the *Fair Unknown* be not Perceval himself, he and Perceval are both representatives of the same primitive
hero, which practically amounts to the same thing." [137]

As Lancelot to Galahad, then, so was Gawain to Perceval (the
Fair Unknown). The two cycles are analogous, save that in the
Lancelot-Galahad redaction a later, strictly sacramental and monastic order of belief is represented. In the figures of the almost
pagan solar hero Gawain and the pure child Perceval of uncorrupted nature, there is no sign at all of the churchly notion of the
force of Original Sin, whereas Lancelot is explicitly fallen man—
and Woman, moreover, Guinevere-Eve, was the cause of his cor-

ruption. By a device of magic, however, that a monk should perhaps not closely scrutinize, he was brought to lie with the virgin daughter of the Grail King, whom he thought by enchantment to be his lady, Arthur's queen—and the moral sense of this begetting of a saint upon a virgin by a sinner who supposed himself to be with someone else's wife is not too easy to explain:

"Lancelot's alter ego," wrote Heinrich Zimmer in his brilliant series of essays interpreting these legends,

the son who bears the name that Lancelot himself received in baptism from his human father (before the Lady of the Lake abstracted, initiated, and renamed him "Lancelot of the Lake"), will achieve the holy adventure of the Grail; for, as in the symbolism of dreams, the child, the son, here connotes a higher transformation of the personality. The child is the self reborn in pristine perfection, the perfect being that we ought to be, that we are striving to become, and that we hoped to become, so to say, when we entered our present body. It is the symbol of the entelechy, or secret model, of our destination.

Thus Sir Galahad, the immaculate, is the redemption of the ambiguous, brilliant father whose "Christian" name he reaffirms and bears. He is the redemption because he is the re-embodiment of the father. The virtues of this triumphant saintly son are those of the essence of the father himself. And so, that father—Sir Lancelot of the Lake, but Sir Galahad of the Baptismal Font—is revealed to have combined in himself the energies of the two spheres, the wordly sphere of desires, and the higher one of the purely spiritual adventure. This is the final secret of his charm.[138]

And in the matter of his night with the virgin whom he took to be Arthur's queen, a like reading can be suggested: namely, that in its spiritual, "intelligible" dimension, as opposed to its social, accidential, his love for the queen was pure: it was the vehicle on this contingent plane of his realization on the spiritual plane of fulfillment.

But let us descend closer to earth and move on, now, to the fourth sphere of development of the *matière* of King Arthur:

D. *The German biographical epics, 1200–1215.* The *san,* the sense, to which the *matière de Bretagne* was here applied was neither political (as in phase A), nor of courtly ideals and manners (phase B), not sacramental-ecclesiastical-ascetic (phase C), but psychological in the modern sense of treating of spiritual initiations generally available in this world and inevitable to anyone seriously sensitive to his own unfolding realizations of the mystery— and impulse—of existence. In the *Queste* the knights entered the forest individually, "there where they saw it to be thickest, in all those places where they found no way or path," and there was great promise in that start. However, it soon appeared that there was actually but one way to be followed, after all: the one "straight path to Paradise," and not the several paths of the variously unfolding intelligible characters of each. Whereas in Wolfram the guide is within—for each, unique; and I see in this the first completely intentional statement of the fundamental mythology of modern Western man, the first sheerly individualistic mythology in the history of the human race: a mythology of quest inwardly motivated—directed from within—where there is no authorized way or guru to be followed or obeyed, but where, for each, all ways already found, known and proven, are wrong ways, since they are not his own.

For each, in himself, is in his "intelligible character" an unprecedented species in himself, whose life-way and life-form (as of a newly sprung plant or animal sport) can be revealed and realized only by and through himself. Hence that sense of yearning and striving toward an unknown end, so characteristic of the Western living of life—so alien to the Oriental. What is unknown, yet deeply, infallibly intended, is one's own peculiar teleology, not the one "straight path to Paradise." The learned Anglo-Indian critic of our civilization, Dr. Ananda Kent Coomaraswamy—who had lived and worked in this country somewhat more than forty years, yet never got the idea nor any sense of the unique majesty of this Occidental style of spirituality—with disparaging intent coined a really telling characterization of the "Faustian soul," when he wrote (using the pronoun "we" to connote not himself, a master of India's "eternal" wisdom, but his Occidental colleagues at the Boston Museum and Harvard University): "We who can call an art 'significant,' knowing not of what, are also proud to 'progress,' we know not whither." [139] And indeed we are—and had better be. For as Spengler has well said: "In Wolfram von Eschenbach, Cervantes, Shakespeare, and Goethe, the tragic line of the individ-

ual life develops from within outward, dynamically, function-
ally." [140]

And so we return from the Vulgate monastic epic of Lancelot
and Galahad, with its subsequent disintegration of the worldly
court of King Arthur, to the earthly Divine Comedy of their nature-
rooted predecessors: Gawain, the model lover, at about the age of
Leopold Bloom, and Parzival, the questing youth, like Stephen,
willing to challenge even God if the mask that he shows—or is said
to have shown—rings hollow when struck.

VIII. The Crowning of the King

BOOK XIV: THE FESTIVAL OF LOVE

Gawain, we have learned,* saw a solitary knight approaching on
the plain in armor redder than ruby. There was a wreath about his
helm plucked from the tree that Gramoflanz guarded, and his
shield was pierced through and through. Gawain recognized the
wreath and, immediately lowering his lance (the other lowered
too), spurred and charged (the other too). They clashed, brought
each other down, steeds and all, and went at it with their
swords—alone on the plain.

Messengers of Arthur, meanwhile, had arrived before Gramoflanz's camp, which they beheld spread out before them as broad
as a mile and a half, guarded by strange knights: Turkish bowmen,
footmen brandishing spears, and beyond those, trumpets blaring
and ladies with bells on their bridles riding in circles around the
king's tent. The ranks parted and the messengers, admitted, saw
the king on a couch beneath a canopy, with gay and pretty
maidens all about him, putting on his greaves.

"Sir," they said, "Arthur asks: How dare you challenge his sister's son? The Round Table knights are his brothers and if need
arise will defend him."

"I have knights of my own," the king answered; "I am not
afraid of number. Never before, however, have I battled only one
man at a time. The ladies are not to praise me when I win."

Returning, the messengers on their homeward way spied the
two battling knights. Gawain was giving ground, and anxious for
his life, they cried out his name, whereupon the other, with a

* Supra, p. 514.

great shout, flung away his sword and cried: "I am betrayed: I am fighting myself!"

"Sir, alas!" then said Gawain, who by now could hardly stand. "Who are you?"

"I am your kinsman," said the other. "I am Parzival."

And so it was, that, when the time arrived for which all these companies had assembled, of the battle of Gawain with Gramoflanz (for whom, because of the wreath, Gawain had mistaken Parzival), the battered knight was so poorly off that the proud king, confronting him on the field, refused to fight and postponed the tournament to the morrow. Parzival, beside his friend, offered to stand in his stead, but Gramoflanz again refused.

And it was then that little Bene, the daughter of the boatman, who had come with Parzival onto the field bearing a token for the king from Gawain's sister, first realized that Gawain was Itonje's brother, and that Gramoflanz, insisting on this tournament, wished to kill him. The oars of sorrow then drew a heavy cargo of grief into her heart, and in anger, fierce words flew from her lips. "You faithless dog! Whose token is this I bring you?" she cried. "Love rejects your service. Love is not to be joined with treachery." Unsettled in his confidence, the king drew her aside, pleading. "You have never learned what loyalty means. Get away from me, you foul thing!" she flung back. And the king turned, mounted, and with his company rode off, while Bene, with Parzival and Gawain, returned to Gawain's pavilion.

Her lord, on the way, made her promise not to reveal the nature of the coming tournament to his sister, who had not yet realized that the champion who was to meet her *ami* was her brother. Moreover, when Parzival tried to persuade Gawain to let him fight in his stead, Gawain refused.

"This morning," Parzival argued, "I found the tree in the grove undefended, broke a branch from it, and came this way to challenge Gramoflanz. I had no idea that you would be here and when I saw you, thought you were he. Let me now face him!"

"God bless you," Gawain answered; "but with fortune, I shall win. I trust my own cause."

Parzival seemed to give in, yet that evening in his quarters, went carefully over his armor, and at dawn rode forth secretly; so that when Gramoflanz arrived early on the field, it was Parzival, already there, who immediately attacked him. And they were at it hard when Gawain, after Mass, arrived to engage his man. Fighting afoot, those two warriors hurled their swords many times high into the air to reverse the cutting edges. Then Gramoflanz began to fail and Arthur rode out with a company of knights to separate the pair. The King of the Tree admitted he was beaten and Gawain said to him courteously: "Sir King, I shall do for you today what you did yesterday for me: we shalt meet tomorrow."

Long before the morrow dawned, however, Itonje noticed that Bene had turned pale and was secretly weeping. "Did the king refuse my token?" she thought. Her ears opened to the gossip of the day and when the message struck her heart, she rushed in terror to her grandmother and mother. "Shall the hand of my own brother cut down my heart's beloved?" she cried; and they too, when they understood what a serious battle was in prospect, were dismayed. Arnive called to a page to go summon Arthur to her tent.

And Gramoflanz on his own side, meanwhile, stung by the tongue of Bene, had begun to feel some anxiety concerning his standing with Itonje, and to set the matter straight had sent two young messengers with a letter to learn what they could of her state of mind. Bene, leaving the ladies' tent when Arthur entered, noticed these two young squires among the tent ropes. "Stand back," she said. "Stand back beyond these ropes." Itonje, within, was crying at Arthur: "Does the Lady Orgeluse then think it proper that my brother, in her service, should murder my *ami?*" and the squires had overheard. They gave the letter from their lord to Bene, who took it into the tent and presently Arthur, coming out, courteously greeted them.

"So what have I done to your king," he asked, "that he should treat my family this way? He cannot regard me very highly. And to pay with hate the brother of a lady one claims to love! Let him think about that! He must realize that if *that* is what he wants, his heart is untrue."

"But the Duchess of Logrois still denies him her good will," they answered. "Gawain is not the only knight of hers that our lord must fear in this camp."

Arthur promised to obtain a truce from her and in turn proposed a meeting midway between the two camps. The truce was readily gained. The Lady Orgeluse was still in sorrow for Cide-

gast, but her anger against his slayer had cooled in the warmth
of Gawain's embraces, while Gramoflanz, on his own side, was
learning to soften as well. Bene had gone to him with his returning
squires, and he never had felt such joy in his life as when she
told him of his lady's love. Arthur, furthermore, had sent along
with her Gawain's young brother Beakurs, and when he looked
upon this graceful lad Gramoflanz thought in his heart: "He rides
so winsomely! And she, after all, is his sister!" While as for the
matter of the wreath: since Parzival, having plucked a branch, had
overcome both himself and Gawain, his quarrel with Itonje's
brother on that score was no longer in point.

Before riding to the meeting, between camps, Arthur saw to
it that a tentful of ladies should be left in attendance on his niece,
and when he had met Gramoflanz in midfield he simply returned
with him to that tent. "If you see among these ladies anyone you
love," he said, "you may greet her with a kiss." And so, as the
poet declares at the close of this festive chapter, no one can say
that there ever took place a more beautiful marriage celebration.
Gawain's second sister was bestowed on Lischois Gwelljus, and his
widowed mother, Sangive, on Florant the Turkoyte. There were
also Gawain and Orgeluse; and with many a fair lady more
thereabout, tenting by the riverside, love and joy among pavilions
were the order of the day.

But Parzival, amidst all this, was brooding alone on Condwiramurs. Would he perhaps greet another in the spirit of this celebration? No indeed! Such loyalty stood guard upon his heart, and
also on his body, that no other woman anywhere would ever dis-
tract his love. He thought: "If I am to keep striving for the Grail,
the dream of her pure embrace it will be that ever spurs me on—
from which I have been too long parted. However, if I am to witness here only joy where my heart knows only sorrow, my eyes
and heart will be ill matched." His armor lay at hand. He had
often donned it alone. "May fortune bear me on," he mused, "to
what I have yet to accomplish." He saddled his steed, and when
dawn broke, galloped away.

BOOK XV: THE ACCOLADE

And he was riding smartly one day toward the line of a great
forest, when he beheld cantering toward him a richly bedizened

stranger. Finest silks caparisoned his mount. Nor would all the wealth of Arthur's Britain have paid for the jewels of his surcoat: salamander worms in the Argremuntin mountains had in hot fires loomed them together; with a brilliant light they blazed. And it had been chiefly noble ladies who had given him these tokens. He wore them now, thus splendidly, in sign of his high heart's striving. Beyond the forest behind him, in a wild bay of the sea, there lay a camp of twenty-five armies, not one of which could understand any language of the others. And he had ridden forth alone from them on adventure.

The lion, they say, is born dead from its dam; its father's roar gives it life: these two men had been born of battle din. They rode immediately charging at each other, and each was amazed and angered when the other held his seat. They battled fiercely and long. And I mourn for this; for they were two sons of one man. One could say that "they" were fighting if one wished to speak of two. They were, however, one. "My brother and I" is one body—like good man and good wife. One flesh, one blood, here battling from loyalty of heart, was doing itself much harm.

The heathen fought for love and gems, and he pressed with them right hard. His battle cry was "Thabronit." And the baptized man fell back. The heathen never wearied of love: his heart, therefore, was great in combat. God shield Gahmuret's son, I say! That is my wish for them both.

The baptized man, since leaving Trevrizent, had cleaved to his trust in God. But the heathen was mighty of limb, and whenever he shouted "Thabronit!"—which is where his queen Secundille was—his battle strength increased. The baptized man now troubles me. More than once he has gone to his knees. However, there is one more thing, brave Parzival, to think upon for courage: those two sweet little boys, Kardeiz and Loherangrin (Lohengrin)—they must not so soon be left orphans—whom your dear pure wife Condwiramurs bore to you after your last embrace.

"Thabronit!" now was answered with "Pelrapeire!" and just in time. Condwiramurs came across the world and filled her knight with the power of her love. Chips flaked and flew from the heathen's valuable shield—many hundred marks' worth, I should say. And with a great crack down upon his ornamented helm, the sword of the Christian broke.

"I see, brave man," said the noble heathen in French, "you would now have to fight without a blade and no fame would I gain from that. Stand still and tell me who you are. Let there be a truce, till we have rested." They sat down, both, upon the grass and the powerful heathen went on: "I have never encountered such a fighter in my life. Be so kind: let me know your name and race, and I shall not have made this journey for nought."

"Am I to tell you then out of fear?" asked Herzeloyde's son.

"I shall give you my own name first," said the other. "I am Feirefiz the Angevin. Many countries pay me tribute."

"How Angevin?" asked Parzival. "Anjou is by inheritance mine. I am told I have a brother, however, in heathendom, who has won great love and praise. If I might see your face, I could tell, sir, if you are the one."

The other flung away his sword. "If there is any fighting to be done now," he said, "our chances will be the same. Tell me, what does your brother look like?"

"He is black and white, they say, like written parchment."

And the heathen said to the baptized man: "I am the one."

Then neither lost time. Both helmets were removed, and indeed he had the markings of the magpie. Kissing, those two concluded peace. Feirefiz, the elder, bade his brother address him now as *tu,* not *vous;* but Parzival, in deference to his age, power, and wealth, demurred. They spoke of their father, and Feirefiz, who had hoped to meet him in Europe, was saddened to learn of his death. "I have seen in this one hour," he said, "both the loss and the winning of joy. You, my father, and I were one; but this one appeared in three parts. I rode against myself and would gladly have killed myself. O Jupiter, write this miracle down! Your power came to our aid." He laughed and tried to conceal his tears; then presently suggested that his brother should come see his army. However, when the Christian spoke of Arthur's host and the heathen heard mention of ladies (they were life itself to Feirefiz), "Take me there," he said, and side by side they rode to Arthur's tents.

Everybody was ready for them; for a messenger from the Castle of Marvels had brought news to the assembled camps of a combat seen reflected in the pillar of the magic tower. Gawain received them in his tent, and when their armor had been removed there was no less amazement at the marvel of a man both black and

white than at the wealth and beauty of his arms. A sumptuous evening was arranged and the noble heathen was praised and admired
all round, the ladies glancing and whispering, wondering what
woman had given him such attire. If he proved unfaithful to her,
his reputation surely would suffer; yet all were so attracted they
would have accepted gladly his service (I suppose, the poet remarks, because of his interesting markings). Arthur, Gramoflanz,
Parzival, and Gawain stepped away to let the ladies have their fill,
and for the following day made plans for another such Round
Table event—spread about a costly circular cloth on the lawn—
as, years before, had seen the visit of the Loathly Damsel.

And behold! When all were settled, a damsel, mounted, was
seen approaching at a canter. Her bridle, saddle, and mount were
splendid, and her face was heavily veiled. Her costly black mantle,
hooded in the French style, displayed in gleaming Arabian gold a
multitude of small turtle doves. She rode around the circle, gave
Arthur greeting, turned to Parzival, sprang from her steed, fell
before his feet, and weeping, pleaded for his greeting; then rose,
tossed away the veil, and, as before, was Cundrie *la sorcière,* as
ugly as ever: muzzle, tusks, and all; yet with dignity she stood and
delivered her say.

"O Crown of Man's Salvation, Parzival: in youth you courted
Sorrow; Joy will now take you from her. You have striven for
the soul's peace, waiting in sorrow for the body's joy. Condwiramurs, and Loherangrin, your son, have also been named to the
Grail. Kardeiz, the other son, is to be crowned King of Pelrapeire.
Greetings I bring, also, from the noble sweet King Anfortas, whom
you now are to heal."

Tears sprang from Parzival's eyes and all about the circle arose
murmuring.

"What am I to do?" he asked.

"Dear my lord," Cundrie answered, "you will choose a male
companion. I shall lead you then on your way."

Parzival asked Feirefiz, who agreed to ride with him in fellowship to the Castle of the Grail; and how it all ended for the rest,
I cannot say; but Cundrie and those two together rode away.*

---

* The Muslim Feirefiz/Aibak, "Mottled, like the Moon" (supra, pp. 502–
503, note), is as worthy to enter the Castle as the Christian. Compare the
two Grail Kings (supra, p. 410).

BOOK XVI: THE NEW KING

Anfortas was still in excruciating pain. His eyes would often close, sometimes for as long as four days. But joy is now to be heard of him.

Parzival and Feirefiz were following Cundrie's lead when a company of armed Templars came riding down upon them, but, recognizing the guide, set up a shout. The heathen, lowering his lance, spurred; but Cundrie caught his reign. "They are wholly in your service," she said. Dismounting, baring their heads, they greeted Parzival afoot, welcomed Feirefiz too, and, again mounting, rode to Munsalvaesche in tears, there to be greeted by a multitude of elder knights, squires, and pages.

We have already heard how the sorrowing Anfortas leaned and seldom sat. His couch was adorned with healing gems. Parzival asked, in tears, "Show me where the Grail is kept, and if God's mercy triumphs in me, this company shall bear witness." He was shown and turning to face the Grail, genuflecting thrice to the Trinity, prayed surcease to the king's pain; then arose, turned again to Anfortas, and asked the long-awaited question: *"Oeheim, was wirret dier? Uncle, what ails thee?"* [141]

Whereupon He that bade Lazarus arise gave help; so that Anfortas was healed, and the luster that the French call *fleur* was seen to come over his flesh. Parzival's beauty, in comparison, now was mere wind. Indeed, no one whose beauty is from birth ever equaled that of Anfortas coming out of his sickness. And since the writing on the Grail had named Parzival its lord, he was there proclaimed its king.

Condwiramurs too was riding hard toward Munsalvaesche, and at the very point where the blood on the snow once had arrested Parzival's heart he was to meet her. He paused, on the way, to visit Trevrizent, who, when he learned of the healing of his brother's wound, was amazed: "Greater marvel," he said, "has seldom come to pass: you have forced God by defiance to make His Trinity grant your will." And he commended Parzival to God, who continued on his way the same night. The escort knew the forest well, and next morning there before him were the tents spread out of the company of his queen. An elder knight came forth, the father of Sigune, Duke Kyot of Catalonia, who, courteously greeting Parzival, brought him to the large tent where Condwiramurs, still asleep with slumbering ladies all about, was in bed with her two little sons. Going directly to the bed, Kyot slapped the covers, calling her to wake and laugh for joy. Her eyes opened: there stood her husband. And though she had nothing on but her smock, she quickly clasped the bedclothes about and hopped out to the carpet. Parzival clasped her in his arms. The children woke, and he kissed them too. Then old Kyot considerately had the little boys carried off, told the ladies in the tent to leave, and closed the tent flaps from outside.

Later that day a priest sang Mass, and Parzival supervised the coronation of his little boy Kardeiz, after which the tents were all struck amid tears and the two companies parted. The old duke had said nothing of his daughter. However, when Parzival and Condwiramurs paused with their escort at Sigune's hermitage, they found her within, kneeling still, but dead. They raised the cover of her lover's grave, where he lay embalmed in all his beauty, placed the virgin gently beside him, closed the cover with a prayer, and pressed on, to arrive in Munsalvaesche that night.

Feirefiz had waited up, and he laughed when little Loherangrin, frightened by the mottled skin, refused his uncle's kiss. Then quickly, preparations were instituted for a ceremony of the Grail. Three great fires of pungent aloe wood were lighted in the middle of the hall; innumerable candles too. And the maidens in the service of the Joy of Paradise appeared, to the number of twenty-five. The Templars all were gathering, and when Condwiramurs had changed from her traveling dress she too came into the great hall. Seats and carpets were set about, and again there was enacted the entire procession of the Grail.

However, something very strange now was observed.

Feirefiz, sitting with Parzival and Anfortas on the seat before which the Grail was set down, saw nothing at all of the stone, but only the eyes of her who carried it, the Queen Repanse de Schoye.

"Do you not see the Grail before you?" Anfortas asked.

"I see nothing but a table," he answered. "But the eyes of that girl go to my heart."

Love's power had turned him pale in the white parts of his complexion. What help now to Secundille the love she had bestowed on him? Or to any of those other ladies of his life the rich rewards

they had granted? Gentle Anfortas perceived that he was in anguish. "Sir, I am sorry if my sister is causing you pain," he said.
"Your brother is her sister's son. He perhaps can give you help."
And he turned to Parzival. "Sir, I do believe that your brother
has not yet seen the Grail."

Feirefiz agreed. He had not. The knights all found this strange,
and word of it reached Titurel, the aged, crippled, bedridden old
man in the neighboring great hall, from which the Grail had been
brought, and back to which it would be returned. "If he is a heathen, unbaptized," so came the word from Titurel, "there is no use
for him to associate with those who do see the Grail. For him there
is a veil around it."

He was urged to be baptized. "Will it help me in this love?" he
asked; and Parzival—addressing him now as *tu,* not *vous*—gave
him to understand that he then might sue for the lady's love. The
baptismal font was sent for: a single beautiful ruby on a circular
jasper step. "If you wish to marry my aunt," said Parzival in warning, "you will have to renounce your gods and Secundille too."

"Whatever I have to do for that girl, I will do," the heathen answered. He was instructed in the doctrine of the Trinity. "Dear
brother," he said, "if your aunt has that god, it is in that god I
believe, and all my own are abjured. For the sake of your aunt's
god, let me be baptized."

And when all had been accomplished, the Grail was uncovered
in his sight, and upon its stone there was now found written the
following charge: ANY TEMPLAR APPOINTED BY GOD'S HAND TO BE
MASTER OVER A FOREIGN FOLK MUST FORBID THE ASKING OF HIS
NAME OR RACE AND HELP THEM TO THEIR RIGHTS. BUT IF THE
QUESTION IS ASKED OF HIM, THEY SHALL NO LONGER HAVE HIS
HELP.

Twelve days later Feirefiz departed with his bride. Messengers
to his army had told of the death of Queen Secundille, and subsequently in India Repanse de Schoye gave birth to the son now
known to the world as Prester John. . . .

IX ENVOY: TO EACH HIS OWN

And so we have heard—the poet claims—at last correctly, how
Parzival, Herzeloyde's child, won the Grail. And he adds: "If
Master Chrétien of Troyes did this story an injustice, there is in-

deed reason for Kyot to be angry, who gave it to us correctly.
. . . From Provence to the German lands the proper story was
sent to us, on up to the adventure's end. And I, Wolfram of
Eschenbach, am going to tell no more of it here than the Master
told of it there." [142]

We need not argue whether Wolfram's references to a Provinçal
master Kyot may be taken seriously.[143] The point for now,
rather, is that in the syndrome of ideas here presented as a unit we
have the earliest definition of the secular mythology that is today
the guiding spiritual force of the European West. Theologians
seem not even to realize that this mythology exists and is the functioning religion of many of their parishoners, mumbling incredible
credos in their pews.

The Grail here, as in the later *Queste,* is the symbol of supreme
spiritual value. It is attained, however, not by renouncing the
world or even current social custom, but, on the contrary, by participation with every ounce of one's force in the century's order of
life in the way or ways dictated by one's own uncorrupted heart:
what the mystics call the Inner Voice. Trevrizent's observation
that a miracle had come to pass, inasmuch as Parzival had forced
God by defiance to make his Trinity grant his will, touched the
quick of the teaching: the anagogy, the metaphysical *san,* of this ex-
emplary Gothic tale. According to its revelation, sprung from the
heart and heartland of the European West, the moral initiative in
the field of time is of man, not God; and not of man as species, or
as member of some divinely ordained consensus, but of each one
separately, as an individual, self-moved in self-consistent action.
That is the meaning in our West of the term "free will." The idea
was announced in Trevrizent's first sermon, where he taught the
lost Parzival that God returns hate for hate and love for love. It is
implicit in the very structure of the plot, where the hero, on his
first visit to the Grail Castle, abiding by instructions, not only fails
to heal the Maimed King but also forfeits the virtue of his own
sweet life and, disoriented, converts everything he touches into
waste: whereas, when he has learned, at last, through solitude in
exile, to become what Nietzsche has termed "a wheel rolling from
its own center," lo, on the Grail stone, his name! In his own life,
his own depth, he has touched the quick of time, in accord with
that twelfth-century hermetic maxim already cited in these

pages,* of God as "an intelligible sphere, whose center is every-where and the circumference nowhere."

For according to this mythology there is no fixed law, no estab-lished knowledge of God, set up by prophet or by priest, that can stand against the revelation of a life lived with integrity in the spirit of its own brave truth. Every so-called "fall," or departure from the "law," is then itself a creative act in which God (to use a mythological term) participates. Hence Joyce's theme from Ro-mans 11:32.† God's initiative is represented in the inborn, sealed-in soul or "intelligible character" of the individual at birth; and the initiative, the freedom to act, must thereafter be one's own, guided not by what other people say, have done, or may tell one is God's will, but by one's own interior voice; for indeed (continuing to speak mythologically) it is in one's sealed-in soul, its hidden, God-given difference from all others, that "God's will" has been secreted, to be found and shown, like an Easter egg: and not by retreat to a bed of rapture either in darkness or in light, but through action here in this mixed world (why, otherwise, be born?), where nothing is foul, nothing pure, but all, like a magpie's plumage, mixed.

Yet in this mythology of the self-moving, self-responsible indi-vidual in time there is a depth-dimension as well, transcending time, transcending space. Gahmuret, Feirefiz, and Parzival are one, as are Parzival and Condwiramurs. The baptized and unbap-tized even in battle are at one, as are in sex play the male and fe-male. We are reminded again of Joyce and his theme at the heart of *Finnegans Wake,* of the battling brothers: "equals of opposites, evolved by a onesame power . . . and polarized for reunion by the symphysis of their antipathies. Distinctly different were their duadestinies." ‡

Still further, again as already remarked, there is a truly mystical sense in this work of that accord between outward event and in-ward readiness recognized by Schopenhauer in his essay on "ap-parent intention." § For, as the last episodes reveal, Parzival had been circling for years within range of a single night's ride of Mun-salvaesche. Only when ready for each did he chance (chance?)

* Supra, pp. 31, 36, 135, and *Occidental Mythology,* p. 522.
† Supra, p. 259.
‡ Supra, p. 308, from *Finnegans Wake,* p. 92.
§ Supra, pp. 340–44.

upon his various adventures in that mystic wood, the forest of this world. It is a law of symbolic life that the god beheld is a function of the state of consciousness of the beholder, and in this work—as in life itself—it is the individual's friends and enemies who function for him as messengers and gods of initiatory guidance and revelation.

But this, after all, is the leading lesson of Arthurian romance in general. Within its fold the gods and goddesses of other days have become knights and ladies, hermits and kings of this world, their dwellings castles; and the adventures, largely magical, are of the magic rather of poetry than of traditional religion, not so much miracles of God as signs of an unfolding dimension of nature: as though in Gafurius's design of the Music of the Spheres (Figure 13) the voice of *Thalia surda,* below ground, were beginning to be heard again, as in pagan times, in her own bucolic song, as the first statement of an accord that should expand through all the inward-outward spheres of the nine Muses. The main purpose of the monk's *Queste del Saint Graal* was to check the trend of this reawakening to nature, reverse its current, and translate the Grail, the cornucopia of the lord of life, into a symbol no longer of nature's earthly grace, but of the supernatural—leaving nature, man, history, and all womankind except baptized nuns, to the Devil.

In total contrast, love, and specifically heterosexual love, with womankind its chief ministrant and vessel, is both the moving and the redeeming power enshrined by the poet Wolfram in his cathedral erected to the virtue of the Grail. Maidens, not invisibles, here bear the talisman, and loves in all variety illuminate the adventure, like saints' lives in the stained glass of Chartres, Amiens, and Beauvais: the loves of families and of couples, mothers for sons, fathers for daughters, a nunlike hermitess for a corpse that her love preserves in all the beauty of youth. Loyalty in service to love is the motivation of the action of this world, where, as the author tells, although all is mixed of black and white, inconstancy augments the black, while "he of steadfast mind trends toward the white." [144] And, as in the love cult and songs of the troubadours, the loves of this world are always personal, specific. They are never, as in the ancient and Oriental cults of *eros* and *agape*—or as in the fashionable antic of the Provençal Valentines *—imper-

* Supra, p. 167.

sonal, orgiastic; unless in the instance of the magpie Feirefiz, who, however, in the Castle of the Grail was smitten specifically—and for good—by a single pair of blue eyes.

Love is born of the eyes and heart: the light world of the godly gift of sight and the dark of the grotto that opens within to infinity (in Figure 3, the realms 16 and 10). Hence, if the goddess Amor is to be served, neither light alone nor darkness can represent her way, which is mixed: neither Galahad's couch to Sarras nor the crystalline bed of Tristan's cave, but as long as life lasts—and life, after all, is her field—Gawain's Marvel Bed of bolts and darts ("Anyone seeking rest," states the author, "had better not come to *this* bed"),[145] or the hard war-saddle of Parzival's turtle-dove-branded charger. At the moment of the wakening to love, an object, apparently without, "passes [in the words of Joyce] into the soul for ever. . . . And the soul leaps at the call. To live, to err, to fall, to triumph, to recreate life out of life!" * Condwiramurs, *conduire amour:* the guide, the summoner, will have opened a prospect to the castle, the passage to which, however, will have to be earned. And, according to this mythology, the one way is of absolute loyalty to that outward innermost object. By this alone can the two worlds be united and the kingship won of one's proper Castle of Life.

"A life so concluded," Wolfram states, "that God is not robbed of the soul, and which yet can with dignity win the world's favor: that is a worthy work." [146] Essentially, this sounds very much like Gottfried's *moraliteit,* of which we have read that "its doctrine is in harmony with God and the world." † However, there the young hero sinned against the Goddess in not recognizing her summons but out of fear acting a role, as Tantris—Tristan reversed—with what results we have seen: shame in the world, disloyalty, and the Amfortas wound unhealed. The ideal, *moraliteit,* kingship of the Grail, was never attained.

Whereas Wolfram solved the spiritual problem of his century first by setting the ideal of love above marriage and, simultaneously, the ideal of an indissoluble marriage beyond love; then by moving his heroes to this end through adventures undertaken, without pretense and with unvacillating courage, on the impulse of

---

* Supra, p. 69.
† Supra, p. 230, from Gottfried, 8010–8014.

their uncorrupted hearts. As far as I know, he was the first poet in the world to put forward seriously this socially explosive ideal of marriage, which has become today, however, the romantic norm of the West, resisted and even despised in the Orient as anarchic, immoral, and insane. For through it are transcended the primitive, ancient, and Oriental orders of tribal and family marriage, where social, political, and economic considerations prevail over personal and romantic, and where the unfolding personality (which in the lore of this revelation is the flower of human life) is bound back, cropped and trained to the interests of a group. Transcended equally here is the desperate courtly answer in adultery to such sociological violations of the claims of the wakening heart, as well as the cold ascetic answer in total escape, by way of a cloister, into Solomon's ship.

And after all the miracles, angelic voices, consecrations, and elevations to the sky of the Cistercian *Queste del Saint Graal,* was it not a lovely thing at last to see a Grail King, newly crowned, proceed immediately to fetch his wife and youngsters from exactly that spot where, in the period of the freshness of his youth, her memory had overpowered him? Further, is it not proper, in the name of life, that the Grail Maiden herself, Repanse de Schoye, should in due time have quit her angelic role for marriage and the bearing of a son? And finally, what are we to say in this year of Our Lord 1968 or so, of that order which appeared, written on the Grail, about the year 1215, directing every knight in its service, who, by God's grace, might ever be appointed master of an alien folk, *daz er in hulfe rehtes,* "that he should help them to their rights"? *

It is not possible for all, or even many, of the noble children of this world, however, to fare into the adventure of life with such aplomb as Parzival. And how many have met their Condwiramurs, once and for all, so beautifully, at just that perfect time? For most, the quest for the ideal to serve will have been rather in the way of Gawain, with his ladies here, ladies there, and finally his life-scarred, dangerously fascinating Lady Orgeluse and her Perilous Bed. For whereas Parzival is the model of an absolute ideal, Gawain is the man of the world. With his noble heart given willingly to Parzival in service, he facilitates the youth's appearances

---

* Supra, p. 563, as in Wolfram, op. cit., XVI. 818:24–819:2.

in the field of history (Arthur's court). The two are like father and son, like Lancelot and Galahad. So that once again we may recognize here, as there, the virtues of the younger knight as of the spirit or essence of his elder. Moreover, the same may be said of their marriages. As Zimmer wrote of Lancelot in relation to his son: the father "combined in himself the energies of the two spheres, the worldly sphere of desires, and the higher one of the purely spiritual adventure," * so, relating these two marriages we may see in that of Gawain and Orgeluse a combination of the energies of both: the imperfect, of marriage in this life on earth, and the perfect, of the ideal it intends; the normal and the supernormal image † of that mystery of love, wherein each is both.

But now, what of that strange farce, the baptism of Feirefiz? The magic of the sacraments had played no significant role in any of the major biographies of the work. Their rites had been associated rather with the ceremonialism of court than with the needs and realizations of the inner life—and then, suddenly, when all was done, a baptism occurred.

One could be tempted to regard the scene as a burlesque of the conversion of heathens by fiat or persuasion, against which stands the fact, however, that following his baptism the mottled heathen (a prefiguration of the modern Anglo-Indian) could actually see—though not greatly appreciate—the Grail. One explanation might be that, since the Roman Church was in Wolfram's time the only authorized public vehicle of the European spiritual heritage, Feirefiz's submission to the rite represented and confirmed an act of willing participation in the moral order of the Christian world. However, there was something rather special about this particular rite.

"The baptismal font," we read, "was tilted a little toward the Grail and immediately became full of water, neither too warm nor too cold." [147] That is, the Grail itself, the philosophers' stone, was the source of the water (*aqua mercurialis*) ‡ poured upon the black-and-white man's head.

Furthermore, the order concerning the need for the rite had

* Supra, p. 552.
† For the idea of the "supernormal image," cf. supra, p. 247, and *Primitive Mythology*, pp. 28–49.
‡ Supra, pp. 272–73.

come from that mysterious beautiful old man—"grayer even than mist"—whom Parzival, on the occasion of his first visit to the castle, had glimpsed reposing on a bed in the neighboring great room.* And who was he?

His name, we have heard, was Titurel, the grandfather of Anfortas. Himself the earliest Grail King, he is here the counterpart of Brons, THE RICH FISHER, in Robert de Boron's *Estoire,* and in Celtic myth, the Welsh god Bran the Blessed (Irish Manannan Mac Lir), lord of the sea and its fish: or once again the Fisher of Men (Figure 3, Station 1).†

The date of this great work, about 1215, represents—as Henry Adams remarked in his studies of cultural dynamics ‡—the apogee of the Gothic Christian arc. "Symbol or energy," he wrote in his chapter on "The Dynamo and The Virgin," celebrating the miracle of the building of Chartres (an exact contemporary of Wolfram's *Parzival*), "the Virgin had acted as the greatest force the Western world ever felt, and had drawn man's activities to herself more strongly than any other power, natural or supernatural, had ever done; the historian's business was to follow the track of the energy; to find where it came from and where it went to; its complex source and shifting channels; its values, equivalents, conversions." [148]

We have already found where it came from: the energy both of the altar of Chartres and of the water (*aqua permanens*) of the Grail (Figures 40–43). We have now, therefore, only to follow what Adams called its "Curve of Degradation," when it burst its Gothic vault and streamed with ever-increasing force to the great "Hall of Dynamos" of the Paris Exposition of the year 1900 and —beyond that—to Hiroshima and the moon.

---

* Supra, p. 446.
† In the cathedral-treasury of S. Lorenzo in Genoa there is an octagonal shallow bowl of green Roman glass (first century A.D.), brought from the conquest of Caesarea (1001–1002), once thought to be a priceless emerald and identified with the Grail in which Joseph caught Christ's blood. "On the rim is an inscription in very fine lines, visible only under a certain light: the writing through which the Grail revealed its commands. Thus at once the most precious stone, a cult vessel, and an oracle!" (Goetz, op. cit., p. 5). The date and form associate this bowl with Figures 3 and 11; the size, with the gem-helmets of Belakane and Gahmuret.
‡ Supra, p. 162.

NEW WINE

✦✦

THE DEATH OF "GOD"

✦✦✦

I. The Crime of Galileo

Whereas you, Galileo, son of the late Vincenzio Galilei, of Florence, aged seventy years, were denounced in 1615, to this Holy Office, for holding as true a false doctrine taught by many, namely, that the sun is immovable in the center of the world, and that the earth moves, and also with a diurnal motion; also, for having pupils whom you instructed in the same opinions; also, for maintaining a correspondence on the same with some German mathematicians; also for publishing certain letters on the sun-spots, in which you developed the same doctrine as true; also, for answering the objections which were continually produced from the Holy Scriptures, by glozing the said Scriptures according to your own meaning; and whereas thereupon was produced the copy of a writing, in form of a letter professedly written by you to a person formerly your pupil, in which, following the hypothesis of Copernicus, you include several propositions contrary to the true sense and authority of the Holy Scriptures; therefore (this Holy Tribunal being desirous of providing against the disorder and mischief which were thence proceeding and increasing to the detriment of the Holy Faith) by the desire of his Holiness and the Most Eminent Lords, Cardinals of this supreme and universal Inquisition, the two propositions of the stability of the sun, and the motion of the earth, were qualified by the Theological Qualifiers as follows:

1. The proposition that the sun is in the center of the world and immovable from its place is absurd, philosophically false, and formally heretical; because it is expressly contrary to Holy Scriptures.

2. The proposition that the earth is not the center of the world, nor immovable, but that it moves, and also with a diurnal action, is also absurd, philosophically false, and, theologically considered, at least erroneous in faith.

Therefore . . . , invoking the most holy name of our Lord Jesus Christ and of His Most Glorious Mother Mary, We pronounce this Our final sentence. . . . : We pronounce, judge, and declare, that you, the said Galileo . . . have rendered yourself vehemently suspected by this Holy Office of heresy, that is, of having believed and held the doctrine (which is false and contrary to the Holy and Divine Scriptures) that the sun is the center of the world, and that it does not move from east to west, and that the earth does move, and is not the center of the world; also, that an opinion can be held and supported as probable, after it has been declared and finally decreed contrary to the Holy Scripture, and, consequently, that you have incurred all the censures and penalties enjoined and promulgated in the sacred canons and other general and particular constituents against delinquents of this description. From which it is Our pleasure that you be absolved, provided that with a sincere heart and unfeigned faith, in Our presence, you abjure, curse, and detest, the said error and heresies, and every other error and heresy contrary to the Catholic and Apostolic Church of Rome. . . .[1]

II. The New Reality

The date of this quaint document is 1630 A.D., midway between Dante and James Joyce; and on the broad canvas of our present study it can be seen to mark the termination of an age of mythic thought that opened in the Near East c. 7500 B.C., with the invention of agriculture, and came to maturity c. 3500 B.C. in Sumer. The symbolic image of the axial World Mountain of the Goddess, with the city of the Lord of Earth on its summit, abyssal waters beneath, and circling celestial spheres above, which we have seen illustrated in the ziggurat of Nippur,[2] recognized again in the Tower of Babel, Mount Sinai, and Olympus, and found developed in Dante's work as a figure of the journey of the soul, represents, from first to last, the world period that Leo Frobenius termed the Monumental Stage of human history. In his view, this age—during the five-thousand-year course of which all the great high cultures arose and in their time expired—was preceded by the long, timeless millenniums of primitive man, foraging for his sustenance in environments dominated not by himself but by the animal and plant worlds. With the development in the nuclear Near East of the arts of agriculture and stockbreeding, however, when a constellation of settled communities of steadily increasing size appeared and, having spread gradually westward and eastward, reached, about 3000 B.C., the Atlantic and Pacific shores, new forms and possibilities of experience were opened to the eyes, mind, sentiments, and organs of action of man: the same old species, *Homo sapiens,* but acquiring now new masteries, creating his own environment, and dreaming his old, inevitable dreams of childhood, youth, maturity, and age through a context of new forms. And it was upon this broadly shared agricultural base that every one of the Monumental high cultures arose—whether in Mesopotamia, Egypt, and the Aegean; India, China, and the New World; classical Greece and Rome; the Magian-Byzantine-Mohammedan Levant; or, finally, Gothic Europe, where, in the period of Heloise and Abelard, the Grail and Tristan poets, Joachim of Floris, Eckhart, Dante, and Cusanus, the beginnings of the next great stage in the evolution of consciousness appeared.

Frobenius called this new age, now upon us, the period of World Culture. Its technical determinants are to be the scientific method of research and the power-driven machine, as were agriculture and stockbreeding (c 7500 B.C.), with the arts of writing and coercive government (c. 3500 B.C.), of the Monumental. And the distinguishing feature of its new mankind—as heralded in the lives and works of those through whom it was announced—has already been suggested in Wolfram's *Parizval:* that is to say, a mankind of individuals, self-moved to ends proper to themselves, directed not by the constraint and noise of others, but each by his own inner voice.

"Who is that 'other,' " asks Ortega y Gasset, "those 'others,' to whom I entrust the task of being me?"

"Oh—no specific person!" he replies to his own question.

"Who is it that says what 'they say'? Who is the responsible subject of that social saying, the impersonal subject of 'they say'?"

"Ah—people! And 'people' is not this person or that person— 'people' is always someone else, not exactly this one or that one —it is the pure 'other,' the one who is nobody. 'People' is an irre-

sponsibile 'I,' the 'I' of society, the social 'I.' When I live on what
'they say' and fill my life with it, I have replaced the I which I myself am in solitude with the mass 'I'—I have made myself 'people.'
Instead of living my own life, I am *de*-living it by changing it to
otherness."

And he concludes: "What I am saying is simply that life has a
reality that is neither goodness nor meritoriousness, but pure and
simple reality in the degree that it is genuine, that each man feels,
thinks, and does what he and only he, in the most individual sense,
must feel, think, and do." [3]

Such a statement could never have been made in Sumer. It
would have been simply meaningless. Authority there was from
aloft, the order of the heavens, translated, interpreted, and administered by priests. The holy spectacle of the Royal Tombs of Ur,
where the entire court of the dead king descended alive into his
grave,[4] tells of the awesome, noble impersonality of lives lived
thus, in dedication to a priestly play: a mythological play, performed in honor of heaven's law, derived from observations of the
mathematically measurable cycling of the moon, the planets, sun,
and stars. That is to say, just as primitive hunters based their social orders upon rites, and the rites upon fancied relationships and
covenants with their animal neighbors; and as primitive planters,
in their gruesome mysteries of sacrifice, burial, and supposed rebirth, imitated the order of the vegetal world, where life springs
ever anew from the womb of earth: so in the great world age of the
monumental ziggurats, pyramids, temple towers, and cathedral
spires ("Thy will be done on earth as it is in heaven!"), the
lesson that man sought to know and to follow was written above,
for all time and for all—either in the stars (as in the earlier Bronze
Age dispensation) or in the pages of a book dictated from "up
there" and the words of one come down from "up there," miraculously "made flesh." Whereas the new center and source of awe,
truth, virtue, and being, made known to us already in the courage
and loyalty of Heloise, the prophecies of Joachim, the Grail Quest
theme, Dante's dream, and Eckhart's birth of Christ in the heart, is
for each his own, made known within. "I like the silent church before the service begins, better than any preaching," Ralph Waldo
Emerson wrote in his esay on "Self-Reliance." [5]

But the finding of this center implies not only courage in one's own truth but also respect for its equivalent in others; once again, the principle of God as an intelligible sphere whose center is everywhere and circumference nowhere. Hence it was perhaps no mere accident, but historically symbolic, that, at the very time when Galileo was on trial, the individualist Roger Williams (c. 1604–1684) sailed away from England to the New World, arrived in Boston in February 1631, and, when banished by the Massachusetts court for expressing and teaching his opinion that the power of a state cannot properly claim jurisdiction over the consciences of men (moreover, that the king's patent to the colonists conveyed no just title to the land, which should have been bought from its rightful owners, namely the Indians), departed and with four companions founded, in June 1636, on land purchased from the Narragansett sachems Canonicus and Miantonomo, as "a shelter for persons distressed for conscience," the first secular state in history, terming himself in religion a "Seeker," and naming his city, in thanks for "God's merciful providence to him in his distress," Providence.

Emerson (1803–1882), New England's own philosopher-sage of the century of Schopenhauer, when celebrating in his spirited style "that Unity, that Over-soul, within which every man's particular being is contained and made one with all other; that common heart of which all sincere conversation is the worship, to which all right action is submission; that overpowering reality which confutes our tricks and talents, and constrains one to pass for what he is, and to speak from his character and not from his tongue, and which evermore tends to pass into our thought and hand and become wisdom and virtue and power and beauty," puts the mystery before us very simply and clearly when he states: "We live in succession, in division, in parts, in particles. Meantime within man is the soul of the whole; the wise silence; the universal beauty, to which every part and particle is equally related; the eternal ONE." [6] Which is exactly, of course, Paul Tillich's "Ground of Being,* and would be India's *brahman*, too, as well as the Buddhist "body of truth" (*dharmakāya*),[7] were it not for a particular and great stress given throughout the works of the Western writers to the personal, individual embodiment of the mystery as a value in itself: as though to suggest that the place to recognize the *per-*

* Supra, p. 25.

sonality of God (so important to theology) is not in transcendence, "out there," beyond thought, beyond personality, but here in this life, in its immanence, in the faces, personalities, loves, and lives all around us, in our friends, our enemies, and ourselves. Or, returning to the language of Wolfram, touching the battle of Parzival and Feirefiz: My brother and I is one body—like good man and good wife. One flesh and blood, here battling from loyalty of heart, and doing itself much harm.

III. Names and Forms

A realization of the catastrophic implications for theology of the idea of "transcendence" was first delivered to Christian Europe through that "Invincible Doctor," as he was called, the nominalist William of Occam (c. 1300–1349), after whose quick keen slash across the whole great big balloon, scholastic "philosophy" collapsed of its own dead weight. Already in the writings of Thomas Aquinas, in whose vast *Summa Theologica* the art of inflating revelation with reason came to culmination, there is at least one great word in recognition of the ineffable as just that, ineffable; namely, in the *Summa contra Gentiles,* the phrase, already cited: * "For then alone do we know God truly, when we believe that He is far above all that man can possibly think of God." [8] However, the Angelic Doctor went on then to expatiate in his *Summa Theologica* on God as Being, First Cause, a Personality, Immutable, et cetera, refuting heresies right and left (other people's concepts of the inconceivable), as far as to the beginning of an exposition of the sacraments—when, saying Mass one morning in the chapel of Saint Nicholas at Naples, he experienced a sort of thunderclap from aloft, a *raptus mentis:*

"He was smitten with a wonderful change," we read in the report of this catastrophe in the *Acta Bollandiana,* based on the words of his closest confidant, Reginald of Piperno, "and after that Mass he neither wrote nor dictated anything more, but suspended his writing in the third part of the *Summa,* in the treatise on Penance."

And when Brother Reginald saw that Brother Thomas had ceased to write, he said to him: Father, why have you put aside

* Supra, p. 189.

so great a work, which you began for the praise of God and the enlightenment of the world? And the said Brother Thomas replied: I cannot go on. But the said Brother Reginald, fearing that he had fallen into madness as a result of too much study, kept on pressing the said Brother Thomas to go on with his writing, and likewise Brother Thomas replied: I cannot do it, Reginald, everything I have written seems as worthless as straw.

Then Brother Reginald, overcome with surprise, so arranged matters that the said Brother Thomas went to visit his sister, the Countess of San Severino, of whom he was very fond; he hastened to her with great difficulty, and when he arrived and the Countess came to meet him, he hardly spoke to her. Then the Countess, in a state of great fear, said to Brother Reginald: What is all this? Why is Brother Thomas all struck with a stupor, and hardly speaks to me? And Brother Reginald answered: He has been like this since about Saint Nicholas's day, and since then he has not written anything. And the said Brother Reginald began to press the said Brother Thomas to tell him for what reason he refused to write and why he was stupefied like this. And after a great many pressing questions from Brother Reginald, Brother Thomas replied to the said Brother Reginald: I adjure you by the living God Almighty and by your duty to our Order and by the love you have for me, that so long as I am alive you will never tell anyone what I am going to tell you. And he went on: Everything that I have written seems to me worthless in comparison with the things I have seen and which have been revealed to me.

And as the aforesaid Countess continued to be very taken aback, Brother Thomas departed and returned to Naples, and then resumed his journey to the Council according to the invitation he had received,* writing nothing whatsoever. And on the road, in the village of Magentia in Compania, he was attacked by the illness from which he afterwards died.[9]

Riding along absent-mindedly on a mule, he had struck his head on a branch and fallen unconscious. In Maezna, where he then remained for a while with his niece Francisca of Aquino, he asked to be taken to the Cistercian monastery of Saint Mary at Fossanova. (We are following in life the legend of Galahad, on his journey in Solomon's ship.) The report continues:

* To the Council of Lyons, January 1274, on the invitation of Pope Gregory X.

And the said witness said moreover, that when the said Brother Thomas began to be overcome with sickness in the said village of Magentia, he besought with great devotion that he might be borne to the monastery of St. Mary at Fossanova: and so it was done. And when the said Brother Thomas entered the monastery, weak and ill, he held on to a door post with his hand and said: This is my rest for ever and ever. . . . And he remained for several days in that monastery in his ill state with great patience and humility, and desired to receive the Body of our Savior. And when that Body was brought to him, he genuflected, and with words of wondrous and long-drawn-out adoration and glorification he saluted and worshiped it, and before receiving the Body he said: I receive thee, viaticum of my pilgrimage, for love of whom I have studied and watched and labored and preached and taught; never have I said aught against thee unless it was in ignorance: nor am I obstinate in my opinion, but if I have said aught ill, I leave it all to the correction of the Roman Church. And then he died, and was buried near the high altar of the church of that monastery, in a marshy place close to the garden of the said monastery, where there is a stream, from which a water wheel takes up water, by which all that place is watered, as the witness himself has often and carefully observed.[10]

Albertus Magnus (1193–1280), the first great master of the very brief period of the scholastics, who had been Aquinas's master, is reported to have felt the moment of his pupil's death telepathically; and whenever afterward Thomas's name was mentioned, he would burst into tears so violently that people thought he had succumbed to senile decay.[11]

One is strongly reminded of Nietzsche's sudden collapse at the height of his powers, 1888–1889, at the age of forty-five, and his eleven years thereafter, in the care of his mother and sister, in a state of torpid, paralyzed insanity. What sets fire to such minds?

"It has not been sufficiently appreciated," states one biographer, "that Saint Thomas Aquinas died from having contemplated God in an ecstatic vision." [12]

The philosopher Karl Jaspers' analysis of Nietzsche's at least superficially similar case indicates both spiritual and physical influences.[13] Nietzsche had lived all his life in a sphere of boundary experiences. However, illness too had been his constant state; and, as Thomas Mann has demonstrated in his "classic dialogue on sickness and health," *The Magic Mountain,* men's spiritual modes and their states of physical health are by no means unrelated. Nietzsche himself, as Jaspers shows, understood the value to him of his Amfortas wound.

"I am sufficiently aware of my general advantage in my variable health over all those sturdy intellectuals," he once wrote. "A philosopher who has made his way through many states of health and makes it again and again, has also gone through just as many philosophies; he simply cannot help constantly transmuting his condition into the most spiritual form and distance. Philosophy is just this art of transfiguration." [14]

"Sickness," comments Jaspers, "points the way to many and opposing sorts of thinking. It becomes 'the teacher of the great suspicion.' " [15]

But exactly this realization of the relativity of thought and spirituality to states of mind, and of these to states of the body, is what has supplied the rationale both of Indian yoga and of Christian monastic asceticism. In both (and they are historically related, derived from a single stock) the physical austerities yield states of mind susceptible to raptures that seem to most ascetics to be of a deeper, greater validity than the experiences of health. Not so, however, to Nietzsche. As Jaspers tells:

> He not only experiences the arrogance of cool clairvoyance, but also the intoxication of recuperation; and in this manner he views the healthy from the perspectives of illness, the sick from those of health. At one time he exposes his thoughts to the pressure of illness in order to see what will become of them, and at another time he subjects the sick thoughts to the criticism of health. [16]

And we have Nietzsche's own words on the influence of Alpine air, upon which theme Mann developed the whole symphony of *The Magic Mountain:*

> No one is able to live everywhere, and for anyone who has great tasks to perform that require all his powers, there is a very narrow choice. The influence of climate on *metabolism,* its retardation, its acceleration, is so great that a mistake in the choice of place and climate can not only alienate a person from

his vocation, but even keep him from knowing what it is: he never discovers it. His animal *vigor* never is great enough to spill over into that spiritual state in which one realizes: *that, only I* can do. . . . Even a little intestinal sluggishness that has become habitual is quite enough to convert a genius into something mediocre, something "German": the German climate itself suffices to fatigue powerful, even heroically gifted intestines. The *tempo* of metabolism stands in an exact relationship to the mobility or lameness of the spirit's *feet:* the "spirit" itself, in fact, is only a kind of metabolism. Just consider the places where men of great spirit live and have lived, where wit, *raffinement,* disdain for comfort belong, where Genius almost inevitably makes itself at home: they all have marvelously dry air. Paris, Provence, Florence, Jerusalem, Athens—these names signify something: that Genius is *conditioned* by dry air, by a clean sky—i.e., by rapid metabolism, by the possibility of gathering to oneself, again and again, great, even prodigious quantities of energy.[17]

In Aquinas's case, the moment of supreme rapture had apparently so diminished his respect for the long, sober, "healthy" labor of his life, that his energies could not return to it. They had passed to another sphere: the same at sight of which Galahad, trembling right hard, as when flesh begins to behold spiritual things, held up his hands to heaven and gave thanks and asked to die. It was ineffable, beyond words, beyond signs: *transcendent.*

In theology the word "transcendence" generally is read to refer (I am quoting Webster) to "the relation of God to the universe of physical things and finite spirits, as being, in his essential nature, prior to it, exalted above it, and having real being apart from it; —opposite to *immanence.*" In a philosophical, specifically Kantian sense, however, the term "transcendent" (again quoting Webster) means: "beyond the limits of all possible experience and hence beyond knowledge"; i.e. (and Kant makes this very clear), beyond all the forms and categories of experience and knowledge: *space and time,* as well as *quantity* (unity, plurality, or universality), *quality* (reality, negation, or limitation), *relation* (substantiality, causality, or reciprocity), or *modality* (possibility, actuality, or necessity). All these are the preconditions or presuppositions of human experience and thought. Hence to imagine a creation (causality) and creator (First Cause) of the universe is only

to project the categories of human experience and reason beyond
their field; that is too say, to become in a rather refined way as
guilty of anthropomorphism as any savage.

And that exactly is what the Invincible Doctor, William of
Occam, demonstrated in his own brilliant way in the early fourteenth century. By simply stating in so many words that there can
be no abstractive cognition where there has not first been a perceptive cognition, Occam disqualified the application of concepts
to the mystery called "God." Concepts are functions of the mind,
i.e., of individual minds. They may be derived from and signify perceptions, perceptions of things in the field of space and time; or they
may derive from and signify acts of the mind, the minds of thinking individuals; but in no case can they signify entities other
than those in the mind or those perceived. The concept "dog,"
for example, is in the mind and signifies certain perceptions of
creatures of a certain alikeness outside. It cannot be assumed to
signify some metaphysical *quidditas,* "whatness," or general substance DOG, as an idea in a "divine" mind somewhere else, of which
all the living and dead individuals classified by analogy as "dog"
are representations. "Dragon," "angel," and "God," on the other
hand, find no referents outside of the mind. *"Essentia non sunt
multiplicanda praeter necessitatem:* Beings or essences are not to
be multiplied beyond necessity." With this formula, known as
"Occam's razor," the Invincible Doctor closed with a single phrase
the book of scholastic "realism," wherein substantial "reality" had
been attributed to ideas; and on September 25, 1339, his "nomin-
alism" was the object of a special censure by the Paris Faculty of
Arts.

In effect, the import of Occam's slash across the field of names
and forms was to convert metaphysics into psychology. The arch-
types of mythology (God, angels, incarnations, and so forth)
could no longer be referred to a supposed metaphysical sphere but
were of the mind. Or if they referred to anything outside the mind
(as, for instance, the crucifixion of Jesus, crossing of the Red Sea,
or serpent in the Garden) it could be only to individual facts, historical events that were once actually perceived in the field of
space and time.

Half a century before Occam, in the Condemnations of 1277,
the point had been made that neither Scripture nor its interpreta-

tion by the Church could be reconciled with reason. One could choose to stand either with reason or with Scripture and the Church, but not with both. The Averroists tried to advocate both (how sincerely, who can say?) in their doctrine of the double truth.* With Occam's stroke, however, reason had been disqualified as a vehicle of substantial truth. Scripture, however, as a record of *historical* events, sheer facts, seemed to many to have escaped untouched from Occam's razor. And if the recorded facts were extraordinary—as they certainly were—well then, that proved the extraordinary claims of both Israel and the Church. Moreover, in Christ's own words and acts, so recorded, he had shown himself to be God. Q.E.D. There followed the absolutely anti-intellectual piety of the so-called *Devotio moderna,* of which the *Imitatio Christi* (c. 1400) and *Theologica Germanica* (c. 1350) are the outstanding documents. The latter, through its influence on Martin Luther (1483–1546), became a contributing force in the inspiration of the indomitable churchly and scriptural positivism of the Protestant Reformation and subsequent centuries of bibliolatry; the sum and substance of the whole movement being epitomized in that supine formula of John Gerson already cited: *"Repent and believe the Gospels,* all Christian wisdom lies in this."†

"The believer," as Nietzsche observed, "is not free to have any conscience at all for the question 'true or untrue': to have integrity on *this* point would be his end. The pathological condition of his point of view turns those convinced by it into fanatics—Savonarola, Luther, Rousseau, Robespierre, Saint-Simon—the opposition-type to the strong spirit who has *become* free. Yet the grand pose of these *sick* spirits, these epileptics of the concept, takes effect on the great mass. The fanatics are picturesque. Mankind would rather see gestures than hear proofs." [18]

But the historicizing miracle-mongering of the scriptural fanatics was not the only response of the time to the slash of Occam's razor. Of more respectable spiritual, though not nearly as great historical, significance was a movement away from reason in the opposite direction: not to scriptural positivism, but to psychological absorption in the stages, spheres, and crises of inward realization

---

* Supra, pp. 140–41.
† Supra, pp. 401–402.

symbolized in the imagery of the Christian mystical heritage—as in the vision of Dante (1265–1321) or in the sermons of Meister Eckhart (1260?–1327). A technical argument soon developed here, however—notably between the two chief followers of Eckhart, Tauler (1300?–1361) and Ruysbroeck (1293–1381)—as to whether an experience of union with the mystery called "God" should be expressed in terms of "identity" (*unitive mysticism*) or "relationship" (*epithalamian mysticism*, the "marriage" of the soul to God),* and Christians generally have made a great deal of this distinction. Eckhart and Tauler spoke in terms of identity, Ruysbroeck of relationship. And since the experiences in question were of the mind, the psyche, and, moreover, intimately particular to each mystic, it is really wonderful that Pope John XXII (r. 1316–1334), who was no mystic at all, should have thought himself qualified to censure as false Eckhart's description of what he had experienced.

In India, where, in yoga, they have had a little more experience of this inward way than we in the West, Eckhart and Tauler would simply have been said to have experienced *nir-vikalpa samādhi*, absorption *without* distinction; and Ruysbroeck, *sa-vikalpa samādhi*, absorption *with* distinction: the former dissolved in *nir-guṇa brahman*, the unqualified absolute, and the latter enjoying *sa-guṇa brahman*, the qualified.

"Do you like to speak of God with form or without form?" the Indian saint Ramakrishna (1836–1886) used to ask those coming to him for instruction. "Once upon a time a sannyasi entered the temple of Jagganath. As he looked at the holy image he debated within himself whether God had a form or was formless. He passed his staff from left to right to feel whether it touched the image. The staff touched nothing. He understood that there was no image before him; he concluded that God was formless. Next he passed the staff from right to left. It touched the image. The sannyasi understood that God has form." [19]

And so, equally, from the lucid spirit of Nicholas Cusanus (1401–1464)—whom Giordano Bruno called "divine"—we have not only the wonderful work on "learned ignorance," *De docta ignorantia* (1440), wherein all knowledge is recognized as

---

* $c \neq = x$, or cRx; cf. supra, pp. 345–47.

conjecture and divinity as one's own transcendent essence (immanent, since God is in all and all is in God, whose center is everywhere and circumference nowhere, yet transcendent of all categories of thought), but also, following that publication, his delightful devotional message to the monks of the Benedictine Abbey of Tegernsee, *De visione dei,* "Of the Vision of God" (1453), in which he wrote of the way to an intuition of the mystery of God through the contemplation of an image.

I will now show you, as I promised you, dearest brethren [Cusanus wrote], an easy path to mystical theology. For, knowing you to be led by zeal for God, I think you worthy of the opening up of this treasure, as assuredly very precious and most fruitful. And first I pray the Almighty to give me utterance, and the heavenly Word who alone can express Himself, that I may be able, as you can receive it, to relate the marvels of revelation, which are beyond all sight of our eyes, our reason, and our understanding. I will endeavor by a very simple and commonplace method to lead you by experience into the divine darkness; wherein, while you abide you shall perceive present with you the light inaccessible, and shall each endeavor, in the measure that God shall grant him, to draw even nearer thereunto, and to partake here, by a sweetest foretaste, of that feast of everlasting bliss, whereto we are called in the word of life, through the gospel of Christ, who is blessed for ever.

If I strive in human fashion to transport you to things divine, I must use a comparison of some kind. Now among men's works I have found no image better suited to our purpose than that of a visage that is omnivoyant—its face, by the painter's cunning art, being made to appear as though looking on all around it. There are many excellent pictures of such faces—for example, that of the archeress in the market place of Nuremberg; that by the eminent painter,. Roger [van der Weyden, 1400–1464], in his priceless picture in the governor's house at Brussels; the Veronica in my chapel at Coblenz, and, in the castle of Brixen, the angel holding the arms of the Church, and many others elsewhere. Yet, lest you should fail in the exercise, which requires a figure of this description to be looked upon, I send for your indulgence such a picture as I have been able to procure, setting forth the figure of an omnivoyant, and this I call the icon of God.

This picture, brethren, you shall set up in some place, let us say, on a north wall, and shall stand round it, a little way off, and look upon it. And each of you will find that, from whatsoever quarter he regards it, it looks upon him as if it looked on no one else. And it will seem to a brother standing to eastward as if that face looked toward the east, while one to southward will think it looks toward the south, and one to westward, toward the west. First, then, you will marvel how it can be that the face should look on all and each at the same time. For the imagination of him standing to eastward cannot conceive the gaze of the icon to be turned to any other quarter, such as west or south. Then let the brother who stood to eastward place himself to westward and he will find its gaze fastened on him in the west just as it was before in the east. And as he knows the icon to be fixed and unmoved, he will marvel at the motion of its immovable gaze.

If now, while fixing his eye on the icon, he walks from west to east, he will find that its gaze continuously goes along with him, and if he returns from east to west, in like manner it will not leave him. Then he will marvel how, being motionless, it moves, nor will his imagination be able to conceive that it should also move in like manner with one going in a contrary direction to himself. If he should wish to experiment on this, he will cause one of his brethren to cross over from east to west, still looking at the icon, while he himself moves from west to east; and he will hear that it moves in a contrary direction, even as with himself, and he will believe him. But, had he not believed him, he could not have conceived this to be possible. So by his brother's showing he will come to know that the picture's face keeps all in sight as they go on their way, though it be in contrary directions; and thus he will prove that that countenance, though motionless, is turned to east in the same way that it is simultaneously to west, and in the same way to north and to south, and alike to one particular place and to all objects at once, whereby it regards a single movement even as it regards all together. And while he observes how that gaze never leaves any, he sees that it takes such diligent care of each one who finds himself observed as though it cared only for him, and for no other, and this to such a degree that one on whom it rests cannot even conceive that it should take care of any other. He will also see that it takes the same most diligent care of the least of creatures as of the greatest, and of the whole universe.[20]

IV. The New Universe

"We believe in something with a live faith when that belief is sufficient for us to live by, and we believe in something with a dead, a sluggish faith when, without our having abandoned it, being still grounded in it, we no longer experience it efficaciously in our lives." So Ortega y Gasset.[21]

The disintegration of the foundations for that faith which, during the centuries of its own collapse, became (ironically!) one of the most influential, simultaneously constructive and destructive, forces in the history of mankind, proceeded, and is proceeding still, from two irresistible influences, the same to which the modern process of cultural transformation as a whole has become irrevocably consigned; namely the scientific method of research and the power-driven machine. The latter, of course, did not become a significant force before the end of the eighteenth century; but already in the early thirteenth, important new inventions were being put to use. From the Orient, paper and the compass arrived about 1260 (the time of the voyages of the Polo brothers). About 1320 gunpowder was applied to the propulsion of projectiles, water power came into use in industry and the stern rudder for ships, the mechanical clock was invented, also the windmill, and with the introduction of Arabic numerals a sudden advance was achieved in mathematics, giving promise of more discoveries to come.

The immediate danger to the faith, however, lay in the astonishingly rapid development, even in the period of Aquinas, of an attitude of independent inquiry in fields that for centuries had been allowed to rest about as Aristotle had left them. Adelard of Bath, in his *Questiones naturales,* proposed as early at 1115, the time of Heloise and Abelard, a series of queries in natural history, beginning with the earth and its plants, and proceeding to the lower and higher animals, then on to human psychology, and concluding with the cosmic phenomena of ocean, air, and sky.[22] Today some of the questions sound ridiculous. They did not, however, in their time. No one knew where such queries might lead.

When one tree is grafted upon another, why is all the fruit of the nature of the grafted portion? Why do some brutes ruminate; why are some animals without stomachs; and why do some that drink make no water? Why do men grow bald in front? Why do some

animals see better in the night than in the day and why can a man
standing in the dark see objects that are in the light, while a man
standing in the light cannot see objects that are in the dark? Why
are the fingers of the human hand of unequal length and the palm
hollow? Why do babies not walk as soon as born, and why are
they first nourished on milk? Why does milk not agree equally with
young and old? Why do we fear dead bodies? Why can the voice
penetrate an iron wall? How is the terrestrial globe upheld in the
midst of space? [23]

In a second work, *De eodem et diverso,* the same inquisitive
author observes: "The senses are reliable in respect neither to the
greatest nor to the smallest objects"; and then he asks: "Who has
ever comprehended the space of the sky with the sense of sight?
. . . Who has ever distinguished minute atoms with the eye?" [24]
And with this, as Professor Lynn Thorndike remarks in his eight-
volume *History of Magic and Experimental Science,* the inevita-
bility is already announced of Galileo's telescope. Moreover, that
the author of these inquiries knew exactly what he was doing to the
mansion of belief is evident from a rather startling rebuke
that he delivers in his *Questiones* to an imagined interlocutor:

> It is difficult for me to talk with you about animals: for I have
> learned from my Arabian masters under the guidance of reason;
> you, however, captivated by the appearance of authority, follow
> your halter. Since what else should authority be called than a
> halter? For just as brutes are led where one wills by a halter, so
> the authority of past writers leads not a few of you into danger,
> held and bound as you are by bestial credulity. Consequently
> some, usurping to themselves the name of authority, have used
> excessive license in writing, so that they have not hesitated to
> teach bestial men falsehood in place of truth. . . . Wherefore,
> if you want to hear anything more from me, give and take rea-
> son. For I am not the sort of man that can be fed on a picture of
> a beefsteak.[25]

It is in the light of inquiries and researches of this kind that one
must understand the effort of Aquinas in the later portion of his
Summa Theologica to keep separate the two fields of science and
the Christian faith. "The reason why science and faith cannot be
about the same object, and in the same respect," he wrote, "is
because the object of science is something seen, whereas the

object of faith is the unseen." [26] However, among the matters
of the faith that he and his Church were proposing for belief, as
touching the unseen, were not only the dogmas of the Athanasian
Creed [27] but also, as defined in the Fourth Lateran Council, 1215
A.D., the doctrine of the Real Presence of Jesus Christ in the
eucharist; and further, behind and supporting all this, the entire
geo- and Judeo-centric fairytale of the Old Testament: of Adam
and Eve, the serpent in the Garden, the universal flood, the Tower
of Babel and plagues of Egypt, Moses' parting of the Red Sea,
Joshua's stopping of the sun, the boys in the fiery furnace, and
Jonah in the whale. So that obviously not only things unseen, but
seeable things as well—quite concrete, historical, and cosmological
things—were being here proposed to faith: things of the past, of
which archaeology presently would tell, and things of the present,
the form of the universe, et cetera, which in Aquinas's time had
already begun to come under investigation.

In England, for example, the Bishop of Lincoln, Robert Grosseteste (1175?–1253?), an older contemporary of Aquinas, and a
clergyman like himself, who in a work entitled *On the Order of the
Emanation of Things Caused by God* had expressed the earnest
wish that men should cease questioning the scriptural account of
the age and beginning of the world,[28] nevertheless, in his own
treatise on the Sphere, was willing to propose that the sphericity of
the earth and all the stars and planets "is made evident both by
natural reasons and by astronomical experiences." [29] And the reference here to *experiences,* instead of to the usual *authority,* is
marvelously important: a word of infinite promise. For it is the
heralding word, at last, of Europe against Asia, future against past,
individual quest, and the sharp cut of "proof" into the grip of
"faith." It marks the beginning of that irretrievable break from un-
tested error that was to uproot and demolish, within the next four
centuries, every support of that age of the monumental arts which
for a period of some five millenniums had held mankind enchanted
in a dream of toil and beauty, misery and wonder, serving gods
abiding in a house of myth only a league or so beyond the moon.
The term defines the first absolutely indispensable requisite of any
sort of science or maturity of mind whatsoever.

Grosseteste himself was experimenting, among other matters,
with lenses; and showing thereby, as he declared, "how to make

things very far off seem very close at hand, and how to make large objects that are near seem tiny, and how to make distant objects appear as large as we choose, so that it is possible for us to read the smallest letters at an incredible distance, or to count sand or grain or grass or any other minute objects." [30] Galileo's telescope (invented 1608 in Holland) and the Dutchman Zacharias Zanger's microscope (1590) are here already on the way, to make things unseen, both up there beyond the moon and in here within the living cell, as visible as necessary to explode the entire space-and-time dimension of the edifice of Scripture. Moreover, the same bold English bishop held that light and all natural objects send forth in all directions, along geometrical lines, virtues, or forces, which act upon the senses and upon matter: space itself, in this way, being a function of light.[31] And of this proposition too the implications were immense; for not personal, spiritual wills, but impersonal energies or forces were now to be regarded as the potencies responsible for the operations of nature, and the way thereby was opened to a technology not of prayer, sacrifice, hells, penances, and incense, but of machines.

Another highly significant English "experimenter" of the time —still the time, by the way, of Aquinas—was "The Admirable Doctor," the Franciscan friar Roger Bacon (1214?–1294), who wrote of experiments with magnets and, at the invitation of his protector, Pope Clement IV (r. 1265–1268), sent to Rome three substantial works reviewing, unmethodically but broadly, the entire field of what he took to be proper to experimental science. Languages, mathematics, optics, and the "noblest" science, "mistress of them all," moral philosophy, are discussed here side by side with magic, astrology, miracles, the potency of well-thought words, and the flights of good and bad Ethiopian dragons. "First one should be credulous," Roger Bacon wrote, in his exposition of his scientific method, "until experience follows second, and reason comes third. . . . At first one should believe those who have made experiments or who have faithful testimony from others who have done so, nor should one reject the truth because he is ignorant of it and because he has no argument for it." [32]

However, as an example of the lengths to which his credulity could extend, without correction from either experience or reason of his own, we may cite his following unqualified report to his patron on Peter's throne: that "there was at Paris recently a sage who asked for snakes and was given one and cut it into small sections except that the skin of its belly on which it crawled remained intact; and that snake crawled as best it could to a certain herb by touching which it was instantly made whole. And the experimenter collected an herb of wonderful virtue." [33] *

By the middle of the following century there was being established in Paris, however, in the researches and writings of the masters of the so-called "mechanistic school" of critics—notably the Rector of the University, John Buridan of Bethune (fl. 1328–1366), and the Bishop of Lisieux, Nicolas Oresme (fl. 1348–d. 1382)—a reasonably substantial base for a dependable order of science. Buridan, hypothetically attributing to the celestial bodies matter of the same order as that of the earth, sought to explain why objects tossed into the air should continue to fly after leaving the hand, and then referred his finding to a theory of the planets. Briefly: at the moment when a stone is tossed, there is imparted to it an *impetus* that is proportionate, on one hand, to the velocity of the movement and, on the other, to the quantity of matter moved: which imparted impetus then maintains the movement until the resistance of the air and the weight of the matter prevail. The imparted impulse continuously diminishes; hence the movement of the stone continuously retards, until, in the end, yielding to gravity, it falls back to its natural place.[34]

"If he who hurls projectiles," Buridan states, "moves with an equal speed a light piece of wood and a heavy piece of iron, these two pieces being otherwise the same in volume and shape, the piece of iron will go farther because the impetus to it is the more intense." [35] As Professor Etienne Gilson comments to this point: "John Buridan got very close to the notion of the *impeto* in Galileo and the *quantity of movement* in Descartes."

However, even more important than the approximate laws proposed in this theory was its very bold extension of the laws of earth to the celestial spheres (also as in Galileo). For now, continuing the argument (as summarized by Gilson): "Assuming that

* Compare with this apparently traditional fantasy the old Babylonian legend of Gilgamesh, the serpent, and the plant of immortality (*Occidental Mythology*, pp. 90–92); also, the Arabian Nights tale of "The Queen of the Serpents" (Joseph Campbell, ed. *The Portable Arabian Nights*, New York: Viking, 1952, pp. 406–15).

God conferred on celestial orbs a certain *impetus* at the moment of their creation, that he preserves it in them as he universally preserves all things, and that no resistance either inner or outer neutralizes that initial impetus, there is no reason why the movement of celestial orbs should not continue by itself." [36] With this, the angelic intelligences formerly supposed to be in charge of maintaining the movements of the heavens (the Muses of Figure 13) were rendered useless, and the laws of this earth were extended outward into spheres formerly reserved for orders only of the more subtle, spiritual kind: of God and his heavenly host.

Nicolas Oresme then extended Buridan's mechanistic theory of impetus inward, to the psychological field: "Just as you see a hammer rebound upward from an anvil several times of itself and then come to rest in the middle," he wrote, "so too in movements and powers of the soul there are sometimes produced at the start impetuses and dispositions that have great effect." [37] Oresme, furthermore, applied rectangular coordinates to the study of falling bodies and in his *Treatise on Heaven and Earth* maintained that experiments should be conducted to determine whether it is the sky that is moved and the earth not, or vice versa—even giving in illustration of the latter possibility, "several fine persuasions to show that the earth is moved in a daily movement and the sky not." [38]

Now one of the most important effects for Western science of the old Levantine mythology of matter and spirit as distinct from each other, and of a god that is not immanent in nature but "out there," was the corollary that matter of itself is inert, and that, consequently, any movement observed in nature must have been communicated to it, either by God, directly or through an angel, or else by some other external spirit—the only other such spirit possible, however, being Satan, or some member of his host. The findings of Oresme and Buridan cleared the field at least of the angels and the devils, completing the work begun by Grosseteste a century before. In their view, the old Sumerian vision of a universe moved by superior beings, intelligences or gods, gave place to a marvelous machine, made and moved by God, the Master of the machine; and this idea remains among us to the present.

However, in the popular view the angels and devils still were at work. The world, indeed, was a machine, and God was its Maker and Master; but Satan, once the prince of angels, knew its secret and through alchemy, necromancy, astrology, and the other sciences was communicating his knowledge to men, both to bind them to himself by offering aid to illegitimate ends, and ultimately to win from God control of the machine. When Satan tempted Christ, he offered him all the kingdoms of the world in return for adoration, whence it is infallibly known that Satan bestows knowledge only on those who render him allegiance. The masters and mistresses of his knowledge and arts were therefore to be "vehemently suspected," not of heresy alone, but even of having bound themselves to the service of the prince of Hell. And with the rapid increase of heresy throughout Europe from 1250 to 1650, together with the knowledge and works of science, the guardians of the authority of Rome and the Scripture were seized with a passion of anxiety that released throughout the Christian world a reign of terror matched in history only by the mass liquidations of the modern tyrant states.

In the year 1233 the Inquisition had been established and assigned to the Dominicans by Gregory IX (r. 1227–1241). In 1250 Frederic II, the principal antagonist and restrainer of the papacy, died, and two years later, May 15, 1252, Innocent IV (r. 1243–1254), in his bull *Ad extirpanda,* authorized the secular authorities to use torture in the scouting out of both heresy and sorcery. Alexander IV (r. 1254–1261) four years later extended this privilege to the clergy, and from April 5 to 9, 1310, at Toulouse, the first of a series of full-scale *autos da fé* was instituted.[39] September 19, 1398, a statement from the doctors of the University of Paris—under the chancellorship at the time of that leading protagonist of the *Devotio moderna,* John Gerson (to whom some scholars now attribute the writing of the *Imitatio Christi*)—declared that there is an implied contract with Satan to be recognized in every superstitious observance of which the expected result cannot reasonably be anticipated from God or from nature, condemning, furthermore, as erroneous the assertion that it is permissible to invoke the aid of demons or to seek their friendship; to enter into compacts with them or to imprison them in stones, rings, mirrors, or images; to use sorcery even for good purposes; or to hold that God can be induced by magic arts to compel demons to obey invocations, that the celebration of Masses

or other good works is permissible in connection with thauma-
turgy, that the prophets and saints of old performed their miracles
by these means, or that by magic arts we can attain the sight of the
divine essence.[40] Joan of Arc, it is recalled, was burned as a witch
in 1431. Five decades later the inquisitor Cumanus gained for
himself a high place in heaven by shaving scrupulously the whole
bodies of forty-seven witches before committing them to the flames;
and as Frazer notes in *The Golden Bough* in comment on this
incident: "He had high authority for this rigorous scrutiny, since
Satan himself, in a sermon preached from the pulpit of North
Berwick church, comforted many of his servants by assuring
them that no harm could befall them 'as lang as their hair wes on.' "
Frazer points to identical customs among the primitive Bhils of
India and the Aztecs.[41] And indeed, reading of the religion of
those years, one has the sense of watching the putrefaction of a
corpse—the body, once so beautiful at Chartres, dissolving in a
horrid stench:

Witches, by the light of the moon, rode on brooms, those nights,
to mountaintops, to consort there in obscene rites with Satan himself in the form of a goat, poodle, or ape. They would lift his
tail and kiss him there, while holding a lighted candle, trample and
spit upon the Cross, turn up their own rear ends to God, and listen
to a sermon preached by His Satanic Majesty to a parody of the
Mass, where they would learn they had no souls to lose and that
there would be no future life. Tables loaded with meat and wine
would then rise from the earth. A dance would follow, with the
women held behind their partners, and when bowing to the demon
they bent backward, lifting a foot forward in the air. Indiscriminate
intercourse would terminate such rites, much in the way of the old
Gnostic love feasts,* and with obliging demons now serving as
either incubi or succubi as required.[42]

Nor was the Protestant world, when its time came, one whit better off. When Luther, in the year 1520, burned at Wittenberg the
papal bull, together with a volume of scholastic philosophy and a
copy of the church canon, shattering the Church Militant into a
galaxy of contending Christianities (all equally opposed both to
Occam's unknown God and to the works of science and reason,
tortured with a Pauline sense of the sinfulness of life, and fighting

* Supra, pp. 159–61.

with fire and brimstone both each other and the rising tide of facts by which their scriptural Rock of Ages was already well nigh engulfed), superstition and violence did not decline but even increased. Luther himself hurled his inkpot at the Devil, spoke often of his struggles against Hell, and hurled the Bible at Copernicus (1473–1543), naming him "an ass who wants to pervert the whole art of astronomy and deny what is said in the book of Joshua, only to make a show of ingenuity and attract attention." He and all about him were as riddled with superstition as those from whom they were revolting. As the one rational Christian of the day, the very learned Erasmus, remarked in his timely work *In Praise of Folly:* "The Christian religion seems to have some relation to Folly and no alliance at all with wisdom." And again: "There are none more silly, or nearer their wits' end, than those too superstitiously religious." [43]

The Protestant legend of the magician Faust who sold his soul to Satan was conceived and born of this madness. Historically, Doctor Johann Faust (1480?–1540?)—or Magister Georgius Sabellius Faustus Junior, as he is said to have called himself—was a contemporary of Erasmus (1466–1536), Luther (1483–1546), Zwingli (1484–1531), Melanchthon (1497–1560), Calvin (1509–1564), and Henry VIII (r. 1509–1547). besides the alchemist Paracelsus (1493–1541) and the rollicking monk Rabelais (1495–1553). The earliest dated reference to him is in a letter, August 20, 1507, from the Benedictine Abbot Johann Tritheim (who was himself reputed to be a magician in league with Satan) to the mathematician Johann Windung, wherein the fellow is named simply a fool, vain babbler, and mountebank fit to be whipped. Philipp Begardi, another contemporary, in his *Index sanitatis* (published in Worms, 1539), ranks him with Paracelsus as a "wicked, cheating, unlearned" doctor: "Since several years he has gone through all regions, provinces and kingdoms, made his name known to everybody, and is highly renowned for his great skill, not alone in medicine, but also in chiromancy, necromancy, physiognomy, visions in crystal, and the like other arts. And also not only renowned, but written down and known as an experienced master. Himself admitted, nor denied that it was so, and that his name was Faustus, and called himself *philosophum philosophorum.* But how many have complained to me that they were deceived by him—verily a great number!"

But it was a Protestant pastor in Basel, Johann Gast (d. 1572), who in his *Sermones convivales* (Basel, 1543) first definitely credited this mountebank with supernatural gifts derived from the Devil, by whom he was ultimately carried off; the performing horse and dog by which he had been accompanied on his rounds having been his familiar evil spirits. "The wretch came to an end in a terrible manner," wrote Pastor Gast; "for the Devil strangled him. His dead body lay constantly on its face on the bier, although it had been five times turned upward." The councilor and historian of Maximilian II, Johann Mannel (d. 1560) reported in his *Locorum communium collectanea* (published in Basel, without date) a conversation of Melanchthon in which the reformer spoke strongly of Faust as "a disgraceful beast and sewer of many devils," who had been killed indeed by the Devil's wringing his neck; while still another witness, Johann Weiher, body physician to the duke of Cleves, described Faust in his *De praestigus daemonium* (Basel, 1563) as a drunken vagabond who had studied magic at Cracow and practiced "this beautiful art shamelessly up and down Germany, with unspeakable deceit, many lies and great effect."

The legend set going by the pastor Gast soon gained in all Protestant lands almost infinite popularity. Ballads, dramas, and puppet plays appeared, as well as a proliferation of Faust books. On the puppet stage, a voice cried from the right: "Faust! Faust! desist from this proposal! Go on with the study of theology, and you will be the happiest of mortals." To which a voice from the left responded: "Faust! Faust! leave the study of theology. Betake you to necromancy, and you will be the happiest of mortals!" Faust deliberately chose the latter, preferring human, satanic knowledge to that of God. "He laid the Holy Scriptures behind the door and under a bench, refused to be called doctor of theology and preferred to be called doctor of medicine"—and so, was justly damned.

The first of the numerous "Faust books" was put forth by Johann Spies at Frankfurt in 1587, with the following descriptive title: *History of Dr. Joh. Faust, the notorious sorcerer and black artist: How he bound himself to the Devil for a certain time:*

*What singular adventures befell him therein: What he did and
carried on until finally he received his well-deserved pay. Mostly
from his own posthumous writings; for all presumptuous, rash and
godless men, as a terrible example, abominable instance and well-
meant warning, collected and put in print. "Submit yourselves
therefore to God: resist the Devil and he will flee from you"*
(James 4:7). This book immediately sold out, and before the end
of the year there were four pirated editions. The very next
year, at Tübingen, a rhymed version appeared; at Frankfurt, a second edition by Spies; and in Lübeck, a Low German version. Re-
prints and amplified redactions continued to pour forth until in
1599 there was published the culminating Faust book, by Georg
Rudolf Widmann,[44] wherein, among other novelties, Luther himself was declared to have been able only with God's help to ward
off the assaults that Faust by his magic put upon him.

The Faust books are marvelously Protestant. Mephistopheles,
Faust's devil, appears in the costume of a monk and when Faust
asks for a wife declares that, since marriage is pleasing to God, it
would be a violation of their contract. The magician's body servant, Wagner, is the son of a Catholic priest. And when wines and
rich meats are desired, they are produced from the cellars and pan-
tries of the clergy. There is, furthermore, no sympathy at all for
the tragedy of the protagonist, torn between the wonders of this
world and the promise of eternity. He was wicked, he was damned,
and let the reader be warned by his fate.

On the other hand, in the play by Christopher Marlowe (1564–
1593), *The Tragical History of Doctor Faustus,* though the incidents of the first Faust book are closely followed, the moral is
totally transformed—from the Reformation, one might say, to the
Renaissance. For along with the rise in these centuries of a respect
for experience and reason there had been unfolding (and not in
Italy alone) that new appreciation of the loveliness of this world
and the arts of its celebration which, even while Luther was hurling
his ink at Devils and the Papal See, had come to culmination in the
masterworks of Leonardo (1452–1519), Dürer (1471–1528),
Michelangelo (1475–1564), Raphael (1483–1520), and Titian
(1477–1576). Already in the period from Buridan to Cusanus—c.
1350–1450)—the Renaissance of delight in this world had begun
to refute, in its own immediate way, the Gothic system of dis-

paragement. Petrarch (1304–1374), directly following Dante (1265–1321) and Giotto (1272–1336), is, of course, the pivotal figure of this inversion. Next follow Boccaccio (1313–1375) in Italy, Deguilleville (fl. 1330–1335) in France, and in England Geoffrey Chaucer (1340?–1400), in whose *Canterbury Tales* the wakening interest in portraiture, the features, character, motives, and delights of living individuals, comes to the foreground, and the Middle Ages echoes only in their words, the folklore, saints' tales, fabliaux, and romances that they recount to each other for entertainment. It is as though the plane of serious interest had shifted from the mysteries within the alchemical *vas* to the lives of the alchemists themselves, from our Figures 38, 41, 42, and 43, of the mystic connubium of the king and queen, to come to rest upon Figure 39.

And so, too, in the visual arts. The symbolic personages of the Christian mythology, of the Fall by the Tree and Redemption by a Savior on Holy Rood, began to assume, more and more distinctly, the weight and tangibility of this physical world. Even the sensuous values of their garments acquired significance, and their settings in landscapes or in buildings became more and more fields of interest in themselves. Many an "Adoration of the Virgin" or "Baptism of Christ" is but an occasion for an interesting arrangement of superb portraits—not of saints, but of Renaissance Florentines. And where the mythological theme is stressed, as it is in Titian's eloquent rendition of "The Fall of Man," now in the Prado, the interpretation is of the *human* moment—rendering a sense at once of the tragical and the beautifully necessary mystery of man, woman, death, and birth, in the joys and sorrows of this world. Only Angelico (1387–1455) retained in his work that sense of a distinction between what the Indians call the "subtle matter" (*sukṣma*) of mythological forms and the "gross matter" (*sthūla*) of this earth. So that when, in the reformed spirit of the Catholic Counter-Reformation, after the Council of Trent (1545–1563), an attempt was made to render mythic themes in relation again to Heaven—as, for example, in "The Immaculate Conception" by Murillo (1618–1682), also in the Prado—the result was of neither Gothic nor Renaissance sincerity but Baroque sentimentality. For look you what had taken place!

By about 1440 the art of printing from movable type had been invented, and, from his press at Mainz, Johann Gutenberg produced in 1454 and 1455 the first dated printed documents, some letters of indulgence made from type cast in a mold; then in 1456 the so-called Mazarin Bible (named from a copy in the library of Cardinal Mazarin, 1602–1661). By 1464 there was a printing press in Italy, near Rome; by 1468 one in Switzerland, with Erasmus as the press corrector; by 1470 there was a press in France, at the Sorbonne; by 1471 one in Utrecht, 1473 in Holland, 1474 Spain, 1476 Manchester (Caxton), 1539 Mexico City, and 1638 Cambridge, Massachusetts. Already in the middle sixteenth century, since the new art seemed to be stimulating too much freedom of thought, repressive measures were introduced by Church and State alike (or rather, now, by churches and by states), and the quality of the work greatly declined; but in the eighteenth century a revival occurred, and the beautiful types of Caslon, Baskerville, and Bodoni were designed.

In 1445 Cape Verde was discovered, exploding the idea that only sand, water, and the mountain of Purgatory lay to the south. In 1486 Diaz rounded the Cape of Good Hope; in 1492 Columbus crossed the ocean blue, and in 1498, Vasco da Gama reached Calicut; in 1512 another bold Portuguese reached Java and the Moluccas; in 1519, Magellan, likewise a Portuguese, circumnavigated the globe, and the same year Cortez conquered Mexico for Spain, in 1530, Pizarro, Peru. So that, besides new worlds geographically, new worlds of mythology had also been discovered, and the problem already was recognized that has been exercising students of religion ever since: of how it is to be explained that so many of the basic themes and patterns of the authorized Christian myths and rites appear also (in Satanic parody, as it were) among the heathens of the Americas, Africa, and Asia.

Then, as we have seen, in 1543 Copernicus published his exposition of the heliocentric universe, and Galileo some sixty years later commenced his celestial researches with a telescope, which led immediately to the condemnation of the new cosmology as contrary to Scripture—which of course it was and is.

v. The Knight of the Rueful Countenance

Henry Adams named the year 1600—the year of the burning of Giordano Bruno—as marking the watershed of the passage from the "religious" to the "mechanical age" of mankind,[45] and, as he notes, the leading spirits of the transit actually did not realize what, in their pursuit of truth, they were doing to the armature of faith.

Society [as he tells] began to resist, but the individual showed greater and greater insistence, without realizing what he was doing. When the Crescent drove the Cross in ignominy from Constantinople in 1453, Gutenburg and Fust were printing their first Bible at Mainz under the impression that they were helping the Cross. When Columbus discovered the West Indies in 1492, the Church looked on it as a victory of the Cross. When Luther and Calvin upset Europe half a century later, they were trying, like St. Augustine, to substitute the *Civitas Dei* for the *Civitas Romae*. When the Puritans set out for New England in 1620, they too were looking to found a *Civitas Dei* in State Street; and when Bunyan made his Pilgrimage in 1678, he repeated St. Jerome. Even when, after centuries of license, the Church reformed its discipline, and, to prove it, burned Giordano Bruno in 1600, besides condemning Galileo in 1630—as science goes on repeating to us every day—it condemned anarchists, not atheists. None of the astronomers were irreligious men; all of them made a point of magnifying God through his works; a form of science which did their religion no credit. Neither Galileo nor Kepler, neither Spinoza nor Descartes, neither Leibnitz nor Newton, any more than Constantine the Great—if so much —doubted Unity. The utmost range of their heresies reached only its personality.

Continuing, Adams then comes to his crucial point, the naming of the new force, the new theme, by which the old, of unity, whether personified or not, was being displaced:

This persistence of thought-inertia is the leading idea of modern history. Except as reflected in himself, man has no reason for assuming unity in the universe, or an ultimate substance, or a prime-motor. The *a priori* insistence on this unity ended by fatiguing the more active—or reactive—minds; and Lord Bacon [1561–1626] tried to stop it. He urged society to lay aside the idea of evolving the universe from a thought, and to try evolving thought from the universe. The mind should observe and register forces—take them apart and put them together—without assuming unity at all. "Nature, to be commanded, must be obeyed." "The imagination must be given not wings but weights." As Galileo reversed the action of the earth and sun, Bacon reversed the relation of thought to force. The mind was thenceforth to follow the movement of matter, and unity must be left to shift for itself.[46]

Essentially what has happened is that in the physical field—the field of matter understood as distinct from spirit—an order of law has been recognized that is apparently not the same as that of the human will and imagination. As in the Freudian view of the forces operative in the structuring of the psyche the *wish* of the growing child is countered by the *prohibition* of the parent, and as in Adler's view the child's *wish* is frustrated by its own *impotence* to achieve, so here the symbols of the soul's dynamic structure, projected upon the universe, are met and broken by an irrefragable order in diametric opposition. Whereas in the soul, or heart, there is the sense of freedom—freedom of choice and to will—out there, in the field of its action, a mechanical determinism prevails. Whereas here there would seem to be intelligence and intention, there there is only blind, irresponsible, unknowing, unfeeling momentum. The desert-field and dust-storm of inert, unconscious matter, set blowing, whether by God, by chance, by itself, or by nothing at all, has welled out from that stone flung upward by John of Buridan to fill, to permeate, and to become the world; and from the hammered anvil of Oresme, driven inward, as well, to the seat of the soul itself.* Galileo and Newton confirmed Buridan's intuition of the stone; Freud and Pavlov, Oresme's of the anvil. Kant's *Critique of Pure Reason* (1781) renewed for the modern mind the slash of Occam's razor, and Flaubert's *Madame Bovary* (1856) assumed upon the modern throne the place of Helen of Troy.

Don Quixote de la Mancha, the Knight of the Rueful Countenance, riding errant on his lean horse Rozinante ("Horse of Once-upon-a-Time"), striving both for the benefit of the public and for the increase of his private honor (just about the year 1600), saw before him, spread across the plain, a phalanx of some thirty or forty windmills.

"Look there, friend Sancho!" he cried. "Those giants! I am going to quit them of their lives."

* Supra, pp. 592–93.

"What giants?" Sancho asked, trotting alongside on his donkey.

"Those ahead!" Quixote replied. "Some of that kind have arms that can reach two leagues." He was already lowering his lance.

"Please," Sancho warned, "take another look! Those are windmills. What you take for arms are their sails."

But the knight had given spur to his nag and, with lance couched, was on his way.[47]

In the language of the troubadours, the contrast of the two world orders of adventure and banality, will and determinism, was epitomized in the imagery of the passage from night—the night of love—to dawn, the day of the watchman's cry and the legally cruel *gilos*. "Oh God! Oh God! This dawn, how quickly it comes!" * Abelard, Clinschor, and Anfortas were not the only gallants in those days whose battle cry of *Amor!* terminated in disaster. But their fate was no more than symbolic of the usual breakage of the will of man, his dream and urge for life, by circumstance: the windmill phalanx of the hard facts of this world. Parzival and Gawain were able to overthrow this weight. The will in them was fulfilled. Don Quixote, on the other hand, was about to encounter in those windmills more than his match.

The wind had risen; the mill sails had begun to move. Covering himself with his shield and recommending himself to the vision of his imagined Lady Dulcinea del Toboso, in whose service he was riding, he charged with Rozinante's utmost speed at the first of the giants before him, running his lance into its sail—which received the blow and, continuing its mechanical round, hurled both the knight and his mount a good way off, splintering the lance.

The question again arises that was posed by Schopenhauer, as to whether, in the fate of any rightly striving man, the weight and impact of sheer circumstance can be such as to vanquish altogether his sense of will, and therefore of being. And so what had Don Quixote to say when his squire, trotting on his donkey as fast as short legs could go, arrived to help his master to his feet?

"God help us!" said Sancho Panza. "Anyone could have seen that these are windmills—not giants—unless he had windmills in his head!"

"Be still, my friend Sancho," said the knight. "Affairs of war,

* Supra, p. 184.

more than any others, are subject to abrupt change. I am sure it
was that necromancer Frestón who transformed these giants into
mills, to deprive me of the honor of this victory. He has *always*
been my enemy, this way. However, his evil arts will have little
force, in the end, against the virtue of my sword."

Miguel de Cervantes Saavedra (1547–1616), living and writing—as Ortega y Gasset points out in his *Meditations on Quixote*
—precisely at that moment in the adventure of man when the
worlds of the inward vision and outward crude reality came ir-
resolvably together, intersecting, "forming a beveled edge," marks
the end in literature of the sheerly imaginative epic and the opening of the present age of the novel. "Reality is coming into poetry,"
Ortega writes, "to raise adventure to a higher aesthetic power."

> The epic plane, on which imaginary objects glide, was until
> now the only one, and poetry could be defined in the same terms
> as the epic. But now the imaginary plane comes to be a second
> plane. Art is enriched by one more aspect; it is, so to speak, en-
> larged by a third dimension; it reaches an aesthetic depth, which
> like geometric depth, presupposes a plurality of aspects. Con-
> sequently, the poetic can no longer be made to consist of that
> special attraction of the ideal past or of the interest which its
> procedure, always new, unique, and surprising, lends to adven-
> ture. Now our poetry has to be capable of coping with present
> reality. . . .[48]

Cervantes looks at the world from the height of the Renaissance. The Renaissance has tightened things a little more, and
has completely overcome the old sensibility. With his physics,
Galileo lays down the stern laws that govern the universe. A
new system has begun; everything is confined within stricter
forms. Adventures are impossible in this new order of things.
Before long Leibnitz [1646–1716] would declare that simple
possibility lacks validity; that only the *"compossible"* is possible; that is to say, what is closely connected with natural laws.
In this way the possible—which shows its crusty independence
in the miracle, in the myth—is inserted into the real as *the adventure* in Cervantes' portrayal of truth." [49]

Reality carried Quixote, that is to say, who carried adventure in
his head. Adventures are impossible, and yet Don Quixote brings
them to pass. In the earlier world of the epic of Parzival and
Gawain, knights in the forest met with adventures in accord with

the movements and readiness of their hearts, dreamlike; Quixote, on the other hand, encountered windmills in a hard, resistant world, unresponsive to his will: yet his will remained—a reality in itself.

> People [as Ortega remarks] may be able to take good fortune away from this neighbor of ours, but they will not be able to take away his efforts and courage. His adventures may be the vapors of a fermenting brain, but his will for adventure is real and true.
>
> Now, adventure is a dislocation of the material order, something unreal. In this will for adventure, in this effort and courage, we encounter, then, a strange dual nature, whose two elements belong to opposite worlds: the will is real, but what is willed is not real. Such a phenomenon is unknown in the epic. The men of Homer belong to the same world as their desires. In Don Quixote we have, on the other hand, a man who wishes to reform reality. But is he not a piece of that reality? Does he not live off it, is he not a consequence of it? How is it possible for that which does not exist—a projected adventure—to govern and alter harsh reality? Perhaps it is not possible, but it is a fact that there are men who decide not to be satisfied with reality. Such men aim at altering the course of things; they refuse to repeat gestures that custom, tradition, or biological instincts force them to make. These men we call heroes, because to be a hero means to be one out of many, to be oneself. If we refuse to have our actions determined by heredity or environment, it is because we seek to base the origin of our actions on ourselves and only on ourselves. The hero's will is not that of his ancestors nor of his society, but his own. This will to be oneself is heroism.[50]

And, as Ortega next remarks, a life lived in these terms is necessarily tragic.

> The tragic character is not tragic, and therefore poetic, merely in so far as he is a man of flesh and blood, but only in so far as he wills. The will—that paradoxical object which begins in reality and ends in the ideal, since one only wants what is not—is the tragic theme; and an epoch for which the will does not exist, a deterministic and Darwinian epoch, for example, cannot be interested in tragedy. . . .
>
> The plain man very sensibly thinks that all the bad things

happen to the hero through his persistence in such and such a purpose. By giving it up, he could make everything turn out well and, as the Chinese say at the end of a tale, alluding to their former nomadism, could settle down and raise many children. . . . The plain man, incapable of heroic acts, is ignorant of that stream of life in which only sumptuary, superfluous activities take place. He is ignorant of the overflow and excess of vitality. He lives bound to what is necessary and what he does, he does perforce. He is always impelled to act; his actions are reactions. . . .

Far from the tragic originating in fate, then, it is essential for the hero to want his tragic destiny. . . . All the sorrow springs from the hero's refusal to give up an ideal part, an imagined role that he has chosen. The actor in the drama, it might be said paradoxically, plays a part which is, in turn, the playing of a part, although this part is played in earnest. . . . And this "act of will," creating a new series of realities which exist only through it—the tragic order—is naturally but a fiction for anyone whose only wishes are those of natural necessity, which is satisfied with what merely exists." [51]

And with this I return to Christopher Marlowe, the father of Elizabethan tragedy; for his *Doctor Faustus* too is a work of this epoch of the "beveled edge." He also was one who looked at the world from the height of the Renaissance: a young genius aware of both the promise for humanity and the marvels of the universe being opened to view in his time by the heroes of this dawning modern age. Francis Kett, the mystic, burned in 1589 for heresy, had been a fellow and tutor of his college at Cambridge. Sir Walter Raleigh was a close friend; so too Thomas Harriott the astronomer, Walter Warner and Robert Hughes, two mathematicians. At Cambridge, furthermore, he had been a student of classical mythology, particularly in Ovid, whose *Amores* he translated. His orientation was totally secular; so that, though he based his drama on an English version of the first Faust book of Spies,* his own sympathy for the yearning, daring hero, and recognition of the tragic force of a life torn between the claims of eternity and time, set him spiritually completely apart from the fiercely moral Christian-Lutheran stand. And it was this humanizing, problematic transformation of the legend that recommended it to Goethe, who when Marlowe's play

* Supra, pp. 597–98.

was mentioned burst into the exclamation: "How greatly it all is planned!"

The hero here is no "sewer of devils," but a man, a living Renaissance man, thirsting for the infinite and willing to risk for it Hell itself—as had been Tristan for Isolt, Parzival for integrity, and Heloise for Abelard. Though in the end he is destroyed, throughout his life we are with him in his joys—which, after all, are innocent enough: in science, in wealth, in world travel, in love, and with a reach of soul and desire beyond anything Satan could appease:

> When I behold the heavens, then I repent,
> And curse thee, wicked Mephistophilis,
> Because thou hast deprived me of those joys.[52]

And his praise of Helen of Troy, furthermore, is of a man worthy of such beauty: the lines themselves are his redemption:

> Was this the face that launched a thousand ships
> And burnt the topless towers of Ilium?
> Sweet Helen, make me immortal with a kiss.
>
> Her lips suck forth my soul: see where it flies!—
> Come, Helen, come, give me my soul again.
> Here will I dwell, for Heaven is in these lips,
> And all is dross that is not Helena.
> I will be Paris, and for love of thee,
> Instead of Troy, shall Wertenberg be sacked;
> And I will combat the weak Menelaus,
> And wear thy colours in my plumèd crest:
> Yea, I will wound Achilles in the heel,
> And then return to Helen for a kiss.
> Oh, thou art fairer than the evening air
> Clad in the beauty of a thousand stars;
> Brighter art thou than flaming Jupiter
> When he appeared to hapless Semele:
> More lovely than the monarch of the sky
> In wanton Arethusa's azured arms:
> And none but thou shalt be my paramour.[53]

It was Lessing (1729–1781) who first recognized that the end of Faust should have been not damnation but salvation, and Goethe (1749–1832) then brought this insight to realization, representing his hero, moreover, as a pattern of the yearning, striving, creative spirit of specifically European man, with Mephistopheles but an agent of that principle of negation, "the dead and the set fast," of which creative reason "makes use" in its "striving toward the divine," the unattainable absolute of fulfillment. *

> *Vom Himmel fordert er die schönsten Sterne*
> *Und von der Erde jede höchste Lust,*
> *Und alle Näh' und alle Ferne*
> *Befriedigt nicht die tiefbewegte Brust.*[54]

> The fairest stars from Heaven he requires,
> From Earth the highest raptures and the best,
> And all the Near and Far that he desires
> Fails to subdue the tumult of his breast.

So Spengler in *The Decline of the West*, following Goethe, termed the Western monumental culture that is unfolding still, the "Faustian," with its impulse to infinity, and its prime symbol, limitless space—in contrast to the "Apollonian" classical, with its accent on the visible; and to the "Magian" Levantine, with its sense of a duality of mysteriously contending forces in this universe, "matter" and "spirit," darkness and light, Devil and God. "The Magian hierarchy of angels, saints and Persons of the Trinity is becoming more and more disembodied," Spengler wrote, "paler and paler, in the lands of the Western pseudomorphosis,† supported though it is, still, by the whole weight of ecclesiastical authority; and even the Devil, the great counterplayer in the Gothic world drama, is disappearing unnoticed as a possibility for the Faustian world feeling. He, at whom Luther still could throw his inkpot, has been passed over, long since, in embarrassed silence by Protestant theologians. For the sense of *aloneness* of the Faustian soul cannot rest in a duality of world powers. Here God himself is the All." [55]

VI. Toward New Mythologies

So let us attempt now to say something of the new prospects for mythology appearing in this fresh world of NOW and HERE, beyond

---

* Supra, p. 383.

† For this term, see supra, pp. 31–32 and *Occidental Mythology*, pp. 398–99.

the scattered ruins—still in fragments among us—of the old Sumerian mansion of five thousand years. As already shown, a complete mythology serves four functions.

1. THE METAPHYSICAL-MYSTICAL PROSPECT

The first function of a living mythology, the properly religious function, in the sense of Rudolf Otto's definition in *The Idea of the Holy,* is to waken and maintain in the individual an experience of awe, humility, and respect, in recognition of that ultimate mystery, transcending names and forms, "from which," as we read in the Upanishads, "words turn back." [56] I would say that in the modern world, outside of the synagogues and churches at least, this humility has been restored; for every claim to authority of the book on which pride of race, pride of communion, the illusion of special endowment, special privilege, and divine favor were based has been exploded. Theology, so called, can now make no claim more than to be a literary exercise in explanation or an archaic text wherein certain historically conditioned, ambiguous names, forms, acts, and utterances are attributed to what (if the term "what" must be used) can be called only "far above all that man can possibly think," i.e., ineffable. The faith in Scripture of the Middle Ages, faith in reason of the Enlightenment, faith in science of modern Philistia belong equally today to those alone who have as yet no idea of how mysterious, really, is the mystery even of themselves.

"Suppose you are sitting on a bench beside a path in high mountain country," suggests the great modern physicist, Erwin Schrödinger.

There are grassy slopes all around, with rocks thrusting through them; on the opposite slope of the valley there is a stretch of scree with a low growth of alder bushes. Woods climb steeply on both sides of the valley, up to the line of treeless pasture; and facing you, soaring up from the depths of the valley, is the mighty, glacier-tipped peak, its smooth snowfields and hard-edged rock-faces touched at this moment with soft rose-color by the last rays of the departing sun, all marvelously sharp against the clear, pale, transparent blue of the sky.

According to our usual way of looking at it, everything that you are seeing has, apart from small changes, been there for thousands of years before you. After a while—not long—you will no longer exist, and the woods and rocks and sky will continue, unchanged, for thousands of years after you.

What is it that has called you so suddenly out of nothingness to enjoy for a brief while a spectacle which remains quite indifferent to you? The conditions for your existence are almost as old as the rocks. For thousands of years men have striven and suffered and begotten and women have brought forth in pain. A hundred years ago, perhaps, another man sat on this spot; like you he gazed with awe and yearning in his heart at the dying light on the glaciers. Like you he was begotten of man and born of woman. He felt pain and brief joy as you do. *Was* he someone else? Was it not you yourself? What is this Self of yours? What was the necessary condition for making the thing conceived this time into *you,* just *you* and not someone else? What clearly intelligible *scientific* meaning can this 'someone else' really have? If she who is now your mother had cohabited with someone else and had a son by him, and your father had done likewise, would *you* have come to be? Or were you living in them, and in your father's father . . . thousands of years ago? And even if this is so, why are you not your brother, why is your brother not you, why are you not one of your distant cousins? What justifies you in obstinately discovering this difference—the difference between you and someone else—when objectively what is there is *the same?*

Looking and thinking in that manner you may suddenly come to see, in a flash, the profound rightness of the basic conviction in Vedanta: it is not possible that this unity of knowledge, feeling and choice which you call *your own* should have sprung into being from nothingness at a given moment not so long ago; rather this knowledge, feeling and choice are essentially eternal and unchangeable and numerically *one* in all men, nay in all sensitive beings. But not in *this* sense—that *you* are a part, a piece, of an eternal, infinite being, an aspect or modification of it, as in Spinoza's pantheism. For we should then have the same baffling question: which part, which aspect are *you?* what, objectively, differentiates it from the others? No, but, inconceivable as it seems to ordinary reason, you—and all other conscious beings as such—are all in all. Hence this life of yours which you are living is not merely a piece of the entire existence, but is in a certain sense the *whole;* only this whole is not so constituted that it can be surveyed in one single glance. This, as we know, is what the Brahmins express in that sacred, mystic formula which is yet really so simple and so clear: *Tat tvam asi,* this is you. Or, again, in such words as "I am in the east and in the west, I am below and above, *I am this whole world.*" [57]

Schopenhauer's oxymoron, "Everything is the entire world as will in its own way," points to this same transcendent sense of mystery; so also the circle of Cusanus; likewise the words of Jesus in the Gnostic Thomas Gospel: "Cleave a piece of wood, I am there." [58] For this indeed is the insight basic to all metaphysical discourse, which is immediately known—as knowable to each alone—only when the names and forms, the masks of God, have dissolved. "Truth is one," states the Indian *Rg Veda,* "the sages call it by many names." [59]

However, as the Invincible Doctor, William of Occam, showed, Kant confirmed, and Henry Adams recalled, the category, or name, of unity itself is of the mind and may not be attributed to any supposed substance, person, full or empty void, or "Ground of Being." Indeed the term "being" itself is but a name; so too "non-being."

Who, then, is to talk to you or to me of the being or non-being of "God," unless by implication to point beyond his words and himself and all he knows or can tell?

2. THE COSMOLOGICAL PROSPECT

The second function of a mythology is to render a cosmology, an image of the universe, and for this we all turn today, of course, not to archaic religious texts but to science. And here even the briefest, most elementary review of the main crises in the modern transformation of the image of the universe suffices to remind us of the fact-world that now has to be recognized, appropriated, and assimilated by the mythopoetic imagination.

First, in 1492 there was the Columbian revolution. Dante, it is recalled, had placed Paradise on the summit of the mountain of Purgatory, which his century situated in the middle of an imagined ocean covering the whole of the Southern Hemisphere; and Columbus at first shared this mythological idea. The earth, he wrote, is shaped "like a pear, of which one part is round, but the other, where the stalk comes, elongated"; or, "like a very round ball, on

one part of which there is a protuberance, like a woman's nipple."
The protuberance, he believed was to be found in the south; and
on his third voyage, when his vessels sailed more rapidly northward than southward, he believed this showed that they had begun
to go downhill. And he was the more convinced of his error since
some weeks earlier, at the southern reach of his voyage, when he
had sailed between the island of Trinidad and the mainland of
South America, the volume of fresh water pouring into the ocean
from the mighty Orinoco, "the roar, as of thunder," that occurred
where the river met the sea, and the height of the waves, which
nearly wrecked his little ships, had assured him that so great a
volume of fresh water could have had its origin only in one of the
four rivers of Paradise, and that he had at last, therefore, attained
to the stalk end of the pear. Sailing north, he was leaving Paradise
behind.[60]

Hardly two centuries earlier Aquinas had sought to show by
reasonable argument that the Garden of Paradise from which
Adam and Eve had been expelled was an actual region of this
physical earth, still somewhere to be found. "The situation of Paradise," he had written, "is shut off from the habitable world by
mountains, or seas, or some torrid region, which cannot be
crossed; and so people who have written about topography make
no mention of it." [61] The Venerable Bede, five and a half centuries before, had sensibly suggested that Paradise could not be a
corporeal place but must be entirely spiritual; [62] Augustine, however, had already rejected such a notion, maintaining that Paradise
was and is both spiritual *and* corporeal; [63] and it was to Augustine's view that Aquinas adhered. Columbus died without knowing that he had actually delivered the first of a series of potent
blows that were presently to annihilate every image not only of an
earthly but even of a celestial Paradise. In 1497 Vasco da Gama
rounded South Africa, and in 1520 Magellan, South America: the
torrid region of the seas was crossed, and no Paradise found.

In 1543 Copernicus published his exposition of the heliocentric
universe, and some sixty years later, as we have already noticed,
Galileo commenced his celestial researches with a telescope. These
led immediately, as we have also noticed, to the condemnation of
the new cosmology as contrary to Holy Scripture. It was contrary
also, however, to the poetic Hellenistic imagery of the Music of the

Spheres (Figure 13), which now, like every other feature of pre-Copernican cosmology, whether of the Orient or of the Occident, must be interpreted solely in psychological terms. The ancient mythic notion of an essential and evident macro-meso-microcosmic harmony is dissolved. Cosmology, sociology, and psychology are of different orders, and the ancient concept also has been lost, therefore, of the hieratic arts as making visible in the "things that are made" the "invisible things of God," those structuring forms by which all things are held in place. Wrote Ananda K. Coomaraswamy:

> Those who think of their house as only a "machine to live in" should judge their point of view by that of Neolithic man, who also lived in a house, but a house that embodied a cosmology. We are more than sufficiently provided with overheating systems: we should have found his house uncomfortable; but let us not forget that he identified the column of smoke that rose from his hearth to disappear from view through a hole in the roof with the Axis of the Universe, saw in this luffer an image of the Heavenly Door, and in his hearth the Navel of the Earth, formulae that we at the present day are hardly capable of understanding; we, for whom "such knowledge as is not empirical is meaningless." Most of the things that Plato called "ideas" are only "superstitions" to us.[64]

And after all, one cannot help asking, why not? Both Plato's universe and that of the neolithic dweller in a little mesocosmic hut were founded, like our own, upon empirical observation, plus the idea of an inward macro-microcosmic unity. The navel of the earth is no longer an adequate popular symbol, however, of the "still point of this turning world," which is to be found within the heart—and everywhere, within every atom, as well as, perhaps, outward, at some inconceivable distance, to which our galaxy itself is but a moon. As in the lines of the poet Robinson Jeffers:

> The atom bounds-breaking,
> Nucleus to sun, electrons to planets, with recognition
> Not praying, self-equaling, the whole to the whole, the microcosm
> Not entering nor accepting entrance, more equally, more utterly, more incredibly conjugate
> With the other extreme and greatness; passionately perceptive of identity. . . .[65]

The meaning of the word "superstition" (Latin, *superstare,* "to stand over," from *stare,* "to stand," plus *super,* "over") is simply "belief in something 'standing over,' as a vestige, from the past." The image of this earth, for example, as a flat revolving plate, covered by a dome through which a golden gate, the sun door, leads to eternity, was not a "superstition" in the eighth millennium B.C., but an image derived empirically from contemporary naked-eye observation. Its spiritual value did not inhere in anything intrinsic to the image, but derived from its power to suggest and support a sense in man of accord with the universe. However, such a cosmic image, taken literally and insisted upon today, would suggest not accord but disaccord, not only with the known facts of the universe, but also with the science and civilization facing those facts—as the trial of Galileo has well shown. Not the neolithic peasant looking skyward from his hoe, not the old Sumerian priesthood watching planetary courses from the galleries of ziggurats, nor a modern clergyman quoting from a revised version of their book, but our own incredibly wonderful scientists today are the ones to teach us how to see: and if wonder and humility are the best vehicles to bear the soul to its hearth, I should think that a quiet Sunday morning spent at home in controlled meditation on a picture book of the galaxies might be an auspicious start for that voyage.

Revolution number three, following the Columbian and Copernican, then, was the Newtonian, of the *Machina Coelestis.* The prelude was announced in the impulse theory of John Buridan, wherein the idea of sustaining intelligences was eliminated from the universe: one good push from God at the beginning would have sufficed to set his entire little geocentric whirligig in motion. Galileo, in his *Discourses and Mathematical Demonstrations concerning Two New Sciences pertaining to Mechanics and Local Motions,* published 1638 in Leiden (beyond reach of the windmill arms of the Inquisition), introduced a mathematically controlled statement of the laws governing movements and inertias, and in Prague meanwhile, independently, Johann Kepler (1571–1630) had broken forever the old classical notion of the circle as the structuring form of the universe, by demonstrating that the orbits of the planets are not circles but ellipses, and establishing a single formula for the calculation of their various speeds of passage.

These findings he announced in 1609 in a work based upon his study of the eccentric orbit of Mars, *Astronomia nova* αἰτιολογικός, *seu Physica coelestis tradita commentariis de motibus stellae Martis.* The precision of his reckoning led him to write of the celestial machine as "something like a clockwork in which a single weight drives all the gears," and—as Dr. Loren Eiseley puts it in his lucid summary survey of the rise of modern science, *The Firmament of Time*—to this clockwork figure of Kepler's, Sir Isaac Newton (1642–1727), with his formulation of the laws of gravity, "supplied the single weight." [66] "God had been the Creator of the machine, but it could run without his interference. . . . Newton, however, remained devout in a way that many of his followers of the eighteenth century did not." [67]

Immanuel Kant (1724–1804) and Pierre Simone Laplace (1740–1827) extended backward in time the laws that Newton had flung into space, and projected the so-called Kant-Laplace theory of the evolution of the universe—which then became the fourth of these modern cosmological revolutions, and perhaps the most dangerous of all. For now the origin of the universal machine was found to have been not as a perfectly formed structure immediately from God's hand, but as a precipitate, by natural laws, from a cloud of rotating gas, a nebula; and there have now been located literally tens of thousands of such nebulae in the infinite reaches of space, in various stages of the process. There is now no necessity, or even possibility, of imagining a point in time past when a personality (somewhere that was nowhere) set up the entire show. In fact, philosophically it is not permissible to speak of a "time" when time was not or when time will cease to be. There is no before or after time that is not itself time. And if the principle of causality is allowed to lead us to seek for a cause in time of this universe that we see, then it must be allowed to lead us to ask, further, for the cause of that cause, and so on, forever backward; which is a form of questioning not to be shut off, finally, simply by saying, "Well, now I am tired, let's stop here and draw the line and name the blank space beyond that line God: * and specifically not Shiva, Ptah, Enki, or Tezcatlipoca, but the one right here, the so-called Living God, the one with the personality, in our cozy family Bible, who sent down to his Chosen People all those interesting

* Supra, p. 365.

rules about not gathering sticks on Saturday or eating butter and meat at the same meal."

Instead let me quote, for a moment, from a rather more recent popular work that arrived in the mail the other day:

> The basic unit of the universe is the galaxy, a great grouping of stars. Millions of galaxies are racing through space out and away from one another. . . . In a single galaxy, stars being born, stars in vigorous life and stars dying in heaving nuclear explosions—the beginning, middle and end of creation—are all present.
>
> The story of a star begins with its birth. . . . A cloud of dust and gas, whirled into pockets of high density, begins to contract around one or more of its gravitational centers. Many centers in one tight cloud can result in a single star plus planets, a multiple star, or a multiple star plus planets. The finished product depends on the density and size of the original cloud and on the degree of rough-and-tumble in its movements. Astronomers believe that they may see unlit protostars in the very act of contracting in the nearby clouds of the Milky Way's spiral arms. They appear as dark globules against the less opaque regions of gas and dust around them.
>
> When a protostar contracts, its central regions are warmed by the release of gravitational energy—the heat of infalling atoms colliding with one another. Eventually the heat becomes so intense that the hydrogen of the core begins to fuse into helium. At first the nuclear fusions of single atoms are infrequent and release little energy but, as the star continues to contract under the weight of its accumulating outer layers, the atoms of the core are pressed closer together and fuse more and more frequently. Eventually they are producing exactly enough outpushing energy to counteract the star's inpulling gravitation. At that point the shakedown is over and the star has arrived at a stable, mature state. . . .
>
> In due course, however—after a few hundred thousand years if it is a hot, blue, massive, fast-burning star; after a few billion years if it is a mild, yellow, sun-sized, temperately burning star; or after a few hundred billion years if it is a cool, red, lightweight, slow-burning star—it consumes about 10 per cent of its original hydrogen and begins to grow overbright and abnormal. The sun is approaching this point but is not expected to reach it for another three to five billion years. . . .

Although stellar evolution's rule of thumb is the smaller they start, the longer they last, eventually even the smallest, most conservatively invested reserves of star stuff will be spent. . . . Up to now, not even the most monstrous supergiants that died in the earliest eons of the Milky Way's history have had time to cool completely and lose all their energy. But, ultimately, the last expiring ghosts of white dwarfs must succumb to the chill of space. One by one they will grow as dark and cold as the voids which reach out from the Milky Way toward other, receding galaxies in the universe beyond.[68]

The fifth revolution Dr. Eiseley has termed the Huttonian, after the Scottish geologist James Hutton (1726–1797), whose paper, delivered in 1785 to the Royal Society of Edinburgh, entitled *Theory of the Earth, or an Investigation of the Laws Observable in the Composition, Dissolution and Restoration of Land upon the Globe,* broached the question of the manner of formation of this earth which the Living God was supposed to have fashioned *ex nihilo* in 4004 B.C. According to Hutton's view, the rocks of the earth's surface are formed largely from the waste of older rocks. These materials were laid down beneath the sea, compressed there under great pressure, and subsequently upheaved by the force of subterranean heat, during which periods of upheaval veins and masses of molten rock were injected into the rents of the dislocated strata. The upraised land, exposed to the atmosphere, became again subject to decay; and the waste again was washed to the sea floor, where the cycle was renewed—as in *Finnegans Wake.*

Conflicting with the short chronology of the Bible, this theory of gradual transformation was opposed by a passionately argued contrary notion of sudden catastrophes. Goethe in his *Faust,* Part II, Act II (the "Classical Walpurgisnacht"), humorously plays the two contending views against each other, letting the Greek philosopher Thales stand for the gradualists—the so-called "Neptunists"—and Anaxagoras for the catastrophism of the "Vulcanists": showing his own preference for the former view, however, by confiding his comical little secondary hero Homunculus (born of the art of Faust's alchemy and still enclosed in his *vas Hermeticum,* Figure 43) to the care of Thales for incorporation, through infusion, in the living, nourishing waters of this evolving world.[69]

Goethe's contemporary, the great French naturalist Baron Georges Léopold Chrétien Frédéric Dagobert Cuvier (1769–1832), having observed "that none of the large species of quadrupeds whose remains are now found embedded in regular rocky strata are at all similar to any of the known living species," had proposed that floods and other catastrophes, all according to God's plan, had brought about an advance toward man by sudden stages. The later forms had not evolved biologically from the earlier, but after each annihilation there had taken place a re-creation of forms on a higher plane, proceeding from Platonic ideas in the mind of God.[70] Jean Louis Rodolphe Agassiz (1807–1873), the great Swiss-American contemporary of Darwin, retained this idea of a succession of creations, which, however, had already been challenged by Charles Lyell (1794–1875) in his celebrated *Principles of Geology* (1830), where "passage beds" were identified, and a theory supporting Hutton's of local transformations, not universal catastrophes, accounted for the changes of the earth: the rise and fall of coastlines, the slow upthrust of river systems, through periods of illimitable time.[71] And so the way was prepared for the sixth great revolution, that to which the name of Charles Darwin (1809–1882) is now attached.

An anticipation of the general theory of organic evolution is already suggested in the notebooks of Leonardo da Vinci (1452–1519), where, writing of comparative anatomy, he studies homologous structures in man and in those which, as he states, "are almost of the same species: the baboon, the ape, and others like these, which are many." [72] Goethe published in Jena in 1786 a famous paper on the intermaxillary bone in the higher mammals, in the ape, and in man; and in 1790 a larger work on the metamorphosis of plants. "The resemblances of the various animals to each other, and in particular those of the higher species," he declared in a lecture introducing the first of these publications, "strikes the eye and is generally recognized by everybody in silence. . . . All of the higher natural organisms—among which are to be named, the fish, amphibians, birds, mammals and, as highest of these last, mankind—have been formed according to a simple pattern, which only varies, more or less, in its various parts and even now, in its procreation, is changing and developing." [73] In his work on the morphology of plants, this theme of continuing transformation then was carried on:

No matter what forms we observe, but particularly in the organic, we shall find nowhere anything enduring, resting, completed, but rather that everything is in a continuous motion.
. . . No living thing, furthermore, is a unit, but a plurality; even though it may seem to us to be an individual, it is nevertheless a collection of living, independent things, which in idea and potential are alike, yet in appearance can become either alike and equivalent or unalike and various. These entities sometimes are joined together in the beginning, sometimes find each other and become linked. They divide and again seek each other, and so bring about an endless course of productivity in all manners and in all directions.

The more imperfect the creature, the more its parts are alike and equivalent, and resemble thus the whole. The more perfect the creature becomes, the more unlike do the parts become. In the former case the whole is more or less like the parts, in the latter, the whole is unlike the parts. The more nearly alike the parts are, the less is one subordinate to another. Subordinations of the parts belong to a more developed creature. . . .

When man compares plants and animals of the least developed stages, they are hardly distinguishable from each other. A point of life, fixed, or else moving or half moving, is there, hardly perceptible to our senses. Whether such a first beginning, susceptible to development in either direction, was to be brought by light to the state of a plant or by darkness to that of an animal, we should hardly presume to decide were there not analogous examples about, to let us know. This much, however, can be said: that the creatures who in the course of time gradually developed from an originally hardly distinguishable condition, on one hand as plants and on the other as animals, perfected themselves in two directions, so that the plants attained their glory in the enduring fixed form of the tree, and the animals in the supreme mobility and freedom of man.[74]

With this the immemorial idea of fixed species, whether in the mind of God or in the order of nature, was transcended, and the principle of life in evolution introduced. It remained only to determine and define precisely the conditions of the process.

The seventh great revolution in the cosmological sciences dates from the turn of the present century, when, on one hand, the shell of the atom was penetrated to reveal a universe within of spinning demons, and, on the other, the philosophically devastating implications of the Michelson-Morley experiment of 1887 were established in Albert Einstein's formulation in 1905 of the basic proposition of relativity: "Nature is such that it is imposible to determine absolute motion by any experiment whatsoever." It was Dr. Max Planck (1858–1947) of the University of Berlin who broke the reign of Newtonian principles in the field of physics, when in 1901 he proposed his quantam theory of the laws of radiation.[75] Sir Ernest Rutherford (1871–1937) in 1911 then showed that the atom is not a solid ball but an almost empty universe of energies, and in 1913 the Dane Niels Bohr (1885–1962), at work in England, applied Planck's quantum theory to a definition of the active structure of the Rutherford atom. We all know what has happened since. As Henry Adams prophesied in a letter written January 17, 1905, to his friend Henry Osborn Taylor:

> The assumption of unity which was the mark of human thought in the middle ages has yielded very slowly to the proofs of complexity. The stupor of science before radium is a proof of it. Yet it is quite sure, according to my score of ratios and curves, that, at the accelerated rate of progression shown since 1600, it will not need another century to tip thought upside down. Law, in that case, would disappear as theory or *a priori* principle, and give place to force. Morality would become police. Explosives would reach cosmic violence. Disintegration would overcome integration.[76]

Some might say the Devil had won and that Faust, caught in Satan's snare, was now self-prepared for extermination through his own science. However, as far as HERE and NOW is concerned (and, my friends, we are still here), the first function of a mythology—to waken a sense of awe, humility and respect, before that ultimate mystery, transcending names and forms, "from which," as we have read, "words turn back"—has been capitally served by every one of these sciences of the second function: the rendition of a cosmology, an image of this universe of wonder, whether regarded in its spatial or its temporal, physical, or biological aspect. For there is nowhere any certainty more, any solid rock of authority, whereon those afraid to face alone the absolutely unknown may settle

down, secure in the knowledge that they and their neighbors are in
possession, once and for all, of the Found Truth.

3. THE SOCIAL PROSPECT

Nor is the situation more comforting in the moral, social sphere
of our third traditional mythological function: the validation and
maintenance of an established order. In the words of the late John
Dewey (1859–1952):

> Christianity proffered a fixed revelation of absolute, unchang-
> ing Being and truth; and the revelation was elaborated into a
> system of definite rules and ends for the direction of life. Hence
> "morals" were conceived as a code of laws, the same every-
> where and at all times. The good life was one lived in fixed ad-
> herence to fixed principles.
>
> In contrast with all such beliefs, the outstanding fact in all
> branches of natural science is that to exist is to be in process, in
> change. . . .
>
> Victorian thought conceived of new conditions as if they
> merely put in our hands effective instruments for realizing old
> ideals. The shock and uncertainty so characteristic of the
> present marks the discovery that the older ideals themselves are
> undermined. Instead of science and technology giving us better
> means for bringing them to pass, they are shaking our confi-
> dence in all large and comprehensive beliefs and purposes.
>
> Such a phenomenon is, however, transitory. The impact of
> the new forces is for the time being negative. Faith in the divine
> author and authority in which Western civilization confided, in-
> herited ideas of the soul and its destiny, of fixed revelation, of
> completely stable institutions, of automatic progress, have been
> made impossible for the cultivated mind of the Western world.
> It is psychologically natural that the outcome should be a col-
> lapse of faith in all fundamental organizing and directive ideas.
> Skepticism becomes the mark and even the pose of the educated
> mind. It is the more influential because it is no longer directed
> against this and that article of the older creeds but is rather a
> bias against any kind of far-reaching ideas, and a denial of sys-
> tematic participation on the part of such ideas in the intelligent
> direction of affairs.
>
> It is in such a context that a thoroughgoing philosophy of ex-
> perience, framed in the light of science and technique, has its
> significance. . . .

A philosophy of experience will accept at its full value the fact that social and moral existences are, like physical existences, in a state of continuous if obscure change. It will not try to cover up the fact of inevitable modification, and will make no attempt to set fixed limits to the extent of changes that are to occur. For the futile effort to achieve security and anchorage in something fixed, it will substitute the effort to determine the character of changes that are going on and to give them in the affairs that concern us most some measure of intelligent direction. . . .

Wherever the thought of fixity rules, that of all-inclusive unity rules also. The popular philosophy of life is filled with desire to attain such an all-embracing unity, and formal philosophies have been devoted to an intellectual fulfillment of the desire. Consider the place occupied in popular thought by search for *the* meaning of life and *the* purpose of the universe. Men who look for a single purport and a single end either frame an idea of them according to their private desires and tradition, or else, not finding any such single unity, give up in despair and conclude that there is no genuine meaning and value of life's episodes.

The alternatives are not exhaustive, however. There is no need of deciding between no meaning at all and one single, all-embracing meaning. There are many meanings and many purposes in the situations with which we are confronted—one, so to say, for each situation. Each offers its own challenge to thought and endeavor, and presents its own potential value.[78]

In sum: the individual is now on his own. "It is all untrue! Anything goes!" (Nietzsche).[79] The dragon "Thou Shalt!" has been slain—for us *all*. Therein the danger! Anfortas too was installed through no deed, no virtue of his own, upon the seat of power: Lord of the World Center, which, as Cusanus knew, is in each. The wheel on the head of the Bodhisattva, revolving with its painful cutting edge: Who can bear it? Who can teach us to bear it as a crown, not of thorns, but of laurel: the wreath of our own Lady Orgeluse?

The nihilist's question, "Why?" [wrote Nietzsche] is a product of his earlier habitude of expecting an aim to be given, to be set for him, from without—i.e. by some *superhuman authority* or other. When he has learned not to believe in such a thing, he goes on, just the same, from habit, looking for *another* authority of some kind that will be able to speak unconditionally and set goals and tasks by *command*. The authority of *Conscience* now is the first to present itself (the more emancipated from theology, the more imperative *morality* becomes) as compensation for a *personal* authority. Or the authority of *Reason*. Or the *Social Instinct* (the herd). Or *History,* with an immanent spirit that has a goal of its own, to which one can *give* oneself. One wants, by all means, to get around having to will, to desire a goal, to set up a goal for oneself: one wants to avoid the responsibility (—accepting fatalism). Finally: *Happiness,* and with a certain tartuffery, the *Happiness of the Majority.*

One says to oneself: 1. a definite goal is unnecessary, 2. is impossible to foresee.

And so, precisely when what is required is Will in its highest power, it is at its weakest and most faint-hearted, in *Absolute Mistrust of the Organizational Force of the Will-to-be-a-Whole.*
. . .

Nihilism is of two faces:

A. Nihilism, as the sign of a heightened power of the spirit: *active nihilism.*

B. Nihilism, as a decline and regression of the power of the spirit: *passive nihilism.*

Attempts to escape from nihilism *without* transvaluing earlier values only bring about the opposite of escape: a sharpening of the problem.[80]

4. THE PSYCHOLOGICAL SPHERE

And so we are brought infallibly to the fourth sphere, the fourth function, of an adequate mythology: the centering and harmonization of the individual, which in traditional systems was supposed to follow upon the giving of oneself, and even giving up of oneself altogether, to some one or another of Nietzsche's authorities named above. The modern world is full of survivals of these reactionary systems, of which the most powerful today is still the old Levantine one of the social order. However, as Loren Eiseley states: "The group ethic as distinct from personal ethic is faceless and obscure. It is whatever its leaders choose it to mean; it destroys the innocent and justifies the act in terms of the future." [81] But the future, as he then points out (and one might have thought such a warning unnecessary), is *not* the place to seek realization. "Progress secularized, progress which pursues only the next invention, progress which pulls thought out of the mind and replaces it with idle slogans, is not progress at all. It is a beckoning mirage in a desert over which stagger the generations of men. Because man, each individual man among us, possesses his own soul [Schopenhauer's 'intelligible character'] and by that light must live or perish, there is no way by which Utopias—or the lost Garden itself —can be brought out of the future and presented to man. Neither can he go forward to such a destiny. Since in the world of time every man lives but one life, it is in himself that he must search for the secret of the Garden." [82]

THE EARTHLY PARADISE

✦✦

I. All the Gods within You

"We of the Occident," declared Heinrich Zimmer at the opening of a course on Indian philosophy delivered in 1942,

> are about to arrive at a crossroads that was reached by the thinkers of India some seven hundred years before Christ. This is the real reason why we become both vexed and stimulated, uneasy yet interested, when confronted with the concepts and images of Oriental wisdom. This crossing is one to which the people of all civilizations come in the typical course of the development of their capacity and requirement for religious experience, and India's teachings force us to realize what its problems are. But we cannot take over the Indian solutions. We must enter the new period our own way and solve its questions for ourselves, because though truth, the radiance of reality, is universally one and the same, it is mirrored variously according to the mediums in which it is reflected. Truth appears differently in different lands and ages according to the living materials out of which its symbols are hewn.
>
> Concepts and words are symbols, just as visions, rituals, and images are; so too are the manners and customs of daily life. Through all of these a transcendent reality is mirrored. They are so many metaphors reflecting and implying something which, though thus variously expressed, is ineffable, though thus rendered multiform, remains inscrutable. Symbols hold the mind to truth but are not themselves the truth, hence it is delusory to

625

borrow them. Each civilization, every age, must bring forth its own.

We shall therefore have to follow the difficult way of our own experiences, produce our own reactions, and assimilate our sufferings and realizations. Only then will the truth that we bring to manifestation be as much our own flesh and blood as is the child its mother's; and the mother, in love with the Father, will then justly delight in her offspring as His duplication. The ineffable seed must be conceived, gestated, and brought forth from our own substance, fed by our blood, if it is to be the true child through which its mother is reborn: and the Father, the divine Transcendent Principle, will then also be reborn—delivered, that is to say, from the state of non-manifestation, non-action, apparent non-existence. We cannot borrow God. We must effect His new incarnation from within ourselves. Divinity must descend, somehow, into the matter of our own substance and participate in this peculiar life-process." [1]

Traditionally, as our survey of the myths of the world has disclosed, the idea of an absolute ontological distinction between God and man—or between gods and men, divinity and nature—first became an important social and psychological force in the Near East, specifically Akkad, in the period of the first Semitic kings, c. 2500 B.C. Then and there it was that the older, neolithic and Bronze Age mythologies of the Goddess Mother of the universe, in whom all things have their being, gods and men, plants, animals, and inanimate objects alike, and whose cosmic body itself is the enclosing sphere of space-time within which all experience, all knowledge, is enclosed, were suppressed and set aside in favor of those male-oriented, patriarchal mythologies of thunder-hurling warrior gods that by the time a thousand years had passed, c. 1500 B.C., had become the dominant divinities of the Near East. The Aryan warrior herdsmen, driving downward from the north into Anatolia, Greece, and the Aegean isles, as well as west to the Atlantic, were also patriarchal in custom, worshiping gods of thunder and war. In contrast to the Semites, however, they never ranked ancestral tribal gods above the gods of nature, or separated divinity from nature; whereas among the Semites in their desert homeland, where nature—Mother Nature—had little or nothing to give and life depended largely on the order and solidarity of the group, all faith was placed in whatever god was locally recognized as patron-father of the tribe. "All Semitic tribes," declares one distinguished authority in this field, the late Profesor S. H. Langdon of Oxford, "appear to have started with a single tribal deity whom they regard as the divine creator of his people." [2] The laws by which men lived, therefore, were not the laws of nature, universally revealed, but of this little tribe or that, each special to itself and derived from its own mythological first father.

The outstanding themes of this Syro-Arabian desert mythology, then, we may summarize as follows: 1. mythic dissociation, God as transcendent in the theological sense defined above,* and the earth and spheres, consequently, as mere dust, in no sense "divine"; 2. the notion of a special revelation from the tribal father-god exclusively to his group, the result of which is 3. a communal religion inherently exclusive, either as in Judaism, of a racial group, or as in Christianity and Islam, credal, for and of those alone who, professing the faith, participate in its rites. Still further, 4. since women are of the order rather of nature than of the law, women do not function as clergy in these religions, and the idea of a goddess superior, or even equal, to the authorized god is inconceivable. Finally, 5. the myths fundamental to each tribal heritage are interpreted historically, not symbolically, and where parallels are recognized to those of other peoples (gentiles), the rationalization applied is: *illis in figura, sed nobis in veritate,* as in the Second Letter of Peter.†

In the earlier, Bronze Age order, on the other hand—which is fundamental to both India and China, as well as to Sumer, Egypt, and Crete—the leading ideas, we have found, were of: 1. The ultimate mystery as transcendent of definition yet immanent in all things; 2. the aim of religion as an experience of one's own identity yet non-identity with that "ground" which is no ground, beyond being and non-being ($c + = x$); ‡ 3. the universe and all things within it as making multifariously manifest one order of natural law, which is everlasting, wondrous, blissful, and divine, so that the revelation to be recognized is not special to any single, supernaturally authorized folk or theology, but for all, manifest in the universe (macrocosm) and every individual heart (microcosm),

---

* Supra, p. 582.
† Supra, p. 155, footnote.
‡ Supra, p. 347

as well as in the hieratic order of the state with its symbolic arts
and rites (mesocosm): consequently 4. women play ritual roles,
and since the universal goddess personifies the bounding power of
māyā within the field of which all forms and thoughts whatsoever
(even of gods) are contained, the female power may be revered
even as superior, since antecedent, to the male. And finally, 5. since
all personifications, forms, acts, and experiences make manifest
the one transcendent-immanent mystery, nothing known, not even
the being of any god, is substatial as known, but all equally are
symbolic in the sense of Goethe's oft-quoted lines from the final
stanza of *Faust:*

> *Alles Vergängliche*
> *Ist nur ein Gleichnis.*

The Aryans entering Greece, Anatolia, Persia, and the Gangetic
plain, c. 1500–1250 B.C., brought with them, as we have amply
seen, the comparatively primitive mythologies of their patriarchal
pantheons, which in creative consort with the earlier mythologies
of the Universal Goddess generated in India the Vedantic, Puranic,
Tantric, and Buddhist doctrines and in Greece those of Homer and
Hesiod, Greek tragedy and philosophy, the Mysteries, and Greek
science. Something similar appears to have occurred in China
when the Shang people arrived—likewise c. 1500–1250 B.C.—to
found the first dynastic house in that area, where formerly only a
comparatively primitive high neolithic order of village civilization
had been known. And in the Near East, where the dominant
peoples were now largely Semitic (Phoenicians, Akkadians, Ca-
naanites, Arabians, et cetera), comparable interactions of the male
and female orders were in process. "Names of deities in Phoenicia
like Melk-'Ashtart, at Hammon near Tyre, Eshmun-'Ashtart at
Carthage, 'Ashtar-Kemosh, of the Moabites, clearly prove," states
Professor Langdon, "that the Mother-goddess of the West Semitic
races held even a greater place in their religion than the local gods
of their most important cults. . . . The entire mythology of
Astarte goes back to the Sumerian Ininni–Ashdar–Ishtar, goddess
of [the planet] Venus and mother, wife, and lover of the Sumerian
dying god Tammuz." [3]
Our reading of the Old Testament Books of Samuel and Kings

has shown, however, that in the Hebrew sphere such interactions were resisted and from time to time severely put down. That they were occurring with support even from the royal house is clear; for of all the kings from c. 1025 to 586 B.C. in both Israel and Judah, not more than half a dozen "did right in the sight of the Lord." The rest "built for themselves high places, pillars, and Asherim on every high hill and under every tree. . . . And the people continued to sacrifice and burn incense on the high places." Yet the reactionary faction represented in the great doings of Elijah and his adjutant Elisha (ninth century B.C.: I Kings 17 through II Kings 10) and, five centuries later, the priestly tyrant Ezra prevailed, and in the end the Jews—in the midst of the mixed and mixing Hellenistic world of secular science and philosophies, syncretistic mysteries, and cosmopolitan culture—retained, or rather reinvented, an exclusive tribal, desert-based mythology, which, with its old Sumerian three-layer image of a god-created flat universe, was already scientifically out of date when put together by its priestly scribes.[4]

Now it can hardly be said of the Christian cult, which sprang into being in this environment and was carried thence to Europe, that it was "brought forth" from the substance, life experiences, reactions, sufferings, and realizations of any of the peoples on whom it was impressed. Its borrowed symbols and borrowed god were presented to these as facts; and by the clergy claiming authority from such facts every movement of the native life to render its own spiritual statement was suppressed. Every local deity was a demon, every natural thought, a sin. So that no wonder if the outstanding feature of the Church's history in the West became the brutality and futility of its increasingly hysterical, finally unsuccessful, combats against heresy on every front! Already in Augustine's time the Irish Pelagian heresy was abroad. And that heresy now has won. For who today, outside of a convent, really believes that every child born of woman throughout the world will literally be sent to an actual Hell unless water is poured on its head to the accompaniment of a prayer? Who accepts today the idea of inherited sin? And since there was no Garden of Eden, no Adam and Eve, no Fall, then what is all the talk about Redemption, unless by "Fall" and "Redemption" the same psychological states of ignorance and illumination are meant that the Hindus and Buddhists also are talking about? In which case, what happens to the doctrine of the unique historical importance of the Incarnation and Crucifixion? The whole myth, to make any sense, must be totally reread—with honest eyes.

"Just as in the period of the deflation of the revealed gods of the Vedic pantheon," declared Zimmer, "so today revealed Christianity has been devaluated. The Christian, as Nietzsche says, is a man who behaves like everybody else. Our professions of faith have no longer any discernible bearing either on our public conduct or on our private state of hope. The sacraments do not work on many of us their spiritual transformation; we are bereft and at a loss where to turn. Meanwhile, our academic secular philosophies are concerned rather with information than with that redemptive transformation which our souls require. And this is the reason why a glance at the face of India may assist us to discover and recover something of ourselves." [5]

The functions of mythological symbols, we have said, are four: mystic, cosmological, sociological, and psychological; and today, as we have seen, not only has science dissolved the claim of the Church and its Book to represent the second of these, the cosmological, but the social order once supposed to have been supported by scriptural authority also has dissolved. Even its social horizon has dissolved. The way in which India might contribute—and indeed already is contributing—to our rescue in this circumstance is through its teaching in the Upanishadic and Buddhist doctrines of the basically *psychological* origin, force, and function of the same symbols that in *our* system have been read as a) revealed from a jealous personal God "out there" and b) historically unique.

On the popular side, in their popular cults, the Indians are, of course, as positivistic in their readings of their myths as any farmer in Tennessee, rabbi in the Bronx, or pope in Rome. Krishna actually danced in manifold rapture with the gopis, and the Buddha walked on water. However, as soon as one turns to the higher texts, such literalism disappears and all the imagery is interpreted symbolically, as of the psyche.

> This that people say [we read in the Brihadaranyaka Upanishad]: Worship this god! Worship that god! One god after another! The entire world is his creation, and he himself all the gods. . . .
>
> He has entered into all this world, even to the tips of one's

fingernails, like the razor in a razor case, like fire in firewood. Him they see not; for as seen, he is incomplete.

When breathing, he is called the vital breath; when speaking, voice; when seeing, the eye; when hearing, the ear; when thinking, mind. These are but the names of his acts. Anyone meditating on one or another of these aspects, knows not; for as in one or another of these, he is incomplete. One should worship with the idea that he is one's Self (*ātman*); for therein all these become one. This—the Self—is the footprint of this All: and just as, verily, one finds cattle by a footprint, so one finds this All by its footprint, the Self.

Whoever knows "I am *brahman!*" becomes this All, and not even the gods can prevent his becoming thus, for he becomes their very Self. But whoever worships another divinity than his Self, supposing "He is one, I am another," knows not. He is like a sacrificial beast for the gods. And as many animals would be useful to a man, so is even one such person useful to the gods. But if even one animal is taken away, it is not pleasant. What then, if many? It is not pleasing to the gods, therefore, that people should know this.[6]

Contrast Genesis 3:22–24!

The same idea appears to have been rendered in the Pyramid Texts of Egypt (c. 2350–2175 B.C.) and the later Book of the Dead (c. 1500), where the soul of him who has died is conceived of as *reabsorbing the gods.* "He is equipped," we read in a Pyramid charm, "he who has incorporated their spirits. He dawns as the Great One, the lord of those with ready hands." "It is he who eats their magic and swallows their spirits; their Great Ones are for his morning meal, their middle-sized ones are for his evening meal, their little ones are for his night meal, their old men and old women, for his fire." [7] And from the Book of the Dead: "My hair is the hair of Nu, my face the face of the Disk. My eyes are the eyes of Hathor, my ears the ears of Ap-uat. . . . My feet are the feet of Ptah. There is no member of my body that is not the member of some god." "I am Yesterday, Today, and Tomorrow, and I have the power to be born a second time; I am the divine hidden Soul who creates the gods. . . . Hail, lord of the shrine that stands in the middle of the earth. He is I, and I am he, and Ptah has covered his sky with crystal." [8]

James Joyce's *Finnegans Wake* is on one level a parody of this

Book of the Dead: "We seem to us (the real Us!), to be reading our Amenti in the sixth sealed chapter of the going forth
by black." [9] "The eversower of the seeds of light to the cowld
owld sowls that are in the somnatory of Defmut after the night of
the carrying of the word of Nuahs and the night of making Mehs to
cuddle up in a coddlepot, Pu Nuseht, lord of risings in the yonder-
world of Ntamplin, tohp triumphant, speaketh." [10] *

"If it were permissible to personify the unconscious," wrote Dr.
Jung in a paper on modern man in search of a soul,

> we might call it a collective human being combining the charac-
> teristics of both sexes, transcending youth and age, birth and
> death, and, from having at his command a human experience of
> one or two million years, almost immortal. If such a being ex-
> isted, he would be exalted above all temporal change; the
> present would mean neither more nor less to him than any year
> in the one-hundredth century before Christ; he would be a
> dreamer of age-old dreams and, owing to his immeasurable ex-
> perience, would be an incomparable prognosticator. He would
> have lived countless times over the life of the individual, of the
> family, tribe and people, and he would possess the living sense
> of the rhythm of growth, flowering, and decay.[11]

Just so was Joyce's hero, H.C.E. ("Here Comes Everybody").
So too the embalmed Pharaoh in his pyramid. So each of us in the
ground of his being. So Christ, the Word made Flesh.

In the course of any manifestation of this unspecified Master-
Mistress Everybody in a field of space and time—in the way of a biological progress from infancy and dependency, through adulthood
with its specific duties, on toward age and a preparation for departure—two main motives are to be recognized: first, in youth,
engagement and commitment to the modes of the local culture (the
ethnic motive), and second, emotional disengagement from the

* Amenti: Egyptian region of the dead; also, amenty, madness. Owl: bird
of death and wisdom. Cow and Sow: animals of Hathor, respectively, and
Epet ("She Who Bears the Sun"). Defmut: Deaf-mute; also, Jeff-Mutt, code
names of the dreamer's contending sons, Shaun and Shem. Nuahs: Shaun re-
reversed. Mehs: Shem reversed. Pu Nuseht: The Sun Up, reversed. Ntamplin: Dublin; also tamp. Tohp: tope, a Buddhist reliquary shrine; a kind
of fish; also to tope (drink hard), and Tophet, Hell.

role one has learned to play and reconciliation with the inward self (the archetypal-individual motive).

In India these two ends were served in the course of the classical order of a lifetime by dividing the life in two: the first half to be lived in the village and the second in the forest, with each half, in turn, divided in two, the first part of each a preparation for the second, as follows: 1. as student, practicing obedience, learning the skills and duties of one's caste (*antevāsin*); 2. as a responsible householder in marriage, fulfilling without question all of one's caste duties (*grhastha*); 3. in middle life, departure to the forest, to undertake seriously meditation (*vanaprastha*); and 4. achievement of the goal of life (*mokṣa:* "release" from the will to live) and aimless wandering thereafter, as a rootless, lifeless mendicant (*bhikṣu, sannyasin*), until the body finally "drops off." [12]

In the West, on the other hand, we have had an altogether different classical view, for which Dante's formulation in the *Convito* of his own ideal of the four stages of life may be taken as an example. The course of a life Dante compares to an arch. "It is hard to say," he concedes, "where the highest point of this arch is . . . ; but in the majority I take it to be somewhere between the thirtieth and the fortieth year. And I believe that in those of perfect nature it would be in the thirty-fifth year": which is where he was himself at that moment "in the middle of the road of his life" when, at the opening of the *Commedia,* he discovered himself to be in a "dark wood" alone, confronted by three beasts. Moreover, his own thirty-fifth year fell precisely in the year of Our Lord 1300, which he took to be the apex year of the history of the world. And finally, Christ, who was "of perfect nature," was crucified, he believed, at the end of his thirty-fourth year, at noon, the apex of the day.

Adolescence, the first stage, in Dante's view, extends to the age of twenty-five. Its virtues are four: obedience, sweetness, sensitiveness to shame, and grace of body. "The adolescent," he writes, "who enters into the wandering wood of this life would not know how to keep the right path if it were not shown him by his elders." The aim of this period of life is increase, it is comparable to spring. The second portion is that of *Manhood,* ten years on either side of the apex, twenty-five to forty-five. Its proper virtues are temperance, courage, love, courtesy, and loyalty, its aim is achievement, and its season summer. Instead of retirement to the forest, however, the next stage is to be of usefulness, bestowal. "After our own proper perfection, which is acquired in manhood," Dante writes, "that perfection should also come which enlightens not only ourselves, but others." The virtues of *Age,* therefore, the autumn of life, from forty-five to seventy, are again four: prudence, justice, generosity, and affability. After which, finally, in the winter of *Decrepitude,* the noble soul does two things: "she returns to God, as to that port whence she departed when she came to enter upon the sea of this life," and "she blesses the voyage she has made. . . . And even as the good sailor, when he draws near to the port, lowers his sails, and gently with mild impulse enters into it, so ought we to lower the sails of our worldly activities and turn to God with all our purpose and heart; so that we may come to that port with all sweetness and all peace." [13]

A very different picture indeed from the Oriental, marked particularly by the contrast of the ideals for period three: retreat from the world, in the first case; service to the world in the second—which accounts in large measure for the contrast in the economic and political institutions, sciences and arts of the Orient and the West. "For, as Aristotle says," declares Dante, " 'a man is a civic animal,' wherefore he is required not only to be useful to himself but also to others." Furthermore, throughout the history of the properly European tradition, from the period of the Greeks onward, the ideal of maturity has nowhere been obedience, which is the virtue rather of adolescence. The ideal is of responsible critical judgment and decision.

But this requires age. As again in Dante's words: "the senior . . . should follow the laws only in so far as his own right judgment and the law are one and the same thing; and he should follow his own just mind, as it were, without any law; which the man in his prime cannot do." [14]

The critical period of the transit, then, from adolescent obedience to the prudence and justice, generosity and affability of age, is the period of the mid-span of twenty years of manhood, at the middle of which, at the apogee, the adventure of the dark wood will occur: the crucifixion, death, descent to Hell, and passage through Purgatory to Paradise—and return, then, to the service of the world. Dante continually cites the paradigmatic history of Virgil's hero Aeneas, who in mid-career, on leaving behind the Asian phase of his life, when about to undertake the task of the founding of European Rome, "hardened himself to enter alone with the Sybil into hell and search for the soul of his father Anchises, in the face of so many perils." [15] Likewise Odysseus, though in a different order of life, on returning from his army duty to the governing of his own palace in his own kingdom, descended first to the Underworld, guided by Circe, and, beyond that, passed to the mythic Island of the Sun. Goethe, also, in *Faust,* divides the work into Parts I and II: the first devoted, as he himself tells, to "the development of a somewhat obscure individual condition, almost wholly subjective," and the second bearing the hero from "the little world" of his individual life, to "the great," of his labors in the field of history; while between the two occur his visits to the mythic realms of the Gothic and great classical Walpurgisnacht scenes. Wolfram's Parzival, we have seen, rode forth to the ordeal of those desert years in his transit from adolescence to the realization of his high social role as King and Guardian of the Grail, and Stephen Dedalus, strolling, brooding, by the sea, was also at what he took to be the meridian of his life. Stephen associated the moment with the Crucifixion: "Come. I thirst." With the fall of Lucifer: "Allbright he falls, proud lightning of the intellect." With Hamlet and Ophelia: "My cockle hat and staff and his my sandal shoon. . . . He took the hilt of his ashplant, lunging with it still." Moreover, the time of day was noon: "Pan's hour, the faunal noon." And the date was June 16, 1904, five days before the summer solstice.

"Yes," thought Stephen, "evening will find itself in me, without me. All days make their end. By the way next when is it? Tuesday will be the longest day. Of all the glad new year, mother, the rum tum tiddledy tum." [16]

But that same June 16 had been in the author's own life the day of his first evening meeting—on that same shore—with Nora Barnacle, the woman who became his wife.

"The appointment was made," Richard Ellmann tells in his biography of Joyce, "and for the evening of June 16, when they went walking at Ringsend, and thereafter began to meet regularly. To set *Ulysses* on this date, was Joyce's most eloquent if indirect tribute to Nora, a recognition of the determining effect upon his life of his attachment to her. On June 16 he entered into relation with the world around him and left behind him the loneliness he had felt since his mother's death. He would tell her later, 'You made me a man.' June 16 was the sacred day that divided Stephen Dedalus, the insurgent youth, from Leopold Bloom, the complaisant husband." [17]

And in Thomas Mann's unassuming Hans, whose family name suggests the mortal member of the classical twins Castor and Pollux (Figure 3, Stations 12 and 13), another life is shown in the attainment of its faunal hour. Mann explicitly compares the sanatorium to the alchemist's *vas Hermeticum*. Already in the course of the two-day railroad journey to the whirling mountain summit, much of the outside world had been left behind; for, as the author tells: "Space, rolling and revolving between Hans and his native heath had possessed and wielded the powers that we generally ascribe to time, yet in a way even more striking. Space, like time, engenders forgetfulness; but it does so by setting us free from our surroundings and giving us back our primitive, unattached state." [18] Like the flakes falling from the dragon of Figure 40, the sentiments of the social setting in which Hans had been reared dropped away, up there, and left him to his own ungoverned self. The Old Adam disintegrated, the Adam of the toils and duties of his temporal condition, and a New came into being—like Homunculus in the *vas* of Goethe's *Faust*.

The pedagogue Settembrini, whom Mann compares to Goethe's Mephistopheles—a dapper rhetorician working to win men's souls to his own purposes—recognized in the young German signs of an increasing fascination for the spectacle of that dissolute Mountain of Venus and both warned and begged him to go home. However, such advice, while prudent, like that of Gurnemanz to Parzival, or of the ferryman to Gawain, was contrary to this young man's sense of life, and in the interest not of prudence but of *wyrd*—his own unfolding adventure—Hans let the beat of his excited heart hold and guide him to his own uncharted way.

The first stage of his adventure, would have to be of social disengagement, with a deep trust thereby both in his own nature, and in the nature of the world. Settembrini feared and rejected nature. "In the antithesis of body and spirit," he said very sternly one day, "the body is the devilish, evil principle; for the body

is Nature, and Nature—within the sphere, I insist, of her antagonism to the Spirit, to Reason—is evil, mystical and evil." [19]
And the second pedagogue, Naphta, the Jewish Jesuit-Communist
due to appear in the story later, would equally, though differently,
be antagonistic to the influence of the principle of nature in the
individual. As he was to say one afternoon to all three, to Hans,
Settembrini, and Joachim:

> "Either Ptolemy and the schoolmen were right, and the world
> is finite in time and space, the deity is transcendent, the antithe
> sis between God and man is sustained, and man's being is dual;
> from which it follows that the problem of his soul consists in the
> conflict between the spiritual and the material, to which all so
> cial problems are entirely secondary—and this is the only sort
> of materialism I can recognize as consistent—or else, on the
> other hand, your Renaissance astronomers hit upon the truth,
> and the cosmos is infinite. Then there exists no suprasensible
> world, no dualism; the Beyond is absorbed into the Here, the
> antithesis between God and nature falls; man ceases to be the
> theater of a struggle between two hostile principles, and be
> comes harmonious and unitary, the conflict subsists merely be
> tween his individual and his collective interest; and the will of
> the State becomes, in good pagan wise, the law of morality." [20]

It has been one of the really painful problems of the modern
Western individual to gain release for his conscience from this
Levantine assurance of a separation of spirit and nature (mythic
dissociation), together with its correlative totalitarian dogma (social identification) of "society"—almost any quorum, it seems,
will do: a "people," a "Church," even a trade union, or anything
calling itself "the state"—as the only vehicle of value, through
association with which an individual life can achieve worth: when
actually the truth is the other way round, that whatever human
worth a social group may claim, it will have gained only by grace
of the great and little individuals of its membership.

It was consequently for Hans a moment of the greatest spiritual
consequence when, together with his cousin Joachim, entering the
laboratory to be X-rayed, he was allowed to see the skeleton of
death in his own living hand held over a fluoroscope. He there
gazed, as it were, into his own grave, but in the normal light of
Settembrini's world, when he again examined his hand, the grave

had closed. And it was after that, that he spontaneously turned from his Italian friend's sociological rhetoric to a study in solitude of the sciences of life, inspired not only, or even principally, by the wonder of his own interesting body, but by that, more fascinating still, of the irritating Russian woman who had slammed the door—and repeatedly did so—at the fish course.

The first phase of the Magic Mountain epic terminates in that grotesque little tragicomic scene, labeled by its author "Walpurgisnacht," where Hans, on his knees, at the end of a silly carnival contest to see who, blindfold, could succeed in drawing a *pig,* declared to his Circe with the braided locks his love in the knowledge of the whole science of her body—which he understood to be one with the science of the earth and stars. "I love you," he told her in French, eyes closed, head bowed to her lap. "I have always loved you; for you are the *Thee* of my life, my dream, my destiny, my wish, my desire eternal. . . ." She caressed the close-cropped hair at the back of his head and, beside himself at her touch, he went on: "Oh love . . . the body, love, and death, these three are together one. For the body is delight and disease: it is what delivers death. Yes, they are carnal both, love and death; therein their terror, their grand magic! . . ." [20a]

The first volume ends in this Walpurgisnacht of loss of control—which is, in its way, analogous to the scene of Bloom's disintegration when he saw himself as a pig, and of Stephen's collapse in the same Walpurgisnacht event, when, following a mad caper and street brawl, he was struck down by a cursing British Redcoat in the role of the Roman who pierced Christ's side or—the pagan who struck Anfortas.

"Like a bridegroom Christ went forth from his chamber," reads a passage from a sermon of Saint Augustine. "He went out with a presage of his nuptials into the field of the world: he ran like a giant exulting on his way and came to the marriage bed of the cross, and there in mounting it he consummated his marriage. And when he perceived the sighs of the creature, he lovingly gave himself up to the torment in place of his bride, and he joined himself to the woman forever." [21]

Here, as in Stephen's mind, the mysteries of marriage and the crucifixion—Tristan's crystalline bed and the altar of the sacrifice —are the same. The state suggested is of the Solar King and Lunar

Queen (Figure 43) united in the tomb. That is the ultimate con-summation—where a deathlike stillness reigns—of the mystic *con-iunctio oppositorum.* "When Adam sinned his soul died," states Gregory the Great; [22] however, in the words of the alchemist Se-nior: "What had been given over to death, comes again, after great tribulation, to life." [23] As in those words of Paul that are the se-cret of *Finnegans Wake*—"For God has consigned all men to dis-obedience, that he may have mercy upon us all"—so in the silence of the tomb, the retort, the cave (again Figure 43):

> There falls the heavenly dew, to lave
> The soiled black body in the grave.*

And in the same order, in both *Ulysses* and *The Magic Mountain,* at the end of the journey into night a change occurs: the dew of divine mercy falls, *caritas,* compassion, *karuṇā,* and the ever deep-ening descent turns into illumination from above.

Stephen's brief impulse of compassion for his mortified elder, Bloom (compare that of Parzival for Anfortas), and Bloom's reciprocally, for a tortured youth struck down by a soldier in the street, break the reign in both lives of the law of death, and each gives to the other in the mutually sympathetic brief fellowship of the following two hours of the night (the only completely un-defensive moment in the course of either's long day) the keys to the resolution of his impasse and the passage of the difficult thres-hold.

In the brothel the ghost of Stephen's dead mother had appeared to him:

THE MOTHER
(*With the subtle smile of death's madness.*) I was once the beautiful May Goulding. I am dead.
STEPHEN
(*Horrorstruck.*) Lemur, who are you? What bogeyman's trick is this?
THE MOTHER
(*Comes nearer, breathing upon him softly her breath of wetted ashes.*) All must go through it, Stephen. More women than men in the world. You too. Time will come.

* Supra, p. 294.

STEPHEN

(*Choking with fright, remorse and horror.*) They said I killed
you, mother. . . . Cancer did it, not I. Destiny.

THE MOTHER

(*A green rill of bile trickling from a side of her mouth.*) You
sang that song to me. *Love's bitter mystery.*

STEPHEN

(*Eagerly.*) Tell me the word, mother, if you know now. The
word known to all men.

THE MOTHER

Who saved you the night you jumped into the train at Dalkey
with Paddy Lee? Who had pity for you when you were sad
among the strangers? Prayer is all powerful. Prayer for the
suffering souls in the Ursuline manual and forty days' indulgence. Repent, Stephen.

STEPHEN

The ghoul! Hyena!

THE MOTHER

I pray for you in my other world. Get Dilly to make you that
boiled rice every night after your brain work. Years and years I
loved you. O my son, my firstborn, when you lay in my
womb.

ZOE

(*Fanning herself with the grate fan.*) I'm melting!

FLORRY

(*Points to Stephen.*) Look! He's white.

BLOOM

(*Goes to the window to open it more.*) Giddy.

THE MOTHER

(*With smouldering eyes.*) Repent! O, the fire of hell!

STEPHEN

(*Panting.*) The corpsechewer! Raw head and bloody bones!

THE MOTHER,

(*Her face drawing nearer and nearer, sending out an ashen
breath.*) Beware! (*She raises her blackened, withered right arm
slowly towards Stephen's breast with outstretched fingers.*) Beware! God's hand! (*A green crab with malignant red eyes sticks
deep its grinning claws in Stephen's heart.*) *

STEPHEN

(*Strangled with rage.*) Shite! (*His features grow drawn and grey
and old.*)

* For the crab, cf. supra, pp. 261–62.

BLOOM

(*At the window.*) What?

STEPHEN

Ah non par exemple! The intellectual imagination! With me all or not at all. *Non serviam!*

FLORRY

Give him cold water. Wait. (*She rushes out.*)

THE MOTHER

(*Wrings her hands slowly, moaning desperately.*) O Sacred Heart of Jesus, have mercy on him! Save him from hell, O divine Sacred Heart!

STEPHEN

No! No! No! Break my spirit all of you if you can! I'll bring you all to heel!

THE MOTHER

(*In the agony of her deathrattle.*) Have mercy on Stephen, Lord, for my sake! Inexpressible was my anguish when expiring with love, grief and agony on Mount Calvary.

STEPHEN

Nothung!

(*He lifts his ashplant high with both hands and smashes the chandelier. Time's livid final flame leaps and, in the following darkness, ruin of all space, shattered glass and toppling masonry.*)

THE GASJET

Pwfungg!

BLOOM

Stop!

LYNCH

(*Rushes forward and seizes Stephen's hand.*) Here! Hold on! Don't run amok!

BELLA

Police!

(*Stephen, abandoning his ashplant, his head and arms thrown back stark, beats the ground and flees from the room past the whores at the door.*) 24

It was then that he met with the Redcoat and, when knocked down, was rescued and taken in charge by Bloom, to be restored in Bloom's kitchen with a cup of cocoa, enriched by the host with "the viscous cream ordinarily reserved for the breakfast of his wife Marion (Molly)." 25 Then on Bloom's side it was to be the bit that he would tell his bedmate Molly of this nighttown adventure with Stephen that would turn her thoughts, eventually, from her galaxy of lovers to himself.[26] And in *The Magic Mountain* it was the gentle touch and sympathetic response of Frau Chauchat to her smitten carnival lover that enabled him to win from her in her grotto, at last, the resolution of his yearning.

In the sanatorium Berghof there were two cynically jovial, rather questionable doctors, one always dressed in shiny black, the other in a surgeon's white belted smock, who controlled the population of that castle of the living dead. The black one, Dr. Krokowski, was a broad-shouldered, short psychiatrist, fleshy and pale as wax, about thirty-five years of age, with a black beard parted in two points. The other, Dr. Behrens, surgeon-director of the institute, three heads taller than his dark subordinate, had unhealthily purple cheeks, goggling bloodshot blue eyes, and wore, under his snub nose, a close-trimmed white mustache. It was he who had introduced Hans to his skeleton at the fluoroscope. And Krokowski, through a series of lectures delivered in the dining room on "The Power of Love as an Agent of Disease," had then turned his thoughts even further inward, to the problem of his strangely thumping heart. For already on arrival, when he stepped forth from the railroad car, his heart had been set racing by the Alpine air; and his associated sense of a general excitement had lacked a proper object until his mind, of itself, after a few days on the mountain, began to return irresistibly and persistently to that female with the reddish-blond braided hair and Asian, Kirghiz eyes.

"All symptoms of disease," Krokowski had declared, "are but disguised manifestations of love; and disease, but love transformed." [27] Repressed, Krokowski explained, the power of love infects the entire system through an effect upon some unknown substance in the body, which, disintegrating, liberates toxins. "One could even believe," Hans later remarked to his cousin in comment on this point, "that there might be something after all in those legends of love-drinks and the like, of which the old sagas tell." [28]

It was Behrens, however, who made clear to Hans—some time after his glimpse of his own body as his living grave—the line between death and life. Living, said Behrens, consists of dying; for living as well as putrefying is a process finally of oxidation, the combustion of cellular albumen: hence the temperature of which one sometimes has too much. "However, there is nevertheless a difference: *Life is the keeping of form through change of substance.*" [29]

And so it was that, toward the close of Hans Castorp's curiously pedantic carnival exposure to Clavdia of his erotic intoxication in the wonder of her dying body, behold! like the sun of a new day, this saving term of Apollonian light came up—*sainte merveille de la forme!*—to be developed to the end of his speech:

"The body and the body's love," he declaimed, "are indecent affairs and troublesome. The body, in fear and shame of itself, blushes and pales on its surface. But it also is a grand and adorable glory, miraculous image of organic life, holy marvel of form and of beauty: and love for it, for the human body, is furthermore an altogether humanitarian interest, a force far more instructive than all the pedagogy in this world!" [30]

Thus, at the high noon of his years, hermetically sealed from history and its occasions, played upon by the vapors of science and philosophy, Life's Delicate Child, as Mann calls him, incubating the fevers of his own body's mystery and devotion, came in his own sweet way to an experience of spiritual centering and dedication. Mann terms such a process, "Hermetic Pedagogy." And the second part of the novel then treats of its hero's maturation around this central ordering point of a life-furthering, self-consistent wisdom; following which—as a "wheel rolling of itself"—Hans voluntarily departs, with a full knowledge of what he is doing, to a literal giving of himself on the field of battle (1914) to his people in loyalty and love. (Compare Dante's age and act of "bestowal.")

Now Carl Jung, during the years when Thomas Mann was at work on *The Magic Mountain* (c. 1912–1921), was arriving in his own way, independently, at interpretations of both the psyche and its mythic symbols that accorded remarkably with those of the novelist—as the latter acknowledged generously in his address on "Freud and the Future," delivered in 1936. For the two were of exactly the same age (Mann, 1875–1955; Jung, 1875–1961) and so were crossing together, in those catastrophic years just before, during, and after the First World War, the meridian of their day. So too, in a way, was Europe itself: or so, at least, thought their contemporary, the historian Oswald Spengler (1880–1936), whose masterwork, *The Decline of the West,* appeared in 1923— just between *Ulysses,* 1922, and *The Magic Mountain,* 1924. Moreover, in the year 1921 Leo Frobenius's *Paideuma* had appeared: an anthropologically documented study in historic depth of the psyche and its symbolic forms, which had opened (both around and beneath the Magic Mountain of Europe) a new and mighty prospect of the spiritual dimension of man.

> The typical motifs in dreams [wrote Jung] . . . permit a comparison with the motifs of mythology. Many of those mythological motifs, in collecting which Frobenius in particular has rendered such signal service, are also found in dreams, often with precisely the same significance. . . . The comparison of typical dream motifs with those of mythology suggests the idea— already put forward by Nietzsche—that dream-thinking should be regarded as a phylogenetically older mode of thought. . . . Just as the body bears the traces of its phylogenetic development, so also does the human mind. Hence there is nothing surprising about the possibility that the figurative language of dreams is a survival from an archaic mode of thought.[31]

In *The Magic Mountain,* the culmination of Hans Castorp's noon-meditation on the mystery of death in life is rendered in the chapter called "Snow," wherein the no longer innocent or young voyager, with both head and heart now full of experience, put on skis and, with a boldness greater than his skill, set forth alone. In the vast Alpine silence he presently realized he had gone astray and, frightened a little, drank a charge of port to give him strength, which, instead, put him to sleep leaning for support against a snowbound mountain hut. And there a beautiful dream came to him, of a landscape he had never seen: a lovely sunlit Hellenic world of people solemnly, gracefully moving among tall Ionic colonnades.

It was a dream that Mann had derived from the last paragraphs of Nietzsche's *Birth of Tragedy,* where it illustrates that work's central theme of a reciprocal relationship between Dionysus and Apollo: the powers, respectively, of the dark impersonal will (Figure 3, at Station 10) and beauty of form (Station 16). "Only so much," wrote Nietzsche, "of the Dionysian ground of existence can enter into the consciousness of an individual as can be controlled by his

Apollonian power of transfiguration. These two prime principles of art consequently unfold their powers reciprocally, according to a law of eternal balance. . . . And that this reciprocity is inevitable, everyone will intuitively know who has ever (even if only in dream) found himself carried back to an Old Hellenic scene." [32]

Like Nietzsche's imagined dreamer, Hans too was carried back to a scene of idyllic nobility and beauty. And as the earlier dreamer had been taught by an Aeschylean guide to realize how great the terrible force must have been of the god of dithyrambic madness, where such radiant beauty was needed to hold it in control, so Hans, exclaiming in his heart at the beauty of his vision, was given to realize that behind him was a temple of darkness, death, and blood, where two gray hags, half naked and with hanging witches' dugs, were in savage silence tearing a child apart over a caldron. And as he waked horrified from this revelation, spellbound still by its beauty, its meaning leapt to his mind, epitomized in a term that he had first heard in his conversations with Naphta and Settembrini, but now in a sense not known to either: *Homo Dei.* "Myth," states Jung, "is the revelation of a divine life in man"; [33] and so was this dream, for Hans.

It is Man, Hans thought, *Homo Dei,* who is the lord of both life and death: he alone is noble, not they. More noble than life is the piety of his heart; more noble than death, the freedom of his thought. And love, not reason, is stronger than death. Love, not reason, gives gentle thoughts, and love and gentleness render form: form and civilization—in silent recognition of the feast of blood. "I shall keep faith with death in my heart," he concluded, "remembering, however, that keeping faith with death and the past becomes malignant, ominously sensual and misanthropic, the instant we let it govern thoughts and deeds. *For the sake of gentleness and love, man shall let death have no sway over his thoughts.* And with this I wake." [34]

"The dream," states Jung, "is a little hidden door in the innermost and most secret recesses of the psyche, opening into that cosmic night which was the psyche long before there was any ego consciousness, and which will remain psyche no matter how far our ego consciousess may extend. . . . All consciousness separates; but in dreams we put on the likeness of that more universal, truer, more eternal man dwelling in the darkness of primordial night. There he is still the whole, and the whole is in him, indistinguishable from nature and bare of all egohood." [35]

In the ancient world, following Hesiod, Parmenides, Socrates, and Plato,[36] the deity symbolic of the creative energy of that whole was Eros:

> Who breaks the limbs' strength
> who in all gods, in all human beings,
> overpowers the intelligence in the breast,
> and all their shrewd planning.[37]

"Eros," Jung writes, in comment on this classical idea,

> was considered a god whose divinity transcended our human limits, and who therefore could neither be comprehended nor represented in any way. I might, as many before me have attempted to do, venture an approach to this daimon, whose range of activity extends from the endless spaces of the heavens to the dark abysses of hell; but I falter before the task of finding the language which might adequately express the incalculable paradoxes of love. Eros is a *kosmogonos,* a creator and father-mother of all higher consciousness. I sometimes feel that Paul's words—"Though I speak with the tongues of men and of angels and have not love"—might well be the first condition of all cognition and the quintessence of divinity itself. . . . Love "bears all things" and "endures all things" (I Corinthians 13:7). These words say all there is to be said; nothing can be added to them. For we are in the deepest sense the victims and the instruments of cosmogonic "love." [38]

In the Orient the Bodhisattva represents this principle in its aspects both of time-transcending wisdom (*bodhi*) and of time-regarding compassion (*karuṇā*), while Shiva, as both the archetypal yogi and personification of the *liṅgam,* is an earlier representation of the same. Dionysus, Orpheus, and the other figures of the mysteries are variant aspects in manifestation of this cosmogonic power, whose mythology in the Christian sphere became focused in the crucified Redeemer (Figure 9). ("Who sees me sees Him who sent me." "I and my Father are one.") [39] Through our humanity (we have been told), we are related to that of Christ, who through his godhood relates us to divinity (*c*R*x*).* In the

* Supra, p. 346.

Bodhisattva, on the other hand, each is to recognize the mirror-to-nature of his own intelligible Buddhahood $(c \neq = x)$.* "Florry Christ, Stephen Christ, Zoe Christ, Bloom Christ, Kitty Christ, Lynch Christ," Joyce wrote in the brothel scene. Feirefiz, Parzival, and their father Gahmuret are one: so Wolfram von Eschenbach. The *Imitatio Christi* proper to the non-dual knowledge of *Homo Dei* must be to recognize the personality of the god or goddess Eros-Amor, Kosmogonos, not where it can be neither sought nor found, "out there" somewhere, in transcendence, but—as Christ did—in oneself. And not oneself alone, but all things, all events: in every individual, just as he is—crude, fine, or superfine—God's mask.

II. Symbolization

1.

The Indian Mandukya Upanishad, in its analysis and exposition of the four elements of the mystic syllable AUM, supplies a touchstone for the classification of symbols.

"AUM," the text begins: "This imperishable sound is the whole of this visible universe. Its explanation is as follows. What has become, what is becoming, what will become—verily, all of this is the sound AUM. And what is beyond these three states of the world of time—that, too, is the sound AUM." [40]

The element A, we are next told, denotes Waking Consciousness and its world (what has become); the element U, Dream Consciousness and its world (what is becoming); the element M, Deep Dreamless Sleep, the unconscious state (what will become); while the fourth element—the SILENCE before, after, and around AUM —denotes that absolute, unqualified, unconditioned state-that-is-no-state of "consciousness in itself" to which Erwin Schrödinger refers in his passage above quoted.†

Expounded in detail: first, *The Element A:*

Waking Consciousness, which is outward-turned, is called the Common-to-All-Men. Its objects are of gross matter and are separate from each other: *a* is not *b*. Perceived by the senses, named by the mind, and experienced as desirable or fearful, they compose the

---

* Supra, pp. 413 and 347.

† Supra, pp. 609–11.

world of what Goethe called "the become and the set fast: the dead," of which the understanding (*Verstand*) is concerned "only to make use." * This is the aspect of experience that Mephistopheles comprehends and controls: the world of empirical man, his desires, fears and duties, laws, statistics, economics, and "hard facts." It is the world, as Stephen Dedalus judged, of the shells left behind by life: "Crush, crack, crik, crick. Wild sea money." [41] Money and securities, banalities and fixed forms. It is the Waste Land, Dante's Hell: the world of naturalistic art and intellectual abstraction. Its order of symbols can best be studied today in Ludwig Wittgenstein's comanding *Tractatus Logico-Philosophicus;* as, for example, in the following selection of his scrupulously dry formulae.

Proposition 2.1 "We picture facts to ourselves." 2.12 "A picture is a model of reality." 2.161 "There must be something identical in a picture and what it depicts, to enable the one to be a picture of the other at all."

Proposition 3 "A logical picture of facts is a thought." 3.1 "In a proposition a thought finds an expression that can be perceived by the senses." 3.31 "I call any part of a proposition that characterizes its sense an expression (or a symbol). . . ." 3.32 "A sign is what can be perceived of a symbol."

Proposition 4 "A thought is a proposition with sense." 4.001 "The totality of propositions is language." 4.11 "The totality of true propositions is the whole of natural science (or the whole corpus of the natural sciences)." 4.111 "Philosophy is not one of the natural sciences. . . ." 4.112 "Philosophy aims at the logical clarification of thoughts. . . . Without philosophy thoughts are, as it were, cloudy and indistinct: its task is to make them clear and to give them sharp boundaries. 4.1121 "Psychology is no more closely related to philosophy than any other natural science. Theory of knowledge is the philosophy of psychology. . . ." 4.116 "Everything that can be thought at all can be thought clearly. Everything that can be put into words can be put clearly. . . ." [42]

Bertrand Russell, in this same tombstone spirit, has summarized in one sentence both his own idea and Wittgenstein's of the aim of symbolization: "The essential business of language is to assert or

* Supra, p. 383.

deny facts." [43] A more usual business of language, however, has been to motivate action and, to this end, to excite fear, rage, or desire, to indoctrinate, to prevaricate, to intimidate, and to brainwash. Indeed, to assert or deny "fact" is about the last thing language has ever been used for. "Fiction," rather, would have been the honest term for this master of clarity to have used—for, as Nietzsche already knew, "whatever can be thought, cannot but be a fiction." "There are many kinds of eyes. Even the Sphinx has eyes. Therefore, there are many kinds of truths—and therefore, there is no truth." [44] "Truth is that form of error without which a thinking subject cannot live." And "Logic rests on presuppositions to which nothing in the actual world corresponds." [45]

The psychological functions chiefly involved in the outward-turned, "objective" order of cognition, "common to all men," are *sensation* and *thinking. Feeling* and *intuition,* on the other hand, lead inward, to private spheres. As Jung declares: "The pain-pleasure reaction of feeling marks the highest degree of subjectivation of the object"; whereas intuition is that mode of perception which includes the apprehension of subliminal factors: "the possible relationship to objects not appearing in the field of vision, and the possible changes, past and future, about which the object gives no clue. Intuition is an immediate awareness," Jung continues, "of relationships that could not be established by the other three functions at the moment of orientation." [46]

In the arts of both Joyce and Mann, such intuited subliminal relationships are indicated by the echoing motifs in which their works abound, suggesting analogies, homologies, significant synchronicities, and so forth; the recurrent "dog" motif in *Ulysses,* for example, or, in "Tonio Kröger," the musically developed contrasting themes of "dark gypsies" and "blue-eyed blonds." *

So we are led to *the Element U, the second element of AUM:* Dream Consciousness, called the Shining One, is inward-turned, where it coincides with the movement of the will, i.e., "what is becoming." Its objects are not of gross but of subtle matter, which, like fire, like the sun, is self-luminous, not, like gross matter, illuminated from without. In the world of Waking Consciousness, the fire of the hearth and of the funeral pyre, as well as the blazing sun door, open to this visionary world, which is beyond all pairs of op-

* Supra, pp. 275–77, 295–96, and 327.

posites. For here, since the dreamer and his dream are the same, the subject-object opposition falls: the visions are of his own motivating powers; their personifications are his gods—or, if improperly served, disdained, or disregarded, become his fiends. Furthermore, since the powers of nature in *this* dreamer, in *that* dreamer, and in the macrocosm of nature itself, are the same, only differently inflected, the powers personified in a dream are those that move the world. All the gods are within: within you—within the world. And it will be according to the inward tensions and resolutions, balances and imbalances, of the individual that his visions will be of either infernal or celestial kind: confused and personal, or enlightening and generic: negative, dark, and monstrous (like Dante's three-headed Satan) or positive and radiant (like his Trinity). For the hells, purgatories, and heavens are within, as but modes of experience of the one terror-joy of Dream Consciousness at the burning point of what Goethe called "the becoming and the changing: the living," through which it is the concern of Reason (*Vernunft*) "to strive toward the divine." Here all pairs of opposites coincide, whether of subject and object, the dreamer and his dream, desire and loathing, terror-joy, or the micro- and the macrocosm.

Freud, in his epochal work *The Interpretation of Dreams* (published 1900), which is based on insights derived from years devoted to the fantasies of neurotics, concentrates all attention upon those distorting *personal* anxieties and fixations of his patients which were, in fact, the "sins" (to use a theological term) that bound them to their hells, from which it was the aim of his compassionate science to release them. And for those self-condemned, tortured wretches, the whole world was an Inferno—as it is in Marlowe's *Doctor Faustus* for his Mephistophilis:

FAUST. Where are you damned?
MEPH. In hell.
FAUST. How comes it then that thou art out of hell?
MEPH. Why this is hell, nor am I out of it:
      Think'st thou that I who saw the face of God,
      And tasted the eternal joys of Heaven,
      Am not tormented with ten thousand hells,
      In being deprived of everlasting bliss? [47]

And again, a little later:

FAUST. Tell me where is the place that men call hell?
MEPH. Under the Heavens.
FAUST. Ay, but whereabout?
MEPH. Within the bowels of these elements,
    Where we are tortured and remain for ever;
    Hell hath no limits, nor is circumscribed
    In one self place; for where we are is hell,
    And where hell is there must we ever be:
    And, to conclude, when all the world dissolves,
    And every creature shall be purified,
    All places shall be hell that is not Heaven.
FAUST. Come, I think hell's a fable.
MEPH. Ay, think so still, till experience change thy mind.[48]

"I believe that a large portion of the mythological conception of the world which reaches far into the most modern religions, *is nothing but psychology projected to the outer world,*" Freud wrote in his early paper on *The Psychopathology of Everyday Life* (1904). "The dim perception (the endo-psychic perception, as it were) of psychic factors and relations of the unconscious was taken as a model in the construction of a *transcendental reality,* which is destined to be changed again by science into *psychology of the unconscious.* . . . . We venture to explain in this way the myths of paradise and the fall of man, of God, of good and evil, of immortality and the like—that is, to transform *metaphysics* into *meta-psychology.*" [49]

So too in Nietzsche's *Human, All-Too-Human* (1878): "In the ages of the rude beginnings of culture, man believed that he was discovering *a second real world* in dream, and here is the origin of all metaphysics. Without dream, mankind would never have had occasion to invent such a division of the world. The parting of soul and body goes also with this way of interpreting dream; likewise, the idea of a soul's apparitional body: whence, all belief in ghosts, and apparently, too, in gods." [50] Compare Occam, supra, p. 583.

Freud, we have said, was concerned in his science primarily with pathology. He read the symbols of dream allegorically, as masked references to the psychological shocks sustained in infancy by the dreamer, chiefly in relation to parental figures; and in turning from dreams to mythologies, he diagnosed these, accordingly, as symptomatic of equivalent shocks in the formative past of the peoples to whom the myths in question appertained. "We base everything upon the assumption of a psyche of the mass," he wrote in *Totem and Tabu* (1913), "in which psychic processes occur as in the life of the individual. Moreover, we let the sense of guilt for a deed survive for thousands of years, remaining effective in generations which could not have known anything of the deed." [51]

Jung, on the other hand, gives stress in his interpretations of both dreams and myth not so much to history and biography as to biology and those initiations into the nature and sense of existence that all, in the course of a lifetime, must endure.

According to my view [he states], the unconscious falls into two parts which should be sharply distinguished from one another. One of them is the personal unconscious; it includes all those psychic contents which have been forgotten during the course of the individual's life. Traces of them are still preserved in the unconscious, even if all conscious memory of them has been lost. In addition, it contains all subliminal impressions or perceptions which have too little energy to reach consciousness. To these we must add unconscious combinations of ideas that are too feeble and too indistinct to cross over the threshold. Finally, the personal unconscious contains all psychic contents that are incompatible with the conscious attitude. This comprises a whole group of contents, chiefly those which appear morally, aesthetically, or intellectually inadmissible and are repressed on account of their incompatibility. A man cannot always think and feel the good, the true, and the beautiful, and in trying to keep up an ideal attitude everything that does not fit in with it is automatically repressed. If, as is nearly always the case in a differentiated person, one function, for instance thinking, is especially developed and dominates consciousness, then feeling is thrust into the background and largely falls into the unconscious.

The other part of the unconscious is what I call the impersonal or collective unconscious. As the name indicates, its contents are not personal but collective; that is, they do not belong to one individual alone but to a whole group of individuals, and generally to a whole nation, or even to the whole of mankind. These contents are not acquired during the individual's lifetime but are products of innate forms and instincts. Although the child possesses no inborn ideas, it nevertheless has a highly developed brain which functions in a quite definite way. This brain

is inherited from its ancestors; it is a deposit of the psychic functioning of the whole human race. The child therefore brings with
it an organ ready to function in the same way that it has functioned throughout human history. In the brain the instincts are
preformed, and so are the primordial images which have always
been the basis of man's thinking—the whole treasure-house of
mythological motifs. . . .[52]

In the course of the six and a half decades of his development of
his theories of the unconscious (1896–1961: exactly the years
during which a formidable company of creative artists and authors—Yeats, Pound, Eliot, Joyce, Mann, Picasso, and Klee, for
example—were exploring the same "dark wood," each in his own
direction and where there was no way or path), Dr. Jung used the
terms "archetype" and "primordial image" interchangeably, to
designate those formative powers of the psyche that have been discussed at length in the first chapters of the opening volume of this
study: *Primitive Mythology*, Chapter I, "The Enigma of the Inherited Image," and II, "The Imprints of Experience." Our pages
chapters, and volumes since have been devoted to a systematic
survey of the changes throughout space and time of these protean,
timeless "forms," which the poet Robinson Jeffers termed "the
phantom rules of humanity / That without being are yet more real
than what they are born of, and without shape, shape that which
makes them:

The nerves and the flesh go by shadowlike, the limbs and the lives
    shadowlike, these shadows remain, these shadows
To whom temples, to whom churches, to whom labors and wars,
    visions and dreams are dedicate.[53]

Adolf Bastian (1825–1905) coined the term "ethnic ideas"
(*Völkergedanke*) for the local, historic transformations of the
archetypes, and the term "elementary ideas" (*Elementargedanke*)
for the archetypes themselves. Leo Frobenius then employed the
term "Culture Monad" to represent an operative constellation of
ethnic ideas in historic manifestation. The constellating force of
such a "Monad" would be, according to his view, an intuiton of
order inspired by some fascinating presence: for instance, among
primitive hunters, the striking presences of the animal world,
where the permanence of each unique species appears through

ephemeral individuals; among primitive planters, the miracle of the plant world, where life springs from decay; and in the city-states of Sumer, the wonder of the night sky, where a mathematically calculable cosmological order was recognized in the passages of the planets, moon, and sun.

Such revelations of subliminal relationships behind and within fields of temporal-spatial observation were received with awe, according to Frobenius, and the associated phenomena themselves, regarded with fascination, then supplied both the imagery and the chief foci of a system of mythology and cult through which the affected social group attempted to bring itself into accord with the intuited principle of order. Frobenius thus gave stress in his studies of the genesis of mythology to the phenomena of the environment, whereas Freud, who in relation to myth also treats chiefly of historical factors, found that in no matter what environment, the nuclear theme of all myth, art, religion, and civilization, up to his own time, had been of the nuclear human family scene of desire, jealousy, and guilt in the inevitable triadic romance of Mother, Father, and Child.

It is reasonable to assume, however, that in the shaping of mythologies *both* environments must have counted. Where such differences appear as between, say, the primitive hunting and planting mythologies, or the Syrian of Astarte and biblical of Yahweh, the larger environmental factor will surely merit prime consideration, whereas in the case of a wealthy Viennese fantasizing on a couch, the family drama of his own half-forgotten infancy may well have built the labyrinth in which his hero soul has become lost.

In any case, whether as a reflex of *a*) the natural environment, *b*) historic tribal or national life, *c*) the family triangle, or *d*) the inevitable biological course of human maturation and aging, together with what James Joyce termed "the grave and constant in human sufferings,"—to which I would add, "in human joy"—it is clear that the actual images and emphases of any mythological or dream system must be derived from local experience, while the "archetypes," the "elementary ideas," the "roles" that the local images serve, must be of an order antecedent to experience; of a plot, so to say, a destiny or *wyrd,* inherent in the psychosomatic structure of the human species.

In the opening pages of the first volume of his great biblical tetralogy, *Joseph and His Brothers,* which in sense and inspiration is an unfoldment—large and beautiful—of the seed of Hans Castorp's dream in *The Magic Mountain,* Thomas Mann writes of the backward thrust of scholarship questing for the origins of those mythic forms that have been the support of all human life and culture whatsoever. And as he there declares: "The deeper we sound, the further down into the lower world of the past we probe and press, the more do we find that the earliest foundations of humanity, its history and culture, reveal themselves unfathomable." [54] He then calls upon the Gnostic myth that we have already considered—of creation as a function of the soul's descent or "fall" before the beginning of time—to suggest that the actual garden of Paradise inheres in the soul itself and antecedes creation. "We have sounded the well of time to its depths, and not yet reached our goal," he writes: "the history of man is older than the material world which is the work of his will, older than life, which rests upon his will." [55]

So, also, Jung: "The deeper 'layers' of the psyche lose their individual uniqueness as they retreat farther and farther into darkness. 'Lower down,' that is to say as they approach the autonomous functional systems, they become increasingly collective until they are universalized and extinguished in the body's materiality, i.e., in chemical substances. The body's carbon is simply carbon. Hence, 'at bottom' the psyche is simply 'world.' " [56]

One cannot help thinking here of the Upanishadic myth of the Self in the form of a man who became this whole creation,[57] and of Schopenhauer's view of the world as will: the will that is all in all of us and in which each of us is the all.

But the "archetypes," which are of this primal order of the psyche, are not to be thought of as of determined content.

Again and again [states Jung] I encounter the mistaken notion that an archetype is determined in regard to its content, in other words that it is a kind of unconscious idea (if such an expression is admissible). It is necessary to point out once more that archetypes are not determined as regards their content, but only as regards their form and then only to a very limited degree. A primordial image is determined as to its content only when it has become conscious and is therefore filled out with the material of conscious experience. Its form, however, . . . might perhaps be compared to the axial system of a crystal, which, as it were, preforms the crystalline structure in the mother liquid, although it has no material existence of its own. This first appears according to the specific way in which the ions and molecules aggregate. The archetype in itself is empty and purely formal, nothing but a *facultas praeformandi,* a possibility of representation which is given *a priori.* The representations themselves are not inherited, only the forms, and in that respect they correspond in every way to the instincts, which are also determined in form only. The existence of the instincts can no more be proved than the existence of the archetypes, so long as they do not manifest themselves concretely.[58]

And so we are led from the sphere of the element U to that of M, Deep Dreamless Sleep, where potentiality, or "what will become," resides:

"Here," states the Upanishad, "a sleeper neither desires anything desirable nor beholds any dream. Undivided, he is an undifferentiated, homogeneous lump or mass of consciousness, consisting of bliss and feeding on bliss, his only mouth being spirit. He is here 'The Knower': the Lord of All, the Omniscient, the Indwelling Controller, the Source or Generative Womb of All: the Beginning and End of beings." [59]

From the point of view of either Waking or Dream Consciousness, Deep Sleep would seem to be darkness, a mere blank; yet dreams pour forth from it, and out of it comes waking. Moreover, back into it, all disappears.

It is the dark into which Stephen Dedalus disappeared, following his kitchen conversation with Bloom in the basement of Bloom's castle, Bloom's temple, his home, where he lived with his goddess Molly, who was at that hour in bed upstairs. It is the dark into which Bloom disappeared, when he had mounted to that second floor and in the grotto of his goddess mounted the bed, his Cross.

How?

With circumspection, as invariably when entering an abode (his own or not his own): with solicitude, the snakespiral springs of the mattress being old, the brass quoits and pendent viper radii loose and tremulous under stress and strain: prudently, as entering a lair or ambush of lust or adder: lightly, the less to disturb: reverently, the bed of conception and of birth, of consummation of marriage and of breach of marriage, of sleep and of death.

What did his limbs, when gradually extended, encounter?
New clean bedlinen, additional odours, the presence of a human form, female, hers, the imprint of a human form, male, not his, some crumbs, some flakes of potted meat, recooked, which he removed.

If he had smiled, why would he have smiled?
To reflect that each one who enters imagines himself to be the first to enter whereas he is always the last term of a preceding series even if the first term of a succeeding one, each imagining himself to be first, last, only and alone, whereas he is neither first nor last nor only nor alone in a series originating in and repeated to infinity.[60]

Molly, the goddess, roused a little, asked sleepily, and was answered, of her returning consort's Odyssey that day. And, just as at the end of Dante's heaven-ascent, *The Divine Comedy,* the poet, beholding the ultimate vision of God, saw above the heads of the Persons Three the marvel of a Living Light, of which the Trinity itself was a reflex, and of which he states that

within the profound and clear subsistence of that lofty Light there appeared three circles of three colors and of one dimension,[61]

so, on the ceiling above the adulterated marriage bed of Marian and Leopold Bloom, there was to be seen, as she listened to his saga,

the upcast reflection of a lamp and shade, an inconstant series of concentric circles of varying gradations of light and shadow.

In what directions did listener and narrator lie?
Listener: S.E. by E: Narrator N.W. by W: on the 53rd parallel of latitude, N. and 6th meridian of longitude, W.: at an angle of 45° to the terrestrial equator.

In what state of rest or motion?
At rest relatively to themselves and to each other. In motion

being each and both carried westward, forward and rereward respectively, by the proper perpetual motion of the earth through everchanging tracks of neverchanging space.

In what posture?
Listener: reclined semilaterally, left, left hand under head, right leg extended in a straight line and resting on left leg, flexed, in the attitude of Gea-Tellus, fulfilled, recumbent, big with seed. Narrator: reclined laterally, left, with right and left legs flexed, the indexfinger and thumb of the right hand resting on the bridge of the nose, in the attitude depicted on a snapshot photograph by Percy Apjohn, the childman weary, the manchild in the womb.

Womb? Weary?
He rests. He has travelled.

With?
Sinbad the Sailor and Tinbad the Tailor and Jinbad the Jailer and Whinbad the Whaler and Ninbad the Nailer and Finbad the Failer and Binbad the Bailer and Pinbad the Pailer and Mindbad the Mailer and Hinbad the Hailer and Rinbad the Railer and Dinbad the Kailer and Vinbad the Quailer and Linbad the Yailer and Xinbad the Phthailer.

When?
Going to dark bed there was a square round Sinbad the Sailor roc's auk's egg in the night of the bed of all the auks of the rocs of Darkinbad the Brightdayler.

Where? [62]

There is an important contrast to be noticed between the attitudes of Joyce and Mann toward the night world and the light: the abyss into which all pairs of opposites disappear, and the day where they subsist, "common to all men." As already remarked, these two masters, in the stages of their progress, though largely unaware of each other, were on parallel courses, step by step. Both commencing at the turn of the century in the mode of the realistic sociological-psychological nineteenth-century novel of the world of Waking Consciousness, each told through his young characters of his own youthful separation from the economic, social, and political interests of his folk: "to find," as Stephen Dedalus put it, "the mode of life or of art whereby his spirit could express itself in unfettered freedom." [63] Tonio Kröger's formula of "erotic irony," stated in his letter to Lisabeta, and Stephen's theory of aesthetics —of proper and improper, static and kinetic art *—represent equally, though from different sides, the sense of aesthetic arrest, where all the faculties of sensation, thinking, feeling, and intuition are dissociated from the service of the artist's personal will, so that, like the Buddha on the Immovable Spot, he is released from fear and desire, because free (for the moment at least) of ego: "beside himself," transfixed by the object. The eye, which normally, biologically, is an organ in the service of an aggressive, lustful organism—scouting the world for prey and estimating dangers—is in the aesthetic moment cleared of personal concerns, so that all is beheld as by the World Eye of Apollo with his lyre on the summit of Mount Helicon. The World Song, the music of the spheres, then is heard ("silent Thalia," singing), and, as Goethe states in a famous poem: "Then life-joy streams from all things." †

Ulysses and *The Magic Mountain* are such world-eye visions of our present much-maligned humanity. The personages and events, ostensibly separate from each other—as in the field of vision of the sociological, psychological, realistic novel—are by the alchemy of art shown to be, as in a field of dream, at one: in Stephen's terms, "consubstantial": essentially the vision is of the Mahayana Buddhist "Net of Gems," the universe as a context of "totalistic harmony mutually relating and penetrating," [64] one in all and all in one; each gem, each jewel of a being, reflecting all, so that "even in a hair there are innumerable golden lions." Or one thinks again of Wolfram's comment on the battle of Parzival and Feirefiz: if one likes, one can speak of them as two, but they are one. Musically

---

* Supra, pp. 311–12, 327–28, and 349–50.
† *Wenn im Unendlichen dasselbe*
Sich wiederholend ewig fliesst,
Das tausendfältige Gewölbe
Sich kräftig ineinander schliesst;
Strömt Lebenslust aus allen Dingen,
Dem kleinsten wie dem grössten Stern,
Und alles Drängen, alles Ringen
Ist ewige Ruh in Gott dem Herrn.
("Zahme Xenien VII." *Werke* in 40 Bänden, 1853; Bd. III, S. 135.)

developed and manipulated motifs of explicit mythological association, echoing and re-echoing, serve in both novels—in the way of
the anamorphoses suggested by Schopenhauer in his essay on the
cosmic dream in which all the dream characters dream too—to reveal within all, within each, the image whole that on the waking
plane is apparently in pieces: Hans Castorp's *Homo Dei;* Stephen
Dedalus's "Florry Christ, Stephen Christ, Zoe Christ, Bloom
Christ, Kitty Christ, Lynch Christ."

The order of the world of Waking Consciousness disintegrates
in these novels and that of Dream breaks through in the scenes,
respectively, of Hans's vision of the Greek landscape and of
Stephen's brothel orgy. However, Hans then is carried further and
more deeply into the awesome sphere of night when, at a later
stage of his adventure—in a chapter labeled by its author *Frag-
würdigstes,* "Highly Questionable"—he allows himself to participate in a series of séances, where, at a climax, Joachim, who has
died some months before, returns, reappears on the summons of
Hans himself, garbed prophetically in the uniform which it was to
be Hans's destiny to wear, of the German Army of World War I.

The dilettante séances had been organized as an upshot of the
lectures of Krokowski and the chance arrival in the sanatorium of
a stoop-shouldered little Danish girl of nineteen who "had things
about her of which no one could have dreamed." She proved to be
possessed of occult powers, and at first simply to pass the time, but
presently more and more seriously, the old guard of the Mountain,
of whom Hans now was one, discovered and exploited these, until,
at the climax of a most amazing sequence of increasingly eerie ap-
paritions in that darkened room, Joachim, who had long been
dead, was summoned and indeed appeared: in that as yet unknown
uniform, he was seen sitting in a vacant chair. Hans stared, appalled. It seemed for one moment as though his stomach would
turn over. His throat contracted and a four-, a fivefold sob went
through and through him. He leaned forward. "Forgive me!" he
whispered to the apparition, his eyes broke into tears and he could
see no more. He stood up, strode in two strides to the door and with
one quick movement turned on the white light.[65]

Stephen Dedalus, on the other hand, overcome by a similar visi-
tation—of his mother—had struck the light *out* and gone wild.*

* Supra, p. 641.

Thus the abyss that Hans refused, and together with Hans his author, Joyce and his characters entered: so that in the following majestic masterworks, *Joseph and His Brothers* and *Finnegans Wake*, where the implications of the dream in the snow and brothel orgy open to full flower and the plane of Waking is let go, to drop to that of Dream (which is to say, of myth), we are presented with opposed experiences and representations of the archetypes of our lives: that of the soul of light, so to say, and that of the soul of darkness; in the language of the Bible: Abel and Cain, Isaac and Ishmael, Jacob and Esau, Joseph and his brothers. Mann identified with Jacob and Joseph, Joyce with Esau and Cain; i.e., Mann with the one who wins in the light world, Joyce with the one who loses there, retreats to his hole, called "The Haunted Inkbottle, no number Brimstone Walk, Asia in Ireland," and there, "dejected into day and night with jesuit bark and bitter bite," "noondayterrorised to skin and bone by an ineluctable phantom," "wrote over everysquare inch of the only foolscap available, his own body, till by its corrosive sublimation one continuous present tense integument slowly unfolded all marryvoising moodmoulded cyclewheeling history (thereby, he said, reflecting from his own individual person, life unlivable, transaccidentated through the slow fires of consciousness into a dividual chaos, perilous, potent, common to allflesh, human only, mortal)." [66]

Jacob and Joseph in the novel of Thomas Mann, as well as in the Book of Genesis, gain God's grace and become a destiny (or, as they think of it, a "blessing") to the world: Hans went down from the Magic Mountain to engage in the course of history. But "history," declared Stephen in *Ulysses,* "is a nightmare from which I am trying to awake." And when the schoolmaster, Mr. Deasy, grandiloquently proclaimed, "All history moves towards one great goal, the manifestation of God," "God," was Stephen's answer, "is a shout in the street." [67]

In Sanskrit, the term *deśi* (pronounced "day-shee"), meaning "local, ethnic, of the region," is used (as remarked in the first volume of this study) [68] to designate the necessarily various historic forms of mythology and ritual: the "ethnic ideas" of Bastian; while the term *mārga,* "way" or "path," is used for the transcendence of these, the passage of the gateless gate toward an experience of the formless forms of Dreamless Sleep. In *Joseph and His Brothers* the sense of enacting mythic roles is brought to the support, magnification, and sophistication of a way of life. "The artist eye has a mythical slant upon life," Mann declared in his address on Freud and the Future, "which makes life look like a farce, like a theatrical performance, a prescribed feast, like a Punch-and-Judy epic, wherein mythical character-puppets reel off a plot abiding from past time and now again present in a jest. It only lacks that this mythical slant should pass over and become subjective in the performers themselves, become a festival and mythical consciousness of part and play, for an epic to be produced such as that of the 'Tales of Jacob.' . . . Joseph, too, is another such celebrant of life: with charming mythological hocus-pocus he enacts in his own person the Tammuz-Osiris myth, 'bringing to pass' anew the story of the mangled, buried and arisen god, playing his festival game with that which mysteriously and secretly shapes life out of its own depths—the unconscious. The Joseph of the novel is an artist, playing with his *imitatio dei* upon the unconscious string." [69]

In *Finnegans Wake,* on the other hand, the mythic forms point, rather, downward. In the final chapter of *Ulysses,* following Stephen's disappearance into the outer night and Bloom's into the inner, the lead has passed to Molly, Gaia-Tellus; in Hesiod's lines:

> Gaia of the broad breast,
> the unshakable foundation
> of all the immortals who keep the crests
> of snowy Olympus. [70]

She is the mother of all beings: "the holy stock of the everlasting immortals came into being out of Gaia," even "starry Ouranos," Heaven, her son and spouse. [71] Figure 56 is from an Indian eighteenth-century manuscript illumination, showing the male divinities of the Hindu pantheon—who neither singly nor together had been able to overthrow a buffalo-demon who had laid waste and was ruling the world—sending back their energies to their source: the Mother Dark, Mother Night, from which, then, the personification appeared of Maya-Shakti-Devi, the Goddess Creatrix of All Forms, who, having taken back from her progeny of sons the powers originally hers, now, with many arms in token of the qualities of those powers, strode forth and in a battle of great fury and

Figure 56. The Summoning of the Goddess; India, c. 1800 A.D.

many miracles overcame and slew the monster, restoring to the
world laid waste its life.

"Yes because . . ." begins Molly Bloom's earth-mother recollection (after Bloom, her spouse, had gone to sleep) of the many
males in her life, no one of them her match. Yet she is remembering, too, her Leo and why she had liked him (because she had
seen he understood or felt what a woman is) and how she had
thought, "well as well him as another": "and first I put my arms
around him yes and drew him down to me so he could feel my
breasts all perfume yes and his heart was going like mad and yes I
said yes I will Yes." [72]

Molly Bloom is the "Yes because" of the world. The minds of
her lovers severally may not be able to understand and feel what
life, what a woman, is, nor their deeds to fulfill the adventures of
their promise (so that the world of Waking Consciousness in

which they hold control is indeed a Waste Land: a world, as we are told in the Bible, of dust), yet, as told in *Finnegans Wake:* "This ourth of years is not save brickdust and being humus the same roturns." [73]

Anna Livia Plurabelle, the counterpart in *Finnegans Wake* of Molly Bloom in *Ulysses,* is the living source becoming, as Molly is the source become; she is of the world of Dream Consciousness, the world as vision, as Molly of the world of Waking, the world as fact. Nor is she a compound of all women; rather, an *a priori* archetype, primordial image of their being—and matched, furthermore, by an adequate consort in the *a priori* tragi-comical manliness of her consort, Here Comes Everybody. Moreover, as in dream, so here: all is here and now, in flux; not in progress, "moving towards one great goal," but kaleidoscopically revolving. "The oaks of ald now they lie in peat yet elms leap where askes lay." "Teems of times and happy returns. The seim anew." "All's set for restart after the silence." The atom "explodotonates"; no minutes, no seconds later, the two annihilated parties are shaking hands again. "Mere man's mime: God has jest. The old order changeth and lasts like the first." "Weeping shouldst not thou be when man falls but that divine scheming ever adoring be" . . . "in the multimirror megaron of returningties, whirled without end to end."

And through all this revolution, the more one labors and broods upon its enigmatic "funforall," its "Hereweareagain Gaieties," the more impressively and ubiquitously do the presences of H.C.E. and A.L.P. come to view as the inhabiting—creating, supporting, and disintegrating—substance, consciousness, and bliss of all things.[74] Dante's idea of Purgatory, as the condition of a soul being purged of its pride and so readied to respond to the radiance of God's love (as Parzival, following his conversation with Trevrizent), is matched in the Orient by the idea of Reincarnation: through many lifetimes release from egoism is achieved and so from the sorrows of rebirth. Joyce, in *Finnegans Wake,* brings the two mythologies together as alternate symbols of that state or plane of experience in which the daylight illusions of separateness dissolve and a single Syllable—Voice—Presence—begins to be heard and perceived through all.

But there is a further depth to be known and realized, within, beyond, before and after that night into which Bloom dissolved—

● —and whence the goddess of many arms, beauties, talents, and names, Anna Livia Plurabelle (Figure 56), arises; that of, namely:

The Fourth Element of AUM: THE SILENCE:

As the last pages of *Ulysses* were of the monologue of Molly Bloom, so the last of *Finnegans Wake* are of Anna Livia Plurabelle—in her character of Old Age, passing out: the river Liffey at the end of its course, sweeping out to sea, to the All-Father, "moananoaning": Manannan. "A way a lone a last a loved a long the   " The last sentence of *Finnegans Wake* breaks off abruptly, in a blank. Thus the ring is broken—if you like! However, turning back to the start of the book, we find there, at the head of the first page, the cut-off remainder of that last sentence, beginning all anew "riverrun . . . brings us . . . back to *Howth Castle and Environs*," i.e., to H.C.E., and the round rolls on.

In Deep Dreamless Sleep, Absolute Consciousness, the Omniscient One, is buried, like a treasure, in darkness. "Just as those ignorant of the spot might pass, time and time again, over a buried treasure of gold and not find it, so do all creatures go daily to that Brahma-world in sleep and not find it." [75] Creatures go there in death also, without finding. The goal of wisdom is to arrive there awake and alive: to carry Waking Consciousness through dream realizations, while awake, to an experience, awake, of identity with THAT (*tat tvam asi*). In *Oriental Mythology* there is a picture (page 335, Figure 21) of the mythic "Isle of Gems," the womb of the universe, showing the world goddess seated on her spouse, who is there beneath her in two aspects: one upward-turned in connubium, the other turned downward and away. The reference of the first is to Consciousness in the state of Deep Sleep, which, as we have read, is "the Source (*yoni:* the Generative Womb) of All: the Beginning and End of beings." Here the world is created, not in the way of an act at the beginning of time, but continuously, forever, as the ground of being; for there was never a beginning of time, there will never be an end, the creative moment is now, in

Deep Dreamless Sleep, the sphere of bliss, of Shiva-Shakti, H.C.E. and A.L.P., Molly Bloom's Yes. Whereas the figure turned away from the goddess, downward, is called Shava, the "corpse," and represents Consciousness transcendent, the fourth portion of the Self, symbolized in the SILENCE.

"What is known as the fourth portion," we read in the Upanishad, "is neither inward- nor outward-turned consciousness, nor the two together; not an undifferentiated mass of dormant omniscience; neither knowing nor unknowing—because invisible, ineffable, intangible, devoid of characteristcs, inconceivable, undefinable, its sole essence being the assurance of its own Self: the coming to peaceful rest of all differentiated, relative existence: utterly quiet: peaceful-blissful: without a second: the Self, to be known." [76]

2.

In our classification of symbolic forms, all four orders of experience represented in the syllable AUM will have to be recognized. On the first level, A, of Waking Consciousness, the references (ideally, as charged by Wittgenstein) will be directly and precisely, *a*) to facts, and *b*) to thoughts. Other symbols on this level (apparently not recognized by Wittgenstein) will be references, however, *c*) to feelings, and *d*) to intuitions of subliminal relationships (analogies, homologies, et cetera); still others *e*) will be to imperatives: stop, go, back up, sit down!

For a symbol to function as intended, certain conditions must be satisfied. First, the code must be understood by both the sender and the receiver. Codes are of two orders: 1. inherited (instinctual) and 2. learned; and of the latter category there are *a*) code elements triggering conditioned reflexes, and *b*) code elements consciously controlled. The code channels generally are of sight, sound, smell, taste, or touch. The sender and receiver may be the same or not the same; and anyone who has forgotten what his own jottings meant on his date pad will be likely to appreciate the possibility of misreading symbols, even when they are one's own.

On the level of U, Dream Consciousness, this possibility of misreading one's own communications is of high significance. For the sender of the message here would be one's own unconscious, and the receiver, the conscious personality. Read in the Freudian way,

as allegories symbolic of forgotten events, the symbols of dream
would then be comparable to the messages on one's date pad in
forgotten or illegible script; while myths would be like that soiled
and mangled letter scratched up in *Finnegans Wake* from an
orangeflavored mudmound by a hen.

But, on the other hand, when the message is not of an occasion
registered in the past, whether of oneself or of one's race, it will be
of another order altogether. It is then something like a bubble
coming up from the bottom of a sea. What or who is the sender?
The sender is oneself. What can the meaning be?

What is the meaning of a bubble from the bottom of the sea?

Well, in the first place, such a message is instinctual. Its source,
ultimately, is of the consciousness below waves, the light folded in
the dark of Deep Sleep. It is not of the order of Waking Consciousness, nor to be read as a conscious thought. Professor
Thomas A. Sebeok, of the Research Center in Anthropology,
Folklore, and Linguistics at Indiana University, in an article in
Science on "Animal Communication," has enumerated a number of
types of instinctual message, of which at least four might be of relevance here. The first is the Monologue, a "vacuum activity" in the
absence of a recipient, delivered without regard to the ability of
other individuals to receive the message: a display, a sort of spontaneous song of life. The second has been dubbed (following Mal-
inowski) "Phatic Communication": messages that serve merely to
establish or prolong communication: a type of speech in which ties
of union are created by a mere exchange. "This," we learn, "is the
first verbal function acquired by human infants and commonly
predominates in communicative acts both within and across species." Next are "Emotive Messages": messages that are action responses to visceral and sensory stimuli, and which chiefly serve to
alert recipient individuals about the condition of the signaling individual. And finally, "Vocatives and Imperatives": messages oriented toward the addressee, devoid of truth value, having a chiefly
conative (or appeal) function: "Look at me!" "Let me out the
door!" [77]

The message of our bubble, then, will be the announcement of a
presence, possibly intentional, possibly addressed to the waking
world, but certainly referring to no *conscious* context of concerns.
Its only meaning, finally, is the announcement of its own presence—

which can have no more "meaning" than the presence somewhere of a stone, a flower, a mountain, or a winding stream. The value of the message to our Waking Consciousness will be to alert us to an unknown aspect of ourselves, which, if we are to "know ourselves," and so realize our destiny, our *wyrd,* will have to be recognized.

Dream Consciousness, then, to summarize and terminate, is the channel or medium of communication between the spheres of M, Deep Dreamless Sleep, and A, Waking Conciousness. In its upper, "personal" strata, the messages are of a code and context derived from the Waking Consciousness of an early, perhaps long-forgotten date, and may be read—though with difficulty—as referring to light-world themes. In its lower strata, however, the messages and codes are of the instincts, the archetypes, the gods: vacuum, phatic, emotive, vocative, or imperative announcements of their existence—requiring to be recognized. And their language is of both-and, neither-nor: like the image of God set up for the brothers by Cusanus, regarding all ways at once.

Figure 57, from a sketch by Picasso, made four years before his "Guernica," for the cover of the first issue of an elegant surrealist review entitled *Minotaure,* provides an interesting supplement to the icon of Cusanus's thought. The moon, the moon-bull, and the dead and risen god, whether as the mild and loving Christ or as this savage mixed monster of the abyss, are of an order of symbolization the "meanings" of which cannot be reduced to light-world, even "dream-world" terms. The knife here is of the form of a leaf and Picasso has arranged beside his sketch three leaves of the same form. The death-life oxymoron is suggested. In Figure 58, from his etching called *Minotauromachy* (1935), the same monster appears from the watery abyss, shading his eyes from the light, in polar contrast to the figure of the sage at the left (Nietzsche's "Socratic Man"), climbing aloft to escape the reality of the Dionysian terror, while the Graces Three with their dove (the bird of Venus-Aphrodite) calmly regard the apparition: the youngest of them, innocent Thalia, holding in one hand the flowers of life-abundance and in the other the light of consciousness, which are here the foci of the composition, equidistant from the eye of the sage and left eye of the bull. The sword of the overcome matador is pointed not at the bull but at the eviscerated horse, and the matador is

Figure 57. Adapted from Pablo Picasso: *Minotaur;* 1933

revealed as a woman. Clearly the "Guernica" (1937) is a reorganization of the same mythological motifs, recognized as implicit in a monstrous act of war and rendered as a moment equally of rapture and of pain (terror-joy), with the figure in flames at the right marvelously falling and rising at once, both from and toward the window at the upper right, which, like the end of *Finnegans Wake,* opens to the void.

"O sweet fire!" sang the Spanish mystic Diego de Estella (1524–1578). "The flames of Thy holy love in Thy most sacred passion mount on high. Thy torments and afflictions are the wood

Figure 58. Adapted from Pablo Picasso: *Minotauromachy*; 1935

wherewith this holy fire burns." [78] And from John of the Cross (1524–1591): "This flame of love is the spirit of its Spouse— the Holy Spirit. And this flame the soul feels within it as a fire which burns within it and sends out flame. . . . In this flame the acts of the will are united and rise upward, being carried away and absorbed in the flame of the Holy Spirit." [79]

"The bull is a bull and the horse is a horse," Picasso is reported to have said. "These are animals, massacred animals. That's all, so far as I am concerned." [80] Which is obviously untrue: horses are not of papier-mâché, nor do bulls have an eye in the middle of the forehead. Such deliberate prevarication is justified, however, by the fact that mythic symbols point beyond the reach of "meaning," and even in the sphere of meaning have many "meanings." To define and fix authoritatively any consciously conceivable set of final "meanings" would be to kill them—which is, of course, what happens in dogmatic and historicizing theology, as in both didactic and pornographic art. Symbols of the mythological order, like life, which they unfold from dark to light, are there, "thus come" from beyond "meaning," on all levels at once.

Accordingly, as James Joyce's title, *Ulysses,* refers us from the Waking level of the action of his novel to the mythic, so Picasso's title "Guernica," from the mythic order of his imagery to the Waking of historical event. Such double-talk, uniting history and geography (*land náma*) and the archetypes of the psyche, is of the essence of creative art-as-myth; the prime function of the Muses being to serve as the channel of communication (U) between the spheres of daylight knowledge (A) and the seat of life (M): in Figure 13, between the earthly order below of silent Thalia, and that aloft of Apollo and the Graces: the Lord of Light (consciousness) and the Goddess of Life (creative energy) in her triadic manifestation as future, present, and past: "Anna was, Livia is, Plurabelle's to be." [81]

In art, in myth, in rites, we enter the sphere of dream awake. And as the imagery of dream will be on one level local, personal, and historic, but at bottom rooted in the instincts, so also myth and symbolic art. The message of an effective living myth is delivered to the sphere of bliss of the deep unconscious, where it touches, wakes, and summons energies; so that symbols operating on that level are energy-releasing and -channeling stimuli. That is their function—their "meaning"—on the level of Deep Sleep: while on the level of Waking Consciousness the same symbols are inspirational, informative, initiatory, rendering a sense of illumination with respect to the instincts touched, i.e., the order subliminal of nature—inward and outward nature—of which the instincts touched are the life.

The question arises as to whether in the human species any of the codes of communication on this pre- or unconscious level are inherited. Among the animals from whose midst our species arose, patterns of controlled behavior comparable to ritual forms appear spontaneously on occasions of social excitation: most notably in the highly stylized courtship exchanges of certain species of bird. And these extensions of action beyond the strictly necessary have been frequently compared to the rites of mankind, not only because of their formality, but also because of their function, which is, in a word, to engage the individual in a superindividual event, conducive to the well-being not of himself but of the race. On all such ceremonious occasions, the cries, attitudes, and movements elicit reciprocal responses from those to whom they are addressed; and these, in counterplay, conduce to the unfoldment of a kind of ritual ensemble, not invented either by the creatures performing it or by any choreographer, but grounded in the species and brought forth by all members everywhere in exactly the same way. The most elaborate of these festivals appear among the species with the best eyes; for the various displays are signals to be seen, depending for effect on correlations between the sending apparatus and a receiving organ—what is technically termed an "instinct crossing" structure. The sign stimuli work automatically as energy-releasing and -directing agents; so that the interlacing sequences, though apparently of the individuals, are actually unwilled, like the procesess of a dream. The performing bees, birds, fish, or quadrupeds are moved spontaneously from centers of memory antecedent to their own lives. Through each, the species speaks. And since in human traditional rites also spontaneous collective responses to formalized displays occur, the earliest creators of the myths and rites of primitive mankind may not have been individuals at all, but the genes of the species. And since in human traditional rites also a certain psychological readiness to respond to certain specific sign stimuli is to be remarked—particularly among primitives—the earliest individual creators of myths and rites must not have been merely freely inventive fantasists, but inward-gazing, inward-listening seers (shamans), responding to some inner voice or movement of the species.

However, already in the animal kingdom, on the higher levels, and particularly among apes, instances have been observed of individual wit and invention, as well as of individual cases (as it were) of fetish-worship. In *Primitive Mythology* I have quoted to this point from Dr. Wolfgang Köhler's *The Mentality of Apes,* where he tells of an adult female chimpanzee named Tschengo who became so attached to a round stone that had been polished by the sea that, as Köhler states, "on no pretext could you get the stone away, and in the evening the animal took it with it to its room and its nest." I have also quoted his description of the spinning game and dance invented by Tschengo and another ape named Chica,[82] where the occasion was mere disinterested play. of no use to the species, no "survival value" whatsoever, but only delight, which might be escalated to rapture: the field, that is to say, of creative art.

At the opening of *Primitive Mythology* I have discussed the old problem of nature and nurture in relation to the forms of myth and rite; and throughout the subsequent chapters of our survey, not only in the Primitive, but also in the Oriental and Occidental volumes, evidence enough has appeared to warrant the statement now that there are indeed universal mythological themes, which in the various provinces have appeared in local transformations appropriate to the differing local scenes; that, furthermore, the ultimate source and references of such enduring themes cannot have been the changing outward environments of geography, history, and belief, but only some enduring inward realities of the species; and finally that, since man, in contrast to the beasts, is endowed with a brain and nervous system not as stereotyped as theirs but greatly open to imprint and to learning, the signals to which the race responds do not remain unchanged throughout the centuries, but are transformed through experience. Basically, the *responses* remain associated with what James Joyce termed "the grave and constant" in human suffering and joy; but the *stimuli* through which such responses have been released have greatly altered in the course of human events. So also have the "meanings" attached to them.

The large human brain, with its capacity for unforeseen experience and unprecedented thought, and the long human infancy, which is longer far than that of any other species, have endowed our race with a capacity for learning that greatly exceeds that of any other creature, and with a danger thereby of disorientation. One of the chief concerns of the ritual lore of primitive and developed human groups, therefore, has always been that of guiding the child to the adult state. The infantile response system of dependency must be transformed to responsibility, and specifically in terms of the requirements of the local social order. The son has to become father, and the daughter, mother, passing from the sphere of childhood, which is everywhere essentially the same, to that of the variously offered social roles, which radically differ according to the modes of human life. The instincts have to be governed and matured in the interests both of the group and of the individual, and traditionally it has been the prime function of mythology to serve this social-psychological end. The individual is adapted to his group and the group to its environment, with a sense thereby of gratitude for the miracle of life. And that I would call the function of *the Mythology of the Village Compound:* the training of the instincts and inculcation of sentiments.

But there is the other function, beyond that: of *the Mythology of the Forest, the Quest, the Individual:* the SILENCE. And there is in Thomas Mann's *Magic Mountain* a charming scene in which the sense of the silence comes through. It is the picnic scene of the last chapter of the epic, where that manly old colonial Dutchman, a retired coffee-planter, Mynheer Pieter Peeperkorn (who had arrived late in the story, together with the much younger Frau Chauchat, when she had returned to the Mountain Palace after a sojourn in the flatland), led an expedition of his friends, one blissful day in May, to enjoy together a picturesque cascade in the valley of the Fluela. I shall leave it to my reader to discover for himself in the novel, if he has not already done so, Mann's affectionate treatment of this sturdy, tragicomic personality, with his way of talking, flourishing his large broad hands with their pointed nails, leading on, it always seemed, to some revelatory climax, which, however, no one ever quite caught. His was a conversation of expectancy, of sentences not completed. And when he chose for his picnic site a spot directly by the waterfall, where the roar of nature's wonder drowned completely all conversation, so that Settembrini and Naphta, that pair of verbal prodigies, were silenced absolutely to nonentity, it was a high moment when he himself stood up, delivering to his company an address of which not a single word could be heard.

On arriving at the romantic spot—Frau Chauchat and five gentlemen—their ears were saluted with the maximum of sound. The tumbling water, foaming white, sent sprays over the rocks, and the visitors moved close in toward the roaring, enveloped in its mist, exchanging glances, headshakes, and gestures of amaze. Their lips formed soundless phrases of admiration and marvel. Then Hans, Settembrini, and the fifth gentleman, a Russian, Anton Karlovitch Ferge by name, began climbing a series of narrow steps up the side of the chute to a bridge that spanned the water just where it arched to pour downward; and, while crossing, they paused midway, to lean on the rail and wave to the party below, then, continuing, climbed laboriously down on the other side of the stream to rejoin their friends. A journey without goal, a circle, for the pleasure merely of itself!

And when they had settled to their picnic, suddenly the old Dutchman, Peeperkorn, began to speak. Extraordinary man!

It was impossible for him to hear his own voice, [declares our author] still more for the others to catch a syllable of what he let transpire without its in the least transpiring. But with the winecup in his right hand, he raised his forefinger, stretching his left arm palm outwards toward the water. They saw his kingly features move in speech, the mouth form words, which were as soundless as though spoken into empty, etherless space. No one dreamed he would continue; with embarrassed smiles they watched his futile activity, thinking every moment it would cease. But he went on, with tense, compelling gesture, to harangue the clamour that swallowed his words; directing upon this or that one of the company by turns the gaze of his pale little weary eyes, spanned wide beneath the lifted folds of his brow; and whoever felt himself addressed was constrained to nod back again, wide-eyed, open-mouthed, hand to ear, as though any sort of effort to hear could better the utterly hopeless situation. He even stood up! There, in his crumpled ulster, that reached nearly to his heels, the collar turned up; bare-headed, cup in hand, the high brow creased with folds like some heathen idol's in a shrine, and crowned by the aureole of white hair like flickering flames; there he stood by the rocks and spoke, holding the circle of thumb and forefinger, with the lancelike others above it, before his face, and sealing his mute and incomprehensible toast with that compelling sign of precision. Such words as they were accustomed to hearing from him, they could read on his lips or divine from his gestures: "Settled" and "Absolutely!" —but that was all. They saw his head sink sideways, the broken bitterness of the lips, they saw the Man of Sorrows in his guise. But then quite suddenly flashed the dimple, the sybaritic roguishness, the garment snatched up dancewise, the ritual impropriety of the heathen priest. He lifted his beaker, waved it half-circle before the assembled guests, and drank it out in three gulps, so that it stood bottom upwards. Then he handed it with outstretched arm to his Malay servant, who received it with an obeisance, and gave the sign to break up the feast.[83]

Once again, the words of Wittgenstein:

Proposition 6.44 "It is not *how* things are in the world that is mystical, but *that* it exists."

Proposition 6.522 "There are, indeed, things that cannot be put into words. They *make themselves manifest*. They are what is mystical."

And finally, Proposition 6.4311 "If we take eternity to mean not infinite temporal duration but timelessness, then eternal life belongs to those who live in the present." [84]

"C'est la personnalité qui conte," the old master sculptor Antoine Bourdelle used to say to the students in his Paris studio; and in the guiding of their work: *"L'art fait ressortir les grandes lignes de la nature."* The imagery of art, that is to say, as of myth and religious ritual, is presentational, beyond "meaning"; hence, of many possible "meanings" simultaneously (many dogmas), on both dream and waking levels, and with effects, as well, in the unconscious. "During the course of the spiritual adventure inward," Heinrich Zimmer remarks in a comment on the syllable AUM, "the emphasis shifts from the outer world to the inner, and finally from the manifest to the unmanifest, and there is a prodigious increase in the powers gained; nevertheless, the inferior, as well as

superior, states remain as constituents of the whole. . . . Each quarter is on an equal footing, somehow, with the others." [85] So too in every mythic symbol: it touches and unites in the actuality of a person the whole range of his living present: the ultimate mystery of his being and of the spectacle of his world, the order of his instincts, of his dreams, and of his thought. And this today in a way of especial immediacy.

For even in the sphere of Waking Consciousness, the fixed and the set fast, there is nothing now that endures. The known myths cannot endure. The known God cannot endure. Whereas formerly, for generations, life so held to established norms that the lifetime of a deity could be reckoned in millenniums, today all norms are in flux, so that the individual is thrown, willy-nilly, back upon himself, into the inward sphere of his own becoming, his forest adventurous without way or path, to come through his own integrity in experience to his own intelligible Castle of the Grail—integrity and courage, in experience, in love, in loyalty, and in act. And to this end the guiding myths can no longer be of any ethnic norms. No sooner learned, these are outdated, out of place, washed away. There are today no horizons, no mythogenetic zones. Or rather, the mythogenetic zone is the individual heart. Individualism and spontaneous pluralism—the free association of men and women of like spirit, under protection of a secular, rational state with no pretensions to divinity—are in the modern world the only honest possibilities: each the creative center of authority for himself, in Cusanus's circle without circumference whose center is everywhere, and where each is the focus of God's gaze.

The norms of myth, understood in the way rather of the "elementary ideas" (*mārga*) than of the "ethnic" (*deśi*), recognized, as in the Domitilla Ceiling (Figure 1), through an intelligent "making use" not of one mythology only but of all of the dead and set-fast symbologies of the past, will enable the individual to anticipate and activate in himself the centers of his own creative imagination, out of which his own myth and life-building "Yes because" may then unfold. But in the end, as in the case of Parzival, the guide within will be his own noble heart alone, and the guide without, the image of beauty, the radiance of divinity, that wakes in his heart *amor:* the deepest, inmost seed of his nature, consubstantial with the process of the All, "thus come." And in this life-creative adventure the criterion of achievement will be, as in every one of the tales here reviewed, the courage to let go the past, with its truths, its goals, its dogmas of "meaning," and its gifts: to die to the world and to come to birth from within.

REFERENCE NOTES
INDEX

REFERENCE NOTES

PART ONE: THE ANCIENT VINE
CHAPTER 1: EXPERIENCE AND AUTHORITY

1. T. S. Eliot, *The Waste Land* (1922), lines 331–58, from *Collected Poems 1909–1962* by T. S. Eliot, p. 66, copyright, 1936, by Harcourt, Brace & World, Inc.; copyright, ©, 1963, 1964, by T. S. Eliot. Reprinted by permission of the publisher.
2. *Taittirīya Upaniṣad* 2.9.
3. *Hamlet* III. ii.
4. Compare *The Masks of God: Primitive Mythology*, pp. 32–33 and 461–72.
5. *The Masks of God: Occidental Mythology*, pp. 255–69.
6. Matthew 4:19; Mark 1:17; Luke 5:10.
7. *Revue d'assyriologie et d'archéologie orientale*, 1905, p. 57; Robert Eisler, *Orpheus the Fisher* (London: J. M. Watkins, 1921), Plate X.
8. John 3:5.
9. *The Masks of God: Oriental Mythology*, pp. 328–31.
10. A. Wünsche, *Aus Israels Lehrhallen*, II, 53, as cited by Eisler, op. cit., Plate XLVII.
11. *Occidental Mythology*, pp. 90–92.
12. Edith Porada, *Corpus of Ancient Near Eastern Seals in North American Collections*, The Bollingen Series XIV (New York: Pantheon Books, 1948), Vol. I, Plate CXVII, 773 E.
13. Genesis 3:19–20.
14. *Primitive Mythology*, p. 101; *Occidental Mythology*, pp. 183–85.
15. I Corinthians 15:36, 42.
16. Romans 7:24.
17. *Occidental Mythology*, Figures 3 and 4.
18. *Occidental Mythology*, Figure 24.
19. *Occidental Mythology*, pp. 9ff.
20. *Oriental Mythology*, Figure 20.
21. The only surviving manuscript of the Abbess Herrad von Landsberg's *Hortulus deliciarum* was destroyed at the siege of Strasbourg, 1870. Many of its illustrations had already been reproduced, however, in a monograph by Christian M. Englehardt, *Herrad von Landsberg und ihr Werk Hortus deliciarum; ein Beytrag zur Geschichte. . . . des Mittelalters* (Stuttgart and Tübingen, 1818).
22. Mark 10:45; Matthew 20:28; also Timothy 2:5–6.
23. For references: Irenaeus, *Adversus haereses* 5.1; Origen, *Exhort. ad martyr.* 12; Gregory of Nyssa, *The Great Catechism*, 26; Augustine, *de Trinitate*, 13. 12–14; Gregory the Great, *Moralia in Librum Job* 33.7. For discussions, see Adolph Harnack, *History of Dogma*, translated from third German edition, of 1900, by Neil Buchanan (New York: Dover Publications, 1961), Vol. II, p. 367 and Note 1; Vol. III, p. 307; also W. Adams Brown, article "Expia-

tion and Atonement (Christian),"
in James Hastings (ed.), *Encyclopaedia of Religion and Ethics*
(New York: Charles Scribner's
Sons, 1928), Vol. V, pp. 642–
643.

24. I have been following Harnack,
op. cit., Vol. VI, pp. 59–67, with
large abridgments and with attention, also, to Brown, op. cit., pp.
643–45. The quotations from Anselm are from *Cur deus homo?* II,
6–11 and 18–19, as translated in
Harnack, op. cit., pp. 64–67.

25. Harnack, op. cit., Vol. VI, pp. 78–
80.

26. Etienne Gilson, *History of Christian Philosophy in the Middle
Ages* (New York: Random House,
1955).

27. Ibid., p. 163.

28. Hans Leisegang, "The Mystery of
the Serpent," in Joseph Campbell
(ed.), *The Mysteries,* Papers from
the Eranos Yearbooks, Vol. 2,
Bollingen Series XXX.2 (New
York: Pantheon Books, 1955),
pp. 257–58.

29. Orphic Hymn XXXIV. Translation by Thomas Taylor, *The Mystical Hymns of Orpheus* (Chiswick: C. Whittingham, 1824), pp.
77–79, as cited in Leisegang, op.
cit., p. 255.

30. The sketch is adapted from Eisler,
op. cit., Plate XXXI.

31. Eisler, op. cit., Plate XXXI.

32. John A. T. Robinson, *Honest to
God* (London: SCM Press, Ltd.,
1963), p. 74.

33. John 15:5.

34. *Oriental Mythology,* pp. 251–52;
Occidental Mythology, pp. 242–
271.

35. Aristotle, *Metaphysics,* Book XII,
Chapter 8, paragraph 1074a.

36. Benedict Spinoza, *Tractatus Theologico-Politicus,* Chapter XX, third
paragraph from end.

37. I am following the exposition of
Bruno's thought in J. L. McIntyre's article, "Bruno," in James

Hastings (ed.), op. cit., Vol. II,
pp. 878–81.

38. Leo Frobenius, *Monumenta Terrarum,* Erlebte Erdteile, Vol. VII
(Frankfurt am Main: Frankfurter
Societäts-Druckerei, 1929), pp.
178–80 and passim.

39. Einstein's key paper, "Zur Electrodynamik bewegter Körper,"
appeared in *Annalen der Physik,*
4. Folge, Bd. 17 (1905), pp. 891–
921; English translation by W.
Perrett and G. B. Jeffery in H. A.
Lorentz, A. Einstein, H. Minkowski, and A. Weyl, *The Principle
of Relativity* (London: Methuen
and Co., 1923). My interpretation
and reference to Newton follow
Sir James Jeans, *The Mysterious
Universe* (New York: The Macmillan Co., 1930), p. 95.

40. Sir Isaac Newton, *Philosophia
naturalis principia mathematica*
(1687), Definition VIII, Scholium
IV; translation by Andrew Motte,
Newton's Principia (New York:
Daniel Adee, 1848), p. 79.

41. *Liber XXIV philosophorum,* Proposition II; Clemens Bäumker, "Das
pseudo-hermetische 'Buch der
vierundzwanzig Meister' (Liber
XXIV philosophorum)," in *Abhandlungen aus dem Gebiete der
Philosophie und ihrer Geschichte.
Festgabe zum 70 Geburtstag
Georg Freiherrn von Hertling*
(Freiburg im Breisgau: Herdersche Verlagshandlung, 1913), p.
31.

42. Oswald Spengler, *Der Untergang
des Abendlandes* (Munich: C. H.
Beck, 1923), English translation
by Charles Francis Atkinson, *The
Decline of the West* (London:
Allen and Unwin, Ltd.; New
York: Alfred A. Knopf, 1926,
1928), Vol. II, p. 227 (German),
p. 189 (English).

43. *Occidental Mythology,* pp. 398ff.

44. Sir Arthur Keith, in the anonymously edited volume, *Living
Philosophies* (New York: Simon

and Schuster, 1931), pp. 142–43.

45. Arthur Schopenhauer, *Über die Grundlage der Moral* (1840), in *Sämtliche Werke* (Stuttgart: Cotta'sche Bibliothek der Weltlitteratur, no date), Vol. 7, pp, 133ff.

46. Arthur Schopenhauer, *Die Welt als Wille und Vorstellung*, Book II, Section 26; *Sämtliche Werke*, Vol. 2, p. 176.

47. Ibid., Book III, Section 45; Vol. 3, pp. 65ff.

48. Ibid., Book II, Section 26; Vol. 2, pp. 175ff.

49. Ibid., Book II, Section 20; Vol. 2, p. 151.

50. Arthur Schopenhauer, *Aphorismen zur Lebensweisheit*, Chapter VI; *Sämtliche Werke*, Vol. 9, p. 260.

51. Schopenhauer, *Die Welt als Wille und Vorstellung*, Book II, section 28 (Vol. 2, pp. 202ff.) and Book IV, section 55 (Vol. 3, pp. 140ff.).

52. *Oriental Mythology*, pp. 243, 317.

53. James Joyce, *A Portrait of the Artist as a Young Man* (London: Jonathan Cape, Ltd. 1916), p. 242.

54. Albert Pauphilet (ed.), *La Queste del Saint Graal* (Paris: Champion, 1949), p. 26, lines 15–19. For an excellent interpretation of this work, see Frederick W. Locke, *The Quest for the Holy Grail* (Stanford: Stanford University Press, 1960).

55. Gottfried von Strassburg, *Tristan und Isold*, 45–66. References are to the lines of the Middle High German text as edited by Friedrich Ranke (Berlin-Charlottenburg: Weidmannsche Verlagsbuchhandlung, 4th ed., 1959).

56. Joyce, op. cit., p. 281.

57. Passages quoted by Peter Gast, "Einführung in den Gedankenkreis von *Also sprach Zarathustra*," in Friedrich Nietzsche, *Werke* (Leipzig: Alfred Kröner Verlag, 1919), Vol. VI, pp. 496–97.

Chapter 2: THE WORLD TRANSFORMED

1. Gottfried, op. cit., 111–18.

2. Ibid., 119–30; 235–40.

3. *Occidental Mythology*, pp. 490–504.

4. Gottfried, op. cit., 16689–16729.

5. Ibid., 16963–17138, abridged.

6. Ibid., 16807–16820 and 16902–16908.

7. Ibid., 15166–15168.

8. Henry Adams, *Mont-Saint-Michel and Chartres*, (Boston and New York: Houghton Mifflin Co., 1904), p. 198.

9. Ibid., pp. 94–95.

10. *Oriental Mythology*, pp. 49–98.

11. *Primitive Mythology*, pp. 404–18.

12. A. R. Radcliffe-Brown, *The Andaman Islanders* (2nd printing: London: Cambridge University Press, 1933), pp. 233–34; cited in *Primitive Mythology*, pp. 33–34.

13. Dante Alighieri, *Paradiso XXXIII.* 1–21. Translation by Charles Eliot Norton, *The Divine Comedy* of Dante Alighieri (Boston and New York: Houghton Mifflin Co., 1902).

14. Spengler, op. cit., Knopf edition, Vol. II, pp. 288–90, Atkinson translation, greatly abridged.

15. Joyce, op. cit., pp. 135ff.

16. Ibid., pp. 142–43.

17. Gottfried, op. cit., 8112–8131.

18. For the full text, *Primitive Mythology*, pp. 351–52.

19. *Occidental Mythology*, pp. 36–40

20. Quotations from the translation of the letters in Henry Osborn Taylor, *The Mediaeval Mind* (Cambridge, Mass.: Harvard University Press, fourth edition, 1925), Vol. II, pp. 30–41. Abelard's *Historia calamitatum* together with the letters will be found in Jacques Paul Migne (ed. and publisher), *Patrologiae cursus completus*, Latin Series (Paris:

1844–1855), vol. clxxviii, columns 113–326.

21. H. O. Taylor, op. cit., p. 41.

22. Ibid., Vol. II, pp. 42, 49. Migne, *Patr. Lat.*, clxxviii, 187, 212.

23. *Occidental Mythology*, pp. 495ff.

24. *Occidental Mythology*, p. 448.

25. Sarahapāda, *Dohakoṣa* 34; cited in Shashibhusan Dasgupta, *Obscure Religious Cults as Background of Bengali Literature* (Calcutta: University of Calcutta Press, 946), p. 95.

26. *Oriental Mythology*, pp. 343–64.

27. *Occidental Mythology*, pp. 440–453.

28. *Occidental Mythology*, pp. 456–473.

29. Philip K. Hitti, *History of the Arabs* (New York: The Macmillan Co., 1951), p. 562. This derivation is clearly preferable to that more usually proposed, from an assumed Vulgar Latin *tropare*, supposed to have meant "to invent." (See, for instance, *Webster's New International Dictionary of the English Language* [Springfield, Mass.: G and C. Merriam Company, 2nd edition, 1937.]) W. Meyer-Lubke's *Romanisches Etymologisches Wörterbuch* (Heidelberg: Carl Winter's Universitäts-buchhandlung, 1924), p. 683, item 8992, derives the word from the Latin *turbare*, "to agitate, disturb, throw into confusion" (cf. English "turbulent"); however, with a discussion conceding considerable doubt.

30. Hitti, op. cit., p. 600.

31. H. A. R. Gibb, article "Literature," in Sir Thomas Arnold and Alfred Guillaume (eds.), *The Legacy of Islam* (Oxford: The Clarendon Press, 1931), pp. 189–190.

32. Hitti, op. cit., p. 562.

33. *Oriental Mythology*, pp. 489–90.

34. *Occidental Mythology*, pp. 449–450.

35. *Oriental Mythology*, pp. 358–61.

36. Dante, *Divina Commedia*, last line.

37. Idries Shah, *The Sufis* (New York: Doubleday and Company, 1964), pp. 322–23.

38. Friedrich Nietzsche, *Also sprach Zarathustra*, 1.3: "Von den Hinterweltlern"; *Werke*, Vol. VI, p. 43.

39. Hakuin's "Song of Meditation," translation from Daisetz Teitaro Suzuki, *Manual of Zen Buddhism* (London: Rider and Company, 1935), pp. 151–52.

40. Nietzsche, *Also sprach Zarathustra*, 1.6: "Vom bleichen Verbrecher"; *Werke*, Vol. VI, p. 53.

41. José Ortega y Gasset, *History as a System*, translated from the Spanish by Helen Weyh (New York: W. W. Norton and Company, 1962), pp. 175–76.

42. Gottfried, op. cit., 17101–17135.

43. Joyce, op. cit., pp. 223 and 242–243.

44. Dante Alighieri, *La Vita Nuova* II, translation by Charles Eliot Norton (Boston and New York: Houghton Mifflin Company, 1867), p. 2.

45. Ibid., XLIII (Norton translation, pp. 89–90).

46. Joyce, op. cit., pp. 194–96.

47. A. T. Hatto, in the introduction to his translation of Gottfried von Strassburg, *Tristan* (Baltimore: Penguin Books, 1960), p. 24.

48. Aug. : Closs, in the introduction to his edition of the Middle High German text of Gottfried von Strassburg, *Tristan and Isolt* (Oxford: Basil Blackwell, 1958), pp. xiv–xv.

49. See Eugène Vinaver, "The Love Potion in the Primitive Tristan Romance," in *Medieval Studies in Memory of Gertrude Schoepperle Loomis* (Paris: Librairie Honoré Champion; New York: Columbia University Press, 1927), p. 79.

50. Eilhart von Oberge, *Tristrant und Isolde*, F. Lichtenstein (ed.), *Eilhart von Oberge*, Quellen und

Forschungen zur Sprach- und Kulturgeschichte der germanischen Völker, 19 (Strassburg: K. J. Trübner, 1877), lines 2288–2300.

51. *Briefwechsel zwischen Wagner und Liszt* (Leipzig: Breitkopf und Härtel, 1900), Vol. II, p. 46.

52. Richard Wagner, *Mein Leben* (Munich: F. Bruckmann, 1911), p. 605.

53. Schopenhauer, *Über die Grundlage der Moral,* Section 16; *Sämtliche Werke,* Vol. 7, pp. 233–234.

54. Wagner, op. cit., p. 626.

55. *Occidental Mythology,* pp. 297, 466–67, 469.

56. *Occidental Mythology,* pp. 440, 447–52, 509.

57. Schopenhauer, *Über die Grundlage der Moral,* Section 22; Vol. 7, pp. 290–94, abridged.

58. Wagner, op. cit., p. 604.

59. Plato, *Republic* 7

60. *Oriental Mythology,* pp. 13f., 177, 184, 237, 254, 335–36.

61. Percy Bysshe Shelley, *"Adonais,"* LII, 462–63.

62. Goethe, *Faust* II. 1, lines 4702–4727.

63. Schopenhauer, *Die Welt als Wille und Vorstellung,* II. 21; *Sämtliche Werke,* Vol. 2, pp. 152–53.

64. Ibid., 22; pp. 154–55.

65. Schopenhauer, *Über die Grundlage der Moral,* Section 22; Vol. 7, p. 293.

66. Gottfried, op. cit., 4862–4895, slightly abridged.

67. Schopenhauer, *Die Welt als Wille und Vorstellung* II. 27, last paragraph; Vol. 2, p. 201.

68. Ibid., III. 34; Vol. 3, p. 17.

69. Joyce, op. cit., p. 242.

70. Schopenhauer, *Die Welt als Wille und Vorstellung,* III. 36; Vol. 3, pp. 24–25.

71. Seneca, *De tranquilitate animi* 15. 16.

72. John Dryden, *Absalom and Achitophel,* lines 163–64.

73. Schopenhauer, *Die Welt als Wille und Vorstellung* III. 36; Vol. 3, p. 31.

74. Richard Wagner, *Tristan und Isolde,* Act. I, conclusion.

75. Gottfried, op. cit., 11708–11870, greatly abridged.

CHAPTER 3: THE WORD BEHIND WORDS

1. José Ortega y Gasset, *Man and Crisis,* translated from the Spanish by Mildred Adams (New York: W. W. Norton and Company, 1958, 1962), p. 113.

2. T. S. Eliot, "The Hollow Men," Part III, last four lines.

3. Ibid., Part I, p. 79: from *Collected Poems 1909–1962,* pp. 80–81, copyright, 1936, by Harcourt, Brace & World, Inc.; copyright, ©, 1963, 1964, by T. S. Eliot. Reprinted by permission of the publisher.

4. Nietzsche, *Also Sprach Zarathustra,* I. 11: "Vom neuen Götzen," *Werke,* Vol. VI, pp. 69–72, abridged.

5. Benjamin Lee Whorf, "Science and Linguistics," *The Technology Review,* Vol. XLII, No. 6 (April 1940); "Linguistics as an Exact Science," Ibid., XLIII, No. 2 (December 1940); "Languages and Logic," ibid., XLIII, No. 6 (April 1941); "The Relation of Habitual Thought and Behavior to Language," *Language, Culture and Personality* (Menasha, Wis., 1941), pp. 75–93; "An American Indian Model of the Universe," International Journal of American Languages, Vol. 16, No. 2 (April 1950).

6. *Taittirīya Upaniṣad* 2.4.

7. *Muṇḍaka Upaniṣad* 2.2.1.

8. Tomás de Villanueva, *Opera* (Salamanco, 1761–64; Bibl., No.

1073), Vol. IV, p. 388; translation from E. Allison Peers, *Studies of the Spanish Mystics* (London: S.P.C.K., 1960), Vol. II, p. 68.

9. Eliot, *The Waste Land*, note to line 411, from F. H. Bradley, *Appearance and Reality* (London: Swan Sonnenschein and Co., 1893), p. 346.

10. *Primitive Mythology*, pp. 386–87.

11. *Occidental Mythology*, pp. 9–17.

12. Eliot, "The Hollow Men," Part V: from *Collected Poems 1909–1962*, pp. 81–82, copyright, 1936, by Harcourt, Brace & World, Inc.; copyright, ©, 1963, 1964, by T. S. Eliot. Reprinted by permission of the publisher.

13. Ernest Robert Curtius, *European Literature and the Latin Middle Ages*, translation by Willard R. Trask, Bollingen Series XXXVI (New York: Pantheon Books, 1953), pp. 12 and 591.

14. *Occidental Mythology*, pp. 255–269.

15. Leisegang, loc. cit., pp. 194–260.

16. Gafurius, *De harmonia musicorum instrumentorum* (Milan, 1518), fol. 93v. I am here following Edgar Wind, *Pagan Mysteries in the Renaissance* (New Haven: Yale University Press, 1958), p. 46, note 5.

17. H. E. D. Blakiston, "Greco-Egyptian Religion," article in James Hastings (ed.), op cit., Vol. VI, p. 377, column 2.

18. Macrobius, *Saturnalia*, Liber I, Caput XX, describing the three-headed animal of the sun-god Serapis in the temple of Alexandria.

19. Gafurius, op. cit., Ch. 92; as cited by Jean Seznec, *The Survival of the Pagan Gods*, Bollingen Series XXXVIII (New York: Pantheon Books, 1953; Harper Torchbook, 1961), pp. 140–41.

20. *Occidental Mythology*, pp. 325–330.

21. *Primitive Mythology*, pp. 412–15.

22. Hesiod, *Theogony* 50–67.

23. Roger Sherman Loomis, *Celtic Myth and Arthurian Romance* (New York: Columbia University Press, 1927), Chapter V, "Curoi, Gwri, and Gawain," and Chapter XVI, "The Grail Heroes."

24. Eleanor Hull, *Early Christian Ireland* (London: David Nutt; Dublin: M. H. Gill & Son, 1905), pp. 253–54.

25. *Occidental Mythology*, pp. 466–467.

26. Harnack, op. cit., Vol. V, Chapter VI, note 1.

27. Dante, *Inferno* I. 1–3, Norton translation.

28. Ibid., 10–18, Norton translation.

29. Ibid., 31–51, Norton translation.

30. Ibid., 113.

31. Ibid., II. 7.

32. Ibid., II, 127–42.

33. *Primitive Mythology*, pp. 173–76.

34. Curtius, op. cit., pp. 18–19.

35. *Occidental Mythology*, pp. 481–482.

36. *The Sutton Hoo Ship-Burial: A Provisional Guide* (London: The British Museum, 5th impression, 1956), p. 62.

37. Bede, *Historia Ecclesiastica Gentis Anglorum*, Book IV, Chapter XXIV. Migne, op. cit., xlv, 212–213. Translation from Vida D. Scudder, Everyman Library, 1910.

38. *Oriental Mythology*, pp. 444–45.

39. *Oriental Mythology*, pp. 447–55.

40. *Oriental Mythology*, pp. 464–5, 466.

41. The dating of *Beowulf* is still uncertain, ranging from c. 700 to the end of the eighth century. See C. L. Wrenn, "Sutton Hoo and Beowulf," in Lewis E. Nicholson (ed.), *An Anthology of Beowulf Criticism* (Notre Dame, Ind.: University of Notre Dame Press, 1963), pp. 325–29.

42. Cf. C. L. Wrenn, *Beowulf* (Boston: D. C. Heath and Co.; London: George G. Harrap and Co., 1953), pp. 32–37.

43. Ibid., pp. 64–65.

44. George K. Anderson, *The Literature of the Anglo-Saxons* (Princeton: Princeton University Press, 1949), p. 230.

45. Translation by Anderson, op. cit., p. 231; from Bede, *Historia* V. 13.

46. *Oriental Mythology*, pp. 228 and 241.

47. Miguel Asín y Palacios, *La Escatologia musulmana en la Divina Comedia* (Madrid: Imprenta de Estanislao Maestre, 1919; 2nd ed., Madrid-Granada: Escuelas de Estudios Árabes, 1943), p. 166.

48. Wrenn, *Beowulf*, p. 83.

49. W. W. Lawrence, *Beowulf and the Epic Tradition* (Cambridge, Mass.: Harvard University Press, 1928), p. 4.

50. Ibid., pp. 7–8.

51. Spengler, op. cit., Vol. II, pp. 101–102; English edition, Vol. II, p. 87.

52. *Beowulf*, lines 700–702, as cited by Marie Padgett Hamilton, "The Religious Principle in *Beowulf*," in Nicholson (ed.), op. cit., p. 112.

53. Werner Speiser, *The Art of China* (New York: Crown Publishers, 1960), p. 36.

54. *Oriental Mythology*, pp. 471–72.

55. *Beowulf*, 2419–2420.

56. *Poetic Edda, Völuspó* 20.

57. Grimm, Tale Number 50; cf. *Grimms Fairy Tales* (New York: Pantheon Books, 1944), pp. 237–241.

58. Grimm, Tale Number 14; cf. ibid., pp. 83–86.

59. Translation largely following Clarence Griffin Child, *Beowulf and the Finnesburgh Fragment* (Boston, New York, Chicago: Houghton Mifflin Company, 1904).

60. This point is made by Levin L. Schücking, "The Ideal of Kingship in Beowulf," in Nicholson (ed.), op. cit., p. 37.

61. *Beowulf* in this connection has been studied in detail and at length by F. Panzer, *Beowulf*, Studien zur germanischen Sagengeschichte I (München, 1910). See also, Johannes Bolte and Georg Polívka, *Ammerkungen zu den Kinder- und Hausmärchen der Brüder Grimm* (Leipzig: Dieterich'sche Verlagsbuchhandlung, 1915), Vol. II, pp. 300–16.

62. *Primitive Mythology*, pp. 339–47.

63. *Occidental Mythology*, pp. 162–177.

64. Ibid., pp. 34ff. and 64–72.

65. Ibid., pp. 291–96.

66. O. G. S. Crawford, *The Eye Goddess* (New York: The Macmillan Company, no date).

67. *Occidental Mythology*, pp. 34–41, 62–72.

68. T. G. E. Powell, *The Celts* (New York: Frederick A. Praeger, 1958), pp. 146–47.

69. Marcel Probé and Jean Roubier, *The Art of Roman Gaul* (Toronto: University of Toronto Press, 1961), Plate 8.

70. *Primitive Mythology*, pp. 183–84.

71. Ibid., pp. 441–51.

72. Ibid., pp. 432–34.

73. Gottfried, op. cit., 13513–13536.

74. Asín, op. cit.

75. *Analecta Bollandiana*, as cited by The Duke of Alba in his Introduction to the English translation, op. cit., pp. IX–X.

76. *Inferno* XV.

77. Asín, op. cit., English translation by Harold Sunderland, *Islam and the Divine Comedy* (London: John Murray, 1926), pp. 253–54.

78. *Opus majus* (Edit. Jebe, 1733), p. 246 (Asín's note).

79. *Opera omnia* III.3, *De Anima* 166 (Asín's note).

80. *Blanquerna* II. 105, 134, 158–160 (Asín's note).

81. Asín, op. cit., translation by Sunderland, op. cit., pp. 256–58.

82. R. A. Nicholson, "Mysticism," in Arnold and Guillaume (eds.), op. cit., pp. 227–28.

83. Asín, op. cit., English edition, pp. 239–44 abridged.

84. *Oriental Mythology*, pp. 321–27; *Occidental Mythology*, pp. 402–407.
85. *Occidental Mythology*, pp. 442–443.
86. *Oriental Mythology*, pp. 338–67; 378; 481–96.
87. Jacobus de Voragine, *The Golden Legend* (London, New York: Longmans, Green, 1941); for the Coptic version, E. A. W. Budge, *Baralâm and Yĕwâsĕf* (London: Cambridge University Press, 1923); for a discussion, J. Jacobs, *Barlaam and Josaphat* (London: David Nutt, 1896).
88. La Fontaine, *Avertissement* to Vol. 2 of his *Fables*.
89. Joseph Campbell (ed.), *The Portable Arabian Nights* (New York: The Viking Press, 1952), pp. 19–20.
90. *Ibid.*, pp. 14–15.
91. *Oriental Mythology*, p. 327; citing Hermann Goetz, "Imperial Rome and the Genesis of Classical Indian Art," in *East and West*, New Series, Vol. 10, Nos. 3–4, Sept.–Dec., 1959, p. 264.
92. Spengler, op. cit., Vol. II, p. 92 (English edition, Vol. II, p. 78).
93. *Ibid.*, Vol. II, p. 62 (English edition, Vol. II, p. 55).
94. For instance, the fine series of articles on "Fate" in Hastings (ed.), op. cit., Vol. V, pp. 771–796.
95. *Koran* 27:48.
96. Quoted from Gilson, op. cit., p. 399, where it is cited without precise reference.
97. Ibn Rushd (Averroes), *Kitāb faṣl al-maqāl wa tagrīr mā bayn ash-sharī 'a wal-ḥikma min al-ittisāl* ("The Book of the Decision of the Discourse, and a Determination of What There Is of Connection between Religion and Philosophy"), Book II, 7:1–18 and 8.11; translation from George F. Hourani, *Averroes: On the Harmony of Religion and Philosophy*, E. J.

W. Gibb Memorial Series, No. 21 (London: Luzac and Co., 1961), pp. 50–51.
98. Averroes, op. cit., 15. 8–15; Hourani, p. 59.
99. Miguel Asín y Palacios, "El Averroísmo Teológico de Santo Tomás de Aquino," in *Homenáje á D. Francisco Codera* (Zaragoza: Mariano Escar, 1904), pp. 307–308.
100. *Quest. disp. de Veritate*, q. XIV, *De fide* a. 10.
101. Jacob Guttmann, *Das Verhaltnis des Thomas von Aquino zum Judenthum und zür jüdischen Litteratur* (Göttingen: Vandenhoeck and Ruprecht, 1891); *Die Scholastik des dreizehnten Jahrhunderts in ihren Beziehangen zum Judenthum und zür jüdischen Litteratur* (Breslau: M. & H. Marcus, 1902).
102. Asín y Palacios, "El Averroísmo," etc., pp. 318–19.
103. St. Thomas Aquinas, *Summa Theologica* I. 14. Art. 8.
104. *Paradiso* X. 136–138.
105. *Inferno* IV. 131–143.
106. *Inferno* XXVIII. 22–45.
107. *Oriental Mythology*, pp. 234–38.
108. *Oriental Mythology*, pp. 276–79.
109. *Oriental Mythology*, p. 294.
110. E.g., Richard Garbe, *Die Sâṃkhya-Philosophie* (Leipzig: H. Haessel, 2nd ed., 1917), Chapter III, "Uber den Zusammenhang der Sâṃkhya-Lehre mit der griechischen Philosophie."
111. *Occidental Mythology*, p. 412.
112. Matthew 19:21 (Mark 10:21) and Matthew 8:22 (Luke 9:60).
113. A. Guillaumont, H. –Ch. Puech, G. Quispel, W. Till and Yassah 'Abd al Masēh, *The Gospel According to Thomas* (Leiden: E. J. Brill; New York: Harper and Brothers, 1959), 91: 30–32; p. 31.
114. *Occidental Mythology*, pp. 403–404.

115. *Oriental Mythology*, pp. 13–14, 254–55, 264–66.
116. *Oriental Mythology*, pp. 447–55.
117. Augustine, *Confessions*, Book III, Chapter 6.
118. Galatians 5:16. Cited by Augustine, *The City of God*, Book XIII, Chapter 13.
119. Augustine, *The City of God*, Book XIV, Chapter 5.
120. Ibid., Book XIII, Chapter 13.
121. Tertullian, *Apologeticus* 7 (Migne, op. cit., i, 506); Aristides, *Apology* 17.2; Justin Martyr, *Apologiae* I. 5, 15, 18, 27, and II. 12 (J. P. Migne, *Patrologiae Cursus Completus, Series Graeca* (Paris: 1857–1860), vi. 335–36, 349–52, 355–56, 369–75, 463–66); Minucius Felix, *Octavian*, 9.6. (Migne, *Patr. Lat.*, iii. 262); the Younger Pliny, *Epist.*, X. 96. See Max Pulver, op. cit., pp. 292–95.
122. Galatians 3:13.
123. I Corinthians 11:20–22.
124. Revelation, 2:19–25.
125. Ibid., 2:14.
126. Jude 4 and 12.
127. Tertullian, *De Jejunis* 17 (Migne, *Patr. Lat.*, ii. 977).
128. "The Gospel According to Thomas," 84:34–85:6; Guillaumont, etc., op. cit., p. 15.
129. Ibid., 87:26–88:1; p. 23.
130. *Occidental Mythology*, pp. 388–394.
131. Epiphanius, *Panarion* 1. 37.5 (272A ff), as quoted by Leisegang, op. cit., p. 231.
132. Leisegang, op. cit., p. 231.
133. John 3:15.
134. Numbers 21:5–9.
135. *Occidental Mythology*, pp. 101–102.
136. II Kings 18:4.
137. Genesis 3:15.
138. *Occidental Mythology*, pp. 362–375.
139. Hippolytus *Elenchos* V. 17. 1–2 and 8, as cited by Leisegang, op. cit., p. 230.
140. *Occidental Mythology*, p. 468.
141. "The Gospel According to Thomas," 99: 16–18 (op. cit., p. 57) and 80: 24–81: 2 (p. 3); cited in *Occidental Mythology*, pp. 367–68.
142. *Oriental Mythology*, pp. 300–303.
143. *Oriental Mythology*, p. 496.
144. *Oriental Mythology*, p. 304.
145. Epiphanius, *Panarion* 26.4.1; from Max Pulver, "Vom Spielraum gnostischer Mysterienpraxis," *Eranos-Jahrbuch* 1944 (Zurich: Rhein-Verlag, 1945), pp. 289–92.
146. Henry Adams, *The Education of Henry Adams* (New York: Random House, The Modern Library, 1931), p. 498.
147. *Occidental Mythology*, pp. 496–500.
148. Innocentii III, *Epist.* Book vii, No. 75, in Migne, *Patr. Lat.*, ccxv, 355–357; as cited by J. Bass Mullinger, article "Albigenses," in Hastings (ed.), op. cit., Vol. I, p. 280.
149. *Occidental Mythology* pp. 386, 464, 492.
150. Rene Fülöp-Miller, *Der Heilige Teufel: Rasputin und die Frauen* (Leipzig: Grethlein and Co., 1927). Translation by F. S. Flint and D. F. Tait, *Rasputin, the Holy Devil* (London and New York: The Viking Press, 1928).
151. Leisegang, op. cit., p. 244.
152. Following J. A. MacCulloch, article "Relics," in Hastings (ed.), op. cit., Vol. X, p. 655.
153. Charles Schmidt, *Histoire et doctrine des Cathares ou Albigeois* (Paris: J. Cherbulier, 1849), Vol. I, p. 31.
154. See Heinrich Zimmer and Joseph Campbell, *The Art of Indian Asia*, Bollingen Series XXXIX (New York: Pantheon Books, 1955), Vol. II, Plates 114–436, passim.

155. *Oriental Mythology*, p. 359 and note.
156. *Oriental Mythology*, p. 361, citing H. H. Wilson, "Essays on the Religion of the Hindus," *Selected Works* (London: Trubner and Company, 1861), Vol. I, p. 263.
157. John Rutherford, *The Troubadours* (London: Smith, Elder, and Company, 1861), Vol. I, p. 195.
158. Zimmer and Campbell, op. cit., Vol. II, Plates 336–43.
159. *Oriental Mythology*, pp. 343–358.
160. Arthur Avalon (Sir John Woodroffe), *The Principles of Tantra* (Madras: Ganesh and Co., 1914; 2nd edition, 1952), pp. lxxi-lxxii.
161. *Oriental Mythology*, pp. 325–27; *Occidental Mythology*, pp. 389–394.

PART TWO: THE WASTE LAND
Chapter 4: THE LOVE-DEATH

1. Denis de Rougemont, *Love in the Western World* (New York: Pantheon Books, 1940, revised and augmented, 1956), passim.
2. See Barbara Smythe (trans.), *Trobador Poets* (London: Chatto and Windus, 1929), p. 152.
3. Malory, *Le Morte Darthur*, Book XI, Chapter IX to Book XII, Chapter IV. Malory's source for these books of his compilation was the early thirteenth-century "Vulgate Tristan" in the enlarged version represented by three manuscripts at the British Museum, viz. Add. 5474, Royal 20 D ii, and Egerton 989. See H. Oskar Sommer, *Le Morte Darthur* (London: David Nutt, 1891), Vol. III, pp. 280ff.
4. Rutherford, op. cit., pp. 124–25.
5. *Occidental Mythology*, pp. 464–466.
6. Matthew 23:39.
7. Erik Routley, *The Man for Others* (New York: Oxford University Press, 1964), p. 99.
8. Guiraut de Borneilh, *Tam cum los oills el cor. . . .* Rutherford, op. cit., pp. 34–35. The rhyme scheme of this poem is as follows: a b c c b b a d d a / b c c b b a e e a.
9. *Oriental Mythology*, pp. 482, 489–90.
10. Bernart de Ventadorn, *Joie d'aimer*, verses I, IV and VII; from Joseph Anglade, *Anthologie des Troubadours* (Paris: E. de Boccard, no date), pp. 39–41. The rhyme scheme of the poem is a b b a c d d c / c a a c b d d b / a b b a c d d c . . . etc.
11. H. O. Taylor, op. cit., Vol. II, p. 57.
12. Carl von Kraus (ed.), *Die Gedichte Walthers von der Vogelweide* (Berlin: Walter de Gruyter & Co., 1962), pp. 52–53, lines 39:11–40:18. The rhyme scheme is as follows: a b c, a b c, d—tandaradei—d.
13. Ibid., p. 165; lines 257:10–13 (*Swer giht daz minne sünde sî . . .*)
14. Ibid., p. 68; lines 48:38–39.
15. H. O. Taylor, op. cit., p. 58.
16. Kraus, op. cit., p. 115; lines 81.31–82:2 (*Diu minne ist weder man noch wêp . . .*). The rhyme scheme here is: a a, b b, c d, c.
17. *Cambridge Medieval History* (Cambridge: Cambridge University Press; New York: The Macmillan Company, 1936), Vol. VI, p. 50.

18. Kraus, op. cit., p. 11, lines 9: 16–27 (*Ich sach mit mînen ougen*).

19. Translation from Dom Gaspar Lefebure O.S.B., *Daily Missal* (Saint Paul, Minn.: E. M. Lohmann Co., 1934), pp. 123–24.

20. Anglade, op. cit., pp. 13–14: the rhyme scheme is a, a, a, refrain; b, b, b, refrain etc. I am giving but three of the five stanzas.

21. Geoffrey of Monmouth, *Historia Regum Britanniae*, Book XI, Chapter 2.

22. Wace, *Roman de Brut*, final passage.

23. Layamon, *Brut*, G. L. Brook and R. F. Leslie (eds.) (London: Oxford University Press for the Early English Text Society, 1963), last lines.

24. *Occidental Mythology*, pp. 9–20.

25. Gottfried, op. cit., 704–758, and 847–853, abridged.

26. Gottfried Weber, *Gottfried's von Strassburg Tristan und die Krise des hochmittelalterlichen Weltbildes um 1200* (Stuttgart: J. B. Metzlersche Verlagsbuchhandlung, 1953).

27. Ibid., Vol. I, p. 34.

28. *Webster's New International Dictionary of the English Language* (Springfield, Mass.: G. and C. Merriam Company, second edition, 1937), p. 1747.

29. *Muṇḍaka Upaniṣad* 2.2.1.

30. *Kena Upaniṣad* 1.3.

31. *Mu-mon*, "The Gateless Gate," 48; in Paul Reps, *Zen Flesh, Zen Bones* (Garden City, New York: Doubleday and Company, Anchor Books, 1961), p. 127.

32. *Oriental Mythology*, p. 303, citing *Aṣṭasāhasrikā Prajñāpāramitā* 1.

33. Nicholas Cusanus, *Apologia doctae ignorantiae*, as quoted in Gilson, op. cit., pp. 538 and 536.

34. Thomas Aquinas, *Summa contra Gentiles* I. v.

35. Werner Heisenberg, *Physics and Philosophy* (New York: Harper Torchbooks, 1958, 1962), p. 49.

36. Nietzsche, *Also sprach Zarathustra*, "Von der Selbstüberwindung"; *Werke*, Vol. VI, p. 167.

37. Gottfried, op. cit., 847–853.

38. Ibid., 915–982.

39. Ibid., 1159–1171.

40. Ibid., 1219–1330; 1337–1362, abridged.

41. Ibid., 1373–1750.

42. Ibid., 3379–3384.

43. Schopenhauer, *Transcendente Spekulation über die anscheinende Absichtlichkeit im Schicksale des einzelnen*, *Werke*, Vol. 8, pp. 208–209.

44. Ibid., pp. 210–11.

45. *Muṇḍaka Upaniṣad* 2.2.5.

46. Wordsworth, "Lines Composed a Few Miles above Tintern Abbey, on Revisiting the Banks of the Wye During a Tour. July 13, 1789," lines 88–102.

47. Schopenhauer, *Transcendente Spekulation. . .*, *Werke*, Vol. 8, p. 211.

48. James Joyce, *Ulysses*, (Paris: Shakespeare and Company, 1922, eighth printing, 1926), p. 204; (New York: Random House, The Modern Library, 1934), p. 210.

49. Ibid., Paris edition, pp. 376–377; Random House, p. 388.

50. Jean-Paul Sartre, *L'Existentialisme est un humanisme* (Paris: Les Éditions Nagel, 1946); translation from Walter Kaufmann, *Existentialism from Dostoyevsky to Sartre* (New York: Meridian Books, 1956), pp. 294–95.

51. *The Journals of Kierkegaard*, translated by Alexander Dru (New York: Harper Torchbooks, 1959), pp. 189 and 203.

52. *Twelfth Night*, I. v. 331–332.

53. Schopenhauer, *Transcendente Spekulation. . .*, *Werke*, Vol. 8, pp. 212–13.

54. Standish H. O'Grady, *Silva Ga-delica* (London: Williams and Norgate, 1892), Vol. II, pp. xiii and 311ff.
55. Gottfried, op. cit., 3721–3739.
56. *Occidental Mythology*, pp. 62–68.
57. *Primitive Mythology*, pp. 151–225.
58. *Primitive Mythology*, pp. 170–171.
59. *Oriental Mythology*, pp. 9–10.
60. *Oriental Mythology*, pp. 168–71.
61. *Primitive Mythology*, pp. 405–413.
62. Gertrude Schoepperle, *Tristan and Isolt* (London: David Nutt; Frankfurt a. M.: Joseph Baer and Co., 1913), p. 227.
63. H. Zimmer, "Zur Namenfor-schung, in den altfranzösischen Arthurepen," *Zeitschrift für fran-zösischer Sprache und Literatur*, Vol. XIII (1891), pp. 58ff.
64. *Primitive Mythology*, pp. 183–190.
65. Sir James G. Frazer, *The Golden Bough*, one-volume edition (New York: The Macmillan Co., 1922), p. 470. See *Primitive Mythology*, p. 184.
66. *Primitive Mythology*, pp. 432–434.
67. *Occidental Mythology*, pp. 36–41.
68. Béroul, *Le Roman de Tristan*, edited by Ernest Muret (Paris: Honoré Champion, 1962), line 1334.
69. *Oriental Mythology*, pp. 190–97.
70. *Nihongi* 19.34; as cited in *Oriental Mythology*, p. 480.
71. Oswald Spengler, *Jahre der Ent-scheidung* (Munich: C. H. Beck, 1933), pp. 36–37.
72. *Occidental Mythology*, pp. 291–334, and pp. 393–94.
73. *Occidental Mythology*, pp. 456–490.
74. José Ortega y Gasset, *Medita-tions on Quixote*, translated from the Spanish by Evelyn Rugg and Diego Marín, copyright, ©, 1961 by W. W. Norton and Company, p. 51.
75. Ibid., p. 136.
76. Ibid., p. 138.
77. Ibid., pp. 138–39.
78. Ibid., p. 164.
79. Ibid., pp. 164–65.
80. G. V. Anrep (trans. and ed.), I. P. Pavlov, *Conditioned Reflexes, an investigation of the physiolog-ical activity of the Cerebral Cor-tex* (London: Oxford University Press, 1927).
81. John B. Watson, *Psychology from the Standpoint of a Be-haviorist* (Philadelphia and Lon-don: J. B. Lippincott Company, 1919, 1924).
82. *Ibid.*, pp. 9–10. The italics are Dr. Watson's.
83. *Satapatha Brāhmaṇa* 10.5.2.13 and 16, as cited by Ananda K. Coomaraswamy, *Hinduism and Buddhism* (New York: Philo-sophical Library, no date), p. 7.
84. *Oriental Mythology*, pp. 52–53.
85. *Bhagavad Gītā* 2:22.
86. James Joyce, *Finnegans Wake* (New York: The Viking Press, 1939), p. 455.
87. *Oriental Mythology*, pp. 23–25.
88. Gottfried, op. cit., 6931–6947, abridged.
89. Ibid., 7051–7059.
90. Ibid., 6732–6752.
91. Ibid., 6611–6616.
92. Ibid., 6594–6598.
93. Ibid. 7165–7195.
94. Nietzsche, "Die fröhliche Wis-senschaft," §87, *Werke*, Vol. 5, p. 120.
95. Gottfried, op. cit., 7275–7299, abridged.
96. *Homeri Hymni* 7.
97. Gottfried, op. cit., 7507–7523.
98. Ibid., 7772–7821, abridged.
99. Ibid., 7835–7859, abridged.
100. *Occidental Mythology*, p. 25.

101. W. B. Yeats, *Irish Folk and Fairy Tales* (New York: The Modern Library, no date), Introduction, p. ix.

102. Gottfried, op. cit., 7911–7924.

103. Ibid., 8002–8018.

104. August Closs, *Tristan und Isolt: A Poem by Gottfried von Strassburg* (Oxford: Basil Blackwell, 1958), pp. xlix–1.

105. Gottfried, op. cit., 8085–8089; 8112–8131.

106. Ibid., 8253–8262.

107. Joseph Anglade, op. cit., p. 30: "Amor de lonh," Stanza IV.

108. Gottfried, op. cit., 8608–8613.

109. Gottfried, op. cit., 8263–8284.

110. Cf. C. G. Jung, *The Archetypes of the Collective Unconscious,* translated by R. F. C. Hull, Bollingen Series XX, Vol. 9, 1 (New York: Pantheon Books, 1959), pp. 25ff. and index under "anima."

111. Gottfried, op. cit., 8505–8509.

112. According to the Middle English translation of Thomas, *Sir Tristram,* Strophe 95.

113. Gottfried, op. cit., 8902–8924.

114. Ibid., 8925–11366.

115. *Occidental Mythology,* pp. 54–55.

116. Gottfried, op. cit., 10885–10898, abridged, and 10992–11005.

117. Curtius, op. cit., pp. 48ff.

118. Gottfried, op. cit., 11556–11580.

119. A. T. Hatto, translator: Gottfried von Strassburg, *Tristan* (Baltimore: Penguin Books, 1960), p. 28.

120. Closs, op. cit., p. lii.

121. Dante, *Inferno* V. 118–120 and 127–138; Charles Eliot Norton translation, slightly retouched.

122. Weber, op. cit., p. 87.

123. Ibid., pp. 89–90.

124. Gottfried, op. cit., 11964–11972.

125. Ibid., 11978–12041, abridged.

126. Ibid., 11435–11444.

127. Ibid., 12106–12133, abridged.

128. Ibid., 12157–12182.

129. Ibid., 12463–12502.

130. Bernard of Clairvaux, *Sermones in Cantica Canticorum* LXXIX. 1. Translation from Terence L. Connolly, S.J., *Saint Bernard on the Love of God* (New York: Spiritual Book Associates, 1937), pp. 224–25.

131. W. O. E. Oesterley and Theodore H. Robinson, *An Introduction to the Books of the Old Testament* (New York: Meridian Books, 1958), p. 217.

132. Bernard, op. cit., IX.2 (Connolly, op. cit., pp. 82–83). The italicized phrases are from, respectively, Psalm 99:4, and the Song of Songs 1:2.

133. *Oriental Mythology,* pp. 352–58.

134. See *Primitive Mythology,* pp. 38–49, 62, 75–76.

135. N. Tinbergen, *The Study of Instinct* (Oxford: The Clarendon Press, 1951), p. 45. The picture is reproduced by kind permission of The Clarendon Press.

136. Bernard, op. cit., XXXII. 2 (Connolly, op. cit., p. 141). The italicized phrase is from Revelation 14:4.

137. William Blake, *The Marriage of Heaven and Hell,* "A Memorable Fancy," and "Proverbs of Hell" (c. 1793).

138. Gottfried, op. cit., 12217–12231 and 12279–12304.

139. Ibid., 12237–12244.

140. Ibid., 12527–12674, abridged.

141. Ibid., 17770–17803, abridged.

142. Ibid., 17858–17906, abridged.

143. Ibid., 16587–16620, abridged.

144. Ibid., 18335–18344.

145. I am here following Weber, op. cit., Vol. I, p. 306.

146. Thomas, *Le Roman de Tristan,* Joseph Bédier (ed.) (Paris: Société des Anciens Textes Français, 1902), Vol. I, p. 317, line 1011.

CHAPTER 5: PHOENIX FIRE

1. Joyce, *Finnegans Wake*, p. 123.
2. Ibid., p. 232.
3. Ibid., p. 383.
4. Ibid., p. 105.
5. Ibid., p. 107.
6. Ibid., p. 32.
7. Genesis 1:27.
8. Joyce, *Finnegans Wake*, p. 261.
9. Ibid., pp. 14, 61, 70, 73, 274, 310.
10. See Joseph Campbell and Henry Morton Robinson, *A Skeleton Key to Finnegans Wake* (New York: Harcourt, Brace and Co., 1944), p. 46.
11. Translation from Lefebure, op. cit., p. 831: "Holy Saturday: Blessing of the Paschal Candle."
12. Joyce, *Finnegans Wake*, p. 536.
13. Ibid., p. 24.
14. Joyce, *Ulysses*, Paris ed., p. 478; Random House ed., pp. 496–97.
15. "The Gospel According to Thomas" 94:24–28; Guillaumont, etc. op. cit., p. 43.
16. *Bhagavad Gītā* 10.8, 20, 36.
17. Joyce, *Ulysses*, Paris ed., pp. 480–481; Random House ed., p. 499.
18. *Rosarium philosophorum. Secunda pars alchimiae de lapide philosophico vero modo praeparando. . . . cum figuris rei perfectionem ostendentibus* (Frankfurt a. M.: 1550), pp. 219, 230, and 274.
My text and pictures are from C. G. Jung, "The Psychology of the Transference," in the volume entitled *The Practice of Psychotherapy*, Bollingen Series XX, Vol. 16 (New York: Pantheon Books, second edition, 1966), pp. 212–13 and 288, note 15.
19. Matthew 7:6.
20. Luke 8:10.
21. Muhammed ibn Umail at-Tamini (known to the Latin world as "Senior"), "The Book of the Silvery Water and Starry Earth" (translated into Latin as *De chemia*), edited by E. Stapleton and M. Hidayat Husain, *Memoirs of the Asiatic Society of Bengal*, Vol. XII. I am quoting from Marie-Louise von Franz, *Aurora Consurgens*, Bollingen Series LXXVII (New York: Pantheon Books, 1966), p. 45, notes 8 and 9.
22. Theobald de Hoghelande, "Liber de alchemiae difficultatibus," in *Theatrum chemicum, praecipuos selectorum auctorum tractatus. . . . continens* (Ursel: 1602), Vol. I, p. 155; as quoted by C. G. Jung, *The Practice of Psychotherapy*, p. 288, note 15.
23. Heinrich Conrad Khunrath, *Von hyleanischen, das ist, primaterialischen catholischen, oder allgemeinen natürlichen Chaos* (Magdeburg: 1597), p. 21; as cited by Jung, *The Practice of Psychotherapy*, p. 288, note 15.
24. Giordano Bruno, *The Expulsion of the Triumphant Beast*, translated and introduced by Arthur D. Imerti (New Brunswick, N.J.: Rutgers University Press, 1964), pp. 235 and 236.
25. Dedicatory epistle to *De l'infinito universo et mondi*, in *Opera italiane* (ed. Giovanni Gentile and Vincenzo Spampanato; Bari: Gius. Laterza & Figli, 1925–1927), Vol. I, p. 156; cited by Arthur D. Imerti, in op. cit., p. 20.
26. Vincenzo Spampanato, *Documenti della vita di Giordano Bruno* (Florence: Leo S. Olschki, 1933), "Documenti romani," XXX. 202, as cited by Imerti, op. cit., p. 64.
27. The Prankquean episode, *Finnegans Wake*, pp. 21–23. Cf. William York Tindall, *James Joyce, His Way of Interpreting the Modern World* (New York: Charles Scribner's Sons, 1950), p. 86.
28. T. S. Eliot, "Burnt Norton" Part

II, in *Four Quartets;* from *Collected Poems 1909–1962* by T. S. Eliot, p. 177, copyright, 1936, by Harcourt, Brace & World, Inc.; copyright, ©, 1963, 1964, by T. S. Eliot. Reprinted by permission of the publisher.

29. C. G. Jung, *Psychology and Alchemy,* translated by R. F. C. Hull, Bollingen Series XX, Vol. 12 (New York: Pantheon Books, 1953), pp. 231–32.

30. Ibid., pp. 235–37, from *Abtala Jurain. Hyle und Coahyl.* Translated from Ethiopian into Latin and from Latin into German by Johannes Elias Müller (Hamburg: 1732), Chapters VIII and IX. The text actually is not old, or of the origin claimed.

31. Ibid., p. 237; quoting Hoghelande, "Liber de alchemiae difficultatibus," in *Theatrum chemicum, praecipuos selectorum auctorum tractatus. . . . continens* (Ursellis, 1602), Vol. I, pp. 121–215.

32. Ibid., p. 239 and note 8.

33. Ibid., Figure 2; from *Mutus liber in quo tamen tota Philosophia hermetica, figuris hieroglyphicis dipingitur. . . .* (La Rochelle: 1677), p. 11, detail.

34. Khunrath, op. cit., p. 59 and passim.

35. Jung, *Psychology and Alchemy,* pp. 299–300.

36. Ibid., pp. 225–28.

37. Kalid, "Liber secretorum alchemiae," in *Artis Auriferae quam chemiam vocant* (Basel: 1593), Vol. I, p. 340; as quoted by Jung, *The Practice of Psychotherapy,* p. 248, note 4.

38. Gottfried, op. cit., 15801–15893, abridged.

39. Jung, *Psychology and Alchemy,* p. 313, quoting Michael Maier, *Symbola aurea mensae duodecim nationum* (Frankfurt: 1617), p. 380.

40. Joyce, *Ulysses,* Paris ed., p. 49; Random House ed., pp. 50–51.

41. Joyce, *Ulysses,* Paris ed., pp. 44–

46; Random House ed., pp. 45–47.

42. Eliot, *The Waste Land,* lines 71–76; op. cit., p. 68.

43. Joyce, *Ulysses,* Paris ed., p. 561; Random House ed., p. 548.

44. Eliot, *The Waste Land,* lines 42–48; from *Collected Poems 1909–1962* by T. S. Eliot, p. 54, copyright, 1936, by Harcourt, Brace & World, Inc.; copyright, ©, 1963, 1964, by T. S. Eliot. Reprinted by permission of the publisher.

45. Ibid., lines 49–56.

46. Ibid., note to lines 46ff., op. cit., pp. 70–71.

47. London. British Museum. MS. Additional 5245. "Cabala mineralis," Rabbi Simeon ben Cantara. Alchemical figures in water-colours with explanations in Latin and English; fol. 2. From Jung, *Psychology and Alchemy,* p. 227.

48. Ovid, *Metamorphoses* I. 5–9; translation by Frank Justus Miller, The Loeb Classical Library (London: William Heinemann Ltd.; Cambridge, Mass.: Harvard University Press, 1916).

49. Ibid., 21–31.

50. Lynn Thorndike, *A History of Magic and Experimental Science* (New York: Columbia University Press, 1923–1958), Vol. I, p. 82, citing Pliny, *Historia naturalis* XX. 33.

51. Ibid., Vol. I, p. 580, citing the Greek edition of his text by Robert Étienne Stephanus (1567), Vol. I, pp. 156–57; and the more recent edition by Theodore Puschmann, *Alexander von Tralles, Original text und Ubersetzung nebst einer einleitenden Abhandlung* (Vienna, 1878–79), Vol. I, pp. 567–73.

52. Ibid., Vol. I, p. 769.

53. Opening paragraph of Joyce, *A Portrait of the Artist as a Young Man.*

54. Joyce, *Ulysses,* Paris ed., p. 376; Random House ed., 388.

55. *Oriental Mythology,* p. 426, citing

Tao Têh Ching 15. Translation from Arthur Waley, *The Way and Its Power* (New York: The Macmillan Co.; London: George Allen and Unwin, Ltd. 1949), p. 160.

56. *Primitive Mythology*, pp. 413–18; quoting S. N. Kramer, *Sumerian Mythology* (*Memoirs of the American Philosophical Society*, Vol. XXI, 1944), pp. 90–95.

57. *Primitive Mythology*, pp. 406–18; *Oriental Mythology*, pp. 42–45.

58. *Oriental Mythology*, pp. 58–72.

59. *Oriental Mythology*, pp. 396–97; 403–406; 463–64.

60. *Oriental Mythology*, pp. 66–67 and pp. 190–97.

61. John 12:24–25.

62. Eliot, *The Waste Land*, lines 395–401; from *Collected Poems 1909–1962* by T. S. Eliot, p. 68, copyright, 1936, by Harcourt, Brace, & World, Inc.; copyright, ©, 1963, 1964, by T. S. Eliot. Reprinted by permission of the publisher.

63. Eliot's reference, *Bṛhadāraṇyaka Upaniṣad* 5.1. is incorrect; the passage is in 5.2.

64. Eliot, *The Waste Land*, lines 400–422; op. cit., pp. 68–69.

65. Joyce, *Ulysses*, Paris ed., p. 37; Random House ed., p. 38.

66. Ibid., Paris ed., pp. 593 and 600; Random House ed., pp. 618 and 625.

67. Ibid., Paris ed., pp. 21, 38, 189, 374 and 638; Random House ed., pp. 22, 39, 194, 385, and 666.

68. Jung, *The Practice of Psychotherapy*, p. 241.

69. *Rosarium*, p. 241; Jung, *The Practice of Psychotherapy*, p. 242.

70. *Rosarium*, p. 239; Jung, *The Practice of Psychotherapy*, p. 244.

71. Jung, *The Practice of Psychotherapy*, p. 244.

72. *Bṛhadāraṇyaka Upaniṣad* 4.3. 19–21, abridged.

73. The translation is by R. F. C. Hull, in Jung, *The Practice of Psychotherapy*, p. 247.

74. Jung, *The Practice of Psychotherapy*, p. 247.

75. A classic of Arabic origin, put into Latin between the eleventh and twelfth centuries. [C. G. Jung's note, ibid., p. 274, n. 7.]

76. Julius Ruska (ed.), *Turba philosophorum* (Berlin: J. Springer, 1931), p. 247; as cited by C. G. Jung, *Mysterium Coniunctionis: An Inquiry into the Separation and Synthesis of Psychic Opposites in Alchemy*, translated by R. F. C. Hull, Bollingen Series XX, Vol. 14 (New York: Pantheon Books, 1963), p. 21.

77. Jung, *The Practice of Psychotherapy*, pp. 268–69.

78. Ibid., pp. 273 and 282–83.

79. *Rosarium*, p. 277; cited in Jung, *The Practice of Psychotherapy*, p. 274.

80. Jung, *The Practice of Psychotherapy*, pp. 286–87.

81. Joyce, *Ulysses*, Paris ed., pp. 527–528; Random House ed., p. 549.

82. Ibid., Paris, ed., pp. 560–61; Random House ed., pp. 583–84.

83. From the translation by Emma Gurney Salter, Nicholas of Cusa, *The Vision of God* (New York: E. P. Dutton and Co., 1928; republished New York: Frederick Ungar, 1960), Chapters III and X, pp. 12–13 and 46.

Chapter 6: THE BALANCE

1. Myrrha Lot-Borodine, "Tristan et Lancelot," in *Medieval Studies in Memory of Gertrude Schoepperle Loomis* (Paris: Honoré Champion; New York: Columbia University Press, 1927), p. 23.

2. *Occidental Mythology*, pp. 471–473; also *Primitive Mythology*, pp. 432–34.

3. A. Glasheen, "Out of My Census," *The Analyst*, No. XVII (1959), p. 23; as cited by Clive Hunt, *Structure and Motif in Finnegans Wake* (Evanston, Ill.: Northwestern University Press, 1962), p. 81.

4. Schoepperle, op. cit., pp. 391–444; John Arnott MacCulloch, *Celtic Mythology*, The Mythology of All Races, Vol. III (Boston: Marshall Jones Company, 1918), pp. 175–78; Lady Gregory, *Gods and Fighting Men* (London: John Murray, 1904), p. 343–99; and, for the full text of one version of the story, Standish Hayes O'Grady (ed.), *The Pursuit after Diarmuid O'Duibhne, and Grainne, the Daughter of Cormac Mac Airt, King of Ireland in the Third Century*, Transactions of the Ossianic Society for the year 1855, Vol. III (Dublin: John O'Daly, 1857), pp. 40–211.

5. Roger S. Loomis (trans.), *The Romance of Tristan and Ysolt of Thomas of Britain* (New York: E. P. Dutton and Co., 1923), following H. Zimmer, op. cit., p. 103.

6. For this identification, see Jessie L. Weston, *From Ritual to Romance* (Cambridge: The University Press, 1920), pp. 130, 180, 185–88.

7. Thomas, *Tristan* 2120.

8. Elucidation 4–9; 12–13.

9. First Continuator.

10. *Primitive Mythology*, pp. 151–215.

11. For the variants and references, see C. Kerényi, *The Heroes of the Greeks* (New York: Grove Press, 1960), pp. 227–34, and notes.

12. Euripides, *Hippolytus* 527–532 and 561–562; translation from David Green, in David Green and Richmond Lattimore (eds.), *The Complete Greek Tragedies* (University of Chicago Press, 1959), Vol. III, pp. 185 and 186.

13. Joyce, *Finnegans Wake*, p. 92.

14. Ibid., p. 259.

15. Sigmund Freud, *Jehnseits des Lustprinzips* (1921); *Gesammelte Werke chronologisch geordnet* (London: Imago Publishing Co., 1940–1952), Bd. 13.

16. Thomas Mann, *Die Forderung des Tages: Reden und Aufsatze aus den Jahren 1925–1929* (Berlin: S. Fischer Verlag, 1930), p. 175.

17. Thomas Mann, "Tonio Kröger," translation by H. T. Lowe-Porter, in Thomas Mann, *Stories of Three Decades* (New York: Alfred A. Knopf, 1936), p. 132.

18. *Oriental Mythology*, pp. 13–34 and passim.

19. Joyce, *A Portrait of the Artist as a Young Man*, p. 281.

20. Thomas Mann, *Betrachtungen eines Unpolitischen* (Berlin: S. Fischer Verlag, 1922), pp. 560–561. The work has not been translated.

21. Ibid., p. 364.

22. Ibid., p. 202.

23. Ibid., p. 445–46.

24. Ibid., p. 227.

25. Mann, *Die Forderung des Tages*, pp. 191 and 193–94.

26. *The New York Times*, December 7, 1951; greatly abridged.

27. *Oriental Mythology*, Chapter 1 and passim.

28. Aldous Huxley, *Brave New World* (1932) (New York: Harper, 1946), motto page.

29. Mann, *Betrachtungen eines Unpolitischen*, p. 431.

30. Thomas Mann, *Bemühungen* (Berlin: S. Fischer Verlag, 1925), pp. 270–74.

31. Mann, *Betrachtungen eines Unpolitischen*, p. 60.

32. Ibid., pp. 60–62.

33. Thomas Mann, *Rede und Ant-*

wort (Berlin: S. Fischer Verlag, 1922), pp. 13–15.

34. Mann, *Betrachtungen eines Unpolitischen*, pp. 604–605 and 608. Another translation of this passage, in Joseph Warner Angell (ed.), *The Thomas Mann Reader* (New York: Alfred Knopf, Inc., 1950), pp. 493–94, 496.

35. Matthew 5:43–44.

36. Matthew 7:1.

37. *Oriental Mythology*, p. 503.

38. Philippians 2:6–8.

39. Galatians 2:20.

40. *Oriental Mythology*, pp. 282–83; 302–03; 319–20.

41. *Vajracchedika* 5.

42. *Madhyamika-śāstra* 15.8.

43. Friedrich Nietzsche, *Die Geburt der Tragödie*, in *Werke* (op. cit.), Vol. I, p. 19.

44. Ibid., pp. 19–25.

45. *Oriental Mythology*, pp. 13f., 177, 184, 237, 254, 335–36.

46. Joyce, *Ulysses*, Paris ed., p. 37; Random House ed., p. 38.

47. Ibid., Paris ed., p. 38; Random House ed., p. 39.

48. Immanuel Kant, *Prolegomena zu einer jeden künftigen Metaphysik, die als Wissenschaft wirdauftreten können*, paragraphs 57–58.

49. Johannes Scotus Erigena, *De divisione naturae*, Liber II, 28; in ed. Monasterii Guestphalorum (1838), pp. 152, 154; Migne, *Patr. Lat.*, cxxii, 594c, 596c.

50. Schopenhauer, *Transcendente Spekulation.* . . , *Werke*, Vol. 8, pp. 220–25.

51. *Chāndogya Upaniṣad* 6.9–16.

52. Joyce, *Ulysses*, Paris ed., pp. 660–61, 693, 735; Random House ed., pp. 688–89, 722, 768.

53. *Māṇḍūkya Upaniṣad*, complete.

54. *Oriental Mythology*, pp. 35–83.

55. Ibid., pp. 98–100.

56. *Primitive Mythology*, passim.

57. Joyce, *A Portrait of the Artist as a Young Man*, pp. 241–43.

58. Ibid., p. 233.

59. *Oriental Mythology*, pp. 15–21.

60. Schopenhauer, *Die Welt als Wille und Vorstellung* III. 34; *Werke*, Vol. 3, p. 18, citing Spinoza, *Ethics* V. prop. 31, schol.; also *ib* II. prop. 40, schol. 2, and V. prop. 25–28.

61. Robinson Jeffers, "Natural Music," in op. cit., p. 232.

62. *Oriental Mythology*, pp. 35–36; 45–47; 461, 478; also *Occidental Mythology*, p. 519.

63. Otto, op. cit., pp. 12–13.

64. Joyce, *A Portrait of the Artist as a Young Man*, pp. 232–33.

65. Schopenhauer, "Zur Rechtslehre und Politik," *Parerga und Paralipomena*, Par. 127; *Werke*, Vol. 10, p. 245.

66. Nietzsche, *Götzen-Dämmerung*. "Streifzüge eines Unzeitgemässen," 8–9; "Was ich den Alten verdanke," 5; *Werke*, Vol. VIII, pp. 122–24 and 173–74.

67. Schopenhauer, *Die Welt als Wille und Vorstellung* III, 52 (last paragraph); *Werke*, Vol. 3, pp. 119–20.

68. Thomas Mann, "Leiden und Grösse Richard Wagners," in *Leiden und Grösse der Meister* (Berlin: S. Fischer Verlag, 1935), pp. 99 and 95–97. Another translation, by H. T. Lowe-Porter, in Thomas Mann, *Essays of Three Decades* (New York: Knopf, 1947), pp. 311–12.

69. Ibid., p. 93. (*Essays* . . . , p. 309.)

70. Ibid., pp. 109–110. (*Essays* . . . , pp. 319–20.)

71. Ibid., p. 99.

72. Wolfgang Golther, *Richard Wagner an Mathilde Wesendonck* (Leipzig: Britkopf und Härtel, 1922), pp. 260–61.

73. Mann, *Leiden und Grösse der Meister*, pp. 136–37. (*Essays* . . . , p. 336.)

74. Ibid., p. 133. (*Essays* . . . , p. 334.)

75. Thomas Mann, *Joseph und seine Brüder*, I. *Die Geschichten*

Jaakobs (Berlin: S. Fischer Verlag, 1933), published in English as *Joseph and His Brothers*, translation by H. T. Lowe-Porter (New York: Alfred A. Knopf, 1936), see Chapter 2, Section 1: "Lunar Syntax".

76. Joseph Campbell, *The Hero with a Thousand Faces*, Bollingen Series XVII (New York: Pantheon Books, 1949).

77. Joyce, *Finnegans Wake*, p. 581.

78. Joyce, *A Portrait of the Artist as a Young Man*, pp. 40 and 48.

79. Jung, *The Archetypes of the Collective Unconscious*, pp. 13–15, abridged.

80. Ibid., pp. 12–13.

81. Joyce, *A Portrait of the Artist as a Young Man*, p. 277.

82. Joyce, *Ulysses*, Paris ed., p. 34; Random House ed., p. 35.

83. Nietzsche, *Götzen-Dämmerung*, Section 8, "Was den Deutschen abgeht," Paragraph 3; *Werke*, Vol. VIII, pp. 110–111.

84. Mann, *Betrachtungen eines Unpolitischen*, p. 395.

85. Nietzsche, *Die Geburt der Tragödie*, Paragraph 13; *Werke*, Vol. I, pp. 95–96.

86. Goethe, in "Geistes-Epochen," *Sämmtliche Werke* (1853), Vol. 3, pp. 327–330.

87. Thomas Mann, *Der Zauberberg*, (Berlin: S. Fischer Verlag, 1924), pp. 526–28, abridged; English transl. by H. T. Lowe-Porter, *The Magic Mountain* (New York: Knopf, 1927), pp. 510–11.

88. Ibid., pp. 537, 538; English, pp. 520, 522.

89. Ibid., p. 515; English, p. 499.

90. Isaiah 24:1–6.

91. *Oriental Mythology*, pp. 505–16.

92. Numbers 15:32–36.

93. Ralph Waldo Emerson, *Essays* (*First Series*), "Self-Reliance"; *Works* (Boston and New York: Houghton, Mifflin Company, 1883), Vol. II, pp. 51–52.

94. Johann Peter Eckermann, *Gespräche mit Goethe in den letzten Jahres seines Lebens, 1823–1832* (Berlin: Deutsches Verlagshaus Bong & Co., 1916), Vol. I, p. 251 (Feb. 13, 1829). Translation by Charles Francis Atkinson, in Oswald Spengler, *The Decline of the West*, Vol. I, p. 49, note 1.

95. *Primitive Mythology*, pp. 226–383.

96. *Primitive Mythology*, pp. 144–150; 404–18; *Oriental Mythology*, pp. 35–102; *Occidental Mythology*, pp. 6–7.

97. Hans Heinrich Schaeder, *Der Mensch in Orient und Okzident: Grundzüge einer eurasiatischen Geschichte* (Munich: R. Piper & Co., 1960), pp. 30–32.

98. *Oriental Mythology*, pp. 422–29.

99. Emerson, "History," in op. cit., p. 7.

100. Ortega y Gasset, *Man and Crisis*, translation by Mildred Adams, op. cit., pp. 98–99.

101. Wagner, *Mein Leben*, Vol. III, pp. 605–606.

102. Chrétien de Troyes, *Li Contesdel Graal*, lines 3507–3524; Alfons Hilka (ed.) (Halle: Max Niemeyer Verlag), p. 158.

103. Wolfram von Eschenbach, *Parzival* IX. 478:8–16. My references are to the lines of the Middle High German text, as edited by Karl Lachmann, *Wolfram von Eschenbach* (Berlin-Leipzig: Walter de Gruyter & Co., 6th ed., 1926).

104. Ibid., IX. 479:1–480:29, abr.

105. James Douglas Bruce, *The Evolution of Arthurian Romance* (Göttingen: Vandenhoeck & Ruprecht; Baltimore: The Johns Hopkins Press, 1928), Vol. I, p. 317.

106. See *Oriental Mythology*, pp. 6–7, 22, 107, 131–32, 392, 500; *Occidental Mythology*, pp. 72–92.

107. Tertullian, *On the Flesh of Christ*, as quoted in Gilson, op. cit., p. 45.

108. I Corinthians 1:21.
109. Abailard, *Dialogus inter philosophum, Judaeum et Christianum,* in Migne, *Patr. Lat.,* clxxviii, 1610ff.
110. Gilson, op. cit., p. 163.
111. Abailard, *Sic et Non,* prologue, in Migne *Patr. Lat.,* clxxviii, 1347.
112. Abailard, *Introducto ad Theologian* ii. c., in Migne, *Patr. Lat.,* clxxviii, 1050. I am following here the article "Abelard," by H. B. Workman in Hastings (ed.), op. cit., Vol. I, pp. 14–18.

113. Abailard, *Historia Calamitatum,* Chapters IX–XIII.
114. Thomas Aquinas, *Summa Theologica* 1.I.2. Art. 2. Translation by Father Lawrence Shapcote, as edited by Anton C. Pegis, *Basic Writings of Saint Thomas Aquinas* (New York: Random House, 1945).
115. Ibid., 2–2. I. 1. Art. 5.
116. Cited from Gilson, op. cit., pp. 392, 397.
117. Ibid., pp. 405–408.
118. *Occidental Mythology,* pp. 503–504.

PART THREE: THE WAY AND THE LIFE
CHAPTER 7: THE CRUCIFIED

1. Roger Sherman Loomis, *Celtic Myth and Arthurian Romance* (New York: Columbia University Press, 1927); *Arthurian Tradition and Chrétien of Troyes* (New York: Columbia University Press, 1949), *The Grail: From Celtic Myth to Christian Symbol* (New York: Columbia University Press, 1963).
2. *Primitive Mythology,* pp. 401–434.
3. Elucidation, 11. 4–5, as cited in Weston, op. cit., p. 130.
4. Matthew 27:57–60; Mark 15:14–46; Luke 23:50–53; John 19:38–42.
5. Weston, op. cit., Chapter IX, "The Fisher King."
6. William A. Nitze, "Perceval and the Holy Grail," *University of California Publications in Modern Philology,* Vol. 28, No. 5 (1949), p. 316.
7. *Oriental Mythology,* pp. 389–92.
8. *The Mabinogion,* translation by Lady Charlotte Guest, in Everyman's Library (London: J. M. Dent and Sons; New York: E. P. Dutton and Co., 1906), p. 185.
9. Weston, op. cit., p. 111.
10. Wolfram, op. cit., IX. 491:1–14.

11. *Oriental Mythology,* pp. 273, 285, 287, 305, 320, 485.
12. Ibid., pp. 318–19.
13. *Pañcatantra,* Book 5, Fable 3; translation by Arthur Ryder *The Panchatantra* (Chicago: The University of Chicago Press, 1925), pp. 434–41.
14. Theodor Benfey, *Pantschatantra* (Leipzig: F. A. Brockhaus, 1859), p. 487.
15. William Blake, *The Marriage of Heaven and Hell,* "Proverbs of Hell," Proverb No. 3.
16. Viktor E. Frankl, *Man's Search for Meaning: An Introduction to Logotherapy* (New York: Washington Square Press, 1963).
17. J. A. MacCulloch, *The Religion of the Ancient Celts* (Edinburgh: T. & T. Clark, 1911), p. 368.
18. Benfey, op. cit., p. 487.
19. *Grimm's Fairy Tales* (New York: Pantheon Books, 1944), pp. 258–264.
20. Johannes Bolte and Georg Polívka, *Anmerkungen zu den Kinder- und Hausmärchen der Brüder Grimm* (Leipzig: Dieterich'sche Verlagsbuchhandlung, 1937), Vol. I, pp. 464–85.
21. *Chāndogya Upaniṣad* 7.15.1.

22. *Bṛhadāraṇyaka Upaniṣad* 2.5.15.
23. *Praśna Upaniṣad* 6.6.
24. *Primitive Mythology*, pp. 141, 257, 328.
25. *Primitive Mythology*, pp. 141, 147, 233–34, 441.
26. *Oriental Mythology*, pp. 211–18.
27. *Mahā-Vagga* 1.21. 1–4.
28. *Oriental Mythology*, pp. 13–23.
29. Pindar, *Pythia* 2.21–48.
30. Virgil, *Aeneid* 6.601.
31. Ovid, *Metamorphoses*, 4.465.
32. Albert Camus, *Le Mythe de Sisyphe* (Paris: Gallimard, 1942), pp. 163–65.
33. Ibid., p. 20.
34. Frankl, op. cit., pp. 187–88.
35. Dante, *Inferno* XXXIV. 2.69. Norton translation, slightly modified.
36. Harnack, op. cit., Vol. VI, pp. 78–79, citing Abelard, on Romans 3:22ff.; 5:12ff.; *Sermons*, V, X, XII; *Theologia christiana* IV; and the Dialogue. All in Migne, *Patr. Lat.*, clxxviii respectively: col. 417–25; 448–53; 479–84; 1259–1516; 1609–82.
37. *Occidental Mythology*, p. 450.
38. Abū Yazīd (Bāyazīd), as cited by R. A. Nicholson, "Mysticism," in Sir Thomas Arnold (ed.), *The Legacy of Islam* (Oxford: The Clarendon Press, 1931), p. 216.
39. Chrétien de Troyes, *Li Contes del Graal*, 11. 66ff.
40. "Among the documents emanating from the bishop's palace at Troyes there is a charter dated 1173 which carries as one of its signatories the name of a certain Christianus or Chrétien. He was a canon of the ancient Abbey of Saint-Loup, in which is now housed the public library and museum of the town. The abbey, established in the fifth century by Saint Bernard, apparently enjoyed the special favor of the house of Champagne. This 'Christianus, canonicus Sancti Lupi,' is perhaps our poet. Certainly the latter was a cleric. . . ." (Nitze, op. cit., p. 282).
41. Wolfram, op. cit., IX. 454: 17–25.
42. Loomis, *The Grail*, p. 29.
43. So Arnold of Villanova (d. 1312?), in the *Rosarium philosophorum* (*Artis Auriferae*, Basel, 1593, Vol. II, Part XII), p. 210; as cited by Jung, *Psychology and Alchemy*, pp. 78, 171, note 117.
44. Wolfram, op. cit., IX. 469: 7–28.
45. Ibid., II. 115–27.
46. Ibid., III. 140: 16–17.
47. Ibid., XVI. 827. 19–24.
48. Ibid., 1:1–14.

CHAPTER 8: THE PARACLETE

1. *in dûhte, wert gedinge daz wære ein hôhiu linge ze disem lêhe hie unt dort. daz sint noch ungelogeniu wort.* (Wolfram, op. cit., III 177:6–9.)
2. *Wer immer strebend sich bemüht, Den können wir erlösen.* (*Faust* II. v. 11936–11937.)
3. Wolfram, op. cit., IV. 199: 23–203:11.
4. Gottfried Weber, *Parzival, Ringen und Vollendung* (Oberursel: Kompass-Verlag, 1948), p. 31.
5. Cf. *Oriental Mythology*, pp. 285–286, citing *Thus Spake Zarathustra*, Part I, "Three Transformations of the Spirit."
6. Karl Jaspers and Rudolf Bultmann, *Myth and Christianity: An Inquiry into the Possibility of Religion without Myth* (New York: The Noonday Press, 1958), p. 19.
7. *Occidental Mythology*, pp. 490–504.
8. Joyce, *A Portrait of the Artist as a Young Man*, pp. 177–78; 183.
9. Ibid., pp. 184–85.

10. Joyce, *Ulysses*, Paris ed., p. 481; Random House ed., p. 499.

11. Ibid., Paris ed., pp. 528–33; Random House ed., pp. 549–54.

12. *Occidental Mythology*, pp. 193–194, 197–98.

13. Weston, op. cit., pp. 71–72.

14. See Heinrich Zimmer, *The King and the Corpse*, edited by Joseph Campbell, Bollingen Series XI (New York: Pantheon Books, 1948), pp. 67–95.

15. Ibid.

16. W. B. Yeats, *A Vision* (New York: Collier Books Edition, 1966, based on revised edition of 1956), pp. 286–87.

17. Wolfram, op. cit., IX. 435:23–25.

18. Ibid., IX. 438:28–29.

19. Ibid., IX. 470:1–8.

20. Joyce, *Ulysses*, Paris ed., pp. 542–45; Random House ed., pp. 564–68.

21. Weber, *Parzival*, p. 63.

22. Joyce, *Ulysses*, Paris ed. p. 40; Random House ed., p. 40.

23. *Occidental Mythology*, pp. 500–501.

24. *Occidental Mythology*, p. 350.

25. *Oriental Mythology*, p. 271.

26. Mark 15:38.

27. Nitze, op. cit., p. 317.

28. Joseph Campbell (ed.), *The Portable Arabian Nights* (New York: The Viking Press, 1952), pp. 95–114.

29. Campbell, *The Hero with a Thousand Faces*, p. 30.

30. *Bhagavad Gītā* 3:35.

31. Ibid., 2:22.

32. Ibid., 2:71.

33. Swami Nikhilananda (translator), *The Gospel of Sri Ramakrishna* (New York: Ramakrishna-Vivekananda Center, 1942), p. 257 and passim.

34. C. G. Jung, *Psychology and Religion: West and East*, translated by R. F. C. Hull, Bollingen Series XX, Vol. 11 (New York: Pantheon Books, 1958), p. 502.

35. Schopenhauer, *Die Welt als Wille und Vorstellung*, Book III, Paragraph 45; *Werke*, Vol. 3, pp. 70–71.

36. Joyce, *Ulysses*, Paris ed., p. 14; Random House., p. 15.

37. Mann, *Der Zauberberg*, Chapters I and II.

38. "The Gospel According to Thomas," 113:16–18; Guillaumont, etc., op. cit., p. 57.

39. See *Primitive Mythology*, pp. 123–25.

40. Joyce, *A Portrait of the Artist as a Young Man*, last paragraph.

41. Joyce, *Ulysses*, Paris ed., p. 528; Random House ed., p. 549.

42. Ibid., Paris ed., pp. 496–500; Random House ed., pp. 515–20.

43. Ibid., Paris ed., pp. 58–59; Random House ed., p. 61.

44. Ibid., Paris ed., p. 59; Random House ed., p. 61.

45. Mann, *Der Zauberberg*, pp. 103–104; English, p. 99.

46. *Occidental Mythology*, pp. 129 and 174.

47. Jung, *The Archetypes of the Collective Unconscious*, p. 32.

48. *Oriental Mythology*, Figure 21 and pp. 343–64.

49. Jung, *The Archetypes of the Collective Unconscious*, p. 29.

50. C. G. Jung, *Aion: Researches into the Phenomenology of the Self*, translated by R. F. C. Hull, Bollingen Series XX. Vol. 9, Part 2 (New York: Pantheon Books, 1959), p. 13.

51. Ibid.

52. See our discussion of the psychology of "imprints" at the opening of this study, *Primitive Mythology*, pp. 30–131.

53. *Occidental Mythology*, pp. 129–130.

54. Jung, *Aion*, p. 13.

55. Thomas Mann, "Freud and the Future," translation by H. T. Lowe-Porter in Mann, *Essays of Three Decades*, p. 418.

56. C. G. Jung, as quoted by W. Y.

Evans-Wentz (ed.), *The Tibetan Book of the Dead* (New York: Oxford University Press, Galaxy Book edition, 1960), p. vi.

57. C. G. Jung, "Psychological Commentary," to Evans-Wentz (ed.), op. cit., p. xl.
58. Mann, "Freud and the Future," p. 419.
59. Aśvaghoṣa, *The Awakening of Faith*, translation by Timothy Richard (Shanghai, 1907), p. 26, as quoted by Evans-Wentz (ed.), op. cit., p. 227.
60. Schopenhauer, *Die Welt als Wille und Vorstellung* IV. 54; *Werke*, Vol. 3, p. 127.
61. Goethe, *Faust* II. 1. 6213–6216.
62. Lefebure, op. cit., p. 831.
63. Shakespeare, *Hamlet* III. i. 79–80.
64. Matthew 26:41; Mark 14:38.
65. *Occidental Mythology*, pp. 90–91.
66. Zimmer, *The King and the Corpse*, pp. 86–87.
67. Frazer, op. cit., p. 9. Question 1 is answered, pp. 9–592; Question 2, pp. 592–711. For discussions of ritual regicide, see *Primitive Mythology*, pp. 151–225, 405–460; *Oriental Mythology*, pp. 42–102, 160–68, 207, 284, 394–95, 396–97; and *Occidental Mythology*, pp. 59–60, 64, 155, 312–13, 321 and 506.
68. Augustine, *The City of God* XXI.4, as cited by C. G. Jung, *Mysterium Coniunctionis*, p. 292, note 134.
69. Angelo de Gubernatis, *Zoological Mythology* (London: Trübner and Co., 1872), Vol. II, p. 323, as cited by Jung, *Mysterium Coniunctionis*, p. 291.
70. Jung, *Mysterium Coniunctionis*, p. 289.
71. *Musaeum hermeticum* (Frankfurt a. M., 1678), p. 693–94; as in Arthur Waite (ed. and transl.), *The Hermetic Museum Restored and Enlarged* (London,

1893), Vol. II, p. 194. Cited by Jung, *Mysterium Coniunctionis*, pp. 288–89.
72. *Occidental Mythology*, p. 167.
73. Genesis 3:24.
74. Wolfram, op. cit., IX. 490. 15–18.
75. See Kerényi, op. cit., pp. 340–41, citing *Diodorus Siculus* 4.59.5; *Pausanias Periegeta* 1.39.3; *Apollodorus Mythographus*, epitoma 1.3; *Hygini Fabulae* 38; and *Bacchylides* 18.28.
76. *Occidental Mythology*, p. 25.
77. Wagner, *Mein Leben*, Vol. II, p. 360.
78. Ibid., Vol. III, p. 649.
79. Wagner, *Tannhäuser*, Act II, Scene iv.
80. Golther, op. cit., p. 191.
81. Mann, *Leiden und Grösse der Meister*, pp. 115–16. Lowe-Porter version in Mann *Essays of Three Decades*, pp. 323–24.
82. *Oriental Mythology*, pp. 15–20.
83. *Occidental Mythology*, p. 264.
84. Nietzsche, *Nietzsche contra Wagner*, "Wie ich von Wagner loskam," §1; *Werke*, Vol. 8, p. 200.
85. Ibid., "Wagner als Apostel der Keuschheit," §3; *Werke*, Vol. 8, pp. 198–200, slightly abridged.
86. *Occidental Mythology*, pp. 490–501, 507, 515.
87. Zimmer, *The King and the Corpse*, p. 86.
88. Roger Sherman Loomis, "Gawain, Gwri, and Cuchulinn," *Publications of the Modern Language Association*, Vol. XLII, No. 2, June 1928, p. 384.
89. For these identifications, see Weston, op. cit., pp. 130, 181, 185–88.
90. Thomas, *Tristan* 2120.
91. Elucidation 4–9; 12–13, Hilka ed., op. cit., p. 417.
92. Second ("Wauchier") Continuation, British Museum MS. additional 36614, Fol. 241 Vᵒ. For a discussion and collation of other manuscript passages, see

Jessie L. Weston, "Wauchier de Denain and Bleheris (Bledhericus)" in *Romania* XXXIV (1905), pp. 100–105; also Roger Sherman Loomis, "The Arthurian Legend before 1134," in *The Romanic Review* XXXII (1941), pp. 16–19.

93. *Occidental Mythology*, pp. 383–394, 456–90.

94. *Occidental Mythology*, pp. 125–140.

95. Nennius, *Historia Britonum* (edition by Josephus Stevenson, English Historical Society, 1838), Paragraph 56.

96. Ibid., paragraphs 40–42.

97. *Annales Cambriae*, John Williams ab Ithel (ed.) (Great Britain, Public Record Office: Chronicles and Memorials of Great Britain and Ireland during the Middle Ages, No. 20, 1860).

98. Nennius, op. cit., paragraph 73.

99. Loomis, *Arthurian Tradition and Chrétien de Troyes*, p. 198.

100. *Primitive Mythology*, pp. 199, 347, 369.

101. William Stubbs (ed.), *Willelmi Malmesbiriensis monachi De gestis regum Anglorum* (Great Britain, Public Record Office: Chronicles and Memorials of Great Britain and Ireland during the Middle Ages, No. 90, 1887–1889), p. 11.

102. Giraldus Cambrensis, *Itinerarium Cambriae* I.5 (*The Works of Giraldus Cambrensis*, Rolls Series, 1861–91, pp. 57–58).

103. Sebastian Evans, "The Translator's Epilogue," in the Everyman's edition of Geoffrey of Monmouth, *Histories of the Kings of Britain* (London: J. M. Dent and Sons; New York: E. P. Dutton and Co., 1912), pp. 241–242.

104. Ibid., p. 243.

105. Roger Sherman Loomis, "Geoffrey of Monmouth and Arthurian Origins," in *Speculum*, Vol. III (1928), p. 16.

106. Layamon, op. cit., lines 6–13.

107. Wace, op. cit., lines 9994ff., 10555, 13675; Layamon, op. cit., lines 22736ff.

108. Wace, op. cit., lines 13681ff., Layamon, op. cit., 23080ff., 28610ff. See discussions in Evans, op. cit., pp. xvii–xx.

109. Bruce, op. cit., Vol. I, pp. 119–120.

110. W. Wiston Comfort, Introduction to *Arthurian Romances of Chrétien de Troyes* (Everyman's Library, No. 698), p. xviii.

111. For the interpretation of this *conte* as an *oral* tale, see Wendelin Foerster (ed.), *Der Karrenritter (Lancelot) und Das Wilhelmsleben (Guillaume d'Angleterre) von Christian von Troyes* (Halle: Max Niemeyer, 1899), pp. LXXVI–LXXVII.

112. Loomis, *Arthurian Romance and Chrétien de Troyes*, pp. 36–37.

113. Bruce, op. cit., Vol. I, pp. 120–122.

114. Loomis, *The Grail*, p. 239.

115. Ibid., p. 179.

116. The sources for this portion of the legend were chiefly the Gospels (Matthew 27:57; Mark 15:43; Luke 23:51; and John 19:38–42), the apocryphal "Gospel of Nicodemus" and two other apocryphal works: the "Vengeance of Avenging of the Savior" (*Vindicta Salvatoris*) and the "Story of Joseph of Arimathea" (*Narratio Josephi*). For these, see Montague Rhodes James, *The Apocryphal New Testament* (Oxford: The Clarendon Press, 1953), pp. 94ff., 161ff.

117. H. Oskar Sommer, *The Vulgate Version of the Arthurian Romances* (Washington: The Carnegie Institute of Washington, 1909), Vol. I, pp. 264, 267, 269–279.

118. Ibid., p. 289.

119. Ibid., p. 285.

120. Ibid., p. 77.

121. Ibid., p. 290.

122. Malory, *Le Morte Darthur*, Book XI, Chapters II and III, in part.

123. Albert Pauphilet (ed.), op. cit., p. 19, lines 12–26.

124. Ibid., p. 26.

125. John 20:19.

126. Acts 2:1–4. This identification of the day of the risen Christ's appearance in the upper room with that of the miracle of Pentecost is made by the author of the Queste (Pauphilet [ed.], op. cit.), p. 78, lines 12–18.

127. *Oriental Mythology*, p. 352.

128. Mansi, *Sacrorum Conciliorum Nova et Amplissima Collectio* (Venice, 1778), XXII. 982; cited by Frederick W. Locke, *The Quest for the Holy Grail* (Stanford: Stanford University Press, 1960), p. 110, note 11.

129. Malory, *Le Morte Darthur*, Book XVII, Chapter XX. The corresponding passage in *La Queste del Saint Graal* appears in Pauphilet (ed.), op. cit., pp. 268–271.

130. Pauphilet (ed.), op. cit., pp. 277–78.

131. Malory, *Le Morte Darthur*, Book XVII, Chapter XXII.

132. Migne, *Patr. Lat.*, clxxxiv, col. 21; cited by Loomis, *The Grail*, p. 187, following Albert Pauphi-let, *Études sur la "Queste del Saint Graal,"* p. 151.

133. Locke, op. cit., pp. 10–11.

134. Ibid., p. 10.

135. Pauphilet (ed.), op. cit., p. viii.

136. *Regula Templi* (ed. Henri de Curzon, Paris 1886), rules 70 and 71; cited by Locke, op. cit., p. 114, note 21.

137. Jessie L. Weston, *The Legend of Sir Gawain* (London: David Nutt, 1897), p. 59.

138. Zimmer, *The King and the Corpse*, pp. 180–81.

139. Ananda K. Coomaraswamy, *Am I My Brother's Keeper?* (New York: The John Day Company, 1947), p. 28.

140. Spengler, *Der Untergang des Abendlandes*, Vol. I, German ed., p. 408; English ed., p. 319.

141. Wolfram, op. cit., XVI. 795:29.

142. Wolfram, op. cit., XVI. 827:1–11.

143. For the negative argument, see Loomis, *The Grail*, p. 197; for the positive, Franz Rolf Schroe-der, *Die Parzivalfrage* (München: C. H. Beck'sche Verlagsbuch-handlung, 1928), pp. 70–71.

144. Wolfram, op. cit., I. 1–14.

145. Wolfram, op. cit., XI. 569. 12–13.

146. Wolfram, op. cit., XVI. 827:19–24.

147. Wolfram, op. cit., XVI. 817:4–7.

148. Adams, *The Education of Henry Adams*, pp. 388–89.

PART FOUR: NEW WINE

CHAPTER 9: THE DEATH OF "GOD"

1. J. J. Fahie, *Galileo, His Life and Work* (London: John Murray, 1903), pp. 313–14.

2. *Oriental Mythology*, p. 105, Figure 13.

3. Ortega y Gasset, *Man and Crisis*, pp. 92–93.

4. *Primitive Mythology*, pp. 405–11.

5. Emerson, op. cit., p. 71.

6. Emerson, "The Over-Soul," op. cit., pp. 252–53.

7. *Oriental Mythology*, pp, 198ff. and 316.

8. *Summa contra Gentiles* 1.5. I note that in Anton C. Pegis, *Basic Writings of Saint Thomas Aquinas*

(New York: Random House, 1945), the chapter containing this passage does not appear.

9. *Acta Bollandiana*, pp. 712f., as cited by Marie-Louise von Franz, op. cit., pp. 424–25.

10. Ibid., p. 713. From von Franz, op. cit., pp. 425–26.

11. Angelo Walz, "De Alberti Magni et S. Thomae personali relatione," *Angelicum* (Rome), II:3 (1925), pp. 299ff. Cited by von Franz, op. cit., pp. 428–29.

12. Henri Petitot, *Saint Thomas d'Aquin: La Vocation—l'oeuvre—la vie spirituelle* (Paris, 1923), p. 154. Cited by von Franz, op. cit., pp. 427–28.

13. Karl Jaspers, *Nietzsche,* translated by Charles F. Wallraff and Frederick J. Schmitz (Tucson, Ariz.: The University of Arizona Press, 1965), Book One.

14. Nietzsche, *Die fröhliche Wissenschaft, Vorrede zur zweiten Ausgabe; Werke,* Vol. 5, p. 8; cited by Jaspers, op. cit., p. 114.

15. Jaspers, op. cit., p. 114.

16. Ibid.

17. Nietzsche, *Ecce homo, "Warum ich so klug bin,"* par. 2; *Werke,* Vol. 15, pp. 30–31.

18. Nietzsche, *Umwertung aller Werthe,* par. 54; *Werke,* Vol. 8, p. 295.

19. Swami Nikhilananda (transl. and ed.), op. cit., p. 858.

20. Nicholas of Cusa, *The Vision of God,* translation by Emma Gurney Salter, op. cit., pp. 1–6.

21. Ortega y Gasset, *History as a System,* translation by Helen Weyl, op. cit., p. 172.

22. I am here citing largely from Lynn Thorndike, *A History of Magic and Experimental Science,* 8 volumes (New York: Columbia University, 1923–1958), Vol. II, pp. 19–43.

23. Ibid., pp. 31–32 and 35.

24. Ibid., p. 9, from Adelard of Bath, *De eodem et diverso:* H. Willner,

Des Adelard von Bath Traktat De eodem et diverso, zum ersten Male herausgegeben und historisch-kritisch untersucht (Münster, 1903), in *Beiträge zur Geschichte der Philosophie des Mittelalters* (ed. C. Baeumker, G. von Hertling, M. Baumgartner, et al., Münster 1891–), p. 13.

25. Thorndike, op. cit., pp. 28–29, citing *Questiones,* cap. 6.

26. Thomas Aquinas, *Summa Theologica* 2–2. Q.1. Art. 5. (Pegis, ed., Vol. II, p. 1062.)

27. *Occidental Mythology,* p. 389.

28. Thorndike, op. cit., Vol. II, p. 439.

29. Ibid., pp. 439–40.

30. Ibid., p. 441, citing Ludwig Bauer, *Die Philosophischen Werke des Robert Grosseteste* (Münster: 1912) in Baeumker's *Beiträge zur Geschichte der Philosophie des Mittelalters,* Vol. IX, 74.

31. Ibid., p. 443, citing Bauer, op. cit., 60.

32. Thorndike, op. cit., Vol. II, p. 657, citing J. H. Bridges (ed.), *The Opus Maius of Roger Bacon,* 3 vols. (Oxford, 1897 and 1900), Vol. II. 202.

33. Thorndike, op. cit., Vol. II, p. 656, citing J. H. Bridges (ed.), op. cit., Vol. II. 208.

34. Gilson, op. cit., p. 515.

35. Ibid., p. 516.

36. Ibid., p. 516.

37. Thorndike, op. cit., Vol. III, p. 450, citing from the Vatican, FL Asburnham 210, fol. 38 v., col. 1.

38. Gilson, op. cit., p. 518.

39. Henry Charles Lea, *A History of the Inquisition of the Middle Ages,* 3 volumes (reprint, New York: Russell and Russell, 1955), Vol. I, pp. 328, 337–39, 421–22.

40. Ibid., Vol. III, 464.

41. Frazer, op. cit., p. 681.

42. Lea, op. cit., Vol. III, pp. 500–501.

43. Desiderius Erasmus (1509), translation by John Wilson (1668),

The Praise of Folly (Oxford: The Clarendon Press, 1913), p. 177.

44. I have followed Bayard Taylor's review of the Faust Legend in his translation of Goethe's *Faust* (Boston and New York: Houghton Mifflin Company, 1870), Vol. I, pp. 337–44, and, almost verbatim, the fine article of Professor W. Alison Phillips of Dublin University in *The Encyclopaedia Britannica* (Fourteenth Edition, 1936), Vol. 9, pp. 120–22, which, in turn, cites Karl Engel, *Zusammenstellung der Faust-Schriften vom 16. Jahrhundert bis Mitte 1884* (Oldenburg: Bibliotheca Faustiana, 2nd ed., 1885) and Carl Kiesewetter, *Faust in der Geschichte und Tradition* (Leipzig: M. Spohr, 1893).

45. Henry Adams, *The Degeneration of the Democratic Dogma,* edited with an introduction by Brooks Adams (New York: The Macmillan Co., 1919, 1947), p. 287.

46. Adams, *The Education of Henry Adams,* p. 484.

47. Miguel de Cervantes Saavedra, *Don Quijote de la Mancha,* Part I, Chapter VIII.

48. Ortega y Gasset, *Meditations on Quixote,* translated from the Spanish by Evelyn Rugg and Diego Marín, op. cit., pp. 136, 137.

49. Ibid., p. 138.

50. Ibid., pp. 148–149.

51. Ibid., pp. 152–55.

52. Christopher Marlowe, *The Tragical History of Doctor Faustus,* Scene VI.

53. Ibid., Scene XIV.

54. Goethe, *Faust,* Prologue in Heaven, lines 304–307, translation by Bayard Taylor (modified).

55. Spengler, *Der Untergang des Abendlandes,* Vol. I, p. 240 (German ed.), p. 187 (English).

56. *Taittirīya Upaniṣad* 2.9.

57. Erwin Schrödinger, *My View of the World* translated by Cecily Hastings (Cambridge: Cambridge University Press, 1964), pp. 20–22.

58. "The Gospel According to Thomas" 94:26 (op. cit., p. 43).

59. *R Veda* I. 164.46.

60. Cecil Jane, *The Voyages of Christopher Columbus; being the Journals of his First and Third, and the Letters concerning his First and Last Voyages, to which is added the Account of his Second Voyage written by Andreas Bernaldez* (London: The Argonaut Press, 1930), p. 36.

61. Aquinas, *Summa Theologica,* Part I, Question 102, Article 1, Reply 3.

62. *Glossa ordin., super Genesis* 2:8 (I, 36F).

63. Augustine, *De Genesi ad Litt.* VIII, I (PL 34, 371); also *De Civit. Dei* XIII, 21 (PL 41, 395).

64. Ananda K. Coomaraswamy, "The Christian and Oriental, or True Philosophy of Art," in *Why Exhibit Works of Art* (London: Luzac and Company, 1943), pp. 32–33.

65. Jeffers, op. cit., p. 24.

66. Loren Eiseley, *The Firmament of Time* (New York: Atheneum Publishers, 1962), p. 14.

67. Ibid., pp. 14, 15.

68. David Bergamini and The Editors of Life, *The Universe,* Life Nature Library (New York: Time Incorporated, 1962), pp. 131–37, greatly abridged.

69. Goethe, *Faust* II. 2. 7495–8487.

70. Eiseley, op. cit., pp. 45–47.

71. Ibid., p. 51.

72. Edward MacCurdy (ed.), *The Notebooks of Leonardo da Vinci* (New York: George Braziller, 1955), p. 191.

73. Goethe, *Vorträge über die drei ersten Capitel des Entwürfs einer allgemeinen Einleitung im die vergleichende Anatomie, ausgehend von der Osteologie* (1796), in *Werke* (1858), Vol. 36, p. 323.

74. Goethe, *Bildung und Umbildung organischer Naturen, Einleitendes zur Metamorphosen der Pflanzen* (1790), *Werke* (1858), Vol. 36, pp. 6–9, abridged.

75. Max Planck, "Über die Elementarquanta der Materie und der Elektrizität," *Ann. der Phys.*, iv (1901), p. 564.

76. Harold Dean Cater (ed.), *Henry Adams and His Friends* (Boston: Houghton Mifflin Co., 1947), pp. 558–59.

77. John Dewey, in *Living Philoso-phies*, a symposium of twenty-two living philosophies (New York: Simon and Schuster, 1931), pp. 25–26, 34–35.

78. Ibid., pp. 26–27.

79. Nietzsche, *Der Wille zur Macht*, Book III, Par. 602, in *Werke*, Vol. 16, p. 96.

80. Ibid., I. "Der europäische Nihilismus," 20, 22, 28, in *Werke* (1922), Vol. 15, pp. 155–56 and 160.

81. Eiseley, op. cit., p. 137.

82. Ibid., p. 140.

CHAPTER 10: THE EARTHLY PARADISE

1. Heinrich Zimmer, *Philosophies of India*, pp. 1–2.

2. Stephen Herbert Langdon, *Semitic Mythology*, in MacCulloch (ed.), *The Mythology of All Races*, Vol. V, p. 11.

3. Ibid., pp. 13 and 14.

4. *Occidental Mythology*, pp. 95–140; 221–26; 271–90.

5. Zimmer, *Philosophies of India*, pp. 13–14.

6. *Bṛhadāraṇyaka Upaniṣad* 1.4.6,7, and 10, abridged. Translation following Robert Ernest Hume, *The Thirteen Principal Upanishads* (London, etc.: Oxford University Press, 1921), pp. 82–84, and commentary, Note 1, p. 83.

7. Samuel A. B. Mercer, *The Pyramid Texts* (New York, London, Toronto: Longmans, Green and Co., 1952), Vol. I, pp. 93–94; texts 398 and 403.

8. E. A. W. Budge, translation, *The Per-em-hru* or "*Day of Putting Forth*," commonly called *The Book of the Dead*, in *The Sacred Books and Early Literature of the East* (New York and London: Parke, Austin, and Lipscomb, 1917), Vol. 2, pp. 190–91 and 196–97.

9. Joyce, *Finnegans Wake*, p. 62.

10. Ibid., p. 593.

11. C. G. Jung, *Modern Man in Search of a Soul.* (New York: Harcourt, Brace, 1956), p. 215.

12. See Zimmer, *Philosophies of India*, pp. 151–60.

13. Dante, *Convivio*, Treatise IV, Chapters 23–28. Translation following Philip H. Wicksteed, *The Convivio of Dante Alighieri* (London: J. M. Dent and Sons, 1903), pp. 341–75.

14. Ibid., IV, 26, v. (Wicksteed, op. cit., p. 363.)

15. Ibid., IV, 26, i–ii. (Wicksteed, op. cit., p. 361.)

16. Joyce, *Ulysses*, Paris ed., pp. 48–50; Random House ed., p. 50–51.

17. Richard Ellmann, *James Joyce* (New York: Oxford University Press, 1959), pp. 162–63.

18. Mann, *The Magic Mountain*, translation by H. T. Lowe-Porter, p. 4. (German, p. 12.)

19. Ibid., p. 317. (German, p. 329.)

20. Ibid., Translation by H. T. Lowe-Porter, p. 505. (German, pp. 521–522.)

20a. Ibid., German, pp. 449–50; English, pp. 432–33.

21. *Sermo suppositus*, 120, 8 (*In Natali Domini* IV), translation from Marie-Louise von Franz, *Aurora Consurgens: A Document Attributed to Thomas Aquinas on the Problem of Opposites in Alchemy*, Bollingen Series LXXVII (New

York: Pantheon Books, 1966), p. 428.

22. Epist. CXIV, Migne, P.L., vol. lxxvii col. 806, cited by Jung, *The Practice of Psychotherapy*, p. 258, note 6.

23. *De chemia*, p. 16, cited by Jung, *The Practice of Psychotherapy*, p. 258, n. 5.

24. Joyce, *Ulysses*, Paris ed., pp. 543–546; Random House ed., pp. 565–568.

25. Ibid., Paris ed., p. 633; Random House ed., p. 661.

26. Ibid., Paris ed., pp. 690–92 and 727 ff.; Random House ed., pp. 719–21 and 759 ff.

27. Mann, *Der Zauberberg*, pp. 170–171; English, p. 165.

28. Ibid., p. 249; English, p. 241.

29. Ibid., p. 351; English, p. 338.

30. Ibid., pp. 449–50; English 432–33.

31. C. G. Jung, *The Structure and Dynamics of the Psyche*, translation by R. F. C. Null, Bollingen Series XX. 8 (New York: Pantheon Books, 1960), pp. 247–48.

32. Nietzsche, *Die Geburt der Tragödie*, conclusion.

33. Jung, *Memories, Dreams, Reflections*, p. 340.

34. Mann, *Der Zauberberg*, pp. 647–648; English, pp, 625–26.

35. Jung, *Civilization in Transition*, pp. 144–45.

36. *Theogony* 116 ff.; Parmenides, fragment 132; *Symposium* 178 b.

37. Translation by Richmond Lattimore, *Hesiod* (Ann Arbor: University of Michigan Press, 1959), p. 130.

38. C. G. Jung, *Memories, Dreams, Reflections*, recorded and edited by Aniela Jaffé, translated from the German by Richard and Clara Winston (New York: Pantheon Books, 1963), pp. 353–354.

39. John 12:45 and 10:30.

40. *Māṇḍūkya Upaniṣad* 1. I am following my own translation, in Heinrich Zimmer, *Philosophies of India*, pp. 372–78.

41. Joyce, *Ulysses*, Paris ed., p. 37; Random House ed., p. 38.

42. Translation by D. F. Pears and B. F. McGuinness, Ludwig Wittgenstein's *Tractatus Logico-Philosophicus* (London: Routledge and Kegan Paul; New York: The Humanities Press, 1961).

43. Bertrand Russell, "Introduction" to Ludwig Wittgenstein's *Tractatus*, Pears and McGuinness (eds.), op. cit., p. x.

44. Nietzsche, *Der Wille zur Macht*, Part III, Section 1, "Der Wille zur Macht als Erkenntnis," Aphorisms Nos. 539 and 540.

45. Nietzsche, *Menschlich Allzumenschliches*, Vol. I, Aphorism, No. 11.

46. Jung, *The Structure and Dynamics of the Psyche*, pp. 123–24.

47. Marlowe, *Doctor Faustus*, Scene III.

48. Ibid., Scene III.

49. Sigmund Freud, *The Psychopathology of Everyday Life*, translation by A. A. Brill in *The Basic Writings of Sigmund Freud* (New York: The Modern Library, 1938), pp 164–65.

50. Nietzsche, *Menschlich Allzumenschliches*, Aphorism No. 5.

51. Sigmund Freud, *Totem and Tabu*, in Brill (transl.), op. cit., p. 927.

52. Jung, *The Structure and Dynamics of the Psyche*, pp. 310–11.

53. Jeffers, "Roan Stallion," in *Roan Stallion, Tamar, and Other Poems*, p. 24.

54. Thomas Mann, *Joseph and His Brothers*, Vol. I, translated by H. T. Lowe-Porter (New York: Alfred A. Knopf, 1936), p. 3.

55. Ibid., pp. 37–38.

56. Jung, *The Archetypes of the Collective Unconscious*, p. 173.

57. *Oriental Mythology*, pp. 9–10.

58. Jung, *The Archetypes of the Collective Unconscious*, pp. 79–80.

59. *Māṇḍūkya Upaniṣad* 5–6.
60. Joyce, *Ulysses*, Paris ed., p. 687; Random House ed., 715–16.
61. Dante, *Divina Commedia*, Paradiso XXXIII, 115–17. Norton translation.
62. Joyce, *Ulysses*, Paris ed., pp. 692–693; Random House ed., pp. 721–722. In both editions the dot is by printer's error omitted. See the German translation by Georg Goyert (Zurich: Rhein-Verlag, no date), Vol. II, p. 354.
63. Joyce, *A Portrait of the Artist as a Young Man*, p. 280.
64. *Oriental Mythology*, p. 485.
65. Mann, *The Magic Mountain*, German, pp. 856–93; English, pp. 822–57.
66. Joyce, *Finnegans Wake*, pp. 182–186.
67. Joyce, *Ulysses*, Paris ed., p. 34; Random House, p. 35.
68. *Primitive Mythology*, pp. 461–472.
69. Mann, "Freud and the Future," op. cit., pp. 425–26.
70. Hesiod, *Theogony* 117, Lattimore translation.
71. Ibid., 106.
72. Joyce, *Ulysses*, last lines.
73. Joyce, *Finnegans Wake*, p. 18.
74. Ibid., pp. 4, 215, 382, 353, 486, 563, 582, 458, 455.
75. *Chāndogya Upaniṣad* 8.4.2.
76. *Māṇḍūkya Upaniṣad* 7.
77. Thomas A. Sebeok, "Animal Communication," *Science*, Vol. 147, pp. 1006–1014.
78. Diego de Estella, *Meditations on the Love of God*, Nos. 18 and 28. Translations from E. Allison Peers, *Studies of the Spanish Mystics* (London: S.P.C.K.; New York: The Macmillan Co., 1951), Vol. II, p. 190.
79. John of the Cross, *Living Flame of Love* I, translation from Peers, Vol. I, p. 213.
80. Cited in Rudolf Arnheim, *Picasso's Guernica: The Genesis of a Painting* (Berkeley and Los Angeles: University of California Press, 1962), p. 138, note to p. 23.
81. Joyce, *Finnegans Wake*, p. 215.
82. *Primitive Mythology*, pp. 358–59, citing Wolfgang Köhler, *The Mentality of Apes* (2nd ed.; New York: Humanities Press, 1927), p. 95.
83. Mann, *The Magic Mountain*, translation by H. T. Lowe-Porter, pp. 781–82; German, 813–14.
84. Wittgenstein, op. cit., translation, Pears and McGuinness, op. cit.
85. Zimmer, *Philosophies of India*, p. 375.

INDEX

FOR THE BEST IN PAPERBACKS, LOOK FOR THE

In every corner of the world, on every subject under the sun, Penguin represents quality and variety—the very best in publishing today.

For complete information about books available from Penguin—including Penguin Classics, Penguin Compass, and Puffins—and how to order them, write to us at the appropriate address below. Please note that for copyright reasons the selection of books varies from country to country.

In the United States: Please write to *Penguin Group (USA), P.O. Box 12289 Dept. B, Newark, New Jersey 07101-5289* or call 1-800-788-6262.

In the United Kingdom: Please write to *Dept. EP, Penguin Books Ltd, Bath Road, Harmondsworth, West Drayton, Middlesex UB7 0DA.*

In Canada: Please write to *Penguin Books Canada Ltd, 90 Eglinton Avenue East, Suite 700, Toronto, Ontario M4P 2Y3.*

In Australia: Please write to *Penguin Books Australia Ltd, P.O. Box 257, Ringwood, Victoria 3134.*

In New Zealand: Please write to *Penguin Books (NZ) Ltd, Private Bag 102902, North Shore Mail Centre, Auckland 10.*

In India: Please write to *Penguin Books India Pvt Ltd, 11 Panchsheel Shopping Centre, Panchsheel Park, New Delhi 110 017.*

In the Netherlands: Please write to *Penguin Books Netherlands bv, Postbus 3507, NL-1001 AH Amsterdam.*

In Germany: Please write to *Penguin Books Deutschland GmbH, Metzlerstrasse 26, 60594 Frankfurt am Main.*

In Spain: Please write to *Penguin Books S. A., Bravo Murillo 19, 1° B, 28015 Madrid.*

In Italy: Please write to *Penguin Italia s.r.l., Via Benedetto Croce 2, 20094 Corsico, Milano.*

In France: Please write to *Penguin France, Le Carré Wilson, 62 rue Benjamin Baillaud, 31500 Toulouse.*

In Japan: Please write to *Penguin Books Japan Ltd, Kaneko Building, 2-3-25 Koraku, Bunkyo-Ku, Tokyo 112.*

In South Africa: Please write to *Penguin Books South Africa (Pty) Ltd, Private Bag X14, Parkview, 2122 Johannesburg.*